THE *ENEADOS*

THE SCOTTISH TEXT SOCIETY

FIFTH SERIES

NO. 17

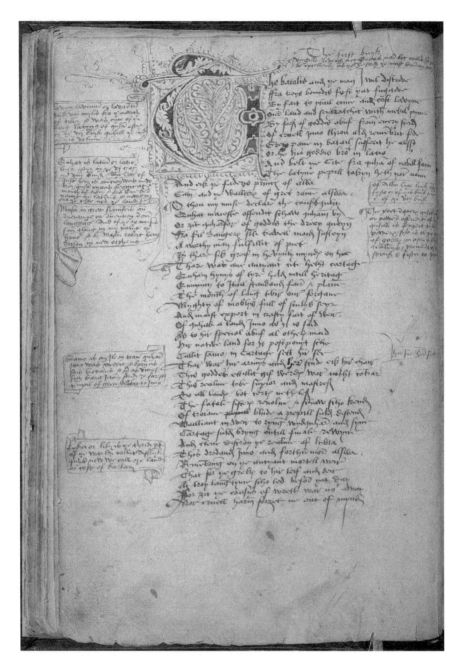

Cambridge, Trinity College Library, MS O.3.12, fol. 9v: incipit of Book 1. Reproduced by kind permission of the Master and Fellows of Trinity College, Cambridge.

THE *ENEADOS*

Gavin Douglas's Translation of
Virgil's *Aeneid*

Volume I
Introduction and Commentary

Edited by
Priscilla Bawcutt
with Ian Cunningham

The Scottish Text Society
2020

First published 2020 by The Scottish Text Society, Edinburgh

ISBN 978-1-89797-642-5

A Scottish Text Society publication
Published by The Boydell Press
an imprint of Boydell & Brewer Ltd
PO Box 9, Woodbridge, Suffolk IP12 3DF, UK
and of Boydell & Brewer Inc.
668 Mt Hope Avenue, Rochester, NY 14620–2731, USA
website: www.boydellandbrewer.com

The publisher has no responsibility for the continued existence or accuracy of URLs for external or
third-party internet websites referred to in this book, and does not guarantee that any content on such
websites is, or will remain, accurate or appropriate

A CIP catalogue record for this book is available
from the British Library

This publication is printed on acid-free paper

Printed and bound in Great Britain by
TJ International Ltd, Padstow, Cornwall

Contents

Preface

This new edition of Douglas's *Eneados* is based upon an earlier one published by the Scottish Text Society between 1957 and 1964: *Virgil's Aeneid Translated into Scottish Verse by Gavin Douglas Bishop of Dunkeld*, edited by David F. C. Coldwell. It was the first edition of the *Eneados* to be organized on modern scholarly principles, and had many virtues, although – as some reviewers noted – it was not wholly without flaws. When it fell out of print, the Council of the Scottish Text Society decided, after much discussion, that a simple reprint would not be adequate. They concluded that substantial corrections and revisions were required, which would preserve the strengths of Coldwell's edition, while eliminating, as far as possible, its weaknesses. This task was undertaken by myself, with the valuable assistance of Ian Cunningham. A full account, both of the characteristics of Coldwell's edition and also of our editorial procedure, will be found in the Introduction to the present volume (see, in particular, p. 35 and p. 38).

The editorial work was largely completed several years ago, but publication was unfortunately delayed, for reasons beyond our control, and chiefly because of the decision to digitize Coldwell's original text, using Optical Character Recognition (OCR). This type of scan could not cope with the vagaries of Older Scots spelling, and produced a badly garbled text. The accurate identification of errors and their correction is not easy and cannot be effected rapidly. We are extremely grateful therefore to Kate Ash-Irisarri and Caitlin Flynn, whose sharp eyes spotted the errors and who possessed the technical competence to carry out their correction throughout this huge work. For the funding to hire them, we wish to thank the University of St Andrews and the Scottish Medievalists (Anderson Dunlop Fund).

Over the years I have received much assistance from the staff of many libraries, particularly the British Library, the Bodleian Library, Oxford, Cambridge University Library, Edinburgh University Library, the Lambeth Palace Library, the National Library of Scotland, the Sydney Jones Library, University of Liverpool, and the Library of Trinity College, Cambridge.

I must pay a special tribute to the classical learning of my colleague Ian Cunningham, who checked and revised all quotations from Latin in the Commentary. I owe warm thanks to other scholars and friends who answered enquiries or who contributed in various ways to my understanding of both Douglas and Virgil: the late A. J. Aitken, the late R. G. Austin, Kate Harris, A. A. MacDonald, Sally Mapstone, Joseph Marshall, Nicola Royan, Sebastiaan Verweij, Emily Wingfield, and Elspeth Yeo. I am particularly grateful to A. S. G. Edwards, who has given me much shrewd advice, and to Rhiannon Purdie, above all, who has been much more than an 'editorial adviser'. In the crucial final stages of preparation her cheerfulness, dynamism, and organizational skills are what have kept this edition on course.

I owe, as always, an incalculable debt to my husband for his constant loving support.

The corona virus pandemic has sadly delayed publication still further. But despite all the difficulties, working from home has continued, and I am very grateful to

Emily Champion and other members of the Boydell & Brewer editorial team. Lastly, my heartfelt thanks go to Janet Hadley Williams: at the proof-correcting stage she miraculously created and sent a hard copy from Australia to England, and has again and again shown her loyalty and friendship.

Priscilla Bawcutt
Liverpool, November 2019

Abbreviations

53	*The xiii Bukes of Eneados of the famose Poete Virgill Translatet out of Latyne verses into Scottish metir, bi the Reuerend Father in God, Mayster Gawin Douglas Bishop of Dunkel & Vnkil to the Erle of Angus. Euery buke hauing hys perticular Prologe.* [William Copland]. London, 1553.
Ascensius	*Aeneis Vergiliana cum Seruii Honorati grammatici huberrimis comme(n)tariis ... Cumq(ue) familiarissima Iodoci Badii Ascensii elucidatione atq(ue) ordinis contextu. Accessit ad hoc Mapphei Veggii liber additicius cum Ascensianis an(n) otatiunculis.* Paris, 1501.
B	Longleat House Library MS 252 A (owned by the Marquess of Bath).
BL	British Library.
C	Cambridge, Trinity College Library, MS O.3.12.
Coldwell	*Virgil's Aeneid Translated into Scottish Verse by Gavin Douglas Bishop of Dunkeld, With Notes and Glossary.* Ed. David F. C. Coldwell. 4 vols. STS 3rd series 25, 27, 28, 30. Edinburgh, 1957–64.
CT	*The Canterbury Tales.*
DOST	*A Dictionary of the Older Scottish Tongue, part of the Dictionary of the Scots Language:* https://dsl.ac.uk/
Dunbar, *Poems*	*The Poems of William Dunbar.* Ed. Priscilla Bawcutt. 2 vols. Glasgow, 1998: references by poem number, and line.
Dundas	*The Aeneid of Virgil, Translated into Scottish Verse. By Gawin Douglas, Bishop of Dunkeld.* [Ed. George Dundas and Andrew Rutherford]. 2 vols. Bannatyne Club. Edinburgh, 1839.
E	The Elphinstoun MS: Edinburgh, Edinburgh University Library, MS Dk.7.49.
EETS ES, OS	Early English Text Society. Extra Series, Original Series.
f	Edinburgh University Library, MS Laing II.655 (fragments)
Henryson	*The Poems of Robert Henryson.* Ed. Denton Fox. Oxford, 1981.
L	London, Lambeth Palace Library, MS 117.
Loeb	*Virgil With an English Translation by H.R. Fairclough,* 2 vols, Cambridge, MA, 1940–2; revised by G. P. Goold, 1999–2000.
Mackail	*Virgil, The Aeneid,* ed. J. W. Mackail. Oxford, 1930.
ME	Middle English.

MED	*The Middle English Dictionary, part of the Middle English Compendium*: https://quod.lib.umich.edu/m/middle-english-dictionary
MLN	*Modern Language Notes.*
MLR	*Modern Language Review.*
Mynors	*P. Vergili Maronis Opera.* Ed. R. A. B. Mynors. Oxford, 1969.
NIMEV	*A New Index of Middle English Verse.* Ed. Julia Boffey and A. S. G. Edwards. London, 2005.
NLS	National Library of Scotland.
NQ	*Notes and Queries.*
ODNB	*The Oxford Dictionary of National Biography*, https://www.oxforddnb.com/
OED	*The Oxford English Dictionary*, https://www.oed.com/
R	The Ruthven manuscript: Edinburgh, Edinburgh University Library, MS Dc.1.43.
RES	*Review of English Studies.*
Ruddiman	*Virgil's Aeneis Translated into Scottish Verse by the Famous Gawin Douglas.* [Ed. T. Ruddiman.] Edinburgh, 1710.
Scots Peerage.	*The Scots Peerage.* Ed. Sir James Balfour Paul. 9 vols. Edinburgh, 1904–14.
SHS	Scottish History Society.
SLJ	*Scottish Literary Journal.*
Small	*The Poetical Works of Gavin Douglas, Bishop of Dunkeld, With Memoir, Notes and Glossary.* Ed. John Small. 4 vols. Edinburgh, 1874.
SRS	Scottish Record Society.
SSL	*Studies in Scottish Literature.*
STC	*A Short-Title Catalogue of Books Printed in England, Scotland and Ireland, and of English Books Printed Abroad 1475–1640*, 2nd ed. begun by W. A. Jackson and F. S. Ferguson, completed by K. F. Pantzer, 1976–91.
STS	Scottish Text Society.
TA	*Accounts of the Lord High Treasurer of Scotland.* Ed. T. Dickson and Sir James Balfour Paul. Edinburgh, 1877–1916.
Tilley	M. P. Tilley, *A Dictionary of Proverbs in England in the Sixteenth and Seventeenth Centuries.* Ann Arbor, 1950.
Whiting	B. J. and H. W. Whiting, *Proverbs, Sentences and Proverbial Phrases from English Writings Mainly before 1500.* Cambridge, MA, 1968.
Whiting *Scots*	B. J. Whiting, 'Proverbs from Scottish Writings before 1600', *Mediaeval Studies* 11 (1949), 123–205, and 13 (1951), 87–164.

Introduction

The *Eneados* and its Author

Gavin Douglas (c. 1476–1522) is a poet who evades easy labels or categories. Employing a language termed 'Scottis' by himself (I.Prol.103), but 'Inglis' by many of his fellow-Scots, he belongs to the literary history of both England and Scotland. The *Eneados* is his major work, a translation of the whole of Virgil's *Aeneid*, completed in 1513. Stylistically, Douglas owed much to the traditions of late medieval poetry. But there is much that is novel and pioneering about the *Eneados*, and it is commonly regarded as one of the first great renaissance translations.

Life and Career

No other early Scottish poet has a life so well documented as Douglas.[1] We have only sparse details about William Dunbar, his great contemporary, or other poets associated with the court of James IV (1488–1513), but much factual information survives about the major events in Douglas's career. The chief sources are legal documents and other public records, but there exists more intimate and valuable evidence in the letters to and from Douglas that have been preserved.[2] We know much about the cultural circles in which he moved: his contacts both with minor clerics, such as his own scribe Matthew Geddes, and men who were internationally renowned, such as Cardinal Wolsey or John Mair [Major] (c. 1467–1550), the distinguished Scottish historian and theologian. Such biographical information has more than a purely intrinsic interest. Douglas's poetic self-portrait in the *Eneados* is not simply a *persona* but closely resembles what we know of his real-life disputatious personality, as it emerges from the records and letters, and the comments, whether friendly or hostile, of those who knew him.

Douglas was the son of Archibald, fifth Earl of Angus, and Elizabeth Boyd, daughter of a former chamberlain of Scotland. Although nothing definite is known of his childhood, it is plausibly conjectured that he was born in Tantallon Castle in East Lothian, one of the chief seats of the Earls of Angus. Douglas was well educated, attending the University of St Andrews, where he matriculated in 1490 and completed his master's degree in 1494. The arts curriculum at St Andrews was closely modelled on that of Paris, and it is possible that, like many of his friends and compatriots, he went on to study at Paris. As a younger son, Douglas was designed from youth for the church, and the fact

---

[1] For detailed information about Douglas's life and cultural background, see Bawcutt 1976, 1–46.
[2] Douglas's letters can be consulted most easily in Small; later references, by volume and page, are embedded in the text. For further discussion, see Bawcutt 1996.

1

that he belonged to a powerful and aristocratic family undoubtedly aided his career. The first known mention of his name occurs in a document discovered fairly recently in the Vatican archives: dated February 1489, it implies that he received a dispensation to hold a benefice while still only 'in his thirteenth year' (Bawcutt 1994, 95–6). During the 1490s Douglas indeed rapidly acquired several minor benefices, and by 1503 he had become provost of St Giles, Edinburgh, a rich and well-endowed collegiate church in the patronage of the king. Both Douglas's major poems belong to this period of his life during the final years of James IV's reign. *The Palice of Honour*, c. 1501, contains an ornate dedication to James, which may have prompted the king's decision to bestow St Giles upon him. According to Douglas himself the *Eneados* was completed on 22 July 1513: 'Apon the fest of Mary Magdelan, / Fra Crystis byrth, the dait quha list to heir, / A thousand five hundreth and thretteyn 3eir' (*Tyme, space and dait*, 2–4). Only a few weeks later James decided to invade the north of England in support of the 'auld alliance' with France, and on 9 September 1513 occurred the disastrous battle of Flodden, in which the king died, along with many of his leading nobles, including two of Douglas's brothers and Henry, Lord Sinclair, the dedicatee of the *Eneados*.

Flodden seems to have been a turning-point for Douglas. Politics and the interests of his family, which had previously competed with literature for his attention, now became more important. During the troubled minority of James V his life was closely involved with the fortunes of his nephew Archibald, who was now the sixth Earl of Angus, and who had married Margaret Tudor, the widow of the late king. Douglas was extremely ambitious, and aspired to high office in the Scottish church. When the bishopric of Dunkeld fell vacant early in 1515, he rapidly took steps to acquire it, writing to Adam Williamson, one of his agents, on 18 January 1515 : 'my self and frendis thinkis nedful I be promovit to that seyt [ecclesiastical seat, see] ... an rycht gud Byschopry of rent and the thryd seyt of the realm' (Small, I, xxxvi). But Douglas did not obtain Dunkeld easily. He had incurred the hostility of John Stewart, Duke of Albany, who was the Governor, or Regent, of Scotland, during the infancy of James V. Charged with infringing the laws that regulated the purchase of benefices at Rome, Douglas was briefly imprisoned in Edinburgh Castle. Even when Douglas arrived at the gates of Dunkeld Cathedral in 1516, after his consecration, he encountered violent armed opposition from supporters of another candidate for the bishopric. The records suggest that Douglas fulfilled his duties at Dunkeld conscientiously, but that he also spent much time in Edinburgh, participating with other Lords of Council in attempting to govern the country justly. In 1517 he was sent on an important diplomatic mission to renew the alliance with France. Towards the end of 1521, however, when the Governor returned after a long absence from Scotland, Douglas's position was increasingly isolated and difficult. Margaret Tudor, whose marriage to Archibald Douglas had broken down, was now his enemy rather than an ally, and Douglas felt obliged to defend the interests of his nephew, despite regarding him as 'a young wytles fwyll [fool]' (Small, I, civ). In December 1521 he fled to London, chiefly to request the support of Cardinal Wolsey at Rome. Some months later, in September 1522 he died, apparently of the plague, in the house of his friend Lord Dacre .

If Douglas had lived only a little longer, it is likely that he would have returned to Scotland. He still had powerful friends and supporters, and the charge of treason against him that sequestrated his Dunkeld estates was soon dropped. It is striking that even during this period of exile in London he held lively conversations with Polydore Vergil, the Italian historian and author of *Historia Anglica*, long resident in England. According to Polydore, he took part in characteristically 'vehement' debate concerning the merits of a very recent book, John Mair's *History of Great Britain*, which had been published in Paris in 1521.[3]

The Eneados

There is some uncertainty as to the exact canon of Douglas's writings. In the *Mensioun* of his three principal works that is placed immediately after the translation of book XII of the *Aeneid* Douglas lists the *Eneados* itself, *The Palice of Honour*, and another mysterious translation – 'Of Lundeys Lufe the Remeid' – that has never been identified. There is no doubt, however, as to Douglas's authorship of *The Palice of Honour*, a long and complex allegorical dream poem on the nature of honour and the different methods by which men have sought to attain it. Works with similar titles and themes were fashionable among French poets in the late fifteenth century, but *The Palice of Honour* is more clearly indebted to the native traditions of courtly allegory that stretch from Chaucer and Lydgate to the author of the *Kingis Quair* and other leading Scottish poets, such as Henryson and Dunbar.[4] There is much in *The Palice of Honour* that fore-shadows the *Eneados*: obvious affinities of style and language, for instance, and a deep love of classical poetry, mythology, and history. Ovid, in particular, had a profound influence upon *The Palice of Honour*, and it is significant that many of its descriptive passages are indebted to a contemporary edition of the *Metamorphoses* containing an explanatory commentary by the Italian humanist Raffaello Regio (d. 1520).[5] Douglas's practice here has clear parallels with his later use of Virgilian commentaries in the *Eneados*.

Douglas tells readers much about the origins of the *Eneados* in the distinctive and extremely interesting Prologues that are attached to each book of the translation, along with a series of valedictory epilogues at its conclusion. We learn at the outset that it was written at the request of Henry, Lord Sinclair, whom Douglas describes as a bibliophile and 'fader of bukis', and also 'neir coniunct [i.e. closely related to him] … in blude' (see notes to I.Prol.79–100). Elsewhere in a more jocular passage, also addressed to Sinclair, he humorously links its composition to *The Palice of Honour*, portraying the work as a fulfilment of a promise made there to appease the wrath of the goddess Venus (*Directioun*, 120–39). Far more serious in tone is a later passage, couched in the form of the traditional envoi by a poet to his book. It begins 'Go, wlgar Virgill', and concludes:

---

[3] On the background, see Vergil 1846, I, 105; Hay 1952, 84; and Bawcutt 1976, 30–1 and 46.

[4] References are to the edition of *The Palice of Honour* published in Douglas ed. Bawcutt 2003. For discussion of the Palice's literary background, see the 'Introduction', and 'Review of Scholarship since 1967' in that volume.

[5] First discovered, and discussed in detail by Cairns (1984).

Now salt thou with euery gentill Scot be kend,
And to onletterit folk be red on hight,
That erst was bot with clerkis comprehend.

(*Exclamatioun*, 43–5)

These words are chosen very carefully. 'Wlgar Virgill' signifies Virgil in the vernacular. The work is designed by Douglas not for 'clerkis', such as John Mair and other learned friends, who were proficient in Latin; nor is it written principally for the unlettered, or illiterate, although he seems to have hoped it might be read aloud to them. Douglas is here addressing himself primarily to 'euery gentill Scot', the cultivated readers of his own language, such as Lord Sinclair, who read Chaucer or Dunbar with ease and pleasure, but were less at home in the world of Virgil. (Cf. also I.Prol.321–3; and *Directioun*, 85–8.)

It is from the Prologues that we learn much about Douglas's critical views, not only on specific books of the *Aeneid* but on other literary topics, ranging from the problems of translation to the subtlety and 'fouth', i.e. copiousness, of classical Latin that he regards as the 'maste perfyte langage fyne' (I.Prol.381–2). Douglas was acquainted with the writings of several of the leading Italian humanists, such as Lorenzo Valla, Poggio Bracciolini, and the Neoplatonist Cristoforo Landino. He shared their antipathy to scholastic theology, their belief in the high importance of ancient classical authors, and ambition to return *ad fontes*, which led to the beginnings of textual criticism in the study both of the classics and the Bible. In the early 1500s no major classic, however, had yet been translated into English. The *Eneados* was a pioneering work, a translation of the whole of the *Aeneid*, based directly on the text, not just a selection or abridgement or free re-telling of the story of Aeneas, such as may be found in the popular medieval works that Douglas forcefully challenged: Chaucer's *Legend of Good Women* (I.Prol.340ff.), Caxton's *Eneydos* (I.Prol.138ff.), and Guido delle Colonne's *Historia Destructionis Troiae* (marginal note to I.v.28).

Douglas proudly asserts his fidelity to 'Virgillis text' (I.Prol.299). Yet in the sixteenth century Virgil's text was rather different from that which we read today. The edition that Douglas is thought to have used was published by the scholar-printer Jodocus Badius Ascensius at Paris in 1501. (For details, see the Appendix to the present Introduction, pp. 41–58.) Its text of the *Aeneid* differed from that found in modern editions, both in wording and also in the fact that it was surrounded by a mass of commentary – principally the ancient and revered commentary of Servius, and also the more elementary commentary of Ascensius himself, which combined both elucidation and paraphrase, designed to introduce Virgil to young beginners. Much in the *Eneados* that may seem extraneous to modern readers derives from the lay-out and contents of this edition: the preliminary list of *The Contentis of Euery Buke*; the marginal 'Comment' that accompanies much of book I in the Cambridge manuscript of the work, and provides a learned exposition of the mythology and geography of the *Aeneid* (see discussion below, p. 10); and, most strikingly of all, the so-called Thirteenth book. This continuation of the *Aeneid* was composed by the Italian humanist Maphaeus Vegius (1407–58), and provoked censure as well as praise from his contemporaries, something which is humorously dramatized in Douglas's Prologue XIII. Nonetheless it was commonly included not only by Ascensius but by many other editors of Virgil from 1470 to the seventeenth century.

Douglas attempted to give his readers a taste of the Virgilian scholarship of his age. But his response to the *Aeneid* was far from pedantic, and he writes of Virgil both with admiration and great affection. As a translator he sought to convey something of Virgil's stylististic 'eloquence', drawing, for instance, on the tradition of native alliterative verse to render the battle scenes in the last six books of the *Aeneid*. Douglas is not always successful, of course. His own style is weakened at times by the over-frequent use of trite 'fillers' or catchphrases, designed – as he himself acknowledges (I.Prol.122–4) – to provide a convenient rhyme, or to shorten or lengthen the line of verse. He is also sometimes over-explicit, out of a desire to render the full implications of Virgil's words, and thus sacrifices the compression of his original, simplifying what is daring in Virgil's handling of language. I would argue that Douglas excels when dealing with scenes of pathos – the grief of Dido in book IV, or the babes weeping on the threshold of the Underworld in book VI, or the death of Nisus and Euryalus in book IX – or portraiture, and descriptions of the natural world, such as occur both in the famous Virgilian similes and also the Prologues. The Introduction to this edition, however, is not the place for a detailed evaluation of the literary merits of the *Eneados*. But the Commentary, both to the translation and the Prologues, provides a wealth of information not only on Douglas's use of Ascensius but also his choice of versification, changes of stylistic register, and creative use of allusions to poets whom he particularly admired – Virgil himself, Ovid, Chaucer, and Henryson.

Douglas's After-Life

Douglas made a bold claim for his literary immortality at the end of the *Eneados* (*Conclusio*, 1–12), and he was widely read in both Scotland and England during the sixteenth century (see below, 'Early Reception'). Yet every generation seems to need to make its own version of foreign masterpieces, and very few translations long outlive their first audience. It is striking therefore that interest in Douglas and the *Eneados* persisted throughout later centuries, even at a time when much early Scottish verse was forgotten or little esteemed. Burns's epigraph to *Tam O'Shanter* – 'Off Brownyis and of Bogillis full is this buke' – is an apt and imaginative quotation from Douglas (VI.Prol.18). It suggests that the great Ruddiman edition of the *Eneados* (1710) made an impact not only on scholars, but poets too (see below, 'Later Editions').[6] In the mid-twentieth century the study of medieval and renaissance Scottish history began to experience a remarkable revival, and this has been accompanied by a huge increase of interest in the literature of the same period. The *Eneados* has thus received far more attention from scholars since Coldwell's edition was completed in 1964. A brief analysis of recent critical trends may therefore be useful to readers, particularly those who are new to the work.

Douglas's literary and intellectual inheritance has been discussed by many scholars. He was undoubtedly the most learned and well-read of the early Scottish poets (Bawcutt 1977; Cairns 1984). Among vernacular poets two that he knew best and

---

[6] Geddie 1912 provides a bibliography of Middle Scots poets, but also contains a valuable history of the fluctuations in their reputation. This is supplemented by Scheps and Looney 1986.

valued highly were Chaucer (Bawcutt 1970) and Henryson (Kratzmann 1980, 255–7; Henryson 1981, cix–cx). His relationship to Dunbar is assessed by Lyall (2001), who sees them as joint founders of the 'high style' in later sixteenth-century Scottish poetry. Douglas had an affinity with the French and Burgundian poets of the later fifteenth century, which is particularly evident in *The Palice of Honour*; but there exists nothing to substantiate the old notion that his translation of the *Aeneid* was influenced by *Les Eneydes de Virgille* of Octovien de Saint-Gelais, a manuscript of which was presented to Louis XII in 1501, and printed posthumously in 1509 (despite Calin 2014, 38–9). Nonetheless it provides an interesting French analogue to the *Eneados*, and further comparison of the two works might be rewarding (Scollen 1977; Brückner 1987). Singerman (1986, 217–85) devotes a large proportion of his study of medieval 're-workings' of the *Aeneid* to Douglas, and stresses his debt to Boccaccio's *Genealogia Deorum Gentilium*. His title, *Under Clouds of Poesy*, interestingly echoes line 193 of Douglas's First Prologue. Blyth (1987) places the *Eneados* within the late medieval chivalric tradition: Douglas's Aeneas is for him an exemplar not of the Prince but the ideal Knight. Baswell (1995) provides a valuable context for the *Eneados* in his survey of the varied medieval attitudes to Virgil, but his treatment of Douglas is brief and unsympathetic (276–9). Tudeau-Clayton (1998) examines the significance to Douglas of the commentary on the *Aeneid* by the humanist Cristoforo Landino. The *Eneados* also figures in the chapter devoted to 'narratives of war' in Simpson (2002: 68–120). Simpson contrasts Douglas's translation, which 'revived ideals of imperial conquest' (68), unfavourably with late medieval works in the Guido tradition, such as the alliterative *Destruction of Troy*. Douglas's ideal of fidelity to the text is by him downgraded to a 'philological project'. Wingfield (2014) considers the *Eneados* 'an advisory text' rather than a political commentary on his age (169, 175). For Royan (2016: 561–82), it is a 'key text in classical reception in Britain'.

More specialized topics include Douglas's diction (Bawcutt 1976, 140–63) and 'notably wide-ranging and eclectic' poetic language (Aitken 1983); the significance of the marginal commentary found in the Cambridge manuscript of the *Eneados* (Pinti 1995; Griffiths 2009; Griffiths 2014, 81–102); the early owners of the 1553 printed edition (Bawcutt 2019); and the extent to which Douglas's poetry expresses his identity as a Scottish aristocrat (Canitz 1996; Terrell 2012; Royan 2012; Royan 2017).

The Prologues have long attracted more discussion than any other aspect of the *Eneados*, perhaps because they are thought to contain Douglas's most 'original' poetry (Coldwell, I, 87). Critics debate their general significance, their relation to the books they introduce, and their over-all 'strategy'. Coldwell considered that some represented earlier poems, 'too good to waste', which were 'draped' on the *Eneados* (I, 88). Fox saw them as 'a series of set pieces intended to demonstrate Douglas's competence in writing in various styles on various subjects' (1966, 191). Later critics are more inclined to argue their relevance to individual books, and to find in them an expression of Douglas's aims and principles as a translator (Bawcutt 1976, 161–94). According to Kinneavy (1974), they promulgate his 'awareness of intricacy and complexity in poetry'; for Ross (1986, 393) they form, in association with the translation, 'a unified long poem'; and Canitz (1990) finds a correspondence between prologues and books arising from Douglas's Christian conception of the *Aeneid*. Two critics see the *Eneados* as unified by an analogy between the journey of Aeneas and that of the poet-narrator, who re-creates the classical text as a 'heroic achievement' (Ebin 1980; Wilson 2012). Fowler (1977 and 2005) finds unity of a different sort in the Prologues, arguing that they have a partly 'calendrical' structure, based on the cyclic progression of the year.

Some Prologues have been singled out for special attention. Prologue IV, for Coldwell (I, 92), was little more than 'a competent exercise in late medieval rhetoric'. Others have found it more complex (Bawcutt 1969; Norton-Smith 1980; Bawcutt 1982). Archibald (1989) discerns 'ambivalence' in Douglas's view of love and also of Dido. A more recent trend is to represent Douglas as a crude misogynist. According to Desmond (1994, 187), Prologue IV 'presents a judgmental reading of Dido: nowhere is the reader invited to sympathize with her plight'. She asserts further that Douglas's 'translation-practices' are shaped by anti-feminist discourse (193). Baswell too considers that Douglas turns the story of Dido into 'a rather disconnected *exemplum* about lust and unregulated love' (1995, 279). Simpson (2002, 91–2) follows this line, and bizarrely states: 'A need to victimize women seems to drive Douglas's own poetic mission'. Such views, however, are challenged by Gray (2000, 115) and Bawcutt (2006, 190–3), who find Douglas's response to Dido compassionate as well as critical. Prologue VIII was long neglected by critics, but receives an interesting analysis from Parkinson (1987), who speaks of its 'Langlandian manner' and 'disturbing interplay of morality and farce'.

Prologues VII, XII and XIII were in the past commonly grouped together as Nature poems, but the notion that they simply portray 'nature for its own sake, as an exercise in realism' is dismissed by Starkey (1973–4, 82–3), and other critics, such as Blyth (1970), or Bawcutt (1976, 175–90). Leahy (2016), however, argues that the depiction of landscape in *The Palice of Honour* 'matured' into the naturalism of the Prologues. Prologue XIII is today rarely treated as a 'nature prologue', but receives more attention for the light it throws on Douglas's critical attitudes. Ross (1981) questions the validity of Douglas's term for Maphaeus Vegius's poem as a 'Christian work'. Pinti (1993) sees Douglas as participating in dialogue not only with Vegius but Virgil, 'distinguishing himself from both ... to his own authorial advantage'. Pinti (1996) takes a similarly Bakhtinian 'multi-voiced' approach to the *Eneados* as a whole: its additions 'highlight the translator's business of orchestrating voices in dialogue' (120). Ghosh (1995, 5) writes of the 'critical duality' underlying Douglas's ostensibly ironized decision to translate the thirteenth book. Cummings (1995) questions why Douglas proceeded 'with a project of which he was suspicious' and considers that he was 'more comfortable with Vegius than with Virgil' (146).

Gray (2000, 114) has suggested that 'nowadays we tend ... to over-privilege the Prologues', partly because 'we have become so interested in [Douglas's] self-consciousness as poet'. In a series of important articles he has to some extent redressed the balance, and provided a sympathetic yet searching assessment of Douglas's powers as a translator. Gray (2000) examines his response to the patterns of imagery and other visual qualities of the *Aeneid*. Gray (2001) is devoted primarily to Aeneas, and argues that 'Douglas does justice to the complexity of Virgil's hero' (32). Gray (2006) stresses his ability as a story-teller: the *Eneados* is 'eminently readable', and 'moves with enormous verve' (159). Gray (2012) explores a less often studied aspect of Douglas, his religious writings, and notes the poetic power of Prologue X, and its 'sheer precision of expression' (89).

Douglas's impact on later poets, particularly in the sixteenth century, continues to receive attention. The indebtedness of the Earl of Surrey's translations of *Aeneid* II and IV to the *Eneados* is illustrated by Ridley (1961 and 1963), but important stylistic differences between Douglas and Surrey are discussed by Emrys Jones (Surrey 1964), Bawcutt (1974), and Kratzmann (1980, 169–89). More recently critics have noted the influence of the *Eneados* upon Scottish poets from the reign of James VI (Bawcutt 1995; Rutledge 2007). It is pleasing that a few twentieth-century poets have also shown an enthusiasm for the *Eneados*. The most famous of these is Ezra Pound, who notoriously claimed, in *How to Read* (1931), that Douglas's translation was better than the original (Thomas 1980). The Scottish poet and critic Edwin Morgan suggests that Douglas's appeal to Pound lay in his 'concreteness' (2000, 95), and elsewhere he contrasts Douglas and Drummond of Hawthornden as translators (1977). W. H. Auden's continuing interest in Douglas, as in other early Scottish poets, is well demonstrated by Leahy (2015 and 2017).

The Text of the *Eneados*

The Witnesses

According to *The Tyme, space and dait of the translatioun*, Douglas completed the *Eneados* on 22 July 1513; elsewhere he often pictures himself at work in his chamber, with a copy of Virgil lying before him on a lectern (VII.Prol.143), or taking out his 'scriptour', a small portable writing case (XII.Prol.305). On each occasion it is early in the morning, before he celebrates mass, or commences the other duties of a busy churchman. Unfortunately Douglas's autograph of the *Eneados* is not extant, but five manuscripts of the complete text survive, dating from the first half of the sixteenth century, together with the fragments of a sixth, and an edition printed in London and dated 1553.

The witnesses are described here in the order of their assumed chronology. Only the three latest can be dated precisely: the Lambeth Manuscript (1545/6), the Bath Manuscript (1547), and the print (1553). The dating of the other manuscripts is more conjectural. The priority of the Cambridge Manuscript largely rests on the scribe's statement that it is 'the first correk coppy nixt efter the translation'; the presence of Dunkeld in the list of Douglas's benefices mentioned in the title-page indicates that it was written after 1515, when he was formally presented to the see of Dunkeld. The watermarks, however, might suggest a later date in the early 1520s. A *terminus ad quem* for the Elphinstoun Manuscript is implied by the date of 1527 placed beside an early owner's inscription. There is little conclusive to date the Ruthven manuscript, except that it must have been written after Douglas's death in 1522, since the title-page describes him as 'vmquhile' (formerly) bishop of Dunkeld. Coldwell considered it 'probably contemporaneous with the Elphinstoun'.[7]

---

[7] *Selections* ed. Coldwell 1964, p. xxii. There has been remarkably little discussion of the dating of these manuscripts. See, however, Coldwell, I, 106; and the brief introduction to Bennett 1938a. Bennett's pioneering thesis has long been unknown to scholars, through a

The Cambridge Manuscript (C)

Cambridge, Trinity College Library, MS O.3.12.

Earlier accounts are found in Small, I, clxxii–clxxiii; James 1902, no. 1184; Coldwell, I, 96–7. A digitized text is now available at https://mss-cat.trin.cam.ac.uk/manuscripts/.

The manuscript contains 330 folios, with extra leaves at the beginning (numbered by Coldwell i–vi) and at the end (vii–x). The binding, which has a stamped pattern of lozenges and flowers, and the remains of brass clasps, contains vellum leaves from service books of the twelfth century. At the base of the first vellum leaf (verso) is written: 'My hart is lenit one the land in lugyne with my lade dere / My body is one the see saland with sorofull hart and seghin so sore'. This forms the opening of an attractive song popular in the sixteenth century: it is mentioned in *The Complaynt of Scotland*, and other texts (one with a musical setting) are known.[8] On the left margin also occurs a version of a common pious couplet: 'In my begynning god me speid / in grace and vertew to [?proceid]' (*NIMEV* 430.5 and 1507.88). This is followed by a third line: 'to lerne to urit (write) I haue greit neid'. There are further pious inscriptions and what appear to be later library numbers on leaf i: 'IHS Heyre begynnis the litill buyk Iesus marea amen Ihus marya.' No. 317. H.3. O.10.17 (cancelled); O.3.12; and at the foot of leaf vi occurs '3e ar my hart'. On the final vellum leaf are notes in Latin. Running down the space between the columns of text, on the verso, is written 'in my begynnyng'.

Folios 1r–330r contain a complete text of the *Eneados*. It is written in one hand, which, although termed 'ugly' by M. R. James, is clear and legible, and laid out with care, in order to aid the navigation of such a large volume. The size of page is 11.5 × 8 inches. Large decorative initial letters, some illuminated in yellow, red, and blue, signal the main divisions of the text, such as books and chapters and sections of Prologue I. There are running titles, usually in red, the chapter headings are numbered, and there is occasional light punctuation. Coldwell notes at least five types of watermark (I, 96–7): '(1) crown on rosette, Briquet 6407, occurring at Paris in 1523–1524, Cologne 1521–1534, Edinburgh 1525, and Rouen 1527; (2) hand, like Briquet 10657 or 10658; (3) hand, Briquet 10659; (4) hand, like Briquet 11169; (5) so faint as to be indistinguishable'.

Fol. 1r contains an informative title-page:

> Heyr begynnys the proloug of Virgyll / prynce of Latyn poetis In hys twelf bukis / of Eneados compilit and translatit furth of / Latyn in our Scottis langage by ane Right nobill / and wirschipfull clerk Master Gawyn Dowglas / provest of Sanct Gylys kyrk in Edinburgh and / person of Lyntoun in Louthiane quhilk eftyr / was bischop of Dunkeld.

Above this is an inscription in italic: 'Iohannes Danyelston Rector a Dysert'. A colophon, immediately beneath Douglas's *Conclusio* (fol. 326v), reads:

> Heir endis the thretteyn and final buke of Eneados quhilk is the first correk coppy nixt efter the translation wrytin be master matho geddes scribe or writar to the translatar.

---

mistaken reference to its author under her maiden name (Edith Bannister) by Coldwell, I, 139; and by her then husband J. A. W. Bennett, in Bennett 1946, 84.

[8] For the full details, see Bawcutt 2002, 193–7.

These words are most plausibly interpreted as those of Matthew Geddes himself, who here stresses both the accuracy of what he has written – it is 'the first correk coppy' – and its closeness to Douglas's original – 'nixt efter the translation'.[9] (Coldwell, I, 106, indeed claims its 'pre-eminence as presumably the author's personal copy'.) It seems likely that Matthew Geddes is the man who was listed as 'Matheus Geddes, pauper' among the *Determinantes* of St Andrews University in 1495–6 (*Acta Facultatis* 1964, II, 254). If so, he would have been similar in age to Douglas, and might have first met him when both studied at St Andrews. It is not known when Geddes entered Douglas's service, but they were co-witnesses to a charter in Edinburgh on 6 March 1511/12.[10] The strongest evidence of their closeness to each other is provided by Douglas's will, of which Geddes was an executor, and in which he received various bequests. He is there termed *magister*, chaplain, and vicar of Tibbermore, a mensal church of Dunkeld, which he probably held through Douglas's patronage.[11]

One of the distinctive features of the Cambridge Manuscript is the presence of a marginal commentary that accompanies Prologue I and the first ten chapters of book I (fols 3r–22v). Coldwell considered that this commentary was written in Douglas's 'own hand', saying that he had compared it with Douglas's surviving correspondence (I, 97). But most of these letters were written by a secretary, and those that are indeed Douglas's autographs were personal documents written in mental turmoil and, as he himself says, 'in haste'.[12] To me the greater part of the marginal commentary appears to be written in the same careful hand as the text itself, and in the same colour of ink. It was certainly composed by Douglas, however, and provides a sustained and learned exposition of mythological, historical, and geographical features in the *Aeneid* that has much in common with the Prologues.[13] References to 'my Palyce of Honour' (I.i.13n), 'my proheme' (I.iii.92n), and 'my prologue of the x buyk' (I.v.2n) are authorial, not those of a scribe or later reader. It is highly probable that these notes represent a work mentioned by Douglas himself in the *Directioun* of the *Eneados* to his patron, Henry, Lord Sinclair:

> I haue alsso a schort comment compilyt
> To expon strange histouris and termys wild.
> And gif ocht lakis mar, quhen that is doyn,
> At ȝour desyre it salbe writtyn soyn.

> (141–4)

These notes are indeed expository, and also 'schort' – covering only a fraction of the *Eneados*. Lines 143–4 suggest Douglas's willingness to add more, but they were possibly never completed because of Sinclair's death at the battle of Flodden on 9 September 1513. My assumption is that they were written after Douglas had finished the translation, and presumably existed for a while on loose sheets. They must have

---

[9] Beal, however, takes the colophon to mean that this manuscript was a copy of that written by Geddes (1980, 3–5).

[10] *Register of the Great Seal*, III, no. 2988. This contains confirmation of the earlier charter.

[11] For Douglas's will, see Small, I, cxix–cxxv.

[12] On Douglas's letters, see Bawcutt 1996. For a facsimile, see Beal 1980, I, plate XI.

[13] For further discussion, see Bawcutt 1976, 86–7, 107–10; Pinti 1995, and Griffiths 2014, 81–102.

been added to this manuscript only after the copying of the text itself had been completed. Where there are only a few on the page, they are placed inside decorative red scrolls, but sometimes the notes are so detailed and copious that they not only occupy the wide outer margins of the page, but have to be squeezed above and below the text. (For an illustration, see the frontispiece to this volume.)

Not all the notes that occur in the margins of Prologue I, however, were written by the scribe. Four of them – to lines 137, 192, 263, and 283 – are in blacker ink, and written in a markedly different rather untidy hand. Jane Griffiths, in a recent article, pointed out that they 'have an exact counterpart' in four notes that are printed at the same points in the 1553 edition. She noted their 'summarizing function', and suggested that their presence might prove that 'the Copland glossator had access to the Trinity manuscript' (Griffiths 2009, 193). To me this seems unlikely. This manuscript is likely to have remained in the possession of its early owner, John Danielston, until his death in 1547, but the 1553 print was certainly available to readers in Scotland, not only in England. It seems more probable that the comments were added to this manuscript by someone who had compared it with the print. There is a slight parallel in the sixteenth-century marginalia added to the National Library of Scotland's copy of the 1579 *Palice of Honour*; many of these appear to derive from comparison with a copy of the London edition of the same work (Douglas ed. Bawcutt 2003, xix and 244–5).

Two other notes – to I Prologue 425 and 437 (fol. 7r and v) – are written in a small and untidy hand. These notes are particularly interesting, because they criticize Douglas's 'argument' and speak of him in the third person: 'Heir he argouis better than befoir'. They challenge Douglas's defence of the conduct of Aeneas, and show a strong partiality towards 'sweit Dido'. They are most plausibly interpreted as a reader's deeply engaged response to the text.[14]

There are many other brief marginal annotations later in the Cambridge Manuscript, most of which were recorded by Coldwell in his 'Appendix: Variant Readings'. These have considerable interest, yet have so far received little attention from scholars. A few of them are written in hands that differ from those of the scribe, and would appear to be the work of readers. There are several instances of *Nota* – e.g. at X.viii.73, X.viii.151, XIII.iii.39. The most important of these marginalia, however, are written in the same hand as the text itself, and their nature suggests that their origin is authorial. They mostly consist of single words, sometimes but not invariably prefixed by *or*, the word in the text often being underlined. These are not explanatory glosses nor emendations, but rather substitutions or alternative readings. They apparently show Douglas in the process of composition, hesitating over the choice of a word. One of the most common motives seems a wish to avoid a clumsy repetition. Thus where the Cambridge MS reads 'Ida forest ... / Thar best belovyt forest' (X.iii.93–4), a note to the second use of *forest* replaces it by *wod*. Similar motivation would seem to underlie the tentative substitution of *breistis* for *pappys* in XI.xi.88, *braid* for *stalwart* in XI.xii.105, and *all creatur* for *euerything* in XIII.Prol.45. Sometimes Douglas apparently wishes to vary the alliteration in a line; so *schap* is substituted for *port* in VI.iv.84: 'Terribill of port and schameful hir presence'. Elsewhere

---

[14] Less possibly these might be read as scribal; so Bawcutt 1976, 108.

Douglas seems to hesitate over whether to introduce an apt but extremely rare word. Thus beside '3on ilk Troiane banyst of Asya' (XII.i.36) is the marginal note *or forhowar*. This noun, meaning 'forsaker' and replacing *banyst*, is an excellent translation of Virgil's *desertorem* (12.15), and Douglas uses the etymologically related verb *forhow* elsewhere in the *Eneados* at VII.vi.21. These are precisely the sort of unusual and archaic words that Douglas often favoured, but he may have wondered whether they would be understood by all readers.

These later marginalia further differ from the Commentary in that they are not wholly peculiar to the Cambridge Manuscript. Most have some kind of equivalent in the other witnesses. I consider that they must have been present in β, the lost intermediate manuscript that Coldwell (see below, p. 23) posits as the ancestor of E, R, L, B, and 53. Sometimes they are recorded as marginal notes, exactly as in the Cambridge Manuscript, but more frequently the other scribes seem to have thought they should be incorporated into the text of the translation. This is the case with *forhowar*, which occurs as a marginal note in L and B, but is part of the text in E, R, and 53. A further illustration is the word *gnawyng*, which in C appears as a marginal alternative to *rungyng* (III.vi.78), but is adopted into the text in other witnesses (E, R, L, B, and 53). (See also editorial commentary to X.xi.39 on *imperiall*.) An extreme example is a rather clumsy quatrain explaining the patronymic *Atrides*: this appears as a marginal note at I.vii,70, in C and also in L and B, but is incorporated into the text of E. It might seem unlikely that Douglas would wish to include such a pedantic piece of verse in the translation, but he does this elsewhere in the *Eneados*. Very occasionally the scribes of other manuscripts seem to have been puzzled as to Douglas's intentions, and rather than choosing between one or other word they included both. The phrase 'Latyn rout' (IX.ix.54) is accompanied in C by the marginal note 'Turnus': in four of the other witnesses this is incorporated into the text as 'Turnus rout', but R's 'Turnus Latin rout' conflates both terms. When translating a line describing Charon's boat, Douglas seems to have hesitated over three possibilities for rendering Virgil's *sutilis* (*Aeneid* 6.14). C's text reads: 'Gan grane or geig full fast the saymyt barge' (VI.vi.62). *Saymyt* is the technical nautical term 'seamed', but above the line is written *ionyt*, 'joined', and in the outer margin occurs *or sewit*, 'stitched together'. The two latter words are both preserved in R's 'ionit or sewit barge'.

The first known owner of the Cambridge Manuscript was John Danielston (the name is also often spelt Deniston), whose signature appears at the top of fol. 1. Danielston was an educated man, who became rector of Dysart in 1531, and archdeacon of Dunblane in 1542, but – to judge from the official correspondence of James V – he was not in holy orders. It is likely that he spent little time in Dysart, since he was a member of the royal household, serving as a *cubicular*, or gentleman of the bedchamber. On 8 February 1540/41 the king made a grant of property in Linlithgow to Danielston and his heirs, and in 1542 Danielston supervised the strengthening of the fortifications of Blackness Castle, near the palace of Linlithgow. He is also known to have acted as one of the Auditors of the Exchequer.[15] Such activities suggest that his interests were secular rather than deeply spiritual, an impression also conveyed by

---

[15] For documentary evidence concerning John Danielston, see *Letters of James V* 1954, 190, 196, 374 and 445; *Register of the Great Seal* III, no. 2274; *Laing Charters* 1899, nos 493 (p. 130) and 526 (p. 138); Thomas 2005, 19, 166, 202 and 227; Murray 1996, 113, 115.

his surviving books, which are not works of abstruse theology but include printed copies of Polydore Vergil, an Epitome of Livy, and Cassiodorus.[16] John Danielston is thought to have died in 1547, when he was succeeded in the benefices of Dysart and Dunblane by a kinsman called Robert Danielston, who may perhaps have also inherited his books, including this manuscript. Nothing is known for certain of its later history, however, until it was acquired by Thomas Gale (1635–1702), dean of York Minster and a learned antiquary, whose large library was bequeathed to Trinity College, Cambridge, by his son Roger Gale (1672–1744).[17] M. R. James noted, interestingly, that 'various manuscripts of Scottish origin' in Class O of Trinity's collection were originally owned by the sixteenth-century Scottish lawyer Henry Scrymgeour. Scrymgeour's manuscripts were bequeathed to his nephew Sir Peter Young; many later passed to his son Patrick Young, librarian to Prince Henry, King James, and Charles I, part of whose collection is known to have been acquired by Thomas Gale.[18]

The Elphinstoun Manuscript (E)

Edinburgh, Edinburgh University Library, MS Dk.7.49.

For earlier accounts, see Small, I, clxxiii–clxxv; Coldwell, I, 97–8; and Lindsay ed. Hamer 1931–6, IV, 8–11.

Edinburgh University Library, Dk.7.49 is a composite, containing two independent sections, separately foliated in a later hand, written at different dates, and probably bound together some time after 1566. The Elphinstoun Manuscript is the first of these parts: it contains a complete text of the *Eneados* (fols 2r–367v), but now lacks any equivalent of a title-page such as is found in the other witnesses. The paper has one watermark throughout both sections: a hand surmounted by a star, in the wrist a fleur de lys and the initials I B. The size of page is 11 × 7.9 inches. Prologue I starts on fol. 2r, above which (in a later hand) is a prayer 'Iesus Iesus Iesus esto mihi Iesus', and at the foot 'W ~ Hay 1527'. The second section of the manuscript, which has a title-page dated 1566, contains texts of Sir David Lindsay's *Monarche* and several of his shorter poems (fols 1r–144v). At the end of this part (fol. 146r–v) is a seventeenth-century verse addition, beginning 'What can confine mans wandring thought'. This has been identified as two Choruses from William Alexander's *Croesus* (Bawcutt 2008, 101–2).

The name of the Elphinstoun Manuscript derives from an inscription at the end of the work: 'Opere finito sit laus et gloria Christo &c. / I. E. / m Iohannes Elphinstoun / M Ioannes Elphynstoun' (fol. 367v). (The two versions of this name appear to be written in different hands.) Elphinstoun's initials I E occur elsewhere in the manuscript, e.g. fols 305v and 341v. At the end of book XIII (fol. 364v) occurs 'quod bocardo et baroco', an apparently jocular use of mnemonics for modes of logic (Small, I, clxxiv; *OED, baroko, bocardo*). Small assumed that Elphinstoun transcribed the whole manuscript, but recent scholars have noted the presence of several hands. It is possible that John Elphinstoun should be regarded as the owner rather than

---

[16] On Danielston's books, see Durkan and Ross 1961, 87–8 and 174.
[17] Gale's ownership of this manuscript was mentioned in William Nicolson's *Scottish Historical Library* (1702). On his distinction as an antiquary, see Duncan 1965, 52–3.
[18] See James 1902, Preface, pp. x–xi, and note on no. 1304 (MS O.5.23).

simply the scribe. He is probably to be identified with the man of this name who was a canon of Aberdeen Cathedral and prebendary of Invernochtie in the middle of the sixteenth century. This John Elphinstoun is recorded as one of a group of 'uenerabiles et egregios uiros' in a document dated 1542, and appears as a witness in another document dated 1547; the same man is likely to have been the prior of Monymusk between 1543 and 1562.[19] It is possible though not certain that this is the same John Elphinstoun who owned a printed copy of Caesar that once belonged to William Elphinstoun, bishop of Aberdeen.[20]

Fol. 1r contains the names of two early owners: Master William Hay, parson of Turriff in Aberdeenshire, and David Anderson, burgess of Aberdeen: 'This buik partinis to dauid andersone burges of Abirdene. be gift of Mr Wm Hay person of turreff. 1563.' Hay's name occurs elsewhere in the manuscript: 'W ~ Hay 1527' (fol. 2r), and 'M. Willelmi Hay' (fol. 62r). He should not be confused with a more famous bearer of the name, who was the friend of Hector Boece and second principal of King's College, Aberdeen. But this William Hay was also an educated churchman, with an interest in collecting books. Like John Elphinstoun, with whom his name is associated in at least one document, he was a canon of Aberdeen Cathedral; he was also rector of Turriff between the dates of 17 June 1551 and 10 Feb 1575.[21] William Hay carefully recorded his ownership of other books, signing them – e.g. 'M. W. Hay a turref 1548' – and sometimes employing a distinctive block stamp or adding a personal motto such as 'patiar'.[22] But these works differ from the Elphinstoun Manuscript in several respects: all are printed books; they are in Latin, not the vernacular; and their subject matter is predominantly liturgical and theological. Their dates suggest that they belong to the latter years of his life, and one wonders whether the possession of the *Eneados* in 1527 reflects Hay's youthful literary tastes, and the later gift of it to David Anderson reveals changed reading habits. Anderson's name occurs again in the second part of the manuscript (e.g. at fols 144v and 145v). He was a prominent and long-lived citizen of Aberdeen, who figures repeatedly in its sixteenth-century burgh records as baillie, dean of guild and master of works at St Nicholas Church, but seems not otherwise noted for his literary interests.[23]

Nothing is known of the manuscript's later history until the seventeenth century when it was owned by the Aikman family of Cairnie, Forfarshire. John Aikman, who donated the manuscript to Edinburgh University Library in 1692 was probably the son of William Aikman of Cairnie (1646–99), laird and advocate, and the elder brother of the portrait-painter William Aikman (1682–1731).[24]

[19] First suggested by Watt (1920, 136); more details are discussed by Wingfield in an unpublished article: 'Gavin Douglas's *Eneados* and its Circle of Scribes, Owners and Readers'. See also Higgitt 2006, 51–2; *Registrum Episcopatus Aberdonensis* 1845, II, 319; Watt and Shead 2001, 158.

[20] See Durkan and Ross 1961, 73. Cf. also Durkan 2006, lxix and note 27; and Durkan and Ross 1961, 164.

[21] See *Registrum Episcopatus Aberdonensis*, I, 456 (for 1552); and Haws 1972, 240.

[22] See Durkan and Ross 1961, 114–15; Durkan 2006, lxvii–lxviii; Takamiya and Linenthal 2014, 178–90.

[23] See *Extracts from the Council Register of the Burgh of Aberdeen* 1844, passim.

[24] See Rosalind Marshall, 'William Aikman of Cairnie 1682–1731', *ODNB*. John Aikman

The Ruthven Manuscript (R)

Edinburgh, Edinburgh University Library, MS Dc.1.43.

For earlier descriptions, see Small, I, clxxv–clxxvi; and Coldwell, I, 98. Denton Fox provides further information in his editions of Henryson's *Testament of Cresseid* (London, 1968), pp. 7–9, and 131, and *The Poems of Robert Henryson* (Oxford, 1981), p. xcvii.

The *Eneados* occupies fols 2r–300v; the size of page is 13.2 × 8.8 inches. The paper is unwatermarked, and the chapters are not numbered. Fol. 2r contains a title very much shorter than that in the Cambridge Manuscript. It corrects the number of books to 'xiii', omits any mention of Douglas's earlier benefices, and replaces 'our Scottis langage' by 'Inglis':

> Here begynnys the buke of Virgile contenand in the self xiii bukis translatit out of Latyne in Inglis be ane reuerend fader in god gawane douglas bischop vmquhile of dunkeld.

The manuscript contains other verse added by later hands. On fol. 1r is a Scottish love poem, beginning 'As Phebus brycht in speir merediane', a shorter version of which occurs in the Bannatyne Manuscript, fol. 230v (*Bannatyne Manuscript* 1928–32, III, 305–7).[25] Fol. 301v contains a version of the opening three stanzas of *The Testament of Cresseid*. A transcript and discussion were first published in Fox's edition of *The Testament*, pp. 7–9, and 131. On fol. 1v are several lines of Latin verse written in a small, neat but very faded script. These were ignored by previous editors, but have been identified by Emily Wingfield as three extracts from Julius Caesar Scaliger's *Epidorpides*, a large collection of moral epigrams first published posthumously in 1573 (Wingfield 2016). These pieces differ interestingly from the additions of Scottish verse. Sententious and hortatory, they instruct how one should live virtuously – *mane accinge, vespere examina … Te tum incipias noscere* – and are the choice of a learned reader with humanist literary tastes.

The text of the *Eneados* is written in one clear large hand, but the scribe is not named nor the manuscript dated, although there are several pointers to its ownership. Fol. 1v contains the inscription 'W DNS Ruthen', i.e. William Lord Ruthven; a facsimile is provided in Small, I, clxxv. At the top of fol. 1r are pen trials that are not easy to decipher, but they include a copy of the opening lines of Prologue I and what appears to be the draft of a letter, beginning 'Rycht honorabill schir … Lord Drummond'. Fol. 301v contains the inscription: 'Partenet Wilhelmo / domino de Ruthven', along with a sketch of the Ruthven arms and the family motto 'Deid schaw'. At the top of the page is written the name 'Patrik Drummond'.

Most scholars follow Small in assuming that the manuscript's owner was William, fourth Lord Ruthven, born around 1543, who became Lord Ruthven in 1566 and Earl of Gowrie in 1581, and was executed in 1584. According to Fox, the 'Italianate signature' on fol. 1v resembles the signature of the fourth Lord Ruthven found in other works,

---

also donated to the library a thirteenth-century Anglo-Norman *Historia Scholastica* (MS D.b.1.4): see Wingfield, 'Gavin Douglas's *Eneados*', and Borland 1916, no. 17.

[25] First noted and described by Bennett 1938a, 2.

and this is supported by the further research of Emily Wingfield.[26] Fox considers that the inscription on fol. 301v, however, is in a different hand. It is worth noting that an earlier and less notorious member of the family also bore the name William: William, second Lord Ruthven, who succeeded to the title in 1528 and died in 1552. His daughter Lilias Ruthven married David, second Lord Drummond (d. 1571), and their son Patrick became the third Lord Drummond (c. 1552–1602).[27] The various references in the manuscript to William, Lord Ruthven, Lord Drummond and Patrick Drummond might perhaps be best explained not in terms of a single owner but rather by a shared family ownership: the manuscript may have been owned by different generations of the Ruthvens, and then passed via Lilias Ruthven to the Drummonds.[28] It was donated to Edinburgh University Library in 1643 (Coldwell, I, 98).

Coldwell noted a high number of 'unfortunate mistakes' in this manuscript. Some were probably accidental, caused by the scribe's unfamiliarity with classical allusions and the Latinate vocabulary: so 'happy' for Harpy (III.vi.27), or 'inhabitatioun' for inhibition (X.i.22); or 'invisible' for invincible (X.v.68). In one case, however, there occurs what seems a deliberate and anachronistic re-writing of the text. Among the followers of Mark Antony at the great naval battle of Actium Douglas mentions:

> The 3ondermast pepill clepit Bractanys
> Quhilk neir the est part of the warld remanys.

> (VIII.xii.31–2; = *Aeneid* 8, 687–8)

The Ruthven scribe, however, substitutes *britanys* and *west* for *Bractanys* and *est*.

The Lambeth Manuscript (L)

London, Lambeth Palace Library, MS 117.

For brief earlier accounts of this manuscript, see Small, I, clxxvi–clxxvii; Coldwell, I, 98–9; and Robinson 2003, I, 44, and vol. II, plate 258 (of fol. 193v). An excellent description by Richard Palmer occurs in the on-line Catalogue of Lambeth Palace Manuscripts (2010), MS 117 (https://www.lambethpalacelibrary.org/).

The text of the *Eneados* occupies fols 1–426. The size of page is 11.9 × 8.2 inches. The manuscript appears to be written in one hand, although the colour of the ink varies. Coldwell (II, 245) suggests that the contents list is in 'a different (?) hand', and identifies the one watermark as Briquet 12661. The title page is verbally almost identical with that of the Cambridge Manuscript. The manuscript has an informative colophon: 'Heir endis the buke of virgill writtin be the hand of Iohanne mudy with maister

---

[26] See Henryson ed. Fox 1968, 8, who refers to J. G. Nichols, *Autographs of … Remarkable Personages* (1829), plate 33, no. 17; *Laing Charters* 1899, no. 125; and Wingfield, 'Gavin Douglas's *Eneados*'.

[27] On the Ruthven family, see *Scots Peerage*, IV, 254 ff; Mary Black Verschuur, 'Ruthven, William, second Lord Ruthven (b.before 1513, d.1552)', *ODNB*; and Sharon Adams, 'Ruthven, William, fourth Lord Ruthven (c.1543–1584)', *ODNB*.

[28] On David, second Lord Drummond, and Patrick Drummond, see *Scots Peerage*, VII, 45–7. On Lilias Ruthven, see *Scots Peerage*, IV, 260; and *Ruthven Family Papers* ed. Cowan 1912, pp. 51ff. and 160–1.

thomas bellenden of auchinovll Iustis Clerke and endit the 2° febrii Anno[rum] etc. xlv' (fol. 426v). A similar inscription on fol. 396v confirms the date of completion as 2 February 1545/6, and uses the same slightly ambiguous preposition, *with*, to link the persons involved in making the manuscript: 'writtin be me Iohnne mudy with mayster thomas bellenden Iustus clerk'. 'I M', the initials of John Mudy, who appears to be the principal scribe, occur on the title page and elsewhere in the manuscript (fols 1r; 9v; 22v; 359v).

John Mudy is likely to be the man of that name who was active as a public notary and witness to various legal transactions in Edinburgh during the first half of the sixteenth century.[29] Thomas Bellenden of Auchnoull is very much better known: serving as Justice Clerk from 1539 to 1546, he was a counsellor to James V and one of the principal law officers of Scotland. What part he played in compiling this manuscript, however, is unclear. It seems unlikely that such a distinguished man would have been its copyist, and he was in any case old and possibly very ill in 1546, the year in which he is thought to have died.[30] Richard Palmer suggests that Mudy 'served under' Bellenden. Interestingly, Bellenden knew Douglas personally, having acted as a witness in 1520 to the contract between Douglas and Elizabeth Auchinleck, widow of his brother William.[31] One might wonder if Bellenden himself possessed a manuscript of the *Eneados*, and wished to have a further copy made. He is not otherwise noted for an interest in poetry, apart from his brief report in 1540 to William Eure, the English commissioner on the Border, concerning the interlude performed before James V at Linlithgow, which has some resemblance to Lindsay's *Satyre of the Three Estates*.[32]

No Scottish owner of this manuscript is known. The inscription 'Edmund Ashefeyld 1596' occurs on fol. 1v, but this person has not been definitely identified. Several Englishmen with this name are known from the reign of Elizabeth, who were educated at Cambridge or Oxford, or members of the Inns of Court (Venn 1922–54, I, 45; Foster 1891, I, 35). Of these perhaps the most likely to have owned the Lambeth Manuscript, since he showed an interest in Scottish affairs, is the Edmund Ashfield who matriculated at St Mary Hall, Oxford, in 1584. He was a Catholic who corresponded with James VI, and in 1599 made a disastrous mission to Scotland, in the course of which the Governor of Berwick, Lord Willoughby, instigated his kidnap and forcible return to England.[33] Some time after 1596 the manuscript was acquired by George Abbot (1562–1633), Archbishop of Canterbury and one of the translators of the King James Bible. According to Palmer, it is listed in the catalogue of his books as: 'Dowglas, Gawin his translation of Virgil's Aenead. MS. fol'. After Abbot's death

---

[29] Mudy is described on 16 April 1530 as a notary and 'presbyter of Glasgow diocese': *Laing Charters* ed. Anderson 1899, no. 380 (p. 100). See also *Protocol Book of John Foular 1514–1528*, nos 160, 222, and 413; and *Protocol Book of John Foular 1528–1534*, no. 252.

[30] See *Scots Peerage*, II, 63; cf. John Finlay's article on his son, Sir John Bellenden of Auchnoull, who succeeded him as Justice Clerk in 1546: 'Bellenden, Sir John, of Auchnoul (d. 1576)', *ODNB*.

[31] See Bawcutt 1976, 20 and note 139, 25 and note 14; Fraser 1885, III, 221.

[32] For the details, see Lindsay ed. Hamer 1931–6, II, 1–6, and IV, 125–9.

[33] For details of this murky event, see *Calendar ... England and Scotland* 1894–6, II, 607–18; and *Calendar ... Mary, Queen of Scots* 1969, xx–xxi, 499ff. and 1128–30.

in 1633 it was presented to Lambeth Palace Library, which had been founded by his predecessor Richard Bancroft (1544–1610).

The Bath Manuscript (B)

This manuscript is owned by the Marquess of Bath, and preserved in the Library at Longleat House, Warminster, Wiltshire (MS 252 A). Its former shelfmark IX.D.54 is late seventeenth or early eighteenth century, closely contemporary with the 1702 catalogue in which the manuscript is first recorded. For earlier accounts, see Small, I, clxxvii; Coldwell, I, 99–100.

The *Eneados* occupies fols 3 to 365. The size of page is 11.6 × 7.6 inches. 'The main watermarks are (1) a hand (with a bracelet and very large little finger) surmounted by a five-petalled flower, and (2) a crowned urn with two bands around the broadest part. The MS. is in one hand, in faded brown ink (a darker ink is used from III, iii to IX, i. The capitals are elaborate, and some are embellished with (later?) grotesque faces and feathers. Chapter headings and some corrections have been added in darker ink' (Coldwell, I, 100). According to Dr Kate Harris, Curator of Longleat Historic Collections, 'the leather roll stamped panel binding is probably contemporary with the manuscript. The spine, most of which survives, has been mounted – the repair looks to be nineteenth century, as do the brown paper pastedowns and possibly the pair of brass clasps on the front edge of the boards. The spine has the remains of what could be an eighteenth century red morocco label. The binding is sewn on five bands'.[34]

The wording of the title-page (fol.3) is identical, apart from spelling, with that of the Cambridge MS:

> Heir begynnys the proloug off /Virgill prince of Latyne poetis In / his twelf bukis of Eneados compilit / and translatit furth of Latyn in our / scottis langage by ane rycht noble / and wirschipfull clerk master gawin / douglas provest of Sanct gelys kirk / in Edinburgh and persoun of Lyntoun / in Louthiane Quhilk eftir was bischope of dunkeld.

The colophon repeats this information, with the addition: 'And als endis the xiii buke translait as said is with the prolougis tharof writtin be me henry aytoun notare publict and endit the twentytwa day of November the ʒeir off god m vc fourtysevin ʒeiris. Finis etc'. Henry Aytoun's activities as a notary public in Edinburgh are known from several sources. On 13 August 1549 he was one of the witnesses to a charter concerning James Bannatyne, father of the compiler of the Bannatyne Manuscript; he witnessed other charters in the 1550s, and is possibly the same man whose labours as a 'writer' between 1559 and 1574 are recorded in *The Treasurer's Accounts*.[35]

---

[34] I am greatly indebted to Dr Harris for much information concerning this manuscript.

[35] See *Bannatyne Manuscript*, I, xliii; and *Register of the Great Seal*, IV, no. 365 (p. 83). For Aytoun's activities as a witness to transactions in Edinburgh on 15 July 1550 and 5 October 1557, see *Laing Charters* nos 569 (p. 148) and 680 (p. 176). For the many payments made to a 'Henry Aytoun', see *TA*, Indices to vols X, XI and XII.

Precisely when the Thynnes acquired this manuscript is uncertain, but it is well known that several members of the family showed an interest in Scottish literature in the sixteenth century, notably William Thynne who included Henryson's *Testament of Cresseid* in his 1532 edition of Chaucer (Henryson ed. Fox 1981, xciv–xcv and ciii). Coldwell noted that Sir John Thynne (1512/13–80), a nephew of William Thynne, acquired a manuscript copy of John Bellenden's translation of Hector Boece's *History of Scotland* during the English invasion of 1544. Upon this manuscript (MS 96) he wrote: 'Founde in Edenburgh at the wyninge and burninge therof / the viith maye beinge wednisday /the xxxvith yier of the Reigne of our souverayn Lorde kinge henry the eight'.[36] Since Sir John also accompanied Somerset on his 1547 campaign against the Scots, Coldwell suggested that he might have acquired the manuscript of the *Eneados* on this later occasion. The suggestion is tempting but unconvincing, since the battle of Pinkie took place on 9–10 September 1547, two months before the copying of the manuscript was completed, and there is no evidence that Sir John Thynne stayed on in Scotland.

An unpublished inventory of books possessed by Sir John Thynne, dated 1577, includes the following item: 'virgills eneodes in skotishe verse by galbin [sic] douglas'.[37] But this, according to Dr Harris, is most likely to refer to the edition of 1553, which is also in the Longleat library. She notes: 'The inventory reasonably consistently refers to manuscript items as 'written' … The earliest firm reference I have to the Gavin Douglas translation is in our catalogue of 1702'.

The MS opens with two unfoliated flyleaves, followed by a narrow flyleaf (foliated f.1), which contains the early shelfmark IX.D.54, and another narrow flyleaf (foliated f.2). This contains what Coldwell termed 'an illegible notation in an Elizabethan hand', but much of this inscription can, with some difficulty, be deciphered.[38] It reads:

Denorben in Southwales ys vj libri per annum
Shotwicke in worall (*words crossed out which read:* both the casle) in the County
of Chestre both howse and parke
in the tenure of Sir John Massye
Ioynt partenour with (*next word uncertain: possibly* Brewe?)

by me Iohne Ty … (*apparently in a different sixteenth-century hand*)

These words appear to derive from a rental of the lands of the earldom of Chester: *partenour* (medieval Latin *parcenarius*) means joint tenant; Dinorben, an Iron Age hillfort, is in North (not South) Wales; and Shotwick is on the north bank of the river Dee in the Wirral. The Masseys were one of the leading families of Cheshire, and the Sir John Massey mentioned here was possibly the knight of that name (d. 1552) who was sheriff of Flintshire and a tenant of the manor of Shotwick in the reign of Edward VI.[39] The significance of this scrappy note, however, is difficult to assess, and

---

[36] See the facsimile of the inscription in [Collins] 1980, 6; also Mark Girouard, 'Sir John Thynne (1512/13–1580)', *ODNB*; and Bawcutt 1998, 63.

[37] Preserved in the Longleat Archives, Thynne Papers, second series, Sir John Thynne senior, 240, 01/09/1577.

[38] In making this transcription I have been greatly aided by Elspeth Yeo.

[39] For information about this area I am indebted to the Cheshire Record Office and the historian Dr Paul Booth. See also Stewart-Brown 1912; and Ormerod 1882, II, 558–63.

its relevance to the Thynnes puzzling. Sir John Thynne and his descendants possessed estates in many parts of the country, including Shropshire, but were not – as far as I know – owners of land in North Wales and the Wirral. If, however, this note had become attached to the manuscript before it was acquired by the Thynne family, it might be a slight but valuable pointer to early ownership of the *Eneados* by someone who lived in the northwest of England, before its acquisition by the Thynnes.

The Fragments (f)

Edinburgh University Library, MS Laing II.655.

These fragments, salvaged by the antiquary David Laing, are all that remain of what appears to have been a complete text of the *Eneados*, similar to the other manuscripts in size, script, and probable date. The folder has a note by Laing (?): 'c. 1530'. They consist of three separate leaves, containing the following sections of text: I.ii.13–I.iii.19 (f1); I.iii.76–I. iv.35 (f 2); and I.viii.7–70 (f 3). There are running titles and chapter headings, decorative capital letters at the beginning of a chapter, and a marginal note at I.iv.22 that also occurs in C, B, and L. One puzzling feature of leaf 2 is that the outer margin contains what appears to be an off-set of some printed words, apparently in Latin but so far unintelligible.

The 1553 Edition (1553, 53)

THE/ xiii Bukes of Eneados of / the famose Poete Virgill / Translatet out of Latyne/ verses into Scottish me-/tir, bi the Reuerend Fa-/ ther in God, May-/ ster Gawin Douglas / Bishop of Dunkel & /vnkil to the Erle / of Angus. Euery / buke hauing hys / perticular / Prologe. / Imprinted at London / 1553.

For earlier discussion, see Small, I, clxxviii–clxxx; Coldwell, I, 101–3.

Little is known for certain about the circumstances of production of this black letter quarto (*STC*, 24797), but it is usually attributed to the press of William Copland. The attribution to Copland is strong, resting on the evidence of printing types and the close similarity of the title page to that of his edition of Douglas's *Palice of Honour* (*STC*, 7073).[40] The motive for publishing the work is unstated, but Copland may have recognized its likely commercial value at a time when no English translation of the *Aeneid* had been printed. The date of publication can perhaps be narrowed down to the first half of 1553. Whereas the print of Copland's *Palice of Honour*, which is undated, bears on its title-page the slogan 'God saue Quene Marye', the title-page of the *Eneados* contains no such profession of loyalty to the new monarch. In view of the Protestant alterations to Douglas's text for which this edition is notorious, it seems likely that its publication – or the preparations leading up to publication – took place in the last months of the reign of Edward VI, who died on 6 July 1553.

Copland's exemplar is unknown. It may have been a manuscript – Coldwell (I, 106) considered that the Ruthven Manuscript was a 'collateral' version, but not a source – or possibly a lost Scottish print. There is a close similarity between Copland's print of the *Palice of Honour* and the fragmentary print of the same poem attributed to the Scottish printer

---

[40] See Isaac 1932, notes to figures 169–71; and McKerrow and Ferguson 1932, no. 49.

John Davidson (*STC*, 7072.8). This led William Beattie, in his study of the fragments, to conclude that Copland's edition was a page-for-page reprint of Davidson's, or one closely related to it (Beattie 1951; Douglas ed. Bawcutt 2003, xv–xvi). It is tempting to wonder whether Copland made similar use of a now lost Scottish print of the *Eneados*, but no evidence survives to support the conjecture. (See however p. 27 below for Denton Fox's hypothesis concerning the source of the extracts in the Bannatyne Manuscript.)

Probably the best-known characteristic of this edition is its Protestantism, evident chiefly in the Prologues. References to the Virgin Mary are commonly altered so as to bring them into line with Protestant doctrine. Whereas Douglas calls upon Mary to be his Muse (I.Prol.463), in the print the invocation reads: 'Thou, Saluiour of mankind, be mye Muse'; and in III.Prol.42 the phrase 'virgine moder but maik' is replaced by 'Christ goddis sone but maik'. (For similar alterations, see also textual notes to I.Prol.456 and 459). Another allusion to Mary in XI.Prol.112 is replaced by an exhortation to study God's word, i.e. the Scriptures: 'And aye vnto his wourd thy mynd be bent'. A whole stanza is omitted from Prologue VI (lines 89–96) that concerns Purgatory and Limbo. The word 'purgatory' is likewise omitted from.Prol.VI. 43, and replaced by 'ane mitigat pane'. Very occasionally the text of the translation has also been purged of offensive-seeming words. 'Purgatory' is omitted from the chapter heading of VI.xii, and 'deuotioune' is substituted for 'bedis' (VI.i.100).[41] Whether this 'anti-Roman Catholic feeling' should be attributed solely to Copland, as Small implies (I, clxxix), is uncertain. Copland is known to have printed many Protestant works in the 1540s, and he took a risk in printing Thomas Cranmer's *Recantation* in 1556.[42] But it is likely that the *Eneados* was brought to his attention by a Scottish intermediary, who may perhaps have co-operated with him in preparing the edition. There were many Scottish Reformers, or 'Evangelicals', present in London during the reign of Edward VI.

Such major modifications of Douglas's text are not confined to religion. In the last lines of the *Conclusio* Douglas bids his readers a jocular farewell:

> Adew, gallandis, I geif ȝou all gud nycht,
> And god salf euery gentill curtas wight.

But the 1553 print inserts an extra couplet, and substitutes 'gud readeris' for 'gallandis'. The tone is far more solemn:

> And wyl derek my laubouris, euer moir
> Vnto the commoun welth, and goddis gloir.
> Adew gud readeris, god gif you al gud nycht
> And eftir deth, grant vs his heueinly lycht.

There are additions of new material elsewhere, notably six lines of verse, beginning 'He hated vice, abhorring craftineis', that are placed between lines 330 and 331 of Prologue I (see below, p. 22). This passage does not radically alter the portrait, of Aeneas, but reinforces Douglas's conception of him as exemplary. Whoever composed these

---

[41] A similar 'expurgation' of *bedis* occurs in post-Reformation texts of Henryson's *Testament of Cresseid*, 363, and line 14 of Dunbar, *Poems*, 11. On the background, see MacDonald 1983.

[42] See Mary C. Erler, 'Copland, William (d. 1569)', *ODNB*; and Blayney 2013, II, 767. On Copland, more generally, see Blayney 2013, II, 611–12, 932, and 970–3; and Duff 1913.

lines possibly also wrote the numerous marginal notes that are a striking feature of the print and differ in kind from those in the Cambridge Manuscript composed by Douglas himself. (More will be said of these marginalia later, p. 28.)

The 1553 print further departs from the manuscripts in its regularization of the book-divisions of the *Eneados*. All the manuscripts have an anomalous and unexplained arrangement of the text: book II thus begins at *Aeneid* 2.13; book VI at 6.9; book VII at 7.25; and book VIII at 8.18. The print, however, follows the long established structure of the *Aeneid*.[43] The disposition of the text in the manuscripts seems to have originated with Douglas himself. This is shown by his references in the Cambridge Manuscript's marginal commentary to book and chapter of the translation. The note to I.v.113 refers to a description of the temple of Janus as being in 'the vii buyk in the X c[ap]'. This passage indeed occurs in chapter 10 in the manuscripts, but not in the print, where it is in the next chapter (numbered as 11 by Small).

All these departures from the text as found in the manuscripts – excising abhorrent traces of papist belief or dogma, or re-inserting the traditional book-divisions of the *Aeneid* – seem to represent a conscious editorial policy. But it would be mistaken to think that the language of the *Eneados* was similarly subjected to a deliberate programme of change, and systematically anglicized. In fact, 1553 usually preserves Douglas's distinctive vocabulary, and also retains many striking features of Scots spelling and grammar, such as *quh-* for English *wh-*, or *scho* for *she*. (It should be remembered that the manuscript versions of the *Eneados* contain many anglicized spellings.) What is more, the additional material in 1553 also contains a somewhat similar admixture of Scots and English. The passage inserted in Prol. I rhymes 'craftineis' and 'grais' in a manner reminiscent of Henryson and other Scottish poets. The language of the marginal notes likewise has many Scottish characteristics, including spellings, grammatical usage, and even rare items of vocabulary. A note to IV.iv.14, for instance, refers to Dido's retinue as 'the quenis trine'. *Trine* was a word employed in this sense in Scots at this time, but its use here cannot be explained as deriving from Douglas himself, since he translates Virgil's *caterva* differently.[44] This kind of linguistic evidence increases the likelihood that a Scot who shared Copland's religious beliefs was also involved, to some extent, in 'editing' the *Eneados*, or preparing it for the press.

Not all copies of the print are identical. Some have an extra leaf in gathering X, which is foliated as clxiii. Coldwell makes no mention of this, but Small speaks of 'a separate leaf … afterwards cancelled' (I, clxxx). In fact, it is the copies without the extra leaf that are defective, since they lack the last two lines of Prol. VII, and 68 lines of the first chapter of the following book. (This corresponds, in the manuscripts, to VI.xvi, because of the differing book-division in the print.) Although the error was recognized and corrected by the insertion of the new leaf, it created a substantial area of empty space on the recto of fol. clxiii. Accordingly there was inserted a piece of prose that served as a 'filler' (printed in the variants). It is clear that this passage, although interesting in itself, has no authorial justification. What is more, it contains some phrases, beginning 'In feates of warre excellyng al

---

[43] Discussion of this topic has been sparse, but see Watt 1920, 144; Coldwell, I, 54; Bawcutt 1976, 139–40; Blyth 1987, 181; and Pinti 1996, 117–20.

[44] Cf. Henryson ed. Fox 1981, 494, note 3; and *DOST*, *Tryn(e*, n.

vderis …', that have a striking similarity to the earlier lines of verse inserted in Prologue I – which suggests that both might have had the same author.

Other errors do not appear to have been noticed and rectified by the printers, such as the omission of a small section of book IV. Small suggested that Copland 'from motives of delicacy omits the account of the adventures of Dido and Aeneas' (I, clxxix), but this is unconvincing. The omission is so clumsy and nonsensical – it runs across two chapters (from IV.iv.65 to IV.v.42) – that it appears to be an accident, perhaps due to turning over two pages of the copy text rather than one. The omitted text runs to 68 lines, which might strengthen the case for the exemplar being a print rather than a manuscript (Copland commonly has 34 lines to a page, whereas the manuscripts are larger and usually fit more lines on to the page.) The omission of Douglas's *Directioun* in 1553 may perhaps have been intentional.

A surprisingly large number of copies of the 1553 print still survive. It is quite mistaken to call it 'one of the scarcest books of Scottish poetry'.[45] In addition to those listed in *STC,* more are owned by private collectors or various great scholarly libraries, principally in England, Scotland, and the United States. Some of them, of course, now provide little evidence of their provenance, but others contain early ownership inscriptions and annotations that usefully enlarge our knowledge of who was handling (if not necessarily closely reading) the *Eneados* in the sixteenth and seventeenth centuries (see below, pp. 26–9).

Coldwell was the first scholar to collate all the early witnesses for the *Eneados.* His succinct account of their relationship (I, 105–6), which derived from an unrivalled intimacy with the texts, is still valuable and is printed below:

> This edition takes into account six texts, the five MSS. (plus the three loose folio pages, which I take as fragments of one text), and the edition of 1553. The Cambridge MS. is the 'authorized' text presumably, since it is the earliest, and the work of Douglas's 'writer', and annotated in Douglas's own hand. None of these texts is directly derived from any other. An inspection of the textual variants reveals the following patterns of divergence from C: a few E R L B 53; many E R 53; many E L B; and many R 53; E R B and L B 53 are so rare as to be accidental. Such filiation of variants suggests the following stemma:

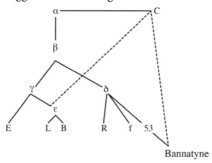

> The primitive text is represented by α ; C is the 'copy next after the translation', β is necessary to explain the variants in which E R L B 53 differ from C and

---

45 See an unsigned note concerning a copy in McGill University, in *SSL* 3 (1965–6), 176.

(sometimes) make nonsense of the text; and to explain the E R 53 parallels. E L B have a common source, but L B must have a separate source in addition, ε, probably corrected by [sic; *read* from?] C. R f 53 are collateral versions of a common original. Each text contains some variants that are not otherwise extant. More intermediaries could of course have existed at any point.

The fact that 53 is not from R is demonstrated by (for example) VII, pro.131– 132 or XI, pro.199. The omission of XII, i, 119– XII, ii, 49, suggests that one folio may have been missing in the source of R, and thus that there was an intervening text between R and δ . XI, ii, 20, is omitted from L but not from B, and thus proves that B is independent of L. XI, vi, 113–114 are run together in E, and show that L B are independent of E. The source of L B was very worn at the end: see the omissions with spaces left in the *Directioun*, lines 24, 25, 96, 97, etc.

Generally speaking, all the variants are so trivial that there is no reason for printing any of the unpublished texts.

(Coldwell, I, 105–6)

The Early Reception of the Eneados

Douglas was very much better known in the sixteenth century than Dunbar or Henryson. There is plenty of evidence to confirm the truth of his prediction that the *Eneados* would be read widely, not only in Scotland but also in England:

> Throw owt the ile yclepit Albyon
> Red sall I be, and sung with mony one.

(*Conclusio*, 11–12)

Non-poetic factors may have contributed to the fame of the *Eneados*, such as Douglas's bishopric and his noble birth, as son of one Earl of Angus and uncle of another. Both of these, revealingly, are mentioned on the title page of the 1553 edition. But the number of good quality manuscripts that survive, dating from not long after the completion of the translation on 22 July 1513, suggests that its merits were recognized early and that there was a demand for copies. The existence of other 'lost intermediate texts, all prior to Copland's Black Letter quarto' was first postulated by J. A. W. Bennett in 1946, from study of the variant readings. One such manuscript was certainly known to Henry Howard, Earl of Surrey, who was executed on 19 January 1547, six years before the print was published. Bennett concluded: 'It seems safe to suppose that at least ten copies of this long work … were made in less than forty years' (Bennett 1946, 84), and his views are lent support by the more detailed textual analysis of Coldwell (see above).

The circulation of these manuscripts is as remarkable as their speed of production. Douglas expected that the first readers of the *Eneados* would belong to the same social group as himself and his patron, Henry, Lord Sinclair. He envisaged

> That Virgill mycht intill our langage be
> Red lowd and playn by ȝour lordschip and me,
> And other gentill companȝeonys quha sa list.

(*Directioun*, 85–7)

Whether Lord Sinclair ever saw a copy is improbable: he accompanied James IV in the invasion of Northumberland, and died at Flodden on 9 September 1513. But other early readers of the *Eneados* – the Earl of Surrey, Sir David Lindsay, and the Ruthvens – were noblemen or moved in courtly circles. Douglas also aspired to bring Virgil to a wider and less privileged audience:

> Now salt thou with euery gentill Scot be kend,
> And to onletterit folk be red on hight,
> That erst was bot with clerkis comprehend.

> (*Exclamatioun*, 43–5)

We have no evidence that the *Eneados* ever reached wholly 'onletterit', i.e. illiterate, members of society. But Douglas's further hope, voiced in *Directioun*, 41–8, that it might be of educational use to teachers in grammar schools and 'thame wald Virgill to childryn expone', may perhaps have been realized.[46] What is known about the owners and copyists of the manuscripts indicates that in the first half of the sixteenth century the *Eneados* was circulating among the educated and professional classes of Scotland: notaries public, such as John Mudy and Henry Aytoun, churchmen, such as John Danielstoun, John Elphinstoun, and William Hay, a lawyer, such as Thomas Bellenden of Auchnoull, and a burgess, such as David Anderson. The geographical provenance of the manuscripts is also interesting: principally Edinburgh and its surroundings, as one might expect, given Douglas's career in church and government; but it is striking that all the early associations of the Elphinstoun manuscript are with locations in or near Aberdeen. Precisely when or how the *Eneados* reached England is not known, and has prompted fanciful conjectures.[47] But it was not a surprising or isolated occurrence. Cultural traffic between the two countries, in both directions, was well established by the later Middle Ages, and was much assisted by the invention of printing. Poems by Dunbar and Alexander Scott are preserved in an Elizabethan lute book, and the very first Scottish poem to be printed, *The Contemplacioun of Synnaris*, was published in 1499 not in Edinburgh but in Westminster by Wynkyn de Worde. A far more famous work, *The Testament of Cresseid*, was first printed (as noted earlier) in Thynne's 1532 edition of Chaucer (Bawcutt 1998; Bawcutt 2000).

The impact of Copland's 1553 edition, just as the manuscript tradition of the *Eneados* was coming to an end, has been neglected by scholars. Yet it played a major part in disseminating wider awareness of the poem in the second half of the sixteenth century, not only in England but in Scotland also, and its influence is visible in later editions up to the present day (see below, p. 33–6). The publications of John Bale illustrate another way in which it contributed to greater knowledge of Douglas and his works. Bale's *Summarium,* a catalogue of British authors,

---

[46] Later in the sixteenth century one Edinburgh schoolmaster borrowed an 'Inglische' version of Ovid's *Metamorphoses*, and others may have welcomed a Scots translation of the *Aeneid*. See Durkan 2013, 76.

[47] Cf. Kratzmann 1980, 173, and Sessions 1999, 282–3. It seems unlikely that Douglas took a manuscript of the *Eneados* with him on his hasty last journey to England, or that one was inherited by Margaret Douglas, daughter of Margaret Tudor and Douglas's nephew, the Earl of Angus.

printed in 1548, mentions Douglas, but the wording shows that he then knew of him only at secondhand through reading Polydore Vergil's *Anglica Historia* (1534). Bale later published an enlarged and updated version of this work in two parts dated 1577 and 1559, the *Scriptorum Illustrium Majoris Britanniae ... Catalogus.* This reveals direct knowledge of the *Eneados*, and quotes the opening line in a latinized form – *Laus, honor, iubilatio.* Bale was highly influential, and his entry on Douglas's translation of Virgil ensured that it entered the bibliographical tradition (Geddie 1912, xliii–liii and 232–4; Bawcutt 1998, 60–2).

Evidence for the circulation of 1553 comes from various sources. Sir Edward Dering (1598–1644) of Surrenden, Kent, an antiquary and MP, carefully listed his fine collection of books, which included 'Virgil: his Aeneads, Scotished by Gawin Douglas Bp of Dunkel London 1553', and recorded that it cost 5s. in an unspecified year.[48] Another copy, owned by an Oxford scholar Edward Higgins (flor. 1576–88), 'late fellowe of Brasenose', was appraised at only 6d. when his collection was inventoried for the purpose of probate.[49] The whereabouts of these books is not known today, but other early owners left their names on copies that still survive. One such, owned by the National Library of Scotland (H.29.b.53), has a title page inscribed 'Thomas Duncombe his booke: Amen'. The same book contains a rhyming inscription in a different and later hand: 'Thomas Baker is my name and with my pen I wrote this same' (sig.C 8r).[50] John Mason donated his copy, probably in the early seventeenth century, to the Library of Corpus Christi College, Oxford. He was probably the student of that college who graduated B.A. in 1599 (cf. Foster 1891, III. 983). Another owner records not only his name but a date, presumably of purchase: 'E Layfield 1559'. He is so far unidentified, but one candidate might be the Edward Layfield (d. 1583), who was a rector of Fulham and prebendary of Holborn in St Paul's Cathedral.[51]

It is possible to say a little more about some early owners. The copy bequeathed to Trinity College, Cambridge by the Shakespearian scholar Edward Capell (Capell 0.2) was first owned by 'Wylliame Belasyse'. He is most probably to be identified with the Sir William Belasise (c. 1524–1604), whose main estates were in Yorkshire, who was appointed High Sheriff of York in 1574, and whose funeral monument may be seen in Coxwold parish church.[52] A particularly interesting signature occurs on the flyleaf of the copy owned by the Pepys Library, Magdalene College, Cambridge (Print 1652): 'Ed. Waterhous: et amicorum'. Edward Waterhouse (1535–91), who was knighted in 1584, was a friend and correspondent of Sir Philip Sidney, and spent much of his career as a public servant and administrator in Ireland, acting for a time as secretary to Philip's father, Sir Henry Sidney.[53] The words *et amicorum* were a humanistic tag, chiefly employed in the sixteenth

---

[48] For full details, see Fehrenbach and Leedham-Green 1992, *PLRE* 4.332 and pp.137–50.

[49] See Fehrenbach and Leedham-Green 2004, *PLRE* 149.63 and pp.149–50.

[50] More details of these and other owners of 1553 will be found in Bawcutt 2019.

[51] This copy of 1553 is one of two owned by the Innerpeffray Library. Edward Layfield was the father of the more famous John Layfield: see R. Bayne, 'Layfield, John (1562/3–1617)', *ODNB*.

[52] See Christine Newman, 'Bellasis Family (c.1500–1653)', *ODNB*.

[53] See Andrew Lyall, 'Sir Edward Waterhouse (1535–1591)', *ODNB*, and *Sidney* ed. Kuin 2012, II, 835.

century by those who owned learned works in Latin or Greek. Its use here suggests that Waterhouse placed a high value on the *Eneados* and was ready to share the book with like-minded friends. His varied literary interests are illustrated by his ownership of two manuscripts in the Harley collection.[54] Another cultured owner was the poet William Drummond of Hawthornden, who donated his copy to Edinburgh University Library in 1628 (De.4.32); a cancelled inscription on the title page shows that it had previously been owned by a 'Iames Levingston'.[55] Another copy in Edinburgh University Library (De.6.63) has the inscription 'Tho: Hudson', who seems likely to be the poet Thomas Hudson, active at the court of James VI and author of *The Historie of Judith* (1584).

Precisely when the 1553 edition reached Scotland is not known, but it supplied George Bannatyne with three items in his celebrated manuscript anthology, completed in 1568: he placed lines 1–18 of Prologue IX in the 'ballatis of moralitie'; Prologue X in the 'ballatis of theologie'; and Prologue IV in the 'ballatis of luve'.[56] He was sufficiently impressed by the marginal notes printed in this edition to draw upon them for his own titles: 'Of godis workis to be incomprehensible be man [sic] wit or ressone' (Prol. X) and 'Of the incommoditie of luve and remeid thairof' (Prol. IV).There are, however, occasional divergences from the 1553 print, not all of which may be explained by Bannatyne's known carelessness as a copyist. A few of these readings appear, according to Coldwell (I, 101), to be 'corrected from some other source'. Denton Fox, however, offered another hypothesis: that Bannatyne's copy-text might have been 'not Copland but another print, no longer extant, which would presumably have been an ancestor of Copland' (Fox 1977, 161–2). Bannatyne's choice of Prologues suggests that he admired Douglas primarily as a moral and devotional poet. Some readers, however, were more interested in Douglas's views on Chaucer. Thomas Speght extracted six lines from Prologue I (339–44) and included them in his 1602 edition of Chaucer's *Works* (sig. cii). By modifying line 339 to read: 'Venerable Chaucer, principall poet without pere', he turned Douglas's nuanced discussion of Chaucer into a free-standing eulogy. A copy of an earlier edition of Chaucer (1550; *STC*, 5072), sold in 2002 at Sotheby's, also apparently contains the very same six-line passage inscribed in an early hand on its title-page. Unfortunately Sotheby's did not recognize the source of the quotation, and printed in their catalogue no more than its rather mangled opening line: 'O venerable Chaucer principall poet and peare'. This English copyist did not understand the Scots phrase 'but peir', which Speght had anglicized.[57]

Detailed critical discussion of poetry was far from common in the sixteenth century, but the *Eneados* attracted a number of brief responses from readers, most of which were laudatory, but a few hostile. The very first – less than eight years after Douglas's death – is Sir David Lindsay's eulogy in the Prologue to *The Testament of*

---

[54]   Cf. Hobson 1949. For more information about the manuscripts, see the British Library's on-line catalogue, *Explore Archives and Manuscripts*, MS Harley 1740 and MS Harley 7334 (http://searcharchives.bl.uk/, last accessed 22 November 2019).

[55]   On Drummond's books, see MacDonald 1971.

[56]   See *Bannatyne Manuscript* 1928–32, II, 113; II, 20–6; and IV, 108–16.

[57]   See Sotheby's sale catalogue for 12 December 2002, Lot 179; and Edwards 2005, 257. The book was bought by Baumann Rare Books of New York, who would not disclose to whom they sold it later.

the Papyngo (composed *ante* 1530). This devotes fifteen lines to Douglas's learning and rhetoric, but singles out for special praise his 'trew translatioun / Off Virgill' (33–4). Lindsay's commendation would have reached many later readers, since his works were very popular and often re-printed; the earliest edition now extant of *The Testament of the Papyngo* itself was printed in London in 1538.[58]

Also interesting, though anonymous and undated, are the occasional brief marginal comments in the manuscripts of the *Eneados*, to which attention has already been drawn. Some of these inscriptions, of course, testify chiefly to the extreme piety of those who wrote them; devout phrases, such as *Iesu Maria Amen*, are scattered throughout the Lambeth Manuscript and closely resemble those that occur at the beginning of the Cambridge and Elphinstoun Manuscripts. The short verses on the flyleaves of the Cambridge, Elphinstoun and Ruthven manuscripts tell us something about the poetic taste of those who inscribed them, but have little bearing on the *Eneados*. More pertinent are the occasional marginalia in the Elphinstoun Manuscript: these highlight *Oratio Didonis* at IV.vi.49 and *Responsio Enee* at IV.vi.105; and note *in propria persona* at several points in II.ii, in an attempt to distinguish the words of Aeneas himself from those of the deceitful Sinon. Moral commonplaces on the inevitability of death or human ignorance are signalled by a marginal *Nota* in various manuscripts (e.g. IV.xi.57, X.viii.73, X.viii.151, and XIII.iii.39). The *nota* beside Latinus's advice not to wage 'wer [war] inoportune' (XI.vii.23–4) suggests that the passage had special relevance for one reader of the Ruthven manuscript. Most striking of all are the comments besides I.Prol.425 and 437 in the Cambridge Manuscript, already mentioned (p. 11), that challenge Douglas's views on Dido, and seem to represent a reader's response to the text.

The marginal notes printed throughout the 1553 edition indicate a strong interest not only in the translation, but in the *Aeneid* itself. Their author (whether Scottish or English) calls attention to the poem's rhetorical features, such as the similes, and different types of oration – consolatory, 'piteous', or 'invective'. The remarks often sound elementary, but their author is far from unlearned. Some of the notes to book VI provide information that is not found in Douglas, but probably derives from Servius. A note on 'the nine cirkillis of hell', placed at the opening of *Eneados* VI.vii recalls Servius's comment on *Aeneid* 6.426: 'novem circulis inferi cincti esse dicuntur'. Other notes (at the opening of VI.xv) precisely identify as Corinthians or Athenians or Egyptians those peoples whom Anchises calls 'mor expert in craftis' than the Romans. These likewise can be traced to Servius's comments on *Aeneid* 6.847. Perhaps the most striking feature of the marginal notes, however, is their stress on the exemplary character of Aeneas. They depict him as a paragon of virtue, and claim more explicitly than does either Virgil or Douglas that he is a type of the good king: an 'exampill and myrrour to euerye prince and nobyl man' (I.Prol.330), one who 'lyk a wyse and constant prynce ouercummis his affectyons' with reason (IV.vii), who is vigilant and 'cairful' for his subjects, and a model in all respects for other rulers (X.v).[59]

---

[58] On the publishing history of *The Testament of the Papyngo*, see Lindsay ed. Hamer 1931–6, IV, 15–18.

[59] For further discussion, see also Griffiths 2014, 81–102.

Although many copies of 1553 survive, only a few of their early owners have left any detailed annotation. The inscriptions in the copy now owned by King's College, Cambridge (M 25.32) consist chiefly of underlinings and elementary comments on the characters in the *Aeneid*. The copy of 1553 acquired in 2008 by Louisiana State University from the Library of the Earls of Macclesfield, however, contains annotations very different in scope and importance.[60] The owner's name is written neatly in the cartouche at the top of the title page: 'W. Barnesley', and above it is written the date '1562' in ink of the same colour. Many pages of the text, both prologues and translation, contain underlinings and marginalia. Those that I have seen suggest a lively and intelligent interest in Douglas's vocabulary, and the differences between Scots and English. In the opening stanzas of Prologue IV, for instance, he has underlined several words, some of which are given glosses in the margin: so *fosteraris* is glossed as 'nurses', *vncorne* as 'not fully ripe', and *fremmit* as 'vncouthe'. Tipped in at the end of the book is a short additional list of notes and glosses, some of which are accompanied by their equivalents from the *Aeneid*: 'hamald goddis' (I.ii.27) – literally 'household gods' – is accompanied by *Penates*.

Barnesley here anticipates the philological interest in the *Eneados* that was to become very common in the seventeenth century. He might be regarded as a less learned and unsystematic fore-runner of the scholar Francis Junius (1591–1677), whose annotated copy of the 1553 edition is now in the Bodleian Library (MS Junius 54), along with his *Index Alphabeticus Verborum Obsoletorum quae occurrunt in Versione Virgilii Aeneadum per Gawenum Douglas* (MS Junius 114). Junius's copy had an earlier owner whose name appears in an abbreviated form in the title page cartouche as 'Rgrs Andrs'. He has been plausibly identified as Roger Andrewes, Master of Jesus College, Cambridge from 1618 to 1632, and – like his more famous brother Lancelot Andrewes – one of the translators of the King James Bible.[61] Junius was a close reader of the text. He made careful cross-references to Douglas's various uses of a word, and occasionally noted Chaucerian parallels to such usages as 'A per se' (I.Prol.8), 'cryis ho' (III.vi.52); and 'Partelot' (XII.Prol.159). He also spotted what he termed the *hiatus* between chapters iv and v of book IV, recognizing it as 'rather the Printers fault than the Translators'.[62] Junius was extremely influential, and later scholars drew heavily upon his work.

Douglas possibly owed his popularity in the sixteenth century in part to the sheer usefulness of the *Eneados* to those who were not fluent in Latin. Until 1573 it was the only complete translation of the *Aeneid* available in England. In the decade following 1553, however, publishers seemed to compete with Copland in producing versions of the *Aeneid*: in 1554 appeared the Day-Owen print of Surrey's book IV, followed in 1557 by Tottel's print of Surrey's books II and IV; the first seven books of Thomas Phaer's translation were published in 1558, followed in 1562 by a

---

[60] This copy is listed in Sotheby's Sale Catalogue, March 2008, no. 4276. I am indebted to Michael L. Taylor, Assistant Curator in Special Collections at Louisiana State University Library, who sent me several digital images of the work.

[61] See Dekker 2016, 3. There is a scathing account of Roger Andrewes in Nicolson 2004, 94–5 and 253.

[62] For an illustration of Junius's annotations, see Mapstone 1996, 20. On his interest in the *Eneados*, see also Bennett 1946, 86, and Duncan 1965, 51–7.

posthumous edition of nine books. Phaer's work was eventually completed in 1573 by Thomas Twyne, who added to it in 1584 his version of Maphaeus Vegius's book XIII. There are a few small signs of an Elizabethan critical debate concerning the rival merits of these works. One occurs in Barnabe Googe's *Epitaph* on Thomas Phaer, published in 1563: although Googe considered Phaer the best translator of Virgil, he nonetheless commended Douglas's 'famous wit in Scottish ryme'. Twyne was less generous than Googe, and, defensive about his own inclusion of book XIII, he commented with a hint of asperity: 'I haue not done it upon occasion of any dreame as Gawin Dowglas did it into the Scottish, but mooved with the worthiness of the worke'.[63] Some years later, in the section of *The Arte of English Poesie* (1589) devoted to stylistic decorum, George Puttenham objected to Douglas's description of Aeneas as 'by fate a fugitive' (see I.i.2–3); because of the low associations of the word *fugitive* he found the phrase 'vndecently spoken' (Puttenham 1936, 273–4 [III, cap.23]). The Phaer-Twyne translation was re-printed several times, and virtually superseded Douglas's version by the end of the century.

The most thoughtful criticism of the *Eneados* in this period comes from two Scots, John Leslie (1527–96) and David Hume of Godscroft (1559–1629). In *De Origine, Moribus et Rebus Gestis Scotorum* (1578) Leslie praised Douglas for his *ingenii acumen acerrimum*, saying that the translation conveyed the sweetness of Virgil's verse (*versuum suauitatem*) as well as its seriousness and gravity (*sententiarum pondera*). But what he stresses repeatedly – perhaps recalling Douglas's own words in Prologue I – is his embellishment of the language: *nostram linguam ... illustrauit*.[64] Hume of Godscroft was a remarkably sensitive and wide-ranging reader, familiar with classical poetry and contemporaries such as Sidney and Daniel, as well as ballads and 'old rude songs'. His comments on the *Eneados* cannot be dated precisely, because they were first printed in a posthumously published work, *The History of the Houses of Douglas and Angus* (1644). The Prologues are singled out for special commendation:

> In his Prologues before every Book, where he hath his libertie, he sheweth a natu-rall, and ample vein of poesie, so pure, pleasant and judicious, that I beleeve there is none that hath written before or since, but cometh short of him.

Hume's appreciation of the Prologues is recorded in even greater detail in a passage preserved in the Hamilton Palace manuscript of the *History*. This records his delight in Douglas's style and diction: his 'choise of significant wordes and sentences, comon or vulgar, and yett not base, but high and sublime and noe wayes affected'. It is evident that Hume was using the 1553 print rather than a manuscript, since he complained that the text was not 'rightly printed and corrected'.[65]

One poet's debt to another is often silent and unacknowledged, and remains long unnoticed by literary historians. This is certainly true of Douglas's effect upon later poets. It was not until 1815 that G. F. Nott suggested that the *Eneados* had influenced the versions of books II and IV of the *Aeneid* made by the Earl of Surrey. Surrey

---

[63] See Googe 1989, 82, and Twyne's Preface 'To the gentle and courteous Readers', in *The XIII Bookes of the Aeneidos* (1584).

[64] *De Origine, Moribus et Rebus Gestis Scotorum* (Rome, 1578), IX, 396; this passage is also reprinted in Geddie 1912, xlii. For a clumsy translation into Scots by James Dalrymple, c. 1596, see Leslie's *Historie of Scotland*, II, 179–80.

[65] The full texts are printed in Hume 2005, I, 27–8, and II, 477–8.

perhaps sought Douglas's translation, in the first place, as an aid to comprehension of the *Aeneid*, but he appears to have found much that was attractive in its style and diction. He adopted many of Douglas's words, phrases, whole lines, and even the greater part of a couplet. Stylistically, however, there are many differences between the poets: Surrey's blank verse contrasts with Douglas's decasyllabic couplets, Surrey's brevity with Douglas's 'fouth'.[66] Surrey could not have seen the 1553 print, but it would have been available to Thomas Sackville, Earl of Dorset. His Introduction to *The Mirror for Magistrates*, which first appeared in the 1563 edition of that work, shows that he had read the *Eneados* attentively, particularly books II and VI, and that, like Surrey, he admired Douglas's alliteration and archaic diction (Bacquet 1966, 179; Bawcutt 1976, 199–200). Some recent scholars have also suggested, vaguely and less plausibly, that Douglas's translation had 'an extensive impact on the diction of Phaer' (Phaer ed. Lally 1987, xxiii–xxvi; Tudeau-Clayton 1998, 517).

The *Eneados* was also influential in Scotland, and gives the lie to over-easy assumptions that poetry from the beginning of the century was rapidly forgotten, displaced by the vogue for French and Italian Renaissance writers. Whenever Lindsay writes in high style, one is reminded of Douglas, sometimes very specifically indeed, as in his eulogy of James I in *The Testament of the Papyngo*:

> patroun of prudence,
> Gem of ingyne and peirll of polycie,
> Well of Iustice and flude of eloquence.

(430–2)

This series of panegyrical topoi recalls the praise of Virgil in lines 4–5 of Douglas's Prologue I, but Lindsay subtly adjusts their wording – 'prudence … polycie … Iustice' – to praise of a king. John Bellenden, who, like Lindsay, may have been personally acquainted with Douglas, is now remembered chiefly for his prose translations of Livy and Hector Boece's *Scotorum Historia*. But in the verse prologues to these works the influence of the *Eneados* (combined with that of *The Palice of Honour*) is clearly visible (Rutledge 2007). In the reign of James VI Douglas's influence seems confined to lesser poets. One of these was Thomas Hudson, who was commissioned by King James to translate *La Judit* of Guillaume de Salluste du Bartas. In the Preface to *The Historie of Judith* (1584), Hudson complains of the heavy burden of bringing 'my half dispaired worke to final end' (Hudson 1941, 4). The phrasing echoes lines that Douglas addressed to his own patron (see I.Prol.92–3). Another translator who shows Douglas's influence was the Edinburgh burgess John Burel. His version of the medieval pseudo-Ovidian poem *Pamphilus* now survives only in a single copy of a print dated shortly after 1590 (*STC*, 4105). Burel had read the *Eneados* very attentively, particularly Prologue I, and his Preface to *Pamphilus* is studded with words and phrases – 'the colour of his propertie' (16) or 'into rethorik flours to flow and fleit' (102) – that unmistakably derive from Douglas.[67]

---

[66] See Nott 1815, I, cciii–ccix. The precise nature of Surrey's debt to Douglas has been much debated: see the careful study by Emrys Jones in Howard 1964, xi–xx and 139–40; also Ridley 1961; Bawcutt 1974; Bawcutt 1976, 197–9; and Kratzmann 1980, 169–89.

[67] See Bawcutt 1995. Line-references are to a forthcoming edition of Burel's poems by Jamie Reid Baxter.

The courtier and landowner Patrick Hume of Polwart (d. 1609) is today over-shadowed by two other poets, his younger brother Alexander Hume, minister of Logie and author of 'The Day Estivall', and Alexander Montgomerie, with whom he engaged in a series of invectives. In 1580, however, Hume published *The Promine* (*STC*, 13956), a short occasional poem celebrating an actual historical event, a dawn hunting excursion from Stirling Castle made by the young king on 12 June 1579. Montgomerie contemptuously accused Polwart of being a pla-giarist – 'Thy scrowis [scrolls] obscuir ar borrowit fra sum buik. / Fra Lyndsay thow tuik, thow art Chawceris cuik' (Montgomerie 2000, 'Invectives', I, 44–5). In the *Promine*, however, it was Douglas to whom Polwart was indebted, and Prologue XII that furnished him with numerous words and phrases. Many of these are extremely learned and aureate: 'rubicound', 'vapouris sweit as sence', or 'sappie subtil exhalatiounis' (cf. XII.Prol.68, 44, and 140). Prologue XII is largely a hymn of praise to the sun, which is visualized as a monarch in triumph; in the *Promine*, by contrast, an actual king is addressed as a *roi-soleil*. It is a work of egregious flattery, but nonetheless displays wit and ingenuity in the re-handling of Douglas's imagery (Bawcutt 1981a).

The title-page of 1553 shrewdly calls attention to the fact that every book of the *Eneados* has its 'perticular Prologe', and it is evident that the Prologues were as popular in the sixteenth as in later centuries. They were anthologized by Bannatyne, praised by Hume of Godscroft, and silently plundered by Burel and Polwart. Readers responded, not to any single aspect of the Prologues, but to their sheer variety – whether they sought 'gude moralitie', ideas on translation, or vivid description of natural scenery. Another distinctive feature of the *Eneados* (both Prologues and translation) is its 'fouth' of language. This too was attractive to a number of poets in the sixteenth century, and was noted by such a discerning critic as Hume of Godscroft. But other readers, it is clear, were beginning to find Douglas's language difficult and obscure. It is telling that in 1614 John Norden substituted his name for that of Lydgate in the traditional trio of great medieval poets:

> *Chawcer, Gowre, the bishop of dunkell,*
> In ages farre remote were eloquent.[68]

It is noteworthy too that by 1633 Douglas was placed among the 'ancient worthies of Scotland' in the pageantry celebrating the visit of Charles I to Edinburgh. His companions on Parnassus included George Buchanan and William Elphinstoun, but only one vernacular poet, Sir David Lindsay (McGrath 1990). From the seventeenth to the eighteenth century it was scholars and philologists – William L'Isle, Sir William Dugdale, George Hickes, Edmund Gibson, and, above all, Francis Junius – who read the *Eneados* most attentively. They kept its reputation alive, less as a translation of Virgil than as an aid to reading Anglo-Saxon, and 'a treasury of ancient words'.[69]

---

[68] See 'The Authors Farewell to his Booke', in *The Labyrinth of Mans Life* (1614).
[69] On the background, see Bennett 1946, 85–8; Duncan 1965; and the classic study, Douglas 1951.

Later Editions

This list comprises editions of the complete *Eneados*. Details of anthologies containing selections from the work up to 1912 may be found in William Geddie's *A Bibliography of Middle Scots Poets* (STS 1912).

The Ruddiman Edition (1710)

Virgil's Aeneis, / Translated into Scottish Verse / By the famous Gawin Douglas / Bishop of Dunkeld. / A new *EDITION*. Wherein The many Errors of the Former are corrected, and the defects supply'd, from an excellent MANUSCRIPT. To which is added A LARGE GLOSSARY, / Explaining the Difficult Words: Which may serve for a Dictionary to the Old SCOTTISH Language./ And to the whole is prefix'd /An exact account of the Author's / Life and Writings from the best / Histories and Records. (Andrew Symson and Robert Freebairn, Edinburgh, 1710)

The credit for this edition is largely attributed to Thomas Ruddiman (1674–1757), the learned Keeper of the Advocates' Library, although his name does not appear on the title-page. It is commonly regarded as a landmark in Scottish publishing, and despite its superficial lack of beauty – printed 'upon course Paper, and in an old worn letter' – the work has great historical importance, and can still be read with profit and enjoyment.[70] The title trumpets the novelty and variety of its contents, but the boast that it is a new edition is not wholly true. According to the unpaginated Preface, 'an old and excellent MS, belonging to the Library of the College of Edinburgh' was consulted, but this was not discovered until 45 pages were in print. These and much else in the volume, including the side notes and other additions, derive from the 1553 edition. The unidentified manuscript was the Ruthven Manuscript, and it was apparently unknown that others existed. One feature of Ruddiman's editing is his 'passion for Correctness' (Duncan 1965, 104). He remarks: 'Our Author ... takes a very great liberty in proper names ... But generally we have followed Virgil himself, where the verse and Scots idiome would allow' ('General Rules for Understanding the Language', signature A1). Yet the edition has very real merits. It contains the first biography of Douglas, accompanied by copious references; this was apparently written not by Ruddiman but by Bishop John Sage. The most important feature, however, is the large Glossary, which many distinguished Scottish lexicographers have drawn upon and treated with great respect (cf. Duncan 1965, 55–7; Aitken 1989). The Preface contains brief but interesting remarks on Ruddiman's methods in compiling the Glossary: he consulted some contemporary authorities, but is disdainful of Francis Junius's manuscript *Index Alphabeticus* of obsolete words (Bodleian, MS Junius 114); he stresses that he himself conversed with 'people of the several Shires' when seeking the meaning of unusual words.

---

[70] Duncan 1965, 48–59, provides an excellent study of the context.

The Aeneid of Virgil Translated into Scottish Verse. By Gawin Douglas, Bishop of Dunkeld [ed. George Dundas], 2 vols, Bannatyne Club (Edinburgh, 1839).

This large handsome edition of the *Eneados* was presented to the Bannatyne Club by the advocates George Dundas and Andrew Rutherford. Its main claim to importance is that it was the first to be based upon the Cambridge Manuscript, and the first therefore to make Scottish scholars aware of its distinctive features, such as the marginal commentary to Prologue I and much of book I. Unfortunately this edition contains a bare transcript of the text, and lacks an introduction or textual apparatus. It has nonetheless had a largely unacknowledged influence upon subsequent editors, who have perpetuated some of its erroneous readings of the text. According to Coldwell (I, 104), the correspondence between George Dundas and David Laing 'throws light on the casual methods of nineteenth-century scholarship'.

The Poetical Works of Gavin Douglas, Bishop of Dunkeld, ed. John Small, 4 vols (Edinburgh, 1874); reprint (Georg Olms, 1970).

John Small (1828–86), who succeeded his father as Librarian to the University of Edinburgh, was the first to publish a 'collected edition' of Douglas's works. The Introduction still has value, chiefly for its detailed account of Douglas's life and inclusion of his surviving letters, but the edition of the *Eneados* is unreliable, outdated, and in no way authoritative. Small was not a scholar of the calibre of David Laing, and his editing of other poems, including Douglas's *Palice of Honour*, has not stood up well to modern scrutiny. A. S. G. Edwards considered Small's text of Dunbar 'a regression, a signal failure to build on Laing's achievements'.[71] According to Small (I, xii), his text of the *Eneados* 'derived' from the Elphinstoun Manuscript, but the transcript is far from accurate.[72] There are revealing discrepancies, in this respect, between his text of Prologues I and VII and that provided by George Gregory Smith in his excellent *Specimens of Middle Scots* (1902), which is based on the same manuscript. One small illustration out of many is seen in Small's version of I.Prol.42: '3it with *your* leif, *Virgill*, to follow the'. Gregory Smith, like the manuscript itself, reads '3it with *thi* leif, *Virgile*, to follow the'. Small at times confuses the readings of the Cambridge manuscript with those of Elphinstoun, and his editorial practice, in general, seems muddled.

Small makes other more intentional departures from the Elphinstoun Manuscript, not all of which are recorded. He includes the marginal 'Comment' from the Cambridge Manuscript (printed in Small, II, 279–95); he takes over from the 1553 print both the extraneous lines of verse in Prologue I, and the prose passage between books VI and VII (see Small, III, 73 and 358); and he also includes what he calls its 'quaint side-notes' (I, clxxx). Small fails to inform readers that he has made alterations to the lay-out of the Elphinstoun Manuscript, in adopting the

---

[71] See Edwards 2001, 60. Douglas Hamer also complains that Small in his edition of *Monarche* recorded only one-sixth of the variants, and 'I could not discover any system upon which he worked in choosing his variants' (Lindsay ed. Hamer, 1931–6, IV, 5).

[72] According to Bennett 1938[a]: xxiii, 'it differs from the manuscript approximately once in every two lines'.

traditional book-divisions of the *Aeneid* (see above, 'The 1553 Edition'). From time to time he also silently 'corrects' the text in another way, here usually following the precedent of Ruddiman. He alters the spelling of proper names, adopting those usually employed in standard editions of the *Aeneid* instead of those found in the manuscripts of the *Eneados*: so *Pristis* for *Pystris* (V.iii.24); *Didymaon* for *Dodymaon* (V.vi.128); and *Numytour* for *Munytor* (VI.xiii.27). In one interesting case he removes a medievalism characteristic of Douglas (and also of Chaucer), when he (like Ruddiman) alters forms such as *Tytane* in dawn descriptions to the more classically correct *Tython* or *Tithone* for Tithonus (IV.xi.2; IX.viii.2; XII. Prol.13). From the perspective of a modern editor, Small thus disguises evidence as to the affiliation of the different manuscripts of the *Eneados*, and removes clues as to which edition of Virgil Douglas might have used.

Virgil's Aeneid Translated into Scottish Verse by Gavin Douglas Bishop of Dunkeld, ed. David F. C. Coldwell, 4 vols (STS, 1957–64).

Coldwell's edition of the *Eneados* was the first modern scholarly edition of the poem. He made a detailed collation of all the manuscripts and the 1553 print, and wisely chose to base his text on the Cambridge Manuscript. He also provided a full apparatus, including an extremely detailed Glossary that benefited from the progress of lexicography in the twentieth century, drawing upon both *OED* and the early volumes of *DOST*. Coldwell was furthermore the first editor to show that Douglas had made systematic use of the Virgil commentary written by the humanist Jodocus Badius Ascensius.[73] Coldwell also published at this time a slightly modernized *Selections from Gavin Douglas* (Oxford, 1964).

Gavin Douglas: The Aeneid (1513), ed. Gordon Kendal, 2 vols, Modern Humanities Research Association (London, 2011).

Kendal mistakenly claims that there is 'no significant difference in textual authority' between Small's edition of the *Eneados* and Coldwell's, and describes his own as a 'word-for-word reproduction of Small, with spelling regularized in order to improve readability' (I, xxxix). The cover, curiously, reproduces the title page of 1553. Dependence upon Small means that Kendal takes over many of his weaknesses, including errors of transcription, inclusion of the spurious verses in Prologue I, and the standardized book-divisions and classical names. The attempt to 'regularize' Older Scots spelling is well-meaning but misguided. It exaggerates and falsifies what Kendal calls the 'mongrel' quality of the *Eneados*. There is also a strange insensitivity to the sound-effects of Douglas's poetry. Many of the spelling changes disrupt the rhyme scheme, as is illustrated repeatedly in Prol. IV (e.g. at lines 11, 72, 149, 201 and 211), and the removal of the *–is* ending in nouns and verbs often has a disastrous effect on the metre. This is, ironically, all too obvious in the following awkward version of Douglas's plea to his scribes not to alter his words (in *Tyme, space and dait*, 22–5):

---

[73] Douglas's use of Ascensius was first noted by Schumacher (1910).

Offend [for *Offendis*] nocht my volume, I beseek,
But read [*redis*] leal, and tak good tent in time
Ye neither maggle nor mismetre my rhyme,
Nor alter nocht my words [*wordis*], I you pray.

The XIII Buiks o Eneados o the famous poet Virgil translatit out o Latin verses intae Scottish metre, by the Reverend Faither in God, Maister Gavin Douglas, Bishop o Dunkeld and uncle tae the Earl o Angus, every buik haein his parteecular prologue. Modrenised by John Law and completit by Caroline Macafee, 2 vols (Scots Language Centre, Perth, 2012).

A brief introduction by Caroline Macafee (pp. ix–xvii) explains the history and wholly linguistic purpose of this work. Its text, unfortunately, is based on Small, and the title derives from the 1553 print.

The Present Edition

Coldwell gives the following account of his 'Method of Editing' (I, 106–10):

The object of a critical edition of a text is to approach as close as possible to the original form of the author's work. The problems in this text are remarkably simple. Three of the texts are exactly dated (L B 53), one can be dated within about five years (C), and the other two (E R) must have been made within ten to twenty years of the time of composition. The Cambridge MS. has pre-eminence as presumably the author's personal copy. There is thus little temptation to conflate, or to emend, or to look for readings that seem best to the critic, though not attributable to the author. Indeed the biggest problem for the critic here is simply the elucidation of what is in the one manuscript.

This is a conservative edition. It aims at an accurate reproduction of the Cambridge MS. with the following exceptions:

1. Punctuation is editorial. The MS. has occasional periods and slanting strokes, capriciously arranged. Punctuation sometimes involves difficult decisions about syntax and an examination of the Latin which the Scots represents, but to omit punctuation is to put an unnecessary barrier between the reader and the poem.

2. Capitals in the manuscript generally follow modern practice, at the beginnings of lines, sentences and proper names. Exceptions in the MS. to modern usage have not been noted.

3. Abbreviations have been expanded in italics. There is no difficulty here except in the case of –ß in plurals, which is sometimes syllabic –sis – when it is so transcribed (it is the metre that determines the form) the manuscript reading is noted among the textual variants. It would seem that –sß stands for –sis, and it has been so transcribed: the rhythm of the line demands the extra syllable.

4. Marginal corrections, linear corrections and interlinings are introduced into the text, but they are noted in the variants.

5. On a few occasions a necessary word, an obvious omission, has been added to the text: each is listed in the variants.

Besides explaining what I have done to the Cambridge MS., the Appendix of textual variants records divergences in the other texts – all of them, I hope, except mere differences in spelling. I do not believe them to be necessary to establish the text Douglas intended, but they have a value for the light they throw on the history of the use and the disuse of words; and on classical scholarship, or rather ignorance, in the distortions of Latin proper names. Copland's text is interesting, as noted above, for its Protestantism. In Book I considerable attention has been paid to spelling variants: 'a / ane'; 'to / til'; 'can / gan' and the like. C makes a practice of running closely related words together into compounds, as 'salbe', 'salbehald', 'forto', 'fortobe', 'tobe', 'tocum', 'ilkane', 'samony', 'solang', 'invayn', 'onfar', 'alsfast', and so on. I should like to believe that these represent a theory of grammar and have preserved them in the text, listed them in the glossary, and recorded the variants in the other texts in Book I. Certain spelling peculiarities recur. Thus C has more y's than the other MSS; E has a taste for final –t's, as in 'witht' and 'furtht'; R doubles final consonants, as in 'sett', 'funerall', 'forgiff' and so on; all the other MSS. have more 'ane's' and fewer 'not's' for 'nocht', and fewer –ß's than C; R likes terminal –z for –s, as in 'termez' or 'rymez'; E R simplify long vowels, as in 'wene' for 'weyn', 'clere' for 'cleir', or 'scule' for 'scuyll'; E R have more –ing's for C's –and's in present participles; E R have fewer qu- forms; L prefers 'cough' for 'couth', and often adds final –e's as in 'amange', 'cummynge', or 'thane'; 53 almost invariably has a comma in the middle of the line, interchanges c and t, and has very few abbreviations – all these are tendencies rather than invariable practices. To record all the spelling variants would be a waste of time. Thus where C has

> Of fresch endyte throu Albion iland braid (I, pro, 343)

R has

> Off fresche endite throw albioun yland brade,

with every word different, though not significantly so. Sometimes, it must be noted, there is a twilight semantic territory where textual variants that are probably simple scribal mistakes can be forced into meaning. Thus 'quhirk' (VII, vi, 88, E: of a top, to move in a sudden or jerky motion: first quotation OED 1821) is probably an error for C's 'quhirl'. Or again, 'lang sumfare' (IV, pro.234, 53) for 'langsum fare' might be taken as 'a long journey somewhere'; or 'command me, lord, away the pryce' (V, vii, 39, R) for 'command me leid …' could be read with 'away' as a transitive verb. This is probably too fanciful, no matter how much it would enrich the English vocabulary.

The glossary must be regarded as an aid to the reading of the poem, not a contribution to Scottish linguistics. It is not complete, but attempts to list every word that might be difficult to the modern reader. Accordingly, I have listed 'hedismen' (V, xii, 175) because it is 'chieftains', not 'headsmen', and 'quhalys' (V, xiii, 132), because it is 'whales', not 'quails', and 'liones' (VI, xvi, 32) because it is 'lions', not 'lioness'. Such a subjective approach involves choices, probably wrong ones, but as the *Dictionary of the Older Scottish Tongue* advances, complete word-lists become more and more unnecessary. Since the glossary is primarily an aid to the reader, words are listed separately under different spellings with rare cross-references. This has meant a considerable expansion of the *size* of the glossary, but it will mean something, I believe, to the reader whose English is Southern. Some interesting words from E R L B 53 have been listed, but no attempt has been made to gloss all their mistakes. There is some overlapping of the glossary and critical notes. The list of proper names is self-explanatory. For Latin proper names I have followed the spellings used in the Loeb edition of Virgil. I have tried to list every name, but I have not recorded every occurrence of each, except for the post-classical names in the prologues. The list of names might have some use as an indication of the relative exactness (compared with Lydgate's, for instance) of Douglas's classical scholarship.

The purpose of the critical notes is two-fold. They show what Douglas has done with the Latin, especially where he has translated not Virgil but the commentary of Ascensius Badius. To show exactly what has been done, the Scots and Latin would have to be interlined: bearing in mind that Douglas must expand a little to fill up his couplets, I have tried to indicate every significant addition and error, and every occasion when Douglas's text probably differed from the modern *textus receptus*. In the second place, the textual [*sic; for* critical?] notes elucidate the poem. Thus they paraphrase passages that seem to me to be obscure, and with reference to the prologues, try to fit Douglas into the pattern of the conventions of his age. I have occasionally called attention to characteristic stylistic devices; whether they are *beauties* is a matter for every reader to decide.

(Coldwell, I, 106–10)

The present edition originated in the recognition that Coldwell's edition, despite its numerous virtues, needed far-reaching corrections and revision. The present editors, although with some reservations, accept the validity of Coldwell's approach to editing. We accept also the 'pre-eminence' of the Cambridge manuscript, but question the notion that it was Douglas's 'personal copy'. One of the chief objectives has been to eliminate, as far as is humanly possible, the major weaknesses in the first edition, some of which were noted by reviewers and other scholars.

Coldwell saw his main purpose as the 'accurate reproduction of the Cambridge MS', but the edition contained a surprising number of mistranscriptions of that text. Some of these were small and trivial – e.g. *but* for *bot*, and vice-versa – and others look like unconscious modernizations, or even anglicisms (*doubt* for *dout*, *sche* for *scho*, *hold* for *hald*, *they* for *thai*). (One wonders whether perhaps the printers were responsible for these, rather than Coldwell himself, and that they were not corrected in proof-reading.) But there was another class of errors that was much more damaging, since these converted sense into absurdity, or suggested that Douglas did not understand Latin. Ascanius, for instance, was described in the marginal commentary to I.v.76 as the *fift*, or fifth, son of Hector, when Douglas in fact used the old Scots and Germanic term, '*sistir* son'.[74] In the storm scene of book I Douglas was likewise credited with a mistranslation of Virgil's *tabulae* as *takillis* (I, iii.44); but the manuscript has *tabillis*, which in this context, like *tabulae*, means 'planks, timbers'. A slightly comic

---

[74] This and other instances are discussed more fully in Bawcutt 1978.

38

example occurs in VIII.ix.123, where a horse appears to have horns: 'hornyt hovyt' was printed instead of the correct 'horny hovyt'. Douglas used the same compound earlier (VII.xii.179) to render Virgil's *cornipedes* (7.779). Several hundred of these misreadings have now been identified and corrected.

A particularly searching review of Coldwell's edition came from the distinguished Virgilian scholar, Professor R. G. Austin, who was a great admirer of Douglas's translation. He noted that many of the Latin quotations were 'riddled with misprints', and commented that no further issue should be published 'until all the Latin has been drastically purged' (Austin 1966, 156). This onerous task was undertaken by Ian Cunningham, who comments:

> Coldwell seems to have been a competent Latinist, and it is difficult to account for the number of these errors. It would appear that a barely legible manuscript was presented to a typist or compositor who did not know Latin, and that Coldwell failed to correct proofs adequately or at all.

Coldwell indeed, in a prefatory note to his volume I, mentions that the printers had to deal with 'a crabbed and intricately-corrected manuscript'. For the present edition all Latin quotations, mainly but not exclusively, of Virgil and Ascensius, have been checked and corrected, and where necessary for clarity more of the contexts have been included. Exact references have been given (book and line for Virgil, folio [in Arabic rather than the original Roman numerals] and column for Ascensius). For further details, see introductory note to the Commentary.

Coldwell was aware that Douglas's translation owed much to an edition of Virgil accompanied by a commentary written by the scholar-printer Jodocus Badius Ascensius. He noted: 'I have used an edition of Vergil's works from the Library of the University of Edinburgh (here called 1507 because the colophon is so dated) … and I have considered it worth while to record in the notes the general agreement of Douglas's chapter divisions with that edition's woodcuts (which were done by Sebastian Brant)' (I, 59–60). Unfortunately this particular edition was a pirated one, printed at Lyons in 1517, long after the *Eneados* had been completed in 1513. Comparison of the *Eneados* with the texts of the different editions of Virgil produced by Ascensius shows that Douglas is most likely to have used an edition published at Paris in 1501, which has no woodcuts. All references therefore in this edition are to Ascensius 1501. A detailed study of the evidence is provided in the Appendix.[75]

The rest of the Apparatus largely follows the framework provided by Coldwell, though it is much revised. Throughout the work the notes have been updated, taking account of new scholarly discoveries, and referring to recent editions of Chaucer, Henryson, Dunbar, and other authors. The notes on the Prologues, in particular, have been completely re-written: they identify, often for the first time, many allusions to or quotations from poets whom Douglas most admired, and they attempt to elucidate

---

[75] Bawcutt 1973, reprinted in the Appendix to this Introduction. For further discussion, see also Bawcutt 1976, 95–102. It should also be noted that a few apparent mistranslations perhaps derive not from Douglas but from his own scribes. Scribal misreadings, especially of minims, might explain odd forms of classical names, such as 'Munytor' for Numitor (VI.xiii.27), 'Momentyne' for Nomentum (VII.xii.15), and 'Munycus' for Numicius (VII.iii.6).

obscurities in his vocabulary (more especially in Prologue VIII). The Glossary has been expanded, and considerably revised: a number of erroneous spellings and line-references have been corrected, and, more importantly, several lexical errors have been weeded out: *lyntquhite*, for instance, is now glossed not as 'thistle finch' but 'linnet'; *onlace* not as 'unlace', but its opposite, 'attach by means of a lace'; and *popland* (of blood) not as 'popping' but 'pouring out in a bubbling stream' (see Glossary headnote for further details). The Index of Proper Names has been revised along similar lines.

The present Introduction replaces Coldwell's seven-chapter Introduction, much of which, despite its livelinesss, now seems eccentric, irrelevant (as in a chapter that gives a summary of *The Palice of Honour*), and inaccurate. The discussion of the 'Text of the *Eneados*' is indebted to Coldwell's chapter 5, but provides a more detailed account of the witnesses and of the poem's early circulation and reception. Also new to this edition is a review of recent trends in criticism, and the Bibliography.

Appendix

Priscilla J. Bawcutt, 'Gavin Douglas and the Text of Virgil'

Originally published in *Edinburgh Bibliographical Society Transactions* 4 (1973), pp. 213–31. Reprinted verbatim with kind permission of the Society.

If we wish to make a correct assessment of the skill and accuracy of Gavin Douglas's translation of the *Aeneid* (1512–13) we must first take into account something that has often been ignored: the nature of his text of Virgil. We are now accustomed to do this in the case of Dryden; J. M. Bottkol has argued that if we compare Dryden's translations from the Latin with the 17th-century editions of their originals, we find that the charge of textual carelessness is unfounded: 'the poet was a much more conscientious scholar than has been admitted by even his friendliest critics'.[1] But 16th-century translators from the classics, unlike Dryden, rarely tell us which edition of their original they used, and in this Gavin Douglas is no exception. Yet in that equivalent of a modern preface, the First Prologue to his *Eneados*, he professes a remarkable concern for textual accuracy; it is this which underlies all his criticisms of Caxton; the word 'text' is one to which he repeatedly returns, sometimes proudly, as in 'Rycht so am I to Virgillis text ybund' (299), sometimes apologetically, as in 'Sum tyme the text mon haue ane expositioun' (347) … 'Sum tyme I follow the text als neir I may, / Sum tyme I am constrenyt ane other way' (357–8).[2] In one of the concluding epistles to his *Eneados*, trying to disarm potential critics, Douglas tells us to compare his translation with the original:

> Bot, gyf I le, lat Virgyll be owr iuge,
> Hys wark is patent, I may haue na refuge.
> (*Exclamatioun*, 19–20, Coldwell's edition, iv, p. 192)

If this interest in the 'text' and this concern for fidelity to his classical original are genuine, it shows Douglas to have been moved by something of the spirit that fired the Humanists. But are they genuine? If we follow Douglas's own advice to let Virgil be his judge, we must play fair and look not only at modern editions of Virgil but at editions produced in his own time. This article does not claim to give a full and definitive account of Douglas's dealings with his Latin original. It is a preliminary investigation, and has precise but limited aims: first, to show that, viewed in the

---

[1] 'Dryden's Latin Scholarship', *Modern Philology*, xl (1942–3), pp. 241–54. See also A. Løsnes, 'Dryden's *Aeneis* and the Delphin *Virgil*' in *The Hidden Sense and other Essays*, Norwegian Studies in English, ix (1963), pp. 113–57.

[2] Quotations from the *Eneados* are taken from David F. C. Coldwell's edition: *Virgil's 'Aeneid' Translated into Scottish Verse by Gavin Douglas*, 4 vols. Scottish Text Society, Ser. 3, xxx, xxv, xxvii–xxviii (1956, 1951, 1953–4) Edinburgh, 1964, 1957–60.

context of early 16th-century classical scholarship, many seeming mistranslations in Douglas's *Eneados* are more apparent than real; secondly, to suggest the probability that Douglas made close use of one particular edition of Virgil, that published in Paris between 1500 and 1501 by the scholar-printer, Jodocus Badius Ascensius.[3]

I.

Non-classical scholars are not always sufficiently aware of how complex is the textual tradition of Virgil. The three main authorities for the *Aeneid* are the Codex Mediceus (5th century), the Codex Palatinus (4th or 5th century) and the Codex Romanus (5th century). Their testimony is supplemented by fragments (such as the Schedae Vaticanae), by a group of later manuscripts, and by the commentary of Servius, whose evidence is sometimes indeed accepted by modern editors even when it conflicts with all three early manuscripts. The most important variants are recorded in good modern editions of Virgil, such as those of R. A. B. Mynors (Oxford Classical Texts, 1969) and H. R. Fairclough (Loeb Classical Library, 1934–5), or J. W. Mackail's edition of the *Aeneid* (Oxford, 1930). But early printed editions of the 15th and 16th centuries have a host of further variants – many of them obvious corruptions – which are not retained in the textual apparatus of modern editions and can only be detected if one examines actual early printed texts. They omit or insert whole lines; they complete half-lines; they insert a punctuation different from that of most modern editors; sometimes they run words together, sometimes they separate them; they often spell personal names and place-names in a very different manner from that now accepted; all this, in addition to numerous lexical variants.

It might thus seem a truism to say that Douglas's text of Virgil would be very different from a 20th-century one; yet it is all too easy to forget this when reading his *Eneados* and comparing it with the most easily available modern editions of the *Aeneid*, and thus to misjudge his care and accuracy as a translator. Even the most recent editor of the *Eneados*, Dr David Coldwell, has fallen into this trap occasionally. He is aware that Douglas's text of Virgil often had readings different from those accepted today (see his Introduction, pp. 55–6, and Notes to VIII.xi.23, VIII.xii.38, and VIII.xii.72); yet he sometimes leads the reader into thinking, quite erroneously, that Douglas has blundered. For instance, at IX.v.27–8 ('The Rutilianys ... Lyggis sowpit, fordoverit' [= exhausted and overcome with sleep]) Coldwell notes Virgil's reading as *conticuere* (IX.237). It is true that that is the reading accepted by most modern editors, but in fact Douglas was translating *procubuere*, which is a reading that derives from the Codex Palatinus, and may be found in numerous early printed editions of Virgil, including those of Ascensius. Again at X.vii.125 Douglas has the personal name 'Lacon', and Coldwell notes Virgil's reading as *Ladona*. But Ascensius's texts (and other 16th-century editions) read *Lacona* at this point (X.413), which explains Douglas's form of the name. There is a similar case in XI.xv.1, where Douglas has 'Choreus', and Coldwell's note implies this is a mistake for *Chloreus* (XI.768). But the mistake is not Douglas's, since Ascensius and other 16th-century editors read *Choreus* too. Similarly Coldwell's note to IX.iii.104–5 ('Quhou mony

---

[3]   Scholars name him variously Badius, Josse Bade and Ascensius. I shall refer to him as Ascensius, since this is what Douglas himself and his latest editor call him.

steill stammyt bargis that ayr / Stude by the costis syde, or thai war fyryt') implies
that these lines derive not from Virgil but from Ascensius's commentary. In fact
Douglas is translating line 121: *Quot prius aeratae steterant ad litora prorae*. Most
modern editors now relegate this line to the footnotes, but Mackail still keeps it
in the text, although he admits that 'this line is not in any good manuscript and
is an insertion from X.223'.

It seems desirable therefore to indicate with greater precision some of the points
where the text of Douglas's Virgil differs from a modern one. The list that follows (it
is by no means a complete inventory) contains passages from the *Eneados* in which
Douglas appears to depart from the text of a good modern edition of the *Aeneid* (my
citations are taken from Mynors' O.C.T. edition), but in fact is translating readings
that had a wide currency in the 16th century. Some occur only in the printed editions,
while some occur in the manuscripts and are quoted by Mynors. To illustrate this,
I have noted readings from the following texts, whose editors differed considerably
in methods and ideals:

1. Asc = Ascensius's Virgil, three editions of which were printed at Paris in the
   early 16th century: 1500–1 (henceforth referred to as 1501, since this is the date
   of the second part in which the *Aeneid* appeared), 1507 and 1512. (For a fuller
   description, see P. Renouard, *Bibliographie des Impressions et des Oeuvres de Josse
   Badius Ascensius*, iii, Paris, 1908, pp. 356–68; also G. Mambelli, *Gli Annali delle
   Edizioni Virgiliane*, Firenze, 1954, nos 93, 111 and 121.) Unless a date is specified,
   the reading is the same in all three editions.

2. Brant = Sebastian Brant's famous illustrated edition of Virgil, printed at Strasbourg
   in 1502. (Mambelli, no 99.)

3. Aldus = the second edition of Aldus Manutius's Virgil, printed at Venice in 1505.
   (Mambelli, no 106.)

Each entry contains, therefore, an extract from Douglas's text, followed by the equivalent passage from Mynors' Latin text, followed by the variant reading in the editions
of Ascensius, Brant and Aldus. It should be noted that I use italics to identify more
readily the words or phrases being compared in the Scots and Latin texts.

1.   II.ii.52–3:
          Quhil in prosperite of the realm he stude,
          And Grekis *ryng* [= kingdom] by counsale was rewlit wysly,
     II.88–9:
          dum stabat regno incolumis *regumque* uigebat
          conciliis,
     Asc, Brant, Aldus: *regnumque*

2.   IV.iv.17–19:
          Hyngand *by hir syde* the cays with arowis grund;
          Hir bricht tressis envolupyt war and wond
          Intil a quayf of fyne gold wyrin threid;
     IV.138:
          cui pharetra *ex auro*, crines nodantur in aurum,
     Asc, Brant, Aldus: *ex humero*

3.   IV.ix.52–4:

> For so the religyus *commandyt* has,
> To omdo and distroy al maner thyng
> Quhilk may ʒon wareit man to memor bring."

IV.497–8:

> abolere nefandi
> cuncta uiri monimenta *iuuat* monstratque sacerdos.'

Asc, Brant, Aldus: *iubet*

4.   V.ii.92–4:

> Lyke to the rayn bow amang clowdis lycht,
> *Drawand* always forgane the son cleir,
> A thousand cullouris of diuers hewis seir.

V.88–9:

> ceu nubibus arcus
> mille *iacit* uarios aduerso sole colores.

Asc, Brant, Aldus: *trahit*

5.   V.xiii.119–20:

> Tho kan this fader of the see, but mair,
> Hys horssis ʒok to draw his *cart or chair*,

V.817:

> iungit equos *auro* genitor,

Asc, Brant, Aldus: *curru*

6.   VI.i.134–5:

> So eftir that to Phebus and Diane
> Of sownd marbill *tempillis* beld may I,

VI.69–70:

> tum Phoebo et Triuiae solido de marmore *templum*
> instituam

Asc, Brant, Aldus: *templa*

7.   VI.xiii.33 ff.:

> Behald quhat maner ʒong gallandis bene ʒon,
> Quhou gret curage thar hart is set apon, ...
> *Bot ʒon*, with coverit hedys by and by
> With ciuile crownys of the strang aik tre,

VI.771–2:

> qui iuuenes! quantas ostentant, aspice, uiris
> *atque* umbrata gerunt ciuili tempora quercu!

Asc, Brant, Aldus: *At qui*, Douglas's repeated 'ʒon' is clearly modelled on the repeated *qui* in his original.

8.   VII.v.99–102:

> Furth of hir set and myrk dongeoun of hell
> Scho dyd provoke, and callys with a ʒell

> Ane of the sory furyus *sisteris* thre,
> Alecto,

VII.324–5:

> luctificam Allecto dirarum ab sede *dearum*
> infernisque ciet tenebris,

Asc, Brant, Aldus: *sororum*

9.   VIII.ix.30:

> To go onto the *land and cost* Tyrrene.

VIII.555:

> ire … Tyrrheni ad *limina* regis.

Asc, Brant, Aldus: *littora*

10.   IX.viii.24–5:

> And as thai stand ful dolorusly, thai *se*
> The twa hedys stikkand on the speris,

IX.471:

> stant maesti; simul ora uirum praefixa *mouebant*

Asc, Brant, Aldus: *videbant*

11.   X.i.39–41:

> "O thou," quod sche,
> "Fader of all, O eternal powste,
> Regnand abufe all men, and *goddis* eik,

X.18:

> 'o pater, o hominum *rerumque* aeterna potestas

Asc, Brant, Aldus: *diuumque*

12.   X.viii.2–4:

> The haly nymphe, clepit Iuturna,
> Hir brother Turnus dyd monys and exhort
> To *succur* Lawsus, and hys folk support;

X.439–40:

> Interea soror alma monet *succedere* Lauso
> Turnum

Asc, Brant, Aldus: *succurrere*

13.   X.x.118–20:

> The tother fey brother, or evyr he stynt,
> Lap fra the cart, and kneland petuusly,
> Vphevand hys *bayr* handis, thus dyd cry:

X.595–6:

> frater tendebat *inertis*
> infelix palmas curru delapsus eodem:

Asc, Brant, Aldus: *inermes*

14.   X.x.137–9:

>   Thys Dardane prynce as *victor* thus in weir
>   Samony douchty corpsis brocht on beir
>   Amyd the planys

        X.602–3:

>   talia per campos edebat funera *ductor*
>   Dardanius

        Asc, Brant, Aldus: *victor*

15.   X.xi.57:

>   *To quham* Iuno on this wys said wepyng:

        X.628:

>   *et* Iuno adlacrimans:

        Asc, Brant, Aldus: *Cui*

16.   X.xiv.43–5:

>   Allace, onto me, wrachit catyve thing,
>   Myne *exill* now at last and *banysyng*
>   Becummyn is hard and insufferabill!

        X.849–50:

>   heu, nunc, misero mihi demum
>   *exitium* infelix,

        Asc, Brant, Aldus: *Exilium*

17.   XI.ii.85–6:

>   Furth haldis syne the drery cumpany
>   Of Troianys, and Tyrrheyn *dukis* thame by;

        XI.92–3:

>   tum maesta phalanx Teucrique sequuntur
>   Tyrrhenique *omnes*

        Asc, Brant, Aldus: *duces*

18.   XI.viii.81–2:

>   Now, O thou *gret* fader and prynce souerane,
>   To the and thy consale I turn agane.

        XI.410:

>   nunc ad te et tua *magna*, pater, consulta reuertor.

        Asc, Brant, Aldus: *magne*

19.   XI.viii.90 ff.:

>   Lat ws beseik for paix at sik distres, …
>   And reke hym furth our ryght hand *bair of armys*.

        XI.414:

>   oremus pacem et dextras tendamus *inertis*.

        Asc, Brant, Aldus: *inermes*

20. XI.xi.92–3:

        With dartis keyn and hedis scharply grund

        Hir fystis and hir handis *chargyt* he;

    XI.574:

            iaculo palmas *armauit* acuto

    Asc, Brant, Aldus: *onerauit*

21. XI.xv.15–16:

        And *clattryng* by hys schuldyr for the weir

        Hys ganȝe cays and goldyn awblaster;

    XI.774:

        aureus ex umeris *erat* arcus

    Asc, Brant, Aldus: *sonat*

22. XI.xv.75–7:

        The *rowtis* can aduert [= notice] and takis tent,

        Turnand thar syghtis, ilk wight, with a blent

        Towart the queyn, thar lady, this Camyll;

    XI.800–1:

        conuertere animos *acris* oculosque tulere

        cuncti ad reginam Volsci.

    Asc, Brant: *acies*; Aldus: *acres*

23. XII.v.98:

        Rutilianys, hynt ȝour wapynnys, and follow me,

    XII.260–1:

            me, me duce ferrum

        corripite, o *miseri*,

    Asc, Brant, Aldus: *rutuli*

24. XII.vi.167–9:

        Quham tho (allace, gret piete was to se!)

        The quhirland quheill and spedy swyft extre

        Smate doun to grond,

    XII.379–80:

        cum rota praecipitem et procursu concitus axis

        impulit effunditque solo,

    Asc, Brant, Aldus: *Quem*

25. XII.viii.1–2:

        Quhen this was said, furth at the portis *hee* [= high],

        Schakand in hand a gret speir, ischit he.

    XII.441–2:

        Haec ubi dicta dedit, portis sese extulit *ingens*

        telum immane manu quatiens;

    Asc, Brant, Aldus: *altis*

26.   XII.xii.59–61:
        For feir the bestis dum all standis by,
        And all in dowt squelys the ʒong ky,
        Quha salbe master of the *catal* all,
    XII.718–19:
        stat pecus omne metu mutum, mussantque iuuencae
        quis *nemori* imperitet,
    Asc, Brant, Aldus: *pecori*

27.   XII.xii.185:
        And tharon eik the clathis *bekend* vpstent.
    XII.769:
        et *uotas* suspendere uestis;
    Asc, Brant, Aldus: *notas*

28.   XII.xiii.189:
        Or quhat now restis to me, *wrachit* wight?
    XII.873:
        aut quid iam *durae* superat mihi?
    Asc, Brant, Aldus: *miserae*

29.   XII.xiii.207–9:
        For, *gif I mortal war*, now, now suythly,
        Thir sa gret dolouris mycht I end inhy,
        And with my reuthfull brother go withall
    XII.880–2:
        possem tantos finire dolores
        nunce certe, et misero fratri comes ire per umbras!
        immortalis ego?
    Asc, Brant, Aldus: *Iam mortalis*; Asc commentary: *si essem iam mortalis
    ego*; Aldus: *Immortalis*

30.   XIII.xi.53–6:
        I sall alsso heich ony of hys kyn,
        Quhilk of thar proper vertu lyst do wyn
        Perpetuall lovyng [= praise] by dedis honorabill,
        And *doith contemp* the wrachit warld onstabill;
    Mapheus Vegius, 617–19[4]:
        Quin si alios sua habet virtus, qui laude perenni
        Accingant sese, gestis praestantibus orbem
        Exornent, illos rursum super aethera mittam."
    Asc, Brant: *Exhorrent*; Aldus: *Exornent*

---

[4]   The text is that of the editio princeps (Venice, Adam de Ambergau, 1471), reprinted, with modernised spelling and punctuation, by A. Cox Brinton in *Maphaeus Vegius and his Thirteenth Book of the Aeneid*, Stanford, 1930.

What may we deduce from a study of these readings? Again and again, they clear Douglas from charges of ignorance, carelessness or downright stupidity as a translator. His spelling of proper names does not show a barbarous indifference to the Virgilian forms but rather a close following of what he found in texts of his own time. (See the discussion above, pp. 42–3; also nos 9 and 13 in section II below, and several of the examples in section III.) Many apparent 'howlers' and comic mistranslations simply disappear, when we realise how different from ours was the reading he had before him: *pecori* not *nemori* (no 26), *notas* not *uotas* (no 27), *iam mortalis* not *immortalis* (no 29), *exhorrent* not *exornent* (no 30). (See also nos 11, 16, 19, 22, 23 and 28.) Sometimes the effect of greater knowledge of Douglas's text is less striking, discernible only if one compares the Latin and Scots very carefully. The effect is to remove small blurs and blemishes in the translation rather than 'howlers' (as in nos 1, 3, 4, 8, 9, 10 and 20), or to explain the presence of small details that one might otherwise think his own interpolation – 'to draw his cart or chair' in no 5, or 'clattering' in no 21. Apparent omissions in the translation may sometimes be accounted for similarly (e.g. of *auro* in no 2). What also emerges clearly is how literal a translator Douglas often is: 'succur' (no 12), 'victor' (no 14) and 'dukis' (no 17) translate, respectively, *succurrere*, *victor*, and *duces*. Similarly, Douglas's closeness to the Latin syntax in nos 7, 15, 18 and 24 is apparent only if we know precisely what was the reading he had before him; it is concealed if we consult a modern edition. I do not assert that Douglas is always an impeccable translator. What these passages show is that if there appears some blur or oddity about his translation, one should not condemn him too swiftly; there may be extenuating circumstances.

II.

Can we identify the particular edition of Virgil that Douglas used? The task might seem an impossibly difficult one, considering the large number of texts available when Douglas was writing. Virgil was consistently one of the most popular of the classical poets. His works were printed and re-printed; over 100 separate editions are listed in Mambelli's *Gli Annali delle Edizioni Virgiliane* between the *editio princeps* (?1469) and 1512. Moreover, manuscripts of his works continued to be copied and illuminated long after the introduction of printing.[5]

But it is possible to narrow the field by various means. Douglas claims to have spent 18 months on his translation, and ended it on 22 July 1513: 'Apon the fest of Mary Magdelan, / Fra Crystis byrth, the dait quha lyst to heir, / A thousand fyve hundreth and thretteyn 3eir;' (*Tyme, Space and Dait*, lines 2–4, Coldwell's edition, iv, p. 194). There is nothing to suggest this statement is false, and it seems unlikely therefore that he would have used an edition published later than 1512. Furthermore, he translated Maphaeus Vegius's 13th book, a 15th-century supplement to the *Aeneid* which is frequently but not invariably found in Virgils of this period. (Aldus Manutius included it in his 1505 edition of Virgil, but not in the editions of 1501 or 1514.) The edition that

---

[5] See C. F. Bühler, *The Fifteenth-Century Book*, Philadelphia, 1960, pp. 33 and 117; B. M. MS. King's 24, which has fine miniatures, was written at the end of the 15th century. For a mid-15th century manuscript in Scottish ownership, see C. P. Finlayson, 'A Glamis Virgil?', *Scottish Historical Review*, xxxii (1953), pp. 99–100.

Douglas used also contained 12 lines of Latin verse, summarising the action of each book of the *Aeneid* (*monosticha argumenta*), which he versified as 'the contentis of euery buke followyng' (Coldwell's edition, ii, p. 18). Perhaps the most valuable clue is that Douglas used an edition containing the commentary of Ascensius, whom he mentions approvingly in VI.Prol.73. Aloys Schumacher seems to have pointed this out first in his dissertation, *Des Bischofs Gavin Douglas Übersetzung der Aeneis Vergils*, Strassburg, 1910, pp. 88 ff. More recently Dr David Coldwell has greatly advanced our knowledge of Douglas's dependence on Ascensius; the notes to his edition of the *Eneados* seem to me to prove unmistakably Douglas's close and continuous use of Ascensius's commentary, which was not published separately but always accompanied the text of Virgil.[6] The first edition was printed for Ascensius by T. Kerver and J. Petit at Paris between 1500 and 1501, and was reprinted several times in the early 16th century (see above, p. 43). It contains the 13th book, and also has the *monosticha argumenta* in the form which Douglas translated. It seems likely that if Douglas used Ascensius's commentary he would also use the text to which it was related, and I think there is ample evidence to support this.

Some scholars, however, have argued that Douglas used Sebastian Brant's edition of Virgil (Strasbourg, 1502). This theory is briefly discussed by Edmund Schmidt in his *Die Schottische Aeneisübersetzung von Gavin Douglas* (Leipzig, 1910), pp. 12–13. His evidence, however, is flimsy. He mentions the presence of the 13th book in Brant; but this and the five readings which he cites as proving Douglas's use of Brant are present in Ascensius also. Four of these variant readings are discussed by Coldwell: for dei not dii, see I.ix.102 and note; for auxilium not augurium, see II.xi.21 and note; for lęti not leti, see IV.iv.83 and note; for extinxi not extinxti, see IV.xii.80 and note. Schmidt's other piece of evidence, that at VI.xiii.36 Douglas was translating a text with At qui not atque, points equally to Ascensius or Brant (see no 7 above). A later scholar, O. L. Jiriczek, was aware that Douglas had used Ascensius's commentary, and modified the argument, suggesting that he might have used both texts: 'Douglas may very well be credited with having had access to more than one edition.'[7] Miss Florence H. Ridley, who has discussed the problem most recently,[8] follows Jiriczek in arguing that in book IV at least Douglas used both Ascensius and Brant. She admits, however, that her evidence is 'meager'; that is, at IV.iv.31–2 'Renewand ryngis and dansys, mony a rowt; / Mixt togidder, his altaris standing about', Douglas translated Virgil's line 145 (instauratque choros mixtique altaria circum), a line which though present in Brant is missing from Ascensius. This might be construed as evidence against Douglas's use of Ascensius, but why should it point so specifically to his use of Brant, when many other editions must, if correct, have contained this line? In fact, although Virgil's line is omitted from Ascensius's text, it is found in full in his commentary, together with an explanatory paraphrase. I think Douglas is following the commentary at this point, even when discrepant with the text, as he does on several other occasions. (See below, pp. 57–8, for further discussion of this

---

6   I shall supply further evidence of this in my forthcoming book on Douglas. [See now Bawcutt 1976.]

7   *Specimens of Tudor Translations from the Classics*, Heidelberg, 1923, p. 3.

8   In *The 'Aeneid' of Henry Howard, Earl of Surrey*, Berkeley and Los Angeles, 1963, pp. 22 ff.

practice.) Neither Jiriczek nor Miss Ridley claims to have studied the textual variants in more than a small portion of the Aeneid; Miss Ridley repeats Jiriczek's assertion that the 'textual tradition of Virgil is rather uniform'.[9] In fact, there are numerous divergencies between the texts of Ascensius and Brant, some comparatively trivial, some far more weighty. If one studies these variants and attempts to relate them to Douglas's translation, there seems no definite evidence that he used Brant's text. I have found no reading in Douglas that could have originated only in Brant, whereas again and again I have found cases in which Douglas is translating a reading that may be found in all editions of Ascensius but not in Brant. Some of these are listed below (again Coldwell's text of Douglas is given first, followed by Mynors' Latin text followed by the Ascensius and Brant readings):

1. II.iii.63–4:
    > Les than agane the land of Arge he socht
    > With *alkyn portage* quhilk was hydder brocht
    II.178:
    > *omina* ni repetant Argis numenque reducant
    Asc: *omnia*
    Brant: *omina*

2. II.iii.100–1:
    > And takyn ar by dissait and *fenʒeit* teris
    > Tha pepil
    II.196:
    > captique dolis lacrimisque *coactis*
    Asc: *coactis*
    Brant: *coacti*

3. II.xii.28–9:
    > Than scho, belyfe, on this wys to me spak,
    > With sic wordis my thochtis to asswage:
    II.775:
    > tum sic adfari et curas his demere dictis:
    Asc: whole line present
    Brant: whole line omitted

4. III.ix.61–2:
    > For he is vgsum and grysly forto se,
    > *Hutyt to speke of*, and *aucht not nemmyt be*.
    III.621:
    > nec uisu facilis nec dictu *adfabilis* ulli;
    Asc: *effabilis* = speakable of
    Brant: *affabilis* = speakable to, affable

---

9   Op. cit., p. 25.

5.   IV.iii.9:

        quhou gret *power* and notabil *mycht*
    IV.94:

        (magnum et memorabile *numen*),
    Asc: *numen*
    Brant: *nomen*

6.   IV.v.84–6:

        With syk wordis Kyng Hyarbas at hame
        Makyng hys prayeris, and grippand the *altar*,
        Him hard onon almychty Iupiter,
    IV.219–20:

        Talibus orantem dictis *arasque* tenentem
        audiit Omnipotens,
    Asc: *aramque*
    Brant: *arasque*

7.   V.xii.96–7:

        The cite salbe, *as was first cunnand* [= covenant, promise]
        Acesta clepyt, eftir Acestes king."
    V.718:

        urbem appellabunt *permisso* nomine Acestam.'
    Asc: *promisso*
    Brant: *permisso*

8.   VII.x.91–2:

        He dryvis furth the *stampand* hors on raw
        Onto the 30k, the chareottis to draw;
    VII.638–9:

            ille *trementis*
        ad iuga cogit equos,
    Asc: *trementes*
    Brant: *frementes*

9.   VII.xii.13–14:

        Of *Mytisca*,[10] quhilk now heicht Tribule,
        Quhar growys of olyve treys gret plente;
    VII.711:

            oliuiferaeque *Mutuscae*;
    Asc: *mitiscᴁ*
    Brant: *mutuscᴁ*

10.   VIII.vi.103–4:

        This *cite* beldit our ald fader Ianus,
        And 30nder cite fundit Saturnus:

---

[10]   Coldwell's *Mystisca* at this point is a misreading or a misprint.

VIII.357:

> hanc Ianus pater, hanc Saturnus condidit *arcem*;

Asc: *vrbem*

Brant: *arcem*

11. VIII.xii.69 ff.:

> In went Discord, …
> Quham followit Bellona of batell,
> With *hir kynd cosyng*, the scharp scurgis fell.

VIII.702–3:

> et scissa gaudens uadit Discordia palla,
> quam *cum sanguineo* sequitur Bellona flagello.

Asc: *consanguineo*

Brant: *cum sanguineo*

12. X.xiii.111–12:

> And eik the travellour 3ond vnder the wald
> Lurkand withdrawys to sum sovir *hald*,

X.805:

> et tuta latet *arce* uiator.

Asc: *arce*

Brant: *arte*

13. XI.xiii.39–40:

> With the formast, *Ewmenyus*, that was one
> Son to *Clysius*;

XI.666:

> *Eunaeum Clytio* primum patre,

Asc: *Eumenium clycio*

Brant: *Euneum clytio*

14. XI.xiii.52–3:

> And the tother present, to kep hym vndir,
> Furth straucht his *febill* arm to stynt his fall,

XI.671–2:

> alter
> dum subit ac dextram labenti tendit *inermem*,

Asc: *inertem*

Brant: *inermem*

15. XI.xiv.51–2:

> This Tarchon, ardent as the fyry levyn,
> Flaw furth swyft as a fowle *vp towart hevyn*,

XI.746:

> uolat igneus *aequore* Tarchon

Asc: *⊠there*

Brant: *aequore*

16.   XI.xvi.23–6:
        Quhat proffitis the in buskis thyne allane
        To haue servyt so lang the blissyt Diane?
        Or by thy syde, or than on schuldir hie,
        So lang our *quavyrris* to haue born?" quod sche.
    XI.843–4:
        nec tibi desertae in dumis coluisse Dianam
        profuit aut nostras umero gessisse *pharetras.*
    Asc: *pharetras*
    Brant: *sagittas*

17.   XII.xiii.25–8:
        Ne suffir not thy hyd sorrow, I pray,
        Na langar the consume and waist away,
        That I na mar sik wofull thochtis se
        Schyne nor appeir in thy sweit face," quod he,
    XII.801–2:
        ne te tantus edit tacitam dolor et mihi curae
        saepe tuo dulci tristes ex ore *recursent.*
    Asc: *coruscent*; Asc commentary: *idest cum coruscatione quadam emineant*
    Brant: *recursent*

18.   XIII.iv.21–2:
        The *remanent* syne of the haill barnage
        Followys wepand,
    Maphaeus Vegius, 197–8:
            tum *extera* pubes
        Flens sequitur.
    Asc: *cetera*
    Brant: *extera*

III.

The evidence, therefore, seems to point towards Douglas's use of Ascensius. But Ascensius published several editions of Virgil; which one did Douglas use? In his Introduction Dr Coldwell says: 'It is my belief that Douglas translated from a text of a common type, with a block of Vergil in the centre of the page ... flanked on one side by the commentary of Servius and on the other by that of Jodocus Badius Ascensius ... I have used an edition of Vergil's works from the Library of the University of Edinburgh (here called 1507 because the colophon is so dated), an edition in which the text is thus laid out on the page, and I have considered it worth while to record in the notes the general agreement of Douglas's chapter divisions with that edition's woodcuts (which were done by Sebastian Brant)' (pp. 59–60). Later he says that this edition was printed at Lyons (p. 143). Coldwell thus implies that this particular edition was early enough to have been used by Douglas. But there is no such thing as a 1507 Ascensius printed at Lyons, and this Edinburgh copy of Virgil's works should be dated 1517, not 1507. None of Ascensius's early editions of Virgil was printed at Lyons; according to Renouard's bibliographical study the first printed at Lyons appeared in 1517.[11] Again, none of the early editions of Virgil published by Ascensius contains woodcuts. Many of the early 16th-century Lyons printers were reputed to have 'blatantly copied the most successful works of the Parisian and Venetian printers',[12] and in this particular edition of 1517 the Lyons printer Jacques Sacon appears to have combined the text and commentary of Ascensius's Virgil with the fine series of woodcuts that first appeared in the famous 1502 Strasbourg Virgil published by Sebastian Brant.[13] Coldwell's mistaken dating seems to have occurred, partly because the dedication of the 1517 *Aeneid* contains the date 1507 (but this date, as was not uncommon,[14] has been repeated from the earlier Paris edition of 1507); and partly because the Edinburgh University copy is defective, lacking the title-page and preliminary leaves of the first part (which contains the shorter poems), and in the second part (i.e. the *Aeneid*) lacking the final leaves and therefore the colophon, which in other copies of the 1517 edition that I have examined reads: *Excussit Lugduni … Jacobus Sacon. Anno … MDXVII ad tertias nonas Decembres.* It should be noted, however, that the colophon of the first part is still extant in the Edinburgh copy, and is clearly dated August 1517: *MDXVII die vigesima mensis Augusti.*

It is important to be accurate in such matters, because these editions of Ascensius's Virgil, whether printed in Paris or Lyons, are by no means identical. They differ in pagination, in spelling, and, what is more crucial, in actual readings. There are three editions of Virgil printed for Ascensius himself that I think Douglas could have used: 1501, 1507, and 1512. (It is highly improbable that Douglas used another of Ascensius's editions, the *Manuale Vergilianum*.[15] Douglas says of his Virgil that 'the volum was so huge' (*Exclamatioun*, 22), but this is a small pocket-sized edition, which contains no full commentary nor does it have the 13th book.) Of these three editions, however, it seems to me unlikely that Douglas used 1512, if we are to accept his own testimony that the *Eneados* was finished in July 1513, and that it was 'compylit in auchteyn moneth space' (*Tyme, Space and Dait*, 12). The colophon of 1512 is dated June, which barely gives Douglas a year to make his translation, even if one assumes that he received a copy of 1512 hot from the press. My study of the variants in 1501, 1507, and 1512 has not been exhaustive, but the evidence, as far as I can see, points to 1501 as being Douglas's working edition. There are several places in the *Eneados* where Douglas's choice of words suggests that he had before him a Latin reading that may be found in *some* of the Ascensius editions but not in *all*. In six of these the reading is invariably found in

[11] Renouard, *Bibliographie des Impressions et des Oeuvres de Josse Badius Ascensius*, iii, Paris, 1908, pp. 370–72.
[12] N. E. Binns, *An Introduction to Historical Bibliography*, 2nd edition, revised and enlarged, London, 1962, p. 67. See also Renouard, i, p. 19 on 'réimpressions lyonnaises'.
[13] For fuller discussion, see A. F. Johnson, 'Books Printed at Lyons in the 16th Century', *The Library*, 4th Series, 3 (1922), pp. 154–7. On the influence of Brant's woodcuts, see also T. K. Rabb, 'Sebastian Brant and the First Illustrated Edition of Virgil', *Princeton University Library Chronicle*, xxi (1960), pp. 196–8.
[14] Cf. R. B. McKerrow, *An Introduction to Bibliography*, Oxford, 1927, pp. 202–3.
[15] The date is uncertain. See Renouard, iii, pp. 365–6; G. Mambelli, *Gli Annali delle Edizioni Virgiliane*, Firenze, 1954, no 108.

1501, but only in one or other of 1507 or 1512. The first of these, the peculiar reading *Cymynyk* in VII.xi.139 (Small normalized it to *Cymynus*[16]), can be explained, for instance, by a misprint or misreading that I have noted only in 1501 and 1507:

1.   VII.xi.137–40:
          And thai that in Flavynya feildis dwell,
          Or that wonnys besyde the layk or well
          Of *Cymynyk*, vndre the montane bra,
          Or ȝit amang the schawys of Capua—
    This corresponds to:
    VII.696–7:
          hi Soractis habent arces Flauiniaque arua
          et *Cimini cum* monte lacum lucosque Capenos.
    1501, 1507: *ciminicum*
    1512 (also 1517): *cimini cum*

Other examples are:

2.   VII.xii.71 ff.:
          Oebalus, …
          Quham Kyng Telon engendrit, as thai say,
          On *Sabetrydes*, the lusty nymphe or may.
    VII.734–5:
          Oebale, quem generasse Telon *Sebethide* nympha
          fertur,
    1501, 1507: *sebetride*
    1512: *sebethide*
    (1517: *sebethride*)

3.   IX.ix.129–31:
          Fostyrrit he was and vpbrocht tendirly
          Within hys *moderis* hallowyt schaw, fast by
          The flude Symethus into Sicill land,
    IX.584–5:
          eductum *Martis* luco Symaethia circum
          flumina,
    1501, 1507: *matris*
    1512 (also 1517): *martis* (This is perhaps a case where Ascensius had second thoughts about the reading. The three primary manuscripts all read *martis*.)

4.   IX.xi.49:
          Wight *Tynarus*, fers myndit to assaill,
    IX.685:
          et praeceps animi *Tmarus*

---

[16] *The Poetical Works of Gavin Douglas*, with memoir, notes, and glossary by J. Small, iii, Edinburgh, 1874, p. 131.

1501, 1507 (also 1517): *tinarus*
1512: *Tmarus*

5. X.vi.125–6:

> With this come *Clawsus*, full of vassalage,
> Confidand in hys 30uth and florist age,

X.345–6:

> Hic Curibus fidens primaeuo corpore *Clausus*
> aduenit

1501, 1512: *Clausus*
1507 (also 1517): *Lausus*

6. X.xii.153–4:

> Aganys hym than went *a man of Arge*,
> Hait Lycyus, bodyn with speir and targe;

X.751:

> pedes et Lycius processerat *Agis*,

1501, 1512 (1517 also): *Argis*
1507: *Agis*

There is one further piece of evidence which seems to point specifically to 1501 as Douglas's text: this is the reading *Lybibe* in

> The dangerus schaldis and cost vppykyt we,
> With al hys blynd rolkis, of *Lybibe*.
> (III.x.99–100)

This translates 'et uada dura lego saxis *Lilybeia* caecis' (III.706). The error, however, is not Douglas's. The reading *libybeia* occurs in 1501, but is corrected to *lilybeia* in subsequent editions of Ascensius's Virgil.

All the evidence seems to point in one direction. Is there anything which might controvert it? There are one or two cases where Douglas seems to translate readings that are not present in the 1501 edition of Ascensius. This might appear disconcerting, but the difficulty can be resolved by remembering Douglas's close use of Ascensius's commentary, and the fact that this commentary sometimes quotes variant readings or even at times glosses readings not actually adopted in the text. Several examples of this may be mentioned. In II.x.99 Douglas speaks of the 'weirlyke weid' of Pallas Athene. This may seem an odd translation of *nimbo*, 'cloud enveloping a god or goddess' (Ascensius's reading at II.616); in fact it corresponds not to this but to *chlamyde militari*, Ascensius's gloss for the variant *limbo* which he mentions immediately after *nimbo* in his commentary. Earlier in book II occurs the famous *Troiaque nunc staret, Priamique arx alta maneres* (56), which appears in Douglas as

> Than suld thou, Troy, haue standyn 3it, but dowt,
> And the prowd palyce of Kyng Priamus
> Suld haue remanyt 3it ful gloryus."

> (II.i.78–80)

Douglas's rendering suggests that in his text the verbs had the form *stares ... maneret.* 1501, however, has *stares ... maneres.* The problem is resolved by the commentary, which reads: *tu stares scilicet incolumis & alta arx priami maneret sup. adhuc: aut & tu o alta arx priami maneres.*[17] A further example may be quoted from VI.xvi.27, where 'hir prowd place of beddis' corresponds to *tectisque superbis* (VII.12) but appears to translate the variant *lectis.* Ascensius's text has *tectis* at this point; his commentary, however, makes no mention of *tectis*, reading only *lectis superbis. idest magnifice extructis.* (See also the discussion above, pp. 50–1)

I do not assert dogmatically that Douglas used one particular edition of Virgil and no other. A man of his education would have studied Virgil both at school and at university; and a man with his interest in books and enthusiasm for poetry would probably have possessed a copy of Virgil long before 1501, when he was aged 26 or 27. Indeed, there are many signs of his reading of Virgil in his early poem, *The Palice of Honour*, which was probably composed by or before 1501.[18] There is, however, a great deal of evidence, drawn evenly from all books of the *Eneados*, which leads me to conclude that, though Douglas may have been acquainted with other editions of Virgil, when he came to translate the *Aeneid*, he chose Ascensius's Virgil and, more specifically, the edition of 1501 as his working text. Many hitherto dark places in Douglas's own text are illuminated when we set them beside Ascensius's text of Virgil; many 'howlers' vanish, and Douglas emerges as an intelligent and responsible, if not a perfect, translator, striving to make the best sense he could of a far from ideal text. I think Douglas may have been led to use Ascensius not only because of the many links at this time between Ascensius's press and Scottish scholars,[19] but because of the similarity between Ascensius's aims and his own. The prefaces to Ascensius's editions of the Latin classics make it clear that they were not intended for advanced students; contrasting him with Aldus Manutius, Renouard says that he was 'surtout un divulgateur et son effort tendait à faciliter aux débutants l'étude des auteurs classiques pour leur permettre d'apprendre le latin aux meilleures sources de latinité.'[20] Douglas says of his translation of the *Aeneid*:

> Now salt thou with euery gentill Scot be kend,
> And to onletterit folk be red on hight,
> That erst was bot with clerkis comprehend.
>
> (*Exclamatioun*, 43–5)

Both Ascensius and Douglas were popularisers, attempting to make more accessible to a wider audience than 'clerks' the classical literature and learning that they themselves valued so highly.

---

[17] It looks as though Ascensius was hesitating over which reading to adopt. 1507 is the same as 1501, but in 1512 the reading has been altered, and the verbs appear as *stares ... maneret.*

[18] See *The Shorter Poems of Gavin Douglas*, ed. Priscilla J. Bawcutt, Scottish Text Society, Ser. 4, iii, Edinburgh, 1967, pp. xxvii–xxix.

[19] Many of John Major's works were printed by Ascensius; for some of his other Scottish connections, see Renouard's Index, under Boece, Caubraith, Lauxius, Lokert and Vaus.

[20] Renouard, i, p. 29.

COMMENTARY

The Commentary is the joint work of Priscilla Bawcutt and Ian Cunningham, but each is primarily responsible for different sections of it. Priscilla Bawcutt has contributed the Commentary on the Prologues. This is essentially a new piece of work, which is not a revision of Coldwell, although it occasionally refers to his views and glosses.

Ian Cunningham has supplied the Notes on the Translation, and writes, as follows, on their complex relationship to Coldwell's original Notes:

> By far the largest and most valuable part of Coldwell's notes consists of data on two related topics: differences between original and translation, and the influence of contemporary texts and commentaries on the translation.
>
> On the former he cites misunderstandings, additions and omissions on the part of the translator, and these notes are (apart from the correction of misprints) here reproduced substantially without change.
>
> On the latter, while his observations are basically sound and important, some misapprehensions have necessitated a thorough revision. Coldwell thought that the edition of Virgil with the commentaries of Servius and Ascensius which he used dated from 1507, but it has since been shown (Bawcutt 1973, reprinted here) to be of 1517, and so later than Douglas's publication; the edition probably used was that of 1501 (ibid.). The citations in the notes have therefore been corrected against a copy of that edition.[1] Its layout perhaps requires explanation. The text of Virgil is printed in one column, next to the inner margin on both recto and verso, and is divided into sections. For each section Servius's commentary follows below the text, and Ascensius's is placed in the outer column, starting beside the beginning of the text; if either extends beyond the other, it

---

[1] In the National Library of Scotland, K.51.c.7 (identified as such during the course of this work). As this is complete for the *Aeneid*, including bk. 13, Coldwell's use of the 1517 edition here, where his principal source was lacking, has also become obsolete. Aeneis Vergiliana cum Seruii Honorati grammatici huberrimis comme[n]tariis, cum Philippi Beroaldi seculi nostri principis doctissimis in eosdem an[n]otationibus suis locis positis. Cum Donati argutissimis subinde sententiarum pr[a]esertim enodationib[us]. Cumq[ue] familiarissima Iodoci Badii Ascensii elucidatione atq[ue] ordinis contextu. Accessit ad hoc Mapphei Veggii liber additicius cum Ascensianis an[n]otatiunculis. Addita praeterea sunt ipsius poet[a]e ac operu[m] eius illustrium virorum pr[a]econia: Aeneidos argumenta & qu[a]edam eiusdem poetae nostri epitaphia. Paris: Quae omnia polite & diligenter a Thielmanno Keruer coimpressa. Venundantur Parrhisiis ab optimis Bibliopolis Ioanne paruo in Leone argenteo regionis diui Iacobi. & Ioanne confluentino ad vicum cytharae in asino intercincto vulgariter a lasne raye.1501.

has from that point the full width. Servius therefore is on ra (recto col. 1) and vb (verso col. 2), Ascensius on rb (recto col. 2) and va (verso col. 1), while both occasionally do not require a column specification. For ease of reference, the folio numbers (as Arabic numerals) have been added, as have references to the lines of the *Aeneid*; while mention of the beginning of sections and woodcuts (regarded as significant by Coldwell) has been removed, as Ascensius's sections do not correspond at all closely with Douglas's chapters and 1501 has no woodcuts.

References to the text and manuscripts of Virgil have been modernized, with information from Mynors's edition. Citations from other authors have been where necessary clarified and updated. 'The translator' is replaced by 'Douglas', and 'Virgil' is written in English (not Vergil). The regrettably large number of misprints throughout have been corrected. Notes which have been substantively modified from Coldwell's are marked with an asterisk *. '—' marks an omission. Apart from standard classical abbreviations, note 's'. for 'scilicet', 'i'. for 'idest'. It should be noted that the abbreviations used here for the major Virgilian manuscripts are: M for Mediceus, P for Palatinus, and R¹ for Romanus. (The latter is employed to distinguish it from R for the Ruthven Manuscript.)

Prologue I

The longest and most important of the prologues, this is an introduction not just to book I but to the translation as a whole. Douglas here expresses his views on Virgil's greatness, the significance of the *Aeneid*, and various problems of a translator. He reverts to some of these topics in later prologues, especially V and VI. The tone is remarkably varied: for the most part colloquial and informal, it ranges from the elevated style of the opening panegyric on Virgil to near-flyting in the attack on Caxton. The verse is the five-stress couplet, which is employed for the translation itself, and several of the later prologues.

1–74. The opening is highly rhetorical; its figures of speech, elevated diction and imagery, drawn from jewels, flowers, and light, are characteristic of contemporary eulogy. Cf. the later praise of Chaucer in lines 339–43.

3. *of Latyn poetis prynce*. This was a common commendation of Virgil. Cf. Boccaccio, *De Genealogia Deorum*, XIV.xiii: 'Virgilium, Latinorum poetarum principem'.

6–7. *palm, lawrer … cedyr tre*. Cf. IX.Prol.38–9, and note.

6. *regester*. 'Register'. This prosaic-sounding term for Virgil is interestingly paralleled by Douglas's reference to Ovid as Calliope's 'Clerk … of Register' in *The Palice of Honour*, 1186–7. Virgil and Ovid were poets whose writings registered, or preserved for posterity, the great deeds of heroes.

7. *charbukkill*. 'Carbuncle', the name for a type of ruby, and also a mythical precious stone believed to emit light. It was a common symbol of excellence. Dunbar calls the young Queen Margaret 'Our charbunkle chosin' (*Poems*, 15.5).

8. *A per se*. 'A standing alone; pre-eminent, unique'. Cf. the application to Chaucer in *Palice of Honour*, 919; and Whiting A 3.

10. *thyne hevynly bell*. The image is a favourite of Douglas's; cf. line 22 below; II.Prol.11; and *Directioun*, 128.

14. Cf. Horace, *Ars Poetica*, 361: 'Ut pictura poesis'.

16–18. A type of hyperbole known as the outdoing topos (Curtius 1953, 162–5). For the rose as surpassing all other flowers, see Whiting R 205. Douglas couples the marigold and daisy similarly in *Palice of Honour*, 37.

16. *Surmontyng … endyte*. The words may echo Dunbar's praise of Chaucer in *Goldyn Targe* (*Poems*, 59.260–1).

19ff. The modesty is traditional, but not insincere. Cf. *Palice of Honour*, 127–35.

33. *Stra for …* A Chaucerian expression of contempt; cf. 'Straw for thy Senek' (*CT.* IV.1567); and IX.Prol.41.

52. *Thyne is the thank and myne salbe the schame. Thank* here means 'credit, merit'. Douglas is slightly varying a modesty topos, employed by English poets from Chaucer to Shakespeare, that derives ultimately from Boccaccio's *Il Filostrato*, I, stanza 5: 'Tuo sia l'onore, e mio si sia l'affanno [labour]'. See further Bawcutt 1984.

57–9. Cf. other allusions to Virgil as a 'flude' and spring of eloquence (4, 9, 310). Douglas employs the traditional theme of the poet who drinks from the Muses' fountain on Mount Helicon; see *Palice of Honour*, 1134ff. *Sugurit tun* then converts the image to that of wine.

60–3. Virgil is a source of illumination for all later poets.

62. *Vesper.* The evening star, similarly linked with the 'stern of day' by Dunbar in *Goldyn Targe*, 1–2.

67–74. *Macrobius.* Macrobius Ambrosius Theodosius (floruit late fifth century), author of the *Saturnalia*, an encyclopedic compilation in dialogue form, much of which is devoted to the praise and discussion of Virgil. Lines 73–4 translate *Saturnalia*, I.24.8: 'haec est quidem ... Maronis gloria ut nullius laudibus crescat, nullius vituperatione minuatur'. See also notes to V.Prol.33–6, and 37; VII.Prol.14.

86. Henry, 3rd Lord Sinclair (d. 1513) was the grandson of William Sinclair, 3rd Earl of Orkney (d. 1480). Henry owned an important manuscript anthology of courtly poetry, Oxford, Bodleian Library Arch. Selden. B. 24, and the Sinclair family included other noted book collectors. See *Scots Peerage*, VII.571–2; Crawford 1985 and 'Sinclair Family (per. 1280–c. 1500)', *ODNB*; and Boffey 2006.

88. *Homeir.* Although there is no evidence that Douglas could read Greek, he knew of Homer's literary eminence (cf. *Palice of Honour*, 895–7). He may have read Lorenzo Valla's Latin version of the first sixteen books of the *Iliad* (1442–4), a copy of which was owned by Walter Ogilvie (Durkan and Ross 1961, 134).

90. *neir coniunct ... in blude.* Douglas perhaps alludes to Elizabeth Douglas, sister of Archibald, 5th Earl of Douglas, and first wife of Henry's grandfather, William, Earl of Orkney (*Scots Peerage*, VII, 569).

100 and marginal commentary. *Ptholome.* Douglas, like others in the Middle Ages, seems to confuse three figures: Ptolomy I (323–283 BC) who founded the great library at Alexandria; Ptolomy II, or Philadelphus (285–246 BC), mistakenly believed to have requested the translation of the Old Testament into Greek known as the Septuagint; and Claudius Ptolemaeus, the Greek astronomer who lived in the second century AD (cf. *Palice of Honour*, 256).

115–24. It was common among writers of this time to contrast the poverty of the vernacular with the copiousness, or *fowth*, of Latin. Cf. *Complaynt of Scotland*: 'oure Scottis tong is nocht sa copeus as is the lateen tong' (1979, 13).

117. *bastard Latyn.* Non-classical Latin, despised by humanists such as Lorenzo Valla, who termed it 'kitchen Latin' (Curtius 1953, 431).

118. *Scottis.* The language of Lowland Scotland was long called 'Inglis', and Douglas was one of the first – though not the very first – to term it 'Scottis'. Earlier uses in this sense are found in a heraldic manuscript dated c. 1494: see *The Deidis of Armorie*

(1994, I, xxxix–xl, and note 17); also the colophon to the Chepman and Myllar print of *The Porteous of Noblenes* (1508).

123. *sayng*. 'Saying, utterance', as also in I.Prol.288. The dissyllabic word is preferable to E's variant *sang*.

127. *Lawrens of the Vaill*. Lorenzo Valla (1407–57), the Italian humanist, author of the influential treatise *De Linguae Latinae Elegantia*. Douglas mentions the exchange of invectives between Valla and Poggio Bracciolini in *The Palice of Honour*, 1232–3, and he was sympathetic to Valla's views on the Latin language and scholastic philosophy. See Broadie 2009.

134–5. The composition of the *Aeneid* is traditionally dated between 30 and 19 BC. For the belief that it took twelve years, see the 'Vita' attributed to Suetonius (Suetonius 1914, II.473).

139–40. Caxton's *Eneydos*, printed at Westminster in 1490, was largely based on the anonymous prose *Livre des Eneydes* (Lyons, 1483); see Caxton's *Eneydos* (1890).

143. This sounds proverbial, but Douglas's is the only citation in Whiting D 179. On Douglas's respect for St Augustine of Hippo, see IV.Prol.218 and VI.Prol.61.

144. 'May he have no credit for it, but lose (i.e. waste) his labour'.

154–72. Douglas objects to the distortion of the proportions of the *Aeneid*; book IV occupies approximately half of Caxton's version.

165. *he fenys to follow Bocas*. Caxton follows his French source in attributing to Boccaccio a version of the Dido story very different from that told by Virgil: see *Eneydos* 1890, 22–38.

173–6. The funeral games in fact are mentioned, but very briefly, by Caxton: see *Eneydos* 1890, 115.

174. *plays palustrall*. Possibly an echo of *Troilus and Criseyde*, V.304, where there is the same rhyme with *funeral*; the phrase was also used by Lydgate in *Troy Book*, IV.3260. But it might simply originate in Virgil: see III.iv.136 (= *Aeneid* 3.281); or VI.x.34 (= 6.642).

177–218. This constitutes a defence of *Aeneid* 6 (which Caxton largely omitted) against possible criticism by churchmen. Prologue VI treats the theme in greater detail.

185–6. Douglas refers to the Orphic-Pythagorean passage in *Aeneid* 6.724–51 concerning the transmigration of souls; cf. also VI.Prol.130.

192–8. Douglas was probably familiar with medieval commentaries on the *Aeneid*, such as those attributed to Bernard Silvestris and John of Salisbury, which discerned a philosophical truth beneath its outer surface. But his views on poetry were particularly influenced by Boccaccio's *De Genealogia Deorum*, a work which he knew well, and whose last two books constitute a virtual defence of poetry as veiled truth. See further Boccaccio trans. Osgood 1956; Bawcutt 1976, 72–3; and Baswell 1995.

193–4. An echo of Henryson's defence of fables as containing 'gude instruction … hid vnder the cloke of poesie' (*Orpheus and Eurydice*, 418–20). For other signs that this work by Henryson was in Douglas's mind, when he was thinking about poetry and poetic inspiration, see notes to I.Prol.460, 468–9, and I.i.13 marginal note.

195–7. Coldwell notes the 'hard' syntax, and absence of a finite verb.

204. This is Douglas's first explicit reference to Boccaccio's *De Genealogia Deorum*. IX.xxxiii. treats of Hercules' descent to the Underworld.

206. *Recolles of Troy.* Editions of Raoul Lefèvre's *Le Recueil des Histoires de Troyes* were published by Caxton, in English (1473–4) and in French (1475–6). See *The Recuyell of the Historyes of Troye* (Caxton 1894). Cf. Douglas's later reference to 'the recollectis of Troy' in a marginal note (I.v.2).

211–12. *Phitones.* The Vulgate term for the Witch of Endor. The marginal note gives the correct Biblical source: Kings I.xxviii.

223. *Tonyr.* Mistakenly transcribed by Coldwell as *Touyr*, but Douglas employs Caxton's spelling throughout this passage. It is not clear, however, what river or tributary is indicated.

239. *Tanais.* The river Don, which is also called the 'merche' between Europe and Asia in *The Sex Werkdayis and Agis* (1990, line 220).

241–4. For Deiphobe as the name of the Cumaean Sibyl, see *Aeneid* 6.36; *Eneados* VI.i.64.

256. *Perfyte symylitudis.* Cf. the marginal note to I.iii.92. On Douglas's response to Virgil's similes, see Gray 2000.

260. *A twenty deuill way fall hys wark.* The sense and syntax are difficult. The context requires a curse, such as: 'May the devil take his work'. But there seems a confusion with another common if vague phrase: *a twenty deuill way*, 'in the devil's name'. This usually occurs as a parenthetic oath (see Whiting D 219; *MED*, *devel*, 6; *OED*, *devil*, II, 19 b.) An easier reading than C's *way* is provided by *mot* (E, R) or *may* (B).

261–2. In Lydgate's 'The Churl and the Bird' (*Minor Poems*, II, 483), the stupid churl cannot discriminate between an owl and a 'popyngay'.

263–4. *besich: be sich.* 'Beseek / beseech: be sik / be such'. This rhyme sounds anomalous, whether pronounced in Scots or English.

269–70. *Franchly leys.* 'Tells lies after the French fashion'. For similar dislike of the French, cf. Dunbar, *Poems*, 67.42.

273. Cf. VI.Prol.17–19.

274. *ded of lait.* Caxton is thought to have died in 1491.

297–8. The image of being bound to a stake derives from bear-baiting: cf. Whiting B 102, S 664, and Tilley B 354. James VI likewise speaks of a translator being 'bound, as to a staik' in 'Some Reulis and Cautelis', chapter 7, which might suggest a debt to Douglas. But the image may have been a translator's commonplace, since it also occurs in Du Bellay's *Epistre to Vers traduits* (1552), a work that was known to King James.

319–20. Possibly proverbial. Cf. *Palice of Honour*, 461–2.

330. At this point 1553 inserts six extra lines of praise for Aeneas. See Introduction.

323. *rebalddaill.* Vulgar readers, literally the lowest class of retainers or foot-soldiers.

339–43. The eulogy of Chaucer echoes that of Virgil in its diction and imagery, but, appropriately, is very much briefer. Cf. Dunbar's praise of Chaucer as 'rose of rethoris all' (*Poems*, 59.253ff).

345. An exact quotation from Chaucer, *Legend of Good Women*, 1002.

350 and marginal commentary. Cf. Servius, on *Aeneid* 1.96: 'oppetere, ore terram petere'; also I.iii.6; and X.viii.122–3.

359ff. and marginal commentary. These reflections on the difficulty of translating from Latin into a vernacular language may possibly be indebted to a passage in the Prologue to Nicole Oresme's translation of Aristotle's *Ethics*, which praises Latin as 'plus parfait et plus habondant' than French, and continues: 'Si comme entre innumbrables examples puet apparoir de ceste tres commune proposicion: *homo est animal*: car *homo* signifie homme et femme et nul mot de françois ne signifie equipellenment. Et *animal* signifie toute chose qui a ame sensitive et sent quant l'en la touche. Et il n'est nul mot en françois qui ce signifie precisement' (Oresme 1940, 100). Oresme's translation was composed c. 1370, but a printed edition was published by Vérard in 1488. A similar passage appears in *The Complaynt of Scotland*, pp. 13–14.

395–8. *Sanct Gregor.* St Gregory (c. 590–604), pope and theologian, expressed his views on translation in several Epistles. Douglas's precise source has not been identified, but perhaps the closest is: 'Dum enim non sunt qui sensum de sensu exprimunt, sed transferre verborum semper propriatem volunt, omnem dictorum sensum confundunt' (Epistle 10).

400–2. Cf. Horace, *Ars Poetica*, 133–4: 'nec verbo verbum curabis reddere fidus / interpres'.

410. *My mastir Chauser.* English poets, such as Hoccleve and Lydgate, frequently termed Chaucer their master. But Virgil was the superlative 'master' for Douglas (I.Prol.9) as also for Dante.

413–14. A precise echo of the opening lines of the 'Dido' tale in *Legend of Good Women*, 926–7. (C's *Quhow* is closer to Chaucer's text than E's *Quhen*.)

415ff. Douglas rebuts the common medieval charge that Aeneas had abandoned Dido callously and treacherously. For Aeneas as a type of the false lover, cf. Douglas himself in *Palice of Honour*, 564; Chaucer, *Legend of Good Women*, 1285–7, and *House of Fame*, 267; Lydgate, *Temple of Glas*, 58, and *Complaint of the Black Knight*, 375.

424. *nocht worth a myte.* A common phrase to indicate worthlessness. Whiting M 611.

452. *prynce of poetis.* Previously used of Virgil (3 and 418), but now applied to Christ.

460ff. This rejection of pagan inspiration was an ancient topos, found in Christian writers as early as the fourth century (Curtius 1953, 235ff). For Douglas's later use, see III.Prol.41–5; V.Prol.55–68; VI.Prol.145–68; X.Prol.151–75.

460. *Calliope.* Muse of heroic poetry, and mother of Orpheus. Cf. Henryson, *Orpheus and Eurydice*, 61ff. She is the poet's protector and guide in *The Palice of Honour*.

468–9. Douglas re-applies to the Virgin Henryson's lines on Calliope in *Orpheus and Eurydice*, 69–70: 'And gart him sowke of hir twa palpis quhyte / The sweit licour of all musike parfyte'.

469. *that hevynly Orpheus.* In the Middle Ages Orpheus was portrayed as a type of Christ in art, and also in hymns and sequences.

478. *in Goddis name.* Probably a rhyme-filler, although Coldwell compares Chaucer, Gen. Prol. *CT*.I. 854: 'a Goddes name'.

481. Reminiscent of Chaucer, Gen. Prol. *CT*.I.308: 'And gladly wolde he lerne and gladly teche'.

484. *brimell.* The word is obscure, and possibly corrupt. Coldwell explains as 'rustic and thorny', taking it as a figurative use of 'bramble'. A better contrast with 'cunnand wight' is provided by the variants *bruitell* (E, R) or *rurall* (53).

490. The sense is difficult. Coldwell paraphrases as: 'Virgil stood so well before that the worse, *i.e.* my translation, can be set aside, beyond the mark, or over the score'. DOST explains *schift our scor* as 'disqualify, reject' (*score*, n. II.2.b).

499–500. Cf. Matthew vii.3; Whiting M 710. Modern readers of the Biblical verse will be familiar with the contrast between mote and beam, which appears in Chaucer as 'stalke' and 'balke' (Reeve's Prol. *CT*.I.3919–20). Douglas's mention of a 'ferry boyt' is startling; but the apparent oddity becomes more explicable, if one knows that *trabem*, the Vulgate reading, not only meant 'beam, plank', but was also used by poets of something made from timbers, such as a ship.

501. Cf. Matthew vii.12; Whiting D 274.

505–10. This translates the four pseudo-Virgilian verses, preserved by Servius, that begin: 'Ille ego qui quondam gracili modulatus avena'. These regularly appeared in medieval manuscripts and early printed texts of the *Aeneid*. For the text, together with discussion, see Virgil ed. Austin 1971, 25–7.

The contentis of Euery Buke Followyng. *These couplets, apart from the thirteenth, correspond to the monosticha argumenta, twelve one-line summaries of the books of the *Aeneid* regularly included in contemporary editions of Virgil. They translate, fairly closely, the version printed by Ascensius in 1501, f.1v; see also Bawcutt 1976, 103.

BOOK I.i; Virgil 1.1–49

1 commentary. (Virgil 1.1) Servius f.3 ra, 'Virum non dicet quem'.

3 commentary. (Virgil 1.2) *Servius f.3 vb, 'Lavina: tria habuit nomina haec urbs. Prius nam Lauinum dictum a Lavino Latini fratre: Deinde Laurentum a Lauro … Postremo Lavinium a Lavinia … Littora atque Lavinum octo milibus distat a mari'.

8 commentary. Cf. Servius's long note to 1.5–6, f.3 vb.

13 commentary. (Virgil 1.8) Ascensius f.5 rb, 'Musa i. dea rerum occultarum inventrix'.

Douglas here interestingly links two passages on the Muses: his own *Palice of Honour*, 851–79, and Henryson's *Orpheus and Eurydice*, 36–63.

14 commentary. (Virgil 1.9) Cf. Ascensius f.5 rb 'deorum regina, & soror & coniunx Iovis …'

23. *full of sculys seyr*. Virgil 1.14, —; suggested by Ascensius f.6 va, 'laus ab arte'?

27–8. **Hir … Samo*. Virgil 1.16, 'Samo'; Ascensius f.7 r, 'Samo in qua nata dicitur'.

37 commentary. (Virgil 1.22.) Ascensius, 'Libyam eandem vocat & Aphricam'.

38. *Iuno*. Virgil 1.23, 'Saturnia'; Ascensius f.7 r, 'Iuno'.

38–59. *Note the structure of this long, sprawling sentence.

45 commentary. (Virgil 1.27) Ascensius f.7 r, 'Fabula de iudicio Paridis notissima est'.

48–9. Virgil 1.28, —; Ascensius f.7 r–v, '… propter Dardanum Iovis ex Electra Iunonis pellice filium'; *Servius f.6 ra, 'Electra pellex fuit Iovis ex qua Dardanus natus est a quo Troiani ducunt originem'.

50. *abuf the sky*. Virgil 1.28, —; Servius f.6 vb, 'inter sydera'.

51. Virgil 1.28, —; Servius f.6 vb, 'ministerium poculorum … est remota Hebe Iunonis filia'.

51 commentary. (Virgil 1.28) *Boccaccio, *De Gen. Deorum*, Lib.IX.cap.ii, '… dea iuventutis … Tandem cum ipse una cum ceteris diis apud Aethyopes comessaturus iuisset, contigit quod ministrante eis Hebe pocula, perque lubricum minus caute incedente caderet, & vestimentis amotis omnibus in casu obscena superis monstraret, quam ob causam factum est ut illam ab officio pincernatus Iuppiter removeret, & loco eius Ganymedem Laumedontis regis Troiae fratrem substitueret'.

57. *Quhilk now is Italy*. Virgil 1.31, —; Ascensius f.7 va, 'Latio i. ab Italia'.

62 commentary. (Virgil 1.36.) *Ascensius f.7 va, 'Ostensis irarum causis docet quo Iuno in Troianos saevit & quod in eos molita est, dicens quod cum iam septimum agerent Troiani in erroribus annum & ex Sicilia ubi Eneas patrem sepeliverat classem ad Italiam appellerent …'

65. *stevynnys*. *Virgil 1.35, 'aere'; Ascensius f.8 v, 'i. rostris aeratis'.

66. *till hir euerlestand schame*. Added by Douglas.

72. Virgil 1.39, 'quippe vetor fatis'.

75 commentary. (Virgil 1.41.) Ascensius f.7 va, 'Nam offensa tum fuit ab Aiace qui … Cassandram oppressit'.

82 commentary. (Virgil 1.46–7.) Boccaccio, *De Gen. Deorum*, Lib.IX.cap.i.

I.ii; Virgil 1.50–91

3 commentary. Boccaccio, *De Gen. Deorum*, Lib.XIII.cap.xx (for the names of the islands and the rational account of Aeolus) and Lib.IV.cap.liv (for the names of the winds).

9. Virgil 1.55, —; Ascensius f.10 rb, 'ventis indignantibus quod inclusi essent'.

12 commentary. (Virgil 1.56.) Boccaccio, *De Gen. Deorum*, Lib.XIII.cap.xx, 'Sunt tamen qui velint hac fictione Virg. eum sublime in arce residentem rationem esse sedem habentem in cerebro. Ventos vero illecebres appetitus in antro humani pectoris tumultuantes …'

12. *chare*. Virgil 1.56, 'arce'.

26. *Tuscane*. Virgil 1.67, 'Tyrrhenum'; Servius f.10 vb, 'Tusciam'.

44 commentary. (Virgil 1.78.) Boccaccio, *De Gen. Deorum*, Lib.IV.cap.liv; so also the commentary to line 57 (Virgil 1.85–6).

46. *consideris*. *Virgil 1.79, 'concilias'. Perhaps E's 'confederis' is the better reading, especially since Ascensius f.12 r has 'confederas'.

58. Added by Douglas.

60. Virgil 1.87, 'stridor rudentum'; *Ascensius f.12 r, 'Stridor: i. strepitus aut fragor rudentum i. chordarum aut funium quibus vela ad malos ligabantur.'

66. *ayr, sey and hevin*. Virgil 1.91, 'omnia'; Ascensius f.12 r, 'omnia s. elementa ignis, aer et aqua.'

I.iii; Virgil 1.92–154

1 commentary. (Virgil 1.92.) *Ascensius f.12 va, 'Servius vult. Frigore i. horore propter metum … nec timuit Aeneas mortem sed genus mortis tam ignobile: nihil autem timere non fortis sed temerarii esset.'

6. *bytand the erd*, and commentary. Virgil 1.96, 'oppetere'; *Ascensius f.12 va, 'oppetere scilicet terram mordicus; nam ne cadentes vocem viro indignam emmitterent opetierunt ore terram eamque momorderunt.' Cf. I.Prol.350 and commentary; and X.viii.121–3.

7. *Diomed*. Virgil 1.97, 'Tydide'; *Ascensius f.12 va, 'i. o Diomedes'.

10. *losit the swete*. Virgil 1.99, 'iacet'.

11. *Achillis*. Virgil 1.99, 'Aeacidae'; *Ascensius f.13 r, 'i. Achillis nepotis Eaci'.

11 commentary. (Virgil 1.99.) Boccaccio, *De Gen. Deorum*, Lib.XIII.cap.lix, 'Laodamia filia fuit Bellerophontis … Iovi placuit … ex ea Sarpedonem peperit, qui postea rex Lyciae fuit'; Ascensius, 'caesus a Patroclo'.

18. *the aris, hechis and the takillis brast*. Virgil 1.104, 'franguntur remi'.

29 commentary. (Virgil 1.109.) *Servius f.13 vb, 'Haec saxa inter Aphricam & Sardiniam sunt & Itali aras appellant quod ibi Aphri & Romani foedus inierunt'; for Syrtes, cf. Boccaccio, *De Maribus*.

35. Virgil 1.113, —; Ascensius f.13 va, 'socios Pandari'.

37. *from the north wynd*. Virgil 1.114, —; Ascensius f.13 va, 'ab Aquilone'.

39. *the skippar clepit Lewcaspis*. Virgil 1.115, 'magister'; Ascensius f.13 va, 'Leucaspis'.

43. *salaris.* Virgil 1.118, 'nantes' misread as 'nautae'?

54 commentary. (Virgil 1.125.) Summary of Boccaccio, *De Gen. Deorum*, Lib.X.cap.i.

58. '... beholds over all the sea ...'

61. Virgil 1.129, 'caelique ruina'; Ascensius f.15 r, 'i. precipitatione imbrium'.

69. *I sal ȝou chastyß.* Virgil 1.135, 'Quos ego — ! sed ...'; Ascensius f.15 r and Servius f.14 vb complete the sense by adding 'puniam'.

69 commentary. *The ultimate source is in a work attributed to Plutarch, *Regum et Imperatorum Apophthegmata*; see Plutarch's *Moralia* (1949, 232–3). The philosopher Athenodorus advised Augustus that whenever he was angry he should not do or say anything before repeating to himself the twenty-four letters of the Greek alphabet (Austin 1966, 157). The anecdote was known to Erasmus, who refers to it in his *Adagia* under the topic 'Festina lente' (II, 1, 1, paragraph 29); for an English translation, see http.www.philological.bham.ac.uk.

75 commentary. (Virgil 1.138.) Boccaccio, *De Gen. Deorum*, Lib.X.cap.i, 'Tridens ... proprietatem ostendit; est enim labilis, nabilis et potabilis.'

85 and commentary. Virgil 1.144, 'Cymothoe simul et Triton'; *Servius f.15 vb, 'Cymothoe conveniens nomen nymphae κυμα enim fluctus est & θειν currere quasi fluctus currens'; Boccaccio, *De Gen. Deorum*, Lib.VII.cap.vii, 'Alii vero bene voluerunt Tritonis maris sonum, sed non eum quem dum se ipsum in se frangit, sed illum tantum quem facit littora percutiens ... Sane Plinius ubi de naturali historia, videtur arbitrari Tritones non solum ficto nomine Poetis deservire, sed etiam veros Oceani pisces existere, dicens de eis sic, Tyberio principi nunciavit Olisiponensium legatio, ob id missa visum auditumque in quodam specu concha canentem, Tritonem, qua noscitur forma.'

92 commentary. *For Douglas's earlier praise of Virgil's similes, see I.Prol.256–7. Here he recalls Servius's comment on *Aeneid* 12.524: 'bellum semper incendio et fluminibus comparat'.

100 commentary. *This is Douglas's first mention of Cristoforo Landino, the Florentine humanist (1424–98), and his influential *Disputationes Camaldulenses*. He summarizes briefly but reasonably accurately books III and IV, which offer a Neoplatonic allegorization of the first half of the *Aeneid*. For a modern edition, see Landino ed. Lohe 1980; for discussion, see Bawcutt 1976, 74–6, and Kallendorf 1983. *Ambesioun.* *'Ambition'. Previously misread by editors as *Avesion*, a ghost word passed over in silence. Douglas refers to a passage in Landino (ed. Lohe 1980, 161) that interprets Juno as a goddess of political ambition: 'vitae civilis cupiditas' and 'honorum ac imperii ardentissima [cupiditas]'.

I.iv; Virgil 1.154–222

7. *arryvit he.* Virgil 1.158, 'vertuntur'.

13. *to se ... is wondir.* Added by Douglas.

19. *forret.* Virgil 1.166, 'fronte'.

22–3. *neuer hewyn with manis hand Bot wrocht by natur.* *Expanded from Virgil 1.167, 'vivo saxo', and Ascensius f.17 r, 'naturali'.

24 and commentary. Virgil 1.168, 'Nympharum'. Cf. Boccaccio, *De Gen. Deorum*, Lib.VII.cap.xiv.

32. *bekit and dryit.* Virgil 1.173, —; Donatus, 'confovebant'.

38. Virgil 1.177, 'Cerealiaque arma'; Ascensius f.17 r, 'idest instrumenta quibus frumentum tractatur'.

39. *For skant of vittal.* Virgil 1.178, 'fessi rerum'; Servius f.16 [XII misprint] vb, 'rerum poenuria fatigati'.

41 commentary. (Virgil 1.180ff.) Cf. Ascensius f.17 rb, quoting Donatus.

49 commentary. (Virgil 1.184.) The idea is also found in Servius f.17 vb. *Douglas refers here not to the *Disputationes Camaldulenses* but to Landino's commentary on the *Aeneid*. Although Ascensius occasionally refers to Landino, the commentary is not included; it is found however in many early editions of Virgil, such as Sebastian Brant's famous illustrated edition of 1502.

66. *Sycilly the cost.* Virgil 1.196, 'litore Trinacrio'; Ascensius f.18 r, 'Siciliensi'.

74. *eschapit.* For Virgil 1.201, 'accestis', approached.

75. Virgil 1.200–1, —; Ascensius f.19 r, '& Charybdim'.

85. *Syk plesand wordis.* Virgil 1.208, 'talia'; Ascensius f.19 rb, 'consolationem'.

90. *it to graith.* Virgil 1.210, —; *Ascensius f.19 va, 'ad praedam parandam'.

98 commentary. (Virgil 1.215.) *Cf. Ascensius f.19 v, 'veteris quod praestantius ab omnibus censeri solet'.

98. *wyne.* Virgil 1.215, 'Bacchi'; Ascensius f.19 v, 'vini'.

I.v; Virgil 1.223–304

1. Virgil 1.223, 'et iam finis erat'; Ascensius f.20 va, 'scilicet sermonis longi … ac diei …'

2 commentary. St Augustine, *De Civ. Dei*, Lib.VII.cap.ix, and Lib.IV (not I), cap. xi and xii; *Lucan, *De Bello Civ.* 9.580 [where in both places 'quodcumque' and 'quocumque' are variants]; Boccaccio, *De Gen. Deorum*. Lib.XI.cap.i, Lib.V.cap.i, Lib. II.cap.ii; Servius f.20 ra, 'felicitas per mulierem ventura'.

Fortuna maior. *'The greater Fortune', not here a figure of geomancy but an astrological term for Jupiter, who, like Venus, is a beneficent planet; they are contrasted with 'frawart' planets, such as Saturn and Mars (known, respectively, as 'Infortuna maior' and 'Infortuna minor'). On the background, see note to Dunbar's mention of 'Fortuna maior' in his *Ballade of Bernard Stewart* (*Poems*, 56.79); and *OED*, *fortune*, 8, and *infortune*). Both Dunbar and Douglas probably recalled Chaucer's use of the term in *Troilus and Criseyde*, III.1420.

17. *drevin from Itale.* Virgil 1.233, 'ob Italiam'; Ascensius f.21 r, 'arceantur ab Italia'.

24. Virgil 1.239, 'fatis contraria fata rependens'; Ascensius f.21 r, 'idest recompensans fata contraria fatis, idest modeste tolerans fata que erant de excidio Troiae ob fata de institutione Romae ... ut pro adversis laeta obtineant Troiani'. 'Fortoun' is the subject of 'follow' — 'that good fortune should follow hard fortune'.

28 commentary. *Guido delle Colonne was the author of the influential *Historia Destructionis Troiae*, completed in 1287, and available in several Middle English translations, the most popular of which was Lydgate's *Troy Book* (1420). This work was largely responsible for the common belief in Scotland that both Aeneas and Antenor treacherously betrayed Troy to the Greeks. The passage from Livy, 1.1.1, is quoted by Ascensius f.21 rb, 'Iam primum omnium satis constat Troia capta in ceteros saevitum esse Troianos, duobus, Aeneae Antenorique, & vetusti iure hospitii & quia pacis reddendaeque Helenae semper auctores fuerunt, omne ius belli Achivos abstinuisse'. The reference to Landino seems to derive from his comment on Antenor in *Aeneid* 1.242 (available in 1502 Virgil, f.134v): 'Glaucum filium: quia sequebatur Paridem abdicauisse: eundem ab Agamennone cesum non fleuisse.'

29 commentary. *Sex. Ruffi Viri Consularis rerum gestarum po. ro. epitome ...* (Basle, 1553), p. 39, 'Habet Illyricus decem & septem provincias ...'. The Timauus passage is from Ascensius f.22 r. *Cf. Landino's comment on *Aeneid* 1.243: 'Illyricos: Est autem dicta illyria ab Illyrio Polyphemi filio' (1502, f.134v).

38. Omits Virgil 1.249, 'nunc placida compostus pace quiescit'.

44. Added by Douglas.

56. *manfull.* Virgil 1.260, 'magnanimum'.

58-9. *schaw ... declair.* Douglas ignores the metaphor of unrolling a scroll implied in Virgil's 'volvens' (1.262).

60. Virgil 1.262, 'longius'.

68 commentary. (Virgil 1.267.) *Ascensius f.23 va, '... divisas facere syllabas ut Iulus trissylabum ...'

70. Virgil 1.268, 'Ilus erat'; suggested by Ascensius f.23 va, 'dignitate & maiestate regali'?

74 commentary. (Virgil 1.270.) *Livy, 1. 3. 2-5, is quoted in Ascensius f.24r.

76 commentary. *sistir son.* *Ascanius was the son of Creusa, Hector's sister. For this idiomatic phrase, see also commentary to I.v.102. Previous editors transcribed it absurdly as 'fift son'.

77. *dochter of a kyng.* Virgil 1.273, 'regina'; *Ascensius f.24 r, 'regis filia'.

81 commentary. (Virgil 1.276) Combination of Livy, 1.3. 10ff.; Boccaccio, *De Gen. Deorum*, Lib.IX.cap.xl and xli; St Augustine, *De Civ. Dei*, Lib.III.cap.xv, and Lib. XVIII.cap.xxi.

85 commentary. *The reference to St Augustine's *De Verbis Domini* derives from Ascensius's note on *Aeneid* 1.127-8, f.24 v: 'numerus nondum completus est cum iam imperium in germanos translatum videamus ... De qua re diuus augustinus, de

verbis domini ser.xxix loquitur … [Virgil replies] non ex persona mea dixerim falsa: sed ioui imposui falsitatis personam. Sicut deus falsus erat; ita vates mendax erat.'

92. Virgil 1.282, 'gentemque togatam'; suggested by *Ascensius f.24 v, 'gentem togatam i. Latinam potissimum Romanam, quae in togis tempore pacis versari solet'?

93. Virgil 1.283, 'sic placitum'; Ascensius f.25 r, 'sup. est deorum concilio'.

94. Virgil 1.283, 'lustris labentibus'.

95. *Anchises of spring*. Virgil 1.284, 'domus Assaraci'; *Servius f.23 vb, 'Assaracus enim Capym, Capis Anchisen … genuit'.

96 commentary. (Virgil 1.284) For the reference to Phthia and Mycene, cf. Servius f.23 vb; for Argos, v. Boccaccio, *De Gen. Deorum*, Lib. IX, cap. xxi and xxii.

102 commentary. (Virgil 1.288) The reference to Virgil is *Ecl.* 9.47. *Cf. Servius, f.25 ra: 'et omnis poetae intentio … ad laudem tendit Augusti'.

111–12. Virgil 1.292, 'cana Fides et Vesta, Remo cum fratre Quirinus iura dabunt'; Ascensius f.26 r, 'Fides cana i. antiqua … & Vesta i. casta religio & Quirinus i. virtus bellica … Romulus legum creator.'

113 commentary. (Virgil 1.294) Ascensius f.25 r, '… Iani portas tertio Augustus clausit … a Numa Pompilio, iterum Tito Manlio consule & ter per Augustum Cesarem …'

113–14. Virgil 1.294, 'claudentur Belli portae'; Ascensius f.26 r, 'i. templi Iani quae apertae bellum significabant …'

116. *wykkyt bargane*. Virgil 1.294, —; Ascensius f.26 r, 'bellicus impius'.

122. *Marcury*. Virgil 1.297, 'Maia genitum'; Ascensius f.26 va, 'Mercurium'.

129. *folkis of Cartage*. Virgil 1.302, 'Poeni'; *Ascensius f.26 va, 'populi Punici hoc est Carthaginenses'.

I.vi; Virgil 1.305–417

15. *athiris*. Virgil 1.313, —; suggested by Ascensius f.27 va, 'altera'?

15 commentary. Servius f.27 ra, 'αχοσ enim cura est quae semper comes est regum'.

16. *schuke*. Virgil 1.313, 'crispans'.

20. *stowt wench of Trace*. Virgil 1.316, 'Threissa'.

20 commentary. Boccaccio, *De Gen. Deorum*, Lib.XI.cap.xxiv.

21. *hir fadir to reskew*. Virgil 1.316–17, —; Ascensius f.27 va, 'patrem a Getis liberatura eos insequebatur'.

23. *eftyr the gyß and maner thar*. *Virgil 1.318, 'de more'; Ascensius f.27 va, 'Ideo autem erat similis Harpalicae.'

25-6. *There is a close echo of Chaucer, *House of Fame*, 229–30: 'As sche had ben an hunteresse / With wynd blowynge upon hir tresse.'

27. Virgil 1.320, 'nuda genu nodoque sinus collecta fluentis'.

42. *Dyane.* Not in Virgil (1.328).

44. *maistreß of woddis.* Virgil 1.328, —; Ascensius f.28 ra, 'venatrix'.

48. *sal we arrive.* Virgil 1.332, 'iactemur', that is 'we are cast'.

53 commentary. Servius f.29 ra.

60 commentary. Ascensius f.29 v.

70–2. Virgil 1.345–6, 'cui pater intactam dederat primisque iugarat ominibus'.

76. Omits Virgil 1.348, 'Quos inter medius venit furor'.

90. *tak the see.* Added by Douglas.

93. Omits Virgil 1.359, 'ignotum'.

107 commentary. Ascensius f.30 v and Servius f.30 vb.

122. *in this cuntre.* Virgil 1.369, —; Ascensius f.30 r–v, 'in istis locis'.

125 commentary. (Virgil 1.375) *Servius f.31 ra, 'Non arrogantia, sed indicium est. non enim scientibus sed nescientibus de re loquitur, vel ut heros loquitur …'

129. *Virgil 1.380, 'Italiam … patriam'; Servius f.31 ra justifies the distinction and the 'and'.

132 commentary. (Virgil 1.382) *Servius f.31 vb, 'Nam Varro in secundo rerum divinarum ait, "ex eo quo a Troia est profectus Aeneas Veneris per diem stellam semper vidisse, donec in Laurentum agrum veniret ubi non est amplius visa; qua re cognovit terras esse fatales."' (B. Cardauns, M. T. Varro, *Antiquitates Rerum Divinarum*, Mainz, 1976, Bk 2, Appendix [k]; however he thinks that, despite Servius, this must be from the Res Humanae section of the work.)

134–5. Virgil 1.383, 'vix septem convolsae undis Euroque supersunt'.

141–2. *drawis … lyfe.* Virgil 1.387–8, 'auras vitalis carpis'; Ascensius f.32 va, 'quibus respirando vivitur'.

151 commentary. (Virgil 1.394) Servius f.32 vb, 'Iovis ales aquila quae dicitur dimicanti illi contra gygantes fulmina ministrasse'.

163, 164. *in May, glitterand brycht and gay.* Douglas's additions.

174. *bot sche is went adew.* Douglas's addition.

183. *into Cypir land.* Virgil 1.415, —; Ascensius f.33 va, 'Cypri'.

I.vii; Virgil 1.418–93

8. Virgil 1. 422, 'strepitum'; *Ascensius f.34 rb, 'strepitum s. ingredientium'.

13. *on hie.* Virgil 1.424, 'manibus'; Ascensius f.34 rb, 'festinantes'.

14. Virgil 1.425, 'pars optare locum tecto'; Ascensius f.34 rb adds 'ad tectum extruendum'.

15. Virgil 1.425, 'concludere sulco'; Ascensius f.34 rb adds 'faciebat ... fossis'.

16. *officeris*. Virgil 1.426, —; *Ascensius f.34 rb, 'ut dicunt nunc officiarios'.

25–35. Note the unusual amount of alliteration.

54. *goldyn statw of the goddes*. Virgil 1.447, 'numine divae'; *Servius f.35 ra, 'numen pro simulachro quod aureum velit fuisse'.

71. *baldar than thame baith*. Virgil 1.458, 'saevum ambobus', which Loeb takes as 'fierce in his wrath against both'; Ascensius f.35 v, 'saevior'.

97. Virgil 1.472, 'ardentis ... equos'; *Ascensius f.36 va, 'idest candore reluctantes, ut Servius dicit; aut feroces et indignantes'.

101. *the fey barn fleand*. Troilus is the 'barn', not Achilles.

104. Virgil 1.476, 'resupinus'.

126. *Vlcanus*. Added by Douglas.

129. *queyn*. Virgil 1.491, —; Ascensius f.37 rb, 'regina'.

131. *for the speir cut away*. Virgil 1.492, 'exsertae'; Ascensius f.37 v, 'exsertae ... ut in pugna expeditiores essent'.

I.viii; Virgil 1.494–578

1. *manfull*. Not in the original.

12. *nymphis*. Virgil 1.500, 'Oreades'; *Ascensius f.38 v, 'montium nymphae'.

15. *Latone hir moder*. Virgil 1.502, 'Latonae'; Ascensius f.38 v, 'matris'.

23. Virgil 1.506, 'saepta armis'; Ascensius f.38 v, 'satellitum stantium circum ipsam'.

39. *as na thing seyn thai had*. Virgil 1.516, —; Ascensius f.39 r, 'se non vidisse socios'.

44. *on raw*. Virgil 1.518, —; Ascensius f.39 r, 'cuncti'.

49. *gretast oratour*. Virgil 1.521, 'maximus'; Ascensius f.40 rb, 'maximus orator'.

54–6. 'We wretched Trojans beseech thee to forbid yon cruel fire ...'

57. *in a rage*. Virgil 1.525, 'infandos', properly applying to 'ignes'.

69. *Kyng Onotryus*. Virgil 1.532, 'Oenotri viri'; *Ascensius f.40 rb, 'viri ab Oenotro rege'.

71. Omits Virgil 1.532, 'minores', i.e. 'a younger race'.

100. *armyt men*. *Virgil 1.550 'arma' R¹ (and Ascensius f.40 v), 'arva' M.

118. Virgil 1.559, 'cuncti simul ore fremebant'; Ascensius f.41 va, 'indignati' (at their unjust treatment by the Carthaginians).

130–1. 'We are not so far away from the centre of the world that we are ignorant of the Trojans.'

133. *quhilk now is Italy.* Virgil 1.569, —; Ascensius f.42 v, 'Italiam'.

134. Virgil 1.570, 'Erycis finis'; *Ascensius f.42 v, 'Siciliam ubi Eryx ... sepultus est'.

140. *hidder from the see.* Virgil 1.573, —; Ascensius f.42 v, 'sursum in terram'.

I.ix; Virgil 1.579-656

23. *quhite polist marbill stane.* Virgil 1.593, 'Parius lapis'; Ascensius f.42 v, 'marmori candidissimo'.

48. *sa nobill a queyn.* Added by Douglas.

53. *conteyn.* Virgil 1.608, 'pascet'; Ascensius f.44 v, 'sustinebit'.

62. *behaldand his bewte.* Virgil 1.613, —; Ascensius f.44 v, 'ad pulchritudinem'.

69. *compacient.* Virgil 1.617, —; Ascensius f.45 rb, 'nobilissimus'.

78. *gave it to Tewcer.* Virgil 1.621, —; Ascensius f.45 rb, 'concessit Teucro'.

82. Virgil 1.624, —; *Ascensius f.45 rb, 'ut Diomedes & alii cum quibus congressus es'.

83. *Tewcer.* Virgil 1.625, 'Teucros', i.e. the Teucrians, the object of 'ipse hostis ... laude ferebat'.

92. *I.e.* 'all who bear adversity'.

95-6. Virgil 1.632, 'divum templis indicit honorem'; *Ascensius f.45 va, '& diem festum agere & ferias seu vacationes facere'.

102. *wyne habundandly.* *Virgil 1.636 'dei' MSS (and Ascensius f.45 r), *i.e.* of the god Bacchus, hence wine; 'dii', *i.e.* of the day, quoted by Aulus Gellius, *Noctes Atticae* 9.14.8, and others.

110. *maste curyus tobehold.* Added by Douglas.

124-5. Virgil 1.649, 'circumtextum croceo velamen acantho'; the same misunderstanding of 'croceo acantho' appears in I.xi.35 (Virgil 1.711). *pliabill.* Virgil 1.649, —; Ascensius f.46 va, 'flexuosum'.

134. Virgil 1.653, —; Ascensius f.46 va, 'quod Ilione collo gesserat'.

I.x; Virgil 1.657-94

12. *tyll hir hart.* *Douglas fails to translate 'sub noctem' (Virgil 1.662), and follows Ascensius, f.47 v in his gloss on 'recursat': 'i. redit celeriter in animum Veneris'. [*Ascensius f.46 v has the correct 'cura', not the misprint 'rura' reported by Coldwell from a later ed. of Ascensius]

18. Virgil 1.665, 'Typhoëa'; *Ascensius f.47 v, 'i.quę Iuppiter in Typhoea gigantem iniecerat'.

29-30. *gestnyng in Cartage, Quhilk is the burgh of Iuno.* *Virgil 1.671-2, 'Iunonia hospitia'; Ascensius f.47 v, 'Carthaginensia quibus Iuno praesidet'.

51. Virgil 1.684, —; Ascensius f.48 va, '... Didonem dolo i. deceptione'.

54. Virgil 1.685, 'gremio'; Ascensius f.48 va, 'inter femora'.

58. Virgil 1.687, 'atque oscula dulcia figet'.

I.xi; Virgil 1.695–756

1–10. Expanded from Virgil 1.695–8.

17. *to mak thar handis cleyn*. Virgil 1.702, —; Ascensius f.50 rb, 'quibus manus tergerentur'.

25. *sik as we call sewaris*. Douglas's explanation.

42–3. *fenȝeand … beyn*. A stricter translation would be 'satisfied the great love of the deceived father'.

51. Omits Virgil 1.720, 'Acidaliae'.

52. *hir first husband*. Virgil 1.720, —; Ascensius f.50 v, 'prioris coniugis'.

67. *Ypocras*. Virgil 1.729, 'mero'.

78–9. 'In time coming, may this day be to our posterity a memorial of our usage (i.e. the treatment of our guests).'

81. Virgil 1.734, 'bona Iuno'; Ascensius f.51 va, 'placata et benigna'.

90. *quhelmyt the gold on his face*. Virgil 1.739, 'pleno se proluit auro'; Ascensius f.51 va, 'involvit totam faciem suam auro pleno'.

92. A comment by Douglas.

94. Virgil 1.741, 'docuit quem maximus Atlas', whom the great Atlas taught.

95. *oblike*. Virgil 1.742, —; Ascensius f.51 va, 'oblique'.

96. Virgil 1.742, 'solisque labores'; Ascensius f.51 va, 'eclipsantem'.

100–2. *Virgil 1.744, 'Arcturum pluviasque Hyades geminosque Triones'. *Hyades*. A cluster of seven stars in the constellation Taurus. *Arcturus* is the brightest star in the constellation Bootes; it is often known as the lodestar, literally, 'guiding star'. *Vrsis*. The two constellations Ursa Major and Ursa Minor, another name given to the Triones. For later astronomical imagery, see III.viii.20–33; and VIII. Prol.149–53.

106. Virgil 1.746, —; *Ascensius f.52 r, 'aestivis … cum dies tantum perdurent'.

132. *of Troy the rewyne*. Added by Douglas.

I.xii; Virgil 2.1–13.
Notice that the beginning of Book 2 is put by Douglas in his First Book.

Prologue II

The shortest of the prologues, this focuses closely on the tragic subject matter of book II. The rhyme royal stanza – *ababbcc⁵* – has Chaucerian associations. James VI called it 'Troilus verse', and thought it particularly suited to 'tragicall materis' (*Reulis and Cautelis*, chapter 8), and Henryson used it for much of his narrative verse, including the 'tragedie' of *The Testament of Cresseid*. Douglas uses it again in Prologue IV, and in the last two stanzas of Prologue V. On the stanza's Scottish popularity, see Goldstein 2012.

2–3. On Melpomene as the muse of tragedy, cf. *The Palice of Honour*, 860–1.

5. *poete principall.* Cf. Virgil, 'of Latyn poetis prynce' (I.Prol.3).

11–12. 'To have one's bell rung' was a common idiom (Whiting B 233), meaning 'to have one's story told, become famous', and usually pejorative. Douglas echoes the wording and the rhyme-pattern of Chaucer's *Troilus and Criseyde* V.1062: 'Thoroughout the world my belle shal be ronge!' On Douglas's liking for bell imagery, see note to I.Prol.10.

13. In the late medieval period and renaissance Saturn was regularly associated with old age, pestilence, death and melancholy. See the striking portraits in Chaucer, *Knight's Tale*, CT.I. 2443ff. and Henryson, *Testament of Cresseid*, 151–68. On the wider background, see Panofsky 1962, 69–93; and Klibansky, Panofsky and Saxl 1964, 127–214.

16. *Mart.* Mars, i.e. battle.

18. The reference is to Sinon's part in the fall of Troy.

20–1. This was one of the most common medieval proverbs. For illustrations, see Dunbar: 'All erdly ioy returnis in pane' (refrain to *Poems*, no. 49); Henryson, *Praise of Age*, 26; and Whiting E 80, J 58 and P 265. For later uses by Douglas, see IV.Prol.220–1; and V.Prol.62–3. Its ultimate Biblical source is Proverbs xiv.13.

BOOK II.i; Virgil 2.13–56

6. *beche.* Virgil 2.16, 'abiete', *i.e.* 'fir'.

10. *walit by cut.* Virgil 2.18, 'furtim', secretly; suggested by Virgil 2.18, 'sortiti', and *Ascensius f.54 va, 'sortes trahantur'.

22. Virgil 2.25, 'nos abiisse rati'.

27. *Grekis.* Virgil 2.27, 'Dorica'; *Ascensius f.54 va, 'hoc est Grecorum'.

39. *cheif palyce.* Virgil 2.33, 'arce'; 'arx' is also translated 'cheif temple' (II.i.53), 'prowde

palice' (II.i.79), 'cheif castell' (II.iii.43), 'hallowit place' (II.iv.47), etc.

49. *Quhat nedis mair?* Douglas's question, not Virgil's.

52. *prest.* Virgil 2.41, —; Ascensius f.55 va, 'sacerdos'.

58. Virgil 2.44, 'dolis'; *Ascensius f.55 va, 'dolis i. fraudibus, & insidiis'.

59. Virgil 2.44, 'sic notus Ulixes?'; Ascensius f.55 va, 'calliditate & fraude illius viri'.

74. *his.* *Loeb wrongly translates, 'had *our* mind not been perverse'; Virgil 2.54 has no pronoun.

II.ii; Virgil 2.57–144

13. *knak and pul.* Virgil 2.64, 'inludere'.

21. *swelly me alyve.* Virgil 2.70, 'accipere'.

24. Virgil 2.71, 'neque usquam locus'; *Ascensius f.56 v, '… tutus aut ubi vivere permittar'.

25. *offendyt.* Virgil 2.72, 'infensi'; Ascensius f.56 v, 'offendi'.

29. *to be bald.* Virgil 2.73–4, —; Ascensius f.57 rb, 'damus animum'.

31–2. Virgil 2.75, 'memoret, quae sit fiducia capto'; Servius f.57 ra, 'meminerit in captivo veriloquium fiduciam esse vitae'.

33. *fenʒeit.* Virgil 2.76, —; Ascensius f.57 rb, 'simulabat'.

47. *stanyt to ded.* Virgil 2.85, —; *Servius f.57 vb, 'lapidibus obrutus est'.

48. *procurit peß.* Virgil 2.84, —; Ascensius f.57 va, 'cohortabatur ad pacem'.

72. Virgil 2.99, 'quaerere arma'; Ascensius f.58 r, 'arma solita hoc est fraudes'.

74. *I mycht rew.* Virgil 2.101, —; *Ascensius f.58 r, 'mala mea et infortunia'.

76. *be na ways.* Virgil 2.101. MSS (and Ascensius f.57 r) read 'nequi(c)quam', *i.e.* 'vainly', but Ascensius f.58 r renders it as 'in nullo aut nullo modo ingrata', and some old texts read 'nequaquam', 'in no wise'.

77. Virgil 2.102, 'quidve moror'; Ascensius f.58 r, 'differo poenas & mortem meam'.

81. Virgil 2.104, 'Ithacus'; *Ascensius f.58 r, 'i. itachensis Vlysses'; cf. lines 115, 127 below and elsewhere.

99. *hattyr.* Virgil 2.112, 'acernis', *i.e.* 'maple'.

101. *preste.* Douglas's explanation, not Virgil's (2.114).

103. *secret oratory.* Virgil 2.115, 'adytis'; *Ascensius f.50 r, 'i. ex oraculis & secretis locis dei'.

133. *page and knycht.* Added by Douglas.

151. *Schir Kyng.* Virgil 2.141, —; Ascensius f.60 rb, 'O rex'.

II.iii; Virgil 2.145–98

1. There is no direct speech in Virgil (2.145).

32. *kepe me thy promyß*. Virgil 2.160–1, 'serves ... fidem'.

47–8. *has ... went*. So in all the texts: 'went' is the past participle of 'wend'.

53. *in thar tempill vpset*. Virgil 2.172, 'positum castris'; suggested by Ascensius f.61 va, 'ablatum', 'taken away violently'?

54. *bittir terys swet*. Virgil 2.173–4, 'salsus ... sudor'; Ascensius f.61 va, 'sudor salsus i. amarus'.

55. *as ony gleid. A popular simile in Douglas and other medieval authors, often used as a rhyme filler. See IV.ii.35; VIII.xii.5; XI.x.1; and Whiting G 139–52.

57. Virgil 2.174, has 'mirabile dictu'.

58. *fell*. Virgil 2.175, 'emicuit'; i.e. 'sprang out'.

60. '... at once, you all must go to sea together'.

64. *alkyn*. *Ascensius f.61 r has 'omnia' in Virgil 2.178, where the MSS have 'omina'. So at 73 *al* some medieval MSS and Ascensius f.62 [LII misprint] r have 'Omnia' for 'omina' of the rest (Virgil 2.182).

75. *lyknes of a horß*. *Virgil 2.184, 'effigiem'; Ascensius f.62 [LII misprint] va, 'scilicet equi'.

80. Omits Virgil 2.186, 'textis'.

89. Omits Virgil 2.191, 'Phrygibusque'.

II.iv; Virgil 2.199–249

2. *be sik hunder*. Virgil 2.199, 'maius ... multoque'; 'a hundred times more'. *For the idiom, cf. Dunbar, *Poems*, 48.27: 'And fassoun him bettir be sic thre'.

4. *Laocon*. Trisyllabic.

24. *athir serpent*. 'Each of the two serpents'.

38. Douglas's addition.

47. *Pallas*. Virgil 2.226, 'Tritonidis'; Ascensius f.63 [LIII misprint] va, 'Palladis'.

49. *boyß*. Virgil 2.227, —; *Ascensius f.63 va, 'umbone'.

57–60. Expanded from Virgil 2.232–3; suggested by *Ascensius f.64 rb, 'conclamant ... simulachrum ducendum sup. esse, ad sedes, s. templi, ad quas destinatum erat, & numina divae, s. Palladis, oranda i. supplicationibus & orationibus placanda sup. esse'.

61. *Quhat wil ȝe mair?* Douglas's question, not Virgil's. Cf. II.i.49; III.iii.59; and III. vii.43. *Similar rhetorical questions are common in Chaucer and other narrative poets.

62. *maid patent*. Virgil 2.234, 'pandimus'; Ascensius f.64 rb, 'patentem viam ... facimus'.

65. *of this ilke bysnyng iaip.* Douglas's addition.

66. *bassyn raip.* Virgil 2.236, 'stuppea vincula'; or hempen ropes, ropes made of bast.

68. Virgil 2.238, 'feta armis'; Ascensius f.64 v, 'pregnans & gravida armis'.

70. *dansand in a ryng.* Virgil 2.239, —; Ascensius f.64 v, 'per circuitum'.

73. *suttell hors of tre.* Virgil 2.240, —; Ascensius f.64 v, 'machina'.

76. *ful of ioy.* Virgil 2.241, —; Ascensius f.64 v, 'dulcis'.

84. *drug and draw.* A common alliterative phrase; cf. Henryson, *Fables*, 2750; Dunbar, *Poems*, 66.10

88–90. Virgil 2.246–7; *Ascensius f.64 v, 'Cassandra … aperit dico ora non credita unquam Teucris i. Troianis iussu i. voluntate dei, s. Apollinis, qui quod promiserat donum vaticinandi illi contulit, sed quia ab ea stupro compromisso fraudatus erat credulitatem & fidem abstulit vaticinio eius: ita ut licet vera diceret ei non crederetur.'

94. *as in May.* The comparison is Douglas's.

95. *fest and ryot maid.* Virgil 2.249, —; Ascensius f.64 v, 'festum agimus'.

96. *for myscheif was glaid.* Virgil 2.249, —; *Ascensius f.64 v, 'extremum gaudii luctus occupat'.

II.v; Virgil 2.250–97

3. *dyrk weid.* Added by Douglas.

17. *fyrryn.* Virgil 2.258, 'pinea'; the Scotch Pine and the Scotch Fir are one, *pinus sylvestris.*

22. *Thersander.* Virgil 2.261. *Ascensius f.64 v, 'Thersandrus', for MSS 'Thessandrus'.

23. *Athamas.* Virgil 2.262. *Ascensius f.64 v, 'Athamas', for MSS 'Acamas'.

24. *Pyrrus.* Virgil 2.263, 'Neoptolemus'; Ascensius f.65 r, 'Pyrrhus'.

29. *liggyng on the wall.* Added by Douglas.

32 and 36. There is nothing in the original corresponding to either line.

47. *of hym Achillys.* Cf. 'hym Iulius', VI.xiii.75. The idiom occurs in Middle English verse; cf. Chaucer, *Knight's Tale*, CT.I.1333: 'For jalousie and fere of hym Arcite.'

50. Virgil 2.276, —; Ascensius f.67 r, '… ignes Phrygios, i. Troianos, puppibus … Grecorum praecipue Protesilai qui … interfectus est ab Hectore.'

78. Virgil 2.292, —; Ascensius f.67 r, 'fata … noluntque patriam defendi'.

82. Douglas's comment.

91. Virgil 2.296, 'Vestam'; *Servius f.67 vb, 'deam ignis que terra est'.

II.vi; Virgil 2.298–360

11. Virgil 2.303, —; Ascensius f.67 va, 'accipio sonitum'.

16. Virgil 2.306, 'sternit agros'.

21. Virgil 2.307, —; Ascensius f.67I va, 'ipse inscius i. nescius causae'.

38. *hait as fyre*. *Douglas often adds this traditional simile, usually for the rhyme. Cf. III.v.30; V.viii.67; others are listed in Whiting F 170.

42. Properly 'Othryades, son of Othrys'.

51. Virgil 2.322, —; *Ascensius f.68 va, 'Quo loco, id est quo statu, aut revera, quo loco est supple res summa, i. sacra & divina …'

56. Virgil 2.324, 'ineluctabile tempus'; Ascensius f.68 va, 'i. nulla lucta [by no struggle] superabile', misunderstood as 'nullo lucto', by no lamentation.

65. *as it war sport*. A comment by Douglas.

77–8. 'Rushing where the Furies and the noise of battle drew me'. Note the enjambment in the opening lines.

82. *Ephitus*. Virgil 2.340. *Ascensius f.69 r, 'Ephitus' for MSS 'Epytus'.

94–103. The order of Douglas's verses differs from Virgil's (2.348–53). *He follows Servius, f.69 r: 'est autem ordo: O iuvenes fortissima pectora frustra succuritis urbi incensae: quia excesserunt dii.'

102. Virgil 2.349, 'audentem extrema', meaning 'follow me who dares the uttermost'.

II.vii; Virgil 2.361–436

12. Added by Douglas.

27. *the spreith of Troy*. Virgil 2.375, 'Pergama'; *Ascensius f.70 ra, 'res Troianorum'.

30. **foyn*. 'Enemies'. Cf. XI.xiii.3. The usual Scots word is 'fais', and this is an anglicized form, found only in poetry.

35. *Seand hir* [i.e. the serpent]. For the gender, cf. II.viii.60–3, 'hir slowch', 'hir body', 'hir nek' and 'hir mouth'. 'Anguis' may be either masculine or feminine.

36. *3allo*. Virgil 2.381, 'caerula'.

40. Expanded from Virgil 2.383, 'circumfundimur armis'.

47. *quhar our manhed has ws taucht*. Virgil 2.388, 'quaque ostendit se dextra', or 'where fortune shows herself favourable'; Ascensius f.70 va, 'qua dextra, i. virtus nostra bellica, ostendit se …'

48. *sen we beyn sawcht*. Added by Douglas.

57. **myself eik*. Virgil 2.394, 'hoc ipse', which Loeb takes as 'so Dymas too'; *Ascensius f.70 va, 'ipse supple facio hoc' (though he prefers to understand as Dymas).

59. *warm.* Added by Douglas.

65. *to hell adown.* Virgil 2.398, 'Orco'; *Ascensius f.71 rb, 'orcum i. ad infernum'.

89–90. Virgil 2.413–14. 'Furthermore, because of the wails of anger (against the Greeks?) spoken by the newly-rescued damsel, the Greeks flock together …' This rendering is supported by Ascensius f.71 va; *Loeb (2nd ed) takes as 'Then the Danaans, with a shout of rage at the maiden's rescue …'

96. Omits Virgil 2.417–18, 'laetus Eois … equis'.

98. *bath ayk, elm and fyr.* Douglas's expansion.

99. Omits Virgil 2.418, 'saevit tridenti'.

113. *Pallas.* Virgil 2.425, —; Ascensius f.72 rb, 'Palladis'.

123. *cuntre folkis.* Virgil 2.431, 'meorum', *i.e.* 'of my kin'.

II.viii; Virgil 2.437–505

11. Omits Virgil 2.442, 'postisque sub ipsos'.

19. *begane.* 'Plated, overlaid, adorned'.

20. *costly stane.* Virgil 2.448, —; *Ascensius f.72 v, 'sublimia & superba decora id est ornamenta'.

32. *desolate and waist.* *This does not correspond to 'infelix', Virgil 2.455, because line 455 is missing from Ascensius; it corresponds to 'relicti' in line 454.

37. *Tharat I enterit.* Virgil 2.458, —; *Ascensius f.73 va, 'per hunc pervium adytum …'

46. *corbalys al to torn.* An addition by Douglas.

74. *master bar.* Virgil 2.480, —; suggested by Ascensius f.74 r, 'cor ianuae'.

106–8. Virgil 2.498–9, 'camposque per omnis cum stabulis armenta trahit'.

111. Virgil 2.500, 'geminosque … Atridas', the Atridan brothers.

117. *gude dochteris.* *Virgil 2.501, 'nurus'; Ascensius f.74 va, 'coniuges filiorum'.

119–24. Expanded from Virgil 2.504–5.

II.ix; Virgil 2.506–58

28. *for it is won.* Virgil 2.522, —; Ascensius f.75 rb, 'cum serum sit'.

33. *but ony threte.* Not in the original.

39. *come to seik reskew.* Virgil 2.528, —; suggested by *Ascensius f.75 rb, 'ad quem se reciperet'?

87–8. Virgil 2.558, 'sine nomine corpus'; *Ascensius f.76 rb, 'corpus sine nomine, id est ignobile id est vulgus ignobile dicitur sine nomine aut ad sui cognitionem mortales invitat, ut cognoscant quia ablato capite etiam regis corpus sit sine nomine, i. non enim agnoscitur.'

II.x; Virgil 2.559–678

9–10. Note the identical rhyme.

17. Virgil 2.569, 'Tyndarida'; Ascensius f.76 va, 'Helenam'.

21. There is nothing like this in Virgil (2.571).

25. Virgil 2.573, 'Troiae et patriae communis Erinys', which Loeb (2nd ed) translates as 'she, the undoing alike of her motherland and ours'; Ascensius f.76 va, 'toti patriae, non suae, sed Troianorum'. The phrase modifies 'scho' in line 26.

27. *onethis seyn*. Virgil 2.574, 'invisa'; *Loeb (2nd ed) translates 'hateful creature'; Ascensius f.76 va, 'non visa sed occultata'. In II.x.76 (Virgil 2.601) Douglas translates 'invisa' as 'Quham thou hatis', following Ascensius f.77 va, 'odiosa tibi'.

49–52. Virgil 2.586–7. Douglas seems to have misunderstood the sense. Loeb (2nd ed) translates, 'It will be joy to have filled my soul with the flame of revenge and satisfied the ashes of my people.'

60. *spretis deificait*. Virgil 2.592, 'caelicolis'; Ascensius f.77 rb, 'celestibus caelum habitantibus'.

74. *smyte to ded*. Virgil 2.600, 'hauserit'; Ascensius f.77 va, 'occiderit eos'.

81. 'For thus I clear the cloud from thy sight …'

99. *in weirlyke weid*. *Virgil 2.616, 'nimbo', with an ancient variant 'limbo'; Ascensius f.78 r, 'aut limbo, i. chlamyde militari'.

100. *into hir scheild*. Virgil 2.616, —; *Ascensius f.78 r, 'in scuto suo'.

101. *fader Iupiter*. Virgil 2.617, 'pater'; *Ascensius f.78 r, 'pater s. Iuppiter'.

118. *ayk*. Virgil 2.626, 'ornum', ash.

123. Virgil 2.628, —; Ascensius f.78 va, 'traxit ruinam & suam & aliarum arborum secum'.

142. *A distructioun*. 'One destruction', *i.e.* that by Hercules after Laomedon deceived him.

147. Added by Douglas.

156. An explanation by Douglas.

161–3. A loose translation of Virgil 2.652–3 'ne vertere secum cuncta pater fatoque urgenti incumbere vellet'.

171. *for ded*. *'For fear of death'.

194. Virgil 2.668, —; suggested by Ascensius f.80 r, 'video … nos ad mortem impelli'. *Adone*. *The equivalent of 'Have done' (II.xi.49).

209. *salbe clepit*. Virgil 2.678, 'dicta'; 'was clepit' would be better.

II.xi; Virgil 2.679–759

1–2. Expanded from Virgil 2.679, 'Talia vociferans gemitu tectum omne replebat.'

21. *help*. Virgil 2.691. *MSS (and Ascensius f.80 r), 'auxilium'; a citation has 'augurium', as in 3.89.

25. Virgil 2.693, 'laevum'; *Ascensius f.80 va, 'pars septentrionalis'.

31. *quhidder at we suld spur*. Added by Douglas.

36. *our bute*. Virgil 2.700, —; Ascensius f.80 va, 'rei bone significativum'.

60. Virgil 2.714, 'desertae Cereris'; that is, 'of the deserted Ceres'.

74. Virgil 2.723, 'succedoque oneri'; Ascensius f.81 va, 'suscipio patrem'.

78. *secret wentis and quyet rewyß*. Virgil 2.725, 'opaca locorum'.

82. *causyt grow*. 'Made me shudder'.

93–4. *I ran Befor the laif*. Virgil 2.737, 'excedo'; *Ascensius f.82 rb, 'excedo id est anteeo insequentes'.

102. *mote of Ceres*. Virgil 2.742, 'antiquae Cereris sedemque sacratam'.

118. *euery streit and way*. An expansion by Douglas.

II.xii; Virgil 2.760–804

4. *thocht it was gyrth*. Added by Douglas.

14–15. *with mony … sayr*. *Ascensius f.83 r completes Virgil 2.767, 'et tacitis implent mugitibus aures'.

38. *sail*. Virgil 2.780, 'arandum'; Ascensius f.83 va, 'navibus non aratro'.

47. *neyce of mychty Dardanus*. Virgil 2.787, 'Dardanis'; Ascensius f.83 va, 'Dardani neptis'.

54. *for ay we mon dissevir*. Added by Douglas.

58. 'And many words *I* would have said'.

63. *or the son beym*. Added by Douglas.

77. *the day starn, Lucifer the brycht*. Virgil 2.801, 'Lucifer'; Ascensius f.84 rb, 'stella matutina lucem ferens'.

84. *Ida hyll*. Virgil 2.804, 'montis'; Ascensius f.84 rb, 'montem s. Idam'.

Prologue III

The main purpose of this elegant introduction to *Aeneid* 3 is to indicate the difficulties facing a reader unfamiliar with the topography of the Mediterranean and Virgil's wealth of mythological allusion. Douglas makes adroit metaphorical use of the dangerous monsters mentioned in book III, such as the Harpies, Cyclops, Scylla and Charibdis (41–5). His nautical language in lines 37–45 similarly foreshadows the wording of the text: cf. 'fronteris' (III.viii.85); 'forland' (III.viii.2); and 'schald bankis' (III.viii.99). The demanding nine-line stanza, *aabaabbab*⁵, is also used in the first two books of *The Palice of Honour*, and (with some variation) in the *Exclamatioun*, which treats several of this Prologue's themes. The stanza, which was first employed in Chaucer's *Anelida and Arcite*, became popular with Scottish poets. Douglas was certainly familiar with earlier uses by Henryson in *Testament of Cresseid*, 407–69, and Dunbar in *The Goldyn Targe* (*Poems*, 59).

1–9. The first stanza consists of a prolonged apostrophe to the moon goddess, bringing together several ancient myths, in which she figured under different names. As Cynthia, she was the sister of Cynthus, the sun god.

1. *Hornyt Lady*. Cf. XIII.Prol.68: 'hornyt Lucyn'; and Lindsay, *Monarche*, 153: 'Synthea, the hornit nychtis quene'. The horns are the pointed extremities of the crescent or waning moon. Douglas may recall Virgil's mention of the moon's 'cornua' (*Aeneid* 3.645; translated at III.ix.103) and also Henryson, *Testament of Cresseid*, 255, where Cynthia is 'buskit with hornis twa'.

2. The line is almost identical with Henryson, *Testament of Cresseid*, 258.

6–7. *Pan*. Virgil alludes to the seduction of the moon goddess by Pan, the rustic Arcadian god, in *Georgics* 3.391–3. *Hyperion*. According to one legend, the moon (under her Greek name Selene) was the daughter of the Titan Hyperion, and lover of Endymion.

7. 'That kissed the sleeping shepherd Endymion'.

10. For similar phrasing, cf. III.vi.47.

11. *althocht my wyt be dull*. For similar self-depreciation, cf. I.Prol.31–2; and *Palice of Honour*, 127–35.

14. *Laborynth*. The Cretan Labyrinth, devised by Daedalus to hold the Minotaur. For Virgil's use in a vivid simile, see *Aeneid* 5.588–91; transl. V.x.77ff.

17. *thar erys to pull*. Literally 'pull their ears', which is best explained not as 'chastise roughly', but as 'pluck their ears, in order to compel attention'. Cf. Latin 'vellere aurem', as in Virgil's *Eclogues* 6.3–4; and *OED*, ear. For other Scottish uses, see *DOST*, pul(l, 4.

18. *Mysknawis*. 'Are ignorant of'.

19. Proverbial. Whiting M 602.

20. Cf. *Fergusson's Scottish Proverbs* 1924, 301: 'He mon have leave to speak that cannot had [hold] his tongue'; Whiting P 66; and *Exclamatioun*, 36.

26–7. The exact sense is not wholly clear. It might be paraphrased as: 'What, my friend, do you really believe that the crow has turned white, even though you are half-blind?' Cf. I.Prol.499–500, IX.Prol.78 and Whiting C 574.

27. *holkis*. An unidentified ailment of the face and eyes that apparently causes blindness.

28. For similar defiance of those who *deym*, i.e. malicious critics, see Dunbar, *Poems*, 18 and 33.

35. *pike … vp*. 'Sail along, hug (the coast)'. The same term is used in III.v.18, and III.x.9.

39. *our barge*. Cf. *Exclamatioun*, 1–6. The ship imagery has a double significance, symbolizing first the work of translation, and later, in line 43, the poet's soul.

41–5. Douglas prays to the Virgin Mary for guidance, addressing her as his *laid star*, i.e. the Pole star by which mariners steer. For a similar use, cf. I.Prol.454. Such imagery for Mary as the star of the sea was traditional in late medieval hymns and religious poetry. Cf. Dunbar, *Poems* 16.1 and note.

42. *virgyne moder*. The 1553 edition substitutes 'Christ goddis sone'. *but maik*. In the double sense, 'without equal' and 'without spouse'.

45. *salue al go not to wraik*. 'Save everything from being wrecked'.

BOOK III.i; Virgil 3.1–68

1. Virgil 3.1–2, 'Postquam … visum'.

3. *empyre*. Virgil 3.1, 'res'; *Ascensius f.85 rb, 'imperium'; Servius f.85ra, 'imperia'.

7. *smoke … reik*. There is no evident distinction, but OED, *reek* 1, suggests that in modern English reek is denser than smoke. Virgil (3.3) has simply 'fumat'.

10. 'By revelations of the gods'. 'Reuelacionys' stands for Virgil 3.5, 'auguriis'.

12. Virgil 3.5–6, 'classemque … molimur'.

14. Omits Virgil 3.6, 'Phrygiae'.

17. *the fresch veir*. Virgil 3.8, 'aestas' (*i.e.* summer); Ascensius f.86 r, 'verna'.

19. Virgil 3.9, 'dare fatis vela iubebat'.

25–6. The interpretation of Virgil 3.12, 'Penatibus et magnis dis' as two groups of gods is sanctioned by Servius f.85 vb and Ascensius f.86 r.

27. *weirly*. Virgil 3.13, 'Mavortia'; Ascensius f.86 rb, 'bellicosa'.

33. Virgil 3.15, 'sociique Penates'; Ascensius f.86 va, 'i. confoederati & amici'.

40. 'Who was daughter of Dione'.

42. *happy helparis*. Virgil 3.20, 'auspicibus'.

46. *hepthorn*. Virgil 3.22, 'cornea', the cornel.

47. Virgil 3.23, 'densis hastilibus horrida myrtus'.

65. *Hamadriades*. Virgil 3.34, 'Nymphas'; *Ascensius f.87 r, 'hamadriades'.

67. *Tarß*. Virgil 3.35, —; Servius f.86 vb, 'Thraciis'.

68. Virgil 3.35, —; Ascensius f.87 r, 'i. Martem qui praesidet arvis geticis, i. getarum populorum'.

72. Omits Virgil 3.38, 'adversae'.

83. Virgil 3.44, 'fuge litus avarum'; Ascensius f.88 rb, 'i. in quo avarus rex imperium tenet'.

93. *quhilk was his son ... Polynestor.* Virgil 3.49, —; Ascensius f.88 rb, 'filius ille Priami ... Polymnestori'.

104. *wrachit.* Virgil 3.57, —; suggested by Ascensius f.88 rb, 'execrabilis'.

105. Virgil 3.56, —; *Ascensius f.88 rb, 'ad omne nefas'.

108. *feirfull wordis quent.* Virgil 3.59, 'monstra'.

109. *noblis and grettast of our men.* Virgil 3.58, 'delectos ... proceres'; Ascensius f.88 rb, 'i. primores & principes populi'.

120. Virgil 3.63, 'stant Manibus arae'.

121. *haw sey hewis.* Virgil 3.64, 'caeruleis'; *Ascensius f.88 v, 'ceruleis aut marinis & in littore lectis'.

123. *Troiane wemen.* Virgil 3.65, 'Iliades'; Ascensius f.88 v, 'i. mulieres Troianae'.

124. Omits Virgil 3.65, 'de more'.

126. Omits Virgil 3.66, 'spumantia'.

127. The burial of the soul (not the body) is determined by Virgil's 3.67, 'animam'.

129–30. Virgil 3.68, —; Servius f.88 ra, '... dicebant Vale, nos te omnes ordine quo natura permiserit cuncti sequemur'.

III.ii; Virgil 3.69–146

3. *wynd.* Virgil 3.70, 'Auster'; Ascensius f.88 va, 'quivis ventus'.

5–6. Virgil 3.71, 'deducunt socii navis et litora complent'.

10. *Delos.* Virgil 3.73, —; Ascensius f.89 rb, 'scilicet Delos'.

12. *Doryda.* Virgil 3.74, —; *Ascensius f.89 rb, 'i. Doridi'.

13. *cheritabil archer, Appollo.* Virgil 3.75, 'pius Arquitenens'; Ascensius f.89 rb, 's. Apollo'; cf. line 33 (Virgil 3.85).

17. *lauborit.* Virgil 3.77, *'coli'; Ascensius f.89 rb, 'habitari'.

26. *withowt the town.* Added by Douglas.

34. *propir.* Virgil 3.85, 'propriam'; Ascensius f.89 rb, 'nobis debitam'.

39. Virgil 3.86–7, 'serva altera ... Pergama'; Ascensius f.89 rb, 'ut Troia periit serva ... serva nos qui sumus altera pergama idest moenia'.

41. Virgil 3.88–9, 'quem sequimur … augurium'; Ascensius f.89 rb, 'significa nobis … intelligere & credere valeamus quem sequimur'.

50. Virgil 3.92, 'cortina'; Ascensius f.90 rb, 'locus secretior'.

70. *weilfair*. Virgil 3.102, 'spes'.

72. Virgil 3.104, 'Iovis … insula'; *Ascensius f.90 va, 'in qua magnus Iuppiter natus dicitur'.

74. Douglas removes the metaphor contained in Virgil's 3.105, 'gentis cunabula nostrae'.

75. *of wyne, oyl and quhete*. Douglas's expansion of Virgil 3.106, 'uberrima'. *The phrasing is Biblical. Cf. also *Palice of Honour*, 1416.

79. *in Phrygy*. Virgil 3.108, —; Ascensius f.90 va, 'idest Phrygias'.

82. *on the feld*. i.e. in the country. An addition by Douglas.

83. *cave*. Virgil 3.110, 'vallibus'; Ascensius f.90 va, 'i. cavernis'.

84. *adornar*. Virgil 3.111, 'cultrix'; Ascensius f.90 va, 'i. exornatrix'.

86. *blast of brasyn trumpettis*. Virgil 3.111, 'Corybantiaque aera', which Douglas has misunderstood. Ascensius f.90 va refers to *Georg*. 4 for an explanation; Douglas has apparently derived the idea that the cymbals were trumpets from *Georg*. 4.67ff.

90. *lyonys suld draw*. Virgil 3.113, 'subiere leones'; Ascensius f.90 va, 'a leonibus traheretur'.

94. *Crete and Gnosia*. Virgil 3.115, 'Gnosia': Ascensius f.90 va, 'i. Cretensia'.

95. *cowrs nor vyage far*. Virgil 3.116, 'cursu'; Ascensius f.90 va, 'i. spacio ad quod percurrendum opus sit'.

101. *for his beheist*. Virgil 3.119, —; Servius f.91 ra, 'propter oraculum'.

110. *with swift cowrs*. Virgil 3.124, —; Ascensius f.91 va, 'celerrime nauigamus'.

111. *iland*. Virgil 3.125, —; *Ascensius f.91 va, 'insulam illam'.

112. *wynys*. Virgil 3.125, 'bacchatam'.

113–14. *marbill*. Virgil 3.126, —; Ascensius f.91 va, 'a colore marmoris … marmor'. *Growis here has the sense 'exists, is found' (see *OED*, grow, 2b and 6c).

118–22. Expanded from Virgil 3.128–9.

118–19. *marynar … thar*. Note the false concord. For 'many' with a singular noun, v. *OED*, many, A 1a.

123. *in our tail*. Virgil 3.130, *'a puppi'; Ascensius f.91 va, 'a posteriore paret navis'.

124. *with bent saill*. Virgil has nothing corresponding to this (3.131).

126. Virgil 3.131, —; Ascensius f.91 va, 'illorum populorum in Creta'.

132. *to graith howsis*. Virgil 3.134, 'amare focos'; *Ascensius f.91 va–92 r, 'aut nouas domos libenter incolere'. *leif in le*: an alliterative tag added by Douglas.

138. Virgil 3.136, 'operata'; Ascensius f.92 r, 'idest sacrificia expleverat'.

141–53. Expanded from Virgil 3.137–42.

149–50. Virgil 3.141, 'Sirius'; Ascensius f.92 r, 'i. sydus illud ardens ore canis'.

155. *Delos*. Virgil 3.143, 'Ortygiae'; Ascensius f.92 r, 'Deli'.

III.iii; Virgil 3.147–210

2. *Desiris rest by kynd*. Douglas's addition.

6. *slepit nocht*. Virgil 3.151. *Ascensius f.92r has 'insomnis', recognized as a variant by Servius f.92 vb, for the MSS 'in somnis'.

12. Virgil 3.153, 'curas'.

23. *to goddis grete*. Virgil 3.159, 'magnis'; Ascensius f.92 va, 'diis'.

33. Virgil 3.165, 'Oenotri coluere viri'; *Servius f.92 vb, 'vel a rege vel a vino'.

37. *brothir*. Virgil 3.168, 'pater'.

42. *Italy*. Virgil 3.170–1, 'terras … Ausonias'; Ascensius f.92 va, 'idest Italicas'.

43. *in Crete neyr Dycteus*. Virgil 3.171, 'Dictaea'; Ascensius f.92 va, 'idest Cretensia, a parte totum'.

47. *nowthir dreym nor fantasy*. Virgil 3.173, 'nec sopor illud erat', where 'sopor' suggests a heavy, drugged sleep like that brought on by opium.

49. Virgil 3.174, 'velatasque comas'.

54. *myne oryson I maid*. Virgil (3.177) has nothing like this.

56. *senß and wyne*. Virgil 3.177, —; Ascensius f.93 rb, 'thus & vinum'.

59. The question is Douglas's, not Virgil's (3.179).

61. Virgil 3.180, 'adgnovit prolem ambiguam', *i.e.* 'He recognized our double or two-fold ancestry'.

66. *contrarius frawart*. Virgil (3.182) has no epithets here.

67. 'How only Cassandra …'

74. *mair than scho had bene dum*. Douglas's addition.

75. '… the words of the prophetess Cassandra'.

86–103. Expanded from Virgil 3.194–202.

95–7. Note the alliteration.

99–100. Virgil 3.201–2, 'ipse … Palinurus'.

100. *'For all his skill in shipman-craft and chart-reading'.

107. Virgil 3.204, —; *Ascensius f.94 v, 'incertos … an dies an nox esset …'

III.iv; Virgil 3.210–83

2. *two*. Virgil 3.210–11, — ; *Ascensius f.94 v, 'quae duę sunt'.

8. *of Arcad*. Virgil 3.213, —; Ascensius f.94 v, 'Arcadie'.

12. *hellis grund*. Virgil 3.215, —; Ascensius f.94 v, 'infernalis'.

16–17. Virgil 3.216–17, 'foedissima ventris proluvies'.

19. *gredy appetite*. Virgil 3.218, —; Ascensius f.94 v, 'voracitate'.

26. *but dreid or aw*. Added by Douglas.

39–42. *Virgil 3.229–30, 'Rursum in secessu longo, sub rupe cavata/arboribus clausi circum atque horrentibus umbris', where 'clausi' of most medieval MSS and Ascensius f.94 v is an emendation of 'clausa(m)' of MP, as in 1. 311, whence 230 has been inserted. This line, however, was deleted by Mynors.

60. *the wait*. Virgil 3.239, —; suggested by Ascensius f.95 v, 'loco editiore'?

75. Virgil 3.248, 'Laomedontiadae'; Ascensius f.96 rb, 'idest perfidi a perfido regi denominati'.

83. *Iupiter*. Virgil 3.251, 'pater'; Ascensius f.96 rb, 'Iupiter'.

91. *Virgil 3.256, 'nostraeque iniuria caedis'; Ascensius f.96 rb, 'i. in boves & iuvencos nostros'.

97. Virgil 3.260, 'cecidere animi'; Ascensius f.96 rb, 'i. labefacti sunt'.

101–2. Virgil 3.262, has 'sive deae seu sint dirae obscenaeque volucres'.

108. *ameyß ʒour wrath and greif*. Virgil 3.265, —; suggested by *Ascensius f.96 va, 'avertite … tam diram famem'?

109. *ankyrris haill*. Added by Douglas.

132. Virgil 3.279, 'lustramur Iovi'; Ascensius f.97 r, 'i. expiamur'.

135. *active*. Virgil 3.280, 'Actiaque'.

III.v; Virgil 3.284–355

4. Virgil 3.286, —; Ascensius f.97 va, 'abiturus'.

5. *tempyl*. Virgil 3.287, —; omits 'adversis'.

6. *of plait*. Virgil 3.286, 'aere'.

7. *maner*. Virgil 3.287, 'rem'.

13. *span aris in hand*. Virgil 3.289, —; Ascensius f.97 va, 'ut remis incumbant'.

14–16. Expanded from Virgil 3.290.

17. *Corsyra*. Virgil 3.291, 'Phaeacum'; Ascensius f.97 va, 'i. Corcyram'.

23. Virgil 3.295, 'Priamiden'.

27. *Achilles.* Virgil 3.296, 'Aeacidae'; *Ascensius f.98 rb, 'genuit … Achilles Pyrrhum'.

35. *as I furth glaid.* Added by Douglas.

87. *Pyrrus.* Virgil 3.326, —; Ascensius f.99 rb, 'Pyrrhi'.

90. *the douchtir of Helena.* Virgil 3.328, 'Ledaeam'; *Ascensius f.99 rb, 'i. Ledae neptem nam … Helene quae est filia Ledae'.

91. *fey wedlok.* Virgil 3.328, 'hymenaeos'; Ascensius f.99 rb, 'infoelices'.

95. Virgil 3.331, 'scelerum'; Ascensius f.99 rb, 's. in matrem quam occiderat'.

98. *in Delphos.* Virgil 3.332, —; *Servius f.99 ra, 'in templo illius Delphico'.

104. *eftir his brodir.* Virgil 3.335, —; Ascensius f.99 v, 'fratre suo'.

112. Virgil 3.340, —; Ascensius f.99 v completes Virgil's unfinished line with 'obsessa est enixa Creusa'.

117. *O Lord!* The exclamation is Douglas's.

139. Virgil 3.353, —; Ascensius f.100 rb, 'rex pervenerat … ad convivium i. pascebat illos'.

III.vi; Virgil 3.356–471

1. Virgil 3.356, 'Iamque dies alterque dies processit'. Douglas's sense is, 'We passed the successive days in pleasure'.

4. *piggeis and our pynsalis.* Virgil 3.357, 'carbasus'.

9–10. Virgil 3.360, 'qui tripodas … sentis'; *Ascensius f.100 va, 'idest revelationem factam apud tripodas Apollinis'.

11. Virgil 3.360, —; Servius f.100 ra, 'tripodes mensae fuerunt in templo Apollinis Delphici in quibus positae Phoebades futura praedicebant'.

16. Virgil 3.361, —; *Ascensius f.100 va, 'sentis augurium … & omina idest portenta aut indicia penne prepetis'.

25–6. Virgil 3.364, 'repostas'; Ascensius f.100 va, 'receptas aut repositas ad adventum nostrum'.

29. *vengeans from the goddis.* Virgil 3.366, 'iras'; Ascensius f.100 va, 'iras deum idest deorum'.

36. *on seyr materis musand.* Virgil 3.372, —; Ascensius f.101 rb, 'attentum'.

42. Virgil 3.376, 'is vertitur ordo'.

59. *Sycil.* Virgil 3.384, 'Trinacria'; *Ascensius f.101 va, '(mari) Sicilo'; cf. lines 142 (Virgil 3.429), 160 (Virgil 3.440), and often elsewhere.

60. *bedyit weill.* Douglas's addition.

63. Virgil 3.386, 'infernique lacus'; *Ascensius f.101 va, 's. Avernus'.

64. *Virgil 3.386, 'Aeaeaeque insula Circae'.

66. *land of Italy.* Douglas's addition.

73. *The first 'white' refers to the sow, the second to the brodmell, or young pigs.

87. Virgil 3.399, —; Ascensius f.102 rb, 'socii Aiacis oilei'.

88. *hill.* Virgil 3.400, 'campos'; *Ascensius f.102 rb, 'campos ... qui sunt iuxta promontorium'.

90. Virgil 3.401, 'Lyctius Idomeneus'; *Ascensius f.102 rb, 'a Lyctio Cretę oppido pulsus'.

94. Added by Douglas.

108. *mont Pelory.* Virgil 3.411, 'Pelori'; Ascensius f.102 va, 'Pelori promontorii'.

109. *vanysys away peyß and peyß.* Virgil 3.411, 'rarescent'.

117–18. Virgil 3.415, 'tantum aevi longinqua valet mutare vetustas'. The metaphors implied by 'kast'and 'mysknaw' are original with Douglas.

123. *baith evyn and morn.* Padding on the part of Douglas.

134. Virgil 3.426, 'prima hominis facies'.

137. Virgil 3.427, 'pistrix'.

143. Virgil 3.430, 'longos et circumflectere cursus'.

147. *in hir wame.* Virgil 3.432, —; *Ascensius f.103 rb, 'quos Scylla in ventre gestare fingitur'.

164. *dedicate to goddis.* Virgil 3.442, 'divinos' (which Loeb translates as 'haunted'); Ascensius f.103 va, 'i. diis consecratos'.

166–86. Expanded from Virgil 3.443–51.

170. *in palm tre leiffis.* Virgil 3.445, 'in foliis'; Ascensius f.104 rb, 'scilicet palmarum'.

192–3. The direct quotation (not in Virgil 3.454) is suggested by *Ascensius f.104 rb, '... socii increpitent idest obmurmurent quod illic moram trahere velis ubi periculum sit ...'

192. *Illyr haill.* *An archaic interjection, meaning not 'hello' but 'bad luck'. The sailors urge Aeneas to sail, because they think it would be disastrous to delay. For a more detailed account of the phrase, see Bawcutt 1971, 48–9.

194. *thocht thine hart betis.* Douglas's addition.

209. *dyvyne answeris.* Virgil 3.463, —; Ascensius f.104 va, 'responsa aut oracula'.

212. *polyst.* Virgil 3.464, 'secto'.

216. *in Epyr land.* Virgil 3.466, —; *Ascensius f.104 va, 'a Dodona Epiri urbe'.

221. *effering to his age.* Virgil 3.469, —; Ascensius f.104 va, 'debita aetati'.

222. Virgil 3.469, —; Ascensius f.104 va, 'conuenientia dona'.

224. *pylotis and lodismen.* Virgil 3.470, 'duces'; *Ascensius f.104 va, 'conductores itinerum'.

III.vii; Virgil 3.472–505

3–4. Virgil 3.473, 'fieret vento mora ne qua ferenti'.

18. Virgil 3.480, 'nati pietate'.

20. Douglas's addition.

27. *prowd*. Virgil 3.484, 'Phrygiam'.

28. Virgil 3.484, 'nec cedit honori', which Loeb takes as 'nor fails she in courtesy'; Ascensius f.105 va, 'nec Ascanius cedit honori … aut forte chlamys non cedit honori'.

29. *nedyll wark*. Virgil 3.484, —; suggested by *Ascensius f.105 va, 'acu pictam', applied to Ascanius's scarf.

34. *vncle Hector*. Virgil 3.488, 'Hectoreae'; Ascensius f.105 va, 'Hectoris avunculi tui'.

37. *O leif is me!* The exclamation is Douglas's.

42. *and hedy peir*. Added by Douglas.

43. *quhat wil ȝe mair?* Douglas, not Virgil (3.492), asks the question.

62. Omits Virgil 3.505, 'animis'.

III.viii; Virgil 3.506–87

7. *chesis rowaris ilke deill*. Virgil 3.510, —; Ascensius f.106 rb, 'per sortes exerciti remis'.

10. *bodeys, feyt and handis*. Virgil 3.511, 'corpora'.

11. *lymmys, lethis and banys*. Virgil 3.511, 'artus'.

15. Virgil 3.513, 'haud segnis'; Ascensius f.106 va, 'diligentissimus … non tardus'.

21–2. *An expansion of Virgil 3.516, a line repeated by Virgil from 1.744; for Douglas's more literal translation, see I.xi.100–2.

21. *Arthuris Huyf*. *Douglas's jocular name for the star Arcturus (Virgil 3.516); see also VIII.Prol.152. An ancient circular building that once stood by the mouth of the Carron near Falkirk was first known as *furnus Arthuri*, 'Arthur's oven'; in later Scots versions of this phrase the word for oven, *one* or *hone*, is thought to have been misunderstood and re-interpreted as *houe*, 'hall, house'. (See the useful account in *DOST, Arthuris hufe*.)

22. Virgil 3.516. *Watlyng Streit*. There is no equivalent for this in Virgil. In the Middle Ages the name was given to the Roman road that led from London to the North West, and later applied figuratively to the Milky Way. Cf. Chaucer, *House of Fame*, 939; Henryson, *Orpheus and Eurydice*, 188; and *OED, Watling-Street*.

Horn. A name for the constellation Ursa Minor, the Little Bear; cf. VIII.Prol.153, and see also *DOST, horn*; and Eade 1984, 164–6. *Charle Wayn*. Literally, Charles's, or Charlemagne's Wain, an ancient term for Ursa Major, the Great Bear (see *OED, Charles's Wain*).

26. *bekyn.* Virgil 3.519, 'signum'; Ascensius f.106 va, 'i. faculam aut tedam incensam'.

27. *went on burd in our the waill.* Virgil 3.519, 'castra movemus'.

34–6. Expanded from Virgil 3.524.

37. *ammyrall of our flote.* Virgil 3.525, —; Ascensius f.107 rb, 'patronus classis'.

42. Virgil 3.525, —: suggested by Ascensius f.107 rb, 'vir prudens atque religiosus sacrorumque peritus'.

50–1. Virgil 3.531, 'templum apparet in Arce Minervae'.

59–60. The first 'wall' is 'wall', the second, 'wave'.

77. *brown.* Douglas's addition.

83–4. Virgil 3.549, 'cornua velatarum obvertimus antemnarum'.

88. Virgil 3.551, 'Herculei'; Ascensius f.107 va, 'i. a Phalanto qui octavus fertur ab Hercule aucti'.

90. *the tempill of Iuno.* *Virgil 3.552, 'diva Lacinia'; Ascensius f.107 va, 'Iunonis'.

108. Virgil 3.561–2, 'rudentem contorsit … proram', which Loeb takes as 'swung the groaning prow'; Ascensius f.108 rb, 'rudente idest fune quo vela diriguntur'.

111. *with mony heyß and haill.* Added by Douglas.

123–4. Virgil 3.569, 'Cyclopum adlabimur oris'.

126. *for schip or barge.* Added by Douglas.

132. *as the hail als thik.* There is no simile in the original (Virgil 3.574). *For similar uses of this popular simile, see X.xii.12; and XII.v.158.

141. 'The rumour is that …'

144–5. Virgil 3.580, 'ruptis flammam exspirare caminis'; Loeb takes with 'Etna', Ascensius f.109 rb, as Douglas, with 'Enceladus'.

III.ix; Virgil 3.588–654

2. *wak nycht.* *This translates not Virgil 3.588, 'primo Eoo', but Virgil 3.589 'umentemque … umbram', glossed as 'noctem humidam' by Ascensius f.109 va.

8. *quhar that we stude in hy.* An explanation by Douglas.

12. Virgil 3.593, 'immissa'; *Ascensius f.110 rb, 'in pectus demissa'.

16. *faderis.* Virgil 3.595, 'patriis', that is, of his country; *Ascensius f.110 rb, 'i. patrię suę aut paternis'.

28. *thar war my hartis eyß.* The sentiment is Douglas's, not Virgil's (3.602).

30. *Troy cuntre.* Virgil 3.603, 'Iliacos … Penatis'.

58. *Poliphemus.* Virgil 3.617, —; *Ascensius f.110 va, 'Polyphemi'.

62. *aucht not nemmyt be.* Virgil 3.621. *P, most medieval MSS and Ascensius f.110 r have 'effabilis'; M, 'affabilis'.

69. Virgil 3.625–6, 'sanieque exspersa natarent limina'; *for 'exspersa' in Ascensius f.110 v, which was the true reading according to Servius f.110 vb, MP and most medieval MSS have 'aspersa'.

91. Virgil 3.637, 'Phoebeae lampadis instar'.

119–20. Virgil 3.654, 'vos animam hanc potius quocumque absumite leto'. Douglas's sense is, 'Rather than having you or me fall into such peril, kill me by whatever means you please.'

III.x; Virgil 3.655–718

11. Virgil 3.661. *Most medieval MSS and Ascensius f.111 v complete the verse with 'de collo fistula pendet', omitted by MP.

12. *for tynsell of hyß e.* Virgil 3.661, —; Ascensius f.112 rb, 'incommodi amissi s. visus'.

30. *for al hys hycht.* Virgil 3.672, —; Ascensius f.112 rb, 'viribus aut gradibus'.

35. Virgil 3.674. 'The round (*curvis*) caverns of Etna …'

41. *elrych.* Virgil 3.678, 'Aetnaeos'.

63. *the mont.* Virgil 3.687, —; Ascensius f.113 rb, 'promontori'.

66. *ile.* Virgil 3.689, 'iacentem'; Ascensius f.113 rb, 'insulam'.

72. *Sycill.* Virgil 3.692, 'Sicanio'; *Ascensius f.113 rb, 'i. Siculo'.

76–7. Virgil 3.694, 'Alpheum fama est huc Elidis'; *Ascensius f.113 r, 'Alpheum Elidis s. civitatis amnem idest qui ab Elide Archadiae nascitur … magna numina locisque illius videlicet Arethuse & Alphei'.

85. Virgil 3.698, —; Ascensius f.113 rb, 'interdum stagna in agris facientis ac inundantis …'

87. *hyrslit.* Virgil 3.700, 'radimus'; Ascensius f.113 rb, 'contigimus'.

88. *Mont.* Virgil 3.699, —; Servius f.113 ra, 'promontorium'.

89. *loch.* Virgil 3.701, —; Ascensius f.113 rb, 'palus'.

90. 'The fates forbid that it should be moved.'

92. *cite.* Virgil 3.703, —; Ascensius f.113 rb, 'urbs'.

95. *hyl.* Virgil 3.703, —; Ascensius f.113 rb, 'mons'.

100. *Lybibe.* Virgil 3.706, 'Lilybeia'; Ascensius f.112v., 'Libybeia'.

109. *in a fremmyt land.* Virgil 3.710, —; Ascensius f.114 r, 'in hoc loco non concesso a fatis'.

112. *as we with hym gan luge.* Added by Douglas.

122. *and rasys.* Added by Douglas.

124. Virgil 3.716, 'intentis omnibus'; *Ascensius f.114 r, '... sed Dido & ceteri Tirii adhuc intenti erant'.

Prologue IV

This fine sustained meditation on the power and complexity of love has the seriousness of a sermon: 'honest' love, guided by reason, is distinguished from 'lufe inordinat' (128), or lust. It is linked to *Aeneid* 4 by a transitional section (215–70), dominated by the tragic figure of Dido. Douglas's attitude to her is far from simple: he is not misogynistic, but – like Virgil himself – critical yet compassionate. The style is highly rhetorical, and abounds in imagery, figures of repetition, oxymoron, puns and word play of various kinds. There is a wealth of literary allusion, notably to the courtly poems of Chaucer, and also Gower, Henryson, Virgil, St Augustine and the Bible. The metrical form is rhyme royal (see note to Prol. II); the reason for switching to a longer eight-line stanza in lines 92–9, 156–71, and 186–93 is not clear. A text of the prologue is included in the Bannatyne Manuscript (fols. 291–4v) which derives from the 1553 edition: see Introduction. Critical responses to this Prologue have differed greatly: see, for instance, Coldwell (I.89–93); Archibald 1989; Desmond 1994, 163–94; Simpson 2002, 91–2; and Bawcutt 2006, 188–93.

1–2. Douglas opens with an apostrophe to *Cytherea*, or Venus, as a planet, 'which alone among the lesser stars casts a shadow'. Norton-Smith (1980) suggested that the source of this piece of astronomical lore was Martianus Capella's *De Nuptiis*, VIII. 883; or else Pliny, *Historia Naturalis* II.6.37. He noted the symbolism: 'a unique and powerful radiance casts a shadow, and so parallels the oxymoron in the attributes of his Cupid'. For a later use of the theme, see Bawcutt 1982.

3. Cupid is commonly depicted as blind and winged by late medieval authors. Cf. Chaucer, *Knight's Tale*, CT.I.1964–5; *Palice of Honour*, 480; *Kingis Quair*, 653–4; and Panofsky 1962, 95–128.

5. *ioly wo.* A Chaucerian oxymoron for love also used in XII.Prol.202. See *Troilus and Criseyde*, II.1099 and 1105; and *Legend of Good Women*, 1192 (of Dido). For similarly paradoxical phrases cf. 'sary ioys' (20) and 'myrry pane' (23).

6. *faynt.* Not 'faint, weak', but 'deceitful, dissembling'. For other uses in this sense, see lines 142 and 254 below, and *MED feint* adj.

8–10. Douglas rhymes, as was permitted, on *saw* = (1) the past participle 'sown'; and (2) the noun 'saying'.

8. *seyd.* The seed of love. Douglas perhaps recalls *Testament of Cresseid*, 137: 'The seid of lufe was sawin in my face', but the ultimate source is *Roman de la Rose*, 1588–9 (Chaucer's *Romaunt*, 1616–17). The metaphor is much elaborated in the following

lines: the seed takes root, produces buds (11), ripens, and produces evil fruits and weeds or wild oats. On the rare *oncorn*, see *DOST, uncorne*, n.

9. On the connection between lust and gluttony, cf. Hoccleve, *Regement of Princes*, 3804–5: 'Glotonye is ful plesant to the fende, / To leccherie redy path is sche'. Cf. also Chaucer's *Parliament of Fowls*, 275–6, and Whiting C 125, W 359.

14. This sounds proverbial: the closest parallels are Whiting C 432 and T 465. Cf. also Matthew vii.17.

20. *sary ioys*. Cf. Chaucer's 'dredful joye' (*Parliament of Fowls*, 3; *Troilus and Criseyde*, II.776).

21. *goddis apys*. 'Fools, dupes'. Cf. the use in VI.Prol.11. The line echoes Troilus's 'Loves servantz everichone / Of nycete ben verray Goddes apes' in *Troilus and Criseyde* I.912–13, where the same rhyme occurs with *iapes*.

26. *30ur traist is bot a trane*. Proverbial. Cf. Whiting T 492.

29–32. These are traditional examples of great men overpowered by love: Solomon, Samson, David, Aristotle, and Virgil. All five appear in Venus's court in Gower, *Confessio Amantis*, VIII.2690ff. Solomon, Samson, and David are Biblical figures: see I Kings xi; II Samuel xi; and Judges xvi.4–20. Aristotle and Virgil, in particular, were paired in medieval legend as examples of famous writers humiliated by women: it was said that Aristotle was bridled and forced to carry his mistress Phyllis on his back; and Virgil was 'crelyt', or suspended in a basket, from his mistress's window. On the background, see Bawcutt 1976, 69–70; and Comparetti 1895, 1997. For further Scottish references, see *The Spectakle of Luf* in *Asloan MS*, pp. 278–9; Gilbert Hay, *King Alexander the Conquerour*, 7163–248; and Rolland, *Seuin Seages*, 2635–45.

36. This is doubly reminiscent of Chaucer's Theseus: speaking of the 'faire cheyne of love' (*CT*.I.2988ff.), and 'The god of love, a benedicite / How myghty and how greet a lord is he!' (*CT*.I.1785–6). Cf. also Clanvowe's quotation of these lines in the opening of *The Boke of Cupide*.

37. Cf. 'Love is he that alle thing may bynde'; and 'Benigne Love, thow holy bond of thynges' (*Troilus*, I.237; III.1261).

38–9. A reference to the Incarnation.

40. The *gyant* is the devil, as in Henryson's *Bludy Serk*, where he is overcome by Christ, the knight and lover of the soul.

41. Cf. Henryson, *Annunciation*, 1: 'Forcy as deith is likand lufe'; also Song of Songs, viii.6; Whiting L 523.

42. *heryit hell*. A brief reference to the Harrowing of Hell, the legend (first told in the apocryphal Gospel of Nicodemus) that between Christ's death and resurrection he descended into hell and released the souls of the righteous who had died before his coming. Cf. also X.Prol.129.

43ff. For similarly idealistic views of love, cf. Chaucer, *Troilus*, III.1–42; Clanvowe, *Boke of Cupide*, 151–60; Gower, *Confessio Amantis*, IV.2296ff.; Dunbar, *Poems*, 24.81–7.

45. On the friendship of David and Jonathan, see I Samuel xviii–xx.

46. For a Scottish account of Alexander the Great's infatuation with Candace, queen of Ethiopia, see Hay, *King Alexander the Conquerour*, 15151ff.; and Martin 2008, 72–4.

47. *Iacob.* On Jacob's fourteen-year service, out of love for Rachel, see Genesis xxix; cf. also *Palice of Honour*, 589–92.

48–9. *Dyonieir.* Deianira. This transcription of the MS is preferable to older readings as *Dyomeir.* In classical myth Hercules was enslaved not by his wife Deianira, who later killed him unintentionally with a poisoned robe, but by Omphale, queen of Lydia, who set him to women's tasks while she assumed his club and and lion's skin.

50. Narcissus fell in love with his own reflection in a spring See Ovid, *Metamorphoses* III.405ff.; and Gower, *Confessio Amantis*, I.2275ff.

51. *Achill.* According to medieval legend Achilles was treacherously slain because of his love for Polyxena. Cf. Chaucer, *Book of the Duchess*, 1067–71; Lydgate, *Temple of Glas*, 94–5, and 785–6.

52. This derives from the altered version of the classical tale of Theseus and Pirithous, told by Chaucer in *Knight's Tale*, CT.I.1198–1200:

> So wel they lovede, as olde bookes sayn,
> That whan that oon was deed, soothly to telle,
> His felawe wente and soughte hym doun in helle.

53. 'The snow white dove often prefers a grey mate'. The disapproving tone resembles similar passages in Alexander Scott, *Poems*, vi.5–6; and xxxiv.105ff.

55–6. Douglas refers to Medea, who killed her children after she had been abandoned by Jason. He translates, fairly closely, Virgil, *Eclogue* 8.47–8: 'saevus Amor docuit natorum sanguine matrem / commaculare manus'.

57–63. *myne author.* Virgil, as in line 92 and elsewhere in the Prologues. These lines are based on *Georgics* 3.250–54.

64–70. Cf. *Georgics* 3.218ff.

71–84. An expansion of six lines from *Georgics*, 3.258–63. Douglas may also recall Ovid's *Heroides* XVIII and XIX.

85–91. The closest parallel is in Lydgate, *Complaint of Black Knight*, 400ff.: 'Lo, her the fyne of loveres seruise. / Lo, how that Love can his seruantis quyte …' This poem was well known in Scotland, but commonly attributed to Chaucer. The repetition of 'Lo' may also recall *Troilus and Criseyde*, V.1849–54.

90–1. A negative version of a well-known proverb. See Henryson, *Fables*, 1033, and Whiting M 170.

91. *leif brothir.* This provides a useful rhyme, but similar phrases were common in moralizing exhortations; cf. Henryson, *Fables*, 2910; and Dunbar, *Poems*, 53.11.

92–9. A free paraphrase of a piece of Latin verse believed in Douglas's time to be the work of Virgil. Like other apocryphal poems, it was included in many early editions of Virgil, including those printed by Ascensius:

Carmen de Venere et vino contra luxuriam et ebrietatem

> Nec veneris nec tu vini capieris amore.
> > Vno namque modo vina venusque nocent.
> Vt venus eneruat vires: sic copia vini
> > Et tentat gressus debilitatque pedes.
> Multos caecus amor cogit secreta fateri:
> > Arcanum demens detegit ebrietas.
> Bellum sepe petit ferus exitiale cupido:
> > Sepe manus itidem bacchus ad arma vocat.
> Perdidit horrendo troiam venus improba bello:
> > Et lapythas bello perdis iacche graui:
> Denique cum mentes hominum furiarit vterque:
> > Et pudor et probitas et metus omnis abest.
> Compedibus venerem: vinclis constringe lyeum:
> > Ne te muneribus ledat vterque suis.
> Vina sitim sedant: natis venus alma creandis
> > Seruit: finem horum transiluisse nocet.

(Do not be ensnared by the desire for either Venus [sexual love] or wine. For indeed wine and Venus are harmful in the same way. Just as Venus weakens bodily strength, so abundance of wine attacks walking and weakens the feet. Blind love compels many people to reveal secrets. Raging drunkenness uncovers what should be private. Wild desire often leads to destructive war. Bacchus often likewise summons hands to fighting. Evil Venus destroyed Troy in horrific war, and you, Iacchus [a name for Bacchus], destroy the Lapiths in harsh battle. In short, when each of you has maddened the minds of men, both shame and uprightness and fear totally depart. Restrain Venus with fetters and Bacchus with chains, so that neither corrupt you with their gifts. Wine satisfies thirst; bountiful Venus presides over the creation of children. To overstep this limit upon their use is harmful.) For more detailed discussion, see Bawcutt 1969.

99. Cf. *Directioun*.88; Whiting D 400.

109. *Ar*. Not an error for 'Is', but sometimes used in Scots with singular sense.

112–34. This section of the Prologue is greatly influenced by St Augustine's teachings on love, both in *The City of God*, XV.xxii (as the marginal note indicates), but also more generally in *On Christian Doctrine*.

114. For love as a flame or fire, cf. *Testament of Cresseid*, 29ff.

117. *as ane onbridillyt hors*. This simile is a focus for a complex pattern of imagery, concerning the control of horses and unruly passions. It looks back to lines 31, 62, and 86; compare also the related uses of the verb *refreyn* in lines 154, 182, and 204.

126. *ane hail manis estait*. 'A healthy man's condition'.

133–8. See Matthew xxii.37–9: 'Thou shalt love the lord thy God with all thy heart … Thou shalt love thy neighbour as thyself'; and cf. Dunbar, *Poems*, 24. 70–1.

141. *dowe nocht a stra*. 'Is not worth a straw'. Whiting S 815.

142–50. Note the ambiguity of line 144 (a prayer either to God or one's mistress), and other word play, especially on the erotic and theological senses of *grace* and *reuth*, 'pity'. This is resumed in lines 201–7.

142. *Faynt*. Both 'weak' and 'deceptive, cheating'.

155. *opynyon*. 'Reputation'. *deyr of a boryt beyn*. 'Not worth a bean'. *Boryt* literally means 'bored, pierced', perhaps here 'worm-eaten'.

156. *skant worth a fas*. 'Hardly worth a tassel, i.e. valueless'. For the idiom, cf. *Want of Wys Men*, 47, a poem once attributed to Henryson; and Whiting F 69.

158. *a fordullyt aß*. Asses were conventionally stupid. Cf. 'doillit aß' (VIII.vi.16), and Whiting A 218.

160. *Venus covrt*. A common trope in love poetry, but the tone here recalls the contempt of *Spectakle of Lufe* (*Asloan Manuscript*, I, 297).

164ff. This draws on the traditional mockery of the *senex amans*, such as the old husband in Dunbar's *Tretis*, *Poems*, 3.89–145.

167. *rovste of syn*. Rust was a common image for sin. Cf. *King Hart*, 930–2.

168. *Venus warkis*. A euphemism for sexual activity. Cf. Chaucer, *Merchant's Tale*, CT.1971; Dunbar, *Tretis*, 127 and 200.

169. *fury rage*. 'Frenzied madness'. Douglas uses this phrase in line 223 below, and often in the *Eneados*. Although Coldwell glossed *fury* as the adjective 'fiery', the words to which the phrase corresponds in the *Aeneid* – e.g. 'furens … femina' (5.6 = V.i.14), or 'impulsus furiis' (10.68 = X.ii.14), or 'furiis agitatus amor' (12.668 = XII. xi.117) – suggest the more powerful sense of 'driven by the Furies, frenzied'. See also Bawcutt 1971, 49.

187. *stynkis in Godis neys*. 'Stinks to high heaven'. A Scots idiom. Cf. *Want of Wys Men*, 62; and *DOST*, *nese*, n.1b.

193. *leche*. This picks up the imagery of love as suffering (192). Bawds act as the devil's physician.

205–6. Cf. Gower, *Confessio Amantis*, VIII.3162ff., for praise of 'thilke love which that is / Withinne a mannes herte affermed / And stant of charite confermed'; Ephesians iii.17; and Minerva's words in *Kingis Quair*, 988–9: 'Desire, quod sche, I nyl it nought deny / So thou it ground and set in Cristin wise'.

208–11. Douglas recalls Henryson's portrait of Venus in *Testament of Cresseid*, 225–8: 'Vnder smyling scho was dissimulait … Angrie as ony serpent vennemous'.

213. *morale Ihonne Gower*. Chaucer's epithet for Gower in *Troilus and Criseyde*, V.1856 rapidly became formulaic. Cf. Dunbar, Poems, 59.262; Douglas, *Palice of Honour*, 920.

215. *dowbill wound*. The wound is both emotional and physical. Virgil repeatedly

alludes to Dido's 'vulnus' (4.2, 67 and 689), but Douglas may also echo Troilus's 'double sorwe' (*Troilus and Criseyde*, I.1 and 54).

218–19. See St Augustine, *Confessions*, I.xiii. Coldwell suggests that Douglas's immediate source was Ascensius: 'Augustinus sese ad lachrymas compulsum Didonis querela confiteatur' (f.cxiv va).

221. Cf. II.Prol.21 and note.

229–35. Such views on love were conventional (see Whiting L 482–4). But Douglas's phrasing is close to Henryson, on the brevity of love: 'Mingit with cairfull ioy and fals plesance' (*Testament of Cresseid*, 236).

234. 'What is all its tedious experience but torment?'

235. Whiting L 517 and L 524.

240. *slycht*. Probably not a noun here, but an adjective, meaning 'crafty'.

243. *swelch*. 'Abyss, whirlpool'.

246. *fendis net*. For lust as a diabolic trap or net, cf. Dunbar, *Poems*, 24.102. Alexander Scott, *Poems*, xxxi.57–8, calls lust 'the verry net that Satane for ws set'.

247. 'What tongue may tell the misery caused by your magic tricks?' *Tryggettis* does not mean 'tragedies' (so glossed by some editors), but represents a Scots form of ME. *treget*, 'enchantment, deceit'. Lust is conceived as a juggling fiend.

248. 'If one struggles with you, you become stronger'. Douglas perhaps recalls the legend of the wrestler Antaeus, whose strength revived on contact with the earth, until he was outwitted by Hercules.

250. *blynd*. Cf. 'blyndyt' (3); and 'caeco … igni' (*Aeneid* 4.2).

254. *mait*. The sense is not certain. It might be construed as the adjective 'vanquished, worn-out' (referring to Dido, with the verb 'was' implicit); or, more plausibly, the verb 'vanquished, triumphed' (with Lust as the grammatical subject).

255. Douglas recalls Dido's own words: 'exstinctus pudor et … fama prior' (*Aeneid* 4.322–3). Cf. also 4.91: 'nec famam obstare furori'.

266–7. *Be the … Be war*. 'By thee (i.e. Dido) … be warned'. The warning to young women recalls *The Testament of Cresseid*, 452–60, but is closer verbally to *Troilus and Criseyde*, V.1772–85, where Chaucer addresses 'every lady bright of hewe': 'Beth war of men'. Cf. also Chaucer, speaking specifically of Dido in *House of Fame*, 269–70; and of Phyllis in *Legend of Good Women*, 2559: 'Be war, ye wemen'.

268–9. Both sense and syntax are difficult. The plural *thar* and *thai* seem more likely to refer to *ladeis* than *strangeris*. *Leir* cannot be glossed as 'glance slyly or immodestly' (so Coldwell), but means 'learn'. The sense is perhaps that if young women take Dido as their model they will achieve nothing but wanton love-making.

BOOK IV.i; Virgil 4.1–53

2. *greyn wound.* Virgil 4.2, 'vulnus'.

14. *and the ayr new schrowd.* An expansion by Douglas.

21. Virgil 4.11, 'quem sese ore ferens', which Loeb takes as 'How noble his mien!'

22. *O God, quhat wondir thing!* The exclamation is Douglas's.

27–8. Expanded from Virgil 4.13, 'degeneres animos timor arguit'.

30–1. Expanded from Virgil 4.14, 'quae bella exhausta canebat'; suggested by Ascensius f.116 rb, 'laboribus ... exhausta i. iam expleta & gesta atque pacta ... gravissima & maxime formidanda'.

36. *dissoverit.* Virgil 4.17, 'deceptam' (*i.e.* Dido); *Ascensius f.116 rb, 'deceptam morte s. prioris coniugis Sichei a Pygmalione interempto [*sic*, misprint for interempti]'.

38. *Genyvs chalmyr.* *Virgil 4.38, 'thalami'; Ascensius f.116 rb, 'i. thori genialis' misunderstood.

40. Virgil 4.19, 'uni ... culpae'; *Ascensius f.116 rb, 'i. ... esset transeundo ad secundas nuptias'.

42. *sory.* 'Wretched' (for Virgil 4.20, 'miseri'), not 'contemptible'.

47. Virgil 4.23, 'veteris flammae'; Servius f.116 ra, 'martialis coniugii ardorem'.

48. *baith corß and spreit.* Added by Douglas.

52–3. *hellis holl ... nycht.* Virgil 4.26, 'Erebi'; Ascensius f.116 rb, 'i. loci obscurissimi in inferno'.

56. *3our.* I.e. of Pudor, named by Virgil 4.27, but not by Douglas.

58. Virgil 4.28–9, 'amores abstulit'; *Ascensius f.116 rb, 'abstulit primos amores s. meos'; *Servius f.116 ra, 'a. cum illo consumpta sunt desideria & voluptates'.

62. *or scho wist.* Added by Douglas.

63. *sa mot I thryve.* This wish is not in Virgil (4.31).

65. *in wedowhed.* Virgil 4.32, 'sola'; *Ascensius f.117 rb, 'i. in viduitate'.

70. Virgil 4.34, 'id ... curare'.

72. *thy lord new ded.* Virgil 4.35, 'aegram'; *Servius f.116 vb, 'idest tristem propter maritum'.

73. *prynce nor duke.* Virgil 4.36, —; Ascensius f.117 rb, 'ductor'.

74. Omits Virgil 4.36, 'non ante Tyro'.

87–8. Virgil 4.42, 'hinc deserta siti regio'; Ascensius f.117 r, 'propter aquarum penuriam'; Servius f.116 vb, 'intelligit Xerolibyen'.

93. *to our supple.* Added by Douglas.

110 and 112. Virgil (4.53) has nothing corresponding to these lines.

IV.ii; Virgil 4.54–89

8. *beneuolence and gude luk.* Virgil 4.56, 'pacem'; Ascensius f.117 va, 'i. pacationem, conciliationem & beniuolentiam'.

13. *Bachus.* Virgil 4.58, 'patrique Lyaeo'; *Ascensius f.117 va, 'seu Baccho patri'.

19. *ontamyt.* Virgil 4.61, —; *Ascensius f.117 va, 'i. mundae et intactae' misunderstood.

20. * *raik on raw.* An alliterative tag, common in Scottish poetry. Cf. VI.xv.36; VIII. vi.109; and Henryson, *Robene and Makyne*, 12.

24. *And rych gyftis geif Troianys.* Virgil 4.63, 'instauratque diem donis'; *Servius f.117 vb, 'aut diis offerebat aut donabat tyriis vel Troianis'.

27. An explanation added by Douglas.

28. Virgil 4.64, —; *Ascensius f.117 va, 'consilium expetit'.

29–38. Expanded from Virgil 4.65–7.

40. *stalkar.* Virgil 4.71, 'pastor'.

45. Omits Virgil 4.73, 'Dictaeos'.

50–1. *offerit … commandment.* *Virgil 4.75, 'urbem paratam'; suggested by Ascensius f.118 va, '… quod signum est coniugalis amoris'?

59. Virgil 4.80, 'post ubi digressi'.

64. Virgil 4.82, 'vacua'; Ascensius f.118 va, 's. amato'.

66–8. *thinkis … be.* Virgil 4.83, 'auditque videtque'; Ascensius f.118 va, 'audit & videt s. per fantasiam & imaginationem illum s. amatum absentem'.

69. *the page.* A gloss by Douglas.

77. *pynnakillis hie.* Virgil 4.88–9, 'minaeque murorum ingentes'; *Ascensius f.119 r, 'i. eminentiae et pinnae murorum'.

78. *towris.* Virgil 4.89, 'machina'; Ascensius f.119 r, 'edificii aut turris'.

IV.iii; Virgil 4.90–128

1. *Iuno.* Virgil 4.91, 'cara Iovis coniunx'.

2. *deir frend.* Taking 'cara' as Ascensius f.119 rb does, 'chara scilicet Didoni'. Loeb (2nd ed) translates, 'Soon as the loved wife of Jove saw that Dido was held in a passion so fatal, and that her good name was now no bar to her frenzy …'

27. *al Lyby land.* Virgil 4.106, —; Ascensius f.120 r, 'in Libyam hoc est in Carthaginem'.

30–1. *the Troiane kynd and werys tocum.* Virgil 4. 106, 'regnum'.

38. Virgil 4.110, 'sed fatis incerta feror', which Loeb translates, 'But the Fates send me adrift'.

65. Virgil (4.125) has nothing corresponding to this.

66. *of stane*. A meaningless expansion by Douglas.

IV.iv; Virgil 4.129–72

2. *as Phebus rayß*. *Not '[a]n additional note of time added by Douglas' (Coldwell), but a translation of Virgil 4.130, 'iubare exorto'.

8ff. *Several details in the description of the hunt show the stylistic influence of Chaucer, particularly his 'The Tale of Dido', in *The Legend of Good Women*.

8. *hovand*. *Cf. *Legend of Good Women*, 1196: 'Hire yonge knyghtes hoven al aboute'.

10–11. *A free translation of Virgil 4.134–5, with echoes of Chaucer's *Knight's Tale* (CT.2506–7): 'The fomy steedes on the golden brydel / Gnawynge'.

16. *Cf. *Legend of Good Women*, 1201: 'Sit Dido, al in gold and perre wrye'.

30. *and ile*. Virgil 4.144, —; Ascensius f.121 rb, 'insulam'.

38. *of lawrer*. Virgil 4.148, 'fronde'; Ascensius f.121 va, 'scilicet lauri'.

46–55. Expanded from Virgil 4.152–5.

46. Virgil 4.152, —; Ascensius f.121 va, '(caprae) compulse a canibus'.

49. Virgil 4.154, —; Ascensius f.121 va, 'transeunt celeriter currentes de alia parte campos patentes'.

52. *herd of hartis*. *Cf. *Legend of Good Women*, 1212.

56. *planys*. Virgil 4.156, 'vallibus'.

57. *startling steid*. *Cf. the 'courser stertlynge as the fyr' ridden by Aeneas in *Legend of Good Women*, 1204.

60. Omits Virgil 4.158, 'votis'.

65–6. Virgil 4.161, 'insequitur commixta grandine nimbus'.

69. *Ascanyus*. Virgil 4.163, 'Dardanius'; Ascensius f.121 va, 's. Iulus'.

72. Virgil 4.164, —; Ascensius f.122 rb, 'i. tegmina & speluncas per agros, i. que & quas intervenire poterant'.

75–6. *al thame alane ... rane*. These lines are added by Douglas.

77. *takyn of wo*. Virgil 4.167, 'signum'; *Ascensius f.122 rb, 'signum s. infelicis coniugii'.

82. *hait Oreades*. Virgil 4.168, 'Nymphae'; Ascensius f.122 rb, 's. Oreades'.

83. *glaidnes*. Virgil 4.169. *Ascensius f.121 v 'lęti' and Ascensius f.122 rb, 'i. laeticie & voluptatis;' editors generally read 'leti', death.

IV.v; Virgil 4.173–278

13. *last.* I.e. 'last-born'.

26–7. *nobillis, princis.* The original (Virgil 4.186–7) is not so specific.

42. *est, west, north and sowth.* Virgil 4.195, 'passim'.

48. Virgil 4.198, 'rapta Garamantide [i.e. Garamantian] Nympha'.

55. Omits Virgil 4.202, 'limina'.

64. *Bachus.* Virgil 4.207, 'Lenaeum'; Ascensius f.123 va, 'Bacchicum'.

79. *Troiane foly hat.* Virgil 4.216, 'Maeonia mitra'; *Ascensius f.123 va, 'Lydia qua etiam Phryges utebantur'.

82. *Becauß.* Virgil 4.218, 'quippe'. 'And yet' would have been a better translation.

83. *invane.* Virgil 4.218, 'inanem'; perhaps misread as an adverb, and influenced by the neighbouring 'frustra' in Servius f.123 vb.

84. *at hame.* Added by Douglas.

85. *altar.* Virgil 4.219. *Ascensius f.124 r, 'aram', for MSS, 'aras'.

99–108. Expanded from Virgil 4.227–31.

109. 'Though the honour of such great things doesn't stir him ...'

122. *weyngis.* Virgil 4.239, 'talaria'; Servius f.125 ra, 'pennae'.

126. *hell.* Virgil 4.242, 'Orco'; *Ascensius f.124 va, 'i. ab inferno'.

128. Virgil 4.243, 'Tartara'; Ascensius f.124 va, 'i. loca profundissima & obscurissima in inferno'.

131. *brekis the stryngis tway.* Virgil 4.244, —; suggested by *Ascensius f.125 rb, '... lumina i. pupillas quas aufert'. See OED *eyestring*: 'The eyestrings were formerly supposed to crack at death'.

138. *fyrryn.* Virgil 4.249, 'piniferum'.

143. *stern and grysly.* Virgil 4.251, 'horrida'.

144. *Mercur.* Virgil 4.252, 'Cyllenius'; Ascensius f.125 rb, 'idest Mercurius', as in lines 151 (Virgil 4.258, Ascensius f.125 va), 185 (Virgil 4.276, Ascensius f.126 rb), and elsewhere. *Virgil has 'paribus nitens Cyllenius alis – Mercury balancing on equal wings'.

160. *brown.* Virgil 4.261, 'fulva'; *Ascensius f.125 va, 'subviridi admixto albo'.

176. *fremmyt.* Virgil 4.271, 'Libycis'; *Ascensius f.126 r, 'inimicis'.

187. *I wait nevir quhar.* Douglas's comment.

IV.vi; Virgil 4.279-361

5. *ful laith*. Contradicts the sense of Virgil, 4.281, 'ardet ... relinquere terras'.

10. *amorus*. Virgil 4.283, 'furentem'.

17. *Cloanthus*. Virgil 4.288. *p* and Ascensius f.126 r have 'Cloanthum' (as 1.510) for most MSS 'Serestum' (as 12.561).

24. Virgil 4.292, —; Ascensius f.126 va, 'abire velit'.

32. *day or nycht*. Added by Douglas.

35. Virgil 4.298, —; Ascensius f.126 va, 'nam res est solliciti plena timoris amor' *(quoting Ovid, *Heroides* 1.12, as is noted by Austin 1966, 161.

41. *nunnys of Bachus*. Virgil 4.302, 'Thyias'; Ascensius f.126 va, 'sacerdos Bacchi'.

42. *bankis, brays and buß*. Added by Douglas.

43. Omits Virgil 4.301, 'commotis excita sacris'.

45. *mont*. Virgil 4.303, —; Ascensius f.126 va, 'mons'.

47-8. *of hir fre will Eftir lang musyng*. Virgil 4.304, *'ultro'; Ascensius f.126 va, 'post longam cogitationem ... non exigentem eius compellationem'.

51. *myne onwyttyng*. Virgil 4.306, 'tacitus'. 'Without my knowing'. For this construction, see *DOST unwittand*.

54. *so cald*. Virgil (4.308) is silent here.

59. *I put the cace*. Virgil 4.311, 'quid'; *Ascensius f.127 rb, 'quid sup. dicere possem'.

61. *will*. An adjective, here meaning 'desolate, unfrequented'. Cf. XI.x.64; and *DOST, will*, adj. 5.

63. *leif this weilfair and ioy*. Virgil 4.311-12, —; suggested by Servius f.127 ra, 'ac si dicat Cartago iam tibi nota est'.

66. Virgil 4.314, 'per has lacrimas'; Ascensius f.127 rb, '... quas effundo'.

85-6. More vivid than Virgil 4.324, 'Hoc solum nomen quoniam de coniuge restat'.

87. Virgil 4.325, 'quid moror'; Ascensius f.127 va, 'i. quid differo mortem'.

88. An expansion by Douglas.

91. *Hyarbas*. Virgil 4.326. *Ascensius f.127 v has 'Hiarbas'; Ascensius f.127 r, as modern editors, 'Iarbas'.

100. *in febil estate*. Added by Douglas.

103. *refrenyt his will*. The parallelism of phrase in this line is due to Douglas.

109. *Dido*. Virgil 4.335, 'Elissae'; Ascensius f.128 rb, 'proprio nomine elisse diceris'.

115. *quhat nedis ʒou sa tofeyn?* Virgil 4.338, —; Ascensius f.128 rb, 'ne dicas eam ex opinione tua fugam'.

118. *ne frendschip in Cartage.* Virgil 4.339, —.

126. *at now fallis.* Virgil 4.343, —; *Ascensius f.128 va, 'post casum'.

136. *delytis.* Virgil 4.348, —; Ascensius f.128 va, 'delectando'.

137. Virgil 4.350, 'invidia'; Ascensius f.128 va, 'invidia i. iniuria'.

146. *ymage.* Virgil 4.353, 'imago', which Loeb (2nd ed) takes as 'ghost', but 'dream' would be better.

IV.vii; Virgil 4.362–407

1. *aggrevit.* Virgil 4.362, —; Ascensius f.129 rb, 'indignata & irata'.

9. *mont.* Virgil 4.367, —; Ascensius f.129 rb, 'mons'.

11–12. Virgil 4.367, 'Hyrcanaeque admorunt ubera tigres'; Servius f.129 ra, 'Arabicae ab Hyrcania Arabiae sylva'.

13. *perswaid.* Virgil 4.368, 'dissimulo'; Ascensius f.129 rb, 'alliciam blando sermone'.

14. Virgil 4.368, 'aut quae me ad maiora reservo'; *Ascensius f.129 rb, 'maiora i. meliora'; Loeb takes 'maiora' as 'wrongs'.

18. *Na, not to ʒeir.* Virgil 4.369, —; *Ascensius f.129 rb, 'etiam modicum … quasi dicat minime'.

22. *querrell.* Virgil 4.372, 'haec'.

36. *on thi passage.* Virgil 4.379, —; *Ascensius f.129 va, 'de avocando Enea'.

42 Virgil 4.383, 'supplicia hausurum'; Ascensius f.129 va, 'idest luiturum & daturum … punitionem perfidie'.

57. Virgil 4.390, 'linquens multa metu cunctantem'.

62. *apon rych carpettis spred.* Virgil 4.392, —; Ascensius f.130 rb, 'tapetibus instratis'.

72. *ballyngar and bark.* Virgil, 4.397–8, does not specify their kind, as Douglas does.

76. *gret mastis.* Virgil 4.399, —; Ascensius f.130 rb, 'pro malis'.

IV.viii; Virgil 4.408–73

4–6. Virgil 4.409, 'cum litora fervere late'.

9. *wytles.* Virgil 4.412, 'improbe'.

17. Virgil 4.417, —; Ascensius f.131 rb, 'unde convenit Annam sororem suam'.

20. Virgil 4.417, 'vocat iam carbasus auras'.

21. *croys.* Virgil 4.418, 'coronas'.

22–4. Douglas changes the tenses; Virgil has 4.419–20, 'potui … potero'.

30–1. Loeb (2nd ed) translates 'You alone will know the hour for easy access to him'.

41. *from hys behufe*. A meaningless addition by Douglas.

56–8. Virgil 4.436. *'dederis' Ascensius f.131 r with the medieval MSS and Servius f.131 vb, 'dederit' the ancient MSS.

57. *weil twentyfald*. Virgil 4.436, —; Ascensius f.131 va, 'copiose'.

59–61. 'With just such tears as she made her request, her sister reports her supplication.'

65. Virgil 4.439, 'tractabilis'; Ascensius f.131 va, 'aut ipse tractabilis s. a natura'.

68. Added by Douglas.

70. Omits Virgil 4.442, 'Alpini'.

84–5. Virgil 4.448, 'magno persentit pectore curas'.

99. * *furth3et*. The participial adjective, 'outpoured'.

106. *carpettis and ensens*. Virgil 4.458, —; Servius f.132 vb, 'laneis vittis … oleo'.

122. *Kyng*. Virgil 4.469, —; Ascensius f.132 va, 'rex'.

124. *fureys*. Virgil 4.469, —; Ascensius f.132 va, 'furiarum'.

128. Virgil 4.471, 'scaenis agitatus'.

129. *Rowpyt and sung*. Virgil 4.471, —; Ascensius f.132 va, 'actus & … exhibitus'.

130. *ourcled*. Virgil 4.472, 'armatam', applied to 'matrem'; Douglas's syntax is ambiguous.

131. *furyis*. Virgil 4.473, 'Dirae'; *Ascensius f.132 va, 'furię'; *grisly goddis fed*. Virgil *ibid.*, —.

IV.ix; Virgil 4.474–521

24. *in the gardyngis*. Virgil 4.484, —; Ascensius f.133 rb, 'quod in hortis … est'.

25. *walkryfe*. Virgil 4.484, —; *Ascensius f. 133 rb, 'draconi s. pervigili'.

26. *goldyn*. Virgil 4.485, 'sacros'; Ascensius f.133 rb, 'aurea'.

28. *to quykkyn his spreit*. Virgil 4.487, —; Ascensius f.133 va, 'conservativum cerebri & humorum draconis'.

47. *sword*. Virgil 4.495, 'arma'; Ascensius f.133 va, 'scilicet gladium'.

49. Virgil 4.496, 'exuviasque omnis'.

56. *as ony wall*. The comparison is Douglas's.

65. *fyrryn*. Virgil 4.505, 'taedis', *i.e.* 'pine'.

76. Virgil 4.510, 'Erebum'; Servius f.134 ra, '… inferiorum profunditatem'.

77. *confundar of elymentis*. Virgil 4.510, —; Servius, note to 6. 265, f.184 ra, 'elementorum confusio'.

78. *Proserpina.* Virgil 4.511, 'Hecaten'; Ascensius f.134 rb, 'i. Proserpina' and so also in IV.xi.50 (Virgil 4.609). She is 'thrynfald' because she is often merged with Diana and Luna.

82. Virgil 4.512, —; Ascensius f.134 va, 'i. lacus ad introitum inferni'.

83. *eftir the courß of the moyn.* Virgil 4.513, 'ad lunam'.

88. Loeb translates 4.516, 'amor' as 'love-charm'; Ascensius f.134 va shares that idea, 'quae nisi caruneulam illam assumpserit pullum, non amat'.

91–2. *bandis ... weyd.* Virgil 4.518, 'in veste recincta'.

95. *gydaris.* Virgil 4.519, 'conscia'.

IV.x; Virgil 4.522–83

13. *onrestles.* Virgil 4.529, 'infelix'.

15. Virgil 4.529–30, 'neque umquam solvitur in somnos'.

23. Virgil 4.534, 'inrisa'.

31–4. Loeb takes Virgil 4.538, 'quiane' as the sign of an ironic question.

42. *a queyn.* Douglas's addition.

49. *and a new rayß.* Another addition by Douglas.

62. *my first husband.* The identification is made by Douglas.

72. *Plesand of cheir.* Virgil 4.558, —; Ascensius f.135 va, 'vocem & colorem'.

79. *quham thou knawys.* Virgil 4.561, —; Ascensius f.135 va, 'tibi nota'.

83. *be nycht.* Added by Douglas.

86. Virgil 4.566, 'turbari trabibus'.

88. *Reddy to byrn thi schippys.* Virgil 4.567, —; Ascensius f.136 rb, 'ad naves tuas comburendas'.

91. *speid hand.* Added by Douglas.

98. *span aris bissely.* Virgil 4.573, 'transtris'; Ascensius f.136 rb, 'transtris ... ubi sedent remiges'.

112. *Virgil 4.581, 'rapiuntque ruuntque'.

116. *haw.* Virgil 4.583, 'caerula'.

IV.xi; Virgil 4.584–641

1. *purpour.* Virgil 4.585, 'croceum'.

2. *Titan.* *Virgil 4.585, 'Tithonus'. It was common in the medieval period to merge

or confuse Titan, the sun god, with Tithonus, the mortal lover of the dawn goddess Aurora. See Dunbar, *Goldyn Targe*, 16–18; Chaucer, *Troilus and Criseyde*, III.1464–70; Dante, *Purgatorio*, 9.1; and elsewhere in the *Eneados*, IX.viii.2; XII.Prol.13.

13. *vavengeour stranger*. Virgil 4.591, 'advena'.

22. *werdis*. Virgil 4.596. *Ascensius f.136 v has 'fata' for the MSS 'facta'.

27. The grammar would be improved if it were 'quha' here and in line 29. The 'quham' may be modelled on Virgil 4.598–9, 'quem … aiunt portare … quem subisse …'

40. *navy*. Virgil 4.604, 'castra'; Ascensius f.137 rb, 'idest classem'.

47. *clengis*. Virgil 4.607, 'lustras' probably should be taken as 'you observe' or 'traverse'.

48. *mediatrix*. Virgil 4.608, 'interpres'; Ascensius, 'idest mediatrix'.

50. *by our gentile lawys*. This in not in Virgil (4.609).

52. *with mony mudy wight*. Virgil 4.609, —; Ascensius f.137 va, 'querentibus frequentatis'.

53. Virgil 4.610, 'Dirae ultrices'; Ascensius f.137 va, 'idest furiae eumenides ultrices s. scelerum'.

55. Virgil 4.610, 'morientis Elissae'; Ascensius f.137 va, 'i. in quarum potestatem ventura est Elissa'.

57–8. Virgil 4.611, 'meritumque malis advertite [*Ascensius f.137 r reads 'avertite'] numen'; Ascensius f.137 va, 'i. a malis quod mali merentur habere infestum : & ita se innocentem indicat'.

61. *portis of Itale*. Virgil 4.612, 'portus'; Ascensius f.137 va, 's. Italiae'.

68. *help*. *Not a misunderstanding of Virgil 4.616, 'complexu' (Coldwell), but translation of Virgil 4.617, 'auxilium'.

76. *hevand vp my handis*. Douglas invents these words for Dido.

80. Virgil 4.622, —; *Ascensius f.138 rb, 'Carthaginenses Tyro'.

93. Virgil 4.629, 'pugnent ipsique nepotesque'; Ascensius f.138 rb, 'sup. inter se'.

101. *broun*. Virgil 4.633, 'ater', i.e. 'black'; the idea of burying is not in Virgil.

110. *Pluto*. Virgil 4.638, 'Iovi Stygio'; Ascensius f.138 va, 'idest Plutoni'.

IV.xii; Virgil 4.642–705

10. *wrocht*. Virgil 4.647, 'quaesitum'; Ascensius f.139 rb, 'comparatum'.

15. Virgil 4.651, 'dulces exuviae'.

17. *blude*. Virgil 4.652, —; *Ascensius f.139 rb, 'i. sanguinem'. *that on flocht is*, added by Douglas.

32. Virgil (4.660) has nothing about this.

34. Virgil 4.660, —; Ascensius f.139 rb, '& eo dicto statim in gladium incubuit'. *Douglas

recalls Chaucer's accounts of the suicide of Dido (*House of Fame*, 373; *Legend of Good Women*, 1351); and also of Pyramus (*Legend of Good Women*, 850).

42. *furthsprent*. Virgil 4.665, 'sparsas', which Loeb takes as 'bespattered'; *Servius f.140 ra, 'resolutas' (as an alternative).

53. *baith but and ben*. A homely touch by Douglas.

77. *with my counsell*. Virgil 4.682, —; Ascensius f.140 rb, 'consilio meo'.

79. *heris*. Virgil 4.682, 'patres'.

80. *[I] distroyt*. Virgil 4.682. *Ascensius f.139 v with the medieval MSS, 'extinxi'; 'exstinxti' the ancient MSS

82. *hald hir in myne arm*. This wish is added by Douglas.

88. *wympil*. Virgil 4.687, 'veste'.

101. *Hir mayd*. Virgil 4.694, —. *from the hevyn*. Virgil *ibid.*, 'Olympo'; Ascensius f.140 va, 'i. caelo'.

105. *natural*. Virgil 4.696, —; Servius f.140 vb, 'naturali'.

117. *to Pluto consecrate*. Virgil 4.702–3, 'Diti sacrum'; Ascensius f.141 r, 'consecratum ... Plutoni'.

Prologue V

Douglas follows Virgil in deliberately juxtaposing images of pleasure and joy with the tragic subject matter of book 4. His remarks on the variety of Virgil's style are highly appropriate at this point, since the principle of variation is not only one of 'the most marked features of the structure of the *Aeneid*', but particularly evident in book 5 (Virgil ed. Williams 1960, xi–xii). The elaborate nine-line stanza *aabaabbcc*[5], which is also used in the third book of *The Palice of Honour*, derives from the inset Complaint in Chaucer's *Complaint of Mars*. A slightly more difficult form of the stanza, which has only two rhymes (*aabaabbab*), occurs in Prologue III.

1–18. This account of the varied ways in which people enjoy themselves is possibly a literary topos. There is a similar but longer treatment in Lydgate's 'Every Thing to his Semblable' (*Minor Poems*, II, pp. 801–8).

1. *Gladys*. Probably in the sense 'gladdens, makes joyful'.

3. Cf. 'The besye hunter is gladde to fynde game': Lydgate, 'Every Thing to his Semblable', 65. *happy*. 'Occurring by good luck'.

4. *rych ryver onto fleyn*. 'To make his way to a river-bank rich in wild fowl'.

5. Cf. 'The famous clerk hathe ioye of his librarye': Lydgate, 'Every Thing to his Semblable', 61.

10. *sterand stedys*. 'Lively horses'. A common alliterative collocation. Cf. *Golagros*, 591 and 893.

12. Proverbial. Cf. Whiting S 131, whose first citation is from Chaucer's *Prologue to the Wife of Bath's Tale*, *CT*.III.552.

13. Religion is not the path to success at court. Cf. Dunbar, *Poems*, 5.17–18.

16. Proverbial. Cf. Whiting H 230.

17. Whiting A 153 treats this as proverbial.

20–1. Douglas closely follows Proverbs xvii.22: 'Animus gaudens aetatem floridam facit'. Cf. Whiting S 633; Tilley H 301.

22–7. The source is Virgil, *Eclogue* 4.60–3:

> Incipe, parve puer, risu cognoscere matrem.
> Matri longa decem tulerunt fastidia menses.
> Incipe, parve puer: qui non risere parentes
> Nec deus hunc mensa, dea nec dignata cubili est.

This passage has long provoked discussion among Virgilian scholars, and there is considerable disagreement as to the identity of the *deus* and *dea* in the last line. Douglas seems to be following Ascensius, who notes the difficulty of explaining the sense, rejects the *Seruianam interpretationem*, and follows instead the argument of Angelo Politian, who – he says – identifies the god with Genius and the goddess with Juno (Ascensius on *Eclogue* 4).

33–6. This probably derives from Macrobius, who commented on Virgil's mastery of all four styles – *copiosum, breve, siccum* and *pingue et floridum* (*Saturnalia*, V.1.7).

37. Cf. Macrobius, *Saturnalia*, I.16.12: [Virgil is] *omnium disciplinarum peritus*.

39–40. The *common weill* often figured in late medieval discussions of the general welfare of a country. See note to Dunbar, *Poems*, 11.48. It is not clear whether Douglas refers to a specific Virgilian passage, but see *Aeneid* 6.845–6 (translated as VI.xiv.100–2), on Fabius who restored 'the common weill'.

49–50. See the earlier criticism of Caxton in I.Prol.138ff, and 173–6.

51. *mank and mutulate*. This alliterative coupling occurs in medieval Latin *manca et mutila*. Cf. also the use by George Bannatyne (*Bannatyne Manuscript* 1928–32, II.1).

52–4. This striking metaphor – cf. also I.Prol.59 and *Directioun*, 88–9 – stresses Douglas's difference from Caxton, whose *Eneydos* was *not* based directly on the *Aeneid*.

52. 'My translation (literally, a ceremonial gift of wine) came straight from the source (literally, the wine press)'.

53. 'Not drawn off from one vessel to another, not poured from tun to tun'. Douglas puns on the last syllable of Caxton's name.

55–68. Douglas switches to rhyme royal, perhaps to signal a change of tone and topic. Cf. his earlier repudiation of pagan inspiration in I.Prol.460–1, and III. Prol.41–5.

55. *Bachus of glaidnes*. Douglas recalls *Aeneid* 1.734: 'laetitiae Bacchus dator' (for

translation, see I.xi.80). *funerall Proserpyne.* Poets commonly couple Proserpina with Pluto, and view her as a 'goddes infernall' (Henryson, *Orpheus and Eurydice*, 111 and 308), but *funerall* is not a stock epithet. Douglas may allude to her mention in Virgil's account of Dido's death (*Aeneid* 4.698).

62. See note to II.Prol.20–1.

BOOK V.i; Virgil 5.1–41

11. *for weil wyst Eneas.* Virgil 5.5, —; Ascensius f.141 va, 'causa … latet s. Aeneam'.

30, 34–5. 58. More precisely nautical than Virgil 5.16, 19, 32–3.

41. Virgil 5.23, 'quoque vocat [Fortuna]'; *Ascensius f.142 rb, 'fortuita et repentina tempestas'.

46. *So haue I seyll.* Virgil 5.26, 'equidem'; Ascensius f.142 rb, 'i. ego certe'.

60. *arryvit.* Virgil 5.34, 'advertuntur'.

64. *als ferß as ony thundyr.* The simile is not in Virgil (5.36).

66. *Affryke.* Virgil 5.37, 'Libystidis'; Servius f.143 ra, 'Africanae'.

V.ii; Virgil 5.42–103

20. Virgil 5.51, 'Gaetulis … Syrtibus'; *Ascensius f.143 rb, 'hoc est in maximis periculis maris qualia sunt apud Syrtes'.

41. Virgil 5.62, 'Penatis'.

52. *or wersyll, and bair the gre.* Virgil 5.67, —; Ascensius f.144 rb, 'luctando caestibus'.

54. *lyke a douchty campioun.* The comparison is not in Virgil (5.69).

55. *baston … or mays.* Virgil 5.69, 'crudo … caestu'; *Ascensius f.144 rb, 'i. armatura manuum a cędendo …' In Douglas's time there was some confusion as to the nature of the *caestus*, a kind of boxing glove loaded with lead or iron. The illustrator of Brant's Virgil (1502), f.240r, showed Entellus and Dares holding curved clubs, suggesting that he pictured it similarly to Douglas.

59. Virgil 5.71, —; Ascensius f.144 rb, 'ostendite favorem'.

68. *in feyr.* 'Together' not 'in fear'.

71. *payane.* Douglas's comment.

80. *thou onlost.* 'With you not lost'.

88. *sweitly and even.* Virgil 5.84, 'lubricus'.

90. Omits Virgil 5.87, 'caeruleae'.

96. *scho.* Virgil 5.90, 'ille'. Douglas makes his 'adder' feminine.

97. Omits Virgil 5.91, 'levia'.

98. *drynk.* Not in Virgil (5.91).

103. *Genyus, the god of that sted.* Virgil 5.95, 'genium loci'; Ascensius f.145 rb, 'genium i. deum … loci'.

105. *fyve.* Virgil 5.96. *PV, the medieval MSS, and Ascensius f.145 r, 'quinas'; MR¹ 'binas'.

111. *in thar degre.* Added by Douglas.

118. *ordanyt for the mulde meyt.* Virgil 5.103, —; *Ascensius f.147 va, 'scilicet ad parentationem faciendam'.

V.iii; Virgil 5.104–58

1. *hys faderis chayr.* Virgil 5.105, —; Ascensius f.147 va, 'auriga solis patris sui'.

4. *of this triumphe.* Virgil 5.106, —; Ascensius f.147 va, 'certaminis'.

13. *gilt.* Virgil 5.110, 'sacri'; Ascensius f.147 va, 'preciosi'.

14. *lawrer.* Virgil 5.111, —; *Pomponius Sabinus (Basle, 1544, p. 381), 'ex lauro'.

16. *of triumphe and myche glory.* Added by Douglas.

22. *squair.* Virgil 5.114, 'gravibus'; cf. V.iii.75; V.vii.107, etc.

38. *sovir sey ship.* *Virgil 5.123, 'caerulea'; Ascensius f.148rb, 'idest cẹrulei coloris: aut qua in mari tute utatur'.

45. *southt est wynd.* Virgil 5.126, 'Cori'; suggested by Ascensius f.148 va, 'ac pluvioso flantes condunt'?

48. *a fair plane greyn.* Virgil 5.128, 'campus'; Ascensius f.148 va, 'campum amoenum'.

49–50. Expanded from Virgil 5.128, 'apricis statio gratissimo mergis'.

52. *aik.* *Virgil 5.129, 'ilice'; Ascensius f.148 va, 'i. quercu'.

80-1. *of wer Or for triumphe.* Added by Douglas.

84. *swete drepand bedeyn.* Virgil 5.146, —; Ascensius f.149 rb, 'spumis abundantia'.

85-6. *'… men [who] yelled so … [who] beheld them'.

87. *Row fast.* The direct speech is Douglas's addition.

90. *'… hit with the noise [that] is so shrill'.

96. Virgil 5.153–4, 'pondere pinus tarda tenet'; Ascensius f.149 rb, 'navis ex pina facta … tarda … mole & magnitudine'.

102. *blont.* Added by Douglas, presumably for the rhyme.

V.iv; Virgil 5.159–243

6. *steirburd.* Virgil 5.162, 'dexter'.

10. *ilk rowth, and waris.* Added by Douglas.

29. Douglas's addition.

31–2. *skyppar, mastir.* Virgil 5.176, 'rector', 'magister'.

39–42. Expanded from Virgil 5.181–2.

46. *for lak of gude steryng.* Virgil 5.184, —; Ascensius f.148 rb, 'quia gubernatorem amiserat'.

57. 'The lattir rewyne of Troy' seems meant adverbially – 'in Troy's last hour'.

60. *of Affryk.* Virgil 5.192, 'Gaetulis'; Servius f.148 vb, 'Africanis'.

62. Virgil 5.193, —; *Ascensius f.148 rb, 'iuxta Charybdin navigarent'.

66. Virgil 5.194, —; Ascensius f.148 rb, 'qui primas partes obtinere soleo'.

68. Virgil 5.195, — Ascensius f.148 rb, 'O quam gloriosum foret in hoc certamine superasse'.

76. *apon athir wail.* Added by Douglas.

77. *mychty.* Virgil 5.198, 'aerea'; *Ascensius f. 148va, 'i. fortis, aut ẹtata'.

78. *brayd bilge of aik.* Douglas's addition.

93. *Cryand, 'Byde, how'.* No direct speech in Virgil (5.207).

95. Douglas's addition.

100. *fludis chyll.* Virgil 5.212, 'prona maria', that is 'sloping sea'.

123–36. Expanded from Virgil 5.227–31.

126. There is no direct speech in Virgil (5.228).

153. *nymphis.* Virgil 5.240, —; Ascensius f.149 va, 'nympharum'.

154. *thai that followis Phorcus.* Virgil 5.240, 'Phorci'; *Ascensius f.149 va, 'i. quibus Phorcus praeest'.

156. *the fader of havynnys.* Virgil 5.241, 'pater'; Ascensius f.149 va, 'portuum deus'.

V.v; Virgil 5.244–85

8. *charge.* Virgil 5.248, 'talentum'; *Ascensius f.149 va, 'i. pondus argenti'.

12–14. Virgil 5.251, 'Meandro duplici Meliboea cucurrit'; *Ascensius f.149 va, 'quod est Meliboensis hoc est Thessala currit meandro duplici i. flexuoso'.

15. Virgil 5.252, 'intextus'.

16. Virgil 5.252, 'puer regius'; Ascensius f.149 va, 's. Ganymedes Trois regis Troianorum filius'.

24. *clappand.* Virgil 5.256, 'tendunt'.

36. 'That was a shelter to save him in battle'.

44. Virgil 5.267, 'Cymbia'; Ascensius f.150 va, 'i. pocula in morem cymbarum facta'.

48. *furth pransand lyke a lard.* Virgil 5.269, —; suggested by the reference in Servius f.150 vb to garlands – 'vt ait Varro magni honoris sunt'.

50. *of the rosys red.* Virgil 5.269, —; Ascensius f.150 va, 'roseis'.

56. This line belongs wholly to Douglas.

57. **hevy schod cart quheill.* Virgil 5.274, 'aerea rota'; Buchanan glosses this similarly as 'a schod quheill', a wooden wheel furnished with an iron rim (Buchanan, George, 1957, 285).

58. *ryvand hir tewch bak.* Douglas supplies this detail.

V.vi; Virgil 5.286–361

6–7. *a playng place ... theatry.* Virgil 5.288, 'theatri'; Ascensius f.151 rb, 'idest locus aptus cursui'.

12. Expanded from Virgil 5.292, 'animos'.

18. *luf sylle*: 'simple, innocent love'. Added by Douglas.

25. *Epyria.* Virgil 5.298, 'Acarnan'; Ascensius f.151 rb, 'de Acarnania, hoc est Epyrota'.

27. *that cite.* Virgil 5.299, —; Ascensius f.151 rb, 'illius oppidi'.

32–3. Virgil 5.302, 'multi praeterea quos fama obscura recondit'; Servius f.151 vb, 'per contrarium illos superiores omnes esse nobiles indicavit'.

40. *wrocht in Creyt.* Virgil 5.306, 'Gnosia'; Ascensius f.151 va, 'idest Cretensia'.

66–7. Douglas is more vivid than Virgil 5.324–5, 'calcemque terit iam calce Diores, incumbens umero'.

69. *skyppyt furth.* Virgil 5.326, 'transeat'.

90. The comment is by Douglas.

97. 'The good will of his friends defends Euryalus'.

99. The comment again is made by Douglas.

107. *rewthfull.* Virgil 5.348. *Ascensius f.152 r has 'pius' for 'pater' of the MSS.

113. Virgil 5.350, 'insontis'; Ascensius f.153 rb, 'qui citra culpam suam dolo nisi lapsus est'.

120. *ran swyft in a lyng.* A pointless addition by Douglas.

124. *for a bourd.* Douglas gives the explanation.

132. *of syk geir as mycht gane.* Added by Douglas.

V.vii; Virgil 5.362–423

4. *mayß or burdon.* See note on V.ii.55.

8. *schakaris.* Virgil 5.366, —; *Ascensius f.153 rb, 'laminis'.

22. *Kyng.* Virgil 5.373, —; Ascensius f.153 va, 'regis'.

69. *harneß and braseris.* Virgil 5.401, —; suggested by Ascensius f.154 va, 'armaturas'.

92. *his.* Virgil 5.414 does not specify whose blood; Ascensius f.154 va, 's. Erycis'.

93. *Hercules.* Virgil 5.414, 'Alciden'; Ascensius f.154 va, 'i. Herculem'.

110. Awkward, and better if 'Hydduus of statur …'; Virgil 5.423, 'ingens'.

V.viii; Virgil 5.424–84

4. Virgil 5.425, 'palmas amborum innexuit'.

6. Virgil 5.426, —; Donatus, 'mox ut arma sumpserunt'.

11–17. Expanded from Virgil 5.429, 'pugnamque lacessunt'.

35–46. Expanded from Virgil 5.439–42.

36. Virgil 5.441, —; Ascensius f.155 va, 'frustratur a primo conatu'.

55. *kosch.* Virgil 5.448, 'cava'.

76. *rayn.* Virgil 5.458, 'grandine'.

86–92. Expanded from Virgil 5.465–7.

95. *dolf as led.* *An expansion of Virgil 5.468. The simile is traditional (Whiting L 120); cf. XI.vii.102, and 189.

96. *For sorow.* Virgil 5.469, —; Ascensius f.156 rb, 'prae dolore'.

102. *abufe in hys mynd.* Virgil 5.473, 'superans animis'.

120. *for now and evir mair.* Virgil 5.484, —; Ascensius f.156 va, 'ad perpetuam requiem'.

V.ix; Virgil 5.485–544

4. *forß of mennys handis.* Virgil 5.487, 'ingentique manu' (*i.e.* his own hand?); Ascensius f.156 va, 'idest multitudine'.

5. *Amyd the greyn.* Added by Douglas. *Sergestus.* Virgil 5.487, 'Serestus'; *Ascensius f.156 va notes earlier mentions of Serestus, but suggests identifying him with Sergestus: 'Sed uidetur idem esse qui & Sergestus ablato g'.

9. *steill.* Virgil 5.490, 'aerea'.

22. *ancyant.* Virgil 5.498, —; Ascensius f.157 rb, 'senior'.

23. *for Eneas sayk.* The explanation is added by Douglas.

26. *at thar feyt.* This detail is supplied by Douglas.

43. *in the ayr.* Virgil 5.512, 'Notos'; Ascensius f.157 va, 'i. ventos'.

78. *of hevyn.* Virgil 5.533, 'Olympi'; Ascensius f.158 rb, 'i. caeli'.

83. *of Trace kyng.* Virgil 5.536, 'Thracius'; Servius f.158 ra, 'rege Thraciae'.

92. Virgil 5.541, —; suggested by the gloss in Ascensius f.158 rb on 'bonus': 'beneficus et amicus'.

V.x; Virgil 5.545–602

4. Virgil 5.546, 'impubis'.

22. *with how and helm.* Virgil 5.556, 'corona'; Servius f.159 ra, 'i. galea'.

32. Virgil 5.562, 'paribusque magistris'; Ascensius f.159 rb, 'i. conformibus'.

40. *rynggyt the forthir e.* Added by Douglas.

41. *on a cursour bay.* Added by Douglas.

47. *Of cullour quhyte.* Added by Douglas.

51. *purchest.* Virgil (5.574) does not say how the horses were acquired from Acestes.

52. *and a maner feir.* Virgil 5.575, 'pavidos', applied to the bashful boys, not the Trojans.

61. *Go togidder.* Direct speech due to Douglas.

62. *ran thai sammyn.* Virgil 5.580, 'discurrere'.

63. *ilkane chesyt hys feir.* Not in Virgil (5.581).

73. *with a crak.* Added by Douglas.

76. *Thar handis schak.* A detail added by Douglas.

80. Douglas's comment, not Virgil's (5.590).

89. *Egyp.* Virgil 5.595, 'Carpathium'; *Servius f.162 ra, 'inter Aegyptum et Rhodum a Carpatho insula'.

V.xi; Virgil 5.603–63

7. Virgil 5.605, 'sollemnia'.

10–11. Expanded from Virgil 5.608, 'necdum antiquum saturata dolorem'.

16. *as a vyre.* *'Swift as a cross-bow bolt'. The simile does not occur in Virgil, 5.609, but is used twice in the Scottish romance *Lancelot of the Laik* (lines 1091, 3288), possibly as an intensification of the more commonplace 'swift as an arrow'.

24. *secret far fra men.* Virgil 5.613, 'in sola secretae;' Ascensius f.160 va, 'i. separatae a viris'.

29–32. Expanded from Virgil 5.615-16, 'heu! tot vada fessis et tantum superesse maris!'

33–4. Virgil 5.617, 'urbem orant'.

42. *Trace.* Virgil 5.620. *Ascensius f.160 v, 'Ismarii'; Ascensius f.161 rb, 'Ismarii i. Thracis;' MSS have 'Tmarii' or 'Mari(i)'

56–7. *schawd sandis … haue we.* Virgil 5.628, 'sidera'; perhaps suggested by Ascensius f.161 rb 'idest tempestates'.

68. *in all my eild.* Added by Douglas.

92. *born a Troiane.* Virgil 5.646, 'Rhoeteia'; Ascensius f.162 rb, 'i. Troiana'.

121. *The flambe.* Virgil 5.662, 'Volcanus'; *Ascensius f.162 rb, 'i. igni'. *at large,* Virgil ibid., —; Ascensius *ibid.,* 'ut libere'.

122. *Virgil 5.663, 'transtra per et remos et pictas abiete puppis'.

V.xii; Virgil 5.664-761

1. Omits Virgil 5.664, 'cuneosque'.

10. *thyddir gan he speid.* Added by Douglas.

16–17. *ayr Onto my fader.* Added by Douglas.

32. Virgil 5.632, 'vomens tardum fumum'.

44. Expanded from Virgil 5.690, 'nunc, pater'.

47. Virgil 5.690, 'tenuis Teucrum res'.

60. Virgil 5.699, 'a peste'.

68. Modifies 'rollyng' in line 65.

69. Virgil 5.704, —; Ascensius f.163 va, 'tunc cum sic dubius esset'.

71. *Mynerve.* Virgil 5.704, 'Tritonia Pallas'; Ascensius f.163 va, 'i. Minerva'.

81. *I.e.* 'To endure fortune is to overcome it'.

84. *wyß and sage.* Douglas adds the tag.

97. *eftir Acestes kyng.* Virgil 5.718, —; Ascensius f.164 rb, 's. ab Aceste'.

100. *cumpaß.* Virgil 5.720. *R¹, the medieval MSS and Ascensius f.163 v, 'deducitur'; MPp, 'diducitur'

103. Added by Douglas.

116. *I tel the thus.* Not in Virgil (5.730).

119. *Pluto.* Virgil 5.731, 'Ditis'; Ascensius f.164 va, 'idest Plutonis'.

122. This assurance is added by Douglas.

127. *plane.* Virgil 5.735, —; Ascensius f.164 va, 'campos'.

133. *as now na langar dwell I may.* Added by Douglas.

135. *wil at I withdraw.* Virgil 5.738, —; Ascensius f.164 va, 'rediturus est'.

144. *Troiane Ingil.* Virgil 5.744, 'Pergameumque Larem'; Ascensius f.165 rb, 'i. ignem perpetuum quem Troiani colebant'.

159–64. Expanded from Virgil 5.752–3.

170–1. Expanded from Virgil 5.756–7, 'haec loca Troiam esse iubet'.

174. *thar merkattis and thar fair.* Virgil 5.758, 'forum'.

V.xiii; Virgil 5.762–826

14. *forß.* *Virgil 5.768, 'numen' (M²P and medieval MSS, Ascensius f.165 v: 'nomen' M¹: 'caelum' R¹).

17. *curtas.* Virgil 5.770, 'bonus'; Ascensius f.166 rb, 'i. Clemens'.

22. *a blak ȝowe.* Virgil 5.772, 'agnam'; Ascensius f.166 rb, 'sicut prius dictum est: Nigram hyemi pecudem'.

22. *god of tempestis fell.* Virgil 5.772, 'Tempestatibus'.

32. *as thai war wode.* The comparison is made by Douglas.

33. *al onflocht.* Added by Douglas.

42. *nor may scho leif at eyß.* The parallelism of phrase here is Douglas's.

48. *Master.* Virgil 5.785, 'media'.

53–4. Expanded from Virgil 5.788, 'causas tanti sciat illa furoris'.

72. *gif so the fatis gydis.* Virgil 5.798, —; Ascensius f.167 rb, 'a diis'.

83–4. Expanded from Virgil 5.801, 'merui quoque'.

108. Virgil 5.812, —; Ascensius f.167 rb, 'i. vellem adhuc liberare Aeneam si necesse esset'.

110. *I salbe ȝit als kynd.* Added by Douglas.

113. *clepit the louch of hell.* This information is supplied by Douglas.

120. *to draw his cart or chair.* Virgil 5.818, *'curru'; Ascensius f.167 va, 'ad currum'.

133. *with his cannos hair.* Virgil 5.823, —; Ascensius f.167 va, 'quia canus est spumis'.

135. *with trump playand thar spryng.* Virgil 5.824, —; Ascensius f.167 va, 'qui concha canunt'.

138. Virgil 5.826, —; Ascensius f.168 rb, 'hoc est nymphae illae quae nereides dicuntur'.

V.xiv; Virgil 5.827–6.8

3–10. Expanded from Virgil 5.828–32.

11. *as lodis man and lard.* Virgil 5.833, —; Ascensius f.168 rb, 's. navitarum aut directorum'.

12. Added by Douglas.

17. *but langar kepe.* Added by Douglas.

21. *god of sleip.* Virgil 5.838, 'Somnus'; Ascensius f.168 va, 'i. deus somniorum'.

54. *the forcy hellys see.* Virgil 5.855, —; Ascensius f.169 rb, 'i. paludis infemalis'.

60. *as that the schip gan helde.* A detail added by Douglas.

71. *that we Marmadynnys clepe.* This explanation is supplied by Douglas.

77. *rok and tailȝeve.* Virgil 5.867, 'errare'.

97. Douglas ignores the metaphor of Virgil 6.6–7 : 'quaerit pars semina flammae abstrusa in venis silicis'.

101–2. Virgil (6.6–8) has nothing corresponding to this.

Prologue VI

The prologue constitutes a defence of Virgil's 'sentence' (27), or high seriousness, and stresses the agreement of many of his beliefs with the tenets of Christianity. In this Douglas was highly traditional: many medieval readers of Virgil, including Bernard Silvestris, John of Salisbury, Dante, Boccaccio, and Chaucer, shared his admiration for *Aeneid* 6. The eight-line stanza, rhyming *ababbcbc⁵*, which resembles that used in Prologue XI, was a common form in the fifteenth and early sixteenth centuries, especially for serious subject matter. When employed by Dunbar and Henryson, it usually has a refrain (see note to Dunbar, *Poems*, 6).

1–6. Douglas first invokes Pluto, ruler of the Underworld, associating him with Acheron, 'hellys flude' (VI.v.2), and the other infernal rivers, Styx, Phlegethon, Lethe, and Cocytus. See also notes to 150 and 167–8.

4. *watyris of oblivie.* An allusion to *Aeneid* 6.715, where the spirits on the banks of Lethe 'longa oblivia potant'.

5. *furyus sistyris thre.* The three Furies, Allecto, Tisiphone, and Megaera, were sometimes invoked by medieval poets as if they were Muses. Cf. line 23 below; Chaucer, *Troilus and Criseyde*, I.6–7 and IV.22–4; and *Kingis Quair*, 129. The mention of their *quhirling*, 'whirling', is puzzling, and Coldwell suggested confusion with the three Fates, and their *spinning*. There may, however, be an over-compressed allusion to passages in Henryson's *Orpheus and Eurydice*, 261–70, and 475–8. Here too the Furies are 'the sisteris thre', who cause the 'quhirlyng', or turning, of the wheel on which Ixion is tortured.

8. *Sibil.* The Cumaean Sibyl, Aeneas's guide in the Underworld.

11. *goddis apis.* 'Fools'. See note to IV.Prol.21.

12–13. Cf. I.Prol.106–8. On the wisdom concealed in 'dyrk poecy', see I.Prol.191–8.

15. *wirk eftir the wiß.* 'Act according to the advice of the wise'. Proverbial. Cf. *Wallace*, VIII.693; and Whiting M 351.

17–24. This is the opinion not of Douglas but of an imaginary critic who finds in book 6 nothing but fantasy and superstition. Cf. also *Directioun*, 25–30.

18. *browneis ... bogillis.* These words are often linked alliteratively; cf. I.Prol.273. In folklore the *bogill* is an ugly terrifying spirit, whereas the *browny* seems helpful and less malevolent. William Birnie, a late sixteenth-century writer, compares the *browny* to the Roman *Lar*, a tutelary spirit, and the *bogill* to the *lemures*, frightening ghosts of the dead (see citations in *DOST*, under *brounie*, *brownie*, and *bogill*).

19. *wow.* An exclamation of horror and disgust.

21. *in the monys cruke.* A time apparently suitable for magical practices, when the moon is crescent or waning. Robert Sempill mentions a charm concerning 'heather ... / Cutted off in the cruik of the moone': *Satirical Poems* 1891–3, I, 363, lines 305–6. Cf. also Henryson, *Sum Practysis*, 46, and Fox's note on the line, referring to *MED*, *crok*, 6a.

23. *plukkit duke.* Pluto is reduced to a plucked fowl by the word play on 'duck' and 'duke'.

24. *deir of a revyn sleif.* The sense is probably 'worth no more than a tattered sleeve'. Cf. Whiting S 378: 'A broken sleeve holds the arm back'. Sleeves were separable items of clothing. There is some slight evidence that such sleeves might be used in witchcraft; see *DOST*, *slef(e*, n 2c.

28. *Seruius.* Maurus Servius Honoratus (*floruit* fourth–fifth century AD), grammarian and author of a famous commentary on Virgil (see Baswell 1995, 49–53), to which Douglas was much indebted. Cf. his comment quoted by Ascensius at the beginning of book 6: 'Totus Virgilius plenus est scientia, in qua hic liber tenet principatum' (f.clxix vb).

32. *ragmentis.* The word is not here pejorative, as in Prol.VIII.147, but probably means 'long complex writings'.

38. *philosophour naturall.* Natural philosophy was a term that might refer to the study of natural phenomena, but might also be applied to humane or moral philosophy; Lindsay wrote of the 'naturall' philosophy of Aristotle and Plato (*Monarche*, 567).

40. *conform ... collaterall.* Perhaps 'in agreement ... parallel'.

41–3. *capital ... venyall.* A theological contrast between mortal, or deadly, sins and those that are pardonable and do not entail spiritual damnation.

43. The 1553 edition modifies this line, omitting the mention of purgatory. It makes similar Protestantizing alterations to lines 88, 89–96 (the whole stanza is omitted), and 167–8. For later changes to the text, see VI.i.100 (omits 'bedis'); VI.ix.23 (omits 'nun'); and VI.xii heading (omits 'purgatory').

44. *plesand plane*. Elysian Fields. Cf. also line 100: 'Camp Elyse'.

46–7. Coldwell compares Matthew vii.13–14, but the primary reference is to *Aeneid* 6.126–9: 'facilis descensus Averno …'

61–4. Douglas is wholly accurate concerning St Augustine's many references to Virgil, particularly *Aeneid* 6, in *The City of God*. Coldwell suggests that Douglas may recall Boccaccio, who remarks similarly in *De Genealogia Deorum* XIV.xviii: 'cum saepissime in suis voluminibus sanctus homo Virgilium aliosque poetas inducat'.

68. 'They ought not to be considered valueless, as if they were lost or straying animals'; cf. *DOST, vagab(o)und*, adj; *waith*, adj.

70. 'For often he modulates his voice according to the Sibyl's words'. Cf. I.Prol.506: 'tonyt my sang'.

71–2. See *Eclogue* 4.6–7: 'iam redit et Virgo, redeunt Saturnia regna; / iam nova progenies caelo demittitur alto'. Cf. also V.Prol.23–7.

73. *Ascencyus*. Jodocus Badius Ascensius (1462–1535), the Flemish scholar and printer, to whose edition of the *Aeneid*, with its detailed commentary, Douglas was much indebted. See Introduction, and Bawcutt 1976, 92–127. For study of Ascensius's publications, see Renouard 1908 and White 2013.

74. The reference is to St Paul, whom Ascensius mentions several times, in his preface to the *Aeneid* and in the commentary on book 6: 'sontibus poenas et iustis praemia tam sancte constituit ut Paulo nostro non indigna que scribit pleraque censeri mereantur'.

77. 'Although some of his writings in part diverge from our faith'.

80, 81 and 154. *a God*. 'One God'.

82. Cf. Hebrews i.7, 14.

87. *Or Criste*. 'Before Christ'.

90. *departingis*. 'Divisions'.

92–3. Douglas alludes firstly to *Limbus patrum*, which was believed to be the dwelling of just patriarchs, such as Abraham, who died before Christ's coming, and secondly, to *Limbus puerorum*, the dwelling of infants, who had died before baptism. Cf. Walter Kennedy, *Passioun of Crist*, 1147; John Ireland, *Meroure of Wyssdome*, I, p. 105.

100–4. In the past this passage was misinterpreted by some editors and critics, who, perhaps because of Douglas's contorted syntax, took *Octauian* to be not the emperor Augustus, known before his elevation as Caesar Octavianus, but the contemporary French poet Octovien de Saint Gelais (1466–1502), also a translator of the *Aeneid*. The subject of the verb *consalis* (102) is not *Octauian* but *He*, i.e. Virgil (as in the preceding lines), and the allusion is specifically to *Georgics*, 1.25, and 36–8. A rough paraphrase is 'Virgil in his *Georgics* counsels Octavian never to desire lordship in hell'.

100. The line is virtually identical with *Palice of Honour*, 1644.

108–11. Based on *Georgics*, 2.336–42.

123

112. It was commonly believed in the Middle Ages that the creation of the world took place at the vernal equinox. Cf. Ascensius on *Georgics*, 2.336: 'consentit ergo cum fide'; Chaucer, *Nun's Priest's Tale*, CT.VII. 3187–8; and Bede ed. Jones 1943, 337–8.

113–18. Cf. *Georgics*, 2.490–2.

120. *hevin empire*. Not 'heaven's empire', but the *coelum empyreum*, or fiery and highest heaven, believed to be the dwelling of God. For this and the similar phrase 'hevyn imperiall', see X.xi.39; *Palice of Honour*, 1878; Dunbar, *Poems*, 58.49; and *DOST*, *empire*, a; *impyre*; *imperiall*, a².

126–8. Douglas recalls several passages in Virgil: *Eclogue* 3.60: 'Iovis omnia plena'; *Georgics* 4.221–4, beginning: 'deum namque ire per omnia'; and *Aeneid* 6.724ff. All three were quoted by St Augustine in *The City of God*: see Bawcutt 1976, 77–8.

130. Cf. I.Prol.186.

132. Cf. I Corinthians xv; and I Thessalonians v.23.

134. See Psalm lxxxii.6; and John x.34–5.

137–9. Douglas draws on ancient Christian traditions that the Cumaean Sibyl and Virgil prophesied Christ's birth and passion; this belief was closely associated with medieval interpretations of Virgil's Fourth *Eclogue* (see also lines 70–3, 145–9, and V.Prol.22–7). Groups of the Sibyls were commonly paired with the prophets of the Old Testament both in art and literature. Cf. *Palice of Honour*, 242–3; and see McGinn 1985.

145–9. A Christianized recollection of Virgil, *Eclogue* 4.4–7: 'Ultima Cumaei venit iam carminis aetas; / magnus ab integro saeclorum nascitur ordo. / iam redit et Virgo, redeunt Saturnia regna; / iam nova progenies caelo demittitur alto'.

149. *the goldin warld*. Alluding to Virgil's 'Saturnia regna'.

150. *Pluto infernall*. Commonly equated by poets with Satan, or the devil. Cf. Dunbar, *Poems*, 59.125–6, and 65.535–6; and Lindsay, *Testament of the Papyngo*, 1125: 'Pluto, the potent prince of hell'.

155. *the errour of Manache*. Manichaeism was a dualistic religion that explained the world in terms of a primeval conflict between light and darkness, good and evil. Douglas may recall St Augustine's denunciation of it in book IV of the *Confessions*.

156–60. These images for Satan are not chosen at random, but owe much to *Aeneid* 8.416ff. (see VIII.vii for translation). The devil resembles Vulcan, god of fire and sooty blacksmith to the gods, who according to some legends was thrown (like Satan) from heaven. The Cyclops were Vulcan's assistants in his underground cave beneath Mount Etna.

163–4. This thought is common in St Augustine. Coldwell compares *In Ioannis Evangelium*, I.i: also 'Peccatum quidem non per ipsum factum est … quia peccatum nihil est' (*Confessions*, III.vii): Evil is no more than mere privation of Good … altogether nothing; and *City of God*, XII.6–7.

165. *Ditis*. The genitive of *Dis*, the Roman equivalent of Pluto. Cf. VI.ix.15.

167–8. A rejection of the earlier invocation of Pluto, and a call for aid to the Virgin Mary.

167. *vail que vailʒe.* 'Whatever befalls'. The phrase has military associations. Cf. Barbour, Bruce, IX.148; and IX.Prol.86.

168. *War at.* The sense is either 'beware of', or the stronger 'make war on'. *sty.* Literally, 'pigsty', here also the filthy lair of the devil, i.e. hell.

BOOK VI.i; Virgil 6.9–80

1. This is a connecting line supplied by Douglas.

3. *tempil.* Virgil 6.9, —; Ascensius f.170 va, 'templum'.

10–12. Virgil 6.13, 'iam subeunt Triviae lucos atque aurea tecta'; *Ascensius f.170 va, 'subeunt iam lucos i. sylvas inceduas Triviae, i. Dianae atque tecta aurea s. Phebi qui illi sunt ubi est lucus Dianae: vocat autem Dianam Triviam quia tris vias habet.'

13. *the wright.* Virgil 6.14, —; Ascensius f.171 rb, 'faber'.

26–30. Virgil 6.20–2; expanded from *Ascensius f.171 va, 'Androgeo … ab Atheniensibus occisi: tum idest deinde Cecropide, idest Athenienses iussi sup. sunt pendere … septena, idest utriusque sexus septem …'

34–5. Virgil 6.23, 'Gnosia tellus'; Ascensius f.171 va, 'i. Cretensis'.

36. *porturit.* Virgil 6.24, —; Ascensius f.172 rb, 'i. sculptura'.

45. *'… having caught, or conceived, pity'.

46–7. *Ariadne, that was the kingis douchtir.* Virgil 6.28, 'reginae'; Ascensius f.172 rb, 'Ariadnes regis filiae'.

52. Virgil 6.31, —; Ascensius f.172 rb, 'fili s. Dedali'.

58. Virgil 6.34, —; Ascensius f.172 rb, 'Aeneas sup. & qui cum eo erant'.

59. *This sculptur.* Virgil 6.33, 'omnia'; Ascensius f.172 rb, 'sculpturam'.

62. *quham thai socht.* Virgil 6.34, —; suggested by Ascensius f.172 rb, 'indagandam'.

63. *Dyane.* Virgil 6.35, 'Triviae'; Ascensius f.172 rb, 'i. Dianae'.

66–7. Virgil 6.37, 'non hoc ista sibi tempus spectacula poscit'; *Ascensius f.172 rb, 'i. non est nunc tempus … spectandi'.

69. *that ʒok bur nevir nane.* Virgil 6.38, 'intacto'; Ascensius f.172 rb, 'i. de iis qui nunquam iugum traxerunt'.

79. Virgil 6.42, 'excisum Euboicae latus …'; Servius f.172 vb, 'hoc est montis Cumani quem Euboici habitaverunt'.

81. *stekit cloß.* Virgil 6.43, —; Ascensius f.172 rb, 'intercludunt'.

86. *the God me steris.* Virgil 6.46, 'deus, ecce, deus'; Ascensius f.172 va, 'invadit me deus'.

93. Virgil 6.49, —; Ascensius f.172 va, 'propter ingressum numinis'.

97–8. Virgil 6.50–1, 'adflata est numine quando iam propiore dei'; *Ascensius f.172 va,

'... propiore i. viciniore: hoc est valde vicino menti & praecordiis [per- misprint] eius.'

100. *bedis.* *This word, with its Catholic associations, is replaced by 'deuotioune' in the 1553 print.

101. 'Unless you pray', not 'unless you cease praying'; the ambiguity is in the Latin, Virgil 6.52, 'Cessas? Neque enim ...'

111. *Achillis.* Virgil 6.58, 'Aeacidae'; Ascensius f.172 rb, 'i. Achilis'.

115. *schald sandys.* Virgil 6.60, 'Syrtibus'.

124. *desist of ʒour fede.* Added by Douglas.

132. Virgil 6.68, 'agitata'; *Ascensius f.173 va, 'profugata'.

138. Virgil 6.71, 'magna penetralia'.

148. *with thyne awin mowth.* Virgil 6.76, —; Ascensius f.174 rb, 'ore edas'.

VI.ii; Virgil 6.81–155

10. *that is determyt be goddis dyvyne.* This assurance is added by Douglas.

13. Virgil 6.86, —; suggested by *Ascensius f.174 va, 'i. qui in Italiam non venerint'.

16. *the gret flude.* Virgil 6.87, —; *Ascensius f.174 va, 'fluvium illum'.

19. *Grekis.* Virgil 6.88, 'Dorica'; Ascensius f.174 va, 'i. grecorum'.

28. Virgil 6.92, —; *Ascensius f.174 va, 'q. d. nullas non oraveris sed omnis'.

29–32. Expanded from Virgil 6.93–4.

50. *Godly.* Virgil 6.103, 'heros'; *Ascensius f.175 rb, 'id est vir providus et quasi divinus'.

59. *Thocht it be rycht difficil.* Virgil 6.109, —; Ascensius f.175 va, '... detur mihi licet difficile sit'.

70. Virgil 6.113, 'omnis pelagique minas'.

73. *as he had beyn a page*: 'As if he were a young man'. A comparison due to Douglas.

83. *Proserpyn.* Virgil 6.118, 'Hecate'; Ascensius, 'i. Proserpina'.

87. *Castor.* Virgil 6.121, —; Ascensius f.176 rb, 's. Castorem'.

87–92. Expanded from Virgil 6.121–2; *Ascensius f.176 rb, '... redemit fratrem s. Castorem morte alterna i. quam alternatim pro illo obit ut ille vicissim pro Polluce & it & redit viam s. ab inferis ad superos'.

95–6. *strang maste dowchty Hercules ... preß.* Virgil 6.123, 'Alciden'; Ascensius f.176 rb, 'i. Herculem magnum ... dicitur ab inferis & cerberum traxisse ad superos ... per violentiam'.

103. *Pluto.* Virgil 6.127, 'Ditis'; Ascensius f.178 va, 'Plutonis'.

110. *equal.* Virgil 6.129, 'aequus'. *deifyit,* Virgil *ibid.,* 'amavit'; *Servius f.178 ra, 'remeare ad superos quos diligit Iuppiter'.

113. *laithly flude.* Virgil 6.132, —; Ascensius f.179 rb, 'idest lacus ille infernalis'.

118. Virgil 6.134–5, 'bis nigra videre Tartara'.

123. *Iuno infernal. I.e.* Proserpina.

142. *wapyn, sword or knyve.* Virgil 6.148, 'ferro'.

149. *lang hame.* *An ancient poetic expression for the grave; see illustrations of its use in Whiting H 422.

151. Virgil 6.153, —; Ascensius f.179 va, 's. ad inferias aut sacrificium funebre'.

154. *clenging graith.* Virgil 6.153, —; Ascensius f.179 va, 'i. purgamina'.

VI.iii; Virgil 6.156–235

18. *martial curage.* Virgil 6.165, 'Martemque'; Ascensius f.180 rb, 'furorem bellicum'.

39. *Tho sped. I.e.* 'he sped'; Virgil 6.177, 'festinant'.

45. Virgil 6.180, 'procumbunt piceae'; Ascensius f.180 va, 'i. arbores illae picis & resinae plenae'.

46. *akis.* Virgil 6.180, 'ilex'; cf. line 100 below.

48. *byrkis.* Virgil 6.181, 'robur'; 'robore' becomes 'ayk' in line 113.

49. *elmys.* Virgil 6.182, 'ornos'.

72. *soyl myghty.* Virgil 6.195–6, 'pinguem … humum'.

74. *that our beild is.* Added by Douglas.

76. Virgil 6.196, —; *Ascensius f.181 va, 'o quae optandi particula est'.

77. *spamen werd.* Virgil 6.197, —; Ascensius f.181 va, 'augurum'.

82. This detail is due to Douglas.

83. Virgil 6.200, 'sequentum'; *Ascensius f.181 va, 'scilicet Aeneae & Achatę'.

90. *'Perched on the tree of diverse natures …'

94. *gum or glew.* Virgil 6.205, 'viscum', *i.e.* mistletoe; *Ascensius f.181 v, 'i. gluten quod secundum Pli[nium, *Nat. Hist.* 16, 247] ex fecibus turdi et palumbis nascitur'. The origin of mistletoe was long found mysterious.

102. Note the change of tense.

114. *als fer as ony seys.* Added by Douglas.

122. This is Douglas's own invention.

123. *schowting, gowling and clamour.* Virgil 6.220, 'gemitus'.

128. *with mony sob and rayr.* Added by Douglas.

146. *Al is done.* *Virgil 6.231, 'novissima verba'; Servius f.182 vb, 'ilicet' [misprint 'silicet' in Ascensius 1501].

150. *prentis.* Virgil 6.233, —; Servius f.182 vb, 'sculpsit in saxo'.

151-2. *vmquhile Aeryus Was clepit.* Virgil 6.234, 'monte sub aërio'; *Servius f.182 vb, 'aerium autem alii altum dicunt, alii nomen antiquum montis intellegunt'.

VI.iv; Virgil 6.236-94

7. *als blak as ony craw.* *The simile, which is not in Virgil, was traditional (Whiting C 565).

14. *or pyt of ded.* This explanation is Douglas's.

15. *Ene.* Virgil 6.244, —; Ascensius f.183 rb, 'ipse'; Loeb takes 'priestess' as the subject.

24. *dym dungeon.* Added by Douglas. *Used earlier in VI.Prol.165.

26. Added by Douglas.

30. *fureys.* Virgil 6.250, 'Eumenidum'; Ascensius f.183 va, 'furiarum'; cf. line 91 (Virgil 6.280).

33. *Pluto.* Virgil 6.252, —; Ascensius f.183 va, 'Plutoni'.

45. *Proserpyne.* Virgil 6.258, —; Ascensius f.184 rb, 'Proserpina'.

58. Virgil 6.265, 'Chaos'; Ascensius f.184 rb, 'origo rerum confusa'.

59. Virgil 6.265, 'Phlegethon'; Ascensius f.184 rb, 'i. ardoris infernalis fluvius'.

66-7. *oneth ... went.* The comment is made by Douglas.

69. *Pluto.* Virgil 6.269, 'Ditis'.

72. *obscure.* Virgil 6.270, 'maligna'; *Servius f.184 ra, 'obscura'.

73. *the kyng etheryall.* The epithet is supplied by Douglas.

80. *Pail Maladeis that causys folk be seik.* Virgil 6.275, 'pallentes ... Morbi'; Ascensius f.184 va, 'i. pallidos facientes'.

85. *at mony ane heß slane.* Douglas is responsible for this commonplace.

86. *diseysful Pane.* Douglas's addition to Virgil's list (6.274-9).

88. Virgil 6.278-9, 'mala mentis Gaudia'; Ascensius f.185 rb, 'i. immodica aut nociva gaudia mentis'.

92. *that wondryng maist crewell.* Added by Douglas.

105. *serpent.* Virgil 6.287, —; Ascensius f.185 rb, 'hydra'.

107. Virgil 6.288, 'flammisque armata'; Ascensius f.185 rb, 'quia mons est cuius cacumen ardet'.

108. *Gorgones thre.* Virgil 6.289, 'Gorgones'; Servius f.185 ra, 'Phorci filiae tres'.

110. Virgil 6.289, —; Servius f.185 ra, 'Eryli & Gerionis'.

VI.v; Virgil 6.295–384

1, 2. *profond, deip.* Virgil 6.295, 'Tartarei'; *Ascensius f.186 rb, 'i. ad profunditatem infernalem tendentis'.

7–18. Expanded from Virgil 6.298–301.

20. Added by Douglas.

22. Virgil 6.304, —; Ascensius f.186 va, 'perpetua & indefatigabilis'.

41. *with brym luyk.* Added by Douglas.

48. *Quhy nyl thai nocht byde.* This question is due to Douglas.

55. Virgil 6.322, 'Anchisa generate'.

72. *and costis thame not a grote.* Information given by Douglas, not Virgil (6.330).

106. Virgil 6.347, 'ille autem'.

108–9. Virgil 6.347, 'neque te Phoebi cortina fefellit'; Ascensius f.188 rb, 'i. locus secretior unde Phoebus responsa dabat'.

134. *spy.* *Obscure. Coldwell suggested that Virgil 6.361, 'praedam' was misread as 'praedonem'; but 'praedo' does not mean 'spy' and 'praedam' is translated by 'pray' (= prey) in 135.

135. Added by Douglas.

159. *thou sary sire.* The epithet is Douglas's.

VI.vi; Virgil 6.384–423

2. *churlych.* The epithet is Douglas's.

17. *Hercules.* Virgil 6.392, 'Alciden'; Ascensius f.190 rb, 'Herculem'.

25. Virgil 6.397, 'dominam'; *Ascensius f.190 rb, 's. Proserpinam deam inferorum'.

28. *Phebus.* Virgil 6.398, —; Ascensius f.190 va, 'i. Apollinea'.

35. Virgil 6.400, 'licet'; Ascensius f.190 va, 'conceditur per nos'.

58. Virgil has 6.412, 'laxatque foros'.

76. *enchantit.* Virgil 6.420, 'medicatis'; Ascensius f.191 rb, 'medica arte paratis'.

VI.vii; Virgil 6.424–76

17. *inquisitour.* Virgil 6.432, 'quaesitor'; Ascensius f.191 va, 'inquisitor'.

18–20. Virgil 6.432, 'urnam movet'; *Ascensius f.191 va, 'movet urnam in qua s. sortes sunt non tamen exeunt mere a casu sed fatis ita disponentibus'.

32. Virgil 6.438, —; Ascensius f.191 va, 'que scilicet vetant reditum'.

39. *all voyd of lycht.* Virgil 6.441, —; Ascensius f.192 rb, 'lucis egentes'.

47. *the spowß of Theseus.* Virgil 6.445, —; Servius f.192 vb, 'uxor Thesei'.

48. *the wyfe of Cephalus.* Virgil 6.445, —; Ascensius f.192 rb, 'uxorem Cephali'.

96. *curage, face nor bre.* Virgil 6.470, 'voltum'.

98. *Mont.* Virgil 6.471, —; Servius f.193 ra, 'mons'.

VI.viii; Virgil 6.477–534

9. *the king.* Virgil 6.480, —; Servius f.194 ra, 'rex'.

36. Virgil 6.493, 'inceptus clamor frustratur hiantis'.

37. *quhilum armypotent.* Lacking in Virgil (6.494–5); perhaps suggested by 'armipotens' in 6.500.

47. Omits Virgil 6.500, 'sanguine Teucri'.

56. Douglas's addition.

58. *neß.* Virgil 6.505, —; Ascensius f.194 v, 'promontorii'.

70. *wers than thou wenyt.* Added by Douglas.

72. Virgil 6.511, 'Lacaenae'; Ascensius f.194 va, 'hoc est Helenae ... Lacena'.

74. *drowreis.* Virgil 6.512, 'monumenta'; Douglas's irony is stronger than Virgil's.

82. Virgil 6.517, 'illa'.

87. *master streyt.* Virgil 6.519, 'summa ... ex arce'.

90. *of irksum weir.* Virgil 6.520, —; Ascensius f.195 rb, 's. longi belli praeteriti'.

91. *for my walkyn mony fald.* Virgil 6.520, —; Ascensius f.195 rb, 'propter praeteritas vigilias'.

103. *or ʒou langar hald.* Virgil 6. 526, —; Ascensius f.195 rb, 'te ... suspensum teneo'.

107. Virgil 6.529, 'Aeolides'; *Ascensius f.195 rb, 'i. nepos Aeoli ... videlicet Ulyxes'.

VI.ix; Virgil 6.535–627

1–5. Expanded from Virgil 6.535–6.

7. *for thar iourne grant.* Virgil 6.537, 'datum'; Ascensius f.195 va, 'concessum eis apud inferos esse'.

8. *sant.* Naturally wanting in Virgil (6.538).

21. Douglas's expansion of the thought.

36. *ravenus flude.* Virgil 6.551, —; Ascensius f.196 rb, 'fluvius'.

45. *furyus monstre wild.* Virgil 6.555, —; Ascensius f.196 rb, 'i. furia infernalis a torquendo'.

55–65. Expanded from Virgil 6.560–3.

66. *Proserpyn.* Virgil 6.564, 'Hecate'; Ascensius f.196 va, 'dea inferorum'.

71. *of Creyt kyng.* Virgil 6.566, 'Gnosius'; Ascensius f.196 va, 'rex Cretensium'.

85. *syne to pyne thame.* Virgil (6.572) does not state the reason.

94. *serpent.* Virgil 6.576, 'Hydra'.

100. *hevynnys.* Virgil 6.579, 'Olympum'; Ascensius f.197 rb, 'celestem'.

102. *gyantis.* Virgil 6.580, —; Ascensius f.197 rb, 'gygantes'.

106. *Othus and Ephialtes.* Virgil 6.582, —; Servius f.198 ra, 'Oethum & Ephialtem'.

116. *secret condytis.* Has Virgil 6.587, 'Lampada' been misunderstood?

117. *Arcad.* Virgil 6.588, —; *Ascensius f.198 va, 'Arcadię'.

119. Virgil 6.589, 'ibat ovans'.

125. Virgil 6.590, 'non imitabile'; Ascensius f.198 va, 'i. quod imitari non licet'.

129. *bleß of thundyr.* Virgil 6.594, 'turbine'; influenced by Ascensius on 6.593, f.198 va, 'fulmen ... fulgure'.

143. Virgil 6.601, —; Servius f.198 ra, 'hi populi Thessalie'.

144. *for gluttony.* Virgil 6.601, —; *Ascensius f.198 va, 'notum est ob gulusitatem ... damnatos esse'.

149. *Tantalus.* Virgil (6.605) does not mention Tantalus and assigns the punishment to Ixion and Pirithous; Ascensius f.198 va, 'Tantalo'.

155. *hungyr in thame blawys.* Virgil 6.606, —; Ascensius f.198 va, 'famem inducens'.

161. Virgil 6.608, 'hic'; Ascensius f.199 rb, 'inclusi expectant poenas'.

164. *throu thar deray and stryfe.* The explanation is given by Douglas.

165. *chasyt in exile.* Virgil 6.609, 'pulsatus'.

179–82. Expanded from Virgil 6.615.

184. Virgil 6.616, —; Servius f.199 vb, 'Sisyphum'.

185–94. The order of appearance of Phlegyas and Theseus is reversed (Virgil 6.617ff.).

187. Virgil 6.618, 'Phlegyas'; Ascensius f.199 va, 'Fuit enim Phlegyas rex Thessaliae'.

190. *all wightis, prynce and kyng.* Added by Douglas.

200–4. Expanded from Virgil 6.623.

208. Added by Douglas.

VI.x; Virgil 6.628–78

5–12. Expanded from Virgil 6.630–2.

6. Virgil 6.631, 'moenia'; Ascensius f.200 va, 'magna moenia'.

12. *goldyn grane.* Virgil 6.632, —; Ascensius f.200 va, 'i. aureum ramum'.

24–8. Expanded from Virgil 6.638–9.

29. *thir feildis beyn largiar.* Virgil 6.640, 'largior hic campos aether ... vestit'.

29. *hevynnys brycht.* Virgil 6.640, 'aether'; Ascensius f.201 rb, 'idest splendor celestis'.

37–46. *Douglas expands and medievalizes Virgil 6.644–6 with carols and ring dances. The depiction of Orpheus as a minstrel may echo Henryson, whose Orpheus likewise plays springs and 'mony suete proporcion'; see *Orpheus and Eurydice*, 144, 268, and 368.

42. *Orpheus of Trace.* Virgil 6.645, 'Threicius'; Ascensius f.201 rb, 'i. Thracius ... Orpheus'.

53. *als Sibilla.* Virgil 6.651, —; Ascensius f.201 rb, 'cum Sibylla'.

64. *be thai man or wyfe.* A pointless remark by Douglas.

72. Virgil 6.657, —; Ascensius f.201 va, 'Apollinem'.

76. *ryver.* Virgil 6.659, —; Ascensius f.202 rb, 'fluvius'.

77. Virgil 6.659, —; *Ascensius f.202 rb, 'unde ad superos ab inferis fluere dicit'.

110–11. *to haue presens Of Anchises.* Added by Douglas.

118. This climax is due to Douglas.

VI.xi; Virgil 6.679–723

2. *full of fence.* Lacking in Virgil (6.679–80). *The variant reading *sence* (E, B, 53), 'fragrance, literally incense', seems preferable to *fence*, which Coldwell glosses as 'defence, places of hiding'.

55. Virgil 6.707–9, 'ac ... strepit omnis murmure campus', that is – the murmur of the bees.

72. 'That water untroubled and without cares'.

85. Virgil 6.719, —; Ascensius f.205 rb, 'ex his tam beatis locis'.

88. *our life.* Virgil 6.721, —; Ascensius f.205 rb, 'vitae'.

92–3. *baith his eyn ... behald.* Expanded from Virgil 6.723, 'suscipit' and Ascensius f.205 rb, 'suscipere i. sursum'.

VI.xii; Virgil 6.724–55

*Note that the 1553 print omits the word Purgatory in the heading,

2. *fyry regioun.* Virgil 6.725, —; Ascensius f.205 va, 'ignem'.

5. Virgil 6.725, 'Titaniaque astra'; Servius f.206 ra, 'aut stellas dicit aut solem'.

7. *dyvyne.* Virgil 6.727, —; Ascensius f.205 va, 'divina'.

10. *clepit vniuersal.* Virgil 6.727, —; Ascensius f.205 va, 'vniuersi'.

18. *quhilk we sawlys call.* *Virgil 6.731, 'seminibus'; Ascensius f.206 rb, 'i. animis'.

21. *Virgil 6.731, 'non tardant'; Ascensius f.206 rb, 'i. deprimunt & offuscant virtutem caelestem'.

29. Virgil 6.733-4, 'neque auras dispiciunt'; Servius f.207 vb, 'nam quia coherent corpori, obliviscuntur naturae suae, quam auras vocavit'.

47. *purgatory.* Virgil 6.743, 'Manis'; *Ascensius f.206 va, 'purgamur apud manes hoc est inferos'.

66. Virgil 6.750, —; Ascensius f.207 rb, 'bonorum … & malorum'.

VI.xiii; Virgil 6.756–807

1–10. Expanded from Virgil 6.756-9.

2. *or thou depart away.* Added by Douglas.

14. *to life.* Virgil 6.761, 'lucis loca'; Ascensius f.207 va, 'id est vitae'.

18. *posthumus.* Virgil 6.763. *Ascensius f.207 r, 'posthuma'; Ascensius f.207 va, 'idest post humationem'; modern editors read 'postuma', last-born. The spelling with 'h' is due to a false etymology.

27. *Munytor.* Virgil 6.768, 'Numitor'.

31. Virgil 6.770, —; suggested by Ascensius f.208 rb, 'quia vix lii aetatis suae anno accepit …'

34. The comment is supplied by Douglas.

38. *to thy honour.* Virgil 6.773, —; Ascensius f.208rb, 'in gloriam tuam'.

43. *New Castell.* Virgil 6.775, 'Castrumque inui'; Ascensius f.208 rb, 'quod castrum novum dicitur'.

53. *Mars.* Virgil 6.780, —; Ascensius f. 208 va, 'Mars'.

63. *moder of goddis.* Virgil 6.784, 'Mater'; Ascensius f.209 rb, 'mater deum'.

74. *Cesar Iulyus.* Virgil 6.789, 'Caesar'; Ascensius f.209 rb, 's. Julius'.

80. *Octauyane.* Virgil 6.791, —; Servius f.209 vb, 'Octavius'.

93. *Assery.* Virgil 6.798, —; Ascensius f.209 va, 'ad fines Assyriorum'.

94. *Scithya.* Virgil 6.799, —; Ascensius f.209 va, 'idest scythica ubi est Meotis'.

98. *Hercules.* Virgil 6.801, 'Alcides'; Ascensius f.209 va, 'idest Hercules'.

100. *wynd swyft.* Virgil 6.802, 'aeripedem', i.e. brazen-footed; Ascensius f.209 va, 'i.

habentem aereos pedes i. veloces'; the phrase should be read 'wind-swift'.

102. *serpent.* Virgil 6.803, —; Ascensius f.209 va, 'hydram'.

103. *Bachus.* Virgil 6.805, 'Liber'; Ascensius f.209 va, 'Bacchus'.

106. *mont.* Virgil 6.805, —; Ascensius f.209 va, 'montis'.

VI.xiv; Virgil 6.808–46

7. *Numa Pompilius.* Virgil 6.810, —; *Ascensius f.210 rb, 'Numam Pompilium'.

8. *haly lays.* Virgil 6.810, —; *Ascensius f.210 rb, 'religiosus'.

13. *Hostilius.* Virgil 6.813, —; Ascensius f.210 va, 'Hostilius'.

19. *Ancus Martyus.* Virgil 6.815, 'Ancus'; *Ascensius f.210 va, 'Ancus s. Martius'.

23. *two.* Virgil 6.817, —; Ascensius f.210 va, 's. Priscum & Superbum'. The whole passage on Brutus is expanded.

27. Virgil 6.818, —; Ascensius f.211 rb, 'vexilla … de … Etruscorum urbe'.

35. Added by Douglas.

38. *quha thame redis.* Added by Douglas.

44. *twa.* Virgil 6.822, —; *Ascensius f.211 rb, 'Livium Drusum & Drusum Tyberii … meminit'.

47. *the vailȝeand capitane.* The epithet is supplied by Douglas.

52. *law degre.* Virgil 6.827, —; Ascensius f.211 rb, 'dum erunt in humili fortuna'.

58. *Cesar.* Virgil 6.829, —; Ascensius f.211 rb, 'Caesar'.

59. *Franch montanys.* Virgil 6.830, 'aggeribus … Alpinis'; Ascensius f.211 va, 'a Galliis'.

60. Virgil 6.830–1, 'arce Monoeci descendens'; Ascensius f.211 va, 'i. a Liguria'.

61. *His mavch Pompey.* Virgil 6.831, 'gener'; Ascensius f.211 va, 's. Pompeius'.

62. *orient.* Virgil 6.831, 'Eois'; Ascensius f.211 va, 'i. orientalibus'.

67. *O thou Cesar.* Virgil 6.834, 'tu'; Ascensius f.211 va, 's. Caesar'.

71–2. *Lucyus … Munyus.* Virgil 6.836, —; Ascensius f.211 va, 's. Lucius Mumius'.

77. *Quintus Metellus.* Virgil 6.838, —; Ascensius f.211 va, 'Quintus Metellus'.

78. Added by Douglas.

81. Virgil 6.839, —; Ascensius f.212 rb, 'Curius & Fabricius'.

82. *Pyrrus.* Virgil 6.839, —; Ascensius f.212 rb, 'Pyrrhum'.

94. Virgil 6.843, 'parvoque potentem', which Loeb (2nd ed) renders as 'in penury a prince'.

97. Added by Douglas.

99. The request is added by Douglas.

101. *slycht and tareyng.* Virgil 6.846, 'cunctando'; *Ascensius f.212 rb adds 'moram trahendo & sic Hannibalem deludendo', which Douglas takes in the medieval sense of 'deceiving, betraying'.

VI.xv; Virgil 6.847–902

3. *lyflyke.* Virgil 6.848, —; Ascensius f.212 rb, 'magis ad vivum'.

10. *geometry.* Virgil 6.850, —; Ascensius f.212 va, 'geometriae'.

16. *modefy.* Virgil 6.852, —; Ascensius f.212 va, 'moderari'.

16. Omits Virgil 6.852 'morem'.

19. *meik.* Not in the original (Virgil 6.854).

21. *Marcus Marcellus.* Virgil 6.855, 'Marcellus'; Ascensius f.212 va, 's. Marcus'.

24. Virgil 6.857, —; Ascensius f.212 va, 'i. principi exercitus inimicorum detractis'.

26. *In bonty.* An addition by Douglas.

31. *Franch.* Virgil 6.858, 'Gallum'.

49. Virgil 6.865, —; Ascensius f.213 rb, 'i. instantiae virilis'.

65. *marcyall.* Virgil 6.872, 'Mavortis', properly applied to 'urbem'; *Ascensius f.213 rb, 'in urbem i. Martis'.

67. Virgil 6.873, 'Tiberine'; Ascensius f.213 rb, 's. deus fluminis Tyberis'.

68. Virgil 6.874, 'funera'.

76. The exclamation is not Virgil's (6.878) but Douglas's.

92. Added by Douglas.

117–18. Virgil 6.897–8, 'his ubi tum … Anchises … dictis'.

VI, xvi; Virgil 7. 1–24.

Douglas is probably justified aesthetically in moving this chapter from the beginning of Book 7, but the shift seems to be original with him.

21. *ille.* Virgil 7.10, 'terrae'.

27. *prowd place of beddis.* *Virgil 7.12, 'tectisque superbis' (MSS and Ascensius f.214 v), 'lectis' Ascensius f.215 rb.

29. *subtil.* Virgil 7.14, 'arguto'; Ascensius f.215 rb, 'subtili'.

32. *Beir*, 'noise', should be distinguished from *beris*, 'bears', in line 35.

Prologue VII

This is probably the most famous of the Prologues, largely because of its vivid description of winter. It is very much a composite picture: many details are clearly drawn from Douglas's own Scottish experience, but others have a more literary origin. Douglas was familiar with Henryson's brief winter scenes in the *Fables*, 1692–1705, 1832–8, and the opening of *Testament of Cresseid*; and his own highly alliterative style suggests that he knew the northern alliterative poetic tradition of describing storms and wintry weather, illustrated in *Sir Gawain and the Green Knight*, 726ff. and *Rauf Coilyear*, 14–36. This Prologue, which stands in striking contrast to the twelfth, marks an important half-way stage in the translation, suggesting the poet's weariness and also his determination to complete an onerous task. Recent criticism includes Blyth 1970; Starkey 1973–4; Bawcutt 1976, 180–6; Nitecki 1981.

1–11. Douglas begins, as was common in descriptive poetry, with an astronomical periphrasis. At the winter solstice the sun is lowest in the heavens (cf. line 2), and the days are shortest (line 14). Several details, such as the mention of Capricorn and the sun's *laton* colour, recall the passage about winter in Chaucer's *Franklin's Tale*, *CT*.V.1244–55, where the sun is similarly 'hewed lyk laton'.

1. *hevynnys e*. 'Eye of heaven'. A traditional image for the sun; cf. Chaucer, *Troilus and Criseyde*, II.904; Spenser, *Faerie Queene*, I.iii.4.

2. 'Entered the area of the zodiac, lying opposite to Cancer, which is the sun's *chymmys*, or mansion at midsummer, when its altitude is highest'.

4. *laton*. Latten is an alloy, an inferior yellowish metal that contrasts with the sun's *goldyn* hue in summer.

7–8. Coldwell mistakenly took the date to be the morning of Christmas Eve, but in this period the sun entered the zodiacal sign of Capricorn on 12 December. But the lines are slightly ambiguous: they may be interpreted as saying that the sun will enter Capricorn in three days' time, and it is now 9 December; or, more probably, that it is already on the eve of its third day in Capricorn (14 December). Cf. Eade 1984: 166–7.

9. *lamp of hevyn*. Cf. Henryson, *Testament of Cresseid*, 197; also Prol.XII.252.

14. *brumaill*. The Latin word *brumalis*, 'wintry', is used by Virgil in *Aeneid* 6.205. But Douglas here refers to the traditional etymology, found in *clerkis*, or learned men, such as Macrobius: 'minimum diei … quod veteres appellavere brumale solstitium: brumam a brevitate dierum cognominantes': i.e. the shortest day, which the men of old called the winter solstice, using the word *bruma* for winter, from the shortness of the days (*Saturnalia*, I.21.15).

15. The phrasing recalls III.v.3, which corresponds to *Aeneid* 3.285. The alliterative *brym blast* occurs in *Golagros and Gawane*, 525 and 536.

16. *Neptunus in his cart*. The sea god was believed to ride in a chariot, drawn by white horses. See Douglas's note on his iconography at I.iii.54.

22. Proverbial images; see Whiting B 123 and L 358.

25–6. Mars was an inauspicious planet, associated with strife and storm; cf. Henryson, *Testament*, 183ff. *Retrograde* indicates that it appeared to be moving backwards, in a direction contrary to the regular order of the signs. *lord.* In astrological use the planet that has dominant influence over an event or period.

27–8. Orion is a constellation associated with storms and rain. Douglas recalls Virgil's epithets for Orion in *Aeneid* 4.52 ('aquosus') and 7.719 ('saevus'), and in *Aeneid* 1.535, where 'nimbosus' Orion shattered the Trojan fleet.

28. *by hys race.* The sense is ambiguous: either 'from the shipman's course', or 'by means of its (i.e. Orion's) onward motion'.

29–32. Saturn is a cold and inauspicious planet, Virgil's 'frigida Saturni … stella' (*Georgics*, 1.336), and commonly linked with disease and 'pestilens'. He is similarly *frawart* in XII.Prol.7, and Henryson, *Testament of Cresseid*, 323. See also II.Prol.13, and note. *progressyve.* 'Moving forward' (in an astronomical sense).

33–4. Hebe, in classical myth, was the daughter of Juno and cup-bearer to the gods; after her fall and subsequent nakedness she was replaced by Ganymede. Douglas here alludes to Boccaccio's symbolical interpretation of the myth in *De Genealogia Deorum*, IX.ii, in which Hebe is linked with spring and its foliage, and her loss of 'array' symbolizes the fall of leaves in autumn. Ganymede, who took over her 'office', is identified with the sign of Aquarius, into which the sun moves after leaving Capricorn. See also I.i.51 marginal commentary.

42. *With frostis hair ourfret.* See line 162 below. Douglas recalls Henryson's description of Saturn in *Testament of Cresseid*, 163: 'ouirfret with froistis hoir'.

44–6. The mention of *hell* and its *gousty schaddois* looks back to book VI. The lines are omitted in 1553.

50. *snypand.* 'Biting, nipping'. The word is rare, but belongs to the alliterative poetic vocabulary. Cf. *Wars of Alexander*, 1560, 'as any snyppand snaw'; and the similar verbal form *snaype* in *Sir Gawain*, 2003; *Awntyrs off Arthure*, 82.

58. 'Animals' coats (literally hair) shivered (or trembled) in the stormy weather'.

59. *red wed.* Literally 'red weed'. According to *OED*, this was a name later given to several plants, such as the corn poppy and knot grass; but *DOST*, *red(e*, sense 14, tentatively glosses *red* as 'dried up, discoloured'.

62. *ische schouchlis lang as ony speir.* The detail echoes Henryson's portrait of Saturn in *Testament of Cresseid*, 160–1.

66. *stripyt of thar weid.* The phrase recalls the image of Hebe in line 34.

67ff. Cf. the bleak winter scene in Henryson's 'Preaching of the Swallow' (*Fables*, 1692–1705).

67. *Boreas.* The North Wind; for his bugle, cf. Dunbar, *Goldyn Targe, Poems* 59.230.

69–70. Cf. *Sir Gawain*, 746–7: [birds] 'That pitously ther piped for pyne of the colde'.

77–8. A wintry transformation of Chaucer's pastoral image of 'thise lytel herde- gromes / That kepen bestis in the bromes' (*House of Fame*, 1225–6).

82. *tuskyt*. The word is rare; cf. Chaucer's similar use in *Franklin's Tale*, CT.V.1254: 'tusked *swyn*', and Lydgate, *Siege of Thebes*, 3597.

89. *stovis*. The sense is not certain: either 'hot air bath, steam room' (*OED* and *DOST*, *stove*, sense 1); or more plausibly, an early instance of *DOST*, sense 3, 'apparatus for producing heat'.

93. *bekyt*. 'Warmed, basking'. Cf. Henryson, *Testament of Cresseid*, 36.

94. *a bed*. 'Abed, on a bed'.

98. *lemand throu the glaß*. Douglas recalls Henryson's sight not of the moon but of the planet Venus, also 'in oppositioun' to the sun (*Testament of Cresseid*, 11–15).

99. *Latonya*. An epithet for the moon goddess, daughter of Latona.

101–4. The moon is moving into the *Crab*, the zodiacal sign of Cancer, her own astrological house or mansion, in which she exercises the most powerful influence. She is *in oppositioun* to the sun; this refers to the relationship of two planets, when they are 180 degrees apart, as seen from the earth.

105–25. Lists of birds formed an ancient literary topos. Douglas treats the theme again in XII.Prol.231–41; he is likely to have been familiar with earlier examples, such as *Georgics* 1.361–4; Chaucer, *Parliament of Fowls*, 330–64; and Holland, *Buke of the Howlat*, 157–234. Douglas's catalogue is striking for its naturalistic setting, and differentiation of the birds through their calls and cries.

105. *Hebowd*. This name for an owl (cf. French *hibou*) is not recorded elsewhere in Scots or English. The long-eared owl, sometimes known as the *horned* owl, has prominent ear tufts and a hooked beak. But the mention of the *elrich screke* (108) fits a barn owl better than the long-eared owl.

113–14. *Phebus crownyt byrd* is a periphrasis for the cock, which was commonly associated with the sun, and had a symbolism similar to that of the lark (cf. XIII. Prol.167–8). Several details are paralleled in Lydgate's 'The Cock and the Jacinth' (*Minor Poems*, II, 568ff.): Lydgate's cock has a crest 'Shape lyke a crowne' (58); he 'Beteth hys wyngis, aforn or he do syng' (71); and his threefold crowing, 'With treble laudes youe to the Trinite, / Slouthe auoydyng, clepeth folk out of ther slombre' (79–80). The use here of the rare word *orlager*, 'time-keeper', recalls Chaucer's 'The kok, that orloge is of thorpes lyte' (*Parliament of Fowls*, 350). Cf. also Henryson, *Fables*, 498.

117. *Synthea*. Cynthia, a name given to the moon goddess, from Cynthus, the mountain in Delos where she was born. Cf. III.Prol.1.

118. *kays keklys*. Cf. Lindsay, *Testament of the Papyngo*, 94: 'kekell lyke ane ka'.

119–20. *Palamedes byrdis*. Cranes, which were still common in Scotland in Douglas's time. The term derives from *Palamedis avem* (Martial, xiii.75). Several classical writers, such as Pliny and Lucan, refer to the reputed invention by the hero Palamedes of letters of the Greek alphabet, including Y, after he had observed the flight-formation of cranes.

121–3. Chaucer also compares a crane's cry to a trumpet (*Parliament of Fowls*, 344), but Douglas's source for this image and for the cranes as weather-prophets may be *Aeneid*, 10.264–6 (= X.v.123ff.).

125. *soir*. 'Sorrel, chestnut-coloured'. The epithet is more commonly applied to horses. *mony a pew*. Henryson mentions a kite, 'pyipand with mony pew' (*Fables*, 2901); cf. also Holland, *Howlat*, 642; and Lindsay, *Testament of the Papyngo*, 93.

136–7. *hailstanys ... Hoppand on the thak*. The observation is precise, but may be partly literary in origin. Cf. Virgil, *Georgics* 1.449: 'tam multa in tectis crepitans salit horrida grando'.

150. Cf. *Palice of Honour*, 1411; Whiting Y 18 records only these citations.

152. This maxim, which originates in Lucan, II.657, occurs also in Barbour, *Bruce*, III.281–2: 'hym thocht he had doyne rycht nocht / Ay quhill to do hym levyt ocht'.

154. *Ourvoluyt*. The sense is not certain. Coldwell glossed as 'laid aside'; *DOST*, following *OED*, suggested that the original might have been *onrevolvyt*, *i.e.* 'did not turn over'.

156. *in the myre*. Proverbial for a state of muddle and confusion (Whiting M 573), and appropriate in the wintry context.

158. *our pleuch*. Douglas now envisages himself as a ploughman, rather than the draught animal of line 150. This image fits aptly into the immediate context (cf. lines 75–6), but ploughing was an ancient figure for prolonged literary labours. Cf. Luke ix.62; Chaucer, *Knight's Tale*, *CT*.I.886–7; Lydgate, *Troy Book*, V.2927–31. See also Curtius 1953, 313–14.

162. *firth and fald*. A popular alliterative phrase; cf. VI.xiii.84; and Henryson, *Robene and Makyne*, 96.

163–8. This self-referential comment constitutes a kind of envoi. In the apparent modesty of tone it contrasts with the rhetorically similar passage that ends Prologue XII.

165–6. Douglas possibly echoes Henryson's *Testament of Cresseid*, 1–2: 'Ane doolie sessoun to ane cairfull dyte / Suld correspond and be equiualent'.

166. *bludy text*. This look ahead to the bloodshed of books VI to XII.

167. *Of sabyll be thy lettyris illumynate*. A sense of literary decorum underlies this notion that a solemn or tragic theme is most fittingly conveyed in *sabyll*, or black, letters. The topos had been earlier used by Lydgate in *Fabula Duorum Mercatorum*, 512–13 (*Minor Poems*, II, 503): 'It sitt the nat enlwmyned for to be / Of othir colour but oonly al of sable'. A similar conceit opens the so-called 'Greneacres' poem (*NIMEV* 524): 'Blak be thy bandis and thy wede also / Thou sorouful book of mater disesparit'. This poem circulated widely, and different versions were associated with both Lydgate and Chaucer: it is attached to the end of several texts of Lydgate's *Fall of Princes*, and also appears at the end of the Selden. B. 24 text of *Troilus and Criseyde*. (For more information, see Boffey and Edwards 1997, 1). The topos was known also to Lindsay, who opens *Monarche* with: 'Thou lytil quair of mater miserabyll / Weil auchtest thou couerit to be with sabyll'.

168. The prose note that appears at this point in some copies of 1553 is not the work of Douglas; see Introduction, p. 21.

BOOK VII.i; Virgil 7.25–101

4. *brovn sanguane.* Virgil 7.26, 'lutea'; *Ascensius f.216 rb, 'subrubeus intermixto s. croceo'.

16. *in the clewis.* Virgil 7.32, —; Ascensius f.216 rb, 'a parte superiori'.

24. Virgil 7.36, 'opaco'; Ascensius f.216 rb, 'umbroso silvis decumbentibus obtecto'.

53. *kyng.* Not so described by Virgil (7.48).

69. *rich of frendis.* Added by Douglas.

71. Virgil 7.56, 'regia coniunx'; Ascensius f.217 rb, 'i. uxor regis Latini Amata nomine'.

81. Virgil 7.61, 'inventam'.

110. *evil at eyß.* Added by Douglas.

117. *with 3yng and ald.* Added by Douglas.

127. Virgil 7.81, 'oracula Fauni'.

151. Virgil 7.91, 'Acheronta'.

VII.ii; Virgil 7.102–47

18. Virgil 7.111, 'pomis agrestibus'.

34. Omits Virgil 7.119, 'numine'.

68. Virgil 7.136, 'genium loci'; Ascensius f.219 va, 'genium i. deum topicum'.

70. *gret moder.* Virgil 7.136, —; Ascensius f.219 va, 'mater deum'.

73. *Virgil 7.139, 'Idaeumque Iovem'; *Ascensius f.220 rb, 'i. qui apud Idam colebatur'.

74. *Cibylla.* Virgil 7.139, —; Ascensius f.220 rb, 'Cybelem'.

76. *hevin and hell.* Virgil 7.140, 'caeloque Ereboque'.

90. *wauchtis.* Virgil 7.147, 'coronant'.

VII.iii; Virgil 7.148–91

6. *Munycus.* Virgil 7.150, 'Numici'; cf. VII.iv.116 (Virgil 7.242).

11. *gay.* Not in Virgil (7.153). Was Douglas thinking of the display of fine clothes made by ambassadors in his own time?

16. *olyve.* Virgil 7.154, —; Ascensius f.220 va, 'olivae'.

19–26. Expanded from Virgil 7.157–9.

34. *Virgil 7.163, 'domitantque in pulvere currus', which Loeb takes as 'break in teams'. It is more likely that 'pulvere' signifies the dust of the race course.

51. Virgil 7.174, 'omen erat'.

52. *crovn.* Virgil 7.173, 'sceptra'.

53. Virgil 7.173, —; Ascensius f.221 rb, 'idest insignia regalia'.

54. Virgil 7.173, 'attollere fasces'.

62. *deambulatour.* Virgil 7.176, —; Ascensius f.221 rb, 'primo introitu'.

64. *with crafty hand.* Added by Douglas.

67. *vndre hys weid.* Virgil 7.179, 'sub imagine'.

75. *cart quhelis.* Virgil 7.184, 'currus'.

76. Virgil 7.184, 'captivi'; Ascensius f.221 va, 'i. quos captivis abstulerunt'.

77–9. Virgil 7.185, 'portarum ingentia claustra'; Ascensius f.221 va, 'i. repagula & vestes ac serae portarum scilicet urbium captarum'.

81. Virgil 7.186, 'rostra'; Ascensius f.221 va, 'i. munimenta aerea aut ferrea'.

82. *fechtand on the see.* Added by Douglas.

85. Virgil 7.187–8, 'parva … trabea'; Ascensius f.221 va, 'i. veste augurali'.

86. Virgil 7.187, 'Quirinali lituo'; Ascensius f.221 va, 'i. baculo augurali'.

90. *fut and hand.* Added by Douglas to eke out the line.

91–2. *clepit … Marcyus.* Virgil 7.189, —; Ascensius f.221 va, 'diciturque Picus Martius'.

VII.iv; Virgil 7.192–283

29. Added by Douglas.

33. *cite Arunca.* Virgil 7.206. *Ascensius f.221 v, 'Aruncos' (modern editions 'Auruncos'); Ascensius f.222 rb, 'ab Arunca civitate'.

37. *the nerrest gait.* Added by Douglas, *to provide a rhyme.

39–40. *the land … Ida.* Virgil 7.207, 'Idaeas Phrygiae … urbes'.

44. *cite.* Virgil 7.209, —; Ascensius f.222 rb, 'oppidi'.

50. *god.* Virgil 7.213, —; Ascensius f.223 rb, 'dei'.

69. Virgil 7.222, 'saevis effusa Mycenis'.

78–80. Virgil 7.226–7, 'extenta plagarum quattuor in medio dirimit plaga'; Ascensius f.223 rb, 'i. zona torrida … regio solis iniqui i. nimium vehementis … temperatam [*i.e.* zonam]'.

106. *takynnys.* Virgil 7.237, 'vittas'; *Ascensius f.223 v, 'in signum'.

125. *tyar hat.* Virgil 7.247, 'tiaras'.

162. *but langar discrepans.* Added by Douglas.

166. *as a gaist.* The comparison is made by Douglas.

174. *fyry levin.* Virgil 7.269, —; Ascensius f.224 va, 'flamma'.

177. *spaymen*. Virgil 7.271, —; Ascensius f.224 va, 'vates'.

180. This line is wholly Douglas's.

189. *mylk quhite*. Virgil 7.275, 'nitidi'; Ascensius f.224 va, 'coloris resplendentis'.

203–4. Virgil 7.282, 'daedala Circe'; Ascensius f.224 va, 'i. ingeniosa ut Dedalus erat'.

VII.v; Virgil 7.284–340

10. *proper regioun*. Virgil 7.287, —; Ascensius f.225 rb, 'in propria regione'.

12. *heland*. Virgil 7.289, —; Ascensius f.225 rb, 'promontorio'.

15. Virgil 7.288, —; Ascensius f.225 rb, 'de prospera legatione'.

20. Virgil 7.291, 'stetit'.

27. *Troy*. Virgil 7.294, 'Sigeis'; Ascensius f.225 rb, 'i. Troianis'.

28–9. The two questions are Douglas's invention.

32. Virgil 7.295–6, —; cf. Ascensius f.225 va, 'quod tamen debuit facere'.

38. Virgil 7.299, —; Ascensius f.225 va, 'perniciosa & vim inferens'.

45. *that sowkand sand*. The explanation is supplied by Douglas.

46. *the swelch is ay rowtand*. The comment is added by Douglas.

51. Virgil 7.304, 'mei'.

59. (Virgil 7.307) *Ascensius f.226 rb, 'neque Lapythis merentibus neque Calidone merente'.

63. *in propir person*. Added by Douglas.

65. *be a man*. Virgil 7.310, —; Ascensius f.226 rb, 'ab uno viro'.

78. *for a 3eir or twa*. Added by Douglas.

83. *effusioun*. Virgil 7.318, —; Ascensius f.226 rb, 'effusionem'.

86. *goddes of batale*. Virgil 7.319, —; Ascensius f.226 rb, 'dea belli'.

88. Virgil 7.320, 'Cisseis'; Ascensius f.226 rb, 'i. Hecuba'.

92. Virgil 7.320, —; Ascensius f.226 rb, '… quia etiam tu: ignes iugales …'

94. *Ene, littill wirth*. Virgil 7.321, —; Ascensius f.226 rb, 'Aeneas raptor'.

101. *thre*. Virgil 7.324, —; *Ascensius f.226 va, 'Alecto … Megera & Tisiphone'.

102–6. Expanded from Virgil 7.325–6, 'cui … cordi'.

114. Added by Douglas.

115–16. Virgil 7.329, 'tot pullulat atra colubris'; Ascensius f.226 va, 'pullulat … quos loco capillorum fruticantes habet'.

117. Virgil 7.330, 'quam'; *Ascensius f.226 va, 'quam s. furiam … perniciosam'.

120–1. *thy proper wark be richt … quhilk is thyne of det.* Virgil 7.331, 'proprium'; Ascensius f.226 va, 'tuae naturae conveniens'.

124. Added by Douglas.

129. *mony ʒeris.* Added by Douglas.

132. *the man agane his wife.* Virgil 7.336, —; Ascensius f.226 va, 'maritum & uxorem'.

134. An addition by Douglas.

135. *in thak and rwys.* Virgil 7.336, 'tectis', i.e. 'under the roof'.

141. *gar all the power.* Virgil 7.338, —; Ascensius f.226 va, 'exeant artes tuae in opus'.

VII.vi; Virgil 7.341–403

6. *his spouß Quene Amatais.* Virgil 7.343, 'Amatae'; Ascensius f.227 rb, 's. reginae coniugis'.

14. *precordialis.* This Latinism is taken directly from Virgil 7.347, 'praecordia'.

18. *thir ladeis.* Virgil 7.350, —, and 'furent*em*' limits the meaning to Amata; Ascensius f.227 rb, 'mulierum'.

22. *serpentyne.* Virgil 7.351, 'viperam'; Ascensius f.227 va, 'i. serpentinam'.

25–7. Virgil 7.352–3, 'fit longae taenia vittae innectitque comas'; *Ascensius f.227 va, 'fit taenia i. extrema pars longae vittae i. fasciae ambientis caput muliebre & innectit comas in morem vittae'.

42. *O fader Kyng Latyn.* Virgil 7.360, 'o genitor'; Ascensius f.227 va, 'O Latine qui pater es'.

48. *in sturt.* Added by Douglas.

51. *be sik a fenʒeit gyrd.* Virgil 7.362, —; suggested by Ascensius f.227 va, 'perfidis … contra fidem'?

52. Virgil 7.363, 'Phrygius … pastor'; Ascensius f.227 va, 's. Paris'.

53. *in Sparta.* Virgil 7.363, —; Ascensius f.227 va, 'in Sparta'.

59. *hald sa gloryus.* Added by Douglas.

66. Virgil 7.370, 'reor'.

69. Added by Douglas.

74. *Twa kyngis of Grece.* Virgil 7.372, —; Servius f.227 vb, 'regis Argivorum'.

75. Virgil 7.372, —; Ascensius f.227 va, 'Mycenae … Turno patria'.

86. Virgil 7.377, 'lymphata'; Ascensius f.228 rb, 'percussa furore nympharum'.

95. *turnyt tre.* Virgil 7.382, 'buxum'; *Ascensius f.228 rb, 'turno rasile buxum'.

98. *Amata the kyngis wife.* Virgil 7.384, —; *Ascensius f.228 rb, 'Amata sup. regina'.

100. *fra hand to hand.* Meaningless addition by Douglas.

109. *god of wyne.* The information is added by Douglas.

113. Virgil 7.390, 'thyrsos'; Ascensius f.228 va, 'hastas'.

114. Virgil 7.390, —; Ascensius f.228 va, 'pampinis'.

122. This detail is not in Virgil (7.394).

124. *vnder the lynd.* Added by Douglas.

130. *fyrrtre.* Virgil 7.397, 'pinum'.

141. Virgil 7.402, 'iuris materni'.

144. *Syng Bacchus sangis.* Virgil 7.403, 'capite orgia'; Ascensius f.228 va, 'i. sacra Bacchi'.

144. *sen na bettir may be.* Added by Douglas. Cf. also VII.ix.128.

VII.vii; Virgil 7.404–74

9. Virgil 7.407, 'vertisse'.

13. *Turnus.* Virgil 7.409, —; Ascensius f.229 rb, 'Turni'.

14. *douchter of Acrysyus.* Virgil 7.410, 'Acrisioneis'; Ascensius f.229 rb, 'Acrisii filia'.

18. Virgil 7.412. *Ascensius f.228 v, 'dictus avi' for MSS 'dictus avis'; Ascensius f.229 rb, 'Ardea ... ab ave'.

20. Virgil 7.413, 'sed fortuna fuit'; Loeb takes as 'but its fortune is fled'; Ascensius f.229 rb, 'fortuna fuit s. que nomen ...'

37. *Latyn, Lavyne.* Virgil 7.423, —; Ascensius f.229 rb, 'Latinus ... Laviniae'.

45. *Hethruria.* Virgil 7.426, 'Tyrrhenas'; Ascensius f.229 va, 'idest Hetruscas'.

53. *portis or havynnys of the see.* Virgil 7.429, 'portis', *gates*, taken as 'portus', *harbour*, suggested by 'flumine pulchro', not translated, in the next line.

70–2. Virgil 7.438–9, 'nec regia Iuno immemor est nostri'; Ascensius f.230 rb, 'ut coepto desistam: nec Iuno regia, quia regnorum dea ... ita non patietur me expelli'.

74. *ourset with hasart hair.* Virgil 7.440, —, as in line 100 (Virgil 7.452) below.

93. Virgil 7.448–9, 'tum flammea torquens lumina'.

104. *consider thir syngis.* Virgil 7.454, —; Ascensius f.230 r, 'indiciis'.

106. Virgil 7.454, —; Ascensius f.230 r, 'furiarum hoc est ab inferis adveni'.

130. *broth.* Virgil 7.466, 'unda'.

148. *to preif his grene curage.* Added by Douglas.

VII.viii; Virgil 7.475–539

4. *infernall.* Virgil 7.476, 'Stygiis'; Ascensius f.231 rb, 'i. infernalibus'.

8. Omits Virgil 7.478, 'insidiis'.

13. Virgil 7.481, 'cervum … agerent'.

21–4. Virgil 7.485–6, 'cui regia parent armenta et late custodia credita campi'.

28. Virgil 7.488, 'ornabat'.

33–4. Virgil 7.490, 'mensaeque adsuetus erili'.

44. *the child.* The epithet is added by Douglas.

47. *Wenand hym wilde.* Virgil 7.493, —; Ascensius f.231 va, 'non debeat putari domesticus'.

52. Virgil 7.499, 'venit harundo'.

67. Added by Douglas.

68. Virgil 7.505–6, 'olli … improvisi adsunt'.

69–70. Virgil 7.506, 'torre … obusto'.

73. Added by Douglas.

75. *the master storour.* *'Chief keeper of livestock'. The description is Douglas's, but cf. l.23 above.

79–80. Virgil 7.510, 'rapta spirans immane securi'.

81. *Alecto.* Virgil 7.511, —; Ascensius f.232 rb, 'Alecto'.

117. Added by Douglas.

131. *hyrdmen.* Added by Douglas.

135. *rurall man.* Virgil 7.535, —; Ascensius f.232 va, 'rusticus'.

VII.ix; Virgil 7.540–600

8. *Italy.* Virgil 7.543, 'Hesperiam'; Ascensius f.233 rb, 'i. Italiam'.

12. *throw a clowd.* Virgil 7.543, —; suggested by the arrangement of Ascensius f.233 rb, 'per auras coeli affatur'.

27. Virgil 7.553, 'armis'.

40. *at my request.* Added by Douglas.

48. *hellis sete.* Virgil 7.562, 'Cocyti … sedem'; Ascensius f.233 va, 'i. infernalis'.

52. *Ansanctus.* Virgil 7.565. *Ascensius f.233 r, 'Ansancti;' modern editors 'Am(p)sancti'.

60. *Pluto.* Virgil 7.568, 'Ditis'; Ascensius f.233 va, 'i. Plutonis'.

62. *that hellis see.* Virgil 7.569, —; Ascensius f.233 va, 'i. fluvio illo infernali'.

93–4. Virgil 7.584, 'perverso numine'; Ascensius f.234 va, 'i. irato s. Iunonis'.

108–10. Virgil 7.593, 'multa deos aurasque pater testatus inanis'.

122. Virgil 7.598, 'omnisque in limine portus'; interpretation suggested by Ascensius earlier f.234 va 'vicinae mortis'.

124. *triumphe riall.* Virgil 7.599, —; Ascensius f.234 va, 'pompa regali'.

127. *cure and charge.* Virgil 7.600, 'habenas'; Ascensius f.234 va, 'absolvit se a gubernaculo'.

128. *sen na better mycht be.* Added by Douglas in order to complete the couplet. Cf. also VII.vi.144.

VII.x; Virgil 7.601–40

2. *ancyent Latyum.* Virgil 7.601, 'Hesperio in Latio'; Servius f.235 ra, 'hoc est in antiquo'.

8. Virgil 7.603, 'movent in proelia Martem'; Servius f.235 ra, '… ancilia commovere'.

9. *with ostis plane.* Virgil 7.604, 'manu'; Ascensius f.235 rb, 'cum novis hostibus'.

10. *Tartareane.* Virgil 7.605, —; Ascensius f.235 rb, 'Tartari'.

16. *Persane.* Virgil 7.606, 'Parthos'.

22. *slottis.* Virgil 7.610, 'robora', *i.e.* strength; Ascensius f.235 rb, 'i. repagula fortia'.

23. Virgil 7.609, 'aeterna'; Ascensius f.235 rb, 'i. inconsumptibilia'.

24. Virgil 7.610, 'custos … Ianus'; Ascensius f.235 rb, 'i. portarum belli'.

25. *this ilk hallowit hald.* Virgil 7.610, —; Ascensius f.235 rb, 'templo'.

28. Virgil 7.613, 'consul'.

29. *rob ryall.* Virgil 7.612, —; Ascensius f.235 va, 'i. regali'.

30. *rich purpour.* Virgil 7.612, —; Servius f.235 vb, 'de purpura'.

31. *fut syde.* Virgil 7.612, —; Ascensius f.235 va, 'circumcingente altera extremitate'.

38. Virgil 7.617, —; suggested by Ascensius f.235 va, 'vir severus & venerandus'.

42. *sa vile a deid.* *Virgil 7.619, 'foeda ministeria'.

43. *nor brek his heist.* Virgil 7.619, —; suggested by Ascensius f.235 va, 'contra foedus & amicitiam fidemque Aeneae datam'.

44. *ganestud thar requeste.* Virgil 7.618, —; Ascensius f.235 va, 'vitavit & refutavit'.

49. *cruell.* Epithet added by Douglas.

50. *Virgil 7.621, 'cardine verso'. *marbill* is Douglas's addition.

54. *into fury bellicall.* Virgil 7.623, —; Ascensius f.236 rb, 's. ardore … bellico'.

56. *vnder scheld.* Added by Douglas.

71. Virgil 7.631, —; Ascensius f.236 rb, 'bene muratae'.

74. This is Douglas's repetition of the previous line.

76–7. Virgil 7.634, 'aut levis ocreas lento ducunt argento'.

78–88. Expanded from Virgil 7.635–7.

90. *Virgil 7.638, 'trepidus'; Ascensius f.236 v, 'anxius, ut in bello tumultuario'.

VII.xi; Virgil 7.641–705

1. *Musys.* Virgil 7.641, 'deae'; Ascensius f.236 va, 's. poetarum musae'.

3. Virgil 7.641, —; Ascensius f.236 va, 'recludite arcana & secreta'.

4–5. Virgil 7.641, 'cantusque movete'; Ascensius f.236 va, 'i. instigate me ut canam & cantu manifestem qui reges …'

12. Added by Douglas.

15. *for the proceß of lang ʒeris.* Not in Virgil (7.646).

19. *the king.* Not in Virgil (7.648).

21. Virgil 7.648. *Modern editors punctuate after 'armat' rather than after 'Mezentius'. Douglas follows Ascensius f.236 v, which has colons after both.

25. Virgil 7.650, 'Laurentis'.

30. *Corete.* Virgil 7.652, —; Ascensius f.237 rb, 'i. cerete oppido'.

31. Virgil 7.653, —; suggested by *Ascensius f.237 rb, 'dignus … imperator esset', picked up from 'dignus quod … beatior patriis imperiis i. que pater illi imperator esset non exul'?

33. *banyst and indyng.* Virgil 7.654, —; Ascensius f.237 rb, 'exul', contrasted with a man 'probus & pius'.

34. Virgil 7.654, —; see the quotation from Ascensius in the note to line 31.

36. *worthy.* Virgil 7.656, 'pulchro'; Ascensius f.237 rb, 'i. honesto & decoro'.

39. *in hys musteris.* Virgil 7.655–6, —; Ascensius f.237 rb, 'in curuli certamine'.

42. *of Larn the serpent gret.* Virgil 7.658, 'serpentibus Hydram'; Ascensius, note to Virgil 1.286, f.185 rb, 'ac belua Lerne i. Hydra'.

47. *went bond.* Virgil 7.661, —; Ascensius f.237 rb, 'concubuerat'.

48. *Hercules.* Virgil 7.662, 'Tirynthius'; Ascensius f.237 rb, 's. Hercules'.

49. *with prowd bodeis thre.* Virgil 7.662, —; Ascensius f.237 rb, 'qui tria dicitur habuisse corpora'.

52. *Spanʒe.* Virgil 7.663, 'Hiberas'; Ascensius f.237 rb, 'i. Hispanicas'.

52. *quhom hym likit best.* Virgil 7.663, —; suggested by Servius f.237 vb, 'admiratio'

from the phrase 'admiratio locorum longinquitate'.

53. Virgil 7.663, 'lavit'.

54. *in Ital strandis*. An explanation added by Douglas.

55-7. *These lines, which correspond to Virgil 7.664-5, appear puzzling at first. But the grammatical subject is *followis*, a rare Scots spelling of *fallowis*, 'companions' (see *DOST, Follow,* n.); *thar* (56) is an emendation of MS *his*.

60. Virgil 7.666, 'ipse'; Ascensius f.237 va, 's. dux eorum Aventinus'.

64. A misunderstanding of Virgil 7.667-8, 'cum dentibus albis indutus capiti'.

72. *eldar*. Virgil 7.671, —; Servius f.238 ra, 'maioris'.

78. 'Generit of the clowd' properly applies to the Centaurs.(cf. Virgil 7.674-5).

84-6. Expanded from Virgil 7.677, 'magno cedunt virgulta fragore'.

102. *in the Sabyne montanys*. Virgil 7.684, —; Ascensius f.238 rb, 'Sabinis'.

106. *in Champanʒe*. Virgil 7.685, —; Servius f.238 vb, 'in Campania'.

106. *flude Amasene*. Virgil 7.685, 'Amasene pater'; Servius f.238 vb, 'est autem fluvius'.

109-12. *Douglas elaborates on Virgil 7.686-7, introducing the *engynys or staf slyng*, i.e. catapult, which may derive from Ascensius f.238 rb, 'e funda iaciendo glandes'. *bla*. This corresponds to Virgil's 'liventis', livid, bluish.

120-30. Expanded from Virgil 7.691-4.

133. *iust*. *Taking Virgil 7.695, 'Aequi' as an adjective, not a proper name, as also Ascensius f.238 r and Ascensius f.238 va, 'aequos i. iustos'.

136. Virgil 7.696, —; Ascensius f.238 va, 's. oppidi Apollini sacri'.

139. *Cymynyk*. *Virgil 7.697, 'Cimini cum'; Ascensius f.238 r, however, has 'ciminicum'.

VII.xii; Virgil 7.706-82

11. Virgil 7.710, 'priscique Quirites'; Ascensius f.239 rb, 'i. Sabini antiqui'.

13. *quhilk now heicht Tribule*. Virgil 7.711, —; Ascensius f.239 rb, 'Trebula dicta est'.

15. *Momentyne*. Virgil 7.712, and Ascensius f.239 r, 'Nomentum'. *The spelling in this line may be a scribal error, since the correct spelling occurs earlier in the text (VI.xiii.39).

16. *rosy*. *Taking Virgil 7.712, 'Rosea' as an adjective, not a proper noun, as also Ascensius 1501 and Ascensius f.239 r; Servius f.239 vb, 'Rosea rura Velini: Velinus lacus est iuxta agrum: qui rosulanus vocatur'.

16. *laik*. Virgil 7.712, —; Ascensius f.239 rb, 'lacus'.

17. Virgil 7.713, 'Tetricae'; Ascensius f.239 rb-va, 'montes asperrimi a quibus omnes rigidi Tetrici nominantur'.

19. Added for effect by Douglas.

24. *that rynnys fresch and cleir*. A comment by Douglas.

38. *Lyde*. Virgil 7.721, 'Lyciae'.

41. Added by Douglas.

44. *bastard*. Virgil 7.723, —; Ascensius f.239 va, 'non legitimus'.

45. *with ferß mud acwart*. Information due to Douglas.

50. *mont*. Virgil 7.726, —; Ascensius f.239 va, 'montes'.

55. *Champany*. Virgil 7.728, —; *Ascensius f.239 va, Servius f.240 ra, 'Campaniae'.

63. Virgil 7.730, 'aclydes'.

66. Virgil 7.731, —; Servius f.240 ra, 'que ita in hostem iaciuntur'.

68. Added by Douglas.

69. *bowand as a syth*. *This comparison is not Douglas's (as Coldwell says), but a literal translation of Virgil 7.732, 'falcati', sickle-shaped.

70. Virgil 7.732, 'comminus'; Ascensius f.240 rb, 'manu conserta'.

76. *ilys*. Not in Virgil (7.735).

85. *Rufa*. Virgil 7.739, 'Rufras'.

86. Virgil 7.739, —; Ascensius f.240 va, 'castella illa Campaniae'.

87. *Celene*. Virgil 7.739. *Ascensius f. 240 v, 'Celennae'; modern editors 'Celemnae'.

88. Virgil 7.739, —; *Ascensius f.240 va, 'Iunoni sacri'.

90. *Nola*. Virgil 7.740, 'Abellae'; Servius f.241 ra, 'multi Nolam volunt intelligi'.

95. *of ful sobir extent*. Added by Douglas.

114. *Marrubya*. Virgil 7.750. *Ascensius f.240 v, 'Marrubia'; modern editors, 'Marruvia'.

116. Expanded from 'king' in the previous line.

120. *ryfe and swell*. Virgil 7.754, —; 'ryfe' might be 'ryse'.

122. *herbis strang*. Virgil 7.754, —; Ascensius f.241 rb, 'herbis potentibus'.

130. Virgil 7.760, —; Ascensius f.241 rb, 's. sacerdos … commiserationem excitet'.

134. There is nothing like this in the original (Virgil 7.760).

137. Virgil 7.762, 'mater Aricia'; Ascensius f.241 rb, 'civitas illa'.

140. *Hymetes*. Virgil 7.763. *P, some medieval MSS and Ascensius f.241 r, 'Hymetia'; MR and others 'umentia'.

140–1. *by Agerya That nymphe … ful tenderly*. Virgil 7.763 'Egeriae lucis' (in Egeria's groves); Ascensius f.241 rb, 's. nymphę'.

152. Virgil 7.767, 'turbatis'; Ascensius f.241 va, 'i. consternatis phocis'.

157. *Asculapyus*. Virgil 7.769, 'Paeoniis', which Douglas in line 158 takes as the name

of a particular herb; Ascensius f.241 va, 'Esculapii'; cf. line 165.

169. *thrynfald Diane.* Virgil 7.774, 'Trivia'; Ascensius f.241 va, 'i. Diana'; cf. line 178.

182. *Hippolitus.* Virgil 7.781, —; Ascensius f.242 rb, 'Hippolytum'.

184. Virgil 7.781–2, 'ardentis ... equos'.

VII.xiii; Virgil 7.783–8. 17.

There is only rhetorical, not bibliographic, authority for running over into Book 8.

1. *of weir the cheif capitane.* Virgil 7.783, —; Ascensius f.242 rb, 'dux & caput belli'.

10. *monstre.* Virgil 7.785, —; Ascensius f.242 rb, 'monstrum'.

11. *sulphureus.* Virgil 7.786, 'Aetnaeos'; Ascensius f.242 rb, 'i. sulphureos'.

12. *that mont peralus.* The comment is Douglas's.

22. Virgil 7.791, 'argumentum ingens'; *Ascensius f.242 rb, 'i. approbatio quae e Graecis oriundus esset'.

27. *thik as the hail schour.* Douglas adds the simile. * See note to III.viii.132.

28. *dryvand vp the stour.* Virgil 7.793, 'nimbus [peditum]'; Ascensius f.242 rb, 'pulverulentam nubem excitans'.

39. *Munycus.* Virgil 7.797, 'Numici'.

44. Virgil 7.799, 'Iuppiter Anxurus'; *Ascensius f.242 va, 'i. ... imberbis'.

46. *Iuno.* Virgil 7.800, 'Feronia'; Ascensius f.242 va, 's. Iuno'.

52. *Tyrrhene.* Virgil 7.802, —; Ascensius f.242 va, 'Tyrrhenum'.

60. Virgil 7.805, —; Ascensius f.243 rb, 'instrumento nendi'.

89. The beginning of Book 8 in Virgil.

90. *quhite as flour.* Added by Douglas.

97. *coniuratioun.* Virgil 8.5, 'coniurat'.

100. Added by Douglas.

107. *a Greik.* Virgil 8.9, —; Ascensius f.244 rb, 'Argivus'.

Prologue VIII

This Prologue belongs to a common medieval genre, the satiric complaint on the evils of the times. Here it forms a grotesque counterpart to the opening of *Aeneid* 8, in which Aeneas falls asleep and has a vision of the river god Tiberinus, who prophesies the founding of Alba by Ascanius. But whereas Virgil stresses the truth of this dream (8.42), Douglas voices scepticism about the reliability of dreams and 'swevynnys' (lines 1 and 171–7). There is a slight similarity to Prologue XIII, where the poet also falls asleep, and has a vision of a stern admonitory figure, but the season and tone are very different. Structurally, Prologue VIII consists of a long monologue by the visitant (7–117), followed by an increasingly angry dialogue between him and the dreamer. Its most striking feature is undoubtedly its metrical form: the thirteen-line rhyming alliterative stanza, with a long ninth line instead of the short line often termed a 'bob'. This was first recorded in the northern Middle English poem, *The Awntyrs off Arthure* (c. 1410–20). In the later fifteenth century it was put to varied use in such Scottish poems as the anonymous *Rauf Coilyear* and *Golagros and Gawane*, Holland's *Buke of the Howlat*, and Henryson's *Sum Practysis of Medecyne*, whose satiric tone resembles that of Douglas. The diction of Prologue VIII, which owes much to the alliterative tradition, is sometimes extremely obscure, which may account for its comparative neglect by critics. David Hume of Godscroft (1559–1629), however, passed a brief but appreciative judgment on it: 'in my opinion, there is not such a piece to be found, as is [Douglas's] Prologue to the 8. Book, beginning (Of Dreams and of Drivelings, etc.)'. For the context, Hume ed. Reid 2005, I, 28, and the related passage from the Hamilton MS of the *History*, Hume ed. Reid 2005, II, 477–8. Cf. also Coldwell I, 88; Bawcutt 1976, 173; and Parkinson 1987, who notes the 'disturbing interplay of morality and farce' in the Prologue (5). On the wider alliterative background, see Turville-Petre 1977; on other Scottish uses of this stanza, see Royan 2010; and Ralph Hanna's introductions to his editions of *Golagros and Gawane* (2008, xxxix–xli), and Holland's *Buke of the Howlat* (2014, 45–50).

1. *dreflyng*. 'Sleeping unsoundly'. The word is a variant of 'dravillyng' (X.xi.96; XII.xiv.52), and is paired with 'sleep' elsewhere: cf. *Sir Gawain and the Green Knight*, 1750; Lindsay, *Satyre*, 2221; and *OED*, dravel v.

2–3. There is a slight resemblance to the opening of the Prologue to *Piers Plowman* (A Text), Langland ed. Skeat 1886, 9–11: 'And as I lay and lened … / I slombred in a slepyng … / Than ganne I to meten a merveillouse sweuene'.

2. *Lent*. In Middle Scots this usually has its ecclesiastical sense and does not mean 'Spring'; cf. Fox's note on *Testament of Cresseid*, 5.

5. *sowpyt in syte*. 'Immersed in sadness'. Douglas may recall *Testament of Cresseid*, 450, although the phrase is traditional.

6. This line is virtually identical with *The Awntyrs off Arthure*, 189: 'Was never wrought in this world a wofuller wight'.

8. *flemyt is in Frans*. 'Is banished to France'. Coldwell comments: 'a place chosen for the alliteration, since Douglas had no great love for the French (I.Prol.270)'.

10. 'Peace is brought to an end'.

15. 'Vexatious study … has taken over the direction of our lives, destroying our sport' (Coldwell).

19–20. 'There is nobody, in short, that refrains from any shameful act, if he may gain his purpose by deception'. For this idiomatic usage with 'schame' and 'schrink', cf. Henryson, *Fables*, 2281, and *Golagros and Gawane*, 1078–9.

22. *wate*. This reading, found only in 1553, seems necessary to the sense.

28–9. 'Lovers long only to entrap lovely ladies, and to embrace them without stop or hindrance'. For the alliterative association of *lace* with love and lovers, see *Eneados* I.x.33; Chaucer, *CT*.I.1817 and 1951.

32–3. The sense is difficult. Perhaps it may be paraphrased: 'The young woman would have a fair face instead of her deformed one, so as to make her seem matchless to her man whom poverty afflicts'. This requires *myscheif is* to be read as the verb *myscheifis*, 'harms, injures'.

34. *grulyng*. 'Grovelling (in prayer)'.

38. *of thrillage*. 'Out of servitude, bondage'.

40. The miller assesses the multure (a toll on grain payable to the owner or tenant of a mill) with a defective measure. Millers were traditionally regarded as thieving. See Fergusson, *Proverbs* 634: 'Millers takes ay the best multur with their own hand'; and *Whiting* M 560. Coldwell compares Lydgate's 'Against Millers and Bakers' (*Minor Poems*, II, 448–9).

42–3. This would seem to imply a traditional rivalry between the *cadgyar*, a peddlar, or itinerant fish-dealer, and the *colȝar*, a charcoal burner.

44. Coldwell suggests this 'might be a contemptuous reference to the Lollards ... but more probably alludes to the friars'.

45. The allusion is to the Latin proverb, 'Dum herba crescit vitulus deficit' (While, or until, the grass grows, the calf is weak). It is quoted by Walter Bower in *Scotichronicon*, XVI.1 (vol. 8, p. 216), and vernacular versions are recorded in *Whiting* G 437. By the time of Shakespeare (*Hamlet*, III.2.335), the proverb was considered 'musty', *i.e.* old and stale.

46. 'One man does not spare (sexually) any woman, whether nun, wedded wife, or aunt (often a term for a prostitute)'.

47. *as God sendis the feir*. Coldwell explains 'as God sends the fixed price'.

48. *gang at*. The sense is obscure. *gait woll*. Goats' wool. Usually a symbol of low value (*Whiting* G 190).

49. 'Some spend in the old way'.

53. *wrach*. Wretch, used here in the common sense 'miser'. *this warldis wrak*. 'This world's dross', a pejorative term for worldly wealth. Cf. Dunbar, *Poems*, 6.10 and note.

54. *mukkyrrar*. 'Money-grubber'.

56. *hereyt*. 'Reduced to poverty, ruined'. Coldwell takes the anomalous singular pronoun *he* to refer to 'peddar' in the previous line, but *thay* (found only in manuscript R) would make easier sense.

57. *byngis*. 'Heaps up'. *the brovne and the blak*. Brown and black cloth.

58. *bane*. Glossed by Coldwell as 'kind of fur', but there is no evidence for a noun of this sense, and it produces awkward syntax. It seems preferable to take *bane* as an adverb, parallel with *bessely*, meaning 'readily'. The same alliterative phrase occurs in *Golagros and Gawane*, 74.

buge, *bevir* and *byce*. Lambskin, beaver, and a dark fur used for lining or trimming garments. (Coldwell and *DOST* mistakenly gloss *byce* as 'dark blue', but see *MED* and *OED*, *byse*.)

59. *for love or for lak*. Probably not 'for love or hate' (Coldwell), but 'for praise or for blame'. This alliterative pair was common in Scottish verse; see *Rauf Coilyear*, 87, and Whiting, L 562.

60. *set apon syß*. Either 'play at dice', or figuratively, 'take risks, act recklessly' (so *DOST*); *syß* signifies the number six on a dice.

66. *ralȝear*. 'Scurrilous critic, slanderer'.

67. *royt* (cf. also *roytast* in 147). *DOST* considers this rare word a variant of the adjective *royet*, and glosses as 'disorderly, incoherent'. *roundalis*. In Scots this sometimes had a precise metrical sense, 'triolets', but here it is a pejorative term for short, muddled verses, as in Montgomerie ed. Parkinson 2000, 99.III.9.

68–71. Cf. Dunbar's similar attack on sturdy beggars in *Poems*, 55.43–6.

71. *thar luffis ar byrd lyme*. The palms of their hands are sticky as bird lime. Cf. Whiting, F 154 and L 433.

72. 'If a bawd, or prostitute, has a baby …'

76. 'With no desire to earn her living'.

77. *Caymis kyn*. The descendants of Cain, allegorically, are evil and unrighteous men. On the background to this and similar terms, see Pearsall's note to X.219 in the C-text of *Piers Plowman* (Langland ed. Pearsall 1994). But Douglas may allude more specifically to the four orders of friars. Cf. 'Of the kynrede of Caym he caste the freres': *Pierce the Ploughmans Crede*, 486, in Barr 1993.

85. *boche*. Previous editors transcribed this word as *bothe*, which resulted in a difficult and nonsensical line, translated by Coldwell as 'Merchants bring home the booth to breed at home …' But there has been a *c/t* confusion, and *boche*, the name of a 'contagious and eruptive disease', makes excellent sense. The burgesses are said to bring back from the market an infectious disease that then spreads within the home – literally 'under the beams, rafters'.

86. *kowhubeis*. 'Boobies, simpletons'. Cf. Dunbar's use in *Poems*, 25.58. *plukkyt crawis*. Common people, robbed of their goods, resemble plucked crows. Douglas may allude to a rough game known as 'Pluk the craw': see *Palice of Honour*, 651 and note; and *DOST*, *pluk*, v. 8.

88. A common proverb: 'A woman will have her will' (Whiting W 519).

89. Apparently proverbial. Cf. Whiting E 117, and Fergusson, 368.

92. The line clearly refers to the forging of false money, but the sense of some words is difficult. Ruddiman's interpretation s.v. *lepis*, followed by both Small and Coldwell, is: 'some, contrary to all law and reason, take mixt metal, Copper or Brass, which they *leep*, i.e. put into molten Tin or Silver, that so it may pass for true Silver, tho truely it be of small value'. *Latton* is a mixed metal, similar to brass (cf. its figurative use in VII.

Prol.4); *latyt* is obscure, but may mean 'heated' or 'bendable' (cf. 'latit sowpill siluer' in VII.x.76); *but lay* might mean 'illegally', if *lay* signifies 'law', but *DOST* prefers to take it as an aphetic form of 'delay'; and *lepys* means 'boils, or heats slightly'. So far this would give support to Ruddiman. But *lawyd lyt* is more likely to mean 'cheap, poor quality dyeing fluid'. *Lawyd* is not the equivalent of 'laud', but a pejorative word related to modern 'lewd' (see *DOST*, *lawit*, a; *lewit*, a; and *OED*, *lewd*, a); and *lyt* is not the adjective 'little, small', but (as the rhyme indicates) the noun *lit* (see *DOST*, *lit*, n., and the related verb *lit*, 'dye, colour', used several times in the *Eneados*).

94–5. An attack on the folly of alchemists, who sought to discover the quintessence, or fifth element, believed to transmute base metals into gold. Cf. Dunbar's similarly satiric tone in *Poems*, 4.58; and 67.55–6.

94. *gowkis*. 'Gazes (in foolish expectation)'. *glas pyg*. 'Glass vessel'.

96. Coldwell paraphrases: 'This one who announces the destruction of the world lives by his wits'. A more plausible interpretation is: 'One miser (*wernour*) who longs for this world's rubbish goes out of his mind'. On *this warldis wrak*, see note to line 53.

97. Coldwell notes: 'Since clipping the coinage was a capital offence, not all the guilty lived in prosperity with their corn stacks'.

98. The line is perhaps corrupt. Coldwell paraphrases as: 'Some haggle for pennies, some flatter with a private promise'. But this seems grammatically and lexically unlikely. It is more plausible to take *prygpenny* and *pyke thank* as compound nouns, meaning respectively 'one who haggles, drives hard bargains' and 'flatterer, sycophant'. The latter word was common in Dunbar and other Scottish poets. One problem with this explanation is the absence of a verb in line 98; a possible solution would be to interpret the nouns as the subject of *kepys* (97), though this is admittedly clumsy.

99. *Ied staf*. Probably the weapon later known as a Jedburgh staff. Jedburgh stands on the river Jed. Cf. John Major [Mair], *History of Greater Britain*, V.iii: 'the iron-knobbed staves of Jedburgh' (Major trans. Constable 1892, 240).

105. *patteraris*. 'Reciters of the paternoster'.

106. 'Seek to have authority over a large (church) estate, and to be prelates'. There is a pun on *patterraris* and *patermon*, 'patrimony'.

107–8. 'The tithes of ten parishes are a mere trifle, but if he can take a kingdom of parish churches and benefices – ah, how fine' (Coldwell). *commendis*. Douglas alludes to the *in commendam* system by which many Scottish abbeys, together with their revenues, were entrusted to 'commendators', often lay members of the nobility.

116–17. 'All would like the present social order to be turned upside-down.'

120. *hed full of beys*. Cf. modern 'With a bee in one's bonnet'.

123. *freik*. An ancient poetic term for a warrior, commonly weakened in sense to 'man'.

124. *I hope thou wald neyß*. 'I believe you would sneeze'. Sneezing was a sign of anger or rashness. Cf. Hay, *King Alexander the Conquerour*, 2535: 'Thay are haistie, thair wit is in thair nois'; and *OED*, *sneeze*, v. sense 1: 'for grete angre he wolde snese at the nose' (*Festiall*, 1493).

126. *ga chat the*. An obscure expression of contempt. Cf. *Christis Kirk*, 35 (*Maitland Folio Manuscript* 1919–27, no. xliii).

133. *Sym Skynnar*. The name is given to a devil in Roule, 'Devyne poware of michtis maist' (in Hadley Williams 2016, B97), and occurs also in Rolland, *Seuin Seages*, 'Address to his Book', 49: 'Sym Skynnar hang thame'. Its origin is unknown, but *DOST* and Coldwell suggest it may be a term for the public hangman.

135. Cf. Carmichaell, *Proverbs*, No.949: 'It is a mirk mirrour ... ane other mans thocht'; Henryson's coarse parodic version in *Sum Practysis of Medecyne*, 90–91; and Whiting, M 35.

137. *Caser*. 'Emperor' (from Caesar), often alliteratively coupled with *king*.

139. 'One longs, on account of liver sickness (*luffyr ill*), to swallow a quart'.

141. *to se the new moyn*. Presumably regarded as a token of good luck. Cf. VI.Prol.21: 'dotage in the monys cruke'. Coldwell refers to Lynn Thorndike, *History of Magic and Experimental Science*, IV (1934), 282.

142. *our buke*. This answers the question put to the dreamer in line 132, and refers not merely to *Aeneid* 8 but the whole translation.

148. *sen God merkyt man*. 'Since God created mankind'. For other uses of this alliterative phrase, see *OED*, *mark*, v. sense 1c.

149–53. Some details in this astronomical passage recall *Aeneid* 1.740–6 (transl. at I.xi.95–106); and 3.515–17 (transl. at III.viii.19–23).

150. *Pleuch*. 'Plough', a common name of the constellation Ursa Major.

151. *Sevyn Starnys*. Sometimes explained as the Pleiades, but the term is earlier used by Douglas to translate Virgil's 'Hyades' (1.744 = I.xi.100). *Charl Wayn*. Literally 'Charles's or Charlemagne's Wain', an ancient term for Ursa Major (see *OED*, *Charles's Wain*).

152. *Elwand*. Literally an 'ell measure', usually explained as 'Orion's belt' (*DOST* sense 2). Cf. 'Kingis Ell' in Montgomerie, *Invectives* II.183. *Arthuris Hufe*. Arcturus, the brightest star in the constellation Bootes; see also I.xi.101. On the interesting history of this term, both as Scottish place name and star, see earlier note to III.viii.21, and *DOST*, *Arthuris hufe, oon*.

153. *Horn*. Not the Unicorn, but a name for the constellation Ursa Minor; see III. viii.22; *DOST*, *horn*; and Eade 1984, 164–6. *Hand Staf*. Literally the handle of a flail, here possibly a term for Orion's sword; Douglas elsewhere refers to Orion's 'goldyn glave' (III.viii.23), translating 'armatumque auro' (3.517).

154. *Prater Iohne*. This refers not to a constellation, but to Prester John, the legendary priest-king of Ethiopia. A fragmentary Scottish translation of the famous 'Letter of Prester John' exists in a Wyntoun manuscript (BL, Royal 17. Dxx, 310 ff). *Port Iaf*. The usual ME name for the Biblical Jaffa, or Joppa.

155. Corn and chaff are proverbially coupled. Cf. Carmichaell, no. 470: 'Everie corne hes the cafe'; and Whiting 428.

163. Poetic dreams often end in shock and disappointment. Cf. P*alice of Honour*, 2089–97.

155

164. *be byke.* 'Wild bees' nest'.

171–8. This returns to the opening theme. Such attacks on the validity of dreams were common. Cf. *Palice of Honour*, 1269: 'Out on dremis quhilks ar not worth ane mite!'; Lichtoun, 'Quha doutis dremis is bot phantasye' (in Hadley Williams 2016, 81–4); and many citations in Whiting D 387 and S 952.

179–82. Cf. the similarly abrupt decision in *Palice of Honour*, 2114: 'Till mak ane end, sittand vnder a tre'.

BOOK VIII.i; Virgil 8.18–67

1–2. Virgil 8.18, 'talia per Latium'.

6. Virgil 8.19, 'cuncta videns'.

23–5. *all on flocht … onglaid.* Virgil 8.29, 'tristi turbatus pectora bello'.

34. *schaip lyke a hempyn saill.* Virgil 8.33, —; Ascensius f.245 r, 'carbasus i. genus lini aut veli'.

37. *but dyn.* A meaningless eking out for rhyme.

54. *sawch.* Virgil 8.43, 'ilicibus'.

62. *of lyme and stanys.* An addition by Douglas.

64. Virgil 8.48, —; cf. Ascensius f.245 va, 'cognominandam ab alba sue inventa'.

65–6. Expanded from Virgil 8.49, 'haud incerta cano'; cf. *Ascensius f.245 va, 'immo certissimis oraculis tibi prius significata …'

89. Virgil 8.59, —; Ascensius f.246 rb, 'cum prima luce'.

96. *with mony iawp and iaw.* Added by Douglas.

98. *fra tovn to tovn.* Added by Douglas.

VIII.ii; Virgil 8.67–96

8. Virgil 8.71, 'nymphae'; *Ascensius f.246 va, 'i. … quae praeestis fontibus'.

11. Virgil 8.72, —; *Ascensius f.246 va, 'fluviis circumnantibus hoc est quibuscumque aquis currentibus'.

15. *to ʒow onbekend.* Not in Virgil (8.73).

18. Virgil 8.76, —; Servius f.246 vb, 'Aeneas pie pollicetur'.

24. *Itall ryng.* Virgil 8.77, 'Hesperidum'; Ascensius f.246 va, 'Italicarum'.

26. Virgil 8.78, —; *Ascensius f.246 va–247 rb, 'post tanta marium pericula'.

27. *promys and orakill.* *Virgil 8.78, 'numina'; Servius f.247 ra, 'oracula & promissa'.

38. *thretty hed.* Virgil 8.82, —; *Ascensius f.247 rb, 's. triginta capitum'.

51. Virgil 8.90, —; *Ascensius f.247 rb, 'quia vident fluvium tam convenientem'.

53. *quhisperyng*. Virgil 8.90, 'rumore'; *Ascensius f.247 rb, 'murmure … secreto sermone'.

62. *as thai war wod*. The comparison is Douglas's.

65. Douglas's addition.

VIII.iii; Virgil 8.97–183

3. Virgil 8.97, —; Ascensius f.247 va, 'i. iam meridies erat'.

6. *bot a few to knaw*. Virgil 8.98, —; Servius f.247 vb, 'nullis obstantibus aedificiis'.

12. *Eneas sort*. Virgil (8.101) gives no subject for his verbs.

13. Virgil 8.102, 'rex Arcas'; Ascensius f.247 va, 's. Evander'.

15. *full hie sacryfyß*. Virgil 8.102, —; Ascensius f.247 va, 'sacrificium'.

16. *Hercules*. Virgil 8.103, 'Amphitryoniadae'; Ascensius f.247 va, 'Herculi'.

17. *fostyr son*. Virgil 8.103, —; Ascensius f.247 va, 'filio putativo'.

18. *I.e.* 'made sacrifice to the other gods …'

22. Virgil 8.105, 'pauperque senatus'.

35. *with a few menȝe*. Virgil 8.111, —; Ascensius f.248 rb, 'cum paucis relictis s. ceteris'.

38. *standis … howe!* Virgil 8.112, has only 'iuvenes'.

50. *man and boy*. Added by Douglas.

54. The purpose is supplied by Douglas.

60. *as Dardanus*. Virgil 8.121, —; Ascensius f.248 va, 'Dardanum'.

71. *best in neid*. Douglas's comment, not Virgil's (8.127).

76. *the branch of olyve tre*. Virgil 8.128, 'ramos'; Ascensius f.248 va, 's. olive'.

77. Virgil 8.128, —; Ascensius f.248 va, 'signum … quia alienis opus habeam opibus'.

82. Virgil 8.130, —; Servius f.249 ra, 'i. Agamemnoni & Menelao'.

93. Virgil 8.135, 'Electra … Atlantide'; *Ascensius f.249 rb, 'i. Atlantis filia'.

94. *be schip*. Douglas's addition.

100. *in Arcad*. Virgil 8.139, —; Ascensius f.249 rb, 'in Arcadia'.

105. *schortlie to conclud*. *A common medieval story-teller's tag. Cf. X.xiv.191; and XI.xiii.44.

108. Virgil 8.143, 'legatos'.

109. *other craft*. Virgil (8.143) 'prima per artem'.

113–14. Virgil 8.146, 'Daunia'; Ascensius f.249 rb, 'id est Rutula a Dauni filio ducta'.

121–4. Virgil 8.149, 'et mare quod supra teneant quodque adluit infra'; Ascensius f.249 rb–va, 'teneant mare quod alluit s. Italiam supra i. ab orientali plaga i. mare Adrianum, & quod alluit infra i. ab inferiore parte s. mare Tyrrhenum'.

145. Hesiona is the sister, not the land (Virgil 8.157 'Hesionae visentem regna sororis').

150. *or berd begouth to spryng*. Virgil 8.160, —; Ascensius f.249 va, 'hoc est barba tenui'.

153. The explanation is given by Douglas, not Virgil (8.162).

154. *blak as hell*. *Proverbial (Whiting H 329).

171. Virgil 8.169, 'dextra'; Ascensius f.250 rb, 'i. fides quam petis'.

173. Virgil 8.169, —; *Servius f.250 ra, 'antiquis … amicitiis'.

189. *fut het*. Added by Douglas.

193. *holyne*. Virgil 8.178, 'acerno', *i.e.* maple.

196. *Hercules altar*. Virgil 8.179, 'arae'; *Servius f.250 ra, 'nondum enim templum Herculis fuerat sed arae modo'.

198. *bakyn breid*. Virgil 8.181, 'dona laboratae Cereris'; Ascensius f.250 rb, 'i. panis confecti artificiosi'.

199. *wynys*. Virgil 8.181, 'Bacchum'; Ascensius f.250 rb, 'i. vinum'.

201. *perpetual oxin fillettis*. Virgil 8.183, 'perpetui tergo bovis', which Mackail takes as 'slices cut the full length of the ox-chine', and Loeb as 'the long chine of an ox'. *Ascensius f.250 rb, 'unde datur perpetuum epulum'.

202. Virgil 8.183, 'lustralibus extis'; Ascensius f.250 rb, 'i. purgativis que ad expurgationem oblata erant'.

VIII.iv; Virgil 8.184–279

25. *hym allane*. Virgil 8.194, —; Ascensius f.251 rb, 'solum'.

26. *a hellis byke̜*. Added by Douglas.

31–2. Virgil 8.197, 'tristi … tabo'.

34. *god of fyre*. Douglas, not Virgil (8.198), gives this information.

43. *Hercules*. Virgil 8.203, 'Alcides'; Ascensius f.251 rb, 'Hercules'; so also in lines 72, 141, 160, etc.

79–81. *Hercules … commonly*. Virgil 8.219, 'Alcidae'; Ascensius f. 266 va, 'i. Herculi …'

82–3. Virgil 8.219–20, 'hic vero Alcidae furiis exarserat atro felle dolor'.

84. *armour*. Not mentioned in Virgil (8.220).

99. *Hercules*. Virgil 8.228, 'Tirynthius'; Ascensius f.252 rb, 's. Hercules'.

111. *cald*. Douglas adds the epithet.

114. Virgil 8.235, —; *Ascensius f.252 rb, 'quae humanis carnibus vescuntur'.

115. Virgil 8.233, 'praecisis undique saxis', transferred from Virgil's order.

116. Added by Douglas.

121. An expansion by Douglas.

128. *demmyt with the rokis*. Virgil 8.240, —; *Ascensius f.252 rb, 'impeditus saxo'.

133. Virgil 8.243, 'vi'.

149. *querral stanys*. *Not 'crossbow bolts' (so Coldwell), but 'quarried stones', translating Virgil 8.250, 'molaribus' (Bawcutt 1971, 51).

168. *ball*. Virgil 8.260, 'nodum'.

VIII.v; Virgil 8.280–312

1. *Hesperus*. Virgil 8.280, 'Vesper'; *Ascensius f.253 va, 'i. stella vespertina que et Hesperus … dicitur'.

6. *the stowt*. Douglas adds the epithet.

13. Virgil 8.285, 'Salii'; Ascensius f.253 va, 'cum hymnis saltantium'; *Servius f.254 ra, 'qui tripudiantes aras circum ibant'.

16. Added by Douglas.

19. Virgil 8.287, —; *Ascensius f.254 rb, 'chorus … canentium & tripudiantium iuvenum'.

21. Virgil 8.287, 'carmine'; Ascensius f.254 rb, 'id est hymno rythmico'.

24. *in creddill*. Virgil 8.289, —; Ascensius f.254 rb, 'in cunis'.

26. *with hys handis tway*. Virgil 8.289, —; Servius f.254 ra, 'manibus'.

35. *Centawres*. Virgil 8.293, 'nubigenas'; Ascensius f.254 rb, 'i. Centauros'.

37. Douglas's expansion of Virgil 8.294, 'manu … mactas'.

40. *bair and bull*. Virgil 8.295, —; Ascensius f.254 rb, 'taurum'.

41. *Nemee forest*. Virgil 8.295, 'Nemeae'; Servius f.254 ra, 'Nemea silva est'.

60. Virgil 8.302, —; Ascensius f.254 v, 'in auxilium veniendo'.

VIII.vi; Virgil 8.313–68

7. An explanation by Douglas for the benefit of his readers.

11. *maneris … nor polecy*. Virgil 8.316, 'mos'; Ascensius f.255 rb, 'i. consuetudo convivendi ab antiquo instituta'.

16. Virgil 8.318, —; Ascensius f.255 rb, 'baccae & acini' misread as 'buculae & asini'?

17–18. *A free version of Virgil 8.318, 'sed rami atque asper victu venatus alebat'.

29. *redis in mony ryme.* Douglas's addition.

39. *war and wyß.* Douglas supplies the adjectives.

78. Virgil 8.346, —; *Servius f.256 vb, 'iurat non sua culpa iura hospitii esse violata'.

81. *mont.* Virgil 8.347, 'sedem'.

96. Virgil 8.353–4, 'nigrantem aegida concuteret'.

98. *that makis thundris beir.* Virgil 8.354, —; *Ascensius f.256 va, '... tonitrua concomitantur'.

99. Supplied by Douglas.

105. *myne awin leif brother.* Douglas's addition. *The phrase is also used in IV.Prol.91.

114. Virgil 8.361, —; Ascensius f.257 rb, 'aedificiis ad modum carinarum factis'.

118. *sobir.* Virgil 8.363, —; Ascensius f.257 rb, 'modica'.

130. *Affrik.* Virgil 8.368, 'Libystidis'.

VIII.vii; Virgil 8.369–453

7. *hir husband and gud man.* Virgil 8.372, —; Ascensius f.257 va, 'maritum suum'.

11. *Grece.* Virgil 8.374, —; Ascensius f.257 va, 'Graeci'.

21. *ontollerabill.* Virgil 8.380, *'durum'; Ascensius f.257 va, 'vix tolerabilem'.

25. *thy ilk spouß and wyve.* Douglas alone makes Venus say this.

26. *derrest to me on lyve.* Virgil 8.382, —; Ascensius f.257 va, 'obseruandum mihi'.

28. Virgil 8.383, 'arma'.

30. *Thetys.* Virgil 8.383, —; Ascensius f.257 va, 'Thetis'.

31. Virgil 8.384, —; Servius f.257 vb, 'quae Achilli arma impetravit'; *Ascensius f.257 va, 'genetrix sc. Achillis'.

33. *Aurora.* Virgil 8.384, —; Ascensius f.257 va, 'Aurora'.

34. Virgil 8.386, —; *Ascensius f.257 va, '... ut Memnoni filio eius arma fabricares ... nigri Memnonis arma'.

36. *in teyn.* Virgil 8.386, —; Ascensius f.257 va, 'ut in gravi bello sit'.

38. Virgil 8.386, —; *Ascensius f.257 va, 'ad excidium i. destructionem meorum'.

53. *myne awin hart deir.* Douglas supplies the term of endearment.

55. This question is not in Virgil (8.395).

58. This question also is not in Virgil (8.396).

61. Virgil 8.397, —; Ascensius f.258 rb, 'i. tunc s. cum Argolici reges vastarent Pergama'.

74. Virgil 8.402, 'liquido ... electro'; cf. VIII.x.68 (Virgil 8.624).

79–80. Added by Douglas.

81. *this hait syre*. Virgil 8.405, —; *Ascensius f.258 va, 'inflammatus'.

86. Douglas it is who supplies this idea.

93. *spynnyng*. Virgil 8.409, 'Minerva'; Ascensius f.258 va, 'hoc est textura'.

99. *lyne*. Virgil 8.412, —; Ascensius f.258 va, 'aut lino seu lanitio'.

100. Virgil 8.412, —; 'lang thredis' is suggested by Ascensius f.258 va, 'stamine'.

101. The explanation is Douglas's.

106. *and hynt his geir*. Added by Douglas.

113. Virgil 8.419, 'antra Aetnaea'.

114. *bront*. Virgil 8.419, —; *Ascensius f.259 rb, 'exesa ... ignibus'.

115. *as quha dyd thunder heir*. Added by Douglas.

118. Omits Virgil 8.421, 'Chalybum'.

128. Added by Douglas.

139. *in maner of gun powder*. Virgil 8.431–2, —. *This seems anachronistic, but Douglas's contemporaries believed that gun powder was known in the ancient world, and invented by Archimedes (see Hale 1966, 116.)

140. *sowder*. The term is Douglas's.

145. *to batale*. Virgil 8.433, —; Ascensius f.259 va, 'in bello'.

146. Virgil 8.434, 'urbes'.

174. *and call*. Added by Douglas.

184. Virgil 8.453, 'in numerum'. *Ascensius f.260 rb, 'i. secundum proportionem rhythmicam'.

VIII.viii; Virgil 8.454–540

1. Virgil 8.454, 'pater ... Lemnius'; Ascensius f.260 rb, 's. Vulcanus'.

6. *the swallow*. Virgil 8.456, —; Ascensius f.260 va, 'praecipue hyrundinum'.

13. *Arcaid*. Virgil 8.459, 'Tegeaeum'; Ascensius f.260 va, 'i. Arcadicum'.

19. Virgil 8.463, 'secreta petebat', *i.e.* sought the secret room of Aeneas, visited his chamber.

30. Added by Douglas.

48. Virgil (8.477) does not have this salutation.

57. *vale, mont and swyre*. Douglas's expansion of 'land'.

66. *speldit furth on breid*. This descriptive phrase is Douglas's own.

107–8. Virgil 8.502, 'tantam subiungere gentem'; Ascensius f.261 va, 'subiugare gentem s. Rutulorum & Latinorum'.

141. Virgil 8.515–16, 'tolerare … militiam'.

149. Virgil 8.519, —; Ascensius f.262 rb, '& ita erunt quadringenti equites'.

170. *brycht as … levin*. *See also X.vi.94; and XI.xiv.51. The simile was very common (Whiting L 211–13).

VIII.ix; Virgil 8.541–96

2–4. *The sense is 'And first he caused to have made up and kindled (*gart … beyt and kyndill*) the extinguished fires and hearths and ingles, raked out the night before.'

6. Virgil 8.543, 'parvosque Penatis'; Ascensius f.263 rb, 'i. deos domesticos'.

24. Virgil 8.552, 'exsortem'; Ascensius f.263 rb, 'equum exortem, i. extra sortem dandum hoc est egregium & non de communi sorte'.

36. *with sair hart*. Added by Douglas.

50. *the gay*. Added by Douglas.

60. *for na weir*. Added by Douglas.

71. Added by Douglas.

73. Virgil 8.574, 'si numina vestra'; Ascensius f.264 rb, 'i. divinae potestates'.

82. *faynt*. Douglas supplies the epithet.

103. Virgil 8.588, 'conspectus'.

104. *in hys tender age*. Added by Douglas.

111. *schene*. Virgil 8.591, 'sacrum'.

113. *for cald dreid*. Virgil 8.592, has only 'pavidae'.

118. Added by Douglas.

124. *dusty streyt*. Virgil 8.596, 'putrem … campum'.

VIII.x; Virgil 8.597–641

3–4. Virgil 8.597, 'Caeritis'; *Ascensius f.264 va, 'i. urbe Agyllinę'.

11–12. Virgil 8.600, 'fama est veteres … Pelasgos'; Ascensius f.264 va, 'i. Graecos'.

26. *lusty, stern and stowt*. The epithets are not in Virgil (8.606).

31. *dyvyne armour cleir*. Virgil 8.609, 'dona'; *Ascensius f.265 rb, 's. arma a Vulcano fabrefacta'.

38. *reward*. Virgil 8.613, 'munera'.

40. *now art thou sovyr and stark.* Virgil 8.613, —; suggested by Ascensius f.265 rb, 'propter virtutem suam bellicam', applied to 'Laurentis'.

62. Added by Douglas.

64. *watry.* Virgil 8.622, 'caerula'; Servius f.265 vb, 'aquosam'.

66. Virgil 8.623, —; Ascensius f.265 va, 'arcum celestem producentibus'.

68. *laton.* Virgil 8.624, 'electro'; cf. VIII.vii.74 (Virgil 8.402).

72. Virgil 8.628, 'Ignipotens'; Ascensius f.265 va, 'i. Vulcanus'.

77. Virgil 8.628–9, 'illic genus omne futurae stirpis ab Ascanio'.

79. Virgil 8.630, 'fecerat'.

81. *furthstrekand breste and vdyr.* Virgil 8.631, 'procubuisse'; *Servius f.266 ra, 'ut inclinatione corporis vbera praeberet infantibus'.

86. *to geif thame sowke* Added by Douglas.

88. *clenge.* Virgil 8.634, 'fingere'; Ascensius f.266 rb, 'i. tergere'.

90. Virgil 8.636, 'sine more'; Ascensius f.266 rb, 'i. nova inventione'.

91–2. Virgil 8.636, 'consessu caveae'; Ascensius f.266 rb, 'i. in loco concavo ubi consederant in circuitu spectantes'.

96. Virgil 8.636, —; Servius f.266 ra, 'dicimus ludos theatrales, ludos gladiatorios'.

98. *Romanys.* Virgil 8.638, 'Romulidis'.

100. Virgil 8.639, 'reges'; Ascensius f.266 rb, 's. Romulus & Tatius'.

VIII.xi; Virgil 8.642–74

1. *thou mycht knaw.* Virgil 8.642, —; Ascensius f.266 va, 'hoc atrox factum videtur'. Throughout the passage Douglas insists more strongly than Virgil that these are pictures on a shield.

1. Omits Virgil 8.642, 'quadrigae'.

2. *Metus Suffytius.* Virgil 8.642, 'Mettum'; *Ascensius f.266 va, 'i. Maetium Suffecium'.

3. *albeit thou thocht this cruelte.* Virgil 8.643, —; Ascensius f.266 va, 'tametsi hoc crudele videtur tibi, O Albane'.

4–5. Virgil 8.643, 'at tu dictis, Albane, maneres !'; Ascensius f.266 va, 'tu maneris … dictis i. promissis & conventis cum Romanis'.

6–7. *war outdraw By command.* Virgil 8.644, 'raptabat'; Ascensius f.266 va, 'i. distrahere faciebat'.

7. *Tullus Hostilyus.* Virgil 8.644, 'Tullus'; Ascensius f.266 va, 's. Hostilius'.

9. This detail is not in Virgil (8.643).

12. Virgil 8.646, 'eiectum'.

19. *Porsen.* Virgil 8.649, 'illum'; Ascensius f.266 va, 's. Porsenam'.

21. *hardy ... darf and bald.* The epithets are once more Douglas's.

22. *that he purposit to hald.* This is added by Douglas.

23. *Chelya.* Virgil 8.651. *Ascensius f.266 v, 'Chloelia'; modern editors 'Cloelia'.

24. *Tibir flude.* Virgil 8.651, 'fluvium'; *Ascensius f.267 rb, 's. Thybrim'.

25-7. Virgil 8.652-3, 'in summo custos Tarpeiae Manlius arcis stabat pro templo'; *Ascensius f.267 rb, 'Manlius ... custos arcis Tarpeiae ... stabat in summo scilicet clypei pro templo i. pro defensione templi Iovis'.

29. *chymmys calendar.* *Ruddiman notes: 'this is what Servius, from whom he has it, calls *Curia Calabra*, built by Romulus on the Capitoline hill. 'Calabra autem dicta est ... quod cum incertae essent Calendae aut Idus, a Romulo constitutum est, ut ibi patres vel populus calarentur, i.e. vocarentur, & scirent, qua die Calendae essent, vel etiam Idus'. [Servius *auctus*, on Virgil 8.654, ed. Thilo 2, 294.]

31. *with stra or gloy.* The detail is added by Douglas.

35. *Franchmen.* Virgil 8.656, 'Gallos'.

37. *to the capitoll.* Virgil 8.656, —; Ascensius f.267 rb, 'Capitolium'.

38. Virgil 8.658, —; Servius f.267 vb, 'alii dicunt tenebris propter cuniculos'.

39. *almaist.* Virgil 8.657, —; *Servius f.267 vb, 'deest paene'.

41. *as ... brycht gold wyre.* Virgil 8.659, 'aurea'. This was a very popular medieval simile (Whiting G 322-8).

43. Omits Virgil 8.660-1, 'tum lactea colla auro innectuntur'.

45-6. Expanded from Virgil 8.661-2, 'duo Alpina ... gaesa' (*Ascensius f.267 r, 'gessa'); Ascensius f.267 va adds 'i. hastilia'.

49. *prestis.* Virgil 8.663, —; Ascensius f.267 va, 'sacerdotes'.

50. Virgil 8.663, —; Servius f.268 r, 'saliant & tripudient'.

51. *Panos prestis.* Virgil 8.664, —; Ascensius f.267 va, 'sacerdotes Panos'.

53. *bowyt.* Virgil 8.664, —; Servius f.268 r, 'rotundum'.

57. *playand ... solace.* Added by Douglas.

60. *Pluto.* Virgil 8.667, 'Ditis'; Ascensius f.267 va, 'i. Plutonis'.

65. Virgil 8.669, 'Furiarumque ora'.

69. *Censorius.* Virgil 8.670, —; Ascensius f.267 va, 'Censorius'.

70. *iust rewardis.* Virgil 8.670, 'iura'; Ascensius f.267 va, 'iusta moderamina'.

72. Omits Virgil 8.672, 'caerula'.

VIII.xii; Virgil 8.675–731

1. *Amyd the seys.* Virgil 8.675, 'in medio'; Ascensius f.268 va, 's. maris'.

2. Virgil 8.675, 'classis aeratas'; Ascensius f.268 va, 'i. bellicas aere munitas'.

4. Virgil 8.677, 'Leucaten'; *Ascensius f.268 va, 'i. montem illum in promontorio'.

7. *On that a party.* Virgil 8.678, 'hinc'; Ascensius f.268 va, 'i. ex una parte'.

8. *Octauyan.* Omitted in Virgil (8.678).

10. *senatouris.* Virgil 8.679, 'patribus'; Ascensius f.268 va, 'i. senatoribus'.

11. Virgil 8.679, 'Penatibus'.

17. *hys frend deir.* Virgil 8.682, —; Ascensius f.268 va, 'i. affinis & amicus Augusti'.

23. *Marcus Antonyus.* Virgil 8.685, 'Antonius'; Ascensius f.268 va, 's. Marcus'.

28. *Perß.* *Virgil 8.686, 'ab Aurorae populis'; Ascensius f.268 va, 's. Parthis'. *Red See.* Virgil *ibid.*, 'litore rubro', *i.e.* Mare Erythraeum, or the Indian Ocean.

29–30. Virgil 8.687, 'viris'; Servius f.268 vb, 'Antonius re comperta collectis ... viribus ... venit ad bellum. Conflictum est navali certamine'.

34. *Queyn Cleopatra.* Virgil 8.688, —; Ascensius f.268 va, 'Cleopatra'.

37. *bensell of the ayris.* Virgil 8.689–90, 'reductis ... remis'; meaning suggested by *Ascensius f.269 rb, 'remis retrorsum ductis'?

38. *raris.* Virgil 8.690. *MP, 'tridentibus'; R¹ and most medieval MSS, and Ascensius f.268 v, 'stridentibus'.

41. *ilandys.* Virgil 8.692, —; Ascensius f.269 rb, 'insulas illas'.

43. *concurrand.* Virgil 8.692, 'concurrere', translated in line 44.

46. *in schip of towr to feght.* Virgil 8.693, 'turritis puppibus'; Ascensius f.269 rb, 'i. propugnacula habentibus'.

47–50. Expanded from Virgil 8.694–5, 'stuppea flamma manu telisque volatile ferrum spargitur'.

51. Virgil 8.695, 'arva ... Neptunia'; Ascensius f.269 rb, 'i. maria'.

52. Virgil 8.695, 'nova ... caede rubescunt'; Ascensius f.269 rb, 'i. effusione sanguinis'.

55. *tympane.* Virgil 8.696, 'sistro'; Ascensius f.269 rb, 'i. tympano'.

58. *that efter hes hir slane.* Virgil 8.697, —; Servius f.269 vb, 'nondum videbat mortem futuram'.

60. Virgil 8.698, —; Ascensius f.269 va, 'deorum Aegyptiorum'.

65. *Mars.* Virgil 8.700, 'Mavors'; Ascensius f.269 va, 'i. Mars'.

68. Virgil 8.701, —; *Ascensius f.269 va, 'ad ulciscendum'.

72. *With hir kynd cosyng.* Virgil 8.703. *Ascensius f.269 r, 'consanguineo'; modern editors 'cum sanguineo'.

74. Virgil 8.704, 'haec'; *Ascensius f.269 va, 'i. hanc commotionem & aleam belli ita quod … anceps esset victoria'.

76. The explanation is added by Douglas.

81. *gang befor the wynd*. Virgil 8.707, 'ventis vocatis'.

82-4. *A free translation of Virgil 8.708. The immediate source of line 84 may be Chaucer's 'Fleth ek the queen, with al hire purpre sayl' (*Legend of Good Women*, 654). The purple sail was a traditional detail, however, in ancient and medieval accounts of Cleopatra's flight, such as Florus, *Epitome Rerum Romanorum*, II. 21, or Boccaccio's *De Claris Mulieribus*, ch. 86 (Boccaccio ed. Branca 1964–, vol. 10).

88. Virgil 8.709, 'inter caedes'.

89. *west wynd*. Virgil 8.710, 'Iapyge'; Ascensius f.269 va, 'i. vento illo illi a tergo flante'.

91. *for thar diseyß*. Added by Douglas.

95. *watry*. Virgil 8.713, 'caeruleum'.

112. *snaw quhite … merbill*. Virgil 8.720, 'niveo'; Ascensius f.270 rb, 'i. de candido marmore facto'.

115-16. *in takynnyng Of hys triumphe*. The explanation is Douglas's.

123. *Vlcanus*. Virgil 8.724, 'Mulciber'; Ascensius f.270 rb, 'i. Vulcanus'.

123. *Numydanys*. Virgil 8.724. *Ascensius f.270 r, 'Numadum'; modern editors 'Nomadum'.

127. *pepill of Sythia*. Virgil 8.725, —; Ascensius f.270 rb, 'populos Scythie'.

128. Virgil 8.725, 'sagittiferosque'; Ascensius f.270 rb, 'i. sagittas quibus plurimum valent in bella ferentes'.

131. *fast by the see*. Virgil 8.727, —; *Ascensius f.270 rb, 'non longe sunt ab oceano'.

134. *Danys*. Virgil 8.728, 'Dahae'.

135. Virgil 8.728, 'Araxes'; Ascensius f.270 rb, 'fluvius Armeniae'.

Prologue IX

Prologue IX divides, thematically and metrically, into two sections. The first is a series of moral maxims, and consists of three six-line stanzas, employing a complex scheme of interlaced final and internal rhymes sometimes called *rime bâtelée*. Parallels occur elsewhere in Scottish verse: one is the short moral piece, 'Remembir man', in the Bannatyne Manuscript (fol. 74v; *Bannatyne Manuscript* 1928–32, II, 182). Bannatyne includes this first part of the prologue in his 'Ballatis of Moralitie' (fol. 45; *Bannatyne Manuscript* 1928–32, II, 113). Unfortunately Douglas's rhyme pattern was corrupted in some witnesses: two of these (the Bannatyne MS and the 1553 print), for instance, have 'versis' instead of 'warkis' in line 1. The second section, which employs the five-beat couplet used for the translation, is longer and, critically, much more interesting. It contains an important statement of some of Douglas's ideas about style, and is closely related to Prologue I.

2. *Agilyte*. 'Intellectual ability'.

3. *merkis*. A command to the reader: 'Note, observe'. Coldwell however interpreted the line differently as 'And therein this agility marks wisdom'.

7–8. Although the ideas are commonplace they find a close parallel in *Palice of Honour*, 1999–2015.

9. *eschew idilneß*. On the evil effects of idleness, cf. Whiting I 6.

10. *hald nathing at is hys*. Perhaps 'keep nothing that is someone else's'.

13. The thought is Scriptural (Luke vi.31), and very common in medieval writers (Whiting D 274). See above I.Prol.501.

15–16. Coldwell comments: 'Notice the political concern with the preservation of class in society'.

16. *Clym nevir our hie*. Proverbial. Cf. Whiting C 296.

21–50. Douglas's critical ideas were largely shaped by medieval rhetoric, and in particular by the doctrine of the three styles, which were thought to be embodied in Virgil's *Eclogues*, *Georgics*, and *Aeneid*, and symbolically represented in John of Garland's *Rota Virgilii*. On the background see Cooper 1977; Laugesen 1962; and Curtius 1953, 201, 231. In practice Douglas, like most medieval writers, is chiefly concerned with the difference between the high and the low style: the first is symbolized by highly valued trees, beasts, and birds; contrasted with these are low-status 'scroggis' and brushwood, and animals and birds held in low esteem, such as goats, buzzards, and kites. Douglas would certainly also be familiar with Horace's views on stylistic decorum (see *Ars Poetica*, 19ff. and 156ff.), and possibly also with the medieval *artes dictaminis*, which taught that the style of a letter should be related to the status of the recipient (cf. Chaucer, Prologue to *Clerk's Tale*, CT.IV.16–18).

21. *The ryall style, clepyt heroycall*. Cf. *Palice of Honour*, 877–8: 'In kinglie stile … Cleipit in Latine Heroicus', where this style is associated with Calliope, muse of heroic poetry.

23. *thewhes*. No satisfactory explanation of this form has been found, but in context it might be a scribal error for *thewles*, 'wanton, dissolute'. *OED* and *DOST* tentatively gloss the variant *tenchis* (E, R, 53) as 'taunts'.

29–37. When Douglas speaks of *myne authour* he usually refers to Virgil (cf. line 53 below). Lines 33–5 directly allude to *Eclogue* 4.2–3: 'Non omnis arbusta iuvant humilesque myricae. Si canimus silvas, silvae sint consule dignae' (Hedgerow and humble tamarisk do not appeal to everyone. If we must sing of woodland, let them be such as may do honour to a consul). The lowly plants and bushes mentioned in line 37 correspond to Virgil's *arbusta* and *myricae*.

30. This line has a rhythmic and thematic resemblance to the opening of *The Testament of Cresseid*.

38–9. On the superiority of the cedar to 'rammale', or brushwood, see *Palice of Honour*, 1879–80. The laurel and cedar were trees traditionally associated with epic, and heroic deeds. Cf. Chaucer, *Knight's Tale*, CT.I.1027; and Dunbar, *Poems*, 56.4 and 67. The palm was a common symbol of triumph or victory in classical antiquity. Cf. XI.Prol.143–4.

41. *gayt*. 'Goats', recalling the common but mistaken etymology of *ecloga* as *caprinus sermo* (see Cooper 1974).

44. *a knychtly taill*. Possibly an allusion to Chaucer's *Knight's Tale*, whose style is more elevated than that of the following 'cherles tales'.

45–8. For a similar contrast between noble birds of prey, such as falcons and goshawks, and those considered inferior, such as kites, see Dunbar, *Poems*, 68.11–14. The knightly classes are represented by falcons and goshawks in Holland's *Howlat*, 321–9.

49–50. The *mastys*, or mastiff, was primarily a guard dog; and Dunbar's references to it are not favourable (*Poems*, 72.17). The spaniel was more esteemed, and used for sporting purposes.

57. *Octauyane*. Augustus. See earlier note on VI.Prol.101.

59–62. See Luke ii.1–5.

63ff. The self-depreciation should not be regarded as merely 'conventional' (so Coldwell). Cf. I.Prol.1ff.

66. *mysfur*. 'Should miscarry, go amiss'. (The earlier reading *myssur* is mistaken.)

76. *mea culpa I cry*. 'I acknowledge my fault'; an expression of contrition from the *Confiteor*.

77–8. This is the first example of the proverb cited in Whiting C 568. Cf. also Whiting *Scots* I 154, and Tilley C 851.

83. *amendis it*. A common modesty or humility topos. Cf. *Exclamatioun*, 39; Henryson, *Fables*, 42; and *Palice of Honour*, 2168.

84. *Stand* is the usual verb in English forms of this proverb (Whiting L 264), but *sit* is found in other Scottish writers (see Whiting *Scots* I 200).

86. *ilk gude deid helpis other*. Cf. Whiting T 533: One good turn (also deed) asks another.

87–9. On Henry, Lord Sinclair, see I.Prol.83–6, and 97–100.

92. *enfors my stile*. 'Lend force to my style'. Cf. VII.xi.1–4.

93. Sharpening one's pen, literally and metaphorically, indicates a writer's resolve to return to work. The trope is common in Lydgate: cf. *Troy Book*, II.5064–5; V.2924.

BOOK IX.i; Virgil 9.1–32

4–5. *that list … iniquyte.* Virgil 9.2, —; Ascensiusf.271 rb, 'inimica Enee'.

7. *malapert and stowt.* Virgil 9.3, —; Ascensius f.271 rb, 'temerarium & confidentem'.

8. *with all his rowt.* Virgil 9.3, —; suggested by Servius f.271 vb, 'consilia capiebat'.

9. *wondyr lovn and law.* Virgil 9.4, 'sacrata'.

10. *at eys.* Virgil 9.4, —; Ascensius f.271 va, 'ociosus'.

12–13. Expanded from Virgil 9.5, 'ad quem sic roseo Thaumantias ore locuta est'; Ascensius f.271 va, 'i. Iris'.

25–6. Virgil 9.10, 'extremas Corythi penetravit ad urbes'; Ascensius f.271I va, 's. montis Thusciae'.

29–30. Virgil 9.12, 'nunc tempus equos, nunc poscere currus'.

33. *in hys presens evin.* Added by Douglas.

41. *thir skyis brovn.* Added by Douglas.

51–2. *with wordis augurall … diuynal.* Virgil 9.22, 'et sic effatus'; Ascensius f.272 rb, 'auguralia verba augurium acceptum significantia'.

63. Virgil 9.26, —. 'Bank and buß' is a common alliterative tag; cf. line 78 below; and Lindsay, *Dreme*, 62.

68. Added by Douglas.

69–71. *Representing Virgil 9.29, 'vertitur arma tenens et toto vertice supra est' (= 7.784), which is found only in some late MSS (and in Ascensius f.272 r).

73. *the flude Indane.* Virgil 9.31, —; Ascensius f.272 rb, 'fluvius ille Indiae'.

74. *efter spayt of rayn.* Virgil 9.32, —; Servius f.272 ra, 'post inundationem'.

75–6. *Douglas expands Virgil's description of the Ganges delta (9.30–1).

78. *bank and buß.* See note to line 63 above.

79. *gret fludis watry rage.* Virgil 9.32, —; Ascensius f.272 rb, 'impetuosus'.

IX.ii; Virgil 9.33–76

12. *Hay, hay, go to!* Virgil 9.38, — ('heia!' is joined to the preceding 'hostis adest').

16. *dredand for thir harmys.* Virgil 9.40, —; Servius f.272 vb, 'qui futura praevideret'.

17. *gif thai assalʒeit wer.* Virgil 9.41, —; Ascensius f.272 va, 'insultus hostilis'.

24. Douglas's addition.

26. Expanded from Virgil 9.44, 'monstrat'.

31. *'Armed *they* stood …'

169

37. *sterand*. Virgil 9.51, —; Ascensius f.273 rb, 'ferocissimi'.

38. *wail fat*. Douglas's addition.

45-6. Expanded from Virgil 9.53, 'campo sese arduus infert'.

55-60. Expanded from Virgil 9.57-8, 'huc turbidus atque huc lustrat equo muros aditumque per avia quaerit'.

82. Virgil 9.67, —; Ascensius f.273 va, 'hoc cogitans'.

86. *as neir owt of dowt*. Added by Douglas.

91. *fyrryn*. Virgil 9.72, 'pinu'.

92. Anacoluthon.

95. *on the schippis slang*. The detail is added by Douglas.

96 and 98. There is nothing in Virgil (9.75) like these lines.

99. *fyre*. Virgil 9.76, 'Volcanus'; Ascensius f.273 va, 'i. ignis'.

IX.iii; Virgil 9.77–167

17. Virgil 9.86, 'in arce fuit summa'; Ascensius f.274 rb, 'hoc est apud Gargara'.

21. *Phrygianys*. Virgil 9.86, —; Ascensius f.274 rb, 'Phrigii'.

43. *so habill to faill*. Virgil 9.96, —; Ascensius f.274 rb-va, 'insensibilibus … submergibilis'.

55. *corruptabill*. Virgil 9.101, —; suggested by *Ascensius f.274 rb, 'corruptibiles', applied to the trees.

57. *immortale*. Virgil 9.101, —; *Servius f.274 vb, 'bene dixit mortalem. nec enim potest fieri ut eadem res et mortalis sit et immortalis; ante est ut desinat esse mortalis'.

59. *Clotho*. Virgil 9.102. *Ascensius f.274 r, 'Clotho' for MSS 'Doto'.

63. *Pluto*. Virgil 9.104, —; Ascensius f.274 va, 'Plutonis'.

71. *werd sisteris*. Virgil 9.107, 'Parcae'.

80. *est*. Virgil 9.111, 'Aurora'; Ascensius f.275 rb, 'i. parte orientali'.

81-3. *The rowtis … of Ideanys … cloß*. Virgil 9.112, 'Idaeique chori'; Ascensius f.275 rb, 'i. qui sunt in tutela matris deorum'.

88. *albeit ʒe mocht*. Added by Douglas.

95. *and swym*. Expanded by Douglas from the sense of the passage.

96. *moder of goddis*. Virgil 9.117, 'genetrix'; Ascensius f.275 rb, 's. deum'.

104-5. Virgil 9.122, 'reddunt se totidem facies'; *Ascensius f.275 rb, 'inquit quot prorae aeratae steterant prius ad litora'.

107. Virgil 9.123-4, 'conterritus … Messapus'.

111. *stop. E's variant stot, 'rebound', is perhaps preferable as a translation of Virgil 9.125, 'revocatque pedem'.

112. for all the feir thai mak. Virgil 9.127, —; Ascensius f.275 va, 'suorum obstupescentium'.

113. Virgil 9.126, 'fiducia'; *Ascensius f.275 va, 'i. confidens, virtus & animositas'.

115. hardy wordis. Virgil 9.127, 'dictis'; Ascensius f.275 va, 'i. verbis consolatoriis'.

117. Virgil 9.127, 'increpat'; Ascensius f.275 va, 'sinit eos turbari'.

118ff. Douglas has found considerable difficulty in Turnus's somewhat incoherent speech, Virgil 9.128–58.

124. withstand. Virgil 9.130, 'exspectant'. for all thar fors is tynt. It is Douglas, not Virgil (ibid.), who says this.

128. feld and cost. Douglas's expansion of Virgil 9.132, 'terra'.

129. Added by Douglas.

132–6. Expanded from Virgil 9.133–4, 'nil me fatalia terrent, si qua Phryges prae se iactant, responsa deorum'; *Ascensius f.275 va, 'fatale eis fuerit in Italiam pervenire'.

147–8. Virgil 9.138, 'Atridas'.

151. Virgil 9.138, —; Ascensius f.275 va, 'me tangit … concessum est'.

152. as that thai schaw. Virgil 9.140, —; *Ascensius f.275 va, 'si dicantur'.

156. Virgil 9.141, —; suggested by Servius f.275 vb, 'Si culpa repetitur, supplicia quoque geminentur'.

157–8. Virgil 9.141–2, 'penitus modo non genus omne perosos femineum', i.e. 'so that henceforth they should loath utterly almost all womankind'.

161. Virgil 9.144, 'dant animos'.

162–3. *Douglas expands Virgil 9.143, 'leti discrimina parva', following Ascensius f.275 va, 'parva distantia … a morte'.

168. Quham I behald. *Virgil 9.146–7, 'quis [some medieval MSS and Ascensius f.276 r: 'qui' FMPR¹ and most medieval MSS] … apparat'.

178. Omits Virgil 9.151, 'late (FR: 'summae' MP) … arcis'.

180. Thame to dissave. Virgil 9.151, —; suggested by Ascensius f.276 rb, 'per insidias'.

187. Virgil 9.157, —; Ascensius f.276 rb, 'imbelli & ignava'.

189. Virgil 9.157–8. *Ascensius 1501 f.276 r, 'lecti … viri'; Ascensius f.276 rb, 'viri lecti i. egregii'; MSS 'laeti … viri'.

193. Virgil 9.158, 'procurate'; Ascensius f.276 va, 'i. reficite corpora vestra'.

195–7. *Ascensius f.276 r and modern editors punctuate line 194 (Virgil 9.158) as the end of Turnus's speech.

206. *ilk man dyd hys det.* Douglas's addition.

207. *of metell bryght.* Virgil 9.165, 'aënos'; Ascensius f.276 va, 'i. aereos'.

IX.iv; Virgil 9.168–223

4. *all that nyght.* Virgil (9.170) does not say this.

7–8. Virgil 9.170, 'explorant pontis'; Ascensius f.276 va, 'explorant … an s. satis firmiter clausae atque munitae sint … ligneos quos sursum trahunt'.

12–13. Virgil 9.171, 'instat'; Ascensius f.276 va, 's. operi i. instanter intendunt'.

14. *at his departyng.* Added by Douglas.

18. Douglas's alternative to Virgil's single 'adversa', 9.172.

20. *bodyn … targe.* A variant of the tag, *'bodyn in feir of weir', added by Douglas.

21–4. Virgil 9.174–5, 'sortita periclum excubat exercetque vices, quod cuique tuendum est'; *Ascensius f.277 rb, 'i. postquam per sortes quilibet quod obiret acceperat … ne simul omnes excubuisse putentur'.

29. *Ida hys moder.* Virgil 9.177, 'Ida'; Ascensius f.277 rb, 's. mater'.

36. Added by Douglas.

39–40. *will, lust, mynd.* Virgil 9.182, 'amor'.

40. *in vniformyte.* Virgil 9.182, —; Ascensius f.277 rb, 'uniformis'.

41. Expanded by Douglas from the two previous lines.

46–50. Virgil (9.184–5) has a direct question.

46. *spretis sylly*, 'blessed spirits'. Virgil 9.184, 'di'; Ascensius f.277 v, 'genii (quem nos angelum ac spiritum nobis deputatum dicimus)'.

49. *god and genyus.* Virgil 9.185, 'deus'; Ascensius f.277 v, 'an genii'.

53. Added by Douglas.

57. Omits Virgil 9.189, 'rara'.

62. *quhat thynkis thou.* Virgil 9.191, 'animo surgat', *i.e.* in his own mind.

64–5. Expanded from Virgil 9.192, 'Aenean acciri omnes'.

66. *sur wittering.* Virgil 9.193, 'certa'. At this point C and the other witnesses have *wrytyng*, but Ruthven's variant *wittering*, 'information', makes better sense and is preferable metrically. The word was common in earlier Scottish poets, such as Barbour, but seems to have become obsolete in the sixteenth century. According to *DOST*, Douglas is the last recorded user, here and in IV.iv.79.

67. *attentik.* Douglas's addition.

68. Virgil 9.194, 'si tibi quae posco promittunt'; Ascensius f.277 v, 'i. cupio promitti i. te mecum proficisci'.

75. Virgil 9.197, 'obstipuit'; Ascensius f.277 va, 's. novitate rei'.

76. *best belovyt.* Virgil 9.198, 'ardentem'.

83. *nor tawcht sik cowardy.* Virgil 9.203, —; suggested by Ascensius f.277 va, 'me socium fugere debeas'.

89. *refusand na pyne.* Added by Douglas.

98–103. Expanded from Virgil 9.208–9, 'ita me referat tibi magnus ovantem Iuppiter aut quicumque oculis haec aspicit aequis'; Ascensius f.278 rb adds, 'ex cuius s. inspirationibus eam mentem conceperat'.

116–17. Virgil 9.211, 'casusve deusve'.

118. Added by Douglas.

127. Virgil 9.217, —; Ascensius f.278 rb, 'mare iterum ingredi'.

131. *ingirand.* Virgil 9.219, 'nectis'; Ascensius f.278 rb, 'ingeris'.

134. *quhar thai lay.* Virgil 9.221, —; Ascensius f.278 rb, 'dormiebant'.

136. *to fulfill hys entent.* Added by Douglas.

IX.v; Virgil 9.224–307

2. *gret and small.* A rhyming tag, added by Douglas.

8. Virgil 9.227, 'summis regni de rebus'; Ascensius f.278 va, 'i. de republica'.

14. Virgil 9.231, 'alacres'; *Ascensius f.278 va, 'i. laeti & prae se ferentes fiduciam'.

22. *equal.* Virgil 9.234, 'aequis'.

24–6. Virgil 9.235, 'neve haec nostris spectentur ab annis', which Loeb (2nd ed) translates as 'and do not let our proposal be judged by our years'; Douglas's sense is in *Ascensius f.278 va, 'i. non iudicentur pro iuvenili aetate nostra, quia iuvenes constat raro esse prudentes'.

28. *lyggis sowpit.* Virgil 9.237, 'conticuere'; Ascensius f.278 v, 'procubuere'. *drunk as swyne.* Douglas intensifies Virgil's 'vinoque sepulti' by adding this traditional simile; see also IX.vi.20; and Whiting, S 955.

43. *watyr of Tibyr.* Virgil 9.245, 'amnem'; Ascensius f.279 rb, 's. Tyberinum'.

48. Virgil 9.246, 'hic'.

51. Virgil 9.248, 'non tamen'; *Ascensius f.279 rb, 'i. tametsi hactenus in summo periculo versamur'.

61. Virgil 9.253, —; Ascensius f.279 rb, 'ignoro'.

68. Virgil 9.255, —; Ascensius f.279 rb, 'Atque si forte Aeneam cito moriturum …'

69–70. Virgil 9.255–6, 'integer aevi Ascanius'; *Servius f.279 ra, 'adolescens; cui adhuc aetas integra superest'.

72. *quhil that he is levand.* Added by Douglas.

74–5. Virgil 9.258, 'excipit Ascanius'; Ascensius f.279 va, 'i. sermonem ex ore loquentis capit'.

76. Virgil 9.258, —; Ascensius f.279 va, '… illius dictum approbat & de se spondet …'

82. Virgil 9. 259, —; Ascensius f.279 va, 'domus Anchise'.

96. *cite Arisban.* Virgil 9.264, 'Arisba'; *Ascensius f.279 va, 'i. civitate'.

97. Virgil 9.265, 'tripodas'; Ascensius f.279 va, 'i. sedes'.

99. *flacconys two.* Virgil 9.266, 'cratera' (singular).

107. *this ʒister nyght.* Virgil 9. 269, —; Ascensius f.280 rb, 'heri'.

108–9. *helm … rede.* Virgil 9.270, 'cristasque rubentis'.

115. Virgil 9.273, 'captivos'; Ascensius f.280 rb, 's. liberos earum aut potius bissex captivos'.

116. Virgil 9.273, 'arma'; Ascensius f.280 rb, '& bona'.

130. *souerane dignyte.* Virgil 9.281, 'fortibus ausis'.

132. *I sal do my best.* Virgil 9.282, —; Ascensius f.280 rb, 'conabor'.

133. Virgil 9.283, —; Ascensius f.280 rb, 'tantum de me polliceri possum'.

135. Added by Douglas.

137. *Within this town.* Virgil (9.285) does not say this.

138. *not comptand hir lyfe.* Added by Douglas.

140. *in Sycyll.* Virgil 9.286, —; Ascensius f.280 rb, 'in Sicilia'.

157. Added by Douglas.

162. *I promyß.* Virgil 9.296. *Some medieval MSS. and Ascensius f.280 v, 'spondeo'; MPR¹ and most medieval MSS, 'sponde'.

165. *quhat so evir scho be.* The doubt is added by Douglas.

171. *owder to weill or wo.* Virgil 9.301, —; Ascensius f.280 va, 'sive incolumis redibis sive non'.

176. This line has no equivalent in Virgil (9.301).

181. *land of Creyt.* Virgil 9.305, 'Gnosius'; Ascensius f.280 va, 'i. Cretensis'.

184. Virgil 9.307, —; Ascensius f.280 va, 'Ascanius gerebat & Euryalo nunc dat'.

186. The comment is made by Douglas.

IX.vi; Virgil 9.308–66

4. Virgil 9.310, 'votis'; Ascensius f.281 rb, 'faciendo pro eorum reditu vota'.

16–18. Expanded from Virgil 9.315–16, '… petunt, multis tamen ante futuri exitio';

*Ascensius f.281 rb, 'i. priusquam castra illa inimica eis sint, i. perniciosa, multis s. Rutulis exitio i. ad exitium & necem'; Servius f.281 ra, 'Castra inimica non tantum hostilia sed pernitiosa'.

20. *as swyne.* *See note to IX.v.28.

23. Virgil 9.317, 'arrectos … currus'; Ascensius f.281 rb, 'i. habentes temones arrectos'.

24. *the hamys abowt thar nek.* Virgil 9.318, —; perhaps suggested by Ascensius f.281 rb, 'lora id est habenas'.

28. *baß voce.* Virgil 9.319, 'ore'; perhaps suggested by *Ascensius f.281 rb, 'ore i. non indicio aut nutu solo sed expressa voce'.

28. *Nysus.* Virgil 9. 319, 'Hyrtacides'.

35. *voyd passage.* Virgil 9.323, 'vasta', *i.e.* 'place wasted by destruction' or (Loeb) 'destruction'; Ascensius f.281 rb, 'i. sine obstaculo pervia'.

51. *luggyng upon the streit.* Added by Douglas.

53. *hys nek.* Virgil 9.331, 'colla' (plural), but note 'thar' in line 55.

66. Virgil 9.337, 'deo victus'; Ascensius f.282 rb, 's. vini Baccho'.

70. *and tyl hym self tane tent.* A comment by Douglas

72. This line is Douglas's addition.

83-4. Is contempt for commons strengthened? Virgil 9.343, 'sine nomine plebes'; Ascensius f.282 rb adds 'i. ignobilem'.

86. *Hesebus.* Virgil 9.344. *Ascensius f.281 v has 'Hebesum' for MSS 'Herbesum'. Douglas's form is presumably his own or the scribe's error.

87. *Arabys.* Virgil 9.344, 'Abarim'.

99-100. Virgil 9.350, 'hic furto fervidus instat'; *Ascensius f.282 rb, 'fervidus s. ex successu instat furto i. furtivę caedi'.

108-9. *dangeris … eft.* Added by Douglas.

116. *for vptakyng quhar it lay.* Added by Douglas.

124. This line is wholly Douglas's.

129-30. Loeb makes the girdle a gift to Remulus; in the Latin (Virgil 9.360) the descent of the belt is obscure; *Servius quoted by Ascensius f.282 va, b gives it up as an 'insolubilem difficultatem'.

137. *ʒongar Remulus.* Virgil 9.362, 'nepoti'; Ascensius f.282 va, 'Remulo iuniori'.

138. *that is heir slane thus.* Virgil 9.363, —; Ascensius f.282 va, 'nunc interfecto'.

141. *suppoß the gold dyd gleit.* Added by Douglas.

IX.vii; Virgil 9.367–458

15. *The comment is an expansion of Virgil 9.374, 'immemorem'.

35. Virgil 9.384, 'tenebrae ramorum'.

37. Virgil 9.385, 'fallitque timor'.

40. *onwar quhar was hys feir.* Virgil 9.386, 'imprudens'; Ascensius f.283 va, 'i. ignarus remanentis Euryali'.

44. Virgil 9.388, 'stabula alta', which Loeb (2nd ed) renders by 'stately stalls'; Ascensius f.283 va, 'stabula s. equorum'.

69. *cousyng.* Virgil 9.399, 'iuvenem'.

76. *afald.* Virgil 9.403, —; perhaps suggested by Ascensius f.284 rb, 'expressa'?

80. Added by Douglas.

88. Virgil 9.408, 'sacra'; Ascensius f.284 rb, 'caput apri ... cornua cervi'.

90–2. *in this ... nycht.* Virgil 9.409, 'rege tela per auras'.

97. *scheild.* Virgil 9.412, 'tergum'; which Loeb renders by 'back'; Ascensius f.284 rb, 's. scutum'.

98. **in schuldir.* 'Asunder, in fragments'. *Schuldir* is a scribal variant of the more usual *schundir* (see *DOST*).

106. Added by Douglas.

109. Virgil 9.416, 'acrior'; Ascensius f.284 rb, 'vehementior hoc i. per hunc talem eventum'.

126. Virgil 9.426, 'perferre dolorem'; *Ascensius f.284 va, 'tantum dolorem quantus erat amicum ... interfeci'.

132. 'Neither might nor durst ...'

138–9. There is nothing in Virgil (9.431) like these two lines.

164. Virgil 9.443, —; 'he' is Nisus.

168. Added by Douglas.

177. *schamful.* Virgil 9.450, —; suggested by *Ascensius f.285 va, 'cum potius victi censendi sint'?

178. *other geir that ganys.* Virgil 9.450, —; Ascensius f.285 va, 'rerum quas exportarant'.

179. *Ioysyng but obstakil.* This is not in Virgil (9.451).

IX.viii; Virgil 9.459–524

2. *Titan.* Virgil 9.460, 'Tithoni'. *See note to IV.xi.2.

12. Virgil 9.464, 'variisque ... rumoribus'; Servius f.286 ra, 'quia duo ausi sunt per

eorum castra transire'.

33. A detail added by Douglas.

35–6. Virgil 9.476, 'excussi manibus radii revolutaque pensa'.

47–8. *This derives from Virgil 9.480, 'dehinc'; Ascensius f.286 rb, 'i. postquam nati ora conspexit'.

51–92. Expanded from Virgil 9.481–97.

96–8. Virgil 9.499, 'torpent infractae ad proelia vires', which Loeb (2nd ed) takes as 'their strength for battle is numbed and crushed'.

111–14. Virgil 9.505, 'testudine'; Ascensius f.286 rb, 'i. coopertura ex clypeis acta sicut testudo testa sua integitur'.

122–46. Expanded from 9.509–20.

IX.ix; Virgil 9.525–89

1. Virgil 9.525, 'vos, O Calliope'; Ascensius f.286 va, 's. musas omnes'.

5. *Virgil 9.526, 'ferro'; Ascensius f.286 va, 'telo aut ense'.

8. Virgil 9.528, 'ingentis oras ... belli'; which Loeb takes as 'mighty scroll of war'; Ascensius f.286 va, 'i. extremitates ... extremas partes belli'.

9–10. *Virgil 9.529 (= 7.645) is found only in R¹ of the ancient MSS, and in Ascensius f.286 v; modern editors omit it.

12. Virgil 9.530, 'pontibus altis', correctly translated in IX.iv.7 (Virgil 9.170).

13. *neir by the ʒet*. Virgil 9.530, —; Ascensius f.286 va, 'ad portas'.

19. *sillys*. Douglas's addition.

22. Virgil 9.535, 'princeps ... Turnus'; which Loeb takes as 'first Turnus ...'; Ascensius f.287 va, 'Turnus princeps s. exercitus & eius oppugnationis'.

39. *with brokyn banys*. A detail added by Douglas.

48. Virgil 9.546, 'serva Licymnia', which Loeb takes as 'Licymnian slave'; *Ascensius f.288 rb, 'Licinia s. nomine'.

52. *onsemly and evill farrand*. Virgil 9.548, 'inglorius', that is, 'unfamed', not 'infamous'.

67–8. Virgil 9.555, —, as the marginal note (in C) points out.

85. *ravanus bludy*. Virgil 9.566, 'Martius'; *Servius f.288 vb, 'aut cruentus: aut Marti dedicatus'.

89. *Rutilianys*. *Virgil 9.567, —; Ascensius f.288 va, 'Rutuli'.

96. *and brak hys nek bone*. Added by Douglas.

99–100. Virgil 9.571, 'Emathiona Liger'.

99–113. The passage is considerably expanded from Virgil 9.571–5.

131. *into Sycill land.* Virgil 9.584, —; Ascensius f.289 rb, 'in Sicilia'.

135. *scheild.* *Virgil 9.586, 'hastis' MP and some medieval MSS, 'armis' (as in 10.52) R¹ and most MSS, and Ascensius f.288 v.

140. Virgil 9.588, 'liquefacto'; *Ascensius f.289 rb, 's. ex celerrimo impetu'.

IX.x; Virgil 9.590–663

18–20. *A free version of Virgil 9.598, 'obsidione … valloque teneri'.

22. Virgil 9.600, 'en qui'; Ascensius f.289 va, 'quales muliebris animi'.

27. Virgil 9.602, 'non hic Atridae'; Ascensius f.290 rb, 'i. lenti illi bellatores'.

35–40. Virgil 9.605–6, 'venatu invigilant pueri silvasque fatigant flectere ludus equos et spicula tendere cornu'; the rest of the speech (41–72, Virgil 9.607–20) is somewhat expanded.

55. Omits Virgil 9.614, 'croco'.

59. Virgil 9.616, 'tunicae manicas habent'; *Ascensius f.290 va, 'i. tegmina ad manus usque protensa que brachia impediunt'.

63. Added by Douglas.

65. *seir.* Virgil 9.618, 'biforem'.

67–70. Virgil 9.619–20, 'buxusque vocat Berecyntia Matris Idaeae'; *Ascensius f.290 va, 'buxus i. fistula ex buxo … Berecynthia idest quae crescit in Berecyntho monte … vocat vos s. ad choreas'.

88. Virgil 9.627, 'aurata fronte'.

89. This line is wholly Douglas's.

106–9. Virgil 9.636–7, 'Teucri clamore sequuntur laetitiaque fremunt animosque ad sidera tollunt'.

117–27. Expanded from Virgil 9.641–4.

133. Virgil 9.648, 'armiger ante fuit'.

142–4. Virgil 9.652, 'atque his ardentem dictis adfatur Iulum'.

161. *in hys cace.* Added by Douglas.

161. Omits Virgil 9.660, 'fuga'.

IX.xi; Virgil 9.664–721

4–5. Virgil 9.665, 'amentaque torquent'; *Ascensius f.292 rb, 'i. tela amentis, hoc est loris quibus mediae religantur & iaciuntur hastae leves seu iacula'.

6. Added by Douglas.

14. *in October.* Virgil 9.668, —; Ascensius f.292 rb, 'in Octobri'.

18–19. *the hevynnys and the ayr With stormy tempest.* Virgil 9.670, 'Iupiter'; Ascensius f.292 rb, 'i. aer horridus'.

19. *northyn blastis.* Virgil 9.670, 'Austris', i.e. southern winds.

22. *that Troiane.* Virgil 9.672, 'Idaeo'; Ascensius f.292 va, 'i. Troiano'.

23. *Hybera.* *Virgil 9.673, 'Iaera;' Ascensius 1501 f.292 r and Ascensius f.292 va, 'hiera'.

28. Added by Douglas.

38. Virgil 9.678, 'armati ferro'.

49. *Tynarus.* Virgil 9.685, 'Tmarus'; *Ascensius f.292 v, 'Tinarus'.

97. *marbill.* Virgil does not specify the material (9.711 'saxea').

99. Virgil 9.710, 'Baiarum'; Ascensius f.293 va, 'urbes'.

103. Virgil 9.712–13, 'ruinam … trahit'; Ascensius f.293 va, 'ut Bytias cecidit'.

107. *ilandis twa.* Virgil 9.715, —; Ascensius f.293 va, 'insula'.

107. Omits Virgil 9.715, 'alta'.

110. *the gyand.* Virgil 9.716, —; Ascensius f.293 va, 's. giganti'.

IX.xii; Virgil 9.722–77

17. Virgil 9.731, 'continuo'; *Ascensius f.294 va, 'i. statim vt receptus atque inclusus est'.

21. *sanguane.* Virgil 9.733, 'sanguineae', applied to Turnus's helmet.

37. *My frend.* Not in Virgil (9.741).

43. *the dynt dyd no deir.* Douglas gives this information.

45–6. *Virgil 9.746 has 'vulnus Saturnia Iuno detorsit veniens, portaeque infigitur hasta', which Loeb translates as 'Saturnian Juno turned aside the coming blow, and the spear lodges in the gate'. The whole episode is very 'hamely' in Douglas's version.

53. *standand on hys typtays.* Virgil 9.749, 'consurgit'.

62–3. Expanded from Virgil 9.754, 'sternit humi moriens'.

87. *onto the corpis ded.* Virgil 9.765, —; Ascensius f.295 rb, 'prostratis'.

96. *in bargan full expert.* Virgil 9.769, 'dexter'; which Loeb renders by 'on the right'; Ascensius f.295 rb, 'i. expeditus bellator'.

108. Added by Douglas.

111–18. Expanded from Virgil 9.775–7.

IX.xiii; Virgil 9.778–818

4. **fleand pail and wan.* Virgil 9.780, 'palantisque'. A double translation: Douglas seems to conflate the correct reading *palantis*, literally 'wandering', with *pallentis*, 'growing pale'.

22. Virgil 9.787, —; Ascensius f.295 va, 'non resistitis'.

57. *spouß and sister.* Virgil 9.804, 'germanae'; Ascensius f.296 rb, 'soror et coniunx'.

Prologue X

George Bannatyne, who derived his text and its title from the 1553 print, aptly included this Prologue in the section of his anthology called 'Ballatis of theoligie' (fols. 9–11v; *Bannatyne Manuscript* 1928–32, II, 20–6). Douglas's exposition of the paradoxes of the Incarnation and the Trinity is learned, subtle, and theologically precise; it has few parallels in the poetry of his contemporaries. Most poems in praise of the Trinity are vague and commonplace: for examples, see James Ryman's carols (in Greene 1977, nos. 279–305); or the anonymous 'O immensa Trinitas' (*Maitland Folio Manuscript* 1919–27, no. lvi); or another poem included in Bannatyne's 'Ballatis of theoligie', John Bellenden's 'The Benner of Pietie' (fols. 1–3v; *Bannatyne Manuscript* 1928–32, II, 3–8). On the text of the latter see Bawcutt 2008, 98–9. Prologue X is linked ingeniously to the following book of the *Aeneid* by a bridging passage (lines 151–75) that re-applies to the Christian God phrases that Virgil uses of Jupiter and his council (see notes to 156–8, and 165ff.). The five-line stanza (*aabba⁵*) is not employed elsewhere by Douglas. On its use by other poets, see Dunbar, *Poems*, 29 and note. For a perceptive analysis of Douglas's 'impressive and remarkable poem', see Gray 2012.

1–20. There is a striking generic resemblance between this passage and the opening of Henryson's 'Preaching of the Swallow' (*Fables*, 1622–1712). Both Henryson and Douglas stress the incomprehensibility of God, who may best be known through his created works, and more particularly by the cycle of the seasons which manifest the order of the universe. For the ancient background to this theme, see Wisdom of Solomon, vii.16–21; and Boethius, *Consolation of Philosophy*, IV, metre 6.

20. *wrocht and bocht.* Cf. XI.Prol.200.

23. *accident.* Coldwell notes: 'Philosophically, the property of a thing which is a contingent attribute, not part of its essential nature'.

35. Note the emphatic use of *a* as 'one', as also in lines 64, 71, 72.

37. The inadequacy of human reason to comprehend God is much stressed; see also lines 50, 87, 91–5, and 101. Simpler verses on this traditional topic, such as the quatrain 'Witt hath wunder that reson ne tell can' (*NIMEV* 4181), were well known in Scotland; see Bawcutt 1986.

42–5. *engendris ... Procedis*. For this orthodox distinction, cf. John Ireland, *Meroure of Wyssdome*, II, 24: 'The sone procedis fra the fader be way of generacioun / and the haly spreit be the way of processioun'.

66ff. The tripartite analysis of the soul was common among medieval thinkers, as was the belief that the soul furnished an appropriate analogy to the Trinity. Douglas may possibly have known St Augustine's discussion of the topic in his treatise *De Trinitate*. This work certainly had readers in late medieval Scotland: see Durkan and Ross 1961, 70 and 117; and Higgitt 2006, S12.149, S18.14b, and S21.6. For a contemporary parallel in Scottish poetry, see Hay, *King Alexander the Conquerour*, 9703 ff: this passage describes the soul as being 'Formit of God ... / Off His substance, and till His semblance like' (9705–6); and having the threefold powers of Wit, i.e. Understanding, Reason, and Memory (9737–47: Hay ed. Cartwright 1986–90).

73–80. For a parallel to this vivid similitude, cf. the elaborate passage in *Piers Plowman* C which begins: 'For to a torche or to a taper the Trinity is likned' (Langland ed. Pearsall 1994, XIX. 167ff.). St Augustine, who may be the ultimate source of the analogy, frequently compared the persons of the Trinity to *ignis*, *splendor*, and *calor* in his sermons: see the quotations in the excellent note on this passage in Langland ed. Skeat 1886, II, 245. Robert Grosseteste likewise wrote that 'Among bodily things the most obvious illustration of the Trinity is fire, or light, which necessarily begets its splendour from itself; and these two reflect on each other a mutual warmth': see Grosseteste trans. Martin 1996, 227.

86. *Frend*. Douglas addresses the reader directly, in the manner of Henryson; cf. *Fables*, 365 and 389.

90. *pretty*. The usual senses at this time were 'clever, fine'. Coldwell takes this use to be ironic.

96. 'Not even *all* matter incloses or comprises God' (Coldwell).

100. 'He is outside everything, yet excluded from nothing' (Coldwell).

101. *investigabill*. 'Inscrutable'.

116–25. A summary of Genesis, i–iii.

129. *hereit hell*. 'Harrowed hell'. Cf. the similar phrasing and rhyme in IV.Prol.41–2.

130. A condensed reference to the Redemption. Jesus paid the *pryce*, or penalty, for Adam's disobedience of God's command in eating from the tree of the knowledge of good and evil (Genesis ii.17). *the forbodin tre*. This term was common; cf. Walter Kennedy, *Flyting*, 293; Lindsay, *Monarche*, 444.

132. *A drop*. 'One drop'. With this hyperbole cf. John Ireland, *Meroure of Wyssdome*, I, 81: 'And thocht a drope of his precius blud had bene sufficient and excedand for the redempcioune of all the waurld, 3it mare haboundanly all his blud and lif he spendit for to wyn thi luf, fyrst schawand the his excellent luf, and kindnes and ardent cherite'. Lindsay expresses a similar thought in *Satyre*, 3470–5.

136–40. Douglas's reference to the mystery of the Eucharist is altered in the 1553 print and the Bannatyne Manuscript: the phrase 'in form of' (137) is replaced by 'luflye with', apparently implying consubstantiation rather than transubstantiation. Bannatyne supplies a further marginal note: 'Commounioun'. Protestant hostility to Catholic doctrines concerning the Eucharist also affected the transmission of Dunbar's religious poetry; see Dunbar, *Poems*, 83.42–5, and note.

145. Explained by Coldwell as: 'Thou art my prize, what I prize; and also my price, the one who paid my debt (cf. line 130); make me a worthy prey'. *Prey* possibly here has the specialized Scriptural sense: 'that which one brings away from a contest' (*OED*, *prey* 1b), with reference to Christ's contest with the Devil.

151–75. At the conclusion Douglas substitutes Christian for pagan inspiration, as in earlier prologues: see I.Prol.452–70; III.Prol.41–5; V.Prol.55–68; and VI.Prol.135–68.

153. *mawmentis*. 'Idols, pagan gods'. The term is strongly pejorative; cf. Lydgate's dismissal of 'fals mawmetrie' in *Troy Book* II.5825; and IV.6948ff.

155. For similar avowals in Chaucer, cf. *Troilus and Criseyde*, II.18; and *Legend of Good Women*, 1352.

156–8. Cf. *Aeneid* 10.2 and 743: 'divum pater atque hominum rex'; also Douglas's marginal note on I.v.2, with its etymological interpretation of Jupiter as 'iuuans pater, the helply fadir', and its cross-reference to this passage: 'bot quham we cleip swa I haf writyn in my proloug of the X buke'.

159. *fudder*. *DOST*, *fudder n²*, glosses as 'loud blast of wind', but the context suggests the ruder 'fart'. For similar expressions, see Whiting F 61 and F 62.

160. Proverbial-sounding, but Whiting gives only this instance (H 346). Coldwell compares Dunbar, *Poems* 3.269.

161. Cf. Deuteronomy x.17: 'Quia Dominus Deus vester ipse est Deus deorum'.

162. Cf. Deuteronomy x. 13: 'Custodiasque mandata Domini'.

165ff. The court of heaven is analogous to Jupiter's pagan 'concilium' (*Aeneid*, 10.2), but its harmony (165, 171) contrast with the 'discordia' of the pagan gods (10.9).

170. Mary is, paradoxically, both spouse of God and queen of heaven, a virgin and mother. Cf. I.Prol.456 and 462. Ireland, *Meroure of Wyssdome*, I, 97, writes similarly of God's 'derrast spous, lady and moder, the virgin glorius'; cf. also *Meroure of Wyssdome*, I, 150.

BOOK X.i; Virgil 10.1–62.

The battle-scenes in this book are considerably expanded, but not from the commentators.

6. *mylky set*. That is, the Milky Way; Virgil (10.3) does not mention it.

11. Virgil 10.5, 'tectis bipatentibus', within the double-doored hall.

18. *Aganys 3our ressonabill oraclys*. Virgil 10.9, —; Ascensius f.297 rb, 'contra placitum & decretum molientibus'.

32. Virgil 10.13, 'Alpis immittet apertas'; *Servius f.297 vb, 'quae ... muri vice tuebantur Italiam'.

43-4. Virgil 10.19, 'namque aliud quid sit, quod iam implorare queamus'; *Ascensius f.298 rb, 'namque ... te alloquor nam quod aliud s. numen aut auxilium sit ...'

58. *nor thame fre of dangar*. Virgil 10.25, —; Ascensius f.298 rb, 'liberari'.

59-60. Virgil 10.26-7, 'muris ... nascentis Troiae'; *Ascensius f.298 rb, 'i. reędificari coeptę'.

64. *into Calabar*. Virgil 10.28, 'Aetolis'; Ascensius f.298 rb, 'in Calabria'.

65. *Diomed*. Virgil 10.29, 'Tydides'; Ascensius f.298 rb, 'Tidei filius Diomedes'.

73. Virgil 10.32, —; Ascensius f.298 va, 'permitto'.

78. Virgil 10.34, 'manis'; Ascensius f.298 va, 'i. inferni'.

84. *Scycilly*. Virgil 10.36, 'Erycino'; Ascensius f.298 va, 'in Sicilia'.

106. *thy nevo*. Virgil 10.47, 'nepotem', which Loeb takes as 'my grandson'; Ascensius f.299 rb has 'meum' and 'tuum' as alternatives.

115. *in Cipyr the cite Amathus*. Virgil 10.51, 'Amathus'; Ascensius f.299 rb, 'civitas illa Cipri'.

137-8. Lacking in Virgil (10.60), but good poetry.

141. Added by Douglas.

X.ii; Virgil 10.62-117

1-96. Juno's speech is expanded from Virgil 10.62-95.

15. *in sport*. Added by Douglas, apparently for the rhyme.

30. *this lady ȝyng*. A most inappropriate addition by Douglas.

31. *ȝister nycht*. Added by Douglas.

38. *pretend tobe kyng*. Virgil 10.75, 'consistere'.

39-40. *god, nymphe*. Virgil 10.76, —; Ascensius f.300 va, 'deus ... nympha'.

51-2. Expanded from Virgil 10.80, 'pacem orare manu'; *Ascensius f.300 va, 'i. indiciis manuum preferendo scilicet ramum olivę: pacem i. concordiam'.

53. *mak reddy for weir*. Virgil 10.80, —; Ascensius f.300 va, 'bellum minari'.

57. *light as lynd*. *Not in Virgil 10.82. Douglas adds this traditional simile (Whiting L 295), probably for the rhyme. Cf. VII.vi.124.

62. '... should we support ...'

64. *as thou allegis*. Added by Douglas.

65. *and quhat iniurys*. Virgil 10.85, —; Ascensius f.300 va, 'que iniuria'.

69–70. An addition by Douglas.

77. *Parys.* Virgil 10.92, —; Ascensius f.301 rb, 'Paris'.

86. Added by Douglas.

90. Virgil 10.93, 'Cupidine'.

97–8. Virgil 10.96, 'talibus orabat Iuno'; *Ascensius f.301 rb, 'i. causas suas defendebat: talibus s. verbis'.

138. Virgil 10.113, 'Stygii per flumina fratris'; Ascensius f.301 va, 'per flumina stygia ... Plutonis'.

X.iii; Virgil 10.118–62

15. *Thybrys.* *Virgil 10.124. MP², the medieval MSS, and Ascensius f.302 r, 'Thybris': P¹RV 'Thymbris'.

17. *Hemon.* *Virgil 10.126. MR¹, the medieval MSS, and Ascensius f.302 r, 'H(a)emon': P 'Thaemon'.

38. *box of tre.* Virgil 10.136, 'buxo', boxwood.

40. *as the geit dois schyne.* Virgil 10.136, —; suggested by Ascensius f.302 va, 'terebynto arbore s. nigra ...' *The simile was traditional (Whiting J 36).

50. *in Lyde cuntre.* Virgil 10.141, —; Ascensius f.302 va, 'Lydia'.

57–8. Virgil 10.145, 'Capys: hinc nomen Campanae ducitur urbi'; Ascensius f.302 va, '... Capua ...'

61–2. Virgil 10.147, 'media ... freta nocte secabat'.

75–6. Virgil 10.152, 'humanis quae sit fiducia rebus'; Ascensius f.303 rb, 'hoc est fragilem esse humanam conditionem cum etiam iusti ab impiis opprimi soleant'.

84. *of the fatys fre.* 'Free of the fate', *i.e.* now having a foreign leader.

89. *as almeral of the flote.* Added by Douglas.

X.iv; Virgil 10.163–214

3. Virgil 10.163, —; Ascensius f.303 rb, 'excitate ... carmina rerum occultarum'.

12. *of hys talent.* Supplied by Douglas for the rhyme.

15. *Tuscane.* Virgil 10.168, —; *Ascensius f.303 va, 'Tusciẹ'.

23–4. Virgil 10.172, 'Populonia mater'; Ascensius f.303 va, 'i. civitas illa ... patria & alumna'.

27. *within the Tuscane see.* Virgil 10.173, —; Ascensius f.303 va, 'adiacens Tusciae'.

28. *steill.* *Virgil 10.174, 'Chalybum ... metallis'; Ascensius f.303 va, 'i. durissimi ferri'.

32. Virgil 10.175, —; *Ascensius f.303 va, 'peritissimus est haruspex … astrologus'.

50. Virgil 10.183, 'Caerete'; Ascensius f.304 rb, 'i. urbe Agilina'.

55. Virgil 10.184, 'intempestae'; Servius f.304 ra, 'sine tranquillitate'; Ascensius f.304 rb, 'pestilentes'.

57. *Cygnus*. Virgil 10.186. *Ascensius f.304 r, 'Cygne' for MSS 'Cinyre' (variously spelt).

60. *suld I be ded*. A not very meaningful addition by Douglas.

66. *al to gay*. Added by Douglas.

70. Virgil 10.190, 'sororum'; Ascensius f.304 va, 'in eas autem finguntur sorores versae'.

77. *in lyknes of a swan*. Virgil 10.192, —; Ascensius f.304 va, 'molli plumi qualem cygni habent'.

78. Douglas's expansion.

81–2. Virgil 10.194 'aequalis comitatus classe cateruas'; *Servius f.305 ra, 'per naues equaliter habens distributas cateruas'. Loeb takes as 'following on ship-board with a band of like age'.

88–90. In Virgil 10.195–7, these lines refer to the centaur-figurehead.

91. *nobill Ocnus*. Virgil 10.198, 'Ocnus'; Ascensius f.304 va, 'nobillissimus'.

93–5. Virgil 10.199, 'fatidicae Mantus et Tusci filius amnis'; *Ascensius f.304 va, 's. nymphae … vaticinantis & amnis Tusci s. Tyberis'.

104. *sobyr*. Not in Virgil (10.202).

112–13. Virgil 10.205–6, 'patre Benaco … Mincius'; *Ascensius f.304 va, 'idest fluvius habens originem ex Baenaco lacu …'

116. *awfull barge*. Virgil 10.206, 'pinu'; Ascensius f.304 va, 'i. navi ex pinu facta'.

124. Added by Douglas.

125. *fludis gray*. Virgil 10.209, 'caerula'.

131–2. Virgil 10.211, 'in pristim desinit alvus'.

138. *bowand bylge of tre*. Douglas's addition.

X.v; Virgil 10.215–86

7. Virgil 10.218, 'ipse'; Ascensius f.305 ra, 'propria manu'.

13. *moder*. Virgil 10.220, —; Ascensius f.305 va, 'mater'.

15. *hand in hand*. Virgil 10.222, 'pariter'.

33–76. Expanded from Virgil 10.229–45.

34. *thy schetis sclaik*. Discussed in Renoir 1956.

36. *fyr and bych tre*. Virgil 10.230, 'pinus'.

185

44. *as we war chaist*. Added by Douglas.

59. Virgil 10.239, —; Ascensius f.306 rb, 'in auxilium misisti'.

77. *with a skyp*. Douglas's addition.

107. Virgil 10.259, 'animos aptent armis ... parent'. Douglas is making a pun. Notice the syllepsis.

116. The description is Douglas's.

120-1. Added by Douglas.

125. *flude of Trace*. Virgil 10.245, —; Servius f.306 ra, 'a fluvio Thraciae'.

145-50. Expanded from Virgil 10.274-5.

175-6. Virgil 10.284, 'audentis Fortuna iuvat'; suggested by *Ascensius f.307 rb, 'quę res in bello saepe probata est'. *The alliterative phrasing recalls Chaucer's *Legend of Good Women*, 1773: 'Hap helpeth hardy man alday'.

X.vi; Virgil 10.287–361

5. *swarffard*. *Glossed by former editors as 'tumultuous', but the word translates 'languentis' (Virgil 10.289). The reference is to spent, weakening waves, and the adjective derives from the verb *swarf*, *swarth*, meaning 'faint, swoon'. Cf. XI.xv.116.

7. *into coggis small*. This detail is Douglas's, *suggested by Servius f.307 vb, 'i. scaphis' on Virgil 10.290, 'remos'.

14. Omits Virgil 10.293 'subito'.

18. *with skyppys*. Added by Douglas.

22. Added by Douglas.

44-5. Virgil 10.307, —; Ascensius f.308 rb, 'quę res eos salvavit'.

50. Virgil 10.310, 'signa canunt'. *Douglas's phrasing recalls Chaucer, *Knight's Tale*, *CT*.I. 2511-12: 'trompes ... / That in the bataille blowen blody sounes'.

58-62. Virgil 10.313-14, 'huic gladio perque aerea suta, per tunicam squalentem auro latus haurit apertum'.

68. The comment is Douglas's.

83. *Greyk*. Virgil (10.325) does not give his race.

94. *forcy as fyry levin*. *Cf. note to VIII.viii.170.

104. 'So that no dart will fly in vain'.

118. Virgil 10.341, 'moribunda'.

139. *cite of Idas*. Virgil 10.351. Idas, as Ascensius f. 309 rb points out, is the father, not the city, so the victims are three fewer than Douglas makes them.

144. *that auld cite*. The explanation is supplied by Douglas.

153–62. Expanded from Virgil 10.356–9.

X.vii; Virgil 10.362–438

15. *suyth as is the creid.* *Proverbial (Whiting C 541), and strikingly anachronistic.

15–16. Virgil 10.367, 'unum quod rebus restat egenis'.

17–47. Expanded from Virgil 10.369–79.

55. *ioggillit.* *This translates Virgil 10.383, 'receptat', tugs at.

66. *Sthenelus.* Virgil 10.388. *The medieval MSS and Ascensius f.310 r, 'St(h)enelum': MP(R), 'Sthenium'.

67. *Prynce of Marrubyanys.* Virgil 10.388, —; *Ascensius f.310 rb, 's. Marrubiorum regis'.

82. Added by Douglas.

102. *ferß as flynt.* A meaningless addition for the sake of the rhyme. *It probably derives from the common alliterative formula indicating great speed: 'as fyre from flint'. Cf. Whiting F 283.1; F 190; and Henryson, *Fables*, 328 and 552.

105–8. Virgil 10.403, 'curruque volutus caedit semianimis Rutulorum calcibus arva'.

125. *Lacon.* Virgil 10.413, 'Ladona'; *Ascensius f.310 v, 'Lacona'.

153. This information is supplied by Douglas.

164–5. Added by Douglas.

190. Added by Douglas.

X.viii; Virgil 10.439–509

2. Virgil 10.439, 'soror alma'; *Ascensius f.311 va, 'i. diva et nympha s. Iuturna'.

33. *quhom thou desyris besyde.* Added by Douglas.

51–2. Virgil 10.459, 'viribus imparibus'.

55–64. Expanded from Virgil 10.460–3.

68. The comment is Douglas's.

69–70. *An expansion of Virgil 10.465, 'lacrimas', perhaps recalling Chaucer, *Prioress's Tale*, CT.VII. 674: 'His salte teeris trikled doun as reyn'.

73–89. Expanded from Virgil 10.467–73.

100. *smyttyn, full of felony.* Added by Douglas.

122–3. Virgil 10.489, —; Ascensius f.313 rb, 'ne screatum aut gemitum viro forti indignum emitteret'.

141–4. Virgil 10.497–8, 'una sub nocte iugali caesa manus iuvenum'; Ascensius f.313

rb–va, 'multitudo iuvenum i. quinquaginta … occisa s. a Danaidibus i. filiabus Danai … sub nocte iugali i. qua primum iuncti erant cum novis nuptis'.

146. *warkman gude.* Virgil 10.499. *Ascensius f.313 r, 'bonus' for MSS 'Clonus'.

163–70. Virgil 10.507–9. *Modern editors punctuate as Virgil's remark; Ascensius f.312 va calls it 'sociorum lamentatio', as it is punctuated in Ascensius f.313 r; Servius f.312 vb gives both possibilities.

X.ix; Virgil 10.510–42

8. *as wod lyon.* Douglas supplies the comparison, *which was common in romance descriptions of knights.

17. *was sa stowt and 3yng.* The epithets are Douglas's.

18. Virgil 10.515, 'Euander'.

24. Added by Douglas.

25. Virgil 10.516, —; Ascensius f.314 rb, 'Ipse capit in huiusmodo ardore'.

27. *the cite.* Added by Douglas.

29. *the flude.* Added by Douglas.

34. The explanation is given by Douglas.

43–58. Expanded from Virgil 10.524–9.

76. *thrynfald Dyane.* Virgil 10.537, 'Triviae'; Ascensius f.314 va, 'i. Dianae'.

78. The explanation is Douglas's.

92. Virgil 10.542, 'rex Gradive'; Ascensius f.314 va, 'id est Mars'.

X.x; Virgil 10.543–605

4. Virgil 10.543, 'instaurant acies'.

16. The comment is Douglas's.

32. Virgil 10. 556, 'inimico pectore'.

53. *kyng of gyandis.* Virgil 10.565, —; Ascensius f.315 va, 'gygas'.

56. Virgil 10.566, —; Ascensius f.315 va, 'in bello giganteo'.

86. Virgil 10.581, —; *Ascensius f.315 va, 'a Diomede … superatus fuisti'.

129. Virgil 10.599–600, 'haud talia dudum dicta dabas'.

130–2. Virgil 10.600, 'Morere et fratrem ne desere frater'.

136. Suggested to Douglas by the previous line.

139. *reddand … large gait.* 'Clearing a wide path'. Douglas much expands the simile

in Virgil 10.603–4. On the sense of *reddand* in this passage, mistakenly glossed in the past as 'making red', see Bawcutt 1971, 52–3; *DOST, red*, v.²

141–2. Added by Douglas.

X.xi; Virgil 10.606–88

12–38. Expanded from Virgil 10.611–20.

15. *that lykis nocht sic bourdis.* Added by Douglas.

26–7. *that our … wald.* Added by Douglas.

39. *imperiall.* *A marginal note in C has 'etherial', which is found in the text of other witnesses, and might seem at first a better translation of Virgil 10.621, 'aetherii'. But *hevyn imperiall* commonly had the sense of 'highest heaven, empyreum' in Scots; see Douglas, *Palice of Honour*, 1878, and note; and *DOST, imperiall*, a.² The gloss in C at this point perhaps indicates authorial hesitation as to which adjective was more appropriate.

41–56. Expanded from Virgil 10.622–7.

45. Virgil 10.622, 'caduco'; Ascensius f.317 rb, 'i. mortali'.

57–64. Expanded from Virgil 10.628–9.

126. *cite.* Virgil 10.655, 'oris'; Ascensius f.317 va, 'civitate'.

167. **fleand paill and wan.* See note to IX.xiii.4.

171. *thocht a thousand tymys I stervit.* Added by Douglas.

175. *sen heir na erth I se.* Not said by Virgil (10.677).

176. Added by Douglas. Cf. Ascensius on 'potius' (676): 'quia terra deest'.

180. *at the warldis end.* Virgil 10.678, —; Ascensius f.318 va, 'ad extrema maris loca'.

200. *Tyll Ardea.* Virgil 10.688, —; Ascensius f.318 va, 'Ardeam'. Douglas omits 'Dauni'.

X.xii; Virgil 10.689–754

6. Virgil 10.690, 'ovantis'; Ascensius f.318 va, 's. de victoria non triumphali'.

12. **thik as haill.* See III.viii.132 and note.

21. Virgil 10.696, —; Ascensius f.319 rb, 'ille dico sic se habens'.

35. *Mynas.* Virgil 10.702. *Ascensius f.319 r, 'Minanta' for MSS 'Mimanta'.

39. *Heccuba.* Virgil 10.705, —; Ascensius f.319 rb, 'Hecuba'.

40. *Dremyt.* Virgil 10.704, —; Ascensius f.319 rb, 'somnians'. *the story tellis thus.* This comment is made by Douglas, *perhaps recalling Chaucer's 'the storie telleth us' (*Troilus and Criseyde*, v.1037), or similar vague appeals to authority in other medieval

narratives.

46. Added by Douglas.

123. Douglas's expansion of the previous line.

148. *Lychåonyus.* Virgil 10.749. *Not taken as a separate person by Ascensius f.320 rb, *pace* Coldwell.

153. *man of Arge.* Virgil 10.751, 'Agis'; *Ascensius f.320 r, 'argis'.

154. *bodyn ... targe.* A common tag; cf. IX.iv.20.

159. *Atronyus.* Virgil 10.753. *Ascensius 1501 f.320 r and Ascensius f.320 va, 'Atronium' for MSS 'at Thronium'.

X.xiii; Virgil 10.755–832

16. Added by Douglas.

21. *all hym allon.* Added by Douglas.

26. *lyke.* Sense misunderstood; Virgil 10.766, pictures Orion as carrying the tree, and is not introducing a new simile.

59. *In Palentyn.* Virgil 10.750, —; *Ascensius f.321 rb, 's. Pallantea'.

111. *ʒond vnder the wald.* Added by Douglas.

166. *or eyß onto thy gost.* Added by Douglas.

173. Virgil 10.831, —; Ascensius f.322 va, 'immorantes levere Lausum'.

X.xiv; Virgil 10.833–908

19. Virgil 10.840, —; Ascensius f.322 va, 'a pugna'.

20. Virgil 10.840, 'maestique ferant mandata parentis'.

32. Virgil 10.845, —; Ascensius f.323 rb, 'non precaturus sed execraturus deos'.

34–65. Expanded from Virgil 10.846–56.

47. Virgil 10.850, —; Ascensius f.323 rb, 'in praecordia'.

105–8. *Virgil 10. 872 (= 12.668) 'Et furiis agitatus amor & conscia virtus' is found in most medieval MSS and in Ascensius f.323 v, but is omitted by modern editors.

126. Virgil 10.879, —; *Ascensius f.324 rb, 'nunc autem quia invitus vivo forte me perdere poteris'.

129. Virgil 10.881, 'desine'; Ascensius f.324 rb, 's. terrere aut minari'.

193–8. Not in Virgil; the marginal note (in CLR) marks 'Additio'.

Prologue XI

This powerful sermon-like Prologue is designed as a Christian equivalent to Aeneas's exhortation to his followers in *Aeneid* 11.14ff: 'Maxima res effecta, uiri; timor omnis abesto'. It has three main sections: the nature of courage in secular warfare (1–55); the spiritual fortitude required of Christians, 'Crystis faithfull knychtis' (56–176); and a short passage, linking the Prologue with the following book, that draws an analogy between Aeneas's 'fatale cuntre of behest' and the promised land 'hecht till Abraham and hys seyd' (177–200). The Prologue is not precisely dated, but, if composed in the spring of 1513 shortly before the battle of Flodden, lines 17–24 might be viewed as oblique advice to James IV not to rush rashly into war (cf. Caughey 2009). The phrasing and imagery draw on medieval chivalric ideals, but more important sources are Aristotle, the Old Testament, St Augustine, and the Epistles of St Paul. The eight-line stanza resembles that used in Prologue VI, but has a different rhyme scheme: *ababbccb⁵*.

3. The euhemeristic conception of the pagan gods – that they originated as heroes, or men of extraordinary abilities – was of great interest to Douglas. For his views, see the marginal commentary to I.i.82, I.ii.3, I.iii.54 and I.vi.1; and for further discussion, Bawcutt 1976, 73–5.

8. 'Let us detest vice and learn virtue'.

10–11. Judas Machabeus, Joshua, and David were the three Old Testament heroes traditionally included in the Nine Worthies. Douglas also mentions them in *Palice of Honour*, 1512, 1525–30, and 1572–4. It was common in the late medieval period for Scots to identify themselves with the 'Maccabees'; see Barbour, *Bruce* I.465–76; Bower, *Scotichronicon* XII.4; and *Complaynt of Scotland* ed. Stewart 1979, 59 and 140. On the historical background, see Goldstein 1993, 145–6.

12–16. On the war in heaven, see Revelation xii.7–11. *Mychael*. The archangel Michael. For the devil as *dragon*, cf. also Dunbar, *Poems*, 10.1.

16. *buge*. Obscure, but probably a kind of long-handled axe.

17–24. The nature of the just war was of great interest to writers in the late Middle Ages. See Douglas's earlier allusion to the subject in *Palice of Honour*, 1964ff.; John Major, *History of Greater Britain*, IV.xv: 'it may be lawful to fight when the cause is just'; and Stephen Hawes, *Pastime of Pleasure*, 3368–74. For a detailed Scottish discussion, deriving from Honoré Bouvet's *L'Arbre des Batailles*, see Gilbert Hay's *The Buke of the Law of Armys*, book IV, in Hay ed. Glenn 2005, II, 93ff. On the philosophical background, see Barnes 1982.

22. *rype*. 'Scrutinize, examine closely'.

29–32. Cf. Psalm cxlvii, 10–11.

33–56. Douglas's ultimate source is Aristotle's *Nichomachean Ethics*, III.6–7, which he may have known in a Latin translation or a vernacular version, such as Nicole Oresme's *Livre de Ethiques d'Aristote* (on this work, see note to I.Prol. 367ff.). It is likely that Douglas was familiar with similar passages in Barbour, *Bruce*, VI.338–60; and Hay, *Law of Armys*, IV.xi (Hay ed. Glenn 2005, II, 110–11).

40. *dolf*. 'Dull, spiritless'. The comparison is more commonly to lead (cf. V.viii.98), and *stane* may owe its presence to the need for a rhyme.

50. *couth he be avyse*. 'If only he could be prudent'.

56. *other chevalry*. The phrase signals the transition to a different type of fortitude.

57. *Crystis faithfull knychtis*. This term is applied to all Christians, but was first used of the apostles. Cf. II Timothy ii.3: 'miles bonus Christi'.

62ff. Cf. I Corinthians ix.25; II Timothy iv.7–8.

68–71. See Matthew xii.30; Mark ix.40; Luke ix.50 and xi.23.

71. *wageour onto Lucifer*. A mercenary soldier in the service of the devil.

73–80. Largely based on the words of St Paul, 'the Apostyll': Ephesians vi.11–12.

73. *armour*. 'Military equipment, both offensive and defensive' (OED). The noun is a collective singular, but here construed as a plural – cf. *beyn thai* (75).

81–96. According to patristic tradition the three enemies of man's soul were the flesh, the world, and the devil. Cf. Dunbar, *Poems*, 21.6–7; *Thre Prestis of Peblis*, 1279–80; Chaucer, *Melibee*, CT.VII, 1421; and *Piers Plowman* C.I.37–8.

84. Cf. Henryson, 'The Paddock and the Mouse', *Fables*, 2959: 'The spreit vpwart, the body precis doun'; and Galatians v.16–17.

98. *Of promyssioun ... the land*. For God's covenant to Abraham and Moses concerning the Promised Land, see Genesis xvii.8; and Deuteronomy xxxiv.4.

99. On the devil's fall from heaven, see lines 12–13 above. Implicit is a reference also to the fall of man.

101–4. The imagery of spiritual armour draws on Ephesians vi.13–17, and I Thessalonians v.8. Faith, hope and charity are the three theological virtues: cf. I Corinthians xiii.13.

102. *onlace*. The sense is not 'unlace', but 'attach by means of a lace' (cf. *DOST*, *lace*, v. sense 1).

108. *on rude was rent*. An alliterative phrase common in references to the Crucifixion. Cf. Henryson, *Prayer for the Pest*, 39; Dunbar, *Poems*, 83.111.

112. 1553 removes the allusion to the Virgin Mary, and substitutes an exhortation to study God's word, *i.e.* the Scriptures: 'And aye vnto his wourd thy mynd be bent'.

120. *cry cok*. 'Confess defeat'. Cf. Dunbar, *Poems*, 65 (*Flyting*), 248.

145–8. The phrasing echoes Chaucer's version of Boethius, *Consolation of Philosophy*, II Prosa 4: 'For in alle adversites of fortune the moost unzeely kynde of contrarious fortune is to han ben weleful'.

151–67. These remarks on free will, merit and grace are theologically orthodox. For some parallels, cf. John Ireland, who frequently discusses the relationship between grace, which originates as a gift of God, and 'werkis of merit': see especially *Meroure of Wyssdome*, I, 48; and II, 130ff. On the background, see Broadie 1990, 68–73.

160. *in arlys of glor*. *Arlys* signifies earnest-money, money given in confirmation of a bargain (*DOST*, *arlis*, n). Here it has a wider figurative sense, 'token, guarantee'.

180. *in rest*. 'Ready for action'. The *rest* for a lance or spear was a fixture on the cuirass or saddle that prevented it from being driven back on impact.

185ff. Coldwell suggested that this passage might refer to *City of God*, xxi.14. J. A. W. Bennett, however, in his review of the edition, identified the precise source in St Augustine's *Sermo ad Catechumenos: de Cataclysmo* (ed. Migne, *Patrologia Latina*, XL. 693): 'Noli esse desertor, nec ut delicatus miles diffluas per voluptates, et te hostis diabolus inermem diffluentemque inveniat: set ut fortis miles, quidquid potes age in hoc bello, ut virtus tua Christus non solum te tueatur, verum etiam alii proficiant ad salutem. Postula a Rege tuo arma spiritualia.' (See Bennett 1967, 312).

199. See 98 and note.

200. *wrocht and bocht*. 'Created and redeeemed'; Cf. X.Prol.20; and Dunbar, *Poems*, 83.98.

BOOK XI.i; Virgil 11.1–58

8. Virgil 11.3, 'funere'; Ascensius f.325 rb, 's. Pallantis'.

9. *the son vpsprent*. Virgil 11.4, 'primo Eoo'; Ascensius f.325 rb, 'i. cum primo ortu solis'.

27. *swerd with evor scawbart fyne*. Virgil 11.11, 'ensem … eburnum'; Ascensius f.325 rb, 'habentem capulum eburnum aut vaginam eburnam'.

62. Virgil 11.26, 'primus'.

72. Added by Douglas. *The word *flottyryt*, 'wet, sodden', is not otherwise found in Scots. Douglas may recall Chaucer's description of the grieving Palamon, 'With flotery berd … ydropped al with teeres' (*Knight's Tale*, CT.I.2883).

75. Virgil 11.31, 'Parrhasio'; Ascensius f.326 rb, 'i. Arcadico' misunderstood.

106–10. Expanded from Virgil 11.47–8 'metuensque moneret acris esse viros, cum dura proelia gente'.

119–24. Expanded from Virgil 11.53–4 'infelix, nati funus crudele videbis! hi nostri reditus exspectatique triumphi?'

129–32. Virgil 11.56–7, 'nec sospite dirum optabis nato funus pater'. Douglas's sense seems to be, 'If he were alive, his father would not have to pray for his death; which the boy would deserve if he had been cowardly; but his conduct was in fact honourable.' Servius has 'quod magis heroicae personae convenit'.

XI.ii; Virgil 11.59–99

10–12. *bot to his estait … se.* Expanded from Virgil 11.63, '… misero sed debita patri'.

13–18. Expanded from Virgil 11.64–5, and made less exact by omitting 'arbuteis'.

20. Virgil 11.66, —; *Ascensius f.327 rb, 'lectos funebres'.

21, 23. Virgil 11.66, 'obtentu frondis'.

39. Virgil 11.73, 'laeta'; *Ascensius f.327 rb, 'cum eius amore capta esset'.

64. Virgil 11.84, —; Ascensius f.327 va, 'trophea'.

74. This detail is added by Douglas.

82–3. Virgil 11.91, 'cetera'; *Ascensius f.327 va, 's. ornamenta ut balteum & paludamentum'.

95–6. *we may nocht … behald and se.* Added by Douglas.

99. *New Troy.* Virgil 11.98–9, 'altos … muros'; *Ascensius f.327 va, 's. Novae Troiae'.

100. *with terys of ennoy.* Douglas's addition.

XI.iii; Virgil 11.100–38

2. *ambassatouris.* Virgil 11.100, 'oratores'; *Ascensius f.328 rb, 'vulgus ambassatores'.

3. Virgil 11.101, 'rogantes'; Ascensius f.328 rb, 'idest gratiam & concessionem'.

12. Omits Virgil 11.105, 'soceris' as Ascensius f.328 rb does in the commentary.

18–43. Expanded from Virgil 11.108–19.

43. Virgil 11.119, 'supponite ignem'.

58. Virgil 11.125, 'caelo'; Ascensius f.328 va, 'i. celestibus diis'.

64. Virgil 11.127, 'haec'; Ascensius f.328 va, 'i. humanitatis tuae indicia'.

76. *sequestrate.* Suggested by Virgil 11.133, 'pace sequestra', *i.e.* under the protection of the truce.

88. *akys.* Virgil 11.138, 'ornos', *i.e.* mountain ash.

XI.iv; Virgil 11.139–81

7. Virgil 11.140, —; Ascensius f.329 rb, 'sermone de morte Pallantis'.

22. *with gret disdene.* Added by Douglas

25. *as his hart wald breke.* Added by Douglas.

27. *with gret difficulte.* *Virgil 11.151, 'vix'; Ascensius f.329 va, 'cum difficultate'.

30–102. Expanded from Virgil 11.152–81.

34. *with harmys at my hart.* Not in Virgil (11.154).

93. *Turnus slauchter*. Virgil 11.178, 'Turnum'; Ascensius f.330 rb, 'id est necem Turni'.

99. Virgil 11.180, —; Ascensius f.330 rb, 'desidero'. 'Only for a moment do I wish to endure here.'

100. Virgil 11.181, —; *Ascensius f.330 rb, 'nuncium de nece Turni'.

XI.v; Virgil 11.182–224

34. Virgil 11.196, —; Ascensius f.330 va, 'infeliciter usi erant cum non prostraverint sed prostrati sint'.

36. Omits Virgil 11.197, 'Morti'.

51–2. Virgil 11.205–6, 'partim finitimos tollunt in agros'.

54. The comment is Douglas's.

59. Omits Virgil 11.209, 'crebris'.

75. *'Whose fathers had been killed'.

76. This is not in Virgil (11.217).

86. *baldly befor the kyng*. Added by Douglas.

91. *gret authoryte*. Virgil 11.223, 'nomen'; Ascensius f.331 va, 'magna auctoritas'.

XI.vi; Virgil 11.225–95

1. Omits Virgil 11.225, 'medio in flagrante tumultu'.

6. Virgil 11.228, 'tantorum impensis operum'.

32. *of thame the gretast man*. Virgil 11.242, —; Ascensius f.332 rb, 'princeps legationis'.

36–7. Virgil 11.243, 'Argivaque castra'; Ascensius f.332 va, 'i. castella ab Argivis in Italia constituta'.

40. Added by Douglas.

44–5. Virgil 11.247, 'Gargani … Iapygis agris'.

46. Virgil 11.247, —; Ascensius f.332 va, 'Apulia'.

65–6. *Douglas mistranslates Virgil 11.259, 'vel miseranda manus', and removes it from the correct position, immediately before the reference to Minerva's constellation.

76. Virgil 11.259, —; Ascensius f.333 rb, 'inimicum & tristitiam efferens'.

77–80. Expanded from Virgil 11.260, 'Euboicae cautes ultorque Caphereus'.

84–5. Virgil 11.262, 'Atrides … Menelaus', one person.

86. Virgil 11.262, 'Protei … columnas'; Ascensius f.333 rb and Servius f.333 vb–334 ra mention their connection with Egypt, but neither suggests they were pyramids. Proteus was king of Egypt at the time of the Trojan War.

92. Virgil 11.264, —; Ascensius f.333 va, 's. Pyrrhi'.

96. Virgil 11.264, —; Ascensius f.333 va, 'ipso pulso'.

97. Virgil 11.265, 'Locros'; Ascensius f.333 va, 'socios Aiacis Oilei'.

98. *waist.* Virgil (11.265) has no epithet.

99. Virgil 11.266, —; Ascensius f.333 va, 'Agamemnon'.

105–6. Expanded from *Virgil 11.268, 'devicta Asia [medieval MSS and Ascensius f.333 r: 'devictam Asiam' MPR] subsedit adulter'.

108. *natyve land.* Virgil 11.269, 'patriis … aris'.

110. *of crymys cleyn.* Virgil 11.270, 'pulchram'; Ascensius f.333 va, 'impollutam adulterio'.

131. Added by Douglas.

143. Added by Douglas.

XI.vii; Virgil 11.296–375

32. Virgil 11.308, —; Ascensius f.335 va, 'cum Diomede in Apuliam'.

50. Virgil 11.316, 'antiquus'; Ascensius f.335 va, 'inutilis mihi'.

52. Virgil 11.317, 'Sicanos'; Ascensius f.335 va, 'i. Sicilienses i. ad Siciliam'.

60. *pynnakillis.* Is this a mistaken translation of Virgil 11.320, 'pinea'?

74. *tymmyr and treis.* Virgil 11.326, 'robore'.

79. *irne.* Virgil 11.329, 'aera'. *warkmen … wrychtis.* Virgil ibid, 'manus'; Ascensius f.336 rb, 'i. operarios'.

80. Virgil 11. 329, *'navalia'; Ascensius f.336 rb, 'atque cetera ad constructionem navium necessaria'.

96. Virgil 11.336, 'infensus'; Ascensius f.336 va, 'molestus Turno'.

102. *dolf as ony led.* The comparison is Douglas's. *See note to V.viii.95.

105–6. Virgil 11.340, 'seditione potens'.

120. *Quhispirand amangis thame.* Virgil 11.345, *'mussant'; Ascensius f.336 va, 'intra dentes murmurant'.

149. Virgil 11.358, —; Ascensius f.337 rb, 'i. metus de Turno … ut non audeamus'.

163. Virgil 11.363, —; *Ascensius f.337 rb, 's. Laviniam'.

169. *gud broder.* Added by Douglas.

189. Virgil 11.372, 'nos animae viles'.

191. That is, '*un*-bewailed'.

197–8. The lines are Douglas's invention.

XI.viii; Virgil 11.376–444

10. Added by Douglas.

35. Virgil 11.392, 'pulsus ego?'; *Ascensius f.338 rb, 'dicisne quod ego pulsus sum?'

45. *his brother*. This information comes from Douglas.

46. Virgil 11.396, 'experti'; *Ascensius f.338 rb, 'experti sunt me haud id est non ita id est talem ut pulsum dicas'.

55. Virgil 11.400, 'proinde'; Ascensius f.338 rb, 'quia sine ratione loqueris'.

57. Virgil 11.400–1, 'magno … metu'.

65. *Diomedes*. Virgil 11.404, —; Ascensius f.338 va, 'Diomedes'; cf. line 126 (Virgil 11.428).

67. Omits Virgil 11.405, 'Hadriacas'.

93. *in this extreme neid*. Added by Douglas.

120. Virgil 11.426, 'melius'; Ascensius f.339 rb, 'i. meliorem exitum quam incepta sint'.

142. *efter Drances menyng*. Virgil 11.435, —; Ascensius f.339 va, 'quantum Drances dicit'.

144. Added by Douglas.

157. *the quhilk sa weil I lufe*. Virgil 11.440, —; Servius f.339 vb, 'bene sibi & favorem'.

166. Virgil 11.443–4, —; Ascensius f.339 va, 'solus Turnus vocetur quia praestantius geret Turnus onus belli'.

XI.ix; Virgil 11.445–85

4. *to the town*. Virgil 11.446, 'aciem'.

6. *as he war chaist*. Added as a graphic touch by Douglas.

23. *febill and agyt*. Virgil 4.454, —; Ascensius f.340 rb, 'seniores'.

43–6. Virgil 11.463–4, 'Tu, Voluse, armari Volscorum edice maniplis, duc … et Rutulos'; *Ascensius f.340 va, 'i. impera & precipe maniplis pro manipulis i. manipularibus hoc est signiferis militibus armari'.

76. Virgil 11.476, —; Ascensius f.341 rb, 'omnis sexus & aetatis'.

81. *Born in hir char*. Virgil 11.478, 'subvehitur'.

98. *that we that sycht may se*. Added by Douglas.

XI.x; Virgil 11.486–531

1. *als fers as ony gleid.* Virgil 11.486, 'furens'. *See note to II.iii.55.

3. Virgil 11.486, 'certatim'; *Ascensius f.341 rb, 'certatim i. cum certamine ipsorum armantium'.

14–15. *A free translation of Virgil 11.491, 'exultatque animis', already rendered more literally in lines 12–13. *Pyn* means 'pin', not 'pain' or 'labour', as glossed by earlier editors. The word forms part of an idiomatic phrase, first recorded in Chaucer's *Merchant's Tale*, CT.IV.1516: 'Youre herte hangeth on a joly pyn!' The sense is 'be in high spirits', and often connotes foolish elation (Bawcutt 1971, 53–4).

27. Added by Douglas.

42. Taking Virgil 11.505, 'manu' in senses of 'hand' and 'band'.

54–6. Expanded from Virgil 11.509–10, 'sed nunc ... mecum partire laborem'.

57. Added by Douglas.

XI.xi; Virgil 11.532–96

1. *Dyan.* *Virgil 11. 534, 'Latonia'; *Ascensius f.342 va, 'Latonae filia Diana'.

3. *nymphe.* Virgil 11.532, —; Ascensius f.342 va, 'nympham'.

11. Added by Douglas.

16. Virgil 11.536, —; *Ascensius f.342 va, 'scil. antiqua & inveterata'.

19–20. *for the cruelte Of his pepill.* Loeb takes Virgil 11.539, 'virisque superbas' as referring to Metabus; *Ascensius f.342 va adds 'civium aut aemulorum'.

20. Omits Virgil 11.541, 'inter proelia belli'.

47. *Weill ybaik.* Virgil 11.553, 'robore cocto'.

58. *knyt to thy schaft.* Virgil 11.558–9, 'tua prima ... tela tenens', which Loeb (2nd ed) takes as 'yours is the first weapon that she clasps'; Douglas's translation is justified by *Ascensius f.343 va, 'tela i. iacula tibi sacra'.

75. *thrynfald Dyane.* Virgil 11.566, 'Triviae'; Ascensius f.343 va, 'Dianae'; cf. XI.xvi.10 (Virgil 11.836).

77. *Virgil 11.567, 'non illum tectis ullae, non moenibus urbes'; Ascensius f.343 v, 'non illum tectis: non ullae ...'; Ascensius f.343 va distinguishes between 'privatis' and 'publicis hospitiis'.

105. *Trace.* Virgil 11.580, 'Strymoniam'; *Ascensius f.344 rb, 'i. Threiciam'.

125. *thir dartis.* Virgil 11.590, 'haec'; Ascensius f.344 rb, 'scil. tela'.

136. Virgil 11.594, 'tumulo'.

140. *clowd.* Virgil 11.596, 'turbine'.

XI.xii; Virgil 11.597–647

14. Virgil 11.603, 'Messapus'.

15. *agill*. Virgil 11.603, 'celeres'; Ascensius f.344 va, 'agiles'.

16. *Catyllus*. Virgil 11.604, 'fratre'; Ascensius f.344 va, 'scil. Catillo'.

17–18. Expanded from Virgil 11.604, 'et virginis ala Camillae'.

37–8. *Tuscane, Rutilyane*. Added by Douglas.

87. *Troiane*. Virgil 11.636, —; Ascensius f.345 va, 'Tuscus'.

92. *als fers as flynt*. Virgil 11.638, 'arduus'. *See note to X.vii.102.

95. Virgil 11.640, 'Catillus'; *Ascensius f.345 va, 'frater s. Core'.

103. Virgil 11.644, 'tantus in arma patet'.

XI.xiii; Virgil 11.648–724

6. *cut and brynt away*. Virgil 11.649, 'exserta'; Ascensius f.346 rb, 'abcisam, aut exustam'.

11. *Turcas*. Nothing in Virgil (11.652) justifies this. *Late medieval authors frequently refer to Turkish bows, which were then very highly esteemed. Camilla is perhaps said to carry one, because of her link with (or comparison to?) the Amazons, who were believed to have lived in an area south of the Black Sea later associated with the Turks. Another Scottish poem, Weddirburn's 'In Praise of Women' (*Bannatyne Manuscript* 1928–32, III, 328), devotes a stanza to the Amazon Queen Penthesilea, who likewise carries 'ane bow torques [Turkish]'.

20. Virgil 11.656, 'aeratam … securim'.

39. *Ewmenyus*. Virgil 11.666. *Ascensius f.346 r, 'Eumenium', for MSS 'Eun(a)eum'.

40. *Clysius*. Virgil 11.666. *Ascensius f.346 r, 'Clycio', for MSS 'Clytio'.

48. *Pegasyus*. Virgil 11.670. *Ascensius f.346 r, 'Pegasum', for MSS 'Pagasum'.

65. *Apulȝe*. Virgil 11.678, 'Iapyge'; Ascensius f.346 va, 'i. Appulo'.

70. *bustuus powis*. This detail is not in Virgil (11.681).

108–9. Virgil (11.699) does not go into such detail.

111. Virgil 11.700, 'filius Auni'; Ascensius f.347 va, 'Aunus filius Auni'.

128. *Leif thy swyft steid*. Virgil 11.706, 'dimitte fugam'; Ascensius f.347 va, 'i. equum fugae praesidium'.

149–56. Expanded from Virgil 11.715–17.

165. *happy goishalk*. Virgil 11.721, 'sacer ales'.

174. *vp to the skyis*. Virgil 11.724, 'ab aethere'.

XI.xiv; Virgil 11.725–67

28. Virgil 11.735, 'tela inrita'; Ascensius f.348 va, 'idest inutilia nobis cum fugiamus omnes unam feminam'.

69. Virgil 11.756, 'luctantem'.

77. Virgil 11.759, 'Maeonidae'; Ascensius f.349 rb, 'i. Lydii'.

82. Virgil 11.759, —; Ascensius f.349 rb, 'destinatus fataliter ad mortem'.

85. Virgil 11.760, 'multa prior arte', which Loeb (2nd ed) takes as 'deep cunning'; Ascensius f.349 rb, 'id est subtilitate honesta'.

98. *payß*. Virgil 11.765, 'habenas', *i.e.* reins.

XI.xv; Virgil 11.768–831

1–2. *Choreus.* Virgil 11.768, 'Chloreus'; *Ascensius f.349 v, 'choreus'. *of gret estait … consecrat.* Added by Douglas.

11. *brovne sangwane.* Virgil 11.772, 'ferrugine'; Ascensius f.349 va, 'purpura'.

13. *wrocht in Creyt.* Virgil 11.773, 'Gortynia'; Ascensius f.350 rb, 'Cretenses'.

14. Virgil 11.773, 'Lycio cornu'.

15. *clattryng by hys schuldir.* Virgil 11.774, 'ex umeris erat'; *Ascensius f.349 v, 'ex humeris sonat'.

16. *cays.* Virgil 11.774, —; Ascensius f.350 rb, 'auro tectus' misunderstood?

18. Virgil 11.775, 'croceam'.

38. Added by Douglas.

45. *smok of sens.* Virgil 11.786, —; Ascensius f.350 va, 'incensum'.

XI.xvi; Virgil 11.832–67

18. *and that is syn.* Added by Douglas.

34. *to Dyane dedicate.* Added by Douglas.

64. *almaste ontil hir eyr.* Added by Douglas.

XI.xvii; Virgil 11.868–915

14. *'With their weapons once made an attempt to stop the Trojans'.

16. Added by Douglas.

50. *with thar hedis.* Virgil 11.890, —; Ascensius f.352 va, 'capitibus suis'.

53. Virgil 11.891, 'summo certamine', which Loeb takes as 'in keenest rivalry'; *Servius

f.353 ra, 'Extremo discrimine ut supra Vocatque labor ultimus omnes'.

99. *occeane*. Virgil 11.913, 'Hibero'; Ascensius f.353 va, 'oceano'.

Prologue XII

There is no false modesty in Douglas's own characterization of this prologue as a 'lusty crafty preambill, perle of May' (307). It is remarkable for its rhetorical catalogues, the jewelled artifice of its style and imagery, the Latinate character of much of its diction, and the presentation of the natural world in terms of classical mythology. It abounds in reminiscences of poets whom Douglas particularly admired: Virgil, Ovid, Chaucer, and Henryson. There are also many echoes, in a Virgilian manner, of his own earlier work, the Prologue to *The Palice of Honour*: see notes to lines 40, 60, 61–72, 133–4, 165, and 244. The very richness of descriptive detail has sometimes obscured the structure of the Prologue. It is primarily a hymn of praise to the sun, and celebrates the rebirth of the world in spring, and the fecundity of 'kynd', or nature (154, 230), in a highly idealized portrait of the month of May. The last section (267–310) is different in tone: conversational and humorous, it provides a transition to book XII and the completion of the translator's task. Recent criticism includes: Blyth 1970; Starkey 1973–4; Bawcutt 1976, 175–80; Nitecki 1981; Fowler 2005; Parkinson 2005; and Leahy 2016.

1–50. A particularly elaborate example of the astronomical opening, or *chronographia*, popular with late medieval poets. See Eade 1984, 166–8.

1. *Dyonea*. 'Daughter of Dione', i.e. Venus, viewed as both goddess and planet.

4–5. Douglas echoes Chaucer, *Complaint of Mars*, 113ff.: 'Now fleeth Venus unto Cilenios tour, / With voide cours, for fere of Phebus lyght … / Within the gate she fledde into a cave'. *Cylenyus* is a name for Mercury, who was born on Mount Cyllene, and the *cave* refers to Mercury's zodiacal house, Gemini.

6. An allusion to Chaucer, *Complaint of Mars*, 130–1, in which Mars pursues Venus 'for al his hevy armure'.

7–10. Saturn was the most baleful of the planets, astrologically, and his absence is propitious. The epithet 'frawart' is also applied to him in VII.Prol.29.

11–12. Nyctimene was changed into an owl by Minerva, as a punishment for incest with her father. Douglas follows closely the account by Ovid in *Metamorphoses* II, especially lines 593–5: 'avis illa quidem, sed conscia culpae / conspectum lucemque fugit tenebrisque pudorem / celat'.

13–20. This dawn description owes several details, such as Aurora's 'safron bed' and the hall 'spred all with rosys', to *Aeneid* 4.584–5, and Ovid, *Metamorphoses* II.112–14. *Tytan*. For this unclassical form of the name of Aurora's lover Tithonus, see note to IV.xi.2.

22. *gold and asur.* The collocation, repeated in line 294, occurs in a similarly height-ened passage in Dunbar's *Goldyn Targe* (*Poems*, 59.41). Azure, or lapis lazuli, was the most precious pigment used in illuminating manuscripts, and signified deep blue in heraldic terminology.

23–4. Cf. Ovid, *Metamorphoses* II.401: 'ingentia moenia caeli'.

25–7. Eous was the second of the four horses who drew the chariot of the sun. Douglas alludes to *Metamorphoses* II.153–4, and also echoes line 30 in his own *Palice of Honour*.

27. *soyr.* 'Reddish-brown'. Henryson employed the same unusual word in describing the sun's steed 'Eoye' (*Testament of Cresseid*, 211). *brovn as berry.* Cf. the Monk's palfrey, 'broun as is a berye' (Chaucer, *CT*.I. 207).

29. Cf. Ovid, *Metamorphoses* II.84–5: 'ignibus illis … naribus efflant'.

30. *Pheton.* Phaëthon, the rash son of the sun god, whose disastrous course through the heavens is described in *Metamorphoses* II.150ff. There is possibly an echo of Chaucer, *Squire's Tale, CT*.V.671.

33. *the blesand torch of day.* Cf. Chaucer, *Complaint of Mars*, 27: 'Phebus with his firy torches rede'.

37. *chrisolyte or topace.* The comparison to chrysolite may have been suggested by Ovid, *Metamorphoses* II.109–10; hair is also compared to topaz in Douglas, *Palice of Honour*, 463.

38. Cf. *Metamorphoses* II.22–3.

39. Cf. *Complaint of Mars*, 95–6, where Chaucer says of Mars, not (as here) Phoebus: 'from his eyen tweyne / The firi sparkes brosten out'.

40. *purge the ayr.* Cf. *Palice of Honour*, 56.

44. *sweit as sens.* 'Sweet as incense'. Cf. the earlier use in VII.viii.28.

46. *stovys.* 'Warm vapours'.

53. The phrasing is very similar to XIII.viii.30 and 32.

55–8. Douglas here much elaborates a line from Chaucer's *Parliament of Fowls*, 189: 'With fynnes rede and skales sylver bryghte'. He adds movement, and distinctive details, such as the chisel-shaped tails, and the comparison to cinnabar, a reddish mineral used for illuminating manuscripts.

60. *beriall strandis.* Cf. *Palice of Honour*, 53 and 1150.

61–72. A similar fascination with reflected light is evident in *Palice of Honour*, 40–2; and Dunbar's *Goldyn Targe* (*Poems* 59, 32–3). It may perhaps be traced to Ovid, *Metamorphoses* II.110: 'clara repercusso reddebant lumina Phoebo'.

73–6. This passage recalls, but re-orders Virgil, *Georgics* II.330–4: 'Zephyrique tepen-tibus auris / laxant arva sinus … nec metuit surgentis pampinus Austros / aut actum caelo magnis Aquilonibus imbrem'.

77. *beris new brerd.* 'Barley's new growth'.

81. *Ceres*, goddess of agriculture; *Pryapus*, god of gardens. Both are fertility deities.

91–4. This closely follows *Georgics* II.201–2: 'et quantum longis carpent armenta diebus / exigua tantum gelidus ros nocte reponet'.

99–100. The absence of the vine and the olive (cf. line 165) from Britain is noted by John Major in his *History of Greater Britain*, I.3, (Major trans. Constable 1892, 12 and 15).

102. *naturis tapestreis*. Echoing *Palice of Honour*, 20.

113ff. The catalogue of flowers is highly idealized – 'ane paradyce it semyt' (149) – but includes close observation of humble flowers, such as the dandelion (119).

113. 'The daisy put on display (*onbreid*) her small coronet'. Douglas recalls Chaucer's celebration of this flower in *The Legend of Good Women*, 218–19: 'ryght as a dayesye / Ycorouned ys with white leves lyte'.

122. Cf. Henryson, 'The Lion and the Mouse', *Fables*, 1336: 'The prymeros and the purpour viola'.

124. *vermel*. The brilliant red pigment vermilion. Cf. 'the vermel rosys red' in XII.ii.40.

133–4. Cf. *Palice of Honour*, 11–12, where Flora's bed is 'powderit with mony a set / Of Ruby, Topas, Perle and Emerant'.

142–8. *Hailsum ... spicery ... electuary ... Seroppis*. Douglas echoes words from Henryson's portrait of Mercury in *Testament of Cresseid*, 246–9, in order to evoke the garden's exotic and health-giving fragrance.

145. *sewane*. Coldwell glosses as 'spice'; *DOST* suggests, rather improbably, that this may be a variant of *sowan*, a Scottish term for a food resembling porridge. But the word seems more likely to represent a variant spelling of *savin* or *savine*, an evergreen herb or shrub with a strong scent (see *MED*, *OED*). This might have had Virgilian associations for Douglas, since it is mentioned in *Culex*, 404 ('herba ... sabina'), in a list of sweet-smelling plants, and is compared to frankincense.

148. *aloes*. Not here the bitter plant, but a fragrant resin, mentioned in the Song of Songs iv.14, and Proverbs vii.16.

152. *rysp and redis*. A common alliterative phrase. Cf. *Eneados* II.ii.142; X.ii.54; and Dunbar, *Goldyn Targe*, 56.

152–68, and 231–51. Cf. the list of birds in VII.Prol.105–25. Such bird-catalogues were traditional in descriptions of spring. Cf. Chaucer, *Romaunt of the Rose*, 655ff. and *Parliament of Fowls*, 330–64. There is a later parallel in *The Complaynt of Scotland* ed. Stewart 1979, 31.

155. *Phebus red fowle*. Cf. VII.Prol.113. The cock is associated with Phoebus, because he crows at sunrise. For his coral crest, cf. Chaucer's Chauntecleer: 'His coomb was redder than the fyn coral' (*Nuns' Priest's Tale*, CT.VII. 2859).

159. *Coppa*. The hen's name might also be read as *Toppa* (so previous editors); for similar variants in Henryson, see *Coppok / Toppok* in *Fables*, 483 (and Fox's excellent note). But in medieval literary tradition the form of the name with initial C is well evidenced, and occurs in several works that Douglas is likely to have read: 'Coppa' is

found in Gower's *Vox Clamantis*, I.545; and 'Coppen' and 'Coppe' occur in Caxton's *Reynard the Fox*, cap. v and vi, where they correspond to French 'Copee' in *Roman de Renart*. 'Coppok' and 'Copok' likewise occur as hens' names in *Colkelbie Sow*, 925, and *The Talis of the Fyve Bestes*, 163. *Pertelot*. This might also be read as *Partelot*, but in view of the Chaucerian context, the spelling of the name employed in *The Nuns' Priest's Tale* seems more likely.

161–4. Cf. Lydgate, *Troy Book* II.2588: 'With Argus eyen enprented in his tail'. Juno punished the giant Argus for his failure to guard Io by placing his hundred eyes in her peacock's tail. The story is told in Ovid, *Metamorphoses* I.622–723.

162. *quheill rym*. Perhaps a proverbial image for the peacock's tail. Cf. *Deidis of Armorie* ed. Houwen 1994, I, 36: 'he dressis wp his tail to mak a quheill'.

165. This line is identical with *Palice of Honour*, 81.

169–72. *Aragne*, or Arachne, angered Athene by competing with her in weaving, and was transformed into a spider; see Ovid, *Metamorphoses* VI.1–145.

174. *Corby*. A common name for the raven.

184. *tayt and tryg*. 'Lively and nimble'. Henryson uses the phrase of mice, not lambs (*Fables*, 1411).

187–8. *Doryda … Thetis*. Doris and her mother Thetis were sea nymphs; *Naedes*. The Naiads were freshwater nymphs.

191. *flowris quhite and red*. A common poetic phrase, but cf. Henryson's use in 'The Lion and the Mouse', 1328.

197–200. Possibly the incipits of love songs. Cf. Bawcutt 2006, 180–2.

202. *ioly wo*. Cf. IV.Prol.5, and note.

209–30. This section strikingly departs from the otherwise idealized picture of the season, and resembles IV.Prol.186–93. The dialogue anticipates Lindsay's *Complaynt*, 237–52.

229. Cf. 'The sesoun priketh every gentil herte' (*Knight's Tale*, 1043).

231. Cf. Dunbar, *Goldyn Targe* (*Poems* 59.8): 'hevyns menstrale'.

234–6. The *merl*, or blackbird, is often coupled with the *mavys*, or thrush, in Scottish verse; cf. Holland, *Howlat*, 712; Henryson, *Fables*, 1338, and Dunbar, *Poems*, 52.164 and 169.

237. *crowdis*. 'Coos', an imitative term for the song of the wood pigeon or ring dove.

244. The line is almost identical with *Palice of Honour*, 1152.

249. *lawdis*. 'Praise', with a further allusion to the service of Lauds, usually sung at dawn. Douglas was probably aware of the stock medieval etymology of Latin *alauda*, 'lark'. See note to XIII.Prol.167–8.

252–66. The birds' song of praise provides a rhetorical summing-up of earlier themes. Structurally, it resembles the bird song that ends Chaucer's *Parliament of Fowls*. With the sustained *repetitio* on 'Welcum', cf. Dunbar, *Poems*, 22 and 56.

266. *sluggardy*. This word introduces the final section of the Prologue, which resembles the transitional passages in Prologues VII and VIII. It implies Douglas's sense of procrastination over the translation, and lightly alludes also to the theme of sluggardy in love and failure of 'observance' (288–90) that is voiced in Dunbar's *Thrissill and the Rose* (*Poems*, 52) and other poems celebrating May.

268. It is daybreak on 9 May. The apparent precision of date and hour (see line 279) may be factual; compare *The Tyme, space and dait*, 1–4. Coldwell found 'no special significance to the day', but it is noteworthy that two other Scottish poems, the anonymous *Quare of Jelusy* and Dunbar's *Thrissill and the Rose* are similarly dated on 9 May (see note to Dunbar, *Poems*, 52.188–9).

282–5. The tragic tale of Philomela, raped by Tereus, the husband of her sister Procne, was well known in the Middle Ages. According to Ovid's version of the myth in *Metamorphoses* VI.424–674, Philomela was changed into a nightingale and Procne to a swallow. Cf. Douglas's allusions in *Palice of Honour*, 569 and XIII.Prol.61–3.

286–7. Aesacus, who pursued the nymph Hesperia, was turned into a *mergus*, a word usually translated as 'diver'; but when Douglas alluded to the story in *Palice of Honour*, 1204–6, he called the bird a *skarth*, or cormorant. Douglas knew Ovid's telling of the story in *Metamorphoses* XI.761–95, and the word *pennance* directly alludes to Ovid's 'piget, piget' (778).

288. *Peristera*. An attendant on the goddess of love who was changed into a dove by Cupid. Her story is not told in Ovid's *Metamorphoses*, but Douglas could have found it in Boccaccio's *De Genealogia Deorum*, III.xx. Boccaccio remarked that doves are birds that have frequent coitus, and Douglas similarly calls them 'wanton' (301). Doves are regularly associated with Venus in art and literature. Cf. *Eneados* VI.iii.63ff.

298. Douglas perhaps recalls Song of Songs ii.12: 'The voice of the turtle is heard in our land'. *I come hydder to wow*. According to Ruddiman (s.v. *Wow*), 'Words which the vulgar fancy to themselves are uttered by the dove'. Small (IV, 243) suggested a connection with a song published in *The Harp of Renfrewshire* (Paisley, 1872), p. liii, that has a similar refrain. But this poem is thought to be a nineteenth-century composition, and is unlikely to have been known to Douglas.

304. *ayr morow*. 'Early morning'.

307–10. This passage forms a kind of envoi to the prologue.

309–10. *with gold … illumnyt*. Douglas here employs a eulogistic topos popular in the late medieval period. Cf. Dunbar's praise of Bernard Stewart, 'Quhoise knyghtli name … /For wourthines in gold suld writtin be' (*Poems*, 56.94–5); and Lydgate's comment that the name of the Roman hero Marcus Manlius ought 'With goldene lettres to been enlumyned' (*Fall of Princes*, IV.371); see also his remarks on Marcus Regulus (*Fall of Princes*, V.821). Dunbar and Lydgate were commending people; it was less common to use the device, as here, to praise the style of a literary work. Expensive manuscripts, however, were quite literally 'illumnyt' with gold; cf. Dunbar's 'bright buke … With mony lusty letter ellummynit with gold' (*Poems*, 3.424–5); and the various references in *The Treasurer's Accounts* to the purchase of

205

gold leaf for the Scottish artist Thomas Galbraith, who illuminated the peace treaty with England in 1502 (Apted and Hannabuss 1978, 40-1). For Douglas's use of the contrasted topos of 'sable' letters, see also VII.Prol.167 and note.

BOOK XII.i; Virgil 12.1-53.

Virgil's fifty-three lines are expanded to one hundred and thirty-two.

4. **tofor onbrokyn*. Douglas correctly translates 'infractos' (Virgil 12.1) as 'Irk … faill' (line 2), but adds a gloss deriving from Servius 'infractos intelligi non fractos olim' (cited by Ascensius f.354 rb)

12. Added by Douglas.

13. *in Trace*. Virgil 12.4, 'Poenorum'.

20. Virgil 12.7, 'fixum [*i.e.* a dart] latronis' misunderstood.

21. *Hym to revenge*. Added by Douglas. *It resembles Servius *auct.* on Virgil 12.6 (ed. Thilo, 2. 575), 'gaudetque': 'gaudetque spe ultionis'; but this could not have been known to Douglas.

32. Virgil 12.13, 'congredior'.

36. **banyst of Asya*. The marginal note *forhowar*, 'one who forsakes' (C, L, B) seems a more accurate translation of Virgil 12.15, 'desertorem Asiae'.

45. *sad and degest mynd*. Virgil 12.18, 'sedato … corde'.

57-8. *Virgil 12.23, 'aurumque animusque Latino est', applying 'animus' to Latinus; Ascensius f.354 v reads 'animusque aurumque Latino', explaining Douglas's taking 'animus' – as does Ascensius f.355 rb – with Turnus.

58. *Liberall and fre*. Virgil 12.23, —; Ascensius f.355 rb, 'liberalis & beneficus'.

64. Added by Douglas.

67. *prent*. Virgil 12.26, 'hauri'; Ascensius f.355 rb, 'i. animaduerte & pondera'.

74. Virgil 12.29, 'cognato sanguine'; Ascensius f.355 rb, 's. sanguini conjugis s. Amatae'.

96. **war … war*. Virgil 12.38, 'if it so were that Turnus were dead and buried'.

113-14. Virgil 12.46, 'aegrescitque medendo'.

126. Virgil 12.52, 'illi'; Ascensius f.356 rb, 'saeuissimo & iniquissimo hosti …'

XII.ii; Virgil 12.54-112

11. *myne awyn knycht*. A medieval touch added by Douglas.

53-6. Virgil 12.74, 'neque enim Turno mora libera mortis'; Servius f.356 vb adds 'venientibus fatis'.

79. Virgil 12.83, —; Ascensius f.357 rb, 'Orithei regis Athenarum filia'.

82. Virgil 12.83, —; Ascensius f.357 rb, 'atavum Turni'.

93. Added by Douglas.

96. *quhitly alcomy.* Virgil 12.87, 'alboque orichalco'; *Ascensius f.357 rb, 'i. illo genere metali albo'.

127. *on hys wifly maner.* Virgil 12.99, —; *Ascensius f.357 va, 'effeminati'.

130. Virgil 12.101, —; Ascensius f.357 va, 'ut hastam alloqueretur'.

137. The colour is added to the scene by Douglas.

145–6. *furour, bellicall.* Virgil 12.108, 'Martem'; Ascensius f.358 rb, 'furorem bellicum'.

152. Added by Douglas.

XII.iii; Virgil 12.113–60

8. Virgil 12.117, 'parabant'.

19. Virgil 12.120, 'verbena'; Ascensius f.358 rb, 'i. herba aut fronde sacra'.

22. The explanation is provided by Douglas.

34. *Virgil 12.127, 'genus Assarici Mnestheus', which Loeb takes as one person; Ascensius f.358 va, 'duo filii eius & …'

48. *flowris.* This comes from Douglas.

102. *Virgil 12.158, 'excute'.

XII.iv; Virgil 12.161–221

2. Virgil 12.162, taking 'procedunt castris' from 12.169, as the parentheses in Ascensius f.359 v '(ingenti … Romae)' and in Ascensius's interpretation (f.359 va) justify.

3. *four quhelit.* Virgil 12.162, 'quadriiugo', four-horsed, correctly translated in line 4. A similar error appears in lines 11–12, in translating Virgil 12.164, 'bigis'.

5–9. Virgil 12.163–4, 'aurati bis sex radii fulgentia cingunt Solis avi specimen'.

13–14. *in athir hand, the braid hed.* For Virgil's (12.165) 'bina manu … hastilia', *i.e.* two spears in one hand.

23–4. *quhamto accordyt mak … contract.* Virgil 12.169, —; *Servius f.360 ra, 'vestis qua festis diebus uti consueuerant sacra celebraturi'.

31. Virgil 12.172, 'illi'; Ascensius f.360 rb, 'i. qui foedus percussuri sunt reges'.

44. *on land and see.* Added by Douglas.

49. *Mars.* Virgil 12.179, 'Mavors'; Ascensius f.360 rb, 'i. Mars', as in XII.vi.53 (Virgil 12.332), Ascensius f.364 rb.

53–8. Expanded from Virgil 12.181–2.

57. Virgil 12.182, —; *Ascensius f.360 rb, 'inferorum'.

67-8. Virgil 12.187, 'sin nostrum adnuerit nobis Victoria Martem'; Ascensius f.360 va, 'si noster Mars annuerit nobis victoriam'.

96. Virgil 12.198, —; *Ascensius f.360 va, 's. Apollinem & Dianam'.

99–100. Virgil 12.199, 'duri sacraria Ditis'; *Ascensius f.260 v, 'diri …'; Ascensius f.360 va, 'loca execrabilia Ditis i. Plutonis diri id est immanis et immitis'.

99. *blak as sabill.* Whiting S 1.

113. Virgil 12.205, 'diluvio'; Ascensius f.361 rb, 'i. inundantia'.

114. Virgil 12.205, 'miscens'; Ascensius f.361 rb, 'i. confundens ea elementa'.

116. Added by Douglas.

130. Virgil 12.210, 'aere decoro'; *Ascensius f.361 rb, 'i. oricalcho [*sic*]'.

142. Virgil 12.215, 'oneratis lancibus'.

150. Added by Douglas.

159–60. Virgil 12.221. *MPR¹, most medieval MSS, and Ascensius f.361 v, 'pubentes'; a few medieval MSS, 'tabentes'; Ascensius f.361 va has both readings.

XII.v; Virgil 12.222–310

11–12. Virgil 12.226, 'ipse acerrimus armis'.

27. Added by Douglas.

42. Added by Douglas.

47. *Omits Virgil 12.240, 'ipsi Laurentes mutati ipsique Latini', as does Ascensius f.362 r. The sense is partly picked up in line 50.

54. *inequale.* Virgil 12.243, 'iniquam'.

62. *fals demonstratioun.* Virgil 12.246, 'monstro'; *Ascensius f.362 rb, 'monstratione falsi augurii'.

91. Virgil 12.258, 'expediuntque manus'; Ascensius f.362 va, 'i. ad pugnam aptant'.

97. Virgil 12.260, 'adgnoscoque deos'; *Ascensius f.362 va, 'favorem deorum erga nos'.

110. Virgil 12.265, 'regem defendite raptum' gives a somewhat different sense.

116. Virgil 12.268, 'certa'; Ascensius f.362 va, 'i. inevitabilis'.

160. Added by Douglas.

165. Virgil 12.286, 'pulsatos … divos'.

184–5. Virgil 12.294, 'telo trabali'.

188. *Ha, art thou hyt?* Virgil 12.296, —; Ascensius f.363 rb, 'percussus est'.

211–12. Virgil 12.306, —; Ascensius f.363 va, 'ubi fugere amplius non poterat'.

214. *akwartly strake.* Virgil 12.308, 'disicit'.

221. Added by Douglas.

XII.vi; Virgil 12.311–82

1. *reuthfull and pacient.* Virgil 12.311, 'pius'.

2. Added by Douglas.

17. *ferm and stabill.* Virgil 12.317, 'firma'; Ascensius f.364 rb, 'i. stabilia'.

20. *to me ded.* Virgil 12.317, 'mihi'; Ascensius f.364 rb, 'i. caput Turni aut vitam eius'.

24. **the bayn.* 'Thigh bone', a detail unspecified by Virgil 12.319. But see later XII. xii.127–9.

42–3. Added by Douglas.

54. *in Traß.* Virgil 12.331, —; Ascensius f.364 va, 'fluvii in Thracia'.

62. *swyftest wyndis tway.* Virgil 12.334, —; Ascensius f.364 va, 'rapidissimos ventos'.

66–8. Virgil 12.335–6, 'atrae Formidinis ora Iraeque Insidiaeque'.

69. Virgil 12.337, 'talis … alacer'.

79. *Sthelenus.* Virgil 12.341. *Ascensius f.364 r, 'Sthelenum' for MSS 'Sthenelum'.

84. *Iasus.* Virgil 12.343, 'Laden'.

100. *Achill.* Virgil 12.350, 'Pelidae'; Ascensius f.364 va, 'i. Achilis'.

103. Virgil 12.351, 'Tydides'; Ascensius f.364 va, 's. Diomedes Tidei filius'.

105. *and hym slewch.* Virgil 12.351, —; Ascensius f.364 va, 'occidit eum'.

128. Omits Virgil 12.361, 'sic moenia condunt'.

131. *Butys.* Virgil 12.362. *Ascensius f.364 v and Ascensius f.365 rb, 'Buten' for MSS 'Asbyten'.

133. *a man of full gret fors.* Added by Douglas.

136. Virgil 12.365, 'Edoni'; Ascensius f.365 rb, 'ab Edone monte Thraciae'.

157–8. Virgil 12.374, 'retectum'; Ascensius f.365 rb, 'nudatum'.

XII.vii; Virgil 12.383–440

22. *son of Iasides.* Virgil 12.392, 'Iasides'; *Ascensius f.365 va, 'i. Iasi filius'.

35. Virgil 12.401, 'Paeonium in morem'; Ascensius f.366 rb, 'i. medicinalem'.

80. *bestis.* Virgil 12.414, 'capris', *i.e.* goats.

87. *lippys*. Taking Virgil 12.417, 'labris' as 'lips', where Loeb takes it as 'ewer'.

96–7. *as thocht … stond*. The comparison is not made by Virgil (12.422).

133. *myne awyn page*. Added by Douglas.

XII.viii; Virgil 12.441–99

7. *quha com behynd*. Added by Douglas.

22. Virgil 12.450, 'atrum rapit agmen'; *Servius f.367 vb, 'pulveris nube coopertum'; *Ascensius f.367 rb, 'propter pulverem'.

28–32. Douglas makes the passage (Virgil 12.453–5) more vivid by direct quotation; Ascensius f.367 rb, however, adds 'ut dicunt agricolae'.

33. *Troian*. Virgil 12.456, 'Rhoeteius'; Ascensius f.367 rb, 'i. Troianus'.

56–8. *virago … offyß*. Virgil 12.468, 'virago'; Ascensius f.367 va, 'i. virile implens officium'.

113. Virgil 12.492, 'poplite subsidens'.

123. Added by Douglas.

XII.ix; Virgil 12.500–53

20. **fled*. This probably derives from Servius on Virgil 12.505, 'ruentis' as 'quos insequebatur Turnus'.

35–6. Virgil 12.515, 'nomen Echionium'; Ascensius f.368 va, 'i. gloriam Thebanam ab Echione rege'.

70. *Kyng Murranus*. Virgil 12.529, 'Murranum'; Servius f.369 vb, 'Murrani … reges fuerunt'.

77–84. Expanded from Virgil 12.532–4.

93. *cumyn from Archad land*. *Virgil 12.538, 'Cretheu'; Ascensius f.369 va, 'fuit ergo Arcas'.

99. *obstant*. *'Resistant'. This renders Virgil 12.541, 'mora', the delaying effect of the shield and armour.

XII.x; Virgil 12.554–613

14. *at quyet man and wyfe*. A pointless addition by Douglas.

25–52. Expanded from Virgil 12.565–73.

64. Virgil 12.578, —; Ascensius f.370 va, 's. in eos qui forte in muris erant'.

81–2. Virgil 12.585. The sense agrees with *Ascensius f.370 va, 'trahunt ipsum s. Aeneam: regem i. ut rex sit in moenia'. Loeb takes it as referring to Latinus.

85. The apology is made by Douglas, not Virgil (12.587).

94–100. Virgil 12.591–2, 'volvitur ater odor tectis, tum murmure caeco intus saxa sonant, vacuas it fumus ad auras', which Loeb takes as still referring to bees; Douglas, following *Ascensius (alternative explanation), reverts to the city; Ascensius f.370 va, 'Sic odor ater i. foedus & a re atra procedens volvitur tectis i. ad tecta urbis & saxa sonant nunc intus murmure caeco i. mussatione populi aut saxa immissa ab oppugnantibus dant incertum crepitum : fumus it ad auras vacuas ubi s. non erant aedificia.'

99. *void.* It should be the *air* that is empty (Virgil 12.592, 'vacuas … auras').

126. Virgil 12.606, —; Ascensius f.371 rb, 'laniatae genas furore feruntur'.

127. *besyde the ded corps standis.* Virgil 12.606, —; cf. line 131, where 'circum' is expanded from Ascensius f.371 rb, 's. cadaver extincte'.

145–50. *Virgil 12.612–13 (= 11.471–2) appear only in some medieval MSS, and in Ascensius f.371 r, 'multaque se incusat, qui non acceperit ante Dardanium Aenean generumque adsciverit ultro'; they are rejected by modern editors.

XII.xi; Virgil 12.614–96

5–8. Virgil 12.616, 'iam minus atque minus successu laetus equorum'.

68. Virgil 12.646, —; *Ascensius f.372 rb, 's. malim inhoneste fugere …'

69. Virgil 12.646, 'Manes'; Ascensius f.372 rb, 'i. dii inferi'.

79. *Sages.* Virgil 12.651. *Ascensius f.372 r, 'Sages' for MSS 'Saces'.

82. More vivid than *Virgil 12.652, 'implorans nomine Turnum'.

95–100. Expanded from Virgil 12.657–8.

119. *schaddois of pertrublans.* Virgil 12.669, 'umbrae'; Ascensius f.374 va, 'hoc est perturbationes'.

181–2. Virgil 12.695, 'foedus luere'.

XII.xii; Virgil 12.697–790.

Note the amount of expansion, two and a half lines of Scots to one of Latin.

6. Virgil 12.700, 'laetitia exsultans'.

9. Virgil 12.701, —; Ascensius f.375 rb, 'tantum eminens'.

10. Virgil 12.701, 'Athos'; *Ascensius f.375 rb, 'mons ille Macedoniae Thraciae imminens'.

11. Virgil 12.701, 'Eryx'; Ascensius f.375 va, 'mons ille Siciliae'.

12. Virgil 12.703, 'pater'; *Ascensius f.375 va, '… montium in … Italia'.

14. *with roky quhynnys hie.* Virgil 12.702, 'ilicibus', *i.e.* oaks, but misunderstood by Douglas.

18–20. Virgil 12.703, —; *Ascensius f.375 va, 'hoc est tantum eminebat Aeneas inter ceteros bellatores quantum hi montes in suis locis inter vicinos colles'.

26–7. 'Also those who before smote the wall as if they were crazy'.

52. Virgil 12.715, 'summove Taburno'; Ascensius f.375 va, 'monte illo Campaniae'.

53. Virgil 12.715, 'ingenti Sila'; Servius f.376 ra, 'mons & sylva est'.

56. Virgil 12.717, 'incurrunt'.

60. *squelys*. Virgil 12.718, 'mussant', which Loeb (2nd ed) takes as 'dumbly wait to see'; Ascensius f.376 rb, 'immurmurantes'.

79. *suld deliuer*. Virgil 12.727, 'damnet'; Ascensius f.376 rb, 'i. liberet secundum Servium [f.376 ra]'.

95. *the wynd*. Virgil 12.733, 'Euro'; Ascensius f.376 va, 'vento rapidissimo'.

111–12. Virgil 12.740, 'mortalis mucro'.

116. *as glaß*. The comparison is Douglas's.

124. *he mycht nocht evaid*. Virgil 12.743, —; Ascensius f.376 va, 'non potuit evadere'.

137–8. Virgil 12.749, 'inclusum'.

140. *of the ern*. Virgil 12.750, —; Ascensius f.376 (bis) rb, 'aquilarum'.

146. *Tuscan hund*. Virgil 12.753, 'Umber'; *Ascensius f.376 (bis) r, 'canis Umber i. Tuscus'.

167. Added by Douglas.

172. The comparison is Douglas's.

184. Virgil 12.769, 'Laurenti divo'.

187. *mysknawand it hallowit was*. Virgil 12.770, 'nullo discrimine'; *Ascensius f.376 (bis) rb, 'sine discretione religionis nescientes arborem sacram esse'.

201. Virgil 12.778, 'Terra'; *Servius f.376 (bis) vb, 'Tellus elementum pro dea posuit'.

206. Added by Douglas.

211. *bytis on his lip*. Virgil 12.782–3, 'morsus roboris', *i.e.* the oaken bite, which Douglas has misunderstood.

217. Virgil 12.785, 'Daunia'; Ascensius f.376 (bis) va, 'i. Iuturna Dauni regis filia'.

XII.xiii; Virgil 12.791–886

4. *tharof na thing prowd*. Virgil 12.792, —; *Servius f.377 vb, 'quasi iam taediantis'.

10–11. Virgil 12.794, 'indigetem'; Ascensius f.377 rb explains 'in diis agentem', and *Servius f.377 vb as an alternative, 'dii sunt ex hominibus facti'.

28. *Schyne nor appeir*. Virgil 12.802, 'recursent'; Ascensius f.377 r, 'coruscent'; Ascensius f.377 rb, 'i. cum coruscatione quadam emineant'.

78. *nor natyve landis*. Added by Douglas.

88. Virgil 12.827, 'Itala virtute propago'; Ascensius f.377 va, 'i. sub titulo virtutis Italice'.

92. *producear*. Virgil 12.829, 'repertor'; Ascensius f.378 rb, 'aut productor'.

102. Added by Douglas.

111. Virgil 12.838, 'hinc genus'; Ascensius f.378 rb, 'i. ex Troianis'.

120. *Fra hir ald wraith*. Virgil 12.841, —; Ascensius f.378 rb, 'ab ira'.

122. *and bad Turnus adew*. Added by Douglas.

129. *wikkit as fyre*. The judgment is Douglas's.

129–30. Virgil 12.845, 'cognomine Dirae'; Ascensius f.378 rb, 'i. execrabiles quasi deorum ira procreate'.

140. *cruell Kyng Pluto*. Virgil 12.849, 'saevi regis'; *Ascensius f.378 va, 'Plutonem intellegat'.

150. *Virgil 12.854, 'omen Iuturnae occurrere iussit'.

151. *to pleß the lard*. A meaningless addition by Douglas.

152. *thuddis*. Virgil 12.855, 'volat'.

156. *Persayn*. Virgil 12.857, 'Parthus'.

168. Expanded from Virgil 12.862–5, 'alitis parvae … quae … nocte sedens'.

175. *maid hym forto grow*. Added by Douglas.

192. *Na, nane wight alyve*. Added by Douglas.

207. **gif I mortal war*. Virgil 12.882, 'immortalis ego'; Ascensius f.378 v, 'iam mortalis ego'; Ascensius f.379 rb, 'i. si essem iam mortalis ego'.

213. *tewch*. The epithet is supplied by Douglas.

XII.xiv; Virgil 12.887–952

10. *this barreß within*. The language of the jousting field.

22. *wordis compt I nocht a stro*. Virgil 12.894–5, 'non me … terrent dicta'. *The wording is proverbial (Whiting S 807).

46. *for feir*. Virgil 12.905, —; Ascensius f.381 rb, 'timoris'.

51–64. Expanded from Virgil 12.908–12.

100. Virgil 12.928, 'gemitu'.

110. *quhat nedis proceß mar?* The question is introduced by Douglas. *Cf. note to II.iv.61.

129. Virgil 12.940, 'cunctantem'.

138. The belt is unfriendly to Turnus because it reminds Aeneas of the death of Pallas; and Turnus was unfriendly to Pallas; the double sense is in the Latin (12.944).

154. *with disdeyn*. Virgil 12.952, 'indignata'.

*The commentary of Ascensius on Book 13 becomes more grammatical and less expository, and hence of less use to Douglas. Douglas does not translate the twelve-line argumentum that precedes the book. Servius of course does not comment on it.

Mensioun of the Pryncipall Warkis

These lines are modelled on Virgil's conclusion to the *Georgics* 4.559–66. They also recall the pseudo-Virgilian lines at the opening of the *Aeneid* (see above, note to I.Prol.505–10).

1. *flowr of poetry*. Virgil.

2. Cf. *Aeneid* 1.1.

4. The avoidance of idleness was a conventional motive for composition, but may here have been suggested by Virgil's 'studiis florentem ignobilis oti' (*Georgics* 4.564). See also *Directioun*, 40.

5. This mysterious early work has not been identified. Ruddiman emended *Lundeys* to *Ovideis* (p. 448), and took the reference to be to Ovid's *Remedia Amoris* (p. 14). No evidence exists that Douglas made such a translation, however, and Coldwell found it discrepant with line 113 of the *Directioun*. He suggested instead that *Lundeys* signifies 'strumpets', and that 'the title could mean "The Remedy of Wanton Love", perhaps something like "The Remedy of Love" in Thynne's edition of Chaucer'. *DOST* provides little support for this interpretation of *lund*, apart from the word *loun* which had a variant spelling *lound*, and highly pejorative senses. Ruddiman's explanation is palaeographically difficult to explain, but it still seems the most plausible.

7–8. Douglas imitates Virgil's echo of the first line of the *Eclogues* in *Georgics* 4.566 by quoting the opening of his own youthful work, *The Palice of Honour*.

Naym of the Translatour

To indicate his name Douglas uses a rebus, a verbal practice that resembles the use of canting arms in heraldry: see Keen 1984, 130 and notes 20–1. For a Scottish instance, cf. the three cockerels in the arms of the Cockburns. Such riddling word-play on a person's name was popular at this time. Cf. the acrostics by Dunbar on 'Barnard Stewart' (*Poems*, 56), or by Robert Sempill on his own name (*Satirical Poems* ed. Cranstoun 1891–2, I, 67).

1. *gaw*. 'Gall', with the usual Scots vocalization of final /l/. Gall was a type of intense bitterness (Whiting G 8). Douglas possibly recalls Matthew xxvii.34: 'Et dederunt ei vinum bibere cum felle mistum'.

2. *dow*. 'Dove'. The spelling indicates the common Scots pronunciation, with vocalization of final /v/. Douglas may recall the pun on the first syllable of the Douglas surname in Holland, *Howlat*, 989–90. *rich in a lyne*. 'Right, *i.e.* straight, in a line'. Cf. *Palice of Honour*, 822.

Prologue XIII

Douglas here humorously attempts to justify the presence in the *Eneados* of the so-called book XIII, the supplement to the *Aeneid* written by the Italian humanist Maphaeus Vegius (1407–58). Although this work was much admired, and included in many manuscript and printed editions of Virgil, Douglas clearly had a divided mind about the propriety of translating it, and his dream dialogue with Maphaeus Vegius dramatizes these doubts vividly and effectively. The interview with Maphaeus has a beautiful and symbolic setting: it begins on a June evening with the poet about to rest, his work on the *Aeneid* apparently concluded; at the end, however, the dawn of a new day brings a resumption of labour for all creatures, including the poet. This type of dream, in which the poet is instructed and sometimes chided by a famous author, has several late medieval antecedents (see Bawcutt 1976, 189); but the closest parallel is Henryson's dream-meeting with Aesop, in the Prologue to 'The Lion and the Mouse' (*Fables*, 1321–1404). For modern editions of Maphaeus Vegius's poem, see Brinton 1930 and Schneider 1985; for criticism of this Prologue, see Bawcutt 1976, 104–5 and 186–90; Rossi 1965; Ross 1981; Pinti 1993; Cummings 1995; Ghosh 1995.

2. *in the Crab Appollo held hys sete*. The sun entered the Crab, the zodiacal sign of Cancer, on 12 June.

3. *ioyus … Iune*. Henryson set his dream similarly 'In middis of Iune, that ioly sweit seasoun' (*Fables*, 1321).

15. Eade (1984, 169) notes that the sun is 'close to its most northerly point of setting'.

16–18. This passage conflates details from three sources: Ovid's account of the horses of the sun (*Metamorphoses* II.153–5), in which the fourth horse is called *Phlegon*; Boccaccio's altered version of the name in *De Genealogia Deorum*, IV.iii: 'Phegon autem quartus ex croceo colore tendit in nigrum', i.e. 'Phegon goes from the colour of crocus (cf. Douglas's *fyry*) to black (cf. *dun*)'; and a single line (217) from Henryson's description of the fourth horse in *Testament of Cresseid*: ' Quhilk rollis Phebus doun into the sey'.

19. *Esperus*. Hesperus, the name given to the planet Venus during the period when it rises after the sun and is visible in the early part of the evening. Milton represents Hesperus similarly as a *forrydar*, or 'advance rider', in *Paradise Lost*, IV.605–6.

26–8. *beryall … cristal … siluer*. Similar imagery for dew drops, drawn from jewels and precious stones, occurs in Dunbar's *Goldyn Targe* (*Poems*, 59.14–17, and 23).

26. *techrys*. 'Drops of liquid'. Cf. *tychirris* (IV.xii.5). This rare and now obsolete word derives not from French *tacher* (so Ruddiman, Small, and Coldwell), but from an Old Northumbrian variant of OE *téar*, 'tear', with medial *h* or 3. It is not recorded in ME, and apparently survived only in sixteenth-century Scottish texts (see *OED*, *tear*, sb.1, Illustration of Forms; *DOST*, *tere*, n. sense 2.)

215

32. *dym*. Either the adjective, or a verb, 'grow dim'. Cf. the similarly alliterative line in *The Destruction of Troy*, 9932: 'The day ouerdrogh, dymmet the skewes' (cited in *OED*, *dim*, v.).

33. *ledderyn flycht*. 'Leather wings'. The bat was traditionally leather-winged. Cf. Spenser, *Faerie Queene*, II.xii.36: 'The lether-winged Bat, dayes enimy'.

35–6. The lark is depicted as taking part in the seven canonical hours, or church services, of which the first is matins, and the last compline. Cf. Spenser, *Epithalamion*, 80: 'The merry Larke hir mattins sings aloft'. A popular belief that the lark flies aloft seven time a day to sing hymns to its creator was recorded by the naturalist Ulisse Aldrovandi (1522–1605) in *Ornithologiae Tomus Alter*, Frankfurt, 1630, p. 362. See also lines 167–8 below.

45. *euery thing*. C's underlining and marginal note 'or all creatur' may indicate an authorial revision, in order to avoid the repetition in line 51.

57. *vrusum*. The word is obscure; earlier editors and *DOST* explain it as an error for *unrusum*, 'restless'.

61–3. *Philomeyn*. Philomela, the nightingale. This image of the bird differs from that in XII Prol.282–5. Many medieval writers saw the nightingale as a joyous bird, associated with spring and love, and proverbially 'merry', despite the belief that it pressed its breast against a thorn (Whiting N 110 and N112). Cf. *Kingis Quair*, 380ff.

64. *vndir a greyn lawrer*. It was common for dreaming poets to sit or slumber beneath a tree of some kind, whether the laurel, as here or in *The Flour of Curtesy*, 45 (Lydgate 1911–34, II) or the hawthorn in Henryson's 'The Lion and the Mouse', 1343. The choice of laurel is peculiarly apt, in view of the part it plays later (see lines 77 and 87), and its poetic associations. Douglas may have known Petrarch's discussion of its symbolism in classical poets, such as Horace, *Odes* II.7 and 15; interestingly, Petrarch notes that it 'may symbolize the rest that is in store for … [poets] after their toils in the study' (Wilkins 1955, 310).

67–8. Douglas observes the Pole star, the constellations of the Great and Little Bear, and the moon.

68. *hornyt Lucyn*. Lucina, a name given to the moon goddess. Cf. Dunbar, *Poems*, 29.1. On the moon's 'horns', see III.Prol.1 and note.

70–2. On Venus as 'goldyn', see Henryson, *Testament of Cresseid*, 13. The term *participate* refers to the proximity, or conjunction, of the planets Venus and Jupiter. This conjunction was considered astrologically auspicious, as Douglas observes in his note to I.v.2, where Jupiter is similarly described as 'gentyll and … full of gud influens'.

76. '… who said'.

77. '… who wishes me no good'.

87–8. Maphaeus's laurel crown is a sign of his poetic distinction. The laurel was particularly associated with epic, and through their own links with Virgil both he and Douglas might aspire to be regarded as epic poets. These lines are indebted to two portraits by Henryson: Aesop, who wears a 'bonat round, and off the auld fassoun' in *Fables*, 1353; and Mercury, who wears a 'croun / Lyke to ane poeit of the auld fassoun' in *Testament of Cresseid*, 244–5. On the details of the iconography, see Bawcutt 1981b.

98. *that sete salbe full salt.* 'That seat (under the laurel) will be most uncomfortable for you'.

102. *I am the sammyn.* Cf. Henryson, *Fables*, 1382: 'I am the samin man'.

104. *red and song.* A poetic formula common in Chaucer. Cf. *Troilus and Criseyde*, IV.799 and V.1797; and *Conclusio*, 11–12.

105. *Albyon.* A poetic term for Britain, employed elsewhere by Douglas: see *Palice of Honour*, 918, and *Conclusio*, 11.

108. *Mastir.* A respectful term also used of Aesop in *Fables*, 1367, 1377, etc.

118. This image derives from Ascensius's note at the beginning of book XIII (fol. 383r): 'unde frustra quidem quadrigis rotam quintam addidit'. Coldwell notes: 'the scribe of R is more familiar with two-wheeled carts'. This appears true also of Carmichaell, in *Proverbs*, No. 1849: 'Ye mister it als meikle as the cart dois the thrid quheill'.

122. *the story of Iherom.* St Jerome (c. 340–420) was famed for his translation of the Bible into Latin. But his conscience was troubled by the deep admiration that he felt for pagan literature; and in a letter to Eustochium (Epistle 22) he describes how he experienced a vision in which he was reproached before the Judgement seat for being not a follower of Christ but a follower of Cicero. This well-known story was also recalled by John Walton, the translator of Boethius: 'Noght liketh me to labour ne to muse / Upon these olde poysees derk / For Cristes feith suche thinges schulde refuse; / Witnes uppon Ierom the holy clerk ...' (Walton ed. Science 1927, 2).

127–8. Psalm xiv.1: 'Corrupti sunt, et abominabiles facti sunt in studiis suis'.

134. Echoing a line from Chaucer's portrait of the Prioress (CT.I.150): 'And al was conscience and tendre herte'.

156. *Iubar.* In Latin this is an abstract noun, 'brilliance, radiance' – cf. the use in IV.iv.2 – but it is sometimes applied, especially by Ovid, to the sun or the planet Venus. *Day star* can similarly refer either to the sun or Venus (cf. Dunbar, *Poems*, 59.1).

157. *Chiron.* One of the Centaurs, here identified with the zodiacal sign of the Archer; according to Boccaccio, *Genealogia Deorum*, VIII.8: 'in celum translatus est, et in zodiaco locatus et Sagittarius appellatus'.

164. *Lucifer.* Another name for the planet Venus.

167–8. Cf. Chaucer, *Knight's Tale*, CT.I.1491–2: 'The bisy larke, messager of day / Salueth in hir song the morwe gray'. The lark, in poetic tradition was commonly 'busy', and its song reproved the indolent for their somnolence; see Bawcutt 1972. Cf. also Dunbar's use in *Poems*, 52.12–14.

171–6. These lines anticipate the imagery of XIII.viii.31–4.

172. Cf. XIII.viii.34: 'To go to laubour of thar husbandry'.

178. *dappill gray.* 'Grey, variegated with darker spots'. Douglas imaginatively re-applies a term more commonly used of horses.

182. *The ioly day now dawys.* For a carol with a similar burden, see Greene 1977, no. 432. Cf. also Dunbar's complaint that the common minstrels of Edinburgh have no other tune but 'Now the day dawis', and 'Into Ioun': *Poems*, 55.30.

187. *vpwark.* 'Completion of a piece of work'. The word's usual context is agricultural, which is apt.

191. Coldwell interpreted this line as 'My speech and my writing are the same, i.e. both vernacular'. But Douglas's point is that his own style of writing is much the same (*efter ane*), whether he is translating Virgil or Maphaeus Vegius.

XIII, i; Maphaeus 1–54

3. *marciall.* Maphaeus 3, 'Mavortius'.

27. The passage (Maphaeus 13) is modelled on Virgil's bull simile in 12.715–22.

31. *onto the batalis fyne.* Not in Maphaeus (15).

50. Maphaeus 22, 'rebus'.

57. *hie Iove.* Maphaeus 25, 'summi tonantis'; Ascensius f.383 v, 'Iovis'; cf. XIII.iii.89 and elsewhere.

63. Not in Maphaeus (28).

88–9. Maphaeus 40, 'omnem deflendae mortis honorem'.

111. *throu the feildis.* Not in Maphaeus (50). Cf. 'our the planys', line 115, Maphaeus 52, —.

112. Maphaeus 50, 'Troia tecta'.

121–2. Maphaeus 54, 'strepit altus plausibus aether'.

XIII.ii; Maphaeus 55–124

9. *fra hand to hand.* Not in Maphaeus (58).

21. *God Bachus.* Maphaeus 66, 'Lyaei'; *Ascensius f.384 r, 'idest Bacchi'.

28. Maphaeus 67, 'magnum tonantem'; Ascensius f.384 r, 'Iovem'.

33–4. Maphaeus 70, 'Mavortem ipsum'; *Ascensius f.384 r, 'i. Martem s. principem bellorum'.

61–2. *Maphaeus 82, 'sublimen … mittam'.

67–108. Expanded from Maphaeus 85–102.

119ff. Maphaeus 107ff. The comparison of Aeneas with a hen seems incongruous, but *Ascensius f.384 v cites a scriptural parallel ('salvator in evangelio'): 'Quotiens volui congregare filios tuos quemadmodum gallina congregat pullos suos sub alas'. (I.e.

Matthew xxiii.37; Luke xiii.34.)

151. In the Latin (Maphaeus 121), Aeneas is properly the subject of the next sentence.

154. Not in Maphaeus (123).

XIII.iii; Maphaeus 125–88

22. *thunderand*. Maphaeus 135, 'fulmineos'.

32. *questyng*. Maphaeus 140, —; Ascensius f.385 r, 'querenti' misunderstood as 'quaerenti'.

39ff. The speech on kingly misery runs counter to Virgil's purpose, of course, though it might apply to the usurper. Indirect references to Fortune and her wheel appear in line 43 (Maphaeus 144, 'turbine'); line 73 (Maphaeus 157, —); cf. XIII.v.48–9, 106–12.

73. Maphaeus 157, .—; Ascensius f.385 v, 'descendunt reges'.

107. *no thyng mycht styntyng the*. Not in Maphaeus (170).

120. *quhar remed was nane*. Not in Maphaeus (176).

121–40. Expanded from Maphaeus 177–84.

134. *caucht in thi bak*. Maphaeus 182, .—; Ascensius f.386 r, 'in tergum'.

XIII.iv; Maphaeus 189–242

11. *the carter*. Maphaeus 194, —; Ascensius f.386 r, 'auriga'.

13. *bedowyn all of swete*. Maphaeus 195, 'rorantem', presumably meaning 'wet with tears', as in the next phrase, 'fletu madidum'.

20. *turnyt down*. I.e. as a token of grief. (Maphaeus 197.) Cf. XI.ii.88.

22. *knycht, swane, man and page*. Maphaeus 197, 'pubes'.

26. This seems to be an improvement over Maphaeus's tautological 'muta silentia' (199)

31. Maphaeus 201, 'funere'.

34. Maphaeus 203, 'urbem' suggests that 'cite' is the object, not the subject.

45. *hait and recent ded*. Maphaeus 209, 'calido … sanguine'.

70. Maphaeus 223, —; *Ascensius f.386 v, 'si cavernula formicę eruatur omnes sarcinulas quas quaeque potest colligunt'.

79. *snaill*. Maphaeus 226, 'testudo', *i.e.* tortoise; v. *OED snail* 1b – though '*on the house side*' seems a curious way to describe a tortoise; *cf. however Ascensius f.386 v, 'animali … pertinaciter parieti domus incensae adherenti', and possibly Douglas had never seen a tortoise.

80. *coppit schell*. Taking Maphaeus 228, 'caput', in the sense of 'top, summit'; 'coppit', i.e. rising to a peak, may have been suggested by the sound.

97. *quham a heron clepe we.* Maphaeus 236, —; for Ardea, see Virgil *Georgics* 1.364.

100. *I.e.* ardea the bird is the namesake and representative of Ardea the city.

113. *fut, tung nor mouth.* Maphaeus 240, 'ora'.

XIII.v; Maphaeus 243–301

2. *of dyseyß.* Not in Maphaeus (243), unless 'praenuntia' embodies the idea of foreboding.

8. Not in Maphaeus (246).

19. Maphaeus 253, 'substitit'.

27–112. *Expanded from Maphaeus, XIII.257–96, a speech much indebted to Virgilian laments, such as those by Euryalus's mother and Evander for their sons (Virgil 9.473–97; 11.152–81).

44. Maphaeus 264, 'afflicto'.

68. Not in Maphaeus (276). *But cf. Chaucer, *Knight's Tale*, CT.2174: 'His voys was as a trompe thonderynge'.

72. *dedis byt.* 'Death's bite'; not in Maphaeus (278), but suggested by 'avidis'.

89. *systir Amata.* Maphaeus 286, 'Amata'.

XIII.vi; Maphaeus 302–401

6, 8. Maphaeus 304, 306. One would expect 'persavand' and 'revoluand' to translate 'videns' and 'volvens' and to improve the syntax. The principal verb is in line 14.

18. *traill syde goun.* 'Trailing voluminous gown'. Cf. Lyndsay's satirical 'Ane Supplicatioun … in Contemptioun of Syde Taillis'.

34–5. Somewhat strengthened in Douglas; Maphaeus 316–17, 'vulgus inerme componit'.

41–2. Maphaeus 319, 'plaudente triumphos'.

43. *lugyngis hie.* Maphaeus 320, 'sublimes domus', creates a different impression; cf. 'tenementis' for 'domos', XIII.x.9 (Maphaeus 539).

73, 76. Maphaeus 334, 335, 'invitus … Latinus'.

85ff. Maphaeus 339ff. The syntax is hard to follow: the meaning seems to be 'Latinus has no resentment, because all the battle was brought about by furious Turnus (who now lies dead), enflamed with such wickedness that he forced the Latins to fight against their will'.

103. *our ardent.* 'Over-ardent'.

106. *Syntactically 'nowder' should precede 'prayeris'.

111. Maphaeus 352, 'talibus ausis'.

123–6. Expanded from Maphaeus 357, 'Tu melior succede bonis Laurentibus haeres'.

141. *newfangill*. 'Ready to take up a new idea', without the usual pejorative sense; Maphaeus 364, 'cupidae'.

147. *Maphaeus 366–7, 'tota … Ausonia'.

151ff. Maphaeus 368ff. The sense is 'Old Latinus believes there is only one way to preserve his life, namely to marry you to his daughter'.

153. *beleif and traste*. Maphaeus 369, 'munera'.

154–9. Expanded from Maphaeus 370–1.

164. *saisyn tak*. A literal translation (< French 'saisir', to seize) of Maphaeus 373, 'cape', but by Douglas's time mostly restricted to legal usage.

189. *I Troian*. An awkward rendering. *Maphaeus 384 has 'mei … Teucri', i.e. my Trojans.

222. Maphaeus 399, 'glandilegos'; *Ascensius f.389 r describes the epithet as inept, as sows do not gather ('legere') nuts but eat them ('devorare').

227. Maphaeus 401, 'enudant'; *Ascensius f.389 r, 'i. spoliant s. pecoribus in eis errare aut pasci solitis'.

XIII.vii; Maphaeus 402–46

21–2. Condensed from Maphaeus 413–14, 'Sublimesque alta statuebant laude trium-phos, Troianam cupido expectantes pectore turbam.'

32–3. Douglas simplifies the language; Maphaeus 420–1, 'Et late regalem oculis spargebat honorem sidereis.'

49. *'Although human wilfullness …' *That* here is not a demonstrative adjective, but should be construed with the preceding conjunction *All thocht*; cf. *DOST thoch(t*, 3.

50. *our*. 'Over'.

60. *sum man*. Maphaeus 432, —; Ascensius f.389 v, 'Turno'.

66. *crop and rutys*. Maphaeus 434, 'origo'.

68. *wyrkaris*. Maphaeus 435, 'auctor'; Ascensius f.389 v, 'Turnus & Amata'.

70. *succeid to heritage*. Not in Maphaeus (436).

71–4. Maphaeus 437, 'Sunt mihi regna, iacent ereptis oppida muris'; the expansion is perhaps influenced by Ascensius f.390 r, quoting Virgil 7.183–4, 'multaque praeterea sacris in postibus arma captivi pendent'.

81–2. Maphaeus 440, 'quem contra bonus Aeneas'.

XIII.viii; Maphaeus 447–89

11–20. Expanded from Maphaeus 451–4.

24. *with hys crukyt beym the plewch.* *Maphaeus 456, 'curvum … aratrum'.

25–34. Expanded from Maphaeus 457–9. *See note to XIII.Prol.172, for Douglas's echoes of this passage.

42. Not in Maphaeus (463).

55–7. Expanded from Maphaeus 468, 'sidereos deiecta oculos'.

64. *na litill apperans.* Not in Maphaeus (472); the idea is if the first glance could astonish Aeneas, long association could well move Turnus.

67–8. The phrasing suggests courtly love in Douglas. Maphaeus simply has 472–3, 'Qui haud parva spe ductus ovans in proelia tantos civisset motus …'

69. *to abbryge our mater.* *A mischievous fiction, in a Chaucerian manner. Lines 69–80 are an expansion of Maphaeus 474–7; 73, Maphaeus —; 75–6, Maphaeus 476, 'plausus fremitusque'; 80–93, Maphaeus 478–82.

XIII.ix; Maphaeus 490–535

1–11. Expanded from Maphaeus 490–2 – the whole chapter shows considerable expansion.

13. Maphaeus 493, 'strato … in ostro'; *Ascensius f.390 v, 'i. purpura'.

16. Not in Maphaeus (494).

30. Not in Maphaeus (500).

46–64. Expanded from Maphaeus 509–15.

73. The reason is not immediately apparent: in the previous line 519 Maphaeus has used the verb 'latere', *i.e.* to hide.

77–8. Maphaeus 521, 'et Bacchi et frugum cultus'.

82. *Atlaß douchter.* Maphaeus 523, 'Atlantide'; Ascensius f.391 r, 'Atlantis filia'.

84. *Hys awyn brother.* Maphaeus 524, —; Ascensius f.391 r, 'fratre'.

85. *in Italy.* Maphaeus 523, —; Ascensius f.391 r, 'urbe Italię'.

91–6. The exact meaning is hard to follow: the sense seems to be, 'Dardanus received the eagle, a known token to the Trojans; so also is it known that the erecting of noble arms and this ensign for the Trojans was first begun by him; and he was chief stock of that blood.' If 'begun' were 'beginner' and a pronoun understood, the sentence would be clearer. Douglas probably stumbled over the Latin, Maphaeus 526–8, 'utque insignem aquilam dono et Iove patre superbus, Hectoreae gentis signum, illustresque tulisset primus avum titulos, Troianae stirpis origo'.

107. *dowbill brangillys and gambatis.* Maphaeus 533, 'sequuntur'.

108–12. Maphaeus 534–5, 'seque agmine toto permiscent, variantque pedes, raptimque feruntur'.

113–18. Added by Douglas, who is perhaps more flippant with Maphaeus than he is with Virgil.

115. *The tone is highly Chaucerian. Cf. *Legend of Good Women*, 1228: 'The autour maketh of it no mencioun.'

118. *subcharge*. Literally 'a second or extra course of food', but chiefly used figuratively. Cf. Henryson, *Fables*, 346.

XIII.x; Maphaeus 536–92

4. Maphaeus 537, 'tum'.

6–8. Maphaeus 538, 'Aeneas urbem curvo signabat aratro'.

13. *at the left hand*. This would be an ill omen. It is not in Maphaeus (541).

17–18. Maphaeus 541–2, 'se nubibus altis Miscentem'; the meaning should be 'the fire rose to the clouds, and yet its base remained on Lavinia's head'.

20. Not in Maphaeus (543).

26. *page, man or syre*. Not in Maphaeus (548).

81. Maphaeus 571, 'penates'.

95–6. *Maphaeus 577, 'O felix, quem tanta manent'; Ascensius f.392 r, 's. ornamenta & dona'. 'Felix' seems rather to apply to Aeneas; Douglas's 'thou' in line 97 is certainly Aeneas.

101. Maphaeus 579, 'Elysias … ad umbras'.

112. Not in Maphaeus (583). *It recalls Chaucer's comment on Arcite's death (*Knight's Tale*, *CT*.2809–10): 'His spirit chaunged hous and wente ther / As I cam nevere, I kan nat tellen wher.'

122–4. Maphaeus 589, 'lataque potens dicione tenebat'.

125. *of fre will*. *Maphaeus 590, 'ultro'.

XIII.xi; Maphaeus 593–630

1–6. Expanded from Maphaeus 593–4.

9. Maphaeus 596, 'res hominum'.

17. *faderis of Italy*. This suggests not the received text of Maphaeus, 601, 'partes', but a reading such as 'patres'.

42–3. Maphaeus 611, 'Iunone secunda'.

53. *of hys kyn*. Not in Maphaeus (617).

56. **contemp.* This is not a misunderstanding of 'Exornent', the standard text of Maphaeus 619, but derives from Ascensius f.392 v, 'Exhorrent'.

73. *recent. I.e.* 'newly dead'.

75-6. *quhar reuthfull Eneas . . . chosyn haß his place.* Not in Maphaeus (629).

80. Maphaeus 630, —; Ascensius 392 v, 'inveníes per tabulam'.

Book XIII is followed by several short pieces of verse that constitute a kind of prolonged leave-taking by the poet of his work: he bids farewell not only to the *Eneados*, but to Virgil, his patron, his readers, and even his critics. Douglas's model for this may have been the conclusion of Chaucer's *Troilus and Criseyde*, 1772-1869. There are few precedents in earlier Scottish poetry, apart from the envois to *Hary's Wallace* XII.1410-64 and *King Alexander the Conquerour*, 19286ff.. It was more usual to end long poems with a short prayer, as in Barbour, *Bruce*, 20.621-30, or *Ratis Raving*, 1799-1814, or *The Buke of the Chess*, 2186-91.

Conclusio

1-12. These lines are a fairly close translation of the proud boast that concludes Ovid's *Metamorphoses*: 'Iamque opus exegi, quod nec Iovis ira nec ignis' (XV.871-9). The theme of poetry's immortality had not yet become a commonplace. See, however, Dunbar in *Poems*, 67.28-34.

6. *not bot.* 'Only'.

8. *bettir part.* A Christianized interpretation of Ovid's 'parte tamen meliore' (XV.875), *i.e.* the soul.

9-10. This recalls the stellification of Aeneas in XIII.xi.73-4.

11. *Albyon*, the poetic term for Britain, here corresponds to the Roman Empire, in Ovid's 'quaque patet domitis Romana potentia terris' (XV.877). For Douglas's earlier use, cf. XIII Prol.105.

12. *Red ... and sung.* See note to XIII.Prol.104.

13-14. The image, that of a votive offering, is classical in origin. Douglas may recall Aeneas hanging a shield on *postibus* (*Aeneid* 3.286-7 = III.v.5-11). When Horace spoke of giving up lyric poetry and turning to philosophy, he compared himself to an old gladiator fixing his armour to the post of Hercules – 'Herculis ad postem' (*Epistles* I.i.4ff.). See Curtius 1953, 306-7; Bawcutt 1976, 171-2.

16-17. Coldwell comments: 'Douglas's muse was subsequently devoted to contemplating the political fortunes of his family'. But Douglas may recall that Virgil, according to the *Vita* attributed to Suetonius (ed. and transl. J. C. Rolfe, 1924), II, 475, intended to devote his life to philosophy after finishing the *Aeneid*.

19-20. The precise date of Douglas's birth is unknown, but these lines suggest that he saw himself as approaching thirty-five in 1513. In 1515 he testified before the Lords of Council that he was 'ane man of forty yeris of age or tharby' (Bawcutt 1976, 4).

Directioun

This address to Henry, Lord Sinclair, Douglas's patron, recapitulates several of the leading themes of Prologue I.

1–4. See the earlier praise of Lord Sinclair, in I.Prol.83–104.

3. *Sanct Geill*. St Giles, Edinburgh, the well-endowed collegiate church of which Douglas was provost.

11–30. The fear of critics may be conventional, since there is no evidence that Douglas was 'chydit' (21) for translating the *Aeneid*. See also I.Prol.485ff. and *Exclamatioun*, 10–18.

17. *this buke*. Douglas refers to the whole translation, as in line 72 also.

24. 'And I have made myself a butt to shoot at' (Coldwell).

28ff. The sense is not wholly clear. Douglas perhaps implies that his translation might be compared to raising the ghosts of pagan authors.

32. *Mea culpa*. A penitential phrase, acknowledging guilt. Cf. IX.Prol.76.

40. *eschew idylnes*. A stock phrase, often used by writers to defend their literary activity. Cf. *Mensioun*, 4; for other Scottish uses, see the Scottish *Legends of Saints, Prologue*, 36; and *Buke of the Chess*, 16. See also Chaucer, *Second Nun's Prologue*, CT.VIII. 1–7; and Lydgate, *Troy Book*, Prologue I.82–3.

46. *word by word*. Contrast I.Prol.395–402.

55–8. These lines develop a favourite image for Virgil's eloquence as a *flude*, 'flood', *surs*, 'source, spring', fountain, and *flum*, 'river'. Cf. line 104 below, and I.Prol.2.

63 and 75. *kyndnes*. 'Kinship, family feeling'.

65. *weriouris*. 'Critics'.

66. Cf. I.Prol.499 and note.

68–9. *Bochas … Genolygy of Goddis*. On the significance of this work to Douglas, see also I.Prol.204. Books 14 and 15 contain an important and influential defence of poetry, and of the study of pagan authors.

76. *cayk fydlar*. No other use is known. Coldwell suggests: 'A parasite, one who sings for his supper'. Fiddlers were held in low esteem. Cf. Walter Kennedy, *Flyting*, 507.

77–80. Coldwell comments: 'The cynic would say Lord Sinclair had more gear than Douglas; but probably this is an expansion of the proverb, "Amicorum communia omnia" (Erasmus, *Adagia*, II, 13F)'.

88. *not bot*. 'Unless'. The allusion is to the proverb, 'Drink but when you are dry' (Whiting D 400). Cf. IV.Prol.99.

89–90. For this image of poetry as wine, cf. I.Prol.59; and V.Prol.52–4.

97. 'I wish others well [that] can speak more skilfully'. For this usage, see DOST, *will*, v. sense 1d.

99. *prefer*. 'Be preferred to'.

103. *said.* Possibly 'assayed, attempted'. Cf. *DOST, say*, v.2.

106. The line is close to Lichtoun's 'My spreit was reft and had in extasye' (see text in Hadley Williams 2016, 81).

113. *Ovid.* Douglas is probably thinking of the *Metamorphoses*, Ovid's longest work.

116. 'For idle people work which consists only of looking is easy'. Henryson uses the proverb very similarly in *Fables*, 102: 'For wyfis sayis that lukand werk is licht'. Cf. also 'Ill workers ar ay gude onlookers': Whiting, *Scots Proverbs*, WORK; and Whiting W 648.

119-24. See *The Palice of Honour*, 991-1000, where Venus charges the poet, not specifically to translate a book but, more generally, to observe her 'nixt ressonabill command'.

128-34. For this defence of Aeneas and rejection of the notion that he was a traitor, see I.Prol.415, and note. The conception of Aeneas as *proditor Troiae*, which was popular in Scotland, was pre-Virgilian. It owed its wide circulation in the Middle Ages to Guido delle Colonne, who described a conspiracy by Aeneas and Antenor to betray Troy to the Greeks in his *Historia Destructionis Troiae*, books 28-30 (see Bawcutt 1976, 82-3; and Wingfield 2014, 48-9, 113).

128. For this imagery, see I.Prol.10 and II.Prol.11.

141. *schort comment.* Most scholars consider that this refers to the marginal commentary, found only in the Cambridge MS, that accompanies Prologue I and much of Book I.

Exclamatioun

The metre changes from the staple five-stress couplet to the nine-line stanza used in Prologue III, with the final lines rhyming either *bb* or *ab*. Douglas also takes over several of the themes and images found in Prologue III.

1-6. The poet envisages his work as a voyage over the open sea, and its conclusion as safe arrival in port. The theme was very ancient. Cf. *Georgics*, 2.41. and 4.116-17. See also Prol.III.37ff.; Chaucer, *Troilus and Criseyde*, II.1-4; *Kingis Quair*, 113-26; Bower, *Scotichronicon*, XVI. 39; Curtius 1953, 128-30.

9. *wlgar.* 'Vulgar, i.e. vernacular', as in line 37.

10-36. A defence against malicious criticism, voiced also in *Directioun*, 11-30.

14. *not worth ane ace.* 'worthless'. The ace, which signified one on a dice, had low value. Cf. Whiting A 26-9.

27. Cf. Whiting, T 142 ('New thing is sweet'). *onassayt.* 'Not put to the test'. Cf. Fergusson, *Proverbs*, 144: 'All thing is good unseyit'.

28. *moyt.* 'Pick out the imperfections'; *DOST* explains as a form of *mute*, v. 1, speak, argue, discuss.

32. *scald thar throte.* Cf. I.Prol.258.

36. Proverbial. See note to III.Prol.20.

37. *Go wlgar Virgill.* This concluding address to one's book was highly traditional, but Douglas is less modest and more confident than many of his predecessors. Cf. Chaucer, *Troilus and Criseyde*, V.1786: 'Go, litel bok'; *Kingis Quair*, 1352: 'Go, litill tretise'; *Hary's Wallace*, XII.1449: 'Go, nobill buk'; and Dunbar, *Goldyn Targe*, 271–9.

39. *corect and amend.* This request was a stock modesty formula; cf. 'pray ilk man til amend the', *Palice of Honour*, 2168; and Henryson, *Fables*, 42.

40. Proverbial and Biblical in origin: see Whiting E 184 and John iii.20. Contrast the tone of *Palice of Honour*, 2167 (and note).

Tyme, space and dait

1–4. Douglas dates his completion of the translation as the Feast of St Mary Magdalene, i.e. 22 July 1513.

12. This implies that Douglas started work early in 1512.

21–5. Douglas's genuine concern for the integrity of his work is evident in this plea to his scribes and readers: *redis leill* (i.e. read and interpret it correctly), do not mutilate or spoil the metre, and do not alter the words. His anxiety recalls that of Chaucer at the end of *Troilus and Criseyde*, V.1795–6: 'So prey I god that non myswrite the, / ne the mysmetre for defaute of tonge'.

24. *maggill.* 'Mutilate, mangle'. For a very similar figurative use of the word, see Dunbar, *Poems*, 64.3.

[Virgil's Epitaph]

The Epitaph appears in the *Vita* attributed to Suetonius, ed. Rolfe, II, 476–7. It is included in many manuscripts and prints of Virgil's works, including those of Ascensius.

Bibliography

Editions of the *Eneados*

Copland. 1553. *The xiii Bukes of Eneados of the famose Poete Virgill Translatet out of Latyne verses into Scottish metir, bi the Reuerend Father in God, Mayster Gawin Douglas Bishop of Dunkel & Vnkil to the Erle of Angus. Euery buke hauing hys perticular Prologe.* [William Copland]. London.

Ruddiman. 1710. *Virgil's Aeneis Translated into Scottish Verse by the Famous Gawin Douglas … A New EDITION. Wherein the many errors of the Former are corrected … To which is added a LARGE GLOSSARY, Explaining the Difficult Words: Which may serve for a Dictionary to the Old SCOTTISH Language …* Symson and Freebairn. Edinburgh.

Dundas. 1839. *The Aeneid of Virgil, Translated into Scottish Verse. By Gawin Douglas, Bishop of Dunkeld.* [ed. George Dundas and Andrew Rutherford]. 2 vols. Bannatyne Club. Edinburgh.

Small, John, ed. 1874. *The Poetical Works of Gavin Douglas, Bishop of Dunkeld, With Memoir, Notes and Glossary.* 4 vols. Edinburgh.

Coldwell, David F. C., ed. 1957–64. *Virgil's Aeneid Translated into Scottish Verse by Gavin Douglas Bishop of Dunkeld, With Notes and Glossary.* 4 vols. STS 3rd series 25, 27, 28, 30. Edinburgh.

Kendal, Gordon, ed. 2011. *Gavin Douglas: The Aeneid (1513).* 2 vols. London.

Law, John and Caroline Macafee, eds. 2012. *The XIII Buiks o Eneados o the famous poet Virgil translatit out o Latin verses intae Scottish metre, by the Reverend Faither in God, Maister Gavin Douglas, Bishop o Dunkeld and uncle tae the Earl o Angus, every buik haein his parteecular prologue.* Modrenised by John Law and completit by Caroline Macafee. 2 vols. Scots Language Centre. Perth.

Primary Texts

Acta Facultatis Artium Universitatis Sanctiandree 1413–1588. 1964. Ed. A. I. Dunlop. 2 vols. SHS, series 3, 54–5. Edinburgh.
Asloan Manuscript, The. 1923–5. Ed. W. A. Craigie. 2 vols. STS 2nd series 14, 16. Edinburgh.
Awntyrs off Arthure, The. 1974. Ed. Ralph Hanna. Manchester.
Bannatyne Facsimile. The Bannatyne Manuscript. 1980. Introduction D. Fox and W. A. Ringler. London.

Bannatyne Manuscript, The. 1928–32. Ed. W. Tod Ritchie. 4 vols. STS 3rd series 5, 22, 23, 26. Edinburgh.

Barbour, John. 1980–5. *Barbour's Bruce.* Ed. Matthew P. McDiarmid and J. A. C. Stevenson. 3 vols. STS 4th series 12, 13, 15. Edinburgh.

— 1997. *The Bruce.* Ed. with translation A. A. M. Duncan. Edinburgh.

Barr, Helen, ed. 1993. *The Piers Plowman Tradition: A Critical Edition of 'Pierce the Ploughman's crede', 'Richard the Redeless', 'Mum and the Sothsegger' and 'The crowned king'.* London.

Bede. 1943. *Bedae Opera de Temporibus.* Ed. C. W. Jones. Cambridge.

Boccaccio, Giovanni. 1511. *De Genealogia Deorum.* Venice.

— 1951. *Genealogie Deorum Gentilium Libri.* Ed. V. Romano. 2 vols. Bari.

— 1956. *Boccaccio on Poetry: Being the Preface and the Fourteenth and Fifteenth Books of Boccaccio's* Genealogia Deorum Gentilium. Trans. Charles G. Osgood. New York.

— 1964-. *Tutte le opere di Giovanni Boccaccio.* Gen. Ed. Vittore Branca. 10 vols. Milan.

Boffey, Julia and A. S. G. Edwards, eds. 1997. *The Works of Geoffrey Chaucer and 'The Kingis Quair': A Facsimile of Bodleian Library, Oxford, MS Arch. Selden. B. 24* Cambridge.

Bower, Walter. 1987–98. *Scotichronicon in Latin and English.* Ed. D. E. R.Watt et. al. 9 vols. Aberdeen and Edinburgh.

Buchanan, George. 1957. 'An Unpublished Commentary by George Buchanan on Virgil'. Ed. Charles P. Finlayson. *Transactions of the Edinburgh Bibliographical Society* 3, 271–88.

Buke of the Chess, The. 1997. Ed. Catherine Van Buuren. STS 4th series 27. Edinburgh.

Calendar of Letters and Papers Relating to the Affairs of the Borders of England and Scotland 1560–1603. 1894–6. Ed. Joseph Bain. 2 vols. Edinburgh.

Calendar of the State Papers Relating to Scotland and Mary, Queen of Scots 1547–1603. 1969. Ed. J. D. Mackie. vol. 13. Edinburgh.

Carmichaell, James. 1957. *The James Carmichaell Collection of Proverbs in Scots.* Ed. M. L. Anderson. Edinburgh.

Caxton, William. 1890. *Caxton's Eneydos.* Ed. W. T. Culley and F. J. Furnivall. EETS ES 57. London.

— 1894. *The Recuyell of the Historyes of Troye.* 2 vols. Ed. H. Oskar Sommer. London.

— 1970. *The History of Reynard the Fox.* Ed. N. F. Blake. EETS OS 263. Oxford.

Chaucer, Geoffrey. 1988. *The Riverside Chaucer.* Ed. L. D. Benson et al. Oxford.

Clanvowe, Sir John. 1975. *The Works of Sir John Clanvowe.* Ed. V. J. Scattergood. Cambridge.

Colkelbie Sow and The Talis of the Fyve Bestes. 1983. Ed. Gregory Kratzmann. New York.

Complaynt of Scotland, The. 1979. Ed. A. M. Stewart. STS 4th series 11. Edinburgh.

Deidis of Armorie, The. 1994. Ed. L. A. J. R. Houwen. 2 vols. STS 4th series 22–3. Edinburgh.

Douglas, Gavin. 1964. *Selections from Gavin Douglas.* Ed. David F. C. Coldwell. Oxford.

— 2003. *The Shorter Poems of Gavin Douglas.* Ed. Priscilla Bawcutt, 2nd edn. STS 5th series 2. Edinburgh.

Dunbar, William. 1998. *The Poems of William Dunbar.* Ed. Priscilla Bawcutt. 2 vols. Glasgow. (References by poem number, and line.)

Extracts from the Council Register of the Burgh of Aberdeen, vol. I (1398–1570). 1844. Ed. John Stuart. Aberdeen.

Fehrenbach, R. J. and E. S. Leedham-Green, eds. 1992. *Private Libraries in Renaissance England: A Collection and Catalogue of Tudor and Stuart Book-Lists*, vol. 1. Medieval and Renaissance Texts and Studies, 87. Binghamton, NY.

— 2004. *Private Libraries in Renaissance England: A Collection and Catalogue of Tudor and Stuart Book-Lists*, vol. 6. Medieval and Renaissance Texts and Studies, 271. Tempe, AZ.

Fergusson's Scottish Proverbs. 1924. Ed. Erskine Beveridge. STS 2nd series 15. Edinburgh.

Fraser, William. 1885. *The Douglas Book*. 4 vols. Edinburgh.

Golagros and Gawane. 2008. *The Knightly Tale of Golagros and Gawane*. Ed. Ralph Hanna. STS 5th series 7. Edinburgh.

Googe, Barnabe. 1989. *Eclogues, Epitaphs and Sonnets*. Ed. Judith M. Kennedy. Toronto.

Gower, John. 1899–1902. *The Complete Works of John Gower*. Ed. G. C. Macaulay. 4 vols. Oxford.

Greene, Richard Leighton, ed. 1977. *The Early English Carols*. 2nd edn. Oxford.

Grosseteste, Robert. 1996. *On the Six Days of Creation: A Translation of the Hexaemeron*. Trans. C. F. J. Martin. Auctores Britannici Medii Aevi, VI.2. Oxford.

Hadley Williams, Janet, ed. 2016. *Duncane Laideus Testament and Other Comic Poems in Older Scots*. STS 5th series 15. Edinburgh.

Hary's Wallace. 1968–9. Ed. Matthew P.McDiarmid. 2 vols. STS 4th series 4–5. Edinburgh.

Hawes, Stephen. 1928. *Pastime of Pleasure*. Ed. W. E. Mead. EETS, OS 173. London.

Hay, Gilbert. 1986–90. *The Buik of King Alexander the Conquerour*. Ed. J. Cartwright. 2 vols. STS 4th series 16, 18 (only vols 2–3 published). Edinburgh.

— 2005. *The Prose Works II: The Buke of the Law of Armys*. Ed. Jonathan A. Glenn. STS 5th series 3. Edinburgh.

Henryson, Robert. 1981. *The Poems of Robert Henryson*. Ed. Denton Fox. Oxford.

— 1968. *Testament of Cresseid*. Ed. Denton Fox. London.

Hoccleve, Thomas. 1897. *The Regement of Princes*. Ed. F. J. Furnivall. EETS ES 72. London.

Holland, Richard. 2014. *The Buke of the Howlat*. Ed. Ralph Hanna. STS 5th series 12. Edinburgh.

Howard, Henry, Earl of Surrey. 1964. *Henry Howard, Earl of Surrey: Poems*. Ed. Emrys Jones. Oxford.

Hudson, Thomas. 1941. *Thomas Hudson's Historie of Judith*. Ed. James Craigie. STS 3rd series 14. Edinburgh.

Hume, David. 2005. *David Hume of Godscroft's The History of the House of Angus*. Ed. David Reid. 2 vols. STS 5th series 4 and 5. Edinburgh.

Ireland, John. *The Meroure of Wyssdome*. (References by volume and page).

1926. vol. I ed. C. Macpherson (books 1–2). STS 1st series 19. Edinburgh.

1965. vol. II ed. F. Quinn (books 3–5). STS 4th series 2. Edinburgh.

1990. vol. III ed. Craig McDonald (books 6–7). STS 4th series 19. Edinburgh.

James I of Scotland. 1981. *The Kingis Quair*. Ed. John Norton Smith. 2nd edn. Leiden.

James VI of Scotland. 1955–8. *The Poems of James VI of Scotland*. Ed. James Craigie. 2 vols. STS 3rd series 22 and 26. Edinburgh.

Kennedy, Walter. 2008. *The Poems of Walter Kennedy*. Ed. Nicole Meier. STS 5th series 6. Edinburgh.

Lancelot of the Laik. 1912. Ed. M. M. Gray. STS 2nd series. Edinburgh.

Laing Charters A.D. 854–1837, Calendar of the. 1899. Ed. Rev. John Anderson. Edinburgh.

Landino, Cristoforo. 1980. *Disputationes Camaldulenses*. Ed. Peter Lohe. Florence.

Langland, William. 1886. *The Vision of William concerning Piers the Plowman*. Ed. Rev. Walter W. Skeat. 2 vols. Oxford.

— 1994. *Piers Plowman: The C Text*. Ed. Derek Pearsall. Exeter.

Legends of the Saints. 1887–95. Ed. W. M. Metcalfe. STS 1st series 13, 18, 23, 25, 35, 37. Edinburgh.

Leslie's Historie of Scotland. 1888–95. Ed. E. G. Cody. 2 vols. STS 1st series 5, 14, 19, 34. Edinburgh.

Letters of James V. 1954. Ed. R. K. Hannay and D. Hay. Edinburgh.

Lindsay [Lyndsay], Sir David. 1931–6. *The Works of Sir David Lindsay of the Mount 1490–1555*. Ed. Douglas Hamer. 4 vols. STS 3rd series 1, 2, 6, 8. Edinburgh.

Lydgate, John. 1924–7. *Lydgate's Fall of Princes*. Ed. H. Bergen. 4 vols. EETS, ES 121–4. London.

— 1911–34. *The Minor Poems*. Ed. H. N. MacCracken. 2 vols. EETS, ES 107; OS 192. London.

— 1906–35. *Troy Book*. Ed. H. Bergen. 4 vols. EETS, ES 97, 103, 106, 126. London.

Macrobius, Ambrosius Theodosius. 2011. *Saturnalia*. Ed. and trans. Robert A. Kaster. 3 vols. Cambridge, MA.

The Maitland Folio Manuscript. 1919–27. Ed. W. A. Craigie. 2 vols. STS 2nd series 7, 20. Edinburgh.

Major [Mair], John. 1892. *A History of Greater Britain*. Trans. Archibald Constable. SHS vol. 10. Edinburgh.

[Maphaeus Vegius]. 1930. *Maphaeus Vegius and his Thirteenth Book of the Aeneid*. Ed. Anna Cox Brinton. Stanford.

— 1985. *Das Aeneissupplement des Maffeo Vegio*. Ed. Bernd Schneider. Acta Humaniora. Weinheim.

Montgomerie, Alexander. 2000. *Alexander Montgomerie: Poems*. Ed. David J. Parkinson. 2 vols. STS 4th series 28–9. Edinburgh.

Nott, G. F. 1815. *The Works of Henry Howard and of Thomas Wyatt*. 2 vols. London.

Oresme, Maistre Nicole. 1940. *Le livre de Ethiques d'Aristote*. Ed. A. D. Menut. New York.

Ovid. 1977. *Ovid III: Metamorphoses, Books 1–VIII*. Ed. F. J. Miller. 3rd edn rev. G. P. Goold. Cambridge, MA.

— 1984. *Ovid IV: Metamorphoses, Books IX–XV*. Ed. F. J. Miller. 2nd edn rev. G. P. Goold. Cambridge, MA.

Paul, Sir James Balfour. 1904–14. *The Scots Peerage*. 9 vols. Edinburgh.

Phaer, Thomas and Thomas Twyne. 1987. *The Aeneid of Thomas Phaer and Thomas Twyne*. Ed. Steven Lally. New York.

Plutarch. 1949. *Moralia*, vol. 3. Ed. and trans. Frank Cole Babbitt. Loeb Classical Library. London.

Protocol Book of John Foular 1514–1528. 1953. Ed. Marguerite Wood. SRS vol. 75. Edinburgh.

Protocol Book of John Foular 1528–1534. 1985. Ed. John Durkan. SRS n.s. 10, Edinburgh.

Puttenham, George. 1936. *The Arte of English Poesie*. Ed. Gladys Willcock and A. Walker. Cambridge.

Ratis Raving and other early Scots poems on morals. 1939. Ed. R. Girvan. STS 3rd series 11. Edinburgh.

Rauf Coilyear. 1987. In *Longer Scottish Poems I: 1375–1650*. Ed. P. Bawcutt and F. Riddy. Edinburgh.

Register of the Great Seal of Scotland. 1882–1914. Ed. J. M. Thomson, Sir J. Balfour Paul, J. H. Stevenson and W. K. Dickson. 11 vols. Edinburgh.

Registrum Episcopatus Aberdonensis. 1845. Ed. Cosmo Innes. 2 vols. Aberdeen.

Rolland, John. 1932. *The Seuin Seages.* Ed. G. F. Black. STS 3rd series 3. Edinburgh.

Ruthven Family Papers, The. 1912. Ed. Samuel Cowan. London.

Satirical Poems of the Time of the Reformation. 1891–3. Ed. James Cranstoun. 4 vols. STS 1st series 20, 24, 28, 30. Edinburgh.

Scott, Alexander. 1896. *The Poems.* Ed. J. Cranstoun. STS 1st series 36. Edinburgh.

Sex Werkdayis and Agis, The. 1990. Ed. L. A. J. R. Houwen. Groningen.

[Sidney, Sir Philip]. 2012. *The Correspondence of Sir Philip Sidney.* Ed. Roger Kuin. 2 vols. Oxford.

Sir Gawain and the Green Knight. 1967. Ed. J. R. R. Tolkien and E. V. Gordon, rev. Norman Davis. 2nd edn. Oxford.

Spenser, Edmund. 1948. *The Poetical Works of Edmund Spenser.* Ed. J. C. Smith and E. de Selincourt. London.

Suetonius. 1914. *Suetonius: with an English translation.* Ed. and trans. J. C. Rolfe. 2 vols. Cambridge, MA (repr. 1924).

Surrey, Earl of. Henry Howard, Earl of Surrey. 1964. *Poems.* Ed. Emrys Jones. Oxford.

Thre Prestis of Peblis, The. 1920. Ed. T. D. Robb. STS 2nd series. 8. Edinburgh.

Twyne, Thomas: see under Phaer.

Vergil, Polydore. 1846. *Vergil's English History.* Ed. H. Ellis. 2 vols. Camden Society 29, 36. London.

Virgil. 1930. *The Aeneid.* Ed. J. W. Mackail. Oxford.

— 1960. *P. Vergili Maronis Aeneidos, liber quintus.* Ed. R. D. Williams. Oxford.

— 1969. *P. Vergili Maronis Opera.* Ed. R. A. B. Mynors. Oxford.

— 1971. *P. Vergili Maronis Aeneidos, liber primus.* Ed. R. G. Austin. Oxford.

Walton, John. 1927. *Boethius: De Consolatione Philosophiae translated by John Walton.* Ed. Mark Science. EETS OS 170. London.

The Wars of Alexander, an Alliterative Romance. 1886. Ed. W. W. Skeat. EETS ES 47. London.

Secondary Studies

Aitken, A. J. 1983. 'The Language of Older Scots Poetry'. In *Scotland and the Lowland Tongue.* Ed. J. D. McClure. Aberdeen, 18–49.

— 1989. 'The Lexicography of Scots Two Hundred Years Since: Ruddiman and His Successors'. In *In Other Words.* Ed. J. Lachlan Mackenzie and Richard Todd. Dordrecht, 235–45.

Apted, M. R, and S. Hannabuss. 1978. *Painters in Scotland 1301–1700.* Edinburgh.

Archibald, Elizabeth. 1989. 'Gavin Douglas on Love: The Prologue to *Eneados IV*'. In *Bryght Lanternis: Essays on the Language and Literature of Medieval and Renaissance Scotland.* Ed. J. D. McClure and M. R. G. Spiller. Aberdeen, 244–57.

Austin, R. G. 1966. Review of Coldwell's *Virgil's Aeneid*, Vol. 1. *Medium Aevum* 35, 154–7.

Bacquet, Paul. 1966. *Thomas Sackville: L'Homme et l'Oeuvre.* Geneva.

Barnes, Jonathan. 1982. 'The Just War'. In *The Cambridge History of Later Medieval Philosophy.* Ed. Norman Kretzmann, A. Kenny and J. Pinborg. Cambridge, 771–84.

Baswell, Christopher. 1995. *Virgil in Medieval England: Figuring the Aeneid from the Twelfth Century to Chaucer*. Cambridge.

Bawcutt, Priscilla. 1969. 'The Source of Gavin Douglas's *Eneados* IV Prol. 92–9', *NQ* 214, 366–7.

— 1970. 'Gavin Douglas and Chaucer', *RES* 21.84, 401–21.

— 1971. 'Lexical Notes on Gavin Douglas's *Eneados*', *Medium Aevum* 40, 48–55.

— 1972. 'The Lark in Chaucer and some Later Poets', *Yearbook of English Studies* 2, 5–12.

— 1973. 'Gavin Douglas and the Text of Virgil', *Transactions of the Edinburgh Bibliographical Society* 4, part 6, 213–31.

— 1974. 'Douglas and Surrey: Translators of Virgil', *Essays and Studies* 27, 52–67.

— 1976. *Gavin Douglas: A Critical Study*. Edinburgh.

— 1977. 'The "Library" of Gavin Douglas'. In *Bards and Makars: Scottish Language and Literature: Medieval and Renaissance*. Ed. A. J. Aitken et al. Glasgow, 107–26.

— 1978. 'Text and Context in Middle Scots Poetry'. In *Actes du 2e colloque de langue et de littérature Écossaises (moyen age et renaissance)*. Ed. J.-J. Blanchot and C. Graf. Strasbourg, 26–38.

— 1981a. 'Source-hunting: Some Reulis and Cautelis'. In *Proceedings of the Third International Conference on Scottish Language and Literature (Medieval and Renaissance)*. Ed. R. J. Lyall and F. Riddy. Stirling, 85–105.

— 1981b. 'Henryson's "Poeit of the Auld Fassoun"', *RES* 32, 429–34.

— 1982. '"Venus Starre" in Donne and Douglas', *NQ* 227, 15.

— 1984. 'A Note on Sonnet 38', *Shakespeare Quarterly* 35, 77–9.

— 1986. 'Dunbar and an Epigram', *SLJ* 13, no. 2, 16–19.

— 1994. 'New Light on Gavin Douglas'. In *The Renaissance in Scotland: Studies in Literature, Religion, History and Culture offered to John Durkan*. Ed. A. A. MacDonald, et al. Leiden, 95–106.

— 1995. '*Pamphilus de Amore* "in Inglish Toung"', *Medium Aevum* 64.2, 264–72.

— 1996. 'The Correspondence of Gavin Douglas'. In *Stewart Style 1513–1542: Essays on the Court of James V*. Ed. J. Hadley Williams. East Linton, 52–61.

— 1998. 'Crossing the Border: Scottish Poetry and English Readers in the Sixteenth Century'. In *The Rose and the Thistle: Essays on the Culture of Late Medieval and Renaissance Scotland*. Ed. S. L. Mapstone and J. Wood. East Linton, 59–76.

— 2000. 'New Texts of William Dunbar, Alexander Scott and Other Scottish Poets', *Scottish Studies Review* 1, 9–25.

— 2002. 'A Song from *The Complaynt of Scotland*: "My Hart is Leiuit on the Land"', *NQ* 247, 193–7.

— 2006. 'Writing about Love in Late Medieval Scotland'. In *Writings on Love in the English Middle Ages*. Ed. Helen Cooney. New York, 179–96.

— 2008. 'The Contents of the Bannatyne Manuscript: New Sources and Analogues', *Journal of the Edinburgh Bibliographical Society* 3, 95–133.

— 2019. 'Gavin Douglas's *Eneados*: The 1553 Edition, and its Early Owners and Readers'. In *Manuscript and Print in Late Medieval and Early Modern Britain: Essays in Honour of Julia Boffey*. Ed. Tamara Atkin and Jaclyn Rajsic. Cambridge, 73–87.

Beal, Peter. 1980. *Index of English Literary Manuscripts I: 1450–1625*. London.

Beattie, William. 1951. 'Fragments of The Palyce of Honour', *Edinburgh Bibliographical Society Transactions* III, part 1, 33–46.

Bennett, Edith. 1938a. 'An Edition of the Prologues to Gavin Douglas's *Eneados*'. Unpublished B.Litt. thesis, Oxford.

— 1938b. 'A New Version of a Scottish Poem', *MLR* 33, 403.

Bennett, J. A. W. 1946. 'The Early Fame of Gavin Douglas's *Eneados*', *MLN* 61, 83–8.

— 1967. Review of vol. 1 of Coldwell's *Virgil's Aeneid, translated into Scottish Verse by Gavin Douglas Bishop of Dunkeld*. In *RES* 18, 310–13.

Blayney, Peter W. M. 2013. *The Stationers' Company and the Printers of London 1501–1557*. 2 vols. Cambridge.

Blyth, Charles R. 1970. 'Gavin Douglas' Prologues of Natural Description', *Philological Quarterly* 49, 164–77.

— 1987. *'The Knychtlyke Stile': A Study of Gavin Douglas' Aeneid*. New York and London.

Boffey, Julia. 2006. '*The Kingis Quair* and the Other Poems of Bodleian Library MS Arch.Selden. B. 24'. In *A Companion to Medieval Scottish Poetry*. Ed. P. Bawcutt and J. Hadley Williams. Cambridge, 63–74.

Borland, C. R. 1916. *A Descriptive Catalogue of the Western Medieval Manuscripts in Edinburgh University Library*. Edinburgh.

Broadie, Alexander. 1990. *The Tradition of Scottish Philosophy*. Edinburgh.

— 2009. 'John Mair's *Dialogus de Materia Theologo Tractanda*: Introduction, Text and Translation'. In *Christian Humanism: Essays in Honour of Arjo Vanderjagt*. Ed. A. A. MacDonald, Z. R. von Martels and J. R. Veenstra. Leiden, 419–30.

Brückner, Thomas. 1987. *Die erste französische Aeneis, Untersuchungen zu Octovien de Saint-Gelais' Übersetzung Mit einer kritischen Edition des VI. Buches*. Düsseldorf.

Cairns, Sandra. 1984. '*The Palice of Honour* of Gavin Douglas, Ovid and Raffaello Regio's Commentary on Ovid's *Metamorphoses*', *Studi Umanistici Piceni* 4, 17–38.

Calin, William. 2014. *The Lily and the Thistle: The French Tradition and the Older Literature of Scotland*. Toronto.

Canitz, A. E. C. 1990. 'The Prologue to the *Eneados*: Gavin Douglas's Directions for Reading', *SSL* 25, 1–22.

— 1991. 'From *Aeneid* to *Eneados*: Theory and Practice of Gavin Douglas's Translation', *Medievalia et Humanistica* 17, 81–99.

— 1996. '"In our awyn langage": The Nationalist Agenda of Gavin Douglas's *Eneados*', *Vergilius* 42, 25–37.

Caughey, Anna. 2009. '"The Wild Fury of Turnus now lies Slain": Love, War and the Medieval Other in Gavin Douglas's *Eneados*'. In *Masculinity and the Other: Historical Perspectives*. Ed. Heather Ellis and J. Meyer. Newcastle upon Tyne, 261–80.

Clancy, Thomas and Murray Pittock, eds. 2007. *The Edinburgh History of Scottish Literature*. 3 vols. Edinburgh.

[Collins, John]. 1980. *A Short Account of the Library at Longleat House, Warminster, Wilts*. London.

Comparetti, D. 1895; 1997. *Vergil in the Middle Ages*, with new introduction by J. M. Ziolkowski. Princeton.

Cooper, Helen. 1974. 'The Goat and the Eclogue', *Philological Quarterly* 53, 363–79.

— 1977. *Pastoral: Mediaeval into Renaissance*. Ipswich.

Crawford, Barbara. 1985. 'William Sinclair, Earl of Orkney, and his Family: A Study in the Politics of Survival'. In *Essays on the Nobility of Medieval Scotland*. Ed. K. J. Stringer. Edinburgh, 232–53.

Cummings, Robert. 1995. "'To the Cart the Fift Quheill": Gavin Douglas's Humanist Supplement to the *Eneados*', *Translation and Literature* 4.2, 133–56.

Curtius, E. R. 1953. *European Literature and the Latin Middle Ages*. Trans. W. R. Trask. London.

Dekker, Kees. 2016. 'The Other "Junius" in Oxford, Bodleian Library MS Junius 74: Francis Junius and a Scots Glossary by Patrick Young', *Scottish Language* 35, 1–42.

Desmond, Marilynn. 1994. *Reading Dido: Gender, Textuality and the Medieval* Aeneid (Medieval Cultures, 8). Minneapolis and London.

Douglas, David. C. 1951. *English Scholars 1660–1730*. 2nd edn. London.

Duff, E. G. et al. 1913. *Handlists of English Printers 1501–1556*, Part IV. Bibliographical Society, London.

Duncan, Douglas. 1965. *Thomas Ruddiman: A Study in Scottish Scholarship of the Early Eighteenth Century*. Edinburgh and London.

Durkan, John and A. Ross. 1961. *Early Scottish Libraries*. Glasgow.

Durkan, John. 2006. 'The Libraries of Sixteenth-century Scotland'. pp. lxv–lxxvi. In *Scottish Libraries*. Ed. John Higgitt. London.

— 2013. *Scottish Schools and Schoolmasters 1560–1633*. Ed. J. Reid-Baxter. SHS, 5th series, vol. 19. Edinburgh.

Eade, J. C. 1984. *The Forgotten Sky: A Guide to Astrology in English Literature*. Oxford.

Ebin, Lois. 1980. 'The Role of the Narrator in the Prologues to Gavin Douglas's *Eneados*', *Chaucer Review* 14, 353–65.

Edwards, A. S. G. 2001. 'Editing Dunbar: The Tradition'. In *William Dunbar, 'The Nobill Poyet'*. Ed. Sally Mapstone. East Linton, 51–68.

— 2005. 'Manuscripts at Auction: January 2002–December 2003', *English Manuscript Studies 1100–1700*, 12, 254–9.

Foster, Joseph. 1891. *Alumni Oxonienses: The Members of the University of Oxford 1500–1714*. 4 vols. Oxford.

Fowler, Alastair. 1977. 'Virgil for "every gentil Scot"', *TLS* July 22, 882–3.

— 2005. 'Gavin Douglas: Romantic Humanist'. In *Rhetoric, Royalty and Reality: Essays on the Literary Culture of Medieval and Early Modern Scotland*. Ed. A. A. MacDonald and K. Dekker. Leuven, 83–103.

Fox, Denton. 1966. 'The Scottish Chaucerians'. In *Chaucer and Chaucerians*. Ed. D. S. Brewer. London, 164–200.

— 1977. 'Manuscripts and Prints of Scots Poetry in the Sixteenth Century'. In *Bards and Makars: Scottish Language and Literature, Medieval and Renaissance*. Ed. A. J. Aitken et al. Glasgow, 156–71.

Geddie, William. 1912. *A Bibliography of Middle Scots Poets*. STS 1st series 61. Edinburgh.

Ghosh, Kantik. 1995. "'The Fift Quheill": Gavin Douglas's Maffeo Vegio', *SLJ* 22.1, 5–21.

Goldstein, R. James. 1993. *The Matter of Scotland: Historical Narrative in Medieval Scotland*. Nebraska.

— 2012. 'A Distinction of Poetic Form: What Happened to Rhyme Royal in Scotland?' In *The Anglo-Scottish Border and the Shaping of Identity 1300–1600*. Ed. Mark P. Bruce and Katherine H. Terrell. New York, 161–80.

Gordon, C. D. 1970. 'Gavin Douglas's Latin Vocabulary', *Phoenix* 24.1, 54–73.

Gray, Douglas. 1994. 'Virgil in Late Medieval Scotland: *Aeneid* and *Eneydos*', *Papers from the 2nd Conference of the Polish Association for the Study of English*. Ed. G. Bystydzienska and L. Kolek. Lublin, 11–22.

— 2000. '"As quha the mater beheld tofor thar e": Douglas's Treatment of Vergil's Imagery'. In *A Palace in the Wild: Essays on Vernacular Culture and Humanism in Late-Medieval and Renaissance Scotland*. Ed. L. A. J. R. Houwen, A. A. MacDonald, and S. L. Mapstone. Leuven, 95–123.

— 2001. 'Gavin Douglas and "the gret prynce Eneas"', *Essays in Criticism* 51, 18–34.

— 2006. 'Gavin Douglas'. In *A Companion to Medieval Scottish Poetry*. Ed. P. Bawcutt and J. Hadley Williams. Cambridge, 149–64.

— 2012. 'Religious Elements in the Poetry of Gavin Douglas'. In *Literature and Religion in Late Medieval and Early Modern Scotland*. Ed. L. A. J. R. Houwen. Leuven, 69–91.

Griffiths, Jane. 2009. 'Exhortations to the Reader: The Glossing of Douglas's *Eneados* in Cambridge, Trinity College, MS O.3.12', *English Manuscript Studies 1100–1700*, 15, 185–97.

— 2014. *Diverting Authorities: Experimental Glossing Practices in Manuscript and Print*. Oxford.

Hale, J. R. 1966. 'Gunpowder and the Renaissance'. In *From the Renaissance to Counter-Reformation: Essays in Honour of Garrett Mattingly*. Ed. C. H. Carter. London, 113–44.

Haws, Charles H. 1972. *Scottish Parish Clergy at the Reformation 1540–1574*. SRS n.s. 3. Edinburgh.

Hay, Denys. 1952. *Polydore Vergil: Renaissance Historian and Man of Letters*. Oxford.

Higgitt, John, ed. 2006. *Scottish Libraries*. Corpus of British Medieval Library Catalogues, no. 12. London.

Hobson, G. D. 1949. 'Et Amicorum', *The Library*, 5th series 4, 87–99.

Isaac, Frank. 1932. *English and Scottish Printing Types 1535–58, 1552–58*, Bibliographical Society, Oxford.

James, Montague Rhodes. 1902. *The Western Manuscripts in the Library of Trinity College, Cambridge: A Descriptive Catalogue*, Vol. III. Cambridge.

Kallendorf, Craig. 1983. 'Cristoforo Landino's *Aeneid* and the Humanist Critical Tradition', *Renaissance Quarterly* 36, 519–46.

Keen, Maurice. 1984. *Chivalry*. New Haven and London.

Kinneavy, G. 1974. 'An Analytical Approach to Literature in the Late Middle Ages: The Prologues of Gavin Douglas', *Neuphilologische Mitteilungen* 75, 126–42.

Klibansky, Raymond, Erwin Panofsky, and Friz Saxl. 1964. *Saturn and Melancholy: Studies in the History of Natural Philosophy, Religion and Art*. London.

Kratzmann, Gregory. 1980. *Anglo-Scottish Literary Relations 1430–1550*. Cambridge.

Laugesen, A. T. 1962. 'La roue de Virgile. Une page de la théorie littéraire du moyen âge', *Classica et mediaevalia* 23, 248–73.

Leahy, Conor. 2015. 'W. H. Auden and Older Scots Poetry', *TLS* July 3, 14–15.

— 2016. 'Dreamscape into Landscape in Gavin Douglas', *Essays in Criticism* 66, 149–67.

— 2017. 'W. H. Auden's Debts to Older Scots'. Unpublished paper.

Lyall, R. J. 2001. 'The Stylistic Relationship between Dunbar and Douglas'. In *William Dunbar, 'The Nobill Poyet': Essays in Honour of Priscilla Bawcutt*. Ed. Sally Mapstone. East Linton, 69–84.

Macafee, Caroline. 2013. 'How Gavin Douglas Handled Some Well-known Passages of Virgil's *Aeneid*'. In *Scots: Studies in its Literature and Language*. Ed. J. M. Kirk and I. Macleod. Amsterdam and New York, 229–44.

McClure, J. Derrick. 2010. 'The Dido Episode in Gavin Douglas's Translation of the *Aeneid*', *The European English Messenger* 19, 47–56.

MacDonald, A. A. 1983. 'Poetry, Politics and Reformation Censorship in Sixteenth-Century Scotland', *English Studies* 64, 410–21.

MacDonald, Robert H. 1971. *The Library of Drummond of Hawthornden*. Edinburgh.

McGinn, Bernard. 1985. '*Teste David cum Sibylla*: The Significance of the Sibylline Tradition in the Middle Ages'. In *Women of the Medieval World*. Ed. Julius Kirshner and S. F. Wemple. Oxford, 7–35.

McGrath, Elizabeth. 1990. 'Local Heroes: The Scottish Humanist Parnassus for Charles I'. In *England and the Continental Renaissance: Essays in Honour of J. B. Trapp*. Ed. E. Chaney and P. Mack. Woodbridge, 257–70.

McKerrow, R. B. and F. S. Ferguson. 1932. *Title-Page Borders Used in England and Scotland 1485–1640*, Illustrated Monographs of the Bibliographical Society 21, Oxford.

Mapstone, Sally. 1996. *Scots and their Books in the Middle Ages and the Renaissance: An Exhibition in the Bodleian Library, Oxford*. Oxford.

Martin, Joanna. 2008. *Kingship and Love in Scottish Poetry 1424–1540*. Aldershot.

Morgan, Edwin. 1977. 'Gavin Douglas and William Drummond as Translators'. In *Bards and Makars*. Ed. A. J. Aitken et al. Edinburgh, 194–200.

— 2001. 'The Legacy of the Makars'. In *The European Sun: Proceedings of the Seventh International Conference on Medieval and Renaissance Scottish Language and Literature, University of Strathclyde, 1993*. Ed. G. Caie et al. East Linton, 91–105.

Murray, Athol L. 1996. 'Exchequer, Council and Session, 1513–1542'. In *Stewart Style 1513–1542: Essays on the Court of James V*. Ed. J. Hadley Williams. East Linton, 97–117.

Nicolson, Adam. 2004. *God's Secretaries: The Making of the King James Bible*. New York.

Nitecki, Alicia. 1981. 'Gavin Douglas's Rural Muse'. In *Proceedings of the Third International Conference on Scottish Language and Literature (Medieval and Renaissance)*. Ed. R. J. Lyall and F. Riddy. Stirling / Glasgow, 383–95.

Norton-Smith, John. 1980. 'Douglas's Venus and Martianus Capella', *NQ* 225, 390–2.

Ormerod, George. 1882. *History of Cheshire*, 2 vols. London.

Panofsky, Erwin. 1962. *Studies in Iconology: Humanistic Themes in the Art of the Renaissance*. 2nd edn. New York.

Parkinson, David. 1987. 'Gavin Douglas's Interlude', *SLJ* 14, 5–17.

— 2005. 'Orpheus and the Translator: Douglas's "lusty crafty preambill"'. In *Rhetoric, Royalty and Reality: Essays on the Literary Culture of Medieval and Early Modern Scotland*. Ed. A. A. MacDonald and K. Dekker. Leuven, 105–20.

Pinti, Daniel. 1993. 'Alter Maro, Alter Maphaeus: Gavin Douglas's Negotiation of Authority in *Eneados* 13', *Journal of Medieval and Renaissance Studies* 23, 323–44.

— 1995. 'The Vernacular Gloss(ed) in Gavin Douglas's *Eneados*', *Exemplaria* 7, 443–64.

— 1996. 'Dialogism, Heteroglossia and Late Medieval Translation'. In *Bakhtin and Medieval Voices*. Ed. T. J. Farrell. Gainesville, 109–21.

Renoir, Alain. 1956. 'A Note on Virgil's *Aeneid*, X, 229'. *NQ* 229, 370–2.

Renouard, Phillipe. 1908. *Bibliographie des Impressions et des Oeuvres de Josse Badius Ascensius: Imprimeur et Humaniste, 1462–1535*. 3 vols. Paris.

Ridley, Florence. 1961. 'Surrey's Debt to Gawin Douglas', *PMLA* 76, 25–33.

— 1963, ed. *The* Aeneid *of Henry Howard, Earl of Surrey*. Berkeley and Los Angeles.

Robinson, Pamela. 2003. *Catalogue of Dated and Datable Manuscripts c.888–1600 in London Libraries*. 2 vols. London.

Ross, Charles S. 1981. 'Maffeo Vegio's "schort Cristyn wark", with a Note on the Thirteenth Book in Early Editions of Vergil', *Modern Philology* 78, 215–26.

Ross, Ian S. 1986. '"Proloug" and "Buke" in the *Eneados* of Gavin Douglas'. In *Scottish Language and Literature, Medieval and Renaissance*. Ed. D. Strauss and H. W. Drescher. Frankfurt am Main, 393–407.

Rossi, Sergio. 1965. 'Il Tredecesimo Libro dell'Eneide nella Versione di Gavin Douglas'. In *Studi di Letteratura Storia e Filosofia in Onore di Bruno Revel*. Florence, 521–32.

Royan, Nicola. 2010. 'The Alliterative *Awntyrs* Stanza in Older Scots Verse'. In *Medieval Alliterative Poetry: Essays in Honour of Thorlac Turville-Petre*. Ed. J. A. Burrow and H. N. Duggan. Dublin, 185–94.

— 2012. 'The Scottish Identity of Gavin Douglas'. In *The Anglo-Scottish Border and the Shaping of Identity, 1300–1600*. Ed. M. P. Bruce and K. H. Terrell. New York, 195–209.

— 2016. 'Gavin Douglas's *Eneados*'. In *The Oxford History of Classical Reception in English Literature 800–1558*. Ed. R. Copeland. Oxford, 561–82.

— 2017. 'The Noble Identity of Gavin Douglas'. In *Premodern Scotland: Literature and Governance 1420–1587. Essays for Sally Mapstone*. Ed. Joanna Martin and Emily Wingfield. Oxford, 127–43.

Rutledge, Thomas. 2007. 'Gavin Douglas and John Bellenden: Poetic Relations and Political Affiliations'. In *Langage Cleir Illumynate: Scottish Poetry from Barbour to Drummond, 1375–1630*. Ed. N. Royan. Amsterdam and New York, 94–113.

Scheps, Walter and Looney, J. A. 1986. *Middle Scots Poets: A Reference Guide to James I of Scotland, Robert Henryson, William Dunbar and Gavin Douglas*. Boston.

Schumacher, Aloys. 1910. *Des Bischofs Gavin Douglas Übersetzung der Aeneis Vergils*. Strassburg.

Scollen, Christine M. 1977. 'Octovien de Saint-Gelais' Translation of the *Aeneid*: Poetry or Propaganda?' *Bibliothèque d'Humanisme et Renaissance* 39, 253–61.

Sessions, W. A. 1999. *Henry Howard, the Poet Earl of Surrey: A Life*. Oxford.

Simpson, James. 2002. *The Oxford English Literary History, II: 1350–1547: Reform and Cultural Revolution*. Oxford.

Singerman, Jerome E. 1986. *Under Clouds of Poesy: Poetry and Truth in French and English Reworkings of the Aeneid 1160–1513*. New York and London.

Starkey, Penelope. 1973–4. 'Gavin Douglas's *Eneados*: Dilemmas in the Nature Prologues'. *SSL* 11, 82–98.

Stewart-Brown, R. 1912. 'The Royal Manor and Park of Shotwick', *Transactions of the Historic Society of Lancashire and Cheshire*, 64, 82–137.

Takamiya, Toshiyuki and R. Linenthal. 2014. 'Early Printed Continental Books Owned in England: Some Examples in the Takamiya Collection'. In *Makers and Users of Medieval Books: Essays in Honour of A. S. G. Edwards*. Ed. Carol Meale and Derek Pearsall. Cambridge, 178–90.

Terrell, Katherine. 2012. '"Kyndness of Blude"; Kinship, Patronage and Politics in Gavin Douglas'. *Textual Cultures* 7, 107–20.

Thomas, Andrea. 2005. *Princelie Majestie: The Court of James V of Scotland, 1528–1542*. Edinburgh.

Thomas, Ronald E. 1980. '"Ere he his Goddis brocht in Latio": On Pound's Appreciation of Gavin Douglas'. *Paideuma* 9, 509–17.

Tudeau-Clayton, Margaret. 1998. 'Supplementing the *Aeneid* in Early Modern England: Translation, Imitation, Commentary'. *International Journal of the Classical Tradition* 4.4, 507–25.

Turville-Petre, Thorlac. 1977. *The Alliterative Revival*. Cambridge.

Venn, John and J. A. 1922–54. *Alumni Cantabrigienses: A Biographical List of All known Students, Graduates and Holders of Office at the University of Cambridge from the earliest times to 1900*. 10 vols. Cambridge.

Watt, D. E. R. and N. F. Shead, eds. 2001. *The Heads of Religious Houses in Scotland from the Twelfth to Sixteenth Centuries*. SRS n.s. 24. Edinburgh.

Watt, L. M. 1920. *Douglas's Aeneid*. Cambridge.

White, Paul. 2013. *Jodocus Badius Ascensius: Commentary, Commerce and Print in the Renaissance*. Oxford.

Wilkins, E. H. 1955. *Studies in the Life and Works of Petrarch*. Cambridge, MA.

Wilson, Emily. 2012. 'The First British Aeneid: A Case Study in Reception'. In *Reception and the Classics: An Interdisciplinary Approach to the Classical Tradition*. Ed. W. Brockliss et al. Yale Classical Studies, no. 36. Cambridge, 108–23.

Wingfield, Emily. 2014. *The Trojan Legend in Medieval Scottish Literature*. Cambridge.

— 2016. 'The Ruthven Manuscript of Gavin Douglas's *Eneados* and a Manuscript Witness of Julius Caesar Scaliger's *Epidorpides*'. *Renaissance Studies* 30.3, 430–42.

— 'Gavin Douglas's Eneados and its Circle of Scribes, Owners and Readers'. Unpublished paper.

Glossary

The glossary is large but not a complete *index verborum*. Its content and layout derive from Coldwell: see pp. 37–8 for his own account of its arrangement and special application of the term *compound*; and p. 40 for the editor's corrections and revisions. It should be noted that the letter yogh usually has the value of modern consonantal *y* and is placed accordingly in the glossary. The scribal practice of interchanging *i* and *y*, and *u*, *v* and *w* is retained, but their order in the glossary follows modern alphabetical conventions.

Abbreviations

adj. adjective.	*v.* verb.
adv. adverb.	*pers.* person.
conj. conjunction.	*inf.* infinitive.
interj. interjection.	*trans.* transitive.
n. noun.	*intrans.* intransitive.
pl. plural.	*pa. p.* verb past participle.
prep. preposition.	*pr. p.* verb present participle.
pron. pronoun.	*vbl.* verbal
quot. quotation.	(e.g. in *vbl.n.* 'verbal noun')
sg. singular.	Vg, Virgil.

C, E, R, L, B, and 53, the Cambridge, Elphinstoun, Ruthven, Lambeth and Bath MSS., and the 1553 printed edition of the *Eneados*.

a *adj.* one (not the indefinite article, with which it can easily be confused) I.Prol.108, 349, 352, 356, 458; I.i.83; I.vi.14; I.viii.4; II.ii.15; II.x.142; II.xi.53; II.xii.56; II.iii.9; III.i.111; III.v.101; III.vi.151, 152; III.vii.62; IV.i.40; IV.iii.40; IV.viii.26, 32; V.xi.28; V.xiii.116; VI.Prol.81; VIII.xii.7; IX.iv.40; X.Prol.35, 64; X.xii.10; XII.xiii.76, 110, 134; XIII.ii.89; XIII.vi.196; XII.x.132

a, ane indefinite article, a, an IX.ii.36

a law *adj.* low down IX.xiii.28

a per se 'A' by itself; hence something unique, a paragon I.Prol.8

abaid *n.* delay I.iv.62; I.vi.96; II.iii.25

abak *adv.* backwards III.ix.20

abandonyt *pa. p.* overcome, conquered I.i.72

abasyt *v.* became amazed, became awestricken V.ii.95

abasyt *pa. p.* abashed, discouraged V.vii.81; VII.vii.89

abaytmentis *n.* diversions V.Prol.45

abhomynabill *adj.* detestable: *the -h- indicates the common renaissance false etymology* III.iv.17

abhorris *v.intr.* feels repugnance I.xii.21

abilʒeit *pa.p.* clothed XII.Prol.34

abone *adv.* or *prep.* above, higher than: in writing, hardly distinguishable from **aboue** I.iv.2; III.iii.87; etc.

aboue *prep.* or *adv.* above VI.ii.108; etc. *See also* **abone**

aboutspech *n.* circumlocution I.Prol.387

absentis *n.* the absent ones IX.ii.68

abufe *adj.* in a high position, lofty, hence vain-glorious. ~ **in hys mynd** (Vg **superans animis**) V.viii.102

abundis *v.* goes at large, extends VII.vii.92

aby *v.* buy, pay for VII.ix.114; XI.viii.161

abylʒeit *pa. p.* equipped XI.xiii.142

accident *n.* philosophically, a contingent attribute X.Prol.23

accord *n.* agreement. **of ane** ~ in agreement IV.v.76; X.Prol.162

accordis *v.* agrees, suits I.Prol.467

accustumate *adj.* accustomed VIII.ii.57; R 53; XIII.vii.83

ace *n.* the lowest throw on a die *Exclamatioun*.14

aclyd *n.* a javelin VII.xii.63

acquart *adj.* turned in the wrong way; hence hostile? IV.vii.2; VI.vii.92

acquyte *v.* pay off (as an obligation) XI.i.12

active *adj.* energetic. **an ~ bow apon hir schuldir** I.vi.24

acton *n.* a leather coat worn under mail XI.Prol.117

acwart *adj.* turned in the wrong way; hence hostile? VII.xii.45

addetyt *pa. p.* obliged (to do something) X.xiv.56

additioun *n.* augmentation, expansion I.Prol.348

addres, addreß *v.* prepare, arrange, direct I.viii.130; III.iv.76; VII.xi.4. dress, array IV.iv.40; XI.x.2. apply oneself to, direct one's energies towards III.iii.18

adekkit *pa. p.* clothed, bedecked XI.xi.140: 53 (C **and dekkit**)

adew *interj.* adieu II.x.145; III.i.129

adew *adv.* departed. **she is went ~** I.vi.174; II.ii.22; IV.Prol.255

adherdand *pr. p.* adhering, sticking to I.Prol.137

adionyt *v.* adjoined IV.iv.26

adiugit *v.* sentenced or condemned to II.ii.129

admonyst *v.* admonished IV.vi.130

admyt *pa. p.* admitted VI.v.72

ado *n.* (from *inf.* **at don**) (something) to do I.Prol.142, 318, 502

adone *phr.* have done II.x.194

adorn *v.inf.* to adore, worship I.i.84

adornar *n.* one who adorns; one who adores (**cultrix**) III.ii.84

adornyt *v.* adored II.xi.37

adoun, adovne *adv.* down, downwards III.vi.106; VII.i.144

adred *adj.* alarmed, afraid III.v.75

adreß *v.* prepare, put in order III.ii.134

aduersar *adj.* adverse, opposing
X.xiii.16

aduersiteis *n.* reverses, misfortunes
XII.i.3

aduert *v.* notice, give heed to VI.xi.49;
XI.xv.75

aduert *v.* give warning of III.x.113

aduertens *n.* heed, attention III.Prol.30

adyll *n.* putrid liquid IV.viii.98

afald *adj.* single, comprising but
one. ~ **godhed** I.Prol.456. sincere,
single-minded. ~ **diligence, ~ and
kynd** VII.Prol.159; IX.vii.76; XIII.
vii.90

afer *v.* certify XII.iv.69: 53 (C **as I
belief**)

affeir *v.* reflexive, be afraid IV.iii.38

afferis *v.* fears IX.iv.86

afferis *v.* befits, is suitable or proper
VIII.v.41

afferyt *pa. p.* feared V.iv.13

affray *n.* state of alarm I.viii.35

affrayit *pa. p.* frightened III.v.49

affrayt *v.* frightened (into flight)
III.x.20

affy *v.* trust XI.viii.83

afor *prep.* before, in front of III.iv.127

agane *prep.* against V.vii.93; etc.

aganestude *v.* resisted VII.x.44: R (C
ganestude)

agast *v.* fill with terror, frighten
IV.vi.146

aggregis *v.* represents as graver, exaggerates XI.v.85

aggregyng *pr. p.* piling up on XI.vii.112

aggrevit *pa. p.* distressed, annoyed
IV.vii.1

agilyte *n.* intellectual ability IX.Prol.2

agryß *v.* frighten IV.vii.47; XII.xiii.195

aik *n.* oak IV.i.112

air *n.* heir VII.i.166

air *n.* oar V.xi.122

ait *n.* oat. ~ **reid** a whistle made of oat-
straw I.Prol.505

aith *n.* oath I.Prol.438

ake *n.* ache VI.xii.41: 53 (C **wak**, watry)

akwart *adj.* perverse, ill-natured III.x.115

akwartly *adv.* backwards, backhand-
edly (Vg **disicit**, struck back)
XII.v.214

akyr *n.* acre VI.ix.132

al *Note* – *phrases beginning* **al**, **all**, *are
alphabetized as words with* **al-, all-**

al and sum all (intensive) II.iii.104; III.
vi.170

alanerly *adv.* only, merely I.Prol.39; III.
vi.26

alang *prep.* along

albayr *adj.* completely bare II.ix.76

albedene *adv.* at once (*a meaningless
poetic tag*) XI.xvii.51

albyrn *v.* burn completely II.ix.81

alcomy *n.* a metallic alloy like gold XII.
ii.96; XII.iv.130

algait, algatis *adv.* always I.Prol.396; III.
iii.65; IV.iii.36. in any case II.ii.80;
IV.viii.43

alhail, alhaill *adj. or adv.* whole, wholly
III.vi.122; III.x.34; IV.i.105; IV.vii.28

alhallow *v.* honour highly VII.iii.183: 53

alichtyn *v.inf.* to illumine XII.Prol.28

alienar *n.* foreigner VII.i.165; VII.vi.61

al infeiris *adv.* altogether, all together
II.viii.78

alkin, alkyn *adj.* all kind of II.iii.64;
V.xi.55; V.xiii.49

all *adj.* every. **adorn that place in ~
degre** I.vii.23

all out *adv.* completely XI.xvi.19

allaik, allake *interj.* alas! III.x.106;
III.i.124

allane *adj.* alone. with possessive pronoun. **myne ~** by myself IX.viii.55

all thar best *compound adj.* best of all
XI.vii.135

alltharlast *compound* last of all V.iv.111

all to baith *v.* inundate, drown XII.xii.67

all tobrok *pa. p.* broken up XIII.iv.75

all tochargis *v.* loads heavily XII.i.93

all to irkyt *pa. p.* very much irked XIII.
iii.10

alltoschakyn, all to schakyng *pa. p.*
quite shaken up XIII.i.15; X.vi.35

all to torn *pa. p.* torn to pieces XII.iii.84

all to trynschit *pa. p.* completely pierced VI.iv.32

alls *adv.* also II.vii.102

ally *n.* alliance VII.iv.136; X.iii.83; in XII.xiii.76 B changes **in a lay** in one law, to **in** ~

allyance *n.* alliance VII.iv.161

allyris *pron. gen.pl.* of all of us XII.i.40

almeral *n.* admiral X.iii.89

aloes *n.pl.* fragrant resin (see OED note) XII.Prol.148

alquhar *adv.* everywhere III.ix.102; etc.

als *conj.* also III.i.89; etc.

als *adv.* as (used interchangeably with **as**) III.vi.136; III.viii.132

alsammyn *adv.* all together V.x.17

alsfast *adv.* straightway VI.vi.75

alsfer *adv.* just as far I.Prol.408

alsmekill *adv.* as much V.vi.103

alsso *adv.* just as. ~ **fast** II.ii.16

alswith, alsswyth *adv.* at once (poetic) I.vi.168; IV.iii.1

altar *n.* author VII.Prol.endnote

altharlast *compound adj.* last of all V.iv.71

al to claif *v.* cut to pieces IX.ix.139

altofruschit, al tofruschit, al to fruschit *v. pa. p.* crushed II.vii.40; II.viii.75, 96; XI.xii.48

all to lorne *pa. p.* quite lost X.vi.63: R 53 (C **al to torn**)

al to rent *pa. p.* torn to pieces X.vi.116

al to schent *pa. p.* quite spoiled XI.xiv.67

al to schuldris *v.* cuts to pieces XI.xii.42

al to schyde *pa. p.* cut up XI.iii.86

alto sparpillyt *pa. p.* sprinkled, spread around X.vii.165

al to torn *pa. p.* torn to pieces II.vii.46; X.vi.63

altotrynschit *v.* pierced X.xii.143

altricatioun *n.* strife XI.ix.1

altyme, altymys *adv.* always IV.v.32; IV.vi.35

aluterly *adv.* completely, entirely IV.vi.99; V.vii.82

aly *pa. p.* allied III.i.33

alycht, alyght, alychtnyng *v.* illumine, illumining IV.i.12; VII.Prol.127; XII. Prol.59

alyftyn *v.inf.* to lift up X.xiv.166

alyt *v.* ailed IV.vii.16

amang *adv.* among. diffused through, as ~ **the ayr** I.ix.13

ambassat *n.* embassy VII.iii.108; XI.vi.27

ambassatouris *n.* envoys VII.iii.11

ambrosian *adj.* ambrosial XII.vii.90

amerant *adj.* emerald-coloured XII. Prol.151; XIII.Prol.9

ameyn *adj.* pleasant, agreeable XII. Prol.54

ameyß *v.* appease, moderate III.iv.108

ammellyt *pa. p.* enamelled VII.x.77: 53 (C **annelit**)

ammeris *n.* embers VI.iii.137

ammovit *pa. p.* excited, disturbed II.ii.148; IV.v.57

ammyral *n.* admiral III.viii.37

amorus *adj.* amorous, without any sense of wanton XII.Prol.233

amouris *n.* love, without sense of frivolity I.xi.54; IV.Prol.109, 132. love-affairs IV.Prol.209

amovit *v.* moved to action I.viii.38

amovyt *pa. p.* excited IX.iii.40

amyabill *adj.* amiable, pleasant (applied, *e.g.*, to wine) I.x.56

and *conj.* if, supposing that I.viii.138; II.ii.77; III.iii.14

ane *adj. and num.* one, a single VI.Prol.126. with **of**, an intensive **thy ancient ennemy werst of** ~ XI.Prol.92. with **in**, continuously IX.xiii.66

anerly *adv.* only, solely IX.iv.124

angyß *n.* anguish II.ii.97

anherdand, anherdyng *pr. p.* adhering II.x.164; III.i.100

animal *Latin n.* a living being, an animal in the widest sense I.Prol.367

annelit *pa. p.* annealed, tempered VII.x.77

annerd, annerdis *v.* consent, give assent to V.ii.59; XI.iii.74

annerdit *v.* agreed XII.xiii.118

anniuersar *adj.* anniversary, annual III.v.38; V.ii.10; V.xi.7

annornyt *v.* adorned, ornamented VI.x.87

anorn *v.* adorn II.iv.95

ant *n.* aunt, with further sense of prostitute VIII.Prol.46

antecessouris *n.* ancestors V.x.100

anys *adv.* once I.ii.56

anys *pron.* one's I.i.74

apertis *v.* comes into the open VI.xv.112: R (C **departis**)

apillis orrange *n.* oranges (Vg **maliferae**) VII.xii.91

apirsmert *adj.* severe I.v.88

apleß *v.* please, satisfy VII.xii.143

appetite *n.* taste, natural inclination (*e.g.* for sleep) I.xii.17

appleß *v.* please V.xiii.41

apposit *pa. p.* opposed XI.viii.162

appoyntment *n.* agreement XII.vi.18

appreif *v.* approve IV.iii.42

approchyng *v.pres.3 pl.* approach XI.xii.57

appunctit *pa. p.* appointed, arranged XII.vi.12

apys *n.* apes, hence fools IV.Prol.21

ar *v.* wander (Vg **erramus**) III.iii.97

arayn *pa. p.* arrayed XIII.vii.17

arbor *Latin n.* tree, as opposed to **lignum**, wood I.Prol.384

arch *adj.* timid, reluctant, faint-hearted XI.vii.119

areik, areke, arekis *v.* reach III.x.29, 44; X.viii.46; X.ix.9

arekit *v.* reached II.ix.42

arest *n.* stopping, delay IV.v.119

arest *v.* stop, stay at rest I.iv.26

argew, argu *v.* accuse, blame XI.iv.57; XI.vii.41; XIII.vi.173

aris *n.* oars I.iii.18; III.v.13; III.viii.7

arlys *n.* earnest money, hence confirmation, guarantee XI.Prol.160

armipotent *adj.* mighty in arms II.vii.113

armony *n.* harmony II.Prol.1

armour pleite *n.* plate-armour III.vi.226: 53

armypotent *adj.* mighty in arms VI.viii.37; XI.i.19

armys *n.* the arms (of the body) V.iii.65; V.vii.3

armys *n.* armour, or armorial bearings (the distinction is hard to make in context) I.i.29

arrace, arraß *v.* remove, rip, tear down, snatch away VI.viii.96; XII.vi.171; XII.xiv.94

arrive *pa. p.* arrived V.ii.31

art *n.* part, neighbourhood, point of the compass I.iv.10; I.vi.46; III.v.3

art *n.* cunning II.iii.16

artik *adj.* arctic VI.i.18

artis *n.* regions, points of the compass III.iv.45

arryve *pa. p.* arrived I.viii.78, 148

arryvyn *v.inf.* to arrive VII.i.30

aryt *v.* cultivated VII.viii.140

as than *phrase*, at that time

ascend *pa. p.* ascended I.vii.2

aschame *v.intrans.* feel shame XII.v.17

askyn *v.inf.* to ask I.x.20

askyn *vbl.n.* asking, request II.ii.109; V.xiii.72

aspect *n.* appearance IV.vi.135. in astrology, the relative position of a planet as it appears from the earth IV.ii.28; V.ix.77; VII.Prol.31

aspergit *v.* sprinkled VI.iii.145 (R **asperdit**)

aspy *n.* spy, observer XII.Prol.265

aspy *v.* look VII.Prol.142

asß *n.* ash VI.iii.135

assail, assaill, assailȝeit *pa. p.* assailed V.x.heading; IV.xi.38, 65

assay *n.* enterprise, trial of courage II.ii.8; II.x.193

assay *v.* test, try III.vi.2; IV.iii.45; IV.iv.57. attempt IV.vi.9, 23

assayit *v.* tested IV.x.96

assayt *pa. p.* attacked (Vg **petitum**) XI.i.24

assegis *v.* besieges VIII.v.28

assentit *pa. p.* agreed, in agreement. **tharto the Grekis ~ ar** II.ii.130

245

assiltre *n.* axle V.xiii.127

assiltre *n.* axis of revolution of earth or heavens VI.ix.3; VI.xiii.77

assis *n.* ashes III.v.40

assolȝeit *pa. p.* absolved VII.i.138

assoverit *pa. p.* saved, made safe VII.v.50

assyngnand *pr. p.* assigning III.ii.140

assys *n.* funeral ashes IV.v.62; IV.xi.83

astabill *v.* establish X.iv.74

astait *n.* estate, condition XII.vii.102

astart *v.* escape from, avoid I.iii.71. leave, depart XIII.Prol.133

astart *v.* spring, start. **dyd ... apon hys aduersar** ~ XII.vi.116

astart *pa. p.* escaped XIII.v.92

astern *adj.* severe, stern X.xii.59

asur *adj.* blue XII.Prol.22

at *conj.* that III.ii.37

at *pron.* that III.i.106

at all *adv. phrase,* in all respects I.Prol.31

at vnder *adv. phrase,* in inferior position, in subjection I.iii.60

atanys *adv.* at once I.Prol.260; I.xii.1; III.viii.12

athir *adj.* both III.vii.62

athir *pron.* each of two, either. **on ~ part; on ~ hand** I.iv.9; I.iv.13. one or other of two III.x.58

athiris *pron.* of each. **in ~ hand the braid steil heid** I.vi.15

atour *prep.* over across VII.Prol.110. as *adv.* all over, everywhere VII.v.68

attachit *pa. p.* tied, fastened I.Prol.297

attantis *v.* accuses X.ii.94

attaynt *v.* accuse, bring charges against XII.Prol.281

attechyng *pr. p.* accusing, arresting XII.Prol.266

attempir, attempyr *v.* moderate IV.Prol.97, 132

attempyt *pa. p.* attempted, attacked, made a hostile attempt against IX.xii.63

attentfully *adv.* attentively VI.xi.5; XIII.viii.13

attentik *adj.* entitled to credit, reliable I.Prol.184; VI.Prol.107; IX.iv.67

atteyn *v.* attain, achieve I.Prol.265

attir *n.* pus, corruption III.x.16

attonys *adv.* at once, together XII.iii.23

aucht *n.* property III.ii.140

aucht *v.* owed VI.viii.67

auchten *adj.* eighth *Contentis*

auchteyn *num.* eighteen. *Tyme, space and dait.*12

augurall *adj.* prophetic IX.i.51

auguriall *adj.* of an augur VII.iii.85

augurian, auguriane *adj.* augural XII.v.58; XIII.x.32

auguriane *n.* augur IX.vi.44

aurial *adj.* golden VI.ii.122

austernly *adv.* sternly IX.xii.28

authorys *v.* authorize, sanction I.Prol.276

autorite *n.* authority I.iii.74

avale *n.* advantage IX.iii.35

avance, avans *v.* encourage, raise in spirit V.iv.134; XIII.ii.126

avansyt *v.* boasted V.vii.22

avant *n.* boast VII.iv.34

avant *v.* preen, glorify oneself IV.Prol.172; IX.iii.136

avantage *n.* **at ~** in superior position, triumphant XII.xi.112

avarus *adj.* avaricious III.i.83

aventour, aventur *n.* chance, accident I.vi.30; III.v.69; IV.xi.37. danger XII.v.19

aventur *v.* venture, risk VI.i.16

avices *n.* counsels, advice XI.vii.116

avisioun *n.* vision III.i.69

avisit *pa. p.* guided by counsel, advised I.Prol.106

avow *v.* make a vow III.ix.115

avowys *n.* vows VIII.ix.31

avyß *n.* advice II.i.43. opinion XII.v.50

avysand *pr. p.* counselling V.viii.46

avysye *adj.* cautious, aware V.ix.35

aw *n.* fear. **stude ~ was afraid (of)** III.ix.19

aw *v.* owned IX.xii.51. owed XI.i.115

awa *adv.* away III.iii.76

awach *v.* watch VII.vi.5

await *v.* lie in wait (for), waylay IX.v.29; XI.vii.128

await *n.* ambush XII.vi.68

awalk *v.* awake IV.x.97

away *adv.* with verb understood. put aside, dispose of. ~ ȝour smart IV.ix.9

awblaster *n.* crossbow XI.xv.16

awondris *v.* marvels, are astonished I.viii.34; I.ix.61

awondrit, awondryt *pa. p.* amazed, astonished I.xi.32; III.v.30; VI.v.25

awowis *n.* vows IX.i.58

awyß *n.* counsel. **on sik** ~ according to such counsel, but probably the reading should be **on sik a wyß**, in such a way I.iii.72

awytnessyng *pr. p.* bearing witness VI.ix.189

axin *vbl.n.* asking, request IX.iii.14

axit *v.pa.t.* asked IV.vi.21

axyng *vbl.n.* asking VII.i.137

ay *adv.* always, ever I.Prol.404, 457

aynd *n.* breath IV.xii.122; V.iv.80; VII.viii.128

ayndyng *vbl.n.* breathing V.xii.136; VII.ix.59

ayr *adv.* earlier IV.ii.55; XI.i.78

ayr *n.* heir V.xii.16; V.xiii.134

ayr *n.* oar (not air, tune) VI.iii.150

ayr morow *n.* early morning XII.Prol.304

ayris *n.* oars VIII.xii.37

bab *n.* babe, child X.ii.20

bad *adj.* poor, of defective quality. **my ~ wyt** I.Prol.294

bad *v.* bade VII.Prol.127

badkyn *n.* embroidered hanging, tapestry I.ix.107 (53 **bandkyn**)

bage *n.* money-bag VIII.Prol.85: 53

baid *n.* wait, delay I.v.23; III.ii.129

bail *n.* beacon-fire II.v.13

baill *n.* sorrow (poetic) VIII.Prol.80; XII.Prol.233

bair *n.* boar IV.iv.61; XIII.iii.21

bair *v.* bore, carried I.viii.17

baissing *vbl.n.* dismay IV.vii.77: R (C

for seizing half onwrocht ...)

baith *v.* bathe. *See* **all to** ~ XII.xii.67

bak *n.* back. **tak the** ~ flee XI.Prol.139

bak *n.* bat I.Prol.320; XIII.Prol.33

bak saill, baksaill *n.* sternmost sail of a ship I.iii.16; V.i.34

bakbyte *v.* slander III.Prol.23

bakyn *pa. p.* baked III.iii.198

baldar *adj.* bolder I.vii.71

baldis *v.* embolden X.vii.90

baldly *adv.* boldly, confidently I.Prol.496

balk *n.* beam XII.x.121

ballance *n.* scales, balance for weighing VI.vii.18

ballancis *n.* plates (Vg **lansibus**) XII.iv.142

ballast *n.* stones in hold of ship, hence weight (Vg **saxum**) X.iv.88

ballen *n.* whalebone VII.xii.67

ballattis *n.* songs (not necessarily narrative poems, nor yet dance songs) VI.x.40; VII.vi.132; XII.Prol.205

ballyngar, ballyngare *n.* ship (originally a whaling-ship, here loosely for any ship) II.i.19; II.iii.65; IV.vii.72; V.xiv.88

balmy *adj.* sweet (used vaguely in aureate language as a term of praise) I.Prol.341

balmyng *v.inf.* to embalm, to anoint IV.iv.39

banareris, banereris *n.* banner-bearers, leaders, literally and figuratively IV.Prol.180; XI.ix.43

band *n.* contract I.Prol.439; IV.vi.117

bandis *n.* bands, bonds I.ii.8

bane *adv.* readily VIII.Prol.58

bane *adj.* comfortable, in good estate, ready to act III.ii.58

bankat, banket *n.* banquet I.ix.106; VI.x.68. sometimes possibly a verb XI.xiv.40

bannys *v.* curses XI.v.78

banwart *n.* a plant, the daisy XII.Prol.115

bar *adj.* bare, leafless VII.Prol.57

barbary *adj.* barbarous, or from pagan lands II.viii.120; XI.xv.23

barbour *adj.* barbarous, rude. **with lewit ~ tong** I.Prol.21

bardis *n.* defensive trappings on horses XI.xii.6; XI.xv.7

bargan, bargane *n.* fight I.vi.116; III.iv.52, 76; V.iii.22

bargannyng, barganyng *vbl.n.* fighting I.vi.61; X.iii.59

barge, bargis *n.* a broad, flat boat, propelled by rowers or sails, larger than a balinger I.iv.45; III.Prol.39; III.iii.81; III.viii.126

baris *n.* boars IV.Prol.70; VI.xvi.35

bark *n.* general term for small ships **schip, ballynger and ~. galay, ~ or barge** I.iv.45; IV.vii.72

bark *v.* bark; figuratively, to speak in a fit of temper III.Prol.19

barknyt *pa. p.* hardened into a crust. of blood, clotted II.v.41

barm *n.* bosom XII.Prol.76

barmkyn *n.* battlement, outer fortification II.iv.61; VIII.vi.101

barn *n.* warrior or hero (or poetic for man) I.vii.101

barn *n.* bairn, child VIII.Prol.72

barnage *n.* body of nobility X.i.142; XII.xi.109

barnage *n.* youth V.Prol.25

barntyme *n.* offspring collectively XII.xiii.133

barrand *adj.* bare of intellectual resources I.Prol.20

barrer *n.* fence or palisade. specifically, the limits of a racecourse or tournament-ground V.iii.79

barreß *n.* enclosure for tournaments XII.xiv.10

barroun *n.* baron, or hero in general (Vg **heros**) VI.vii.58; X.x.92

barys *n.* boars VII.Prol.82

baß *adj.* low (in volume, not pitch), soft (Andromache **with a ~ voce**) III.v.76; IX.vi.28

basnet *n.* small, light helmet XII.viii.114

bassyn *adj.* made of bass or woven fibres II.iv.66

baston *n.* club or staff V.ii.55

bastard *adj.* figuratively, adulterated, corrupt I.Prol.117

batalis *n.* battle-arrays, battalions II.vi.70

bate *n.* boat IV.xi.8

batelling, batellyng *n.* battlements XII.xi.132; IX.ix.12

bath *adj.* both II.i.62

bathing *v.inf.* to bathe VII.xi.53

battalyng *n.* battlements II.viii.14

battil, battill *adj.* of grass, thick, luxuriant VI.x.25; XII.Prol.115

bawbord, bawburd *n.* larboard, or left side of ship III.vi.143; III.viii.110

bawdry *n.* lewdness, immorality IV.Prol.186; XII.Prol.210

bawgy *n.* heraldic badge II.vii.55

bawkis *n.* wooden cross-beams IX.vii.86

bawkis *n.* ridges of unploughed land in fields VIII.Prol.85

bawne *v.* anoint? III.viii.10 (E **bawm**)

bawsand *adj.* of horses, with a white face V.x.40 (R **bawsane**)

bay *n.* song of birds VIII.viii.5; XII.Prol.232; XIII.Prol.166

bay *adj.* of horses, reddish brown V.x.41

bay *n.* curve, a bay of the sea III.iv.29

bayand *pr. p.* curving III.i.35

bayn *n.* bane, death, destruction IX.xii.104

bayt *n.* boat II.viii.106

be *prep.* by IV.iii.24. the phrase **~ sik hunder** to the extent of a hundred such II.iv.2. the phrase **~ tyme** betimes, at the right time VII.Prol.94

bean, beand *pr. p.* being I.v.81, marginal note. VIII.iii.25

beaw *adj.* as a form of address, fair (sir) I.Prol.105

beche *n.* beech-wood II.i.6

becum, becummyn *pa. p.* come VI.v.160. come to, arrived at III.iv.4

bedelvyn *pa. p.* buried XI.v.66

bedelvys *v.* buries XI.v.50

bedene *adv.* straightway, continuously, quickly (usually padding) I.ix.heading; IV.iv.73; V.iii.85

bedettit *pa. p.* indebted VIII.vii.20

bedeyn *adv.* straightway I.ii.33; V.v.6. *See also* **bedene**

bedis *n.* prayers VI.i.100

bedoif *pa. p.* immersed, buried XI.xvi.72

bedone *v. compound,* be done VII.vii.56

bedovyn, bedowyn, bedoyf *pa. p.* immersed V.vi.125; VII.Prol.60; XII. Prol.136

bedowyt *v.* subdued XIII.i.42

bedrall *adj.* bed-ridden XII.vii.32

bedraw *v.* intensive, draw forth thoroughly VII.xi.130

bedy *v.* stain, dye XII.xii.67

bedyit *pa. p.* dyed, stained, soaked I.iv.31; III.vi.60, 83; V.vi.77

befaw *v.* befall IX.i.48

befor *prep.* preceding in rank, excelling in quality, beyond III.v.77

beforn *adv.* before I.Prol.427

beft *pa. p.* beaten II.x.78; XIII.Prol.123. hence, of metals, forged IX.vi.118

befundyn *compound* be found II.ii.24

begane, begone *See* **gold begane**

begeif *compound* be given IX.xii.30

beget *pa. p.* begotten IV.v.47

begouth *v.* began I.Prol.504; I.vii.52; III.i.36

begrat *v.* wept, bewailed VI.vii.64

begravyn *pa. p.* buried XI.iii.8

begunnyn *pa. p.* begun III.vii.53

behald *pa. p.* beheld IV.xii.23

behaldyn *v.inf.* to behold VI.v.73

beheist, behest *n.* promise, vow III. ii.101; IV.ix.97

behufe *n.* advantage, benefit IV.viii.41; VI.xiii.69

behuffis, behuffyt, behufis, behufyt *v.* behooves (with reflexive pronoun) I.Prol.116, 445; I.iii.69; III.vii.43

behwyt *v.* behoved VIII.ix.54; X.iv.72

beik *n.* beak of a bird; hence, ugly nose III.x.43; VI.ix.135

beild *n.* shelter, protection, sheltering-place II.ix.16; IV.iv.72; V.v.36

beild *v.* build I.vii.ii; IV.v.158

beilding *pr. p.* building IV.Prol.259

beir *n.* funeral-bier VI.iii.127

beir *n.* noise produced by rushing movement III.iv.32; VI.ix.50; VII.vii.98. any rasping noise, such as the cry of an owl IV.viii.113

beir *n.* barley VIII.Prol.63

beir *v.* to carry by impact. **leß thai [winds] suld ~ with thar byr the skyis** I.ii.15

beis *n.* bees VII.i.97

beis *v.pres.3 pl.* are VI.xiii.4

beis *v.* imperative, be I.iv.84; I.vi.44

beist *n.* animal, especially farmstock (Vg **pecudem**) III.ii.102

beit *v.* amend, repair VIII.vii.84. prepare I.viii.105; V.xii.159

bekend *pa. p.* known, familiar III.x.4

bekend *pa. p.* instructed II.vi.94; III. viii.122

bekis *v.* enjoys warmth, basks V.iii.50

bekit *v.* warmed, exposed (the body) to heat I.iv.32

beknyt *pa. p.* laced? (cf. Golding *Ovid Met.* **Hir filthy arms beknit with snakes**) VIII.vi.96

bekyn *n.* beckoning, signal, beacon III. viii.26; XII.xi.173

bekyt *pa. p.* baked, exposed to warmth VII.Prol.93

belch *n.* abyss III.vi.127; VII.v.110

beld *n.* shelter, protection II.ix.24; XI.i.134

beld *v.* build VI.i.135

beleif *n.* hope. VI.xv.72

beleif *v.* hope, expect V.vi.105

beleif *v. compound,* give up, relinquish X.xi.166; X.xiii.164

beleve *n.* hope, trust I.viii.109; IV.viii.52

belive *adv.* at once, immediately I.iii.1; I.v.3

bellan *n.* baleen, whalebone V.vii.73

bellettis *n.* songs VII.xi.142

bellicall *adj.* warlike VII.x.54; XI.iii.61

bellis *n.* bubbles VII.vii.129

bellyng *vbl.n.* of stags, roaring. hence, mating-time IV.Prol.68

bellys *n.* bellows VIII.vii.176

belowkit *v.* enclosed IX.vii.64: R (C **lowkyt**)

belt *pa. p.* built I.i.9; VII.iii.47

belt *pa. p.* belted I.vii.132

belyf, belyfe, belyve *adv.* at once I.iv. heading; II.vii.60; III.vi.116

bemand *pr. p.* resounding XI.ix.31

bemyng *vbl.n.* sounding, buzzing VII.i.88

bemys *v.* resounds V.iii.90; V.vii.41

ben *adv.* in inner part of house. **but and** ~ IV.xii.53

benar *adj.* more pleasant VI.v.36

bend, bendis *n.* band, fillets II.ii.138; III. ii.25; IV.viii.106

bend *n.* bound, leap V.vi.58

bene *v.pres.1 pl.* of 'be' are I.iv.70

benedicite *Latin imp.* bless you. used as a mild oath IV.Prol.36

benkis *n.* benches *Directioun*.48

bensell *n.* bending, straining VIII.xii.37

bent *pa. p.* of **bind** in original sense of bind, stretch. **with** ~ **saill** etc. I.i.64; ii.124; V.v.68

benyng *adj.* benign, gracious IV.viii.67

berdyt *pa. p.* bearded I.xi.93

beris *n.* barley XII.Prol.77

beris *n.* bears VI.xvi.35

beris *v.* roars, cries out IV.v.19

bern, bernys *n.* man, warrior (poetic) VIII.Prol.23, 120; VIII.iii.61; VIII.x.25. applied to Pallas Athene VIII.viii.146

berong *compound* be rung II.Prol.11

beryall *adj.* crystal XIII.Prol.26

beschorn *compound* be shorn, harvested IV.Prol.14

beseik *v.* beseech IV.xi.68

besekyng *pr. p.* beseeching III.i.69

besekyng *v.pres.3 pl.* beseech XI.xvii.38

besekyng *v.inf.* to beseech VIII.iii.74

besene *compound* be seen VIII.xi.54

beseyn *pa. p.* arrayed, equipped III.ix.7; IV.v.78

besmottyrit *pa. p.* spattered V.vi.124

besocht *v.* begged, implored III.vi.6

besowth *v.* besought II.x.161

besprent *pa. p.* spotted, sprinkled II.v.39; IX.vi.58

best *n.* beast XIII.i.36

bestad *pa. p.* situated, circumstanced X.xi.17

bestiall *n.* animal-kind VII.Prol.79; XIII.Prol.59

bestis *n.* animals, especially farm stock V.xii.130

besyde *adv.* **go** ~ go to one side or astray I.Prol.301

bet *v.* prepared, repaired I.iv.94; V.xii.143

bet *v.* beat II.iii.95

bet *pa. p.* prepared II.iv.85; III.iv.44; III. viii.144; IV.i.112; IV.v.162

bet *pa. p.* beaten II.viii.72

betald *compound* be told XI.xvi.32

betane *compound* be taken VII.v.30

betauch, betaucht *v.* entrusted II.xi.113; III.ix.115; V.xiii.19

betauch, betaucht *v. pr p.* yielded, entrusted to another XI.xi.124; XII. xii.221

bete *v.* strike, overcome by blows, hence to hunt I.iv.59

bete, betis *v.* beat, hammer, strike I.vii.22; IV.ii.41

betraisit, betrasit *pa. p.* betrayed I.v.42; I.vii.94

betrappyt *pa. p.* entrapped X.xii.56

betrump *v.* deceive, trick II.xi.105; IV.xi.14

betweyn *adv.* among other things. **tyne nocht ʒour laubour and ʒour thank** ~ XI.Prol.176

betyd *pa. p.* betided, happened V.vi.123

betyde *v.* happen I.Prol.440

bevir *n.* beaver fur VIII.Prol.58

bew *adj.* fine IX.Prol.79

bewave, bewavit *pa. p.* stirred up, blown away I.iv.44; III.vi.184

bewch *n.* bough VI.ii.121

bewchit *pa. p.* branched (of anchor) V.xiv.92

beweip *pa. p.* stained with tears XI.i.72

bewis *n.* boughs I.iv.17, 58; IV.ix.68

bewry *v.* turn aside, twist, distort X.i.80

bewry *pa. p.* surrounded IV.iv.16

bewys *n.* boughs II.iv.94

beyk *v.* warm III.viii.10

beym *n.* beam (of a plough) XIII.viii.24

beyn *adj.* gracious, mild, pleasant VI.x.25; VII.Prol.89; VIII.ii.67

beyn *v.* be, are IV.i.17; VI.x.29

beynge *v.* bow XII.Prol.292

beyr *n.* bier, tomb III.i.116; III.i.124

beyr *v.* bear V.i.66

beyt *v.* strike, overcome by blows; hence, of harts, to hunt V.v.19

beyt *v.* prepare, repair IV.ii.23; XII.Prol.233

bigane *pa. p.* surrounded, overlaid. **with gold** ~ VI.i.12

biggingis *n.* buildings VIII.viii.80

biggit *v.* built I.v.36

biggit *pa. p.* built III.viii.88

bilappit *pa. p.* enveloped, surrounded III.iv.40

bilge *n.* lower part of ship's hull V.iv.78

bilgeit *pa. p.* large-hulled II.iii.65

birl *v.* pour out for drinking VIII. iv.200

bisme *n.* abyss (aphetic form of abysm) VII.v.47

bissy *adj.* diligent I.Prol.109

bla *adj.* blue, bluish or livid from cold or a blow VII.Prol.130; VII.xi.112; VII.xiv.10

blabryng *vbl.n.* babbling I.Prol.33

blag *n.* boasting falsehood VIII.Prol.80: E (C **bost gret brag blowis**)

blaiknyt *pa. p.* blackened III.i.122

blait *adj.* dull, stupid I.viii.129

blaith *adj.* blith IV.iii.52: L

blaitly *adv.* dully, stupidly I.Prol.251

blaknyt *v.* became pale XI.xv.119. made pale VIII.iv.32

blanchit *pa. p.* bleached VII.Prol.57; XII.Prol.108

blandit, blandyt *pa. p.* blended, mixed III.ix.83; VI.i.39

blank *adj.* white XII.Prol.118

blason *v.* praise, extol I.Prol.329; VI.xiv.38 (R **blissing**, L **blosum**, B **brason**)

blastrand *pr. p.* blowing in blasts, blustery I.iii.15

blaw *pa. p.* blown, scattered by wind I.i.59; I.vi.6; I.viii.54, 143; IV.ii.5

blawis *n.* blows, blowings, blasts I.iv.15

blawys *v.* stirs up (as hunger) VI.ix.155

bled *n.* bleeding. **fell doun for**~ (E, R, 53 **forbled** perhaps should be taken as bled dry, exhausted by bleeding) VI.viii.56

blenk *n.* glance, brief look I.Prol.108; I.vii.114; III.v.50

blenkit *v.* glanced I.viii.4

blent *n.* glance II.ii.18: E, R, 53 **with ane** ~ **about** (C **with ene**) XI.xv.76

blent *v.* glanced I.vi.3; II.ii.18; II.x.9

bleß, blesys *n.* blaze, bright fire V.ix.66; V.xi.85

blist *n.* blast of a trumpet II.vi.31

blith *adj.* blithe. Of inanimate things, pleasing I.xi.28

blok *n.* scheme, plot V.xi.12

blokkis *n.* blocks of wood, clubs VII. viii.108

blomyt *v.* flourished, came forth vigorously, bloomed literally or metaphorically XI.xii.103

blont *adj.* not sharp V.iii.102

blowt *adj.* barren, bare VII.Prol.65; XI.xvii.8; XIII.vi.227

blud fyre *n.* fever, frenzy IV.i.3: 53 (C **blynd fyre**)

bludy *adj.* bloody I.v.120. hence, monstrous III.iii.98: R

bludyand *pr. p.* making bloody XI.ii.71

blundir *n.* trouble, distress I.Prol.390

blunt *adj.* in intellectual matters, lacking force or point I.Prol.314; XI.Prol.60. barren XI.xvii.8: R; XII. Prol.95, 98: R

blyn *v.* cease, stop IV.Prol.178; VI.i.99; VIII.Prol.23

blynd *adj.* not seeing, or unseen (Vg caeco) IV.i.3. concealed, covered, hidden I.iii.28, 87; III.x.87. hence, of waves, lacking discernment, mindless, implacable III.iii.98 (R **bludy**, 53 **wyndy**)

blyndlyngis *adv.* blindly II.vi.74

blyndyt *pa. p.* blinded, blind IV.Prol.3

blyß *v.* bliss, to rejoice, with pun on bless XII.Prol.303

blyssit *v.* blessed XI.xi.56; XI.vii.12

boche *n.* contagious disease VIII. Prol.85

bocht *v.* bought, redeemed X.Prol.20; XI.Prol.200

boddum *n.* low-lying stretch of ground, pasture VII.Prol.57

bodword *n.* message, report VII.v.4, 15; VIII.iii.44

body *n.* body. person I.Prol.484

bodyn *pa. p.* provided, equipped VII. xi.116; IX.iv.20; XI.xiii.139

bogill *n.* a supernatural creature I.Prol.273; VI.Prol.18

boir *pa. p.* born X.Prol.41; Epitaph.1

boistyt *v.* threatened VIII.xi.20: 53

boith *n.* booth VIII.Prol.57

bok, bokkis *v.* pour, belch forth III. viii.136; III.ix.82

bokkand *pr. p.* belching X.iv.134: R, 53 (C **sey wallis bulrand**)

boldnyt *v.* swelled, flooded I.viii.73

boldyn *pa. p.* swollen, distended II.vii.36

boldynnand *pr. p.* swelling V.iii.43

boldynnys *v.* swells III.iii.91; III.viii.99

boldynnyt *pa. p.* swollen II.v.42

bolm, bolmys *n.* boat-pole V.iv.93; VI.v.15

bond *pa. p.* tied, restrained; hence, figuratively, pregnant VII.xi.47

bondage *n.* servitude IV.Prol.47

bondis *n.* bond-slaves X.Prol.127

bonk, bonkis *n.* bank (poetic) VII. xii.83; XII.Prol.62

bonnettis *n.* additional pieces laced to sails V.xiv.4

bontay *n.* gift VII.Prol.140; XII.vi.127

bonte *n.* goodness I.Prol.331; VI.xv.26

bor *n.* boar X.xii.47

bor *pa. p.* born IX.ix.46

boryt *pa. p.* bored, pierced IV.Prol.155

boß *adj.* hollow, concave I.ii.50; IX.ii.30

bost *n.* threatening, menace, arrogant speech or manner III.iv.107; III. viii.98; V.vii.56; VIII.Prol.80

bost *v. trans.* threaten VIII.Prol.18

bostand *pr. p.* threatening VIII.xi.20; X.iv.88

bosum *n.* of river or ocean, a gulf or bend I.iv.11; VI.ii.114

bosys *n.* shield-bosses IX.xiii.72

bot *adv.* only I.viii.4

bot *conj.* unless I.Prol.279

bot *prep.* without V.Prol.65

bote *n.* wine cask IX.vi.91

botynys *n.* boots (Vg **cothurno**) I.vi.57

boun *pa. p. adj.* ready, prepared IV.vi.38

boundis *n.* limits, literally and figuratively I.Prol.378; I.i.2. in plural form used as a singular. **to a ~ constrenyt** I.Prol.293

bourd, bourdis *n.* joke I.Prol.125; V.vi.124; VII.ii.29

bourd *v.* joke IX.Prol.24

bovn *pa. p. adj.* ready VIII.viii.115

bow *n.* arch, as of a bridge or gate VI.x.10

bow, bowis *n.* herd of cattle VI.i.70; VII. viii.22, 139

bow *v.* bend, curve VII.x.73

bowand *pr. p.* bending, curving III.v.6; XI.xvi.60

bowbardis, bowbartis *n.* sluggards, louts I.Prol.317; IV.i.28 (E **bowbaris**); XI.xiv.18

bowbart *adj.* sluggish I.vii.33

bowellit *pa. p.* disembowelled IV.xi.25: R 53

bowght *n.* sheepfold IX.ii.64

bowit *pa. p.* bent, curved III.iii.81

bowkis *n.* carcass (of a slaughtered animal) I.iv.91; I.ix.100; VI.iv.35

bowkit *pa. p.* of large bulk III.vi.127

bowland *pr. p.* curving, twisting III.iv.15; VI.ix.135

bowle *n.* bowl-shaped basin. **the fludis heß ... maid ~ or bay** III.viii.55

bown *pa. p. adj.* ready, prepared (e.g. to go) III.iii.80; V.x.12; VI.ix.28

bownyng *pr. p.* making ready (to go) II.x.200

bownys *v.* prepares, makes oneself ready (to go), betakes oneself II.viii.68; IV.vii. heading; V.i.2; VII.Prol.97

bowr *n.* inner chamber, bower (Vg **thalamo**) VI.vi.26

bowrd *n.* joke II.iv.89

bowrdyng *vbl.n.* joking XII.xii.174

bowsum *adj.* obedient, complaisant; hence, pleasant, agreeable I.v.134

bowsumly *adv.* humbly, obediently VIII. vi.124

bowtis *v.* bolts, darts, springs V.vi.58

bowys *n.* herds XII.xii.62

bowyt *pa. p.* curved; of ships, built (with curved sides) X.v.36

boyn *n.* boon, prayer IX.vii.76; VIII. Prol.140

boynd wench *n.* woman bound by contract to domestic service (Vg **serva**) IX.ix.49

boyr *n.* hole made by boring, any hole I.iii.51; IV.xi.41

boyr *pa. p.* born. **he that was immortal get and** ~ VI.ii.88

boyß *adj.* hollow, concave II.i.73; II.v.20; VI.iii.27

boyß *n.* boss of shield II.iv.49; VII.xii.97

bra *n.* hillside, bank of stream I.iv.19; I.vi.109; III.vi.70

brace *n.* band of supporting stonework VI.x.10

brace *v.* embrace IV.ii.71

bradand *pr. p.* springing, bursting forth X.viii.43

brade *v.* rushed, burst out I.ii.51

bradis *v.intrans.* bursts forth I.iv.36; IV.x.20; V.viii,12; V.xii.140

bradis *v.trans.* throws out, puts forth suddenly IV.Prol.61

brag *n.* boast, defiant sound VII.x.86; VIII.viii.164; XIII.vii.51

braid *adj.* plain, clear I.Prol.110

braid *adv.* broadly, freely I.ii.73

braid *n.* sudden movement, leap II.iv.22

braid *v.* of speech, spreads abroad IV.vii.5

braid *v.* of speech, burst out, spread abroad II.ii.128

braid syde *n.* broadside, the side of a ship I.iii.20

brais *n.* hillsides I.iv.12

braith *n.* breath I.viii.94; V.iv.79

braithly *adj.* violent I.ii.7

brak *adj.* salty. **large seys** ~ V.iv.147; V.xiii.28

brak *v.* broke (resistance), overcame by persuasion VIII.vii.33

brand *n.* sword (poetical) X.xi.118

brandysis, brandysys *v.intrans.* acts conspicuously or violently IV.v.105; IV.x.82

brane *adj.* mad, furious **Turnus half myndles and** ~; E **in** ~ XII.xii.117

brangillys *n.* a lively dance XIII.ix.107

branglis, branglys *v.* shakes II.x.119; VIII. iv.122 (**brangillis** VIII.Prol.125: 53)

brankand *pr. p.* tossing the head, prancing XI.xii.7

brasand *pr. p.* embracing II.viii.89; V.xiii.10

braseris *n.* pieces of arm armour V.vii.69, 85

brast *v.* burst, broke I.iii.18

brasyng *pr. p.* tying, binding IX.vi.140

bratland, bratlyng *pr. p.* rattling VII. Prol.133; XII.xiv.89

brattill *v.* rattle IX.xi.96

brawland *pr.p.* contending, quarrelling XII.viii.84

brawlys *v.* 2 *sg.* quarrels VIII.Prol.125

brawnys *n.* muscles of arms or legs V.vii.73, 108

bray *n.* harsh cry or sound of animals I.v.34; III.iv.47; III.x.32. Or of humans X.x.72

bray *v.* roar, make a harsh sound I.v.120; IV.xii.47

brayand *pr. p.* clamouring V.i.34; V.xiii.127; VIII.viii.92

brayn *adj.* furious, mad XI.xvii.73

brayn pan *n.* skull X.vii.137

brayng *pr. p.* roaring I.ii.11; I.iii.15

brayng *vbl.n.* roars III.viii.98

bre *n.* eyebrow VI.vii.96

brederyng, bredyr *n.* brothers III.x.41; VII.xi.69

bredyrly *adj.* brotherly, belonging to a brother V.xi.61

breid *n.* breadth. **on** ~ abroad IV.Prol.175; IV.iii.56; IV.v.2

breid *v.* breed, make profit VIII.Prol.85

breistis *n.* breast, as seat of feelings I.Prol.321; hence, courage, aspirations, etc. V.iv.134

breithfull *adj.* angry, full of rage XI.xiv.6; XII.viii.133

brek *n.* breach of peace, outbreak of disorder II.vi.15; XI.vii.105; XIII.vi.85

breke *v.* disband XIII.vi.100

brent *adj.* straight VIII.xii.14

brerd *pa. p.* burgeoned, sprouted II.viii.60

brerd *n.* first shoots (of grain) XII. Prol.77

brethir *n.* brothers IX.xi.heading; XII.v.125; XII.v.139

brethfull *adj.* angry, raging XII.ix.63

briggantis *n.* brigands I.v.81, marginal note

brimell *adj.* obscure (see note) I.Prol.484

brittyn *v.* cut to pieces (poetic) III.iv.26

broch *n.* pointed rod; hence, curling iron XII.ii.126

brochand *pr. p.* pricking, as with spurs VI.xv.82

broche, brochis *n.* pins on which wool is wound VII.xiii.59; IX.viii.36

brochit *v.* skewered I.iv.93; XIII.ii.19

brochyt *pa. p.* pierced V.ix.53

brod *n.* prod, goad VI.Prol.64; VI.ii.47

broddis *v.* prods IX.x.48

brodir *n.* brother II.viii.111

brodmell *n.* offspring, litter III.vi.73; VIII.i.58

brokkaris *n.* panders IV.Prol.186

brokkettis *n.* young stags XII.Prol.179

bromys *n.* broom plant VII.Prol.78

bront *n.* attack, onrush III.x.64; hence, front rank of army IX.viii.19

bront *pa. p.* burnt III.viii.142

bronys *n.* twigs XI.ii.16; XII.Prol.165

broustar *n.* brewer VIII.Prol.63

brovn *adj.* brown; hence, of skies, dark, threatening IX.i.41

browdyn *pa. p.* embroidered IX.ii.45

browny, browneis *n.* brownies, benevolent supernatural spirits I.Prol.273; VI.Prol.18

broym *n.* broom plant IX.Prol.37

broyndis *n.* brands, burning sticks I.iii.94

bruchis *n.* ornamental fastenings, buckles VII.iv.194

brudy *adj.* prolific, fruitful I.ii.4; VI.ix.137; VI.xiii.61

bruke *v.* enjoy, use IV.v.112; IV.xi.73; VI.xiv.11; hence, brook, endure, put up with III.Prol.40

brukkill *adj.* brittle XII.xii.114

brumaill *adj.* wintry VII.Prol.14

brusch *n.* violent onrush II.viii.103

bruschand *pr. p.* rushing IX.vii.144

bruschit *v.* rushed IX.xi.78

brusery *n.* embroidery XI.xv.24

brusyt *pa. p.* embroidered I.xi.30; III.vii.25; IV.iv.15; IV.v.62

brutal, brutale *adj.* pertaining to animals VIII.i.20; hence, opprobriously, of persons, brutish IV.Prol.153

brute *n.* good or ill fame IV.Prol.257; VII.v.7

brute *n.* noise I.vii.8; V.iii.90; V.x.20

brutell *adj.* brutish IV.Prol.225

bruthir *n.* brother (**brodir** is the more usual spelling) XII.viii.83

bruyt *n.* fame VII.ix.51

bruyt *n.* clamour, uproar VI.ix.59

brybry *n.* wretchedness, rascality, triviality (not bribery in modern sense) VIII.Prol.144

bryg *n.* bridge VIII.xii.136

brym *adj.* fierce, furious, violent IV.iii.22; V.v.41; VII.Prol.15

brym, brymly *adv.* savagely, fiercely XII.xii.58, 215

brymmyll *n.* bramble III.ix.110

brynt *pa. p.* burned III.ix.86

bryntstane *n.* brimstone I.ii.3, marginal note; II.xi.34

bryth *n.* birth I.v.113, marginal note

brythnes *n.* brightness III.iii.93

brytnyt, **bryttnyt** *pa. p.* cut up, hewed down (poetic) III.iv.78; IV.ii.11 (R **brikkynnyt**, 53 **briknit**); IV.xi.44; V.ii.105

bub, **bubbys** *n.* blast, squall I.iii.15; IV.iv.65; V.xii.56

buge *n.* a kind of bill, a warlike instrument XI.Prol.16

buge *n.* lambskin VIII.Prol.58

bugill *n.* bugle VII.Prol.67

bukclaris *n.* bucklers, small round shields VII.xii.97

buke *v.* baked I.iv.40

bukleir *n.* buckler, small round shield II.iv.49

bull *n.* boil, state of boiling XII.viii.23: E

bullerand, **bullyrand** *pr. p.* bubbling, flowing impetuously I.iii.51; III.iv.112; IX.vi.53

bullir, **bullyr** *n.* bubble, boiling III.iv.112: R; V.iii.78; VII.vii.127

bullyrrit *v.* boiled I.iii.26

bulrand *pr. p.* boiling XI.xii.70 (E, R **bukand**)

bulyng *pr. p.* boiling VII.vii.126

bund *pa. p.* joined together, as in marriage IV.iii.26. ~ **with child** pregnant VII.v.89

bundis *n.* bounds, limits, place of residence XI.iii.63

bur *v.* bore, carried VI.i.69

bural, **burall** *adj.* rustic, rude I.Prol.48; *Directioun*.52

burd *n.* edging, border XI.ii.36

burd *n.* the side of a ship III.x.21

burdis *n.* boards, tables I.vi.25; III.iv.93; III.vi.11

burdon, **burdonys** *n.* club, cudgel III.x.7; V.vii.4, 68, 88

burely *adj.* strongly made, sturdy IV.iv.16 (from R: C **the burdour al bewry**)

burgeonys *n.* sprouts, branches IV.Prol.11; IV.viii.107

burgeß, **burgessis** *n.* citizen of a burgh VII.Prol.57, 85

burgh *n.* city I.x.130; VIII.ix.64 sometimes fortress, castle, citadel IV.iii.15; IV.vi.133

burgions, **burgyonys** *n.* swelling buds III.i.50; VI.xiii.104

burgionyt *pa. p.* budded, sprouted IV.vii.75

burn *n.* brook III.v.131

burnet *adj.* dark brown XII.Prol.106

burrel *adj.* rude, rustic VII.xi.56

buß *n.* bush IV.vi.42; hence, figuratively, a bunch or clump VII.xi.77

buschboun *n.* boxwood IX.x.67 (53 **buschbome**)

buschement *n.* ambush IX.viii.113: R; XI.x.44: R, 53 (C **enbuschment**)

buskis *n.* bushes III.i.46; III.ix.111; hence, wild places XI.xvi.23

buskit *v.* made ready to go, proceeded VI.iv.94

buskyt *pa. p.* prepared, arranged V.vii.9

bussart *n.* buzzard hawk IX.Prol.45

bustuus *adj.* rough, rude, violent I.Prol.48; III.ix.58; IV.Prol.62; V.ii.55

bustuusly *adv.* rudely I.ii.53

bustuusneß *n.* rude violence XI.vii.140

buustuus *adj.* rude, violent V.vii.12

but *prep.* without I.Prol.339; III.i.115; III.iii.112; III.vi.187

but *adv.* in outer part of house ~ **and ben** IV.xii.53

bute *n.* help, remedy, advantage II.vi.106; II.xi.36; V.xii.80; V.x.20: R (C **for brute and ioy**)

button *n.* knob or stud VII.xiii.82; IV.iv.20

buttonys *n.* buds XII.Prol.101

buyr *v.* bore, gave birth to VI.Prol.142

by *adv.* against VII.ix.109

by *prep.* by. ~ **and** ~ straightway, presently I.vi.48

by *prep.* with regard to IV.Prol.220

by *v.* buy IV.vii.42

byce *n.* dark fur used for lining garments VIII.Prol.58

bych *n.* beech tree X.v.36

byd *v.* request, ask for **I ~ nothir, of ʒour turmentis nor ʒour glorie** V.Prol.59

byd, byde *v.* bide, stop, remain III.iv.38; V.iv.93; V.v.65

byde *v.trans.*, await, wait for III.ix.42

byrdyng *n.* burden XI.xi.39

byg *v.* build I.vii.52; III.ii.128; IV.v.71

bygane *v.* began IV.viii.114

bygareit *pa. p.* striped, ornamented VIII.xi.43

byggit *pa. p.* built II.i.61

byggyngys, byggynnys *n.* buildings II.i.62; II.viii.32

bygrave *v.* bury VI.v.174

bygravit *pa. p.* laid in grave I.vi.83

byke *n.* hive, den IV.vii.81; VIII. Prol.164; VIII.iv.26; XII.x.86

byleip *v.* leap on, cover VII.iv.206

bylappis *v.* encircles VI.vii.35

bylappit *pa. p.* enclosed, encircled V.i.25

bylgis *n.* lower part of ship hulls; hence, any ship-like containers II.i.11

byng *n.* heap, pile IV.vii.80; IV.ix.45, 64; especially a funeral pyre VI.iii.40

byngis *v.* heaps VIII.Prol.57

bypast *pa. p.* having past by II.i.1

byr *n.* wind, strong rush (and accompanying wind) I.ii.15; II.vii.97; III.iv.47

byrd lyme *n.* sticky substance to entrap birds VIII.Prol.71

byrdyngis *n.* burdens I.vii.31

byreft *pa. p.* stolen III.v.96

byrkis *n.* birch trees VI.iii.48

byrl, byrlis, byrlys *v.* pours out for drinking I.iv.67; III.v,138; VIII.iii.199

byrne *n.* cuirass VII.x.95

byrnyng *pr. p.* burning IV.Prol.117

byrnyst *pa. p.* burnished V.v.29

byrrand *pr. p.* flying with a whirring noise IX.ix.134; XI.xv.80

byrsillit, byrslyt *pa. p.* scorched, burned, charred VII.viii.109; VII. xii.36; XI.v.64

byrsit *pa. p.* covered with bristles VI.xvi.35

byrsy *adj.* bristly X.iv.127

byrsys *n.* bristles VIII.iv.181

byrsyt *pa. p.* bruised, crushed IX.xiii.69 (R **birssin**)

byrth *n.* burden, carrying capacity of a vessel V.iii.31

byrun *compound* run by VIII.i.61

byrunnyn *pa. p.* encircled, encompassed V.v.13. past by V.xi.54

byß *v.* hiss VIII.vii.119

bysme *n.* abysm; hence, belly III.vi.127; VI.v.3; VIII.iv.138

bysmer, bysmeyr *n.* bawd or pander IV.Prol.191; VIII.Prol.72

bysmyng *pr. p.* yawning, abysmal VII.v.110

bysnyng *pr. p.* foreboding, portenteous II.i.69; II.iv.65; VI.xi.105

byspark *v.* bespatter XII.ii.37

bysparkyt *pa. p.* bespattered VII.ix.74

bysprent *pa. p.* sprinkled, spotted II.viii.114; IV.xii.5; V.vii.96

byssand *pr. p.* hissing VIII.vii.178 (R **bissy**)

byssy *adj.* busy. **~ weyngyt** with flapping wings V.iv.109

byt *n.* bite, of teeth and figuratively of arrows II.iv.25; IV.ii.95; XIII.v.72

byvaue *v.* turn aside VI.xiv.42. *See also* **be-wave**

bywaif, bywave *pa. p.* blown about, wafted away IV.i.30; IV.x.38; VI.v.110

bywed *pa. p.* married III.v.74

bywent *pa. p.* bygone I.iv.70; VI.xii.40

byworn *pa. p.* worn out *Conclusio*.18

cabyr *n.* caber, pole or spar XII.v.185

cace *n.* case. **on ~** by chance III.i.45. situation, matter for consideration IV.vi.59

cach *v.* catch, take. figuratively, as **to ~ haist** III.x.51

cach *v.* chase, drive IV.x.48

cachit *v.* drove, chased I.iii.31; I.viii.74

cachit *pa. p.* caught up, involved, seized I.v.26; I.vi.50; III.v.94; V.xi.116

cachkow *n.* cow catcher? VIII.Prol.136

cadens *n.* metre, song I.Prol.46

cadgyar *n.* peddler VIII.Prol.42

caf *n.* chaff VIII.Prol.155

cage *n.* cage, place of confinement such as hell VI.vii.21

cahuttis *n.* small enclosed areas, separate rooms III.Prol.15

cald *adj.* cold in sense of temperature IV.xi.70; V.vii.60; VIII.x.34. with sense of sinister or menacing I.xi.111; VI.i.104; VIII.ix.113; XI.xv.139. either cold or sinister IV.xii.40. cool-headed XI.vii.104

caldronys *n.* cauldrons (translating **lebetas**, cauldrons, especially decorative ones given as prizes) III.vi.215

calendar *adj.* connected with calends VIII.xi.29

call *v.* drive with blows; hence hammer VIII.vii.174

callour *adj.* fresh VII.Prol.87; VII.xii.110

cammamyld *n.* camomile plant XII.Prol.116

campe *n.* field XIII.x.101

campion *n.* champion V.vii.18; V.viii.66

camscho *adj.* crooked, deformed III.x.43; VII.Prol.107

camy *adj.* comb-like, serrated, rugged VII.xiii.42

camys *n.* honey-combs I.vii.29

can *v.* is able; sometimes used to form the past tense (**can ceß**, 'ceased') I.viii.116

canicular *adj.* of the dog star III.ii.150; X.v.149

cannos *adj.* hoary, grey V.xii.144; V.xiii.133; X.iv.76

cant *adj.* brisk, lively VIII.Prol.42

canus *adj.* hoary, grey V.vii.97

capill *n.* horse VIII.Prol.42

capital *adj.* affecting life or forfeiture of life VI.Prol.41

capitale *n.* canopy I.xi.7

cappit *v.* sailed III.viii.125

caraland *pr. p.* dancing or singing carols VII.vi.143

caralyng *vbl.n.* dancing or singing VI.xvi.25; VII.vi.115

carcage *n.* carcass XI.v.35

careit *v.intrans.* made (one's) way, travelled VII.v.9

carion *n.* dead body VIII.iv.176

carnail *adj.* fleshly, carnal IV.Prol.4

carp, carpis, carpys *v.* speaks, discourses I.v.heading; III.ix.46; IV.v.19, 185

carpand *pr. p.* speaking, with no sense of complaint ~ **blythly** I.iv.85; I.xi.88

cart *n.* chart, map III.iii.100

cart *n.* chariot (more usually **char** or **chariot**) I.vii.103, 119

cartage *n.* transport, process of conveying by cart **of thare** ~ **oxin** XI.v.35: R (C **carcage of thir oxin**)

carvellis *n.* small ships VIII.ii.61

cary *pa. p.* carried VI.ii.24

caryoun *adj.* carrion VIII.viii.67

cast, castis *n.* device, stratagem, tricks of a trade I.Prol.255, 308. aim, objective VIII.Prol.20

castell *n.* elevated structure on ship, quarterdeck III.viii.41; V.i.23

casys *n.* events, happenings III.v.33

catale *n.* livestock, or property in general (**praedas**) X.ii.45

catchit *pa. p.* driven, tossed I.i.59; I.ix.66; X.i.138; XII.xiii.30

catcluke *n.* bird-foot trefoil XII.Prol.116

catyfe, catyve *adj.* wretched, wicked II.ii.22, 134; III.ix.26

catyfly *adv.* basely IX.xiii.22

catyve, catyvis *n.* wretch II.iv.2; IV.vi.70

caucht *v.* catch I.x.35; IV.ii.70; IV.xi.31; XI.xvi.52; XII.Prol.172

caucht *pa. p.* caught V.v.22

cawch *v.* catch. variant or error for **caucht** I.x.33. *See also* **kauch**

causyng *v.inf.* to cause IV.i.106

cauld *adj.* ominous II.ii.113. cold V.iv.139. *See also* **cald**

causay *n.* causeway, piece of paving VII.Prol.137

cavis *v.* falls helplessly XI.xiii.43

cawcht *v.* conceived, became affected by. **Dedalus** ~ **piete of ...** VI.i.45

cawß *n.* subject of litigation, action, process I.iv.heading

cayk fydlar *n.* parasite *Directioun*.76

Caymis kyn Cain's kin, the wicked VIII.Prol.77

cayrful *adj.* full of care, dismal IV.xi.70; VI.ii.155

cayß *n.* case. **on** ~ by chance I.vi.99

celestiall *adj.* heavenly V.xi.110

celicall *adj.* heavenly XII.Prol.42

cens *n.* incense VI.iii.132

ceptour, ceptre *n.* sceptre I.ii.13, 44; III.v.25

cepturyt *pa. p.* sceptred XI.vi.25

certane *n.* a certain quantity or amount VIII.ix.14. certainty I.vi.145

certifeis *v.* assures definitely XII.ii.20

certis *adv.* certainly I.i.32; I.vi.54

chaffit *pa. p.* of wheat, heated by damp I.iv.37

chaftis *n.* jaws III.iv.92; VII.ii.23

chair *n.* chariot I.vii.91; V.xiii.120, 125

chaist *adj.* chaste, morally pure (without any sexual sense) III.vi.104

chaist *pa. p.* chased III.x.52; VII.vi.122; X.v.44

chak *n.* in chess, check; hence any turn, trick or advantage V.viii.14

chak *v.* examine, arrest VIII.Prol.126: R (C **ga chat the**)

chakkis *v.* clashes, clicks XII.xii.152

challance, challancis *v.* challenge, urge defiantly III.vi.191; V.xiii.7

chalmer, chalmyr, chalmeris, chalmyris *n.* private chamber, bedroom IV.i.38; VIII.vii.8; VIII.viii.28. chamber, room in general I.xi.21; IV.ii.63; VI.iv.91; VIII.ix.96

chancis *n.* things happening by fortune I.xii.19

chancy *adj.* fortunate, lucky III.ii.103; X.vi.66; XII.vii.128

chapyt *v.* escaped IX.vii.39

char *n.* chariot (Douglas also uses **cart**; **chariot** X.x.66; **chariote** X.x.74; **charyot** X.x.104, etc.) III.ii.90

char *adv.* **on** ~ ajar III.vi.177

charbukkill *n.* carbuncle stone. figuratively, something excellent I.Prol.7

chare *n.* chair, throne I.ii.12

charge *n.* load, burden III.vi.214. load, responsibility. **vndir his** ~ in his care I.Prol.443. commandment, order IV.vi.6

chargeand *pr. p. adj.* burdening, oppressive XIII.v.94

chargis *v.* commands III.iv.109; III.vii.2. loads I.vi.100; V.ii.114

charris *v.* turns aside, causes to turn back II.iv.43; V.viii.14

chastiand *pr. p.* chastising VI.ix.73

chat *v.* hang? **ga** ~ **the** VIII.Prol.126 (R **chak**)

chawmeris, chawmyr *n.* bedroom II.viii.116; IV.iv.9; IV.vii.60; IV.ix.48; IV.x.58. rooms in general II.viii.88

chayr *n.* chariot (Douglas also uses **char, cart, chariot**) V.iii.3

cheir *n.* mood, feeling I.iv.68

cheir *v.* rejoice, of men or animals XI.xii.31

chekis *n.* cheeks. hence, side-pieces, side-posts of doors II.viii.96; VII.x.51

chenȝeis *v.* chains I.v.118

cheping *vbl.n.* cheeping, making a bird-sound VII.Prol.70 (E **clepyng**; R **weping**)

cheptour *n.* chapter. one of the sections into which Douglas divides the *Aeneid* I.i.heading

cheritabil *adj.* charitable (for **pius**) III.ii.13

chery *adj.* cheerful XII.vi.69

cherysyt *v.* treated kindly V.i.74

chesbo, chesbow *n.* poppy plant IV.ix.28; IX.vii.150

chesis *v.* chooses I.vii.16; III.viii.7

chesit, chesyt *v.* chose III.i.58; V.x.63

chevaleris *n.* knights, heroes (**heroum**) VI.v.26

chevalre *n.* chivalry, translating **viris**, strength VI.xiii.35

chevalrus *adj.* chivalrous II.iv.77. applied to horses, strong and brave VII.xii.184

chevalry *n.* warfare **from that weirfar and cursyt** ~ XI.vi.81

cheyr *n.* mood, temper I.iv.87

chide *v.* dispute, scold III.Prol.21

chidyng *v.inf.* to chide VI.v.6

chiftane *n.* military leader, captain (no notion of clan chief). XII.ix.38 (53 **chif captane**)

child *n.* youth of gentle. birth **heynd** ~ VI.v.55; VII.viii.44

childering *n.* children V.x.101

chirt *v.* started, sprang out VIII.iv.169

chirtand *pr. p.* squirting, springing out III.ix.72

chop *v.intrans.* strike forcibly against I.iii.32

choppand *pr. p.* striking V.iv.88; V.vi.66

choppyt *v.trans.* pushed, struck IX.xii.46

choß, choyß *adj.* choice, select, chosen II.i.10; IV.iv.3

chosit *pa. p.* chosen VI.iii.139

chowpis *v.* ? mumbles, talks indistinctly I.Prol.153

chrisolyte *n.* chrysolite, an olive-coloured, semi-precious stone XII.Prol.37

churlych *adj.* churlish, rude VI.vi.2

churlys *n.* churls, rustics VI.viii.76 (E **churris**; R **carlis**; 53 **karllis**)

chydis *v.* argues, speaks sharply V.vi.103

chymmys *n.* dwelling houses, mansions VI.x.6; VII.Prol.2; VII.iii.30

chyngill *n.* shingle, beach X.vi.34

chyp *v.* of buds, burst open XII.Prol.124

chyrm *n.* bird-song, chirp III.vi.14

chyrmyng *vbl.n.* chirping VII.Prol.70

chyrmys *v.* chirps XII.Prol.239

chyssell *n.* chisel XII.Prol.58

chyvaler *n.* knight (**heros**) VI.iii.24

chyvirrand *pr. p.* shivering VII.Prol.139

circulat, circulyt *pa. p.* encircled, surrounded X.xi.77. formed into a circle XII.Prol.10

circumfait *v.* spread about, circulated V.xii.20: E (C **contyrfait**)

circumlocutioun *n.* roundabout language I.Prol.386

cirkillettis *n.* fillets III.iii.49

ciuile *adj.* civic VI.xiii.37

claking *n.* clacking cry (echoic) VII.Prol.109

claif *v.* cut up. *See* **al to** ~ IX.ix.139

clam *v.* climbed II.iv.heading; IV.xii.8

clan *n.* tribe, race (**stirpem**) IV.xi.81

clap *n.* blow X.vi.68

clap *v.trans.* strike smartly VI.i.91

clappys *v.intrans.* moves sharply, with a clap IV.iv.79

clasche *n.* resounding impact IX.xii.59

claspit *pa. p.* fastened, enclosed in general sense I.v.115

clausis, clausys *n.* clauses, stipulations VI.Prol.30

clavyr *n.* clover XII.Prol.116

clawcht *pa. p.* caught in claws IX.ix.82 (**claucht** for **caucht** V.v.22: E, B, 53)

clawis *n.* claws III.iv.48

clawß *n.* clause, short sentence; hence, exclamation II.Prol.17; IV.i.heading

cleith *v.* clothe I.x.52

clekkyt *v.* gave birth to, brought forth IV.vii.9

clemens *n.* clemency (**pietas**) V.xii.42

clene *adv.* completely I.i.37; I.i.70

clenge, clengis, clengit *v.* cleanse III.iv.132; VI.ii.154; VI.iii.139; VI.xiv.86

clenging graith, clengyng graith *n.* cleansing equipment IV.xi.105; VI.ii.154. **Purgit entralis, clepit** ~ **meit** VIII.iii.202

clep, clepe *v.* call out I.v.108; II.v.57; III.v.41; VII.vi.134. name III.Prol.161

clepand *pr. p.* naming I.Prol.140

clepit *pa. p.* named I,iii.39; III.i.39; III.ii.150

clepyng *v.pres.1 pl.* we name VIII.vi.7. we call XI.vi.46

clerkis *n.* scholars I.Prol.375

clethyng *n.* clothes IV.ix.49, 71

cleuch, clewchis *n.* gorge, valley VIII.x.7, 35

clewis, clewys *n.* valleys, gorges I.iv.18; IV.iv.47; VII.Prol.40

clewis, clewys *n.* claws III.iv.15; V.v.22; V.vi.116

cleyn *adj.* clean, pure, chaste I.vi.71; III. iii.55; III.vi.202; XI.xi.113

cleyn *adv.* wholly I.Prol.113; II.ix.71

clippis *v.* cuts off XII.iv.28. catch hold of XI.xiii.169

clokkand *pr. p.* clucking XIII.ii.133

clokyng *vbl.n.* cloaking, deception VIII. Prol.20

clokyt *pa. p.* cloaked, concealed IV.iv.90

cloß *adj.* ? close-fitting. **the ~ or dow-bill crown** I.ix.135

cloß *adv.* closely III.iv.41

cloß *n.* close, courtyard IV.ix.43, 66

closeris *n.* bars, enclosing walls II.v.17; II.viii.93

closettis *n.* closed or private places III. ii.51

closing *v.inf.* to enclose VII.iii.26

closouris *n.* bars, barriers I.ii.11

clowdis *n.* clouds; figuratively, obscurity I.Prol.193

clowis *n.* claws VII.xi.64

clowit, clowyt *pa. p.* nailed III.vi.217; V.v.30

clufe *n.* cloven hoof VIII.Prol.156

clukis *n.* claws IX.ix.82; XII.v.85 (E **crukis**)

clummyn *pa. p.* climbed I.iv.42

clynk *v.* sing, make a clinking sound XII.Prol.236

clynkit *v.* rattled, chinked II.iv.81

clynschis *v.* limps V.v.65

clynty *adj.* stony VII.Prol.40

clyp *pa. p.* clipped XII.iv.28 (R **clippit**)

cobill *n.* small, flat-bottomed boat VI.v.15

coetern *adj.* coeternal X.Prol.82

coffyngis *n.* pie crusts VII.ii.24

coggis *n.* small boats X.vi.7

cognycens *n.* armorial bearing, heraldic device XI.xiii.64

coif *n.* cave I.iv.21; VIII.iv.68

coil *n.* coal V.xii.32

coissing *pr. p.* exchanging IX.v.2: 53 (C **thar bissy thochtis sessyng**)

cok *n.* used as an *interj.* sign of surrender, acknowledging someone to be cock or leader XI.Prol.120

colis *n.* coals V.ii.116

collateral *adj.* parallel, in agreement VI.Prol.40

columby *n.* columbine XII.Prol.118

colȝar *n.* charcoal burner VIII.Prol.43

come *n.* arrival III.iv.59; VII.vi.8

command *pr. p.* coming VI.ii.129

commend *n.* commendation VII.iii. heading

commendis *n.* benefices VIII.Prol.108

commixit *pa. p.* mixed together VI.xiii.16

common *v.* commune, have dealings with VIII.iii.158

common weill *n.* commonweal V.Prol.40

commonyng *vbl.n.* talk, communing IV.i.21; VIII.iii.69

commonys *n.* the mass of people I.iii.92

commovit, commovyt *pa. p.* excited, disturbed I.iii.56; I.vi.94; IV.v.11

compace *v.* ponder, consider V.xii.64

compaciens *n.* compassion VIII.ix.69

compacient *adj.* compassionate I.ix.69

compar *n.* comparison; equal or rival I.Prol.381, 491

compaß *n.* circle or ring XII.xii.121

compaß *v.* consider, plan I.vi.2

compasing, compasyng *pr. p.* considering, planning IV.i.15; IV.vi.12; IV.ix.5

compeir *n.* equal, something comparable X.viii.52

compendyus *adj.* concise I.Prol.124

compilar *n.* compiler, author. *Naym of the Translatour*.6

compile *v.* compose I.Prol.388

complenys, complenyt *v.* complains, laments I.iv.108; I.viii.118. makes a formal statement of grievance, lodges a complaint I.iv.heading

complexioun *n.* combination of humours, temperament VII.Prol.29

complicis *n.* accomplices VIII.viii.78. associates XI.xv.87

complyng *n.* compline, the last service of the day XIII.Prol.35

compone *v.* compose, bring to a state of composure VIII.vi.121

comprasyt *v.* lay hold of, comprehended XIII.viii.15

comprehend *v.* include, contain VI.Prol.30

compt *n.* reckoning, account IV.v.116

compt *v.* count, consider III.Prol.19

concernans *n.* matters appertaining to X.xi.91 (E **contynens**)

concordis *v.* agrees V.Prol.17: 53

concur *v.* rush together X.i.20

concurrand *pr. p.* running together VIII.xii.43

condampnyt *pa. p.* condemned VI.ix.79

conding *adj.* suitable, fitting I.iii.79; VI.Prol.59

condiscend, condiscendyt *v.* descend, stoop. be gracious to I.Prol.467; III.ii.44; IV.viii.13; V.xiii.38

condyng *adj.* worthy, of great value I.Prol.50; III.vi.103; V.vi.119

condyngly *adv.* suitably II.ix.53

condytis *n.* conduits VI.ix.116

confectioun *n.* medicinal or aromatic preparation XII.Prol.148

confederate *pa. p.* federated III.i.33

confider *v.* confederate, ally (**foedere**) X.ii.118

confiderans *n.* confederation XII.xiii.76

confiding *pr. p.* having confidence VIII.vii.49

confluence, confluens *n.* crowding together, concourse IV.xii.56; V.xi.20

conform *adj.* identical, in agreement, corresponding to I.ix.10; VI.Prol.40

confortyve *adj.* comforting VII.Prol.91

confoundar *n.* destroyer, confuser IV.ix.77

confundyng *v.inf.* to confound XII.ix.128

congelit *v.* congealed, froze III.iv.96

conionyt *pa. p.* joined, united III.vii.8

conioyn *v.* unite IV.iii.69

coniugall *adj.* matrimonial IV.ix.50

coniunct *pa. p.* connected, joined, associated I.Prol.90; VIII.iii.81

coniune *v.* join I.ii.36

coniurations, coniuratioun *n.* conjuring up of spirits I.Prol.216. sworn league VII.xiii.97

connysans *n.* heraldic device X.iv.66

conpaß *n.* circle XII.xii.122

conqueß, conquyß *v.* conquer VI.xiv.78; IX.v.102

conquest *v.inf.* to conquer IX.v.102: R, 53

consait, consate, consatis *n.* idea, fancy, stratagem I.Prol.338; I.x.2, 37; I.xi.38; IV.Prol.12; V.Prol.16. power of judgment, understanding I.Prol.315; II.ii.71; V.xiii.36; VII.vi.66; IX.vi.7; X.xi.90

consave *v.* comprehend VI.ii.41

consavyt *pa. p.* conceived (offspring) IV.vi.94

conseil *v.* conceal VI.ix.77

considerance *n.* consideration VI.vi.43

consideris *v.* meditates, takes counsel or thought I.ii.46

constrenys *v.* drives, impels, forces IV.viii.10

constrenyt *pa. p.* compelled I.Prol.303, 358; II.ii.127. restrained, restricted I.Prol.293

constreyn *v.* restrain, restrict I.Prol.197

consuler *n.* consul VII.x.28

contagius *adj.* causing moral infection XII.Prol.227

contak *n.* conflict IV.iii.17

contegwyte *n.* contiguity, close proximity I.i.82, marginal note

contemp *v.* despise VIII.vi.120

contempnar *n.* scorner VII.xi.20

contrar *adj.* unfavourable, hostile I.i.30; V.i.35; V.viii.5 (E **contra**)

contrar *n.* opposite. **in thy** ~ in opposition to you V.viii.91

contrar *v.* go against, oppose IV.vii.37

contrarius *adj.* hostile, full of opposition III.iii.66

contrary *adj.* opposed (perhaps a verb, to speak in opposition) I.Prol.278

contrary *n.* opposition **in ʒour** ~ in opposition to you VI.ii.23

contrarying *pr. p.* opposing IV.iii.72

contrauersy *n.* dispute, debate XII.xiv.32

controvar *n.* contriver XI.viii.70.

controvit, controvyt *pa. p.* cunningly contrived II.iii.98; IV.iii.74; V.i.13

contyr *n.* encounter XI.xii.22

contyr *n.* the breast of a horse XI.xii.44

contyrfait *adj. pa. p.* counterfeited, feigned, falsely supposed III.v.129; IV.ix.81

contyrfait *v.* counterfeit IV.ix.heading

contyrfait *v.* counterfeited V.xii.20

contyrmont *adv.* uphill VI.x.77; XI.viii.68

conuenient *adj.* suitable, fitting IX.Prol.30

convenabill *adj.* suitable, fitting IV.iii.49

convene *n.* covenant, agreement VII.iv.167

convenient *adj.* agreeing in opinion, in accord I.i.82, marginal note

convenys *v.* meets I.vi.97. agrees I.v.81, marginal note

convoyar *n.* leader, escort I.Prol.245

convoys *v.* accompanies, guides. *Contentis*

convyne *n.* compact, company VII.xi.29

cop owt To play ~ to drink the cup empty I.xi.92

coppit *pa. p.* rising to a peak XIII.iv.80

corall *adj.* red XII.Prol.155

corbalys, corbell *n.* projections jutting out from walls II.viii.46; VIII.xii.109

corby *n.* raven XII.Prol.174

corn, cornys *n.* cereal plants in general (**seri**, things sown) III.ii.142; III.iii.32. kernels I.iv.39; IV.vii.85

corpsys *n.* bodies **ded** ~ V.xiii.96

corruppit *pa. p.* morally spoiled III.iv.38

corß *n.* body III.ix.10; IV.i.48

corsis *n.* corpses I.v.15

corsy *adj.* large-bodied, weighty XII.viii.34

cortyne *n.* curtain. hence, any enclosed or secret place VI.v.109

corvyn *pa. p.* carved V.vii.77

cost, costis *n.* side of person or animal II.v.18; IV.ii.65; V.viii.22; IX.vi.94; XII.xiv.150. coast, beach V.xii.62. tract of land V.viii.72

costage *n.* outlay, expense VI.xv.91

cosyt *v.* exchanged IX.v.188

cotage *n.* small dwelling with accompanying land I.vi.6

cotarmour *n.* coat of arms XI.ii.84

cote *n.* cottage XII.ix.47

courtyng *n.* curtain, secret place, representing **cortina**, glossed by Ascensius as **locus secretior** III.ii.50

cousyng *n.* cousin, kinsman VI.iv.87; IX.vii.69

covatyce, covatyß *n.* covetousness VI.xi.87; XI.Prol.86

cove *n.* cave, recess VIII.iv.19

covert *n.* hiding place II.i.77

covert *v.* hide, cover up IV.ix.heading

covertouris *n.* coverings IX.viii.141

cowardy *n.* cowardice IX.iv.83

cowchit *pa. p.* covered with layers laid down successively, inlaid V.vii.79; X.viii.111; X.xiii.68. put in place VII.i.142

cowp, cowpe, cowpis *n.* cup I.xi.66, 85; III.v.141

cowrsis *n.* courses (of food) I.xi.24

cowschet *n.* wood-pigeon XII.Prol.237

coyrbulʒe *n.* leather hardened by soaking XI.xv.9

crachour *n.* one who scrapes up, a hoarder VIII.Prol.97

craft, craftis *n.* handicraft, skills I.vii.66; III.iii.100; VIII.Prol.69

crafty *adj.* artistic, characterized by craftsmanship I.Prol.335, 423. wrought with skill IX.v.99. skilful I.i.24

crag *n.* neck XI.xv.142

craggy *adj.* rocky VII.ix.56

craik *n.* a large ship, carrack III.Prol.39

craik, crak *n.* sharp noise like thunder III.viii.138; V.vi.56. croak XII.v.68

crak *n.* loud noise III.viii.138

crakkis *pl.n.* shouts, boasts VIII.Prol.42

crakkis *v.* cracks, breaks VIII.Prol.95

crakkyt *pa. p.* broken VIII.Prol.102

crammysyn *n.* crimson (stain or velvet) XII.Prol.15

cran, crannys *n.* crane XI.xi.105; X.v.123

crap *v.* crept II.iv.48, 51

craw *n.* crow III.Prol.26

crawdoun *n.* recreant, coward XI.Prol.119

crawin *pa. p.* crowed VII.Prol.114

credans, credens *n.* credentials, evidence of being properly accredited XI.vi.29, 34, 52; XII.ii.58

credlys *n.* cradles III.ii.74

Creid *n.* the Creed III.Prol.18

creisch *n.* grease, tallow VII.x.61

crelyt *v.* basketed, hoisted in a basket IV.Prol.32

crepar *n.* grappling-iron I.iii.54, marginal note

creyß *v.* of hair, to curl XII.ii.125

cristit *pa. p.* crested II.vii.53

croftis *n.* small fields II.viii.105; X.xiii.110

crokit *pa. p.* made crooked IV.iv.90: R

cronys *n.* bellows, roars XII.xii.56

crop, croppis, croppys *n.* top, tops I.iii.91; III.x.46; IV.viii.75, 79

croß *n.* elliptic for cross-sail, square-sail V.xiv.3

crosyt *v.* crossed, made the sign of the cross VII.Prol.97

crovn *n.* crown of head XII.v.179

crowd, crowdis *v.* of birds, coo XII.Prol.237, 293

crownell *n.* crownlike flower XII.Prol.113. coronet VII.i.111; X.iii.35

crowplyng *vbl.n.* of birds, harsh crying X.v.123 (E **crouping**, R, 53 **crowping**)

crowpyng *pr. p.* of birds, crying harshly VII.Prol.119; VII.xi.156

croyn *v.* groan, rumble VI.iv.40 (cf. IX.x.91: R **with horneʒ crvne**, where C has **with hornis fuyn**, push, shove)

croys *n.* elliptic for cross-sail, square-sail IV.viii.21

crudelyte *n.* cruelty XII.ix.10

crukit *pa. p.* curved, bent I.vii.128; VI.v.130

crum *n.* particle I.Prol.281

cruyk *n.* blemish, crooked place, deformity. *Exclamatioun.*15

crymys *n.* crimes VIII.Prol.69. accusation or charge of crime II.ii.68

crynys *v.* clips, reduces in size, diminishes (as by stealing) VIII.Prol.62, 97

crysp *adj.* curly, curling I.ix.17

cryspand *pr. p.* curling XII.ii.124

cuchill *n.* grove IX.iii.20 (53 **cuthil**). *See also* **cuthill**

cullage *n.* ? shape, markings X.iv.128

cullour *n.* colour; hence, semblance, sense flavour I.Prol.121; pretence, pretext I.Prol.265; literary grace, embellishment I.Prol.348

culmas *n.* curved sword XI.xiii.72

culron *n.* rascal VIII.Prol.43

cultyr, cultyris *n.* coulter of plough VII.x.79; VII.xiii.40

culʒe, culʒeis *v.* cuddle, caress, cherish I.x.28; VI.xv.90; VIII.x.86

culʒeand *pr. p.* caressing IV.xii.87

cum trew *pa. p. phrase* **althing … ar ~** are come about VI.iii.61: E (C **ar our trew**)

cummyn *pa. p.* come III.iii.1; III.vi.163; IV.iv.44; IV.v.34, 107

cummyn *v.inf.* to come VIII.iii.73; XIII.vii.78

cummyn *vbl.n.* coming, arrival XII.Prol.141

cummyrris *v.* harasses I.v.89

cummyrryt *pa. p.* distressed, afflicted V.xii.94

cumpas *n.* circle, circuit IV.ix.18; VIII.iii.104; X.xiv.135

cumray *v.* discommode, throw into disorder V.x.70

cumryt *pa. p.* irritated X.xiv.145

cun *v.* learn, know VIII.Prol.69

cundyt, cundytis *n.* conduit III.x.79. figuratively, well-spring, source I.Prol.341. a passage in the body XI.v.28; XII.ix.17

cunnand *adj.* knowing, learned
I.Prol.482; V.viii.2

cunnand *n.* understanding, covenant, agreement IV.x.61; VIII.Prol.102; VIII.iii.160 (53 **couenand**)

cunnyng *n.* skill, knowledge III.iii.100

cuntre *n.* encounter VII.viii.123 (53 **compter**)

cunʒe *n.* coinage VIII.Prol.97

cuplyng *vbl.n.* uniting (in marriage) IV.iv.79

cuppil *v.* unite, join IV.i.35

cuppillys *n.* leashes for dogs IV.iv.46

cupplys *n.* pair of sloping rafters I.vii.56

cur *n.* care III.vi.8. office, function, charge VI.v.146, 176

curace, curas *n.* cuirass, breastplate X.v.107; XII.vi.172

curage *n.* mind, disposition III.iii.12; V.Prol.9; VI.vii.96. stoutness of heart, bravery IV.vii.66; V.iv.59

curageus *adj.* great-spirited (**magnanime**) V.i.31

curbulle *n.* leather hardened by boiling V.vii.77

curche *n.* kerchief VII.vi.25

cure, curis, curys *n.* care, anxiety I.Prol.195; I.i.60; I.v.7; I.xi.19

curß *n.* course I.Prol.433; I.viii.131

cursyt *pa. p.* accursed IV.vi.36

curtas *adj.* courteous V.vii.100

curtesly *adv.* courteously XIII.iii.18

cury *n.* cooking, concoction VIII. Prol.95

curyus *adj.* elegant, subtle, abstruse, involved I.Prol.255, 295; I.ix.110; IV.Prol.16

cut *n.* chance, lot I.iii.76; I.viii.27; II.i.10

cuthill, cuthyll *n.* grove VIII.iv.191(53 **cuchil**); VIII.x.10 (53 **cuchil**). *See also* **cuchil**

cuyr *n.* care, office, function I.Prol.423; IV.Prol.236; IV.ii.15. care, anxiety VI.Prol.114. cure, remedy (with pun on sense of anxiety?) I.Prol.333

cuyrbulʒe *n.* leather hardened by boiling VII.x.74

cwatyce *n.* covetousness I.vi.76

daill *n.* dealings with others, doings XII.iv.161. **rebald** ~ ribald doings IX.Prol.47

dalis *n.* valleys VII.Prol.68

dalphyn *n.* dolphin V.x.88

damp *v.* damn, condemn VI.xiv.34

dampnyt *pa. p.* damned VI.ix.20

damycellis *n.* young women, especially female attendants I.xi.18; IV.vii.58

Dan Dominus, title of respect VI.x.1 (53 **dame**); XII.Prol.271

dang *v.* struck III.ix.68; VII.x.48

dangeir *n.* danger, peril III.vi.200

dangerus *adj.* dangerous, perilous I.ix.68; III.x.99. proud, disdainful III. vi.82

dansyng *v.inf.* to dance VI.x.39

dant *v.* daunt, subdue I.v.98; I.viii.52

dante *n.* esteem, regard, favour IV.viii.28; IX.iii.18

danteis *n.* dainties, desserts I.x.56; III.v.140

danter *n.* subduer, controller IV.Prol.226

danting *pr. p.* subduing V.xiii.121

dantit, dantyt *pa. p.* vanquished, subdued IV.Prol.46; VII.Prol.79. of animals, broken in, tamed VII.iii.34

dappill *adj.* dappled, spotted grey IX.ii.38

darf *adj.* active, bold VIII.xi.21; IX.ix.22

darn *adj.* dark (poetic) III.vi.131; III. viii.154. secret V.iv.103

darnly *adv.* secretly, with concealment III.iv.57

darryn *v.inf.* to dare V.ii.55

darth *n.* dearth VIII.Prol.82

dasyt *pa. p.* dazed, stupefied V.vii.58

daw *n.* sloven XIII.Prol.184

daw *n.* day. **brocht of** ~ deprived of life, killed II.ii.58; VI.vii.68

dawyn *pa. p.* dawned VII.Prol.126

dawyng *vbl.n.* dawning, dawn III. viii.29; IV.i.13

daynte *n.* esteem, regard XI.i.56

days *n.* does XII.Prol.181

deambulatour *n.* place to walk in VII. iii.62

debait *n.* strife, contention IV.iii.35; V.v.30

debait, debate *v.* fight, dispute, maintain by argument I.Prol.273; IV.xi.90, 93. abate, reduce XIII.iii.35

debatyng *v.inf.* to debate, to contend IV.i.78

debowellit *pa. p.* disembowelled IV.ii.25

decern *v.* decide, settle XII.xiv.31. distinguish I.xi.102

declaryt *v.* declared, announced I.Prol.436

declyne *v.* decline, sink to a lower level XIII.vi.128

declyne *pa. p.* declined, fallen VIII.iv.17

declynyng *vbl.n.* descent, declination I.xii.16

decreit, decrete *n.* decree VI.v.168; VI.vii.31; X.i.15

decretit *pa. p.* decreed IV.xi.64: R, 53

ded, dede *n.* death, slaughter (not deed) I.ii.68; I.iv.103; II.ii.49; II.x.168, 180; IV.Prol.41; IV.i.43; IV.vi.87; IV.vii.45; IV.viii.132; VII. vii.108; IX.vi.18, etc.

dedenyt *pa. p.* deigned IV.v.36

deden3eit *v.* deigned X.xii.105

dedeyn *v.* deign X.xiv.93

dedicait, dedicate *v. pa. p.* dedicate. dedicated I.Prol.20; III.vi.164

dedis *n.* death's X.vi.68

dedly *adj.* mortal X.vii.38. deathly, death-producing X.vi.118. concerned with death, funereal, dismal II.Prol.3; III.i.122. dying IV.xii.89

dedthrawis *n.* death throes V.vii.20

defaid *pa. p.* faded XI.ii.34

defait *n.* defeat IX.v.53 (53 **deface**)

defame *n.* disgrace, ill repute X.xiv.104

defend, defendis *v.* protect, guard X.i.113. forbid I.Prol.282; III.vi.50; IX.v.176; XII.i.104

defendit *pa. p.* forbidden I.viii.81

defens *n.* **at ~** on guard I.Prol.278

deficill *adj.* difficult I.Prol.290

defowlyt *pa. p.* defiled by immorality X.vii.69

defund *v.* pour down, diffuse IX.viii.4 (E **to fund**)

defundand *pr. p.* pouring down VII. xiii.26; XII.Prol.41

defynd *pa. p.* defined, predetermined, arranged V.viii.101

degest *adj.* grave, serious XII.i.45

degre *n.* stage in elevation, position in rank V.ix.80

deid *n.* deed IV.x.34

deificait *pa. p.* deified, godlike XII.iv.52

deil, deill *n.* part, portion III.Prol.31; VI.v.77

deing *v.pres.1 sg.subjunctive*? die. **it is 3it sum comfort that I of mennys handis ~ at schort** III.ix.36

deir *adv.* dearly, at high cost XIII. Prol.145

deir *n.* harm, injury II.vii.105; II.xi.52; X.vi.95

deir *v.* lurk, hide. **na man suld stop or ellis ~** I.vi.179

deir *v.* harm, injure II.iv.55; XII.iv.66

deit *pa. p.* died (*rhymes with* **Diomed**) I.iii.8

deite *n.* divinity, state of being a god XII.iv.71

dekeit *pa. p.* decayed XI.Prol.147

dekkis *v.* covers, shelters, protects XI.v.92

dekkyt *v.* adorned, arranged XII.ii.127

delait *v.* dilate, extend I.v.100; VI.xiii.85

delicat *adj.* self-indulgent, indolent XI.Prol.186

delvand *pr. p.* digging I.vii.46

delytabill *adj.* delectable IX.iii.61

delyte *n.* physical pleasure IV.Prol.4; IV.v.40

delyuerly, delyvirly *adv.* actively, smartly (poetic) V.viii.60; VIII.v.77

delyver *adj.* quick, agile IX.ix.51

demane *v.* lead (one's life) III.iii.29: 53 (C **remane**)

demanyt *pa. p.* treated (with harshness) IX.viii.52

demmyt *pa. p.* dammed up VIII.iv.128; XI.vii.9

demyng *v.inf.* to judge III.Prol.28

demyng *pr. p.* judging XI.vii.4

demyt *v.* adjudged II.ii.119

dent de lyon *n.* dandelion XII.Prol.119

denude *v.* strip off XIII.ii.1

denudyt *pa. p.* made empty, cleared VIII.ix.65 (B **devidit**)

deny *pa. p.* denied XIII.iii.74

denyis *v.* refuses VII.vii.39

den3e *v.* deign, condescend I.vi.53

den3eing *pr. p.* deigning (with reflexive pronoun) III.vi.183

depart *v.* allot, distribute V.xii.169

depart *pa. p.* varied in colour XII.Prol.111

departingis *vbl.n.* divisions VI.Prol.90

depayntar *n.* painter XII.Prol.261

depechit *v.* rid (oneself of someone) I.v.28, marginal note

deplumand *pr. p.* stripping off feathers XI.xiii.173

depul3e *v.* dispoil IV.vii.80

deput *pa. p.* ordained, assigned VI.ix.181

deray *n.* disorder, disturbance, revelry I.xi.heading; VI.ix.164; VII.ix.31, 77

dere *v.* trouble, annoy I.vi.179

derene *v.* decide by contest XII.xi.184

derenys, deren3eis, dereyn *n.* contests, encounters V.iii.heading; V.vii.49; V.x.1, 87

dereyn *v.* engage in battle, undertake (an enterprise) V.viii.109; X.viii.14; XII.xiv.12; XIII.viii.65

derf *adj.* bold, daring (poetic) IX.x.29

deris *v.* injures, harms V.xii.heading

dern *adj.* secret, concealed (poetic) I.vi.10; III.iv.40

dern *adv.* secretly, in secret VII.Prol.68

derth *n.* scarcity, famine IX.vii.103: 53 (C **cald of deth**)

deß *n.* raised platform in hall on which high table was placed; hence, the table itself I.xi.6; X.viii.56

descend *pa. p.* descended VI.v.56

descryve *v.* describe IX.Prol.33

desert *adj.* desert, uninhabited II.i.20

desert *pa. p.* deserted II.i.29

deserve *pa. p.* deserved XII.xiv.107

desolat *adj.* desolate, abandoned IX.i.21

destane *n.* destiny IV.xii.16

destany, destinat, destinate *v. pa. p.* destined, ordained III.iii.71; IV.v.184; VIII.vii.13; XII.xiii.9

desys *n.* high tables (dais) III.iv.30

det *n.* obligatory action, duty VII.v.121; VIII.i.92; IX.iii.184, 206

detbund *pa. p.* bound by obligation XI.iv.62 (53 **detborne**)

determ *v.* decide formally I.Prol.217

determyn, determyt *pa. p.* decided, determined IV.ix.3; VII.vii.58

detful *adj.* due, naturally required III.iv.105

deth *n.* death II.ii.26

deuote *adj.* virtuous (representing **pias**) III.i.79

devaill, davalis *v.* descend, fall VII.Prol.24; XIII.Prol.30

devalyt *v.* descended, stooped X.vii.58

devill *n.* devil, pagan god VI.Prol.161

devoid *v.* cast out, eject XIII.i.10

devyce, devyß *n.* plan. **at al ~** skilfully, properly V.iv.20; IV.v.167; V.vi.100

devyn *adj.* divine VIII.iii.84

devyß *v.* examine, survey VI.i.67

dew *adj.* dewy, moist. **hait fyry power, warm and ~** VI.xii.16

dewillich *adj.* diabolical I.Prol.216

dewing *vbl.n.* sprinkling VI.iii.143

dewly *adj.* proper XIII.viii.103

dewyte *n.* duty XI.vii.154

deym *v.* judge III.Prol.28

deyr *n.* deer VII.Prol.68

deyß *n.* dais, high table III.ix.58; IV.xi.36

dichis *n.* ditches VII.Prol.51

dicht *pa. p.* prepared III.iv.43

dichtis *v.* prepares XII.iii.8

dicist *v.* cease from XI.Prol.8: R (C **all vyce detest**)

diffame *n.* ill fame, evil repute IV.Prol.176

diffend *pa. p.* defended X.xiii.101

difficil *adj.* difficult VI.Prol.47

diffundit *pa. p.* poured out VI.xii.8

diffynys *v.* describes, gives an account of IV.ii.30

digest *pa. p. adj.* settled, grave XIII.ix.36

digestly *adv.* gravely IX.v.48

dight *pa. p.* prepared, arranged I.vii.120

digressioun *n.* deviation from the subject in writing I.Prol.306

diligens *n.* diligence. **dyd** ~ made a diligent effort I.Prol.419

directrix *n.* directress IX.vii.80

dirking *pr. p.* making dark or confused III.vi.172: R

dirkit *v.* darkened VII.Prol.47: R

discend *pa. p.* descended I.v.104; I.vi.60; IV.iv.62. descended (from ships), disembarked VII.xiii.110

discens *n.* descent III.iii.38; III.ii.68

discrepans *n.* disagreement, divergence in opinion I.Prol.457; VII.iv.162

discrive, discryve, discryvis *v.* describe, record I.Prol.327, 511; I.i.1; III.vi.173

discumfist *pa. p.* defeated XIII.v.8

discumfyst *pa. p.* defeated XIII.vi.4

discur *v.* watch, reconnoitre IX.iii.196

discurriouris *n.* scouts I.viii.124

disdene, disden3e, disdeyn *n.* scorn, contempt I.Prol.475; I.ii.9; IV.Prol.256; XI.iv.22; XI.xv.146. vexation, indignation XII.xiv.154

disiunct *n.* disjointed state, confusion XII.xiii.30

disosyt *pa. p.* unaccustomed VI.xiv.16

dispers *pa. p.* dispersed, scattered VIII.iii.6; XII.Prol.90

dispittuusly *adv.* cruelly XII.v.71

dispituus *adj.* merciless X.xiv.169

displayt *v.inf.* to display. **thar baneris to** ~ perhaps from the conventional phrase **with baneris displayit**, or perhaps **displat** X.v.106 (R, 53 **display**)

displesant *adj.* unpleasant IV.i.37

displesour *n.* thing that displeases IV.viii.24

disponys *v.* arranges, sets in order XII.xiii.144

dispositions *n.* decisions VII.ix.91

dispul3eit *pa. p.* despoiled XI.ii.78

dispyß *v.* scorn I.Prol.275

dispyte *n.* scorn, contempt I.Prol.150, 271; II.Prol.22. indignation V.xii.27

dissait, dissate *n.* deceitfulness, deceit I.iii.62; IV.Prol.240

dissauyt *v.* deceived VII.iv.54

dissave *pa. p.* deceived VI.v.109. forsworn IV.viii.45

dissemblit, dissemlyt *pa. p.* dissembled I.xi.34; II.ii.90

disseuerance *n.* separation VI.xv.76

disolait, dissolat, dissolate, dissolet *adj.* desolate, deserted, abandoned III.i.21; III.ii.105; IV.vi.99; XII.xii.92

dissolvyt *v.* put an end to V.viii.93

dissoverit *pa. p.* sundered, separated, kept apart IV.i.36

dissymyll *v.* dissemble I.viii.39

dissymulance *n.* dissimulation IV.vi.49

dissyverance *n.* separation III.v.46

dissyveris, dissyvir *v.* separates, puts apart or asunder III.vi.58

disteyn *v.* stain, discolour I.Prol.45, 47; IV.Prol.195

distillit *v.* trickled, oozed, fell in drops III.i.54

distinit *pa. p.* destined VI.Prol.88

distrubbill *v.* disturb, molest VII.vii.8

dittam *n.* the plant dittany XII.vii.74 (R **dittane**)

dittit *pa. p.* stopped up, closed up V.xiii.96

diuersyte *n.* diversity, distinction I.Prol.372

diuinationys *n.* divinations, revelations III.vi.10

diuinyte *n.* divinity, quality of being divine I.Prol.429

diurnall *adj.* of the day XII.Prol.61

diuynal *adj.* divining, pertaining to divination IX.i.52

do *pa. p.* done III.i.105; IV.viii.9; VI.vii.61

do *v.* place, put (in a position or state) I.iii.80; III.x.90; V.vii.104

docht *v. past tense of* **dow**. availed, was of use or value XI.vi.7

doillit, dollyt *adj.* spiritless, dull VIII. vi.16; XI.xiv.18

dok *n.* dock, landing-place X.vi.22

dolf *adj.* sluggish I.xi.55; III.iv.97; V.vii.59

dolf *n.* place dug out, pit? VIII.Prol.160

dolfnes *n.* lack of spirit XI.xiv.21; XII. xiii.178

dolly *adj.* sad, dismal VI.ix.80; VII.Prol.51

dolour *n.* expression of grief, lament VI.iii.36

dolp *n.* cavity. **e** ~ eye-socket III.x.15

dolyve *adj.* d'olive, olive VI.iii.134

domesticall *adj.* belonging to a house-hold XIII.vi.192

domys *n.* dooms, judgments, laws I.viii.24; VII.iv.124

domysday *n.* doomsday XII.Prol.308

done *pa. p.* consigned to a state or place V.vii.106; VI.iii.10

dongion *n.* dungeon VI.iv.69

donk *adj.* damp, wet I.xii.15; III.ix.3; IV.i.13

donkis *n.* wet places VII.Prol.60

donky *adj.* damp, wet XII.viii.78

dont *n.* heavy blow V.vii.72

dortyneß *n.* pride, hauteur III.v.86

dosk *adj.* dusky, dark VII.Prol.63

dotage *n.* folly, foolishness (not nec-essarily connected with old age) VI.Prol.21; IV.Prol.225

dotall *adj.* pertaining to a dowry XI.vii.182

dotand *pr. p.* acting foolishly IV.viii.122

doubill *adj.* double. two-faced, deceit-ful, false IX.Prol.14

douk *v.* duck, dive under water VIII.i.104

dour *adj.* resolute, stern, hard. **a** ~ **pepill** (**dura gens**) V.xii.117

dout *n.* doubt IV.vi.14. **but** ~ assuredly II.xii.74

doutsum *adj.* doubtful IV.ii.4; IV.xi.38

dovn *n.* hill (poetic) XII.iii.53

dovyrrit *pa. p.* sunk in sleep VI.vi.12

dow *n.* dove IV.Prol.53; V.iv.102; V.ix.7

dow, dowe *v.* to be of worth or value IV.Prol.141; VIII.Prol.1

dowchty *adj.* doughty, valorous VI.x.48

dowkand *pr. p.* ducking, diving IX.iii.100

dowkis *v.* ducks, dives under water V.xiii.126

dowkit *v.* ducked, dived under water XIII.Prol.17

downebet *pa. p.* beaten down. *Contentis*

downlat *compound v.* let down II.v.21

downys *n.* down, under-feathers of bird XI.xiii.174

dowr *adj.* stern, resolute, hard (**duri** used figuratively) II.v.23; III.ii.54; XII.x.56

dowry *n.* dowry VII.v.85 (E, R, 53 **drowry**); IX.xii.30 (E **drowre**, R **drowry**); XI.vii.182 (E, R, L, 53 **drowry**)

dowreis, dowreys *n.* endowment I.vii.53 (E **drowreris**; R **drowryis**, B **drowreiß**, 53 **drouryis**). gifts in broad sense III.vii.301

dowt, dowtis *n.* state of danger or difficulty I.vi.65; III.Prol.25; V.viii.80; IX.ii.86. fear V.xii.60. **but** ~ assur-edly IX.ii.11

dowt *v.* waver in opinion, hesitate (V **dubitamus**, we hesitate) VI.xiii.107

dowtsum *adj.* doubtful, ambiguous, uncertain II.iii.51; VI.ii.41

dowtyng *pr. p.* fearing II.ii.101

doym *n.* judgment, opinion VI.vii.16; XIII.Prol.93

doyng *pr. p.* doing VI.iii.97

draglit *pa. p.* bedraggled VII.Prol.76

dram *adj.* melancholy, sad IV.Prol.157

draucht trumpet *n.* war trumpet, one drawing to war VII.x.86

drauchtis *n.* draughts. pullings, strokes (of oars) V.iii.75

drave *v.* drove onwards; in metaphorical sense of driving time, using it to the utmost III.vi.1

dravillyng *vbl.n.* dreaming, confused thinking in sleep X.xi.96; XII.xiv.52. *See also* **dreflyng**

draw *v.* contrive, plan, arrange VIII.vi.68

draw *v.* drove XI.xiv.9

draw *pa. p.* drawn II.v.71; XIII.x.100

draw briggis *n.* drawbridges (V **pontis**) IX.iv.7

drawin *pa. p.* brought together, collected I.iv.100

dre *v.* endure I.xi.91; V.iv.24; X.ix.72

dre *pa. p.* endured X.iii.104

dreddour, dredour *n.* fear, dread VI.v.67: E (C **dreid**); IX.xii.67: R, 53 (C **raddour**)

dredely *adj.* dreadful VI.v.165: 53 (C **dreidfull**) **dredis** *v.* be afraid I.x.28

dreflyng *n.* confused thinking in sleep VIII.Prol.1. *See also* **dravillyng**

dreich *n.* **on** ~ at a distance IX.iii.107; X.xii.64. *See also* **ondreich**

dreid *n.* doubt, uncertainty IV.x.33. reverence IV.Prol.96; IV.ii.5

dreid *v.* fear (not so strong as modern dread) III.Prol.16

dreidfull *adj.* inspiring dread II.xi.11

drery *adj.* gloomy, inspiring melancholy III.iv.heading, 73. cruel, horrid I.i.15. melancholy, sad II.ii.17

dreß *v.* array, clothe XII.Prol.303. deal with harshly X.x.18. put into order, arrange IV.x.108

dressit *v.* betook (oneself) I.vi.4

dressit *pa. p.* prepared III.viii.66

drewch *v.* drew II.v.43

dreys *v.* endures IV.x.heading

drive *pa. p.* driven I.vi.47

droggis *n.* drugs XII.Prol.144

drond *pa. p.* drowned I.iii.42; IV.Prol.82: L, B

droukyt *pa. p.* drenched, soaked X.vi.44

drowreis, drowry, drowryis *n.* dowry (q.v.) III.vii.30: E, R, 53; IV.iii.28: E, R, 53; VII.v.85: E, R, 53

drowreis, drowry *n.* love service, affection V.x.48; VI.viii.74

drug *v.inf.* to drag II.iv.84

drumly *adj.* cloudy, gloomy V.xii.55; VII.Prol.47. muddy VI.v.4

drynchit *pa. p.* drenched; figuratively, overwhelmed, buried VI.iv.64

drynkabyll *adj.* capable of being drunk I.iii.75, marginal note

drynking glasß *n.* drinking glasses XIII.ix.25: R (C **drynkyn tassis**)

drynt *pa. p.* drowned IV.Prol.82; VI.v.97

dryve *pa. p.* driven I.ix.90; III.v.108; III.x.119; IV.x.23; VI.ii.5

dub, dubbis *n.* puddle, stagnant pool VII.Prol.54; VIII.ii.49

dubbyt *v.* consigned, condemned (Vg **damnaverat**; modelled on dubbing, a knight?) IV.xii.109

duel *v.* dwell VIII.vi.46

duke *n.* leader, military captain, representing **dux** III.iii.35; III.vi.92; IV.iii.64

dul *adj.* slow to hear, slow of perception IV.viii.40

dulce *adj.* sweet I.Prol.2; I.x.70; XII.Prol.245

dun *adj.* brown (Vg **fulva**) V.vii.19; VIII.ix.26

dung *v. pa. p.* struck IX.x.148; XIII.Prol.121

dunt *n.* blow XI.xvii.60

durris *n.* doors III.ii.47

dusch *n.* heavy blow V.iii.82

duschit *pa. p.* struck heavily II.viii.95; V.viii.114

duyl, duyll *n.* grief, sorrow I.ii.25; IV.i.71; IV.x.51

duylful, duylfull *adj.* doleful (Vg **lacrimabilis**) II.iv.93; III.i.75

duylfully *adv.* dolefully, dismally IV.xii.76

dwawmyng *vbl.n.* swooning, fainting fit III.v.55 (E **dwalmyng**, 53 **dualmyng**)

dwynys *v.* fades away, becomes weak

IX.vii.149; XIII.Prol.159

dyall *n.* dial indicating time of day, clock XII.Prol.278; hence, figuratively, a standard of measurement, symbol of value I.Prol.341

dychit *pa. p.* ditched, moated VII.ii.62 (E, 53 **dicht**, R **dykit**)

dycht *v.* array, put into good shape, set in order III.i.49; V.iv.38

dycht *pa. p.* prepared I.xi.21; V.iii.17; V.v.52

dyd *v.* inflicted upon, afflicted with. **till Ene … ~ gret wo** III.iv.heading

dyght *pa. p.* prepared, equipped, arrayed V.iii.61

dymynew *v.* diminish I.Prol.74

dyn *n.* din II.i.72. noise, not necessarily unharmonious. **~ of silly sawlys** VI.xi.54

dyndlys *v.* rings, vibrates XII.xii.46

dyndlyt *v.* rang, shook XI.xvii.20

dyng *adj.* worthy VII.x.5

dyng *v.* strike I.iii.16; III.iv.79

dyngly *adv.* worthily II.Prol.7

dynnys *v.* resounds III.v.62

dynnyt *v.* resounded I.xi.61

dynt *n.* blow I.iii.5; III.Prol.25; IV.xii. heading

dyrk *adj.* dark III.iii.86; figuratively, obscure I.Prol.193

dyrk *adv.* in darkness VI.iv.66

dyrk *n.* darkness II.vi.109

dyrknyt *v.* darkened VII.Prol.47

dyrlyng *vbl.n.* slight scratch or piercing XII.vii.97

dysdeyn *n.* indignation, vexation V.vi.99

dyseyß *n.* discomfort, hardship I.xii.23; II.ii.158; IV.vii.65

dysmall *n.* unlucky person, wretch V.iv.15

dyssavouris *n.* deceivers II.Prol.18

dyssvsit, **dysvsit** *pa. p.* unused (to), unaccustomed I.xi.56. disused, neglected VII.xi.127

dyttit *v.* closed, stopped up IV.viii.67

dyuulgat *pa. p.* spread abroad, made widely known VIII.iii.86

dyvyne *n.* diviner III.x.113

dyvynour *n.* prophet, diviner II.ii.116;

III.x.112: L

dyvynys *n.* diviners IV.viii.115; IV.ii.29

dywlgait, **dywlgat**, **dywlgate** *pa. p.* made widely known, made common knowledge V.vii.53; VII.ii.83; XII. Prol.225; XII.x.136

e *n.* eye I.Prol.499; I.ii.68

e dolp *n.* eye-socket III.x.15

eclipsis *v.* eclipsis I.xi.96

edder, **edderis**, **eddir**, **eddyr** *n.* adder. any snake (**anguis**, **serpens**) II.iv.9; II.viii.57; V.ii.86; V.v.55

edgit *pa. p.* sharpened, fitted with an edge XII.iv.126: R, 53

edify *v.* construct, raise (as an edifice) I.Prol.230

effectuous, **effectuus** *adj.* effective, earnest VII.vi.141; XII.v.60

effeir *n.* fear III.i.57

effeir *n.* situation, condition, appearance III.iv.65

effek *n.* effect. **in ~** in reality IV.v.92, 117

effer *v.* frighten XI.xii.102

effering *pr. p.* belonging, suitable III. vi.221

efferis *n.* affairs, concerns I.iii.97; V.xii.89

efferis *v.* is suitable, is fitting IV.v.110; IV.x.44

effray, **effrays** *n.* fear, fright III.i.107. cause for alarm III.Prol.12

eft *adj.* aft, rear. **~ schip**, **~ casteill** III. viii.26; V.i.23

eft *adv.* after, afterwards I.viii.41; III.v.97

eft casteill, **eftcastellis** *n.* elevated structure at rear of ship III.viii.41; V.iii.58; X.v.25 (53 **est castell**)

egge *n.* edge. **~ lumys** edged tools XII. iv.126

eggis *v.* incites, urges V.viii.17

egill *n.* eagle I.vi.151

egis *n.* edges XI,xiv.26

eichyrris *n.* ears (of corn) VII.xii.35

eik *adv.* also (poetic) III.ii.87

eik, **eikis** *v.* add, augment II.x.51; III.

vi.223; VIII.vii.96

eild *n.* age (without any notion of oldness) V.vii.96; VIII.ix.41. old age V.xi.68

eildis *n.* ages, eras VIII.x.13

eildit *pa. p.* aged VI.v.19

eir *v.* cultivate, plough VIII.vi.12

eith *adj.* easy IV.viii.24; VI.ii.101

ekill *n.* a little addition *Contentis*.25 (from L: C **ekit**). *See also* **eik**

ekis *v.* adds VII.iv.46

elbok *n.* elbow IV.xii.94; IX.vii.145

eld *n.* age I.xi.22

eldfader *n.* father-in-law VI.xiv.58; VII.v.81

eldmoderis, eldmodir *n.* mother-in-law II.viii.112; XI.v.72

eldris *n.* ancestors III.x.74; VII.i.70

electuary *n.* medical syrup XII.Prol.144

eleuate *pa. p.* elevated, exalted I.Prol.29

elf *n.* a malignant supernatural being, taken as an object of heathen worship X.Prol.154

elike *adj.* like VI.Prol.98

eligant *adj.* graceful, comely VII.xiii.4

eliment *n.* upper air I.vi.128; IV.v.172. one of the four elements XII.iv.113

eliphantyne *adj.* of elephant's tusk, ivory VI.xv.114 (R **elephantis**)

ellis, ellys *adj.* previously I.Prol.491; XI.vi.136. otherwise IV.iv.10

ellis quhar *adv.* elsewhere VII.viii.93

eloquens *n.* eloquence, utterance in general I.Prol.4, 307, 393

elrich, elrych *adj.* weird, uncanny, strange III.x.41 (53 **ebrich**); VI.Prol.17; VII.Prol.108

elvys *n.* elves VIII.vi.7 (E, L, B **elphis**)

elyke *adj.* alike V.iii.97

elyke *adv.* equally I.xi.23

embrace, embraß *v.* embrace V.ix.74. encircle, invest XI.Prol.104

embuschment *n.* ambush IX.viii.114

emmotis *n.* emmets, ants IV.vii.79; XIII.Prol.58

empar *v.* damage VII.ix.103

empire *adj.* empyrean. *See* **hevin**

empire

emptive *adj.* empty I.Prol.20; X.x.42: R, 53 (C **empty**, *which is rare in Scots, though appearing in* III.vi.139 *and* IX.vi.71)

empyre *n.* imperium, right of jurisdiction III.iii.22; V.iv.143

emyspery *n.* hemisphere XII.Prol.28

enarmouris *n.* armour VIII.ix.57

enbalmys *v.* makes fragrant XII.vii.88

enbalmyt *pa. p.* made fragrant XII.Prol.136

enbrace *v.* enclose, invest V.vii.73

enbrasyng *v.inf.* to embrace VIII.vii.82

enbrovd *pa. p.* embroidered XII.Prol.65 (E **enbrouth**, R **enbrowdit**, 53 **enbrede**)

enbusch *v.* ambush XI.x.84

enchewys *v.* eschews, avoids V.viii.34.

end *n.* end. **at** ~ to extremities I.v.14

endland, endlang *adv.* beside, along III.ii.117; VI.vi.57; VIII.iv.51

endlang, endlangis *prep.* alongside III.iv.129; V.ii.116, 53

endite *pa. p.* composed VI.i.141

enduryng *pr. p.* used conjunctionally, while. **that tyme** ~ **the sege lay about Troy** III.v.113

endyng *v.inf.* to end IX.viii.92

endyt *pa. p.* endited IX.Prol.57

endyte *n.* writing, composition I.Prol.2, 16, 28, 343; III.vi.173

endyte, endytis *v.* write, compose IV.Prol.5, 217; V.Prol.22

endyte *pa. p.* endited, composed I.Prol.494; V.Prol.48

eneuch, enew *adj.* enough II.v.44; XI.vii.175

enforcyng *pr. p.* exerting, applying (oneself) XII.Prol.236

enforcys, enforsys *v.* strives VI.i.153; XII.vii.11

enfors, enforsis *v.* reflexive, exert, apply (oneself) I.iii.86; III.ii.127

enfyrit, enfyryt *pa. p.* set on fire, glowing V.iv.84; XIII.Prol.12

engendrit *v.* engendered I.i.48

engenyus *adj.* ingenious VII.iv.203

engrave, engravyn *pa. p.* engraved I.i.44; V.ix.81; XIII.viii.96

engrevyt *pa. p.* annoyed, injured X.xiii.19

engyne *n.* ingenuity I.Prol.2, 20, 147, 291; V.Prol.28; VI.x.86. ingenious or complex structure VI.xii.8

engynys *n.* (siege) engines V.viii.39

engyre *v.* reflexive, obtrude (oneself) X.ii.9

eniosyt *pa. p.* enjoyed X.xiii.162

enioys *v.* enjoy, use XIII.vi.98

ennoy *n.* hardship (stronger than annoyance) I.ix.91; VI.viii.79. annoyance, anger XI.ii.100; XI.iv.54

ennoy *v.* annoy V.xii.188

ennoyus *adj.* bothersome XIII.ii.148

enoynt *v.* anoint IV.iv.39

enoynt *pa. p.* anointed IV.v.80

enparyng *vbl.n.* imparing *Conclusio*.10

enragent *adj.* raging, filled with rage X.x.60 (R enragit, 53 enrageing)

enragit *v.* became furious XI.xii.91

enragyt *pa. p.* made furious IV.vii.5, 29

ensenȝe, ensenȝeis *n.* war cry VII.x.87. insignia, distinguishing emblem III.v.48; VII.iii.53

ensew *v.* pursue, seek to obtain III.vi.25 (L enschew). follow II.Prol.7; IX.Prol.72

ensewit *v.* followed, chased III.v.89

ensewys *v.* follows, comes behind II.xi.77

ensuris *v.* trusts V.viii.19

entechment *n.* instruction XI.iv.41

enterprit *v.* interpret IX.Prol.74

entertenyr *v.* entertain (from the French entretenir) XIII.viii.105

entres *n.* entry, permission or right to enter IV.viii.30; VI.ii.56

entring *v.pres.3 pl.* enter VII.i.23

enty *adj.* empty? *Obscure.* VIII.vii.94 (R entive, 53 empty)

entyre *n.* interment VI.ii.151

entyrit *pa. p.* buried X.xiii.164

entyrment *v.* interment VI.iii.heading

entyrmyddill *v.* intermingle XII.xiii.107

enveroin *prep.* around VI.ii.115

enveron *adj.* around V.iii.6

enveronyt *pa. p.* surrounded, encircled I.iv.9

enveroun *adv.* around I.ix.136

envnte *pa. p.* anointed III.iv.137

envolupyt *pa. p.* enveloped, wrapped up in IV.iv.18

envoluvt *pa. p.* enveloped, enwrapped VI.iv.66

envy *n.* grudge IV.vi.137

envynt *pa. p.* anointed IV.v.80. *See also* envnte, invnct

equal, equale *adj.* just, impartial VI.ii.110. level, on a line V.xi.111

equale *adv.* equalling in height III.x.31

equaly *adv.* equitably, justly II.vii.5

equiualent *adj.* equal VI.vii.103

er *v.* err, wander V.x.81

erd *n.* earth I.iii.25; III.ii.52

erd quake, erdqwkyng *n.* earthquake. I.iii.54, marginal note; VII.iv.133

erdyt *v.* buried V.ii.12

eris *n.* ears I.iii.98

ern *n.* eagle XI.xiv.72; XII.v.63

errand *pr. p.* wandering, errant (not modern erring or errand) VI.i.131; VII.viii.39

errant *adj.* wandering I.xi.124

errit *pa. p.* erred, made mistakes X.ii.130

errour *n.* wandering, straying II.v.88. mistake VI.Prol.165

erst *adv.* formerly *Exclamatioun*.45

ery *adj.* fearful VIII.iv.91; VIII.vi.87

eschame *v.* be ashamed IV.Prol.194

eschape *pa. p.* escaped VIII.iv.81

escheif *v.* achieve, accomplish II.x.163

eschew, eschewis *v.* avoid, eschew III.vi.18, 94; IV.ii.44 (B enschew). escapes, gets away I.xii.23

eschewit *pa. p.* achieved, accomplished IV.i.31

eschewyt *v.* escaped IV.iv.76 (B enschewit)

eschin *adj.* made of ash-wood VI.iii.47

eschis *n.* ash-trees XI.iii.80

essens *n.* perfume, scent VIII.iii.23: R (C **ensens**)

essonȝeis *v.* excuses XIII.Prol.133

estabill *v.* settle, establish VI.i.52

estait, estate *n.* personal position or rank I.Prol.316. high rank XI.Prol.86. state of affairs V.ix.64. physical condition or state IV.vi.100

estonyst *pa. p.* astonished I.viii.35; III.i.89; V.xi.115

etand *pr. p.* eating VI.iii.80

etern *adj.* eternal I.i.67; I.v.10

etheryall *adj.* heavenly, celestial VI.xv.73; XII.Prol.41

etland, etlyng *pr. p.* aiming, intending V.vi.57; V.ix.37; IX.vi.101

etlys *v.* plans, intends, attempts II.iv.34; V.i.26; VI.vi.8

ettill, etyll *v.* intend I.iv.81; IV.x.41. direct one's course V.i.47

ettillit *v.* intended I.i.30

euere *adj.* every II.v.6

eueron *adj.* everyone II.vi.65

euery *adj.* every, all. with plural, in ~ **ȝeris**, ~ **sydis** V.ii.34; VIII.i.7

eueryane *compound* everyone III.viii.24

euerystand *adv.* everywhere, in every station or post IX.xi.1

evadit *v.* escaped, got away II.vii.102

eveir *n.* ivory III.vi.212

evil *adj.* evil. ~ **at eyß** indisposed VII.i.110

evil willy *adj. phrase* ill-disposed V.xi.105

evinly *adj.* level, regular VII.ix.2

evir, evoir *n.* ivory I.ix.20; XII.Prol.14

evyn *n.* evening I.vi.119; IV.ii.54

evyn *adv.* evenly, smoothly III.vii.72; III.x.62. **full** ~ exactly (padding) I.v.121; III.viii.14. to the same degree. ~ **eild** of the same age V.viii.64

evyneild *adj.* of the same age III.vii.42

evyneild *n.* one of the same age II.x.4

evynly *adj.* equal in size V.viii.2

evyr *n.* ivory VI.x.46

eweris *n.* ewers, vessels I.xi.26

excellens *n.* excellence. **be** ~ par excellence I.i.1.marginal note

excellent *adj.* excelling. **Eneas ~ all the leve** XIII.vii.30

except *p.p.* accepted V.iv.152

exceppit *v.* accepted IX.x.93 (E **acceptit**, R accept, L **exceppis**, 53 **acceppit**)

excerß, excersis *v.* perform, do, practise III.iv.136; IV.ii.74; V.xiii.61

excersyt *pa. p.* practised, carried on V.iii.21. occupied in, employed in IV.v.168

execut *v.* executed, performed IV.vii.70

exem *v.* examine XII.vii.48

exemplis *n.* typical instances I.Prol.256

exemyn *v.* examine XII.i.52

exequeys *n.* funeral rites V.ii.24

exercit *pa. p.* exercised, made expert and knowing V.xii.109

exortyng *v.inf.* to exhort X.v.157

expart *adj.* skilled, trained by experience III.iii.99

expedient *adj.* expedient (without the idea of being based on hope of advantage rather than principle) III.i.1

expert *adj.* skilful, knowing by experience I.iv.77. aware, knowledgeable XI.viii.46

expert *v.* experienced VI.xv.10: 53 (C **exerß**)

expert *pa. p.* experienced, known by experience VI.xi.17

expone *v.* expound I.Prol.390; IX.Prol.97. expend, apply XII.i.103

exponyt *pa. p.* translated, explained I.Prol.366

expreme *v.* explain, state, name II.vii.2; IV.vi.107; VI.Prol.26

express *adj.* particular, definite, explicit VI.ii.22

expreß *adv.* expressly, definitely III.iv.74; III.vi.168

expreym *v.* explain, express in words XII.i.116

extasy *n.* ecstasy, mystic or prophetic

trance *Directioun*.106

extre *n.* axle-tree XII.vi.168

extremyte *n.* most aggravated degree of discomfort or suffering III.v.67

eyge *n.* ridge of hill, crest VII.xiii.42

eyldis *n.* ages, eras VII.xi.89

eyn *n.* eyes I.iii.37; III.vii.39; IV.v.17

eyr *adv.* earlier IV.x.68

eyr *v.* cultivate XIII.ix.78

eyrdit *v.* buried I.v.81, marginal note

eyt *v.* ate III.ix.71

eyt *pa. p.* eaten III.ix.79

fa *n.* foe IV.viii.33

fabill, fablis *n.* fictitious statement or tale I.Prol.190; III.Prol.16

face *n.* face. **forgane the ~ of the flude** opposite the mouth of the river III.x.72

facheonys *n.* falchions VII.xi.57

facil *adj.* easy to do or deal with VI.ii.101

facund *adj.* eloquent I.Prol.39; *Directioun*.93

fader *n.* uninflected possessive, father's I.Prol.209; VI.v.29

fader broder *n.* uncle VI.vi.37

faggottis *n.* faggots V.xi.119

faid *n.* company of hunters IV.iii.56

faik *v.* grasp, grip X.vii.88

faikand *pr. p.* grasping V.viii.6

faill *n.* sward, turf XII.Prol.88

faill *n.* failure. **but ~** certainly I.Prol.118

faill *v.* break down, come to nothing IX.iii.43

failȝe *v.* fail VI.Prol.162; VI.ii.23

fair *n.* course, journey VIII.Prol.100; X.iv.90. activity, actions V.ii.24. experiences **ȝour weil ~** V.xii.15

fair *n.* fair, market V.xii.174

fair *v.* travel IV.vii.77

fairfolkis *n.* fairies VIII.vi.7

falt *n.* feat I.i.24; XI.xiv.85

fal *pa. p.* fallen II.vi.27; V.xiv.82

fald *n.* fold IX.x.18. **be firth and ~** by forest and fold, everywhere VI.xiii.84; VII.Prol.16

fald *pa. p.* folded V.iii.65. second element of compounds meaning multiplicity

thyk ~, mony ~ II.v.49; V.xii.4

faldyn *pa. p.* folded XII.xiv.98

fall *n.* a fall in wrestling I.Prol.32

fall *v.* befall, happen I.Prol.444; VII.v.77

falloschip, falloschippis *n.* followers, company, band *Contentis*; III.iv.62. friendships V.xiii.66

fallow, fallowis *n.* associate, companion I.iii.35; IV.Prol.52

fals *v.* violate (an oath or promise) VI.v.60

falt *v.* commit a fault I.iii.72

faltit *pa. p.* been at fault, sinned IX.iii.155

falȝeit *v.* failed I.Prol.496

fame *n.* report I.viii.70; III.ii.104

fame *n.* foam I.i.65; III.iii.92; III.viii.118

famen *n.* foe-men IX.ii.53

famyl *n.* family VI.xiii.23

fang *n.* a rope for steadying the gaff of a sail V.xiv.8

fang, fangis *v.* seize, take VI.ix.138. draw or pull in III.viii.52

fant *adj.* weak, feeble VII.v.51

fant *adj.* feigned X.xi.89

fantasy *n.* mental apprehension of an object or perception IV.ix.2. opinion, product of the imagination without basis in fact III.iii.47; V.Prol.36; VII.vi.66. habit of deluding oneself by imaginary perceptions IV.Prol.109

fanys *n.* flags, pennants XII.Prol.47

fararis *n.* farers, travellers V.xiii.30

farcis *n.* farces IV.viii.128

fard *n.* rush, flight, force, onslaught (*very common in Douglas*) I.v.127; II.viii.103; IV.v.23, 124, 145; VI.i.23

farly *n.* wonder, marvellous thing VII.i.100

farly *v.* marvel X.Prol.87; X.viii.21

farnys *n.* ferns VII.Prol.55

farrand *pr. p.* faring, appearing VII.vii.147. handsome, comely VIII.ix.103

fars *v.* stuff VIII.Prol.52

fary *n.* dismay, dazed state of mind X.xiv.31

faß *n.* tassel, trifle; something of small value IV.Prol.156; V.vii.84; X.xiv.100

fasson *n.* fashion III.ii.89; IV.iv.85

fast *adv.* persistently, strongly I.vii.7.
close or nearby I.iv.54; I.viii.134

fastby *compound.* nearby IX.ii.84

fat *adj.* fat; rich, productive, plenteous
I.xi.58; IV.v.54; VI.iii.110

fatale *adj.* of fate, pertaining to the Fates
I.i.33; V.xi.82. fateful, fated II.iii.40;
IV.i.29; V.ii.81. death-dealing (**fat-
iferum**) VIII.x.59

favour *n.* good will V.vi.97

faw *adj.* variegated VIII.x.16

fawch *adj.* pale brown or yellow
VI.vi.68; VII.Prol.37; VIII.i.34; XII.
Prol.108

fax *n.* hair II.v.51. face (derisively, of a
woman's face, one disfigured by a
moustache?) VIII.Prol.32

fayn *adj.* glad, pleased XIII.Prol.102

fayn *n.* weather vane XII.pro

faynt *adj.* weak, feeble, scant, spiritless
I.vii.33; IV.Prol.6; IV.iv.60; XI.vii.58

fayr *n.* doings, experiences IV.Prol.234

fayt *n.* feat VIII.viii.141

fe *n.* cattle, sheep or goats III.iv.22

febillit *pa. p.* enfeebled IX.xiii.80

feblyng *vbl.n.* enfeebling IV.Prol.15

fed, fede *n.* hostility, enmity, anger
II.ix.48; III.vi.33; IV.viii.131; VI.vii.25;
XII.v.142. continued state of hostility,
feud I.i.6

feddyrame *n.* feathers, plumage IV.v.93

fedlar *n.* fiddler VIII.Prol.64

fedrame *n.* feathers, plumage VI.i.15

fedyng *v.inf.* to feed VI.x.62

fee master *n.* shepherd, keeper of livestock VII.viii.21 (R **fey maistir**; L, B
fee; 53 **hie maister**)

feid *n.* enmity, hatred I.v.41; II.ii.65

feil *adj.* many I.i.16; II.vii.20; III.ii.117. ~
sys many times, often II.xii.20

feilabill *adj.* capable of being felt, producing emotion I.Prol.13

feild *n.* field VIII.Prol.163. field of battle,
battle V.x.72. field, race-course V.iii.79

feill *n.* consciousness, apprehension, knowledge III.Prol.32; V.Prol.37

feill *adj.* many I.i.83

feir *adj.* fair IX.iv.98

feir *n.* fear V.x.52; IX.iii.112

feir *n.* companionship. **in** ~ together
I.viii.143; V.iii.80; XII.vi.129

feir *n.* comrade, companion V.i.27; V.v.63;
VIII.iii.137

feir *n.* fare VIII.ix.75

feir *n.* fixed price VIII.Prol.47

feldis *n.* fighting forces, armies in the field
VII.xiii.55

fell *adj.* fierce, ruthless, cruel I.xi.18; II.iii.94;
III.iv.53. unfortunate, painful II.ii.145

fell *v.* befell. ~ **thame fair** befell fortu-
nately for them V.iv.82

fellon, felloun *adj.* fierce, savage,
cruel I.vi.98; III.x.32; IV.iii.60. very
great, very loud III.ii.64. monstrous
I.Prol.390. gigantic (**ingentis**)
VI.iii.49

felony *n.* fierceness, cruelty X.viii.100;
XII.vi.16: R (C **villany**)

feltrit *pa. p.* of hair, matted or tangled
VI.v.11 (E **feltat**)

fen *n.* marsh VII.Prol.76. filth, dirt III.
iv.17; V.vi.81

fence *n.* defence, places of hiding.
grene vaill full of ~ VI.xi.2 (E, B, 53
full of sence)

fendit *pa. p.* defended II.v.80

fendlich *adj.* devilish III.ix.78

fens *n.* defence, fences, enclosures
(**feildis lauborit ful of** ~; *see* **fence**)
III.i.28

fensabill *adj.* able-bodied, able for
defence II.viii.67

fenystar, fenystaris *n.* window IX.ix.20;
XII.Prol.169

fenyt *pa. p.* pretended, falsified
I.Prol.294

fenʒe *v.* feign IV.i.107. deceive
I.Prol.476

fenʒeand *pr. p.* feigning II.i.7

fenʒeit *pa. p.* feigned, false I.Prol.179;
I.i.87; I.vii.83; II.Prol.6. feigned,
mimic, contrived III.v.37

ferd *adj.* fourth III.x.ending; IV.xii.

ending

ferd *v.* fared, behaved XII.i.22

ferely *adv.* nimbly XII.vi.115

feris *n.* comrades I.iv.63, 69; III.ii.120

feris *n.* bearing, demeanour III.ix.14; IX.vi.107

feris *n.* fears, things frightening IX.iii.136

feris *v.* fares, happens I.vi.54

ferleis *n.* marvels, wonders VII.vi.96

ferleis *v.* wonders, becomes amazed XII. Prol.80

ferleit *v.trans.* wondered at I.vii.7

ferly *n.* marvellous or uncanny occurrence II.vi.22; III.v.49

ferm *adj.* firm I.ii.36.

ferm *v.* make firm X.v.174. shut up, blockade X.v.181

fermand *pr. p.* making firm III.x.8

fermans *n.* enclosure XII.Prol.176

ferreit, ferreyt *pa. p.* of a sow, farrowed VII.i.56; VIII.ii.37

ferry boyt *n.* ferry-boat I.Prol.500

ferryar *n.* ferryman VI.v.63

ferryit *pa. p.* of a sow, farrowed III.vi.72

fersly *adv.* fiercely; of a dove, suddenly, quickly (**subito**) V.iv.105

fertyrris *n.* biers VI.xv.68 (53 **fercyns**)

fery *adj.* active, nimble VI.v.20

festual, festuale *adj.* connected with a religious festival VI.i.136. festive II.iv.94; IV.viii.107

festyng *v.pres.3 pl.* they feast XIII.x.1

fet *v.* fetch VIII.vi.17

fet *pa. p.* fetched VI.v.38 (E,R, L, B, 53 **set**)

fettysly *adv.* elegantly IV.v.163

fewlume *n.* kind of bird. Gaelic **faoileann**, gull? IX.Prol.47

fewtyr *v.* lock together (as in combat) X.xi.166

fey *adj.* unhappy, unfortunate (translating **infelix, infelices**) III.i.91; III.v.91. doomed by fate, fated to die I.vii.101; I.xi.36; IV.viii.89; IV.x.13; V.xi.71. bringing evil fortune II.vi.86; X.Prol.124

feyn *v.* feign I.Prol.198; IV.Prol.240;

XII.Prol.209

feyr *n.* companionship. **in** ~ together V.ii.68

feys *n.* fees I.viii.25

figur *n.* image III.iii.50. face V.xiii.13

figuris *n.* figures of speech I.Prol.196

figuryt *pa. p.* embroidered, decorated with pictures III.vii.26

fild *pa. p.* defiled IV.x.60

fillok *n.* wanton girl VIII.Prol.32

filyt *v.* defiled X.xiv.51

fireflaucht *n.* lightning flash IV.v.67: E, B. *See also* **fyreflaucht, fyreslaucht**

firmament *n.* vault of heaven IV.viii.92

firth *n.* wood (poetic). **be** ~ **and fald** by wood and fold, everywhere VI.xiii.84; VII.Prol.162

flacconys, flacon, flaconys *n.* flagon, bowl V.ii.72; VII.ii.89; XII.v.161

flaf *v.* flap, flutter XII.xiii.175

flaffand *pr. p.* flapping, fluttering X.vii.63

flaggis *n.* flashes of lightning I.iii.61; VII.Prol.49

flakis *n.* pieces of framework XI.ii.14

flane *n.* arrow IV.ii.41; VII.viii.50

flankartis *n.* thigh armour VII.x.76

flappys *n.* flaps, light blows V.vii.26

flat, flattis *n.* piece of level ground, flat place, plain II.vi.13; II.viii.105

flat *v.* flatter IV.Prol.240; XII.Prol.209

flatlyngis *adv.* prostrate V.viii.54

flaucht *see* **fyre flaucht** IX.xii.22

flaw *n.* blast, squall of wind VII.Prol.49

flawmand *pr. p.* flaming I.i.79

flawmys *n.* flames II.vii.122

flawys *n.* flashes, sparks VII.i.112

flayn *n.* arrow X.x.94

fle *v.* flee I.Prol.320

fleand *pr. p.* flying I.iv.54

flechand *pr. p.* cajoling, speaking insincerely II.ii.56

flechyng *vbl.n.* flattery XI.xiii.heading

fleit *v.* flow I.Prol.69

flekit, flekkit, fleklit *pa. p.* flecked, maculate. hence deceitful IV.Prol.191: 53 (C **slekit speche**).

V.ii.90: R, 53 (C **freklit**); V.ii.90: E

flekkir *v.* flicker, quiver VI.i.98

flekkyrand *pr. p.* flickering, quivering V.viii.115

flemyt *pa. p.* put to flight, expelled VII.iv.57; VII.v.41; VIII.Prol.8

flendris *n.* fragments, pieces V.iv.90

flet *v.* floated I.iii.45; V.xii.57

fleur, flewyr *n.* odour, smell III.iv.38; VII.i.134; XII.v.199

fley *v.* frighten, scare IV.v.68

fleyce *n.* fleece; figuratively, a covering of verdure XII.Prol.80

fleyis *v.* puts to flight VI.ix.160

fleyit *pa. p.* frightened, put to flight XI.xv.107

fleym *v.* expel, put to flight VII. Prol.140

fleyn *v.inf.* to fly a hawk V.Prol.4

fleys *v.* flies away I.Prol.398; I.iii.94

fleyt *pa. p.* frightened XI.viii.71

flocht *n.* on ~ in a state of excitement or dismay IV.xii.17; VII.vi.8; VIII.i.5, 23

flodderit, floddyrrit *pa. p.* flooded, overflowed VII.Prol.52; XI.ii.80

flokkyng *v.pres.3 pl.* flock II.xii.73

florist, floryst *pa. p.* flourished, flowery I.vii.25; V.Prol.1

floschis *n.* watery swamp, marsh VII. Prol.54

flot, flote *n.* fleet I.viii.102; III.viii.112; V.xi.21

flotterand *v. pres. p.* flowing XIII.iv.14

flottyryt *pa. p.* wet with tears XI.i.72

flour *n.* flour V.xii.146

flour dammes *n.* auricula XII.Prol.118

flour delyß *n.* iris or lily XII.Prol.117

flowand *pr. p.* flowing (i.e. in a state of hesitation and uncertainty, representing **fluctuat**) VIII.i.5

flowr *n.* flour VII.ii.15

flowris *n.* blossoms XII.iii.48

floyt *n.* fleet I.vi.134; V.xii.14

floyt *n.* troop XII.v.191

flude *n.* overflow of water II.vi.14. river I.Prol.236. figuratively, onrush, state of abundance I.Prol.3

flum *n.* river. *Directioun.*58

flur, flurys *n.* floor III.i.117; VIII.iv.27; XIII.ix.20

flycht *n.* flight X.iv.79. wing-feathers XIII.Prol.33

flycht *n.* act of fleeing from enemies II.x.138

flychtir, flychteris *v.* flutter V.ix.33; VI.iii.81

flyghterand *pr. p.* fluttering VIII.xi.33

flykerand, flykkerand *pr. p.* trembling, quivering I.iv.93; III.ix.73

flyt *v.* depart, pass IV.Prol.88

flyte *v.* wrangle, scold, quarrel I.Prol.153, 272; III.Prol.20; IV.Prol.188

foill *n.* foal X.xiv.89

foke *n.* folk V.vi.12

fold *suffix* used as separate word, denoting multiplication or increase. **mony** ~ V.v.12, 39

folk *n.* folk, people I.vi.60; I.viii.53

folkis *n.* people I.vii.17; II.ii.154; III. ii.63; III.v.14; IV.i.7, etc.

followis *n.* fellows, companions? VII. xi.55

foly hat, foly hattis *n.* hat resembling a fool's cap IV.v.79; VI.Prol.16; IX.x.60

folys *n.* foal's IV.ix.87

fomy *adj.* foaming I.vi.34; XIII.iii.21

for ded *phrase* indeed II.x.171

for out *prep. phrase*, without I.vi.62

for thy *adv. phrase*, for that reason I.Prol.267

forbearis *n.* ancestors III.ii.74; XII. xi.76: E (C **forfaderis**)

forbled *pa. p.* exhausted by bleeding VI.viii.56: E, R, 53 (C **for bled**, for bleeding)

forbodyn *pa. p.* forbidden I.ix.128; VI.ix.203; IX.ix.50

forbreist *n.* breast of a cloak or gown XI.xv.19

forcastell *n.* forward part of a ship V.xiii.25

forcely *adv.* strongly, forcibly I.v.74

forcy *adj.* strong, full of force I.iii.7

forcyly *adv.* strongly X.vi.162

fordell *n.* precedence, first place V.iii.99

fordoverit, fordovirrit *pa. p.* overcome by sleep II.v.35; V.xiv.35; VI.viii.93; IX.v.28; IX.vi.20

fordrunkyn *pa. p.* overcome by drinking III.ix.81

fordryvis *v.* drives away or astray I.i.56

fordullyt *pa. p.* made dull or stupid IV.Prol.158

fordward *adj.* inclined to action, enterprising IX.v.70

fordward, fordwert *n.* covenant VIII. iii.161; X.iii.82

fordyn, fordynnys *v.trans.* fill with din VI.vi.70; VI.ix.60

fordynnys *v.intrans.* resounds VII.vi.125

fordynnyt *pa. p.* deafened III.x.36; IV.xii.48

foresteris *n.* keepers of a forest VII. viii.62 (E **fosteris**)

forfeblit *pa. p.* rendered feeble VII. Prol.10; XII.xiv.59

forfochtin *pa. p.* exhausted by fighting VI.viii.53

forgaddir *v.* come together, assemble VII.ix.26

forgaderit *v.* assembled IV.iv.22

forgane *prep.* over against I.i.22; I.vi.4; III.viii.56, 89

forge *v.* manufacture by smithwork VI.xv.3

forgit *v.* manufactured by smithwork VI.xv.110

forgrandschir *n.* great, or great-great, grandfather XIII.ii.82 (R **ferde grantschir**, 53 **ferdgrantseir**)

forgyar *n.* maker II.v.26

forgyng *v.inf.* to forge VIII.vii.170

forgyt *pa. p.* manufactured, made, formed II.i.6

forhow *v.* abandon, forsake VII.vi.121

forhowar *n.* deserter XII.i.36, C, L, B marginal note, E, R, 53 (C MS **banyst**)

forkyt *pa. p.* having forks (of a road) IV.xi.52

forland, forlandis *n.* cape or headland, coasts III.Prol.37; III.viii.2

forlane, forlayn *pa. p.* shamefully brought to bed VI.i.38; X.vii.70

forleit *pa. p.* abandoned, forsaken XIII. Prol.130

forloppyn *pa. p.* runaway, vagabond VII.ix.80

forlor *pa. p.* forlorn, lost VI.v.62; XIII. Prol.114

forlost *pa. p.* utterly lost IX.vii.101

formaste *adj.* first in number IV.iv.83

fornycht *n.* early evening IX.iii.209

forray *v.* make a foray into a country or area, ravage XI.x.62

forret, forrettis *n.* forehead VII.vii.26; XII.iv.34. *figuratively, as* **the ~ of a bra** I.iv.19

forrowth *prep.* before V.v.2

forrydar *n.* forerunner, one riding in advance of others XIII.Prol.20

forryn *v.* outrun, run ahead of XII. ii.86; XII.vi.61, 90

forß *n.* strength, exertion, impetus I.i.5; V.viii.32. regard, account IX.iv.128. **of ~** of necessity III.x.95

forschame *interj.* fy, **~ !** be ashamed V.iv.6

forschip *n.* prow, bow I.iii.16; III.iv.128; III.viii.109

forsis *v.intr.* be of importance, matter IX.Prol.45

forstam, forstammys *n.* prow V.iii.78; V.iv.52

forsuyth *compound.* in truth, to be sure I.Prol.109; I.viii.146; III.ix.74

forswer *v.* swear falsely XII.xiii.64

forswiftit *pa. p.* swept away III.iii.97

forsychtis *n.* foreseeing (possibly a verb, **you foresee**) VIII.ix.75

fortaleß *n.* fortress III.ii.133

forthir *adj.* of a horse, pertaining to the offside V.x.40

forthir *adv.* moreover III.vi.95

for thy *adv.* for that reason I.Prol.267; IX.xii.34

fortil, fortill, forto *compound.* sign of the infinitive, to I.ii.93; II.Prol.3; III.

iv.37, 64

forto- *first element in compounds.*
~**be** II.ii.4. ~**begile** I.x.51. ~**behald**
I.ix.20. ~**beit** VIII.vii.91. ~**beld**
XI.ii.15. ~**ber** XI.iii.71. ~**cum** III.
vi.169. ~**do** XI.v.11. ~**tak** V.x.59. ~**tell**
III.iv.54

fortop *n.* forehead IV.xii.109

fortunabill *adj.* fortunate I.xi.75; IV.iii.37

fortyfying *vbl.n.* strengthening a person XII.Prol.236: R (C **Enforcyng**
thame quha mycht clynk it best, R
In fortyfing …)

forvay, forvayis, forvays *v.* err III.
Prol.18; IV.Prol.153; IV.i.45; V.Prol.30,
50

forvayit *pa. p.* gone astray IV.x.76

forvayt *v.* went wrong I.Prol.224;
Exclamatioun.26

forworthyn *pa. p.* rendered ugly or
worthless VIII.iv.21

forwrocht *pa. p.* exhausted, ruined
I.iv.6; III.viii.120; X.vi.44

forȝeld *v.* repay II.ix.53

forȝet *v.* forgot III.iii.101

forȝet *pa. p.* forgotten I.ix.44; III.ix.53;
IV.x.12; V.xii.68

fosteraris *n.* breeders, encouragers
IV.Prol.4

fosteris *n.* foresters VII.viii.15 (R
forstaris)

fosterit *v.* gave nourishment I.Prol.469

fostir *n.* child, offspring VI.xv.75

fostyr *n.* fosterer XII.Prol.253 (R, 53
fosterare)

found *v.* establish, base IV.Prol.206. lay
the foundations of IV.v.167

foundand *pr. p.* laying foundations for
IV.v.157

foundment *n.* beginning, foundation
III.i.37

foundris *v.* stumbles X.xiiii.157

four squarit *pa. p.* squared VII.viii.78

fouth *n.* abundance I.Prol.58

fow *adj.* full VI.v.16; VIII.Prol.138

fowcy *n.* fosse, ditch IX.ii.24

fowely *adv.* foully I.Prol.422

fowlis *n.* birds of any kind I.Prol.376

fowne, fownys *n.* fawn VII.vi.126; XII.
Prol.181

fows *n.* fosse, moat, ditch VIII.iv.16 (E
fousy, R **fowsyis**)

fowsy, fowsys *n.* moat, ditch I.vii.15;
VII.ii.52; VII.iii.25

fowth *n.* abundance, plenitude
I.Prol.120

foyn *v.* thrust, feint V.viii.17. *See also*
fuyn

foyn *n.* foes II.vii.30; XI.xiii.3

fra *prep.* from. as soon as, indicating
point of departure in time (**ubi**) III.
vi.106; III.ix.17

fragil *adj.* morally weak IV.Prol.8

fragilyte *n.* weakness of character
IX.Prol.6

frakkis *v.* moves swiftly (*poetic*) I.i.62;
V.iv.101; V.xiii.124

frakly *adv.* nimbly VIII.vii.164

franacy *n.* frenzy, mental derangement
II.ii.61

franand *pr. p.* questioning (*poetic*)
X.iii.102

franches *n.* asylum, sanctuary VIII.vi.69

frane *v.* ask, question, inquire (*poetic*)
III.ii.65; VII.vii.116

frasyng *vbl.n.* grating, creaking VI.ix.52

fraward *adj.* contrary XI.vii.124

frawart *prep.* away from I.i.57; I.iii.19;
II.iii.50

frawart *adj.* adverse, perverse I.v.62;
II.ii.40; III.ii.149

frawartis *prep.* away from IV.Prol.131

fray *n.* fear VII.v.50

frayit *pa. p.* frightened II.viii.87

frays *v.* grate. **cabillis can fret and** ~
I.ii.60

frayt *pa. p.* frightened IV.iv.60

fre *adj.* of noble character VI.Prol.14

fredom *n.* open-hearted generosity,
quality of being noble or generous
I.Prol.98

freik *n.* fighting man (*poetic*) VIII.
Prol.123

freith *v.* exempt from harm X.ii.131

freklyt *pa. p.* spotted, flecked IV.xii.5

frelage *n.* freedom, privilege of sanctuary IX.iii.47

fremmyt *adj.* strange, unfamiliar, unfriendly I.i.58; I.vii.113; IV.Prol.17; IV.vi.75; VI.ii.30

fremmytly *adv.* strangely I.viii.130

frenasy *n.* frenzy IV.ix.1

frendfull *adj.* friendly V.i.43 (53 **freyndlie**)

frendfully *adv.* in a friendly manner V.xiv.29 (R, B, 53 **freyndly**)

frendly *adj.* friendly II.iii.5

frendly *adv.* amiably I.viii.59

frendschip *n.* kinship XII.i.63

frenettical *adj.* feverish VII.vi.35

frensches *n.* freedom VI.xiv.35

fresh *adj.* fresh, blooming I.Prol.254

fresyng *vbl.n.* freezing VII.Prol.140

fret *v.* gnaw IV.Prol.70; VII.ii.47. rub against, be injured by friction I.ii.60

frog stad *n.* with *pa. p.* weighted down by a heavy frock or cloak VI.v.132

front, frontis *n.* face, forehead III.ix.89; XIII.vii.24. foremost part of anything, as of a cliff VII.Prol.40, 61

fronteris *n.* frontiers, borders III. Prol.39

fructuus *adj.* fruitful, fertile I.viii.68; III.iii.32

fruitis *n.* fruit of trees. **cornys and ~** III.ii.142, 153

frusch *v.* smash, break in pieces XI.xvii.50

frustrait, frustrat *pa. p.* frustrated IV.iii.52; V.viii.36

frute *n.* profit, reward VI.xvi.4: R (C **bruit**, fame)

fudder *n.* loud blast of wind X.Prol.159

fuf *v.* puff VIII.vii.120

ful *adv.* fully, completely III.iii.60. very III.vi.58

fulderis *n.* thunderbolts XII.xiv.88

fulfillit *pa. p.* filled completely I.i.17

full *adv.* very IV.iv.7

fulychly *adv.* foolishly IX.ix.118

fulychneß *n.* foolishness IV.Prol.27

fulȝeis *n.* leaves XII.Prol.89

fumy *adj.* vaporous III.v.16, 53

fundament *n.* foundation I.vii.20

funderand *pr. p.* stumbling, falling XI.xv.90

fundir *v.* stumble, fall XI.xiii.51

fundment *n.* foundation VII.i.56

fundrit *v.* stumbled II.ix.75

fundyt *pa. p.* founded, smelted VIII. vii.169

funeral, funerale, funerall *adj.* funereal I.Prol.173; III.i.47; IV.Prol.216; IV.ix.73

fur *n.* furrow II.xi.32; VII.iii.20

furdys *n.* fords of a river IX.xi.17

fureys *n.* the furies IV.viii.124

furnys *n.* furnace. hence, volcano III.x.35

furoll *n.* St Elmo's fire XII.xi.125: R (C **a sworll of fyre**)

furour *n.* fury IV.viii.50

furris *n.* furrows IV.vii.86

furth- *first element in vbl. compounds.* **~bryng** I.vii.28. **~followand** I.Prol.188. **~rekkynnys** VI.xiv.heading. **~schet** XI.xvii.43. **~schew** VII. xi.12. **~stracht** VI.xi.13. **~ȝet** I.iii.55; III.v.121; IV.ii.18

furthstrekit *pa. p.* of a weapon, put forth, launched II.xi.41

fury *phr.* **~ rage** frenzied, driven by the Furies IV.Prol.169, 223; V.i.14; X.ii.14

furyis *n.* the Furies IV.viii.131

fut *v.* dance XIII.ix.110

fut braid *n.* foot-breadth VII.v.128

fut syde *adj.* of a garment, reaching to the feet VII.x.31

fute hait, fute hoyt *adv.* in great haste, rapidly IV.xii.9; V.Prol.52; V.vi.65; V.xii.7

fuyn *v.* thrust, feint (as with the horns) IX.x.91

fuyr *v.* fared, passed, went IX.iii.46

fy *interj.* fie! IV.xi.12; XIII.i.118

fyall *n.* cupola, finial XII.Prol.71 (R, 53

phioll)

fygurate *pa. p.* decorated with figures of speech I.Prol.29: 53 (C **scharp sugurate sang**)

fykkil *adj.* fickle, changeable IV.Prol.8

fyle *v.* defile III.i.79; IV.Prol.56; IV.i.55

fylit, fylyt *v.* defiled II.iii.45; II.v.67

fynd *pa. p.* refined, purified VI.xii.57

fyndar *n.* discoverer, inventer II.iii.39

fyne *n.* end II.iii.10; IV.Prol.130; XI.viii.120

fynysith *v.* finishes II.Prol.21

fyre fangit *pa. p.* set on fire XII.v.201

fyre flaucht, fyreflauch *n.* flash of lightning II.x.156; IV.iv.80: E, R, B; VIII. vii.129; IX.xii.22; X.x.57; XIII.x.14

fyreslauch, fyreslaucht *n.* flash of lightning IV.iv.80; IV.v.67; VIII.viii.160; X.x.57: L, 53

fyrryn *adj.* made of fir II.v.17; IV.v.138; IV.ix.65

fyrth *n.* estuary, inlet, bay II.i.18; III. vi.123; III.viii.87; XII.Prol.54

fysching *v.inf.* to fish XII.ix.46

ga *v.* go II.ix.68

gabbyng *vbl.n.* lying I.Prol.203

gad wandis *n.* goads IX.x.47

gaddis *n.* rods VIII.xii.50

gaistis *n.* ghosts I.Prol.274; VI.Prol.17

gait *n.* way or path V.iv.156; IX.Prol.8. gait, mode of progress III.iv.24

gait *n.* goat IX.ix.88; VIII.Prol.48

gaitis *n.* **thus** ~ in such a manner VIII. viii.177

galay, galeys *n.* galley I.iv.45; V.iii.23

gall *n.* rancour, bitterness VIII.iv.83

gallyart *adj.* gallant, sprightly VIII. Prol.31

galys *v.* of the cuckoo, calls or sings XII.Prol.241

gal3art *adj.* gallant, sprightly XI.xii.6

gam *n.* sport IV.Prol.159

gambattis *n.* leaps in dancing XIII.ix.107

gammys *n.* jaws V.viii.98; X.xii.98

gan *v.* began, did (poetic) III.ii.65; III. vi.37

ganand *pr. p.* fitting, suitable I.Prol.355,

364; I.i.69; IV.vi.139

gane *adj.* suitable, appropriate. **seand thair tyme maste** ~ IX.v.14

gane *n.* ugly face VIII.iv.180

gane *v.* be suitable or fitting V.vi.132

gane *pa. p.* gone III.v.131

ganer *n.* gander VIII.xi.33

ganestand *v.* resist, oppose I.x.17

gang *v.* go VIII.Prol.48

gangat *n.* entrance. **sum glasteris at the** ~ VIII.Prol.48: R (C **sum glasteris and thai gang at**)

gant *n.* gape, yawn VI.viii.36

gant *v.* yawn III.viii.144.

ganys *v.* is suitable or fitting I.Prol.316, 322

gan3e, gan3eis *n.* arrow, crossbow bolt IX.viii.145; IX.xi.6; X.v.82

gan3eld *n.* return, recompense IX.v.62

gar *adj.* eager, ready, keen VI.xiv.30

gar *v.* cause (something to be done) III. ix.120; VI.i.142; VII.v.141

gardeys, gardis, gardy *n.* the arms from elbow to wrist V.iii.75; V.viii.4; X.vi.113; X.viii.95; XI.xi.64

garet *n.* watch-tower III.iv.60

garmond *n.* garment I.xi.35

garnys *v.* furnish with some addition. **with vennom to** ~ **the steil hedis** IX.xii.107 **garnysons** *n.* garrisons VII.xiii.33 (R **garisonis**)

garrand *pr. p.* causing (something to be done) IV.v.158

garrat *n.* watch-tower IX.ii.6

gart *v.* caused (something to be done) I.viii.26; III.viii.26; VIII.ix.2

garth *n.* yard or garden XIII.Prol.64

gastis *n.* ghosts, spirits IV.i.52

gat *n.* hole in the earth III.vi.116

gat *v.* got III.x.1

gat *v.* begot XIII.Prol.144

gatis *n.* ways VIII.viii.50

gaw *n.* gall. *Naym of the translatour*.1

gawd *n.* deceitful trick X.ii.27

gay *adj.* high-spirited, beautiful, cheerful I.Prol.254; VIII.ix.50

gaynsay *v.* oppose, deny I.Prol.96

gaynstand *v.* withstand, resist VI.i.123

gaynȝeld *n.* return, recompense VII.vii.43

gays *v.pres.3 pl.* go III.vi.187

gayt *n.* way, method VI.v.148. way, path, course V.vi.66

geif *pa. p.* given III.vi.149; IV.iii.28; V.vii.1; VII.vi.44

geiffyn *v.inf.* to give V.vi.39

geig *v.* creak VI.vi.62

geir *n.* possessions or articles of any kind I.x.42

geit *n.* jet X.iii.40

gem, gemme, gemmys, gemys *n.* game III.iv.135; IV.Prol.23; V.Prol.44; V.iii.21; V.x.101

gemel *adj.* twin X.vii.71

gemmyt *pa. p.* covered with buds XII. Prol.101

gendir *v.* engender VII.i.166

gendrit *pa. p.* engendered VI.ii.111

genealogy *n.* race, family III.vii.60; IV.v.107; V.iii.27. line of descent from ancestors I.ix.112; III.iii.39

gener, generis *v.* engender VII.i.166: E, 53 (C **gendir**); X.Prol.38

generacioun *n.* fact of begetting, line of a race. **baith fader and son, with haill** ~ IV.xi.43

genitryce *n.* genetrix, female parent VIII.viii.182

genology *n.* race I.xi.70

gent *adj.* graceful, delicately nurtured (poetic) V.x.heading, 16

gentil, gentill *adj.* noble (of horses, hence not gentle in the modern sense) III.vi.224. of good birth or breeding I.Prol.450, 263, 321, 331

gentil, gentile *adj.* racial, of a family or kindred, gentilitial IV.xi.50; VII.iii.56

gentile, gentiles *n.* pagan VI.Prol.53, 58, 79

gentre *n.* generosity, behaviour natural to the gently-born XI.iii.7 (R, 53 **gentrice**)

gentryce, gentryß *n.* behaviour, of the well-born X.viii.130; XI.iii.60

gentyles *n.* gentiles XI.Prol.194

gentyll *adj.* well bred (**pius**) V.vi.1

genus *Latin n.* an assemblage of objects which are related or belong together in consequence of a resemblance in natural qualities I.Prol.371

germane *adj.* having the same parent IV.ix.9; IV.x.52; V.vii.90

gerraflouris *n.* gillyflowers XII. Prol.121

gers *n.* grass I.iv.97

gersis *n.* grasses VII.Prol.64

geß *n.* guess V.i.10

gest *v.* guessed, supposed VIII.vi.80: R

gestis *n.* joists II.ii.99; II.viii.19, 119; V.xii.160

gestis *n.* guests I.xi.74

gestis *n.* deeds I.xi.94; II.vii.heading; hence, stories of deeds IX.xii.113; XIII.ix.heading

gestnyng *vbl.n.* residence as a guest I.x.29

get *n.* offspring. *not pejorative*: **Saturnus** ~, **Iuno**; **O gentil** ~ II.iii.38; V.xi.9; VIII.i.38; IX.i.4

get *pa. p.* begotten VI.ii.88; IX.ix.46

get *pa. p.* got III.vi.159

gevillyng *n.* javelin IX.vii.74

gevin *v.inf.* to give III.Prol.30

geyf *pa. p.* given I.vi.106

giddir *second element of* 'together', *spelled as a separate word* VI.ii.158

gif *conj.* if

gild *n.* noise, clamour V.iii.85

gilt *pa. p.* gilded I.Prol.149

giltin, giltyn *adj.* gilded VII.ii.82

girgand *pr. p.* jarring, creaking VII. xi.33 (*see* XI.iii.87: 53 **girgirand** where C has **iargand**)

girne *v.* show teeth, snarl VIII.iv.82: R (C **begouth to byrn and fry**)

githornys, gittarnys *n.* citherns XIII. iv.8; XIII.ix.105

gittarnys *n.* small flags XIII.iv.8

gladys, glaid *v.* makes glad, gladden V.Prol.1, 60

glaid *n.* gladness, joy. **father ringis of** ~ III.i.66: 53 (C **ryngnys** ~)

glaid *v.* gladden V.Prol.60

glaid *pa. p.* glided, passed smoothly without any idea of sneaking furtively II.iv.17; III.v.35; V.iv.159; VII.iii.18

glaidar *n.* one who makes glad III. Prol.4

glans *n.* flash of light VIII.x.62; XII. Prol.48

glar *n.* mud, slime VI.vi.67; X.vi.42

glasteris *v.* bawls, boasts VIII.Prol.48

glave, **glavys** *n.* sword II.vii.82; III. viii.23; IV.xi.19

gled *n.* a bird, the kite VII.Prol.125; IX.Prol.47

gledis *n.* coals II.vii.27; III.viii.132

gledy *adj.* glowing hot VIII.vii.108: R (C **gledis**)

gleid *n.* coal II.iii.55

gleid *n.* kite XI.x.1

gleit, **gletis** *v.* glitter, shine (poetic) II.vi.70; VII.i.109; IX.vi.141

glevyn *v.* glow VIII.iv.165

glew *n.* viscous sap, especially of the mistletoe VI.iii.94

gleyd *n.* coal IV.ii.35

gleyt *v.* glisten (poetic) XII.x.108

glifnyt *v.* gazed, looked quickly VIII. Prol.165

glor *n.* glory XII.Prol.51

glosys *v.* veils, covers up, disguises VIII.vii.54

glotnyt *pa. p.* clotted, clogged V.vi.74 (R, 53 **glouit**); V.xiv.55

glowrand *pr. p.* staring, gazing VII.vii.93

gloy *n.* straw VIII.xi.31

gloyr *v.* glory IV.Prol.174

glymmyrand *pr. p.* glittering X.xi.118

glystnyt *v.* for gliffen? glanced, looked quickly started **I ~ of sleip** II.vi.8 (*see* III.viii.17: L, B, **glisnyng about**; C **lysnyng**)

gnappar *n.* one who bites or snaps, a boor VIII.Prol.121

gnassing *pr. p.* gnashing VIII.iv.103, 53

gnaw *pa. p.* gnawed VIII.v.45

gnyppand *pr. p.* nipping, biting III. viii.64 (R **grippand**); IV.iv.11, mar-ginal note, R, L, B, 53

go to *v.* fall to get to work. **with equale wapynnys lat ws ~ sone** V.vii.105

gobbettis *n.* little pieces of raw flesh I.iv.93; IV.xi.32

god, **goddas**, **goddes** *n.* goddess II.iii.50, 87; II.x.15; III.v.58

godhed *n.* Godhead, divinity, divine essence I.Prol.457

godly *adj.* sacred, divine III.vi.99. god-like III.vi.167

godlyke *adj.* devout, pious I.v.45. god-like, divine II.ix.18

goif *v.* inspect, examine closely VIII. iv.67

goishalk *n.* goshawk XI.xiii.165

goith *v.pres.3 pl.* they go III.ii.142

gold begane, **begone** *pa. p.* overlaid with gold II.viii.19; III.vi.218

goldspynk *n.* goldfinch XII.Prol.240

goldyn *adj.* having the excellence of gold I.Prol.149

golf *n.* abyss VI.iv.11; X.ii.140

gone *v.pres.3 pl.* they go IV.vi.46

gone *v.trans.p.p.* **Bot quhat wyndis thi cowrß has hydder ~?** III.v.107

gorgeit *pa. p.* choked up VI.ii.58

gorget *n.* throat-armour X.vii.127; XI.i.26

goshalk *n.* goshawk IX.Prol.48

gost *n.* spirit, soul X.ix.133

gottin, **gottyn** *pa. p.* got I.ix.129; IV.iii.20; V.v.46

govand *pr. p.* gazing, staring VI.i.67; VIII.ix.117

gove *v.* stare, gaze VII.xiii.78

governall *n.* government. rule of conduct or behaviour X.Prol.5

gowkis *v.* gawks, stares VIII.Prol.94

gowl *n.* yell XI.ii.74

gowl *n.* throat, maw IX.ix.86

gowling *vbl.n.* yelling, howling IV.xii.46

gowlyng *pr. p.* yelling II.vi.53

gowlys *n.* colour red in heraldry XII. Prol.107

gowsty *adj.* vast, dismal, dreary I.ii.6; III. ix.56 (E **goustly**); V.viii.22 (E **goustly**)

goyf *v.* gaze, stare V.vi.126

graf *n.* grave IV.viii.37; V.ii.85

graif *pa. p.* buried. **sal be** ~ VI.v.174: R (C **salbe bygrave**)

graif *pa. p.* engraved VIII.vii.74

graip *n.* iron fork for digging I.iii.54, marginal note

graip *v.* grope (one's way) III.x.6

graith *n.* equipment IV.xi.105; V.xii.47; VI.v.120; figuratively, items of (spiritual) value VI.Prol.69

graith *v.* prepare, build, make ready I.iv.90; II.iii.69; III.ii.132

graithly *adv.* carefully, attentively I.v.6; III.iii.8; VIII.Prol.166

gram *n.* gloom, sorrow IV.Prol.162

grammys *n.* sorrows VIII.Prol.31 (R, B **gammys**; 53 **games**)

granand *pr. p.* groaning XI.iii.82

grand *v.* ground I.iv.40

grane *n.* branch of a tree, a fork, an offshoot VI.iii.95

grane *v.* groan VI.vi.62

grangis *n.* barns, granaries II.viii.108

grank *n.* hoarse groan VII.viii.56

grank *v.* groan, creak VI.vi.62: R (C **grane or geig … the barge**)

granscher *n.* grandsire, grandfather IV.v.152

grant *pa. p.* granted I.v.86; VI.ix.7

granting *v.inf.* to grant III.iii.44

granys *n.* branches IV.viii.73. prongs I.iii.89; II.x.90

granys *n.* groans XI.xii.80; XII.xii.56

granyt *pa. p.* having branches or prongs I.iii.75; III.iv.42; VI.vi.44

granyt *pa. p.* of cloth, dyed in grain XII.Prol.15

granyt *v. see* **to** ~ IX.xi.95

grape *v.* search, examine I.Prol.497

grapyt *v.* gripped VIII.Prol.166

graslis *v.* makes a grating noise I.ii.60

grassilland *pr. p.* gnashing III.x.17

grat *v.* greeted VI.vi.5; VI.viii.46; XIII.viii.7

grathand *pr. p.* being made ready. **the schippis ar** ~ IV.vi.38

grathis *v.* prepares, makes ready

I.vii.14; I.x.39

grauity, grauyte *n.* dignity or weight of meaning I.Prol.54, 365

grave *adj.* heavy (*from Latin* **gravis**, *physically ponderous*) V.viii.52

grave *v.* bury VI.v.145

grave *pa. p.* engraved I.ix.110; VIII.x.79

gravis *n.* groves I.iv.50

gravis *n.* graves (not groves, since it represents **bustis**) XII.xiii.109

gravyn *pa. p.* engraved I.iv.88

gravys *n.* groves IV.ii.45; IV.iii.57

grayn *n.* branch VI.ii.128; VI.iii.103. branch of a stream I.Prol.237

grayth *n.* grey-headed person II.ix.6 (E, R, L, B, 53 **gray**)

gre *n.* degree, pre-eminence. first place or prize I.Prol.407; V.ii.52; V.iii.14

greif *n.* displeasure, anger, resentment I.i.18; I.iii.95; VIII.iv.79

greif *n.* steward, overseer of a farm XIII. Prol.171

greis *n.* steps in ascent VIII.Prol.121. degrees of descent in relationship VII.vi.75. degrees in astronomy VII. Prol.32

greit *n.* gravel XII.Prol.55

greking, grekyng *vbl.n.* dawn, break of day IV.xi.4; VII.Prol.115

grene *adj.* green, alive I.ix.54. fresh, lively. ~ **curage** V.vi.12: 53

grene guß *n.* young goose, gosling VIII. Prol.51: E

grenys *v.* desires earnestly, longs VIII. Prol.45, 51

gresy *adj.* grassy VI.x.33

gresys *n.* grasses III.viii.64

gret *adj.* pregnant X.xii.40

gret *v.* greeted VI.xi.heading

grete *n.* weeping XII.ii.49 (E, R, 53 **gretand**)

gretis *v.* greets VI.v.95

gretis *v.* weeps VIII.Prol.34

grettumly, gretumly *adv.* greatly V.vii.81; VII.iv.135; IX.i.56

gretyng *vbl.n.* weeping IV.xii.46

grevit *pa. p.* annoyed, angered

I.Prol.418; I.vii.110

grewouß *adj.* grievous, sorrowful I.iv.86

grews *adj.* grievous X.iv.55; XII.xiv.135

grewsly *adv.* to a grievous extent XI.xiv.73

greyce *adj.* gray XII.Prol.107

greyn *adj.* green. fresh, lively I.Prol.325; I.i.67; I.x.6; IV.ix.88

greys *n.* degrees VI.Prol.97

greyt *n.* weeping VI.viii.10

greyt *v.* weep XI.v.73

gripis *n.* vultures I.v.81, marginal note

grippill *adj.* gripping, tenacious XII.xii.193

grisly *adj.* horrible, terrible (poetic) I.iii.11; I.v.117; III.viii.128

grome, gromys *n.* man (contemptuously), fellow VIII.Prol.165. manservant VII.Prol.77

grond *n.* ground, in the sense of a portion of the earth's surface, a land or coast III.vii.14; VI.v.182

grondyn *pa. p.* ground, sharpened I.ii.49

grope *v.* grasp for; figuratively, understand, apprehend mentally XI.vii.36

groß *adj.* rude, gross I.Prol.139, 312. used as a *n.* something gross or uncultivated I.Prol.43

grote *n.* groat, fourpenny piece VI.v.72

ground spere *n.* earth VI.xiii.90: R (C **round speir**)

grow *v.* shudder, shrink in fear II.xi.82; XII.xiii.175

grow *pa. p.* grown XII.xii.177

growf *n.* **on** ~ face downwards XI.iv.24

growis *v.* exists III.ii.113

groym *n.* man VIII.Prol.31

grub *v.* dig around, cultivate XIII.ix.77

gruch *v.* complain of III.vi.77

gruflyngis *adv.* prostrate III.ii.52; III.ix.65; V.vi.81

grulyng *pr. p.* grovelling III.ix.37; V.vi.85; VIII.Prol.34

grund *n.* ground, shore, land I.viii.133; II.iv.17

grund *pa. p.* ground, sharpened IV.iv.17

grundit *pa. p.* based, set on a foundation I.Prol.480

grundyn *pa. p.* ground, sharpened I.iv.58; IV.iv.41

grunschis *v.* grumbles VIII.Prol.31. objects, refuses X.xi.61

grunschit *v.* grumbled VIII.Prol.165

grym *adj.* grim, stern, harsh III.ix.108

grype *n.* vulture VI.ix.135

gryß *v.intr.* become terrified I.xii.21

gryß *v.trans.* frighten, terrify II.ii.135; VI.ii.52; VIII.v.47

grysis *n.* young pigs III.vi.72

grysly *adj.* horrible (*poetic*) III.ix.61; IV.v.143; IV.xii.91

grysys *n.* young pigs VIII.i.56; VIII.ii.38

gubernakil *n.* helm of a ship VI.v.113

gud douchtir *n.* daughter-in-law XI.xi.108

gud fader *n.* father-in-law XIII.vi.187

gud man *n.* woman's husband VIII.vii.7

gudwif *n.* woman, mistress of a household VIII.Prol.34

gukgo *n.* cuckoo XII.Prol.241

gum, gummys *n.* viscid liquid from trees VI.iii.94; XII.Prol.147

gum, gummys *n.* mist VII.Prol.131; XIII.Prol.31

gun powder *n.* VIII.vii.139

gurdis *v.* pushes forward with energy or jerkily? VIII.Prol.121

gurl *adj.* stormy VII.Prol.58

gustand *pr. p.* smelling, fragrant XI.iii.86

gy *v.* guide II.Prol.14

gyand *n.* giant I.x.18

gydar *n.* guide I.Prol.454

gydyng *vbl.n.* guiding IV.v.100

gyiß *n.* guise, customary behaviour III.vi.31

gyld *n.* noise, clamour I.xi.107

gyll *n.* ravine VIII.Prol.167

gylty *adj.* gilded, golden VII.Prol.10; VII.ii.82: R, 53 (C **gilten**)

gym *adj.* neat, smart XII.Prol.161

gymp *adj.* nimble, graceful VI.x.45;

XII.Prol.121

gymp *n.* trivial point, quibble I.Prol.125

gyn *n.* trap, cunning contrivance VII.
iv.66, 94

gynglyng *pr. p.* jingling IV.iv.11

gyrd *n.* trick, stroke of policy VII.vi.51
(V.iii.85: E, **for gird and rerd of
men**, for sudden movements and
clamour; C **for gild and rerd**)

gyrd *v.* make a stroke (*see* **throw** ~
II.vii.118) X.viii.103

gyrnys *v.* snarls IX.ii.65

gyrß *n.* grass VI.x.25

gyrth *n.* place of sanctuary, refuge
II.xii.4

gyrthit *pa. p.* surrounded XII.xiii.49

gyß *n.* guise, manner, mode III.ii.89,
100; III.iii.110

gyssarn *n.* gisarme, a battle-axe VIII.xi.45

habill *adj.* fit; suitable, able (to do
something) III.ii.1; IV.iii.50; IV.vi.25;
IX.iii.56

habirgyon *n.* habergeon, a short coat of
mail (*v.* **habyrgeon**) V.v.29

habitis *n.* garments, attire III.ix.18

habundance, habundans *n.* abundance
III.iv.31; VI.ii.17

habyrgeon *n.* short coat of mail,
etymologically a diminutive of the
hauberk, but Douglas uses the two
terms as synonyms III.vi.217 (R, 53
habir Iohne, habirihone)

habyte *n.* clothing, garment IV.xii.15

had *v.* took, brought II.x.38

hadbe, hadbene *compound.* had been
II.vii.23; II.x.73; III.vii.42

haddir *n.* heather plant IX.Prol.23

hail, haill *adj.* all, the whole II.Prol.13;
X.ix.88

hail *adv.* fully, entirely VI.xi.6

haill *n.* hail II.viii.132

haill *v.* drag or pull (especially nautical) III.i.48; III.iv.109; V.i.29

hailskarth *adj.* unhurt, without scratch
II.x.33; V.v.72; VI.v.103 (L **harskarth**)

hailsum *adj.* wholesome I.vi.3, 141; III.

ix.25

hailsyng *v.inf.* to hail, to greet III.viii.36

hailsyng, hailsyngis *vbl.n.* salutation,
greeting V.vi.89

hair *adj.* hoary, grey-haired VII.Prol.42;
X.xiv.142. of weather, frosty VI.vii.79.
of stones or woods (vaguely), grey
VII.Prol.130; X.xiiii.142

hait *adj.* hot IV.ii.35; V.viii.38. hot, with
possible pun on hate III.v.96; figuratively, of the passions IV.Prol.4, 11, 74.
recent XIII.iv.45

hait *adv.* hotly VIII.vii.168

hait *v.* to be named I.ii.58; III.ix.49

hait *pa. p.* named III.v.106

haitrent *n.* hatred II.ii.55; IV.Prol.147

haitsum *adj.* hateful XI.iv.89

hak *pa. p.* hacked VIII.vii.154

hald, haldis *n.* place of protection or
refuge, fort I.iii.79; III.vi.76

hald, haldis *v.* continue (along a course)
I.viii.107. consider, regard I.Prol.397,
403

hald, haldyn *pa. p.* held III.viii.165;
IV.viii.105

halely *adv.* wholly I.xi.27; V.x.28

half *n.* side, one of two sides of something V.vi.15; VIII.viii.39

half *n.* behalf. **in thi ʒong sonnis ~ garde**
for the sake of guarding your young
son XII.Prol.96: R (C **sonnis salfgard**)

halfdeill *adv.* halfway (poetic) II.ix.47

halffettis, halfhedis *n.* sides of the head,
temples II.xi.10; IV.v.78; IV.xi.107;
V.viii.30

hallowis *v.* reverences, consecrates III.
Prol.4; III.iv.105

hals, halß *n.* neck, throat, throats
I.ix.134; II.iv.12, 33; III.Prol.21; hence,
a narrow inlet I.iv.8.

hals *v.* embrace I.x.57

halshand *pr. p.* embracing V.xiii.10

haltand *adj.* haughty VI.ix.119; X.vi.80;
XI.viii.1

haltand *pr. p.* halting, lame X.Prol.160

haltandly *adv.* haughtily X.xi.98; XII.vi.40

haly *adj.* holy VIII.ii.13

haly *adv.* wholly XI.vii.130

halyday *n.* vacation, holiday (not holy day) I.ix.95

halyly *adv.* wholly XIII.iv.48

halyng *pr. p.* flowing I.vii.85

halys *v.* pulls, draws III.viii.108

halyt *pa. p.* drawn V.ix.36

hame *n.* home VII.viii.133

hamehald, hamhald *adj.* domestic I.ii.27, marginal note

hamys *n.* hames, part of the collar on a draught horse IX.vi.24; XII.Prol.25; XII.vi.156

hand *n.* hand. **at ~, neir ~** close by I.Prol.487; III.vi.203. the hand, as given in pledge, **thar is my ~** IV.vi.131: E

handland *pr. p.* laying hands on hostilely V.viii.38

hank *v.* make fast by means of a looped rope VII.ii.8

hankis *n.* twists, loops II.iv.34

hansell *n.* reward, present IX.x.104

hant *n.* haunt, lair, habitat IV.Prol.249

hant *v.* frequent IV.Prol.99; IV.i.38; V.x.94

hantyng *v.inf.* to frequent VI.ix.204

hantyt *v.* was accustomed to use V.x.92

hantyt *pa. p.* accustomed, habituated V.vi.31

hap *n.* chance, fortune II.iv.52

happely *adv.* by chance II.x.102

happit *v.* happened, chanced II.ii.62

happy *adj.* fortunate VI.Prol.118; VI.i.15. coming by chance V.Prol.3

har *adj.* hoary. of weather, frosty VII. Prol.130

har *n.* hinge II.viii.72. **out of ~** in a state of disorder III.vi.178

harbry *n.* harbour, shelter VII.iv.22

hard *pa. p.* heard I.vi.122; II.Prol.12

hardis *n.* oakum, tow VIII.xii.48

hardyment *n.* hardihood, resolve V.xi.81

haris *n.* hair (plural perhaps under the influence of **comas**; **hair** of course appears: e.g. IV.vi.2; VII.Prol.58) III. vi.98; I.vi.164

harknys *v.trans.* heed IV.x.78

harl *v.* drag, especially forcibly or violently II.x.204

harland *pr. p.* drawing, dragging I.vii.103; II.ii.1

harlotry *n.* ribaldry IX.Prol.52

harlyng *pr. p.* drawing, dragging II.vi.48

harlyt *v.* drew, dragged I.vii.116

harlyt *pa. p.* dragged V.xi.50

harmys *n.* injuries XI.xv.90. pain, suffering, grief, especially in the phrase ~ **at the hart** I.Prol.146; IV.xi. heading; VII.v.22; VIII.vii.84

harn pan *n.* skull V.viii.113

harnasyng *n.* trappings, harness III. viii.74; IV.iv.12

harnes, harneß *n.* armour IV.xi.15; V.viii.43; VIII.vii.28 (R **harnek**)

harnys *n.* brains III.ix.68; V.vii.92; XI.xiii.110

harpeys, harpies, harpyes *n.* harpies III.iv.heading, 7, 33, 59

harro *interj.* a cry of alarm VII.xiii.110

harsk *adj.* harsh, rude III.iv.42

hartly *adj.* heartfelt, hearty III.ii.28; VI.vii.64

harys *n.* hair I.vii.106. *See also* **haris**

hasard, hasart *n.* grey-haired man IV.Prol.164; IV.v.141; VI.v.17; X.xiv.29

hasart *adj.* grey VII.Prol.132

hasartouris *n.* gamblers VIII.Prol.56

hastand *pr. p.* hastening, urging forward I.vi.21

hattyr *n.* maple tree II.ii.99; IX.iii.24

hauchis *n.* pantings VII.viii.79

haue *v.* take, carry, convey VI.ii.149; VI.v.67, 151

havyngis *vbl.n.* behaviour, deportment X.vii.15

havynnys *n.* harbours V.iv.156

haw *adj.* bluish, livid, dull III.i.121; III. iii.114; IV.x.116; XII.xiii.218

hawbrig, hawbrik *n.* coat of mail III. vi.218; XI.xiii.95. *See also* **habyrgeon**

hawchis *n.* alluvial flats, meadows XIII. Prol.21

hay *interj.* ho! VI.iv.48; IX.ii.12

haylscarth *adj.* whole, unscratched XI.xiii.155

haymcom *n.* homecoming XI.ii.122

haymly *adj.* simple, blunt, outspoken II.vii.24

hayß *adj.* hoarse III.Prol.21; V.xiv.75

hayt *pa. p.* hated VIII.iv.137

he *adj.* high XI.xi.78

hechis *n.* hatches on a boat I.iii.18; III.v.13; V.xi.122; V.xii.159

hecht, hechtis *v.* assure, promise I.vi.94; IV.ix.29

hecht *v.* promised II.ii.64

hecht *pa. p.* promised IV.x.62

hecht *v.* named I.Prol.127; I.i.190

hed, hedis *n.* head. individual animal in a flock III.vi.72. a person, individual IV.xi.61. top, extremity of various objects II.vi.9; II.viii.69; V.xii.163; VIII.iii.5. **magre thar** ~ against their will IV.v.129. head (as something to be cut off in an execution) VIII.iii.111 the head as the seat of opinion or the mind II.ii.69; V.Prol.16

heding *vbl.n.* beheading VI.xiv.30, 46

hedismen *n.* head-men, elders (for **patribus**, and hence not headsmen) V.xii.175

hedlys *n.* heddles of a loom, the small cords through which the warp is passed VI.xvi.29

hedy *adj.* of the head. ~ **peir** of equal height III.vii.42

heich *adj.* adv. high I.iii.2; I.viii.22; III.iv.69; VI.Prol.16; XIII.i.132

hell, heill, hele *n.* health III.Prol.29: B; III.v.114: E, R, 53

heild *v.* take cover, hide XII.i.132

heildit *pa. p.* covered IV.v.140

heir *n.* lord, master, hero (*poetic*) V.vi.8; VI.x.102 (*replaced by lord*); VIII.viii.19

heirintil *compound.* herein VI.Prol.28

heiron *compound.* hereon I.iv.79

heist *n.* promise II.x.84

heit *n.* heating XIII.Prol.129

heland *n.* promontory VII.v.12

helde *v.* tilt V.xiv.60

heldit *v.* veiled, covered VIII.iv.202

helm *n.* helmet (*poetic*) V.vii.10

helmstok *n.* tiller V.xiv.47; VI.v.91

helply *adj.* helping, helpful X.Prol.158

hely *adj.* haughty, arrogant IX.x.13

henwyffis *n.* women who keep hens. **Venus** ~ bawds IV.Prol.188

heppis *n.* the hips of the wild rose III.ix.111

hepthorn *n.* the tree with hips, the wild rose III.i.46

herber *n.* flower garden XII.Prol.150

herbis *n.* grasses, without any allusion to medicinal qualities III.v.44

herbry *n.* dwelling-place I.iv.86; III.i.31; III.viii.85. shelter, lodging I.xi.74

herbry *v.* take shelter I.viii.81

herbryit *pa. p.* come to harbour I.vi.159

herd *n.* shepherd XII.x.56

herdis *n.* herds I.vi.51

hereit *v.* harrowed, harried X.Prol.129

hereyt *pa. p.* harried, plundered VIII.Prol.56

heretage *n.* possession of lands by heritable right I.vi.73

heris *n.* lords, chiefs (**ductores, patres**) IV.i.75; IV.xii.79

heris *v.* imperative, hear IV.vi.112

heritage *n.* hereditary succession I.i.20

heroner *n.* heron-catcher. **falcon** ~ falcon trained to fly at the heron IX.Prol.46

heroycall *adj.* heroic, epic IX.Prol.21

hervist *n.* autumn VII.Prol.84; X.Prol.14

herys *n.* lords, chiefs (senior) V.xii.70

hesit *v.* raised, hoisted I.iii.23

hespis *n.* hasps for securing a door VII.x.21

heste *n.* command VI.iii.38

hesyng *v.inf.* to lift, to hoist I.iii.88; VIII.vii.183

het *adj.* hot IV.viii.84

heth *v.pres.3 pl.* have I.i.10

hething, hethyng *n.* scorn, derision IV.x.23, 38

hevand *pr. p.* raising, stretching (without any sense of straining) III.iv.103

hevely *adv.* heavily, mournfully VI.iii.55

hevin *n.* heaven. ~ **empire** empyreum VI.Prol.120, note

hew *n.* appearance, aspect XII.Prol.281

hewch, hewchis, hewis *n.* precipice, crag I.iv.13; III.iv.40 (53 **hench**); III. viii.59; VIII.iv.13

hewmet *n.* helmet IX.vii.194 (R **hew-mound**; 53 **hewmond**)

hewys *n.* cliffs, crags III.iv.119; VII.xii.19

hey, hey how *interj.* hey! VII.vi.109; XI.i.134. used as *n.* a cry of greeting **with ~ and haill** III.viii.36

heynd *adj.* agreeable, courteous (*poetic*) I.Prol.450; V.xii.113; VI.v.85; IX.xii.109

heys, heyß *n.* a sailor's cry III.ii.120; III. viii.111

heyß *v.* lift V.vii.3

heyt *n.* heat, ardour VI.ix.121; XI.vi.59

hiddertill *adv.* in this place I.vi.50

hiddertillis *adv.* until now VI.i.118

hidlis *n.* hiding-places VII.Prol.71

hie *adj.* high; hence lofty, important, of exalted character I.Prol.192; III.ix.58; VI.Prol.75. **on ~** aloft I.i.18; I.iv.41

hight *n.* height I.x.46

hirst *n.* doorsill, threshold, or perhaps hinge VI.ix.88; VII.x.33, 50

hirstis *n.* hillsides VII.Prol.134

hissillis *v.* hisses V.v.64: R (C **hyssis**)

history *n.* narrative I.Prol.305

ho *interj.* stop! III.vi.52; IV.Prol.182

ho *v.* cease, desist V.xi.10; XII.ii.47; XIII.ii.80

hoill *n.* hole, cave VIII.xi.38

holk *n.* large ship or transport IV.vii.74

holk *v.* dig II.viii.47

holkand *pr. p.* digging II.x.92

holkis *n.* small holes. an ailment of the face III.Prol.27

holkis *v.* digs I.vii.18

holkit, holkyt *pa. p.* hollowed I.vi.11; II.i.47; III.viii.116

holl *adj.* hollow, sunken, deep II.viii.84; III.x.35; IV.i.52; VI.ix.98. ~ **sydis** the

body cavity V.viii.26

holl *n.* the hold of a ship V.iii.96

holtis *n.* wood, copse (*poetic*) IV.iv.47

holyne *n.* holly VIII.iii.193

homo *Latin n.* a human being I.Prol.367

hone *n.* delay (*poetic*) VII.vii.55

honest *adj.* honorable, of good character IX.vii.72

honeste *n.* worth of character, good repute. chastity IV.Prol.96, 110, 200; V.iv.27; VIII.vii.102

hoppys *v.* moves rapidly, with no suggestion of frivolity I.Prol.186. dances VIII.xi.49

hornyt *pa. p.* of the moon, having horns III.Prol.1

hostit *v.* coughed up or out XIII.i.10

hosyng *n.* hose, stockings XI.xv.23

hote *adv.* eagerly VIII.viii.10

hovand *pr. p.* remaining stationary (*poetic*) IV.iv.8

hoverand *pr. p.* halting, remaining stationary I.iii.23

hovir *n.* **on** or **in ~** in a state of hesitation or indecision V.xi.106; XII.xiv.129

hovit *v.* remained stationary (*poetic*) XII.viii.110

hovit, hovyt *pa. p.* hoofed VII.xii.179; VIII.ix.123 (L **howy**, hoof-y)

hovyr *n.* **on ~** in a state of indecision XII.xiv.80

how *adj.* hollow VI.ix.38; VIII.x.65

how *n.* cap V.x.22

how *n.* cry (of mariners or owls) III. ii.120; XII.xiii.176

how *n.* the hull of a ship IX.ii.98

howbeyt *conj.* although V.iv.68

howch, howchis, howchys *n.* the hough of an animal IX.xii.82; XII.viii.113; XII.xiv.98

howe *n.* hull V.xii.33

howe *interj.* hey! III.viii.101

howgh sennonys *n.* the hamstrings at the back of the knee X.xii.29

howk, howke *n.* a large ship III.Prol.39; X.iv.123

howlet *n.* owl XII.xiii.168

howsouris *n.* coverings, housing VII.
iv.192

howt *n.* wood, copse (*poetic*) VII.
Prol.66

howys *n.* the hulls of ships III.vi.213

hoyt *adj.* hot IV.ii.37; V.v.43. **full ~**
eager IV.v.127

huddon *n.* a species of whale III.vi.137;
X.iv.132

hufand *pr. p.* waiting, remaining stationary V.x.59

hug, huge *adj.* huge II.i.47; III.iii.91

huge *adv.* hugely V.vii.21; V.xi.113. very
IV.v.49

hukis *n.* sickles IV.ix.84; VII.x.80

hukit *pa. p.* tormented with a hook III.
viii.146: E (C **irkit**)

huly *adj.* moderate, gentle IX.xiii.45

huly *adv.* gently, slowly VI.v.127

humour, humouris *n.* moisture, damp-
ness XII.Prol.91, 137

hundir *n.* hundred I.Prol.389

hundreth *adj.* hundredth I.Prol.247

hungyn *pa. p.* hung. *See* **to hungyn**
XII.xii.76

huntryce *n.* huntress IX.ix.29

hurd, hurdis *n.* hoard, treasure I.vi.92;
VIII.Prol.161

hurkylland *pr. p.* crouching X.xii.97

hurl *v.intr.* rush impetuously IV.x.112

hurland *pr. p.* rushing III.x.39; XI.v.30

husband, husbandis *n.* farmer
I.Prol.508; VII.Prol.75; X.vi.53

husbandry *n.* farming XIII.Prol.172

huslyng *vbl.n.* rattling XII.xii.7

hutit, hutyt *pa. p.* hated III.ix.62 (R, 53
hatit); VII.ix.65; VIII.iv.33

huvis *v.* remains still XI.xiii.114

hwny *n.* honey I.vii.29, 35

hy *n.* haste I.v.128; III.i.16. **in ~** at once
(*generally padding*) III.v.125; III.
vi.197; III.vii.1

hy *v.* hie, hasten VI.iv.48

hychis *n.* the hatches of a ship X.xi.129

hychit *v.* walked jerkily IV.xi.114

hycht *n.* height II.vi.20

hyddyllis *n.* hiding-places III.vi.131

hyddus, hydduuß *adj.* hideous I.iii.38;
III.ix.67

hyddyrtyllys *adv.* hitherto, until then
V.xi.1

hyde *n.* human skin XII.xi.162

hydlys *n.* hiding-places IV.vii.84;
VI.vii.43; IX.viii.143

hydwys *adj.* hideous I.v.61

hyghty *adj.* high, lofty VII.vii.21

hym, hyme *pron.* him, it I.iv.109;
IV.xi.57

hymeneus *n.* marriage, wedlock I.ix.128

hynder, hyndir *adj.* later, recently past
IV.ix.48; XI.vi.130

hyne *adv.* hence III.vii.15; V.vi.38;
Directioun.148

hyne *n.* peasant VIII.Prol.62; XI.v.38.
person. **euery ~** everyone V.xiii.1

hynger *n.* necklace, pendant X.iii.35

hynt *v.* took I.iv.53, 91; IV.x.110

hynt *pa. p.* taken I.ix.122

hynys *n.* peasants, farm labourers
X.xiii.109. people in general I.i.20

hyrd, hyrdis *n.* shepherd II.ii.2; II.vi.19;
III.x.3. ~ **gromys** shepherd boys VII.
Prol.77

hyre *n.* payment, reward VIII.vii.92

hyregang *n.* lease. **in ~** on hire XII.
ix.50

hyrn, hyrnys *n.* recess, hiding-place
II.i.48; VII.Prol.71; X.x.133

hyrslit *v.* grated III.x.87

hyrstis *n.* bare hillsides XI.vii.56 (E, B
hirskis)

hyrsyl *v.* grate V.iv.10

hys *pron.* its I.vii.43; I.viii.66

hyt *pron.* it XI.xvi.61

hyyddir *adv.* hither V.xi.98

I wys for **gewis, ywis**, certainly, *perhaps
misunderstood as* **I wist** (*common
padding in poetry*) I.vi.159; I.xii.6;
III.v.36; V.xi.70

iacynthyne *n.* hyacinth XI.ii.30

iag *v.* pierce, prick VIII.Prol.99

iaip *n.* trick, artifice II.iv.65

iakkis *n.* jackets, jerkins VIII.Prol.99

iangill *v.* find faults, backbite *Exclamatioun*.33

ianglyng *vbl.n.* grumbling, fault-finding IV.Prol.20

iape *v.* joke, jest II.ii.57

iapis, iapys *n.* jokes, nonsense IV.Prol.20; VI.Prol.9

iargand *pr. p.* creaking, grating VI.ix.88; XI.iii.87

iargis *v.* turns (on a hinge), grates I.vii.57

iarris *v.* pushes? VIII.Prol.99

iaschis *n.* waves, the dash of waves XI.xii.70

iasp *n.* jasper IV.v.160

iavillyng, iavillyngis *n.* javelin V.x.23

iaw *n.* dashing or breaking wave I.iii.21; VIII.i.96

iawp, iawpe, iawpis, iawpys *n.* dashing wave III.viii.97; V.iii.44; V.xiv.74; VIII.i.96

iawpyng *pr. p.* of waves, dashing, splashing VII.ix.101

iawyn *pa. p.* poured, dashed V.Prol.53

ichane *interj.* alas! IX.viii.63; XI.v.76 (R **ilkane**; 53 **ych ane**)

ied staf *n.* Jedburgh staff, a bill made at Jedburgh VIII.Prol.99 (E **ged**)

iestis *n.* gestes, deeds VIII.xii.144

ievillyng *n.* javelin XII.iv.14

ilandis *n.* islands III.iv.4

ilis *n.* isles III.iv.2

ilk *adj.* same I.Prol.505; III.i.97; III.ix.17

ilk deill every part III.iii.61

ilkane *pron.* each one I.iv.40; III.i.130; III.ii.140

ilke *adj.* same I.Prol.191; I.ii.51; I.vii.51. each I.Prol.482. ~ **deill** altogether, every part III.viii.7

ilkman *pron.* each man, anyone I.vi.92

illummyn *v.* shed light upon I.Prol.335

illumynat *v.* illumined VI.x.87

illumynate *pa. p.* illumined VII.Prol.167

illusionys *n.* hallucinations I.Prol.215

illustir *adj.* illustrious I.Prol.84;

VI.xiii.7

illyr haill *interj.* bad luck, ill-omened III.vi.192

imperfite *adj.* defective, faulty I.Prol.359

imperiall *adj.* empyreal X.xi.39

importurate *pa. p.* portrayed VIII.x.79: R, 53

impugnand *adj.* repugnant XII.Prol.228: R (C **repugnant**)

impyre *n.* sovereignty, dominion XIII.x.25

in *n.* dwelling (*poetic*) II.vi.4; XII.ii.74

in ane *adv.* anon, continuously V.xiii.51

in cace gif *phrase.* whether III.iv.101

inbrokkyn *pa.p.* broken XII.vii.12

inbryng *compound v.* bring in V.ii.113

incayß *adv.* in case III.Prol.19

incestuus, incestuusly *adj. adv.* incestuous; incestuously VI.ix.203; X.vii.71

incluß *v.* enclose, shut up I.vii.29

inclusit *v.* enclosed VI.xi.3

inclusyt *pa. p.* enclosed (of a sound, enclosed and throwing back an echo) V.iii.89

incommixt *adj.* unmixed X.Prol.27

incompetabill *adj.* incompetent VIII.Prol.110

inconsumptive *adj.* eternal, incapable of being consumed VII.x.23

incontinent *adv.* at once, immediately I.vi.162; I.xii.1; V.x.65

incontrar *prep.* against VII.vii.heading

incovert *adj.* uncovered, bare-headed X.iii.31

indegest *adj.* undigested. figuratively, precipitate, hasty XI.vii.104

indekkyt *pa. p.* bedecked, clothed XI.xi.140: R (C **and dekkit**)

indifferent *adj.* different, unlike X.vii.179

indigites *n.* a deified hero XII.xiii.11; XIII.xi.80

induelleris *n.* inhabitants XI.vii.177

induryng *v.inf.* to endure II.v.78

indwellis *v.* lives in, resides in VII.vi.69

indyng *adj.* unworthy VII.xi.33

inextingwybill *adj.* inextinguishable

IV.Prol.244

infangis *v.* draws in V.i.30

infatigabill *adj.* indefatigable VI.v.22

infect *pa. p.* infected VII.vi.2

infectiue, infective *adj.* contagious, infectious IV.Prol.123, 53; XII.Prol.227

infeir *adv.* together I.ii.31; II.iii.60; II.iv.8

infek *v.* infect III.iv.50

inferis *adv.* together I.Prol.249

infest *adj.* hostile VII.viii.9

infest *v.* attack, assail II.v.27; VI.i.155

infinyte *adj.* large (but not strictly speaking infinitely so) IV.Prol.258

inflambit *v.* caught fire I.i.52

influence *n.* influx V.xi.20: R

influent *adj.* exercising (astrological) influence XII.Prol.42

inforß *v.intr.* use force, strive V.i.37. exert oneself VIII.iv.121

inforß *v.trans.* strengthen I.ii.31

infyryt *pa. p.* set afire, inflamed V.xii.3; VI.i.23; VII.i.112

ingil, ingill *n.* hearth, altar V.xi.117; VI.iv.21. fire VII.vii.123

ingirand *pr. p.* introducing, pressing on the attention IX.iv.131

ingynys *n.* genius, abilities I.Prol.321

inhabit *v.intrans.* dwelt III.iv.3

inhabit, inhabyt *pa. p.* inhabited III.ii.71; III.iii.33

inhaist *adv.* compound, in haste, hastily IV.v.92; VI.ix.12

inherdand *pr. p.* adhering X.xiii.57

inhibitioun *n.* prohibition X.i.22

inhy *adv. compound*, in haste I.ix.25; I.viii.108

inimicall *adj.* hostile X.vi.20; XII.xiii.52

iniquite *n.* want or violation of equity or justice; inequality (not wickedness) IV.xi.72 unrighteousness II.ii.88

iniuris *n.* injuries, injustices III.iv.91

inkirly *adv.* earnestly, eagerly VI.i.106

inlike *compound.* in like, alike XII.iv.94

innarmar *adv.* further in V.iv.7

innatyve *adj.* inborn, innate I.Prol.97

inoportoyn, inoportune *adj.* untimely

XII.xiii.172

inpacient *adj.* impatient IV.vi.39

inpast *compound v.* passed in I.vii.8

inquisitour *n.* investigator VI.vii.17

inran *v.* ran in II.viii.54

inrowand *pr. p.* rowing to shore X.vi.28

insaciabil *adj.* insatiable III.vi.126

insaciall *adj.* insatiable (*rhymes with* **marcyall**) IX.xii.78 (R, 53, **vnsaciable**)

insaciate *adj.* insatiable VII.v.37

inslip *compound v.* slip in VII.vi.13

insondir *adv.* apart III.vi.124

inspiris *v.* breathes in VI.v.140

insprent *compound v.* sprinted in II.viii.98

inspyre *v.* breathe, blow V.xi.15

inspyre *v.* to infuse by breathing I.x.60

instance *n.* urgency, insistence I.Prol.87

instant *adj.* present VIII.i.70

instant *adv.* immediately VIII.iii.186

institut *pa. p.* instituted, ordained VI.ii.129

instrument *n.* weapon of war II.iii.61

insufficiens *n.* insufficiency I.Prol.406

insylde *pa. p.* hidden XIII.Prol.42: R (C **in tha schaddois warryn syld**)

interchangabill *adj.* admitting of interchange, fitful XI.viii.121

intermyddill *v.* intermingle XII.xiii.107: R

interpreter, interpretour *n.* one who expounds I.Prol.401; III.vii.5

interprit *v.* explain I.Prol.367

interpryß *v.* undertake I.Prol.77

intertrike *v.* disarrange I.Prol.484

inthrou *prep.* through III.iii.10

intill *prep.* into I.Prol.362

intitillit *pa. p.* ascribed I.Prol.148

intricate *adj.* involved I.Prol.288

inuolvit *v.* enveloped, wrapped up III.iii.94

inuolwand *pr. p.* concealing VI.ii.44: 53

invadit *v.* attacked II.iv.27

invaid *v.* attack VI.v.133

invane *adv. compound*, in vain I.iii.14;

III.vi.180; IV.vi.85

invasibill *adj.* offensive, used in attack IX.xiii.35

invayd *v.* attack III.iv.62

invayn *adj.* idle, empty X.v.73

invayn *adv.* idly, without purpose (**incassum**) III.v.121

inveroin, inveroum, inveroun *adv.* around, round about IX.xiii.33; X.i.61; X.ix.11; XII.x.135; XIII.v.4

inveroin *v.* surround, encircle X.iii.4

investigabill *adj.* without vestige or sign, inscrutable X.Prol.101

inveterat *adj.* obstinate VI.xii.40

invnct *v.* anoint IX.xii.106

invnct *pa. p.* anointed VI.iii.121

invnctand *pr. p.* anointing X.iii.47

invnctment *n.* ointment XII.Prol.146

invndatioun *n.* inundation XII.iv.113 (E, L **invadatioun**; B **inadatioun**)

involue *v.* twist, wind V.ix.86

involup *v.* envelop VII.iii.67

involupand *pr. p.* enveloping, wrapping VI.ii.44

involuyt *v.* surrounded, beset VIII.vi.155

inwaist *adv.* compound, in vain II.viii.39

inȝet *pa. p.* poured in VII.vi.30

ioggillit *v.* joggled, shook X.vii.55

iolely *adv.* handsomely, finely I.vi.155

ioly *adj.* jolly, gay, splendid (*vague expression of admiration*) I.vi.182

ionand *pr. p.* joining VI.iii.22

ionyngis *vbl.n.* joints II.i.70; II.viii.45

iournay, iourne, iourneis *n.* journey XI.vi.40. day labour IX.iii.192. task VIII.v.30; X.vi.87; X.viii.59; XI.iv.95

iowell *n.* jewel. a costly article IX.vi.139

iowis *n.* jaws (of wolf) XI.xiii.69

iowk *n.* twist, turn, quick movement XI.xiii.101

iowke *v.* bend, twist VIII.iv.120

iowkit *v.* twisted, bent, ducked down X.ix.38

iowkyng *vbl.n.* evading, twisting out of the way X.xiv.144

ioy *n.* joy. the thing that produces delight III.v.112

ioys *v.* enjoy VII.i.149; VIII.viii.125

ioyvs *adj.* joyous III.iv.139

irk *adj.* weary. **thocht** ~ became weary IV.vii.88

irk *v.intrans.* become vexed or weary V.Prol.32

irk *pa. p.* irked V.xii.88

irkit *v.* grew tired II.xi.98; IV.viii.91

irkit *pa. p.* wearied (representing **fessis**, and stronger than modern irk) II.i.1; III.ii.36; XI.xiii.9 (R **ilkit**). disquieted, troubled III.iii.65

irne *n.* iron I.i.77; XI.vii.79. ~ **hewit**, iron-coloured VI.v.15

irny *adj.* hard as iron X.xii.140

irus *adj.* wrathful II.vii.89

ische schouchlis *n.* icicles VII.Prol.62

ischis *v.* issues IV.v.142

ise schokyllis *n.* icicles IV.v.142

isillys *n.* embers, brands X.i.135

ithand *adj.* eager IV.vii.77, 90

ithandly *adv.* eagerly, persistently V.xii.100

iugement *n.* judgment I.i.45

iunct *n.* joint VI.iii.122

iuncturis *n.* joints IV.xii.103

iuperte, iuperty, iupertyis *n.* warlike engagement V.x.91. risk, jeopardy, peril IX.iii.162. stratagem XI.xiii.120

ius *n.* juice XII.vii.90

iustyng *vbl.n.* jousting VIII.x.96

kach *v.* chase, drive V.viii.72

kan *v.* can IV.Prol.241

kankyrrit, kankyrryt *pa. p.* corrupt, depraved V.iv.72; V.xi.12

karellyng *vbl.n.* singing and dancing VI.viii.84

karrellis *n.* carols II.iv.70

karvell, karvellis *n.* light and fast ship III.vi.213; V.iv.77; VII.vii.56

kast *n.* contrivance, device, trick III.vi.117; V.iv.72

katchit *v.* drove I.i.4

kauch *v.* suffered VI.v.78

293

kaucht *v.* catch VI.vii.84

kavill, kavillys *n.* chance, lot (that is cast), especially in phrase **be kut or ~** I.viii.27; II.iv.5; III.ix.84; V.ix.17. the response of an oracle IV.vii.31

kays *n.* jackdaws VII.Prol.118

keill *n.* ochre used for marking sheep, etc. X.vii.82

keip *n.* care, attention IV.v.23; XIII. Prol.124

keip *pa. p.* kept VI.v.105

keklyt *v.* cackled, laughed V.iv.40

kell, kellys *n.* caul, head-dress IV.Prol.195; VII.xiii.82

kem *v.* comb VII.viii.30

kempand *pr. p.* striving, contending III.x.24; V.xiii.32

kempys *n.* champions V.vii.heading, 68

ken *v.* know V.xi.23

kend *v.* knew I.Prol.409; I.iii.62; III. ii.27: E (C knew). instructed IV.v.52

kend *pa. p.* known I.x.52. made known III.ii.92

kendillit *v.* kindled, ignited III.iv.133

kep *v.* intercept, receive III.viii.18.

keparis *n.* guardians (in this case, dogs, not soldiers) VIII.viii.16

kepe *n.* charge. **evill ~** by neglect of duty I.vii.93

kepit *v.* left intact, preserved I.Prol.394

keppit, keppyt *pa. p.* caught (something falling) I.iv.34; VI.iv.27. parried (a blow) X.vii.70; X.xiii.97

keppys *v.* wards off, parries (a blow) V.viii.16

kerf *v.* carve VI.xv.3

keyll *n.* the keel of a ship IV.vii.74

keyp *n.* attention, care IV.x.76

kiltit *pa. p.* tucked up around the body I.vi.27

kith *v.* make known VI.xv.40

kittil *v.* tickle V.xiv.2

knaip *n.* knave, rascal IX.ix.77

knak *n.* taunt, jibe *Directioun*.22

knak *v.* mock, taunt II.ii.13; IX.x.101

knappar *n.* rustic boor VIII.Prol.121: E, R, 53 (C **gnappar**)

knapys *n.* grooms, men-servants XII.ii.87

knaw *pa. p.* known I.ix.80; V.ix.62; VI.xi.23

knollys *n.* a small rounded hill, a hillock or a mound V.ii.5

knoppis, knoppys *n.* flower heads IX.vii.151; XII.Prol.123

knoppit *pa. p.* having protuberances IX.vii.85

knorry *adj.* knotted, gnarled VII.viii.71; VIII.iv.85

know *n.* knoll, hillock VIII.iii.37

knycht *n.* applied to the Romans, a military hero I.Prol.332; IX.xi.48. **~ wageor** mercenary soldier I.xii.12

knyp *pa. p.* nipped XII.Prol.94 (R 53 **gnyp**)

knyttyng *v.inf.* to knit XIII.vi.184

kosch *adj.* hollow V.viii.55

kouth *v.* could IV.vi.27; IV.viii.22

kowhubeis *n.* simpletons? VIII.Prol.86 (see note)

kowth *adj.* known, familiar III.ii.131

koy *adj.* quiet, still II.x.26, 107; X.ii.5

kut, kuttis *n.* the action of drawing pieces of straw cut to various lengths to decide something by chance III.v.81; V.iii.56

ky *n.* cows VIII.iv.50; XII.Prol.185

kyddis *n.* young roes XII.Prol.182

kynd *adj.* native III.v.84; IV.Prol.209; V.xi.49, 65; V.xiii.82; VII.viii.54. of the same race III.vii.36; IV.x.33? gentle, sympathetic I.v.134

kynd *n.* nature, natural inclination, inborn qualities I.vii.28; III.iii.2. species, sort, variety IV.i.83; VI.xii.12. race IV.iii.30. manner, way IV.i.15

kyndly *adj.* natural, innate IV.Prol.114. belonging to one by virtue of one's race II.v.84

kyndnes *n.* nature (with double meaning of benevolence?) IV.Prol.233. kinship *Directioun*.63, 75

kynrayd, kynrent *n.* race, family III. ix.40; IV.xi.81

kynryk, kynryke *n.* kingdom I.v.46; IV.v.183

kyrkmen *n.* clergy VIII.Prol.112

kyrnellis, kyrnellys *n.* battlements

IX.ix.12; XII.Prol.69

kyth *n.* body of people, nation VII.ii.59

kyth *v.* make known I.vi.167; VI.i.55; XII.Prol.124; XII.xii.82

kythit *v.* made known VII.Prol.56

kythyng *pr. p.* making known VII.Prol.5

kytlys *v.* excites, rouses XII.Prol.229

la *v.* lay. ~ **to myne eyr** listen I.Prol.488

laborus *adj.* laborious III.vi.201

lace *n.* snare I.x.33; VIII.Prol.28

lachit *pa. p.* neglected, slighted XII.x.146

ladis *v.* loads (a ship) III.vi.211

laggerit *pa. p.* bemired VII.Prol.55

laid ster, **laid stern** *n.* a star that shows the way, a guide I.Prol.8, 454; I.xi.101; III.Prol.42

laif *n.* rest, remainder I.viii.14; I.ix.39

lair *n.* place for (domestic) animals to rest XIII.Prol.44

lair *n.* learning, knowledge I.Prol.85

laith, **laithly** *adj.* loathsome II.ii.128; III.iv.71; III.viii.130

lak *n.* disgrace, shame II.x.46; VI.viii.44; X.xi.186; XI.i.130. deficiency V.vi.112

lak *v.* reproach, blame VI.Prol.14

lakar *adj.* more inferior I.Prol.346

lakest *adj.* worst XI.xiii.117

lakkyn *v.inf.* to blame or reproach I.Prol.275

landbrist *n.* surf VII.Prol.21

landwart *adj.* rustic VII.viii.107; VII.xi.92

lang hame *n.* grave VI.ii.149

langage *n.* language I.Prol.382

langand *pr. p.* belonging, pertaining to VI.ix.153

langang *pr. p.* longing XII.i.10

langar, **langeir**, **langer**, **langeyr** *adv.* a while ago V.Prol.35; V.iv.111; X.x.129; XII.xi.40, 51

langgis *prep.* alongside III.iv.134

langis *adv.* along, beside IV.vii.73

langour *n.* lassitude, ennui IV.Prol.25;

VIII.Prol.14

langsum *adj.* tedious, long-lasting I.xi.111; III.iii.25; IV.Prol.234

langsyne *adv.* long ago V.i.47

langyng *pr. p.* belonging VI.x.23

lanrent *n.* land-rent, income XI.vii.107: R (C **nobill kynrent**)

lanssand *pr. p.* hurling oneself, launching forth IX.ix.74

lansys *v.* leaps, hurls oneself XI.xii.92

lap *v.* embrace XIII.vii.38

lap *v.* leaped IV.Prol.84; V.iv.90; XII.xii.114

lap, **lappit** *pa. p.* lapped, surrounded, enclosed VII.vi.25; IX.ii.8

lappit *v.* surrounded, enclosed II.iv.24; II.vi.44; III.ix.38

lappys *n.* folds XI.xv.19

lappyt *pa. p.* clothed, enwrapped IV.iv.15

lard *n.* lord V.v.48. pilot V.xiv.11. Lord, Jupiter XII.xiii.151

large *adj.* of size, big; of moral qualities, generous, abundant, unrestrained II.ii.64; III.vi.206; IV.i.6; V.xiii.130; V.xiv.87

laß *n.* cord, rope XII.x.122

lasch *adj.* relaxed, loose IX.xiii.81

lasch *v.* strike out, lash XII.ix.67

laser *n.* leisure IV.x.84; IX.viii.60

lat *v.* let I.Prol.379

latit *pa. p.* of metal, forged, plated VII.x.76

laton *n.* brass VII.Prol.4; VIII.x.68

lattir *adj.* far away, in place, not time VI.viii.4. faraway in time II.iv.93; VI.viii.75. latest, final III.vii.24, 35

latton *n.* brass VIII.Prol.92

latyt *pa. p.* heated, bendable? VIII.Prol.92

lauborit *pa. p.* cultivated, ploughed III.ii.17

laubour *v.* cultivate III.ii.136

lauchand *pr. p.* laughing I.ix.19

lauchfull *adj.* lawful, legitimate III.v.23

laucht *v.* capture, obtain VIII.Prol.27

laucht *pa. p.* captured, obtained V.v.22: E, R

lauchtir *n.* laughter V.Prol.23

lauchyng *pr. p.* laughing IV.iii.74

lavd *n.* laud, honour, praise IV.v.177; IV.vi.81

lave *n.* rest, remainder III.ix.118; IV.x.111; V.i.55

law *adj. adv.* low III.viii.32; VII.Prol.104. **a** ~ low down IX.xiii.28

law *n.* law. ~ **ledar** lawgiver IV.ii.12. **lawis**, laws, including the decrees of pagan deities

law *v.* lower, abase XI.Prol.82

lawd, lawdis *n.* praise IV.iii.6; XII. Prol.247

lawly *adv.* humbly I.ii.24; III.vi.158; IV.x.25

lawrer *n.* laurel I.Prol.6; VII.i.77

lawte *n.* fidelity, loyalty II.ii.153; IV.vii.23; VI.v.105

lawyd *n.* obscure: see note to VIII.Prol.92

lawyst *v.pres.2 sg.* lowers, humbles IV.Prol.43

lay *n.* law XII.xiii.76

lay *n.* delay? VIII.Prol.92

lay *v.* **dar I** ~ (*poetic tag*), dare I wager I.Prol.261. lay eggs? XII.Prol.154

layd *pa. p.* of a fire, set and lit VII.vii.124

layis *n.* songs IV.Prol.142

layr *n.* a night's rest VIII.iv.70

lays *n.* laws, especially religious laws VI.xiv.8

layß *n.* tie, ribbon VII.vi.27

le *n. adj.* lee, the side sheltered from the wind V.i.30; V.xiv.7. shelter, protection (without any nautical flavour) III. vi.76. sheltered X.iv.120. **leif in** ~ live in security III.ii.132

lear *n.* liar II.ii.42

lech, leche *n.* leech, physician IV.Prol.193; XIII.Prol.80

led *n.* lead V.viii.98

led *n.* guidance, leading, direction VIII. ix.23

led *v.* lead. of a style of life, live or possess VII.iv.142

ledderyn *adj.* leather XIII.Prol.33

leddyris *n.* ladders IX.viii.116, 154

ledis, ledys *n.* peoples, nations, races.

everyone IV.Prol.107; VIII.Prol.27, 59

lege *n.* superior to whom one owes feudal allegiance XII.Prol.247

legharnes *n.* armour for the legs XII. vii.114

leid *n.* speech, language I.Prol.372, 384; III.iv.1

leif *adj.* dear I.i.40; III.vii.37; IV.vi.72

leif *v.* live III.v.66; IV.Prol.159

leif *v.* allow, permit to do something X.xi.46

leiffy *adj.* leafy VIII.i.35 (L, B **leiffly**)

leil, leill *adj.* loyal, honest, lawful I.Prol.476; II.ii.153; III.viii.81

leill *adv.* accurately, exactly *Naym of the Translatour*.5

leir *v.* teach III.ii.156; XIII.iv.12

leir *v.* learn I.Prol.481; IV.Prol.269

leisk *n.* groin X.x.103

leit *v.* permitted I.Prol.310

lekkis *n.* leaks VI.vi.63

lekkit *v.* leaked I.iii.50

lemand *pr. p.* shining, gleaming IV.ix.19; IV.x.88; V.i.5

lemman *n.* sweetheart, not in a bad sense III.Prol.6

lemys *v.* gleams VI.xii.4

len *v.* grant, lend *Tyme, space and dait*.11

lenar *adj.* leaner III.ix.6

lend *v.* tarry, remain IX.vi.112

lent *pa. p.* arrived, came VIII.Prol.14

lent *pa. p.* lent, given IV.xii.20

lenth *n.* length. **on** ~ all along I.iv.95

lenth *v.* lengthen II.x.139

lenyt *v.* leaned, reclined VIII.Prol.2

lenʒe *adj.* fine, thin, slender VIII.i.33

lepyng *v.inf.* to leap XII.vi.115

lepys *v.* see note to VIII.Prol.92

lerand *pr. p.* learning V.iv.115

lern *v.* teach XII.iv.80

lernyng *v.inf.* to learn XII.vii.125

leß *conj.* unless I.Prol.495; II.ii.10

leß *n.* lies. **but** ~ to be sure (padding) II.ii.47; II.v.83; III.v.26

lest *impersonal v.* choose, care, desire I.ii.16; III.Prol.28; VI.i.156

lest *v.* last, exist X.v.50

lest *pa. p.* lasted VI.xv.63

lesum *adj.* lawful, permissible IV.iii.25; IV.v.139; XII.xiii.48

lesyng *vbl.n.* losing, loss III.v.116

let *n.* hindrance, delay IV.v.90; V.xii.142; VIII.Prol.29

lethis *n.* joints I.iv.31; III.viii.11; IV.xii.103

lettron *n.* lectern VII.Prol.143

levand *pr. p.* living VI.ii.156

levand *pr. p.* leaving VI.iii.2

levin *n.* flash of lightning I.ii.65; II.x.155; III.iii.96

levingis *n.* remains IV.xi.85

levir *adv.* rather, preferably IV.iii.34; V.iv.132

levis *v.* lives III.v.58

levit *v.* lived V.xii.108

levit *pa. p.* given leave or permission I.viii.102

levyn *n.* lightning I.xi.99; hence, any bright light VII.Prol.10

levyng *pr. p.* living III.vii.38

levyngis *n.* those left, survivors III.ii.40

levys *n.* the folding parts or leaves of a door or gate IX.xii.5

levyt *pa. p.* permitted III.vi.205

levyt *pa. p.* lived IV.xii.19

lew warm *adj.* lukewarm IV.xii.81; VIII. iii.25; VIII.iv.27

lewit, lewyt *adj.* unlearned, untaught I.Prol.21, 323, 406, 476

lewytnes *n.* ignorance IX.Prol.71

ley *n.* sheltered place VIII.Prol.2

leyd *n.* man, person VIII.Prol.118

leyd *n.* language I.Prol.364

leyis *n.* leas, pastures VII.Prol.55

leym *n.* gleam, glitter III.iii.106

leyn *v.pres.3 pl.* lie, err I.Prol.233

leynd, leyndis *v.* dwell, remain IV.x.9; VII.ii.39; VIII.viii.108

leyndis *n.* loins XII.ii.90

leyr *v.* learn III.ii.70; V.Prol.44

leys *n.* lies VI.Prol.10

leys *v.* lies, prevaricates I.Prol.270

leys *v.* was deprived of III.x.104

leyt *pa. p.* let, allowed II.v.30

lichour *n.* lecher, debauchee IV.Prol.164

lichtly *v.* treat lightly, disparage VII.iv.103

lichtnes *n.* lightheartedness V.x.52: R

lift *n.* sky V.xii.178; XIII.Prol.11.

ligging, liggyn, liggyng *pr. p.* lying II.v.29; VI.iii.13; VI.vi.80

lignum *Latin n.* wood, firewood I.Prol.384

like *adj.* like or near to doing something VII.v.heading

lilly *adj.* pure, lily-like VI.xi.54: R (C **silly**)

liltis *v.* lifts up the voice shrilly or harshly VII.viii.88

liones *n.* lions VI.xvi.32

lippiris *n.* of the waves, surges, ripples VII.viii.119

lippyn *v.* trust, confide II.i.65

lippynnyt *v.trans.* entrusted V.xiv.46

lippynnyt *v.intrans.* trusted V.xiv.83

lippyrrand *pr. p.* rippling VIII.xi.73

list *v. personal* or *impersonal.* wish, wished I.Prol.503; I.vii.114; I.viii.130; III.ix.75

listyng *v.pres.3 pl.* they list, wish XI.xvii.37

lite *adj.* as *n.* a little VIII.Prol.3

lith *n.* joint VII.vii.115

littis *v.* colours, stains VII.ix.35

littit, littyt *pa. p.* stained VII.ix.6; XIII. iv.45

lodis man, lodismen, lodysman *n.* pilot, steersman III.vi.224; V.xiv.11; VI.v.120

loft *n.* air, upper region III.iii.91

logicianys *n.* ones skilled in reasoning I.Prol.377

loif *n.* praise XI.iv.37

loif *v.* praise I.Prol.421

lok *v.* lock VIII.Prol.28

lokkerit *pa. p.* curled V.vi.116

lokyrrand *pr. p.* curling VII.xi.63

lomys *n.* tools or implements VII.x.82

longeour *n.* lounger, idler VIII.Prol.122

longis *n.* lungs X.vii.63

loppin *pa. p.* leaped II.x.12

loppirrit, loppyrrit *pa. p.* curdled,

coagulated III.ix.64; VII.viii.128

lorn *pa. p.* lost XII.vi.9

losanger *n.* sluggard VIII.Prol.178; XII. Prol.281

lossyt *pa. p.* lost III.i.98

louch *n.* lake V.xiii.113

louk *v.* enclose VIII.Prol.28

lovabill *adj.* praiseworthy II.x.44; VIII.v.22

lovit *v.* praised I.ix.84

lovit *pa. p.* praised II.x.47

lovn *adj.* calm, quiet VIII.ii.49; IX.i.9

lovn *n.* rogue, boor, clown VIII. Prol.122

lovyng, lovyngis *vbl.n.* praising, praise I.Prol.73; VII.xii.72. with possible pun loving/praising I.Prol.447

lovyt *pa. p.* praised *Exclamatioun.*7

low *n.* flame II.xi.132

low *v.* of cattle, moo VIII.vi.112

lowand *pr. p.* uttering a cattle-like noise IV.Prol.66

lowch *n.* lake VIII.ii.19; IV.ix.82

lowe, lowis *n.* flame V.xii.34; VII.i.108

lowis *v.* loose IV.xii.118

lowke *v.* fasten, join, grapple (as in joining battle or ranks) V.x.85

lowkyt *pa. p.* locked, shut VI.vii.44

lown, lowne *adj.* calm, unruffled III. viii.60; XII.Prol.54

lownyt *v.* calmed X.ii.113

lownyt *pa. p.* calmed V.iv.107; VII.i.5

lowp *n.* vault, leap XII.v.169

lowpit, lowpyt *pa. p.* looped, twisted II.iv.9; V.v.13

lowr *v.* lurk, skulk VII.vi.5

lowsyt *pa. p.* loosed III.viii.137

lowt, lowtis *v.* bows, stoops X.ix.84. stoops to examine V.viii.44

lowuß *adj.* loose IX.Prol.25

lowyn *adj.* calm, unruffled V.iii.47

lowys *n.* lakes IV.x.8; XII.Prol.153

lowyß *v.* loose, free IV.xii.102

lowyt *v.* reverberated III.x.36

loyß *n.* praise XIII.iii.51; XIII.vi.180

loyß *n.* loss IV.viii.22; V.xi.25

loyß, los *v.* lose, waste I.Prol.144. lose

V.iv.131; XI.viii.76

luf *n.* the side next the mast or stay to which a fore-and-aft sail is attached V.xiv.7

luffar, lufler *n.* lover IV.vi.32, 35

lufis, luffis *n.* the palms of the hand V.v.24; VIII.Prol.71; VIII.ii.5

luffit *v.* praised IV.v.58

luffyr *n.* liver VIII.Prol.139

luge *v.* take up residence III.x.112

luge *pa. p.* lodged VII.v.48

lugyn, lugyng *vbl.n.* lodging I.ix.88; III.viii.65; IV.iii.14; VI.iv.79

lugyng *pr. p.* lodging, remaining VIII.v.24

lugyngis *n.* lodgings, houses III.ii.107

lugys *n.* small dwellings III.ii.83

luk *n.* the act of looking (at one with favour or disfavour) IV.ii.8

luk *n.* fortune IV.Prol.96

lukand *pr. p.* looking at, examining? *Directioun.*116

lukkit *v.* chanced, happened II.vii.43

lumys *n.* tools. **egge** ~ cutting tools XII. iv.126

lurdane *n.* worthless person VI.viii.82

lurdanry *n.* rascality VIII.Prol.9 (E, R **lurdanly**)

lurkis *v.* is concealed or latent I.Prol.378

lurkit *v.* hid, lay in concealment III.ix.89. peered out furtively XIII.Prol.78

lust *n.* pleasure, delight, desire IV.v.38; IV.vi.131; V.Prol.15; IX.iv.40

lustely *adv.* prettily, handsomely, a general sign of praise V.v.13

lustris *n.* periods of five years I.v.94

lusty *adj.* lively, pleasing I.Prol.174, 308; I.viii.7; IV.Prol.34, 266; IV.iv.42. pleasure-loving (without any suggestion of lustful) I.ii.34. strong, powerful IV.Prol.270. lustful IV.ii. heading

lustyhed *n.* vigour XIII.v.63

luyffis *n.* the palms of the hand XII.ii.89

lwme *n.* tool VI.iii.53

lyam, lyamys *n.* tie, leash, cord V.ix.40, 94; IX.xi.5; XII.viii.59

lyard *adj.* grey VI.v.11; VI.xiv.5; VII.vii.27
lycht *v.* alight, land V.vi.86
lychtis *n.* lungs IX.xi.80
lychtly *v.* treat lightly, disdain IV.v.74; XI.viii.62
lychtlyit *v.* slighted, treated lightly IV.i.74; IV.x.27
lydder, lyddir, lyddyr *adj.* lazy, sluggish XI.xiv.29. **cum ~ speid** make slow headway I.Prol.383. ill-conditioned VI.v.13
lyft *n.* sky IV.v.3; IV.viii.125; V.v.26
lyftyng *v.inf.* to lift VI.xi.93
lyge *n.* league III.vii.63; IV.iii.43; VIII.i.82
lyggand *pr. p.* lying VIII.Prol.118
lyggyn *v.inf.* to lie III.vi.73
lyght *adj.* frivolous IX.Prol.14
lyk *v.* lick II.iv.20. drink VIII.Prol.139
lykand *pr. p.* likeable, agreeable IV.i.79; IV.xii.15
lykandly *adv.* in a pleasing manner VIII.vi.31
lyke *adv.* as IV.iv.27
lykewalkis *n.* watches kept over dead bodies X.ix.31
lykis, lykyt *v. impersonal.* ~ **me** I like XI.vii.81; ~ **me** XI.iv.68; ~ **ws** XI.iii.69; **thame** ~ III.iv.98
lykly *adj.* resembling, similar VI.xi.48
lykly *v.* make (a rhyme) true or exact I.Prol.124
lymmouris, lymmowris, lymowris *n.* the shafts of a cart or chariot IX.vi.23; XII.vi.156; XII.viii.63
lynd *n.* lime or linden tree VII.Prol.73; VII.vi.124
lyne *n.* linen VIII.vii.99
lyng *n.* line V.vi.120; VII.xiii.76
lynnyn *n.* linen X.xiii.68
lynnys *n.* waterfalls VII.Prol.73; XI.vii.9
lynt *n.* flax scraps used as tinder VIII.xii.48
lyntquhite *n.* linnet XII.Prol.240
lynȝe *adj.* thin VI.xvi.30
lynȝellis *n.* thin cords IX.xi.5: R (C

lyamys)
lyppin, lyppyn *v.* trust, confide VII.i.164; X.vii.28
lyppyrryng *pr. p.* rippling X.vi.11
lyre *n.* flesh I.iv.93; IV.ii.38; VI.iv.35
lyß *v.* lessen, mitigate VIII.Prol.145; XII.Prol.202
lysch *n.* leash V.ix.94
lysnand, lysnyng *pr. p.* listening III.viii.17; V.iii.66
lyssouris *n.* pastures, meadows XII.Prol.183
lyst *n.* hem XIII.Prol.38
lyst *n.* desire, appetite IX.ii.69
lyst *v.* impersonal, be pleasing to. **ȝou ~** I.viii.135. **hym ~** IV.v.123
lyt, lyte *adj.* little VI.x.46. of stars, recently arisen IV.Prol.2
lyt *n.* dyeing fluid VIII.Prol.92
lyve *n.* life. **on ~** alive III.viii.41

ma *adj.* more III.ix.42
mad *adj.* beside oneself XI.viii.55; XII.vi.147
maggill *v.* mangle, maul *Tyme, space and dait.*24
maglit, maglyt *pa. p.* mangled VI.viii.39; IX.viii.77 (53 **manglit**)
magnyfy *v.* glorify, extol I.Prol.421
magre *prep.* in spite of, notwithstanding IV.v.129
maik *n.* peer, match, equal III.Prol.42
maik *v.* mate IV.Prol.53
maikles *adj.* matchless or peerless, mateless or husbandless VIII.Prol.33
mail *adj.* evil. ~ **eyß** discomfort, malaise XII.i.114
mail *n.* chain-mail II.viii.55
mailtalent *n.* ill-will, malevolence I.i.heading
mailȝeis *n.* chain-mail V.ii.91; V.v.29
mair atour *adv.* moreover III.vi.148
mait *adj.* vanquished, worn out III.v.50; IV.Prol.254
mait *n.* mate XI.Prol.78
mait *v.* overcome, destroy IX.x.37
makerellis *n.* procurers, bawds

IV.Prol.193

makly *adv.* evenly, easily V.xiv.32

makyng *v.pres.3 pl.* they make VIII.
xii.102

malancoly *n.* melancholy, ill-temper,
sullenness II.Prol.13

malapert *adj.* impudent IX.Prol.73; XIII.
vii.50. outspoken, bold, apparently in
a favourable sense IX.i.7

malewrus *adj.* unhappy, unfortunate
XI.Prol.150

maleyß *n.* malice ill-will IV.iii.1

malgre *n.* displeasure, spite IX.Prol.17

malgre *prep.* in spite of. ~ **thyne**, ~ **my
wyl** VI.vii.74; X.x.113

malivolus *adj.* disposed to ill-will
XI.Prol.150: R (C **malewrus**)

maltalent *n.* ill-will, malevolence X.xii.103

malyce *n.* wickedness I.Prol.228

man *n.* mankind, the human race. **all
~ may knaw** IX.iii.163 (E, R, L, B, 53
men)

man *v.* must IV.xii.116

mane *n.* strength, power III.x.24

mangeory *n.* banquet, feast VII.iii.57;
VIII.iii.32; XIII.ix.5

mangit *pa. p.* gone astray, confused,
confounded III.v.52; VI.Prol.20 (53
manglit); VIII.Prol.16

manhed *n.* manliness, courage
I.Prol.330

maniory *n.* feast, luxurious, eating
I.x.28; V.ii.42; VI.ix.151

mank *adj.* maimed, mutilated V.Prol.51

mankyt *pa. p.* ruined, maimed X.vi.117

mannans *n.* menace IV.i.91

mannasis *v.* menaces IV.vi.145

mannasit *v.* menaced I.ii.67

mannykillis *n.* manacles II.iii.3

mannysand *pr. p.* menacing II.iv.74

manß *n.* mansion VIII.vi.118; VIII.
viii.76

mansioun *n.* place of residence, settle-
ment, encampment VII.iii.23; VII.
iv.83. astrologically, a twelfth part of the
heavens, or a sign of the zodiac considered as the seat of the greatest influence

of a particular planet VII.Prol.103

manswete *adj.* gentle, mild VII.xii.142

mantemys *v.* maintains IV.v.81

mantill wall *n.* outer wall; rampart; figuratively, a bank of clouds IX.iii.159;
XII.Prol.24

manuyr *v.* till, cultivate IV.v.72

mapamond *n.* map of the world, or the
world itself VIII.Prol.149

mar *adj.* greater VII.i.100; VII.vi.104

maratour *adv.* moreover II.ii.25

marchis, marchys *n.* borders, edges,
starting-places I.vi.61; III.v.110; III.
ix.54; V.iii.71

marcial *adj.* martial I.v.82

mariolyne *n.* marjoram I.x.69

mark *adj.* dark, murky VI.iv.43

mark *v.* aim, make my way
Exclamatioun.1

mark *pa. p.* fashioned VI.i.42

markis *v.pres.3 sg.* directs, aims
VI.Prol.63

markyt *pa. p.* observed XII.v.132

marraß, marrasis *n.* marsh II.ii.141;
XIII.Prol.54

marrow *n.* companion, mate VI.ix.9

marryt *pa. p.* confounded, put into
disorder X.vii.173

marthyrit *pa. p.* killed, slain, without any religious sense II.vii.14;
VI.viii.49

masterful *adj.* violent, overwhelming
V.xiii.57

mastreß *n.* mistress I.i.31

mastys *n.* mastiff IX.Prol.49

mater *n.* material of thought, sub-
ject-matter I.Prol.289, 402, 497

mattok *n.* mattock (for Neptune's trident)
II.x.90

mavch *n.* male relation by marriage, as
son-in-law or brother-in-law VI.xiv.61

mavyß *n.* song-thrush XII.Prol.234

mawch *n.* see **mavch** VII.i.165; VII.v.81
(E **magh**); XII.x.150 (E **maigh**, 53
maich)

mawis *v.* mows X.ix.10

mawmentis, mawmontis *n.* idols,

pagan gods X.Prol.153; XII.v.165

mawys *n.* bellies III.vi.139

may *n.* maiden (poetic) III.v.89; VII. vi.43

mayk *n.* mate, equal VI.vi.18; XI.vii.106

mayn *n.* moan III.v.120

maynsweryng *vbl.n.* perjury IV.x.40

maynsworn *pa. p.* forsworn, perjured I.Prol.422, 428, 440; II.iii.98; V.xiii.107

mayr *adj.* used as *n.* more. **but** ~ without more ado I.vi.100

mayratour *adv.* moreover I.xi.27

mayß *n.* heavy club V.ii.55; V.vii.4; VIII. iv.85

mayt *adj.* overcome, vanquished X.ix.46; XI.xvii.11

mea culpa *Latin* my fault IX.Prol.76

mediatrix *n.* female mediator IV.xi.48

medicyner *n.* physician XIII.Prol.80

meid *n.* reward VI.ix.198; XI.Prol.65

meik *adj.* gentle, courteous (not easily put upon, not humble) I.xi.81; VI.xv.19

meirswyne *n.* dolphin or porpoise VII. Prol.23

meit *adj.* suitable II.vi.116; III.vi.67

meith *n.* landmark, boundary, end X.xiii.45; XIII.v.45

mekil, **mekill** *adj.* large I.i.4; I.iv.51. much I.vi.107

mel *v.* mix or associate with, engage in conflict V.vii.82

meldir, **meldyr** *n.* a quantity of meal ground at one time, used to translate **mola**, the ceremonial meal and salt of sacrifices II.ii.137; IV.ix.90; XII. iv.33

melle *n.* skirmish, hand-to-fight or crowding together I.vii.124; I.xi.116; II.vi.73

melody *n.* beautiful or happy sounds in contrast to **murnyng** V.Prol.35

membris *n.* limbs I.iii.1; III.i.56

memor *n.* memory I.v.38; I.vii.77. posthumous repute I.Prol.317

men *n.* mien, deportment VIII.xi.20

menand *v. pres.p.* lamenting IX.v.157

mendis *n.* remedies, means of obtaining reparation III.ii.158 (E **a mendis**, R **ane mendis**, 53 **our mendis**, for **amendis**)

menskleß *adj.* ungracious IV.v.41

menstrale *n.* minstrel VI.x.41

ment *pa. p.* mingled, mixed V.xi.18; XII.Prol.22

menyng *vbl.n.* intention VIII.Prol.135

menyt *pa. p.* mourned VI.viii.11

menʒe *n.* train, company I.viii.6; II.i.42; III.ii.4

menʒeit *pa. p.* maimed, wounded VI.viii.40; X.xiii.87

merch *n.* marrow IV.ii.38; VIII.vii.43

mercy *n.* mercy. ~ **cry** cry for mercy from I.Prol.452

merely *adv.* merrily I.i.64; I.xi.89; XIII. vi.45

meris *n.* mares VII.iv.206

meritory *adj.* meritorious, praiseworthy VI.Prol.94

merkattis *n.* markets V.xii.174

merkis *v.* heed, observe carefully IX.Prol.3

merkyt *pa. p.* fashioned, framed VIII. Prol.148

merl *n.* blackbird XII.Prol.234

merswyne *n.* dolphin or porpoise VII. xii.152

mervellit *v.trans.* marvelled at, admired I.xi.31

mery *adj.* pleasing, agreeable (not necessarily hilarious) I.Prol.338; IV.x.43

meß *n.* serving of food (with pun on mass?) XII.Prol.304. dishes of food, meal III.iv.35; III.v.140; VII.ii.16

mesit *pa. p.* calmed, appeased II.iii.66; III.ii.2

mesyng *v.inf.* to calm V.viii.85

mesyng *pr. p.* calming IV.x.11

mesys *v.* calms I.v.49

mesys *n.* dishes of food I.xi.24

mesyt *v.* calmed I.vii.59; II.ii.106

met *n.* measure VIII.Prol.40

met *pa. p.* measured out XI.vi.38

mete *adj.* suitable III.ii.98

mete *adv.* suitably, completely III.vi.89

mete *n.* repast VIII.v.9

methis, methys *n.* end, measures, landmarks X.viii.86; XII.ix.109. thing measured out, courses V.i.45; V.xiv.16

metis *v.* dreams. **in thar swewynnys ~ quent figuris** II.v.36

metyr *n.* composition in meter, verse VII.xii.72

meyd *n.* prize, reward V.vii.66

meyn *adj.* poor, mean, despicable V.xii.47; X.Prol.90. occupying a middle space. **~ quhile** the meantime. **this ~ sesson** just now I.iii.52; IV.ii.35; VI.viii.96

meyn *n.* instrument, method, agency, means III.vi.19; IV.Prol.239; XII. Prol.210

meyn *v.* have in mind, remember, intend to indicate a sense I.Prol.385; I.viii.127; II.i.30, 55; IV.Prol.100; X.vii.94

meyn *v.* bemoan, lament V.ii.16

meyr *n.* mare IV.Prol.60

meyrswyne *n.* dolphin or porpoise III. vi.138

meyß *n.* feast, a single dish of food III. ix.57; IV.xi.35

meyß *v.* calm, assuage I.ii.13, 30; I.iii.69; IV.Prol.192

meyth *n.* boundary, mark V.iv.1

minister *n.* minister, one who acts on the authority of another. Vulcan is '~ **of thundring**' as a servant of Jove VI.Prol.157 (E **minster**)

misteris *n.* religious truths VI.Prol.54

mitigat *pa. p.* alleviated, moderated VI.Prol.43 : 53

mo *adj.* more I.Prol.368; III.iv.6

mobillis, mobiis, moblys *n.* moveable goods, property I.i.23; IV.Prol.258; VIII.iii.9, 178; VIII.vi.15 (R **movblis**)

modefy, modyfy *v.* limit, keep within bounds, influenced by Scottish legal sense of assess or determine

IV.vi.121; VI.xv.16

modywarp *n.* mole VIII.Prol.167

moich *adj.* moist, damp XII.Prol.46

mok *n.* mockery VI.i.146

mokkit *pa. p.* held in derision IV.x.23

mold *n.* earth VIII.Prol.148

molest *adj.* troublesome, vexatious XI.vii.96

mollettis *n.* studded bits for horses VII. iv.196

mon *v.* must I.Prol.278, 379

money *adj.* many XII.v.76

monicioun *n.* warning II.iii.74

monstre, monstreis, monstris *n.* wonderful occurrence, thing or event III. Prol.12; III.viii.150; V.ix.61; VII.i.126

month *n.* mountain XII.ix.56; XII.xii.52

monyfald *adv.* in many different ways V.ix.48

monysis *v.* admonishes III.vi.154

monyst *v.* warned, admonished III. iii.77; IV.x.73

monysyngis *vbl.n.* admonitions, warnings IV.viii.115

mor *adj.* more. **but ~** without more ado I.vi.59

morcell *n.* morsel, bite II.iv.26

morrow *n.* morning, day IV.iv.84

mortale *adj.* mortal, death-causing *Contentis.* doomed to death X.xi.45

mortfundeit *pa. p.* chilled, benumbed with cold VII.Prol.136

morysis *n.* morris-dances, grotesque or riotous dances XIII.ix.112

most *v.* must IV.Prol.5; XII.ix.84

moste *adj.* moist VI.iii.87

mot *v.* might V.xii.107

mote, motis *n.* hill, mound III.i.45; VI.xii.74 (L, B **mont**; R **montane**); VI.xvi.13; VIII.i.76 (E, L, B **montis**)

movyng *v.inf.* to move XI.vi.61

mowe *n.* heap, funeral pile IV.ix.69

mowp *v.* chew VII.ii.22

mowthis *n.* mouths. **pail al tyme thar ~ for ora**, faces III.iv.18

mowys *n.* tricks, jests VIII.Prol.148

moy *adj.* mild, gentle XIII.xi.2

moyt *n.* speck, spot, blemish I.Prol.499

moyt *v.* pick out imperfections *Exclamatioun*.28

moyte *n.* mound, hillock IX.iv.71

mud *n.* mud, mire VI.v.4

mud, **mude**, **mudis** *n.* mood, frame of mind I.v.130; V.viii.82; V.xiii.118; VII.xii.45

mudy *adj.* ill-humoured, complaining: Asc. **quaerentibus** IV.xi.52

muggis *n.* earthenware vessels, here used in an alchemist's laboratory VIII.Prol.95

mukkyrrar *n.* miser, hoarder VIII.Prol.54

mulde meyt *n.* funeral banquet V.ii.118

muldis *n.* funeral ashes IV.viii.38

multiply *v.trans.* pile up, accumulate XIII.ii.21

multyr *n.* multure, toll on grain VIII.Prol.40

munge *n.* mingling, mixture VI.iii.112 (C *marginal note and* E, R, L,B, 53 **have heip or hepe**)

mural3eis *n.* walls X.i.53

murdryß *v.* murder III.Prol.22 (53 **murdir**)

muris *n.* moors VII.Prol.56

murnand *pr. p.* lamenting, uttering sounds of grief I.vii.84; IV.ix.82

murtherit, **murthuryt** *pa. p.* killed barbarously or wickedly I.vii.14: 53 (C **marthyrit**); X.viii.143

musardry *n.* idle dreaming, sloth IV.Prol.16

muse *n.* muse, not limited to the Nine Muses, but also any inspirer, as in I.Prol.454, 463

musis *v.* **al for batal** ~ wait or look expectantly VII.x.heading

must *adj.* musty VI.vii.79

must *n.* musk, a basis for perfume XII.Prol.148

musterand *pr. p.* showing itself, appearing VI.i.34

musteris *n.* assemblings of soldiers VII.xi.39

musturis *v.* shows oneself, appears XII.vi.41

mutulate *adj.* having some part destroyed or wanting V.Prol.51

muyd, **muyde** *n.* mood, disposition I.ii.13; V.iv.84; XII.ix.87 (E, R, L. B, 53 **mynd**)

mych *adj.* much I.xi.8

mychtful *adj.* mighty, powerful VI.iv.24

myd *adj.* denoting the middle part (used as a separate word) III.iv.142

myddil erd *n.* the earth, between heaven and hell VI.xi.4

myddillit *pa. p.* mixed, blended IV.iv.66

mydland *pr. p.* mingling, joining, blending XIII.i.29

mydlerd *n.* the world between heaven and hell VI.viii.11

mydlit *pa. p.* mingled I.vii.123; IV.iii.60. having had sexual intercourse with VII.xi.47

mydschip *n.* the middle part of a ship V.iv.52

mygeis, **myghe** *n.* midge, gnat XII.Prol.172 (E **myght of**, R, **nymphe**, 53 **mige**); XIII.Prol.57

myghtis *n.* power (plural representing Latin plural **opes**) III.i.98

myghtyn *v.pres.3 sg.* might III.ix.77 (E **mycht tyne**)

mylky *adj.* soft, gentle, smoothly flowing I.Prol.342

mynd *n.* mind, intention IV.vi.75

mynd, **mynde** *v.* mine, undermine II.viii.47; V.viii.42

myndles *adj.* mad (not inattentive: representing **demens**) IV.vii.26

myne *pron.* mine; for construction with *pres.p.* **onwytting** IV.vi.51. ~ **alane** by myself IV.iii.48

mynt *n.* threatening gesture or movement V.viii.11

mynt *v.* intend, think, aim VI.ix.158; XII.xiv.49

mynyß, **mynnys** *v.* lessen, diminish I.Prol.365; IV.Prol.249

mynysteris *v.* furnishes, supplies I.iii.95

myr *n.* myrrh XII.Prol.148; XII.ii.128

myr tre *n.* myrtle VI.vii.heading, 44

myrk *adj.* obscure; hence, of degree, lowly IV.iii.59; VI.xiv.52

myrknys *v.* darkens XI.xv.131

myrrely *adv.* merrily V.i.71

myrrour *n.* mirror; hence pattern or example, paragon I.Prol.8

myrthis *n.* delights, joys V.Prol.46; VIII.xi.57

myrthus *n.* myrtle III.i.47; V.ii.62

myryt *pa. p.* bogged down; figuratively, perplexed IX.iii.106

myß *n.* miss, mistake I.Prol.455

mysbyleve *n.* false belief X.xi.56

myscareit *v.trans.* led astray, perverted I.Prol.486

myscaryit *pa. p.* brought to harm or woe II.xi.107

myschaip *pa. p.* misshapen III.x.5

myschancy *adj.* unlucky II.iv.85

myscheif, myscheve *n.* evil plight or condition VI.v.112

myschewsly *adv.* harmfully, destructively (stronger than modern mischievously) V.iv.87

myscunnandnes *n.* ignorance VIII. Prol.87: R

mysfortunate *adj.* not favoured by fortune III.i.37

mysfur *pa. p.* miscarried IX.Prol.66

myskennys *v.* is ignorant of I.viii.126

mysknaw *pa. p.* unknown III.vi.118

mysknawand, mysknawyng *pr. p.* being ignorant of I.v.125; II.ii.86

mysmetyr *v.* spoil the meter of *Tyme, space and dait.*24

myssemand, myssemyng *pr. p.* unbecoming, unseemly I.Prol.403; XII.i.63

mysseym *v.* misbecome IV.vi.108

myssour *n.* measure, moderation VII.v.59; X.viii.154. extent, length (as of a shot) IX.vii.91

myssour *v.* curtail XII.iv.35

myssyttand *pr. p.* inappropriate, unbecoming to I.iii.6, marginal note

myster *n.* need; used as an *adj.* in need

of VIII.Prol.33

myster *v.* need XII.ii.117

mysterfull *adj.* needful, in need I.vi.136; IV.iii.25

mysteris, mystir *n.* need, necessity I.viii.105; V.xiv.101; IX.iii.27, 173

myte *n.* very small unit of money, hence a trifle I.Prol.424; III.Prol.13

mythis *v.* marks, makes clear IX.vii.14. measures VIII.Prol.40 (E **mynschis**, diminishes)

mytir, mytyr *n.* mitre, headband or fillet IV.v.79; X.ix.78

nait *adj.* deft, agile XII.vii.47

naitly *adv.* properly, thoroughly (poetic) VI.iii.139

nakyn *adj.* no kind of XIII.vi.183

nalys *n.* nails, rivets XI.xv.9

name couth, name kouth *adj.* well known by name, famous VI.i.43; XII.v.35

nanys, for the ~ *phr.* for that purpose I.v.81, note. Common as a rhyme tag I.Prol.259; II.viii.47; V.iii.63; V.xiv.101

nar *adj.* nearer V.iv.18

nate *n.* purpose, use, advantage IV.xii.10

natly *adv.* properly, thoroughly (poetic) VI.xvi.30; VIII.vii.99

natyve *adj.* of the same nation, from the same birthplace III.v.125

navyn *n.* navy, fleet IV.vi.18

ne *adv.* nigh, near X.xiv.5; XII.iii.82

ne *n.* neigh XI.x.24; XI.xvii.94

ne *conj.* nor I.i.43

ne ... nocht *adv.* indeed not, truly not VIII.iv.57

necessar *adj.* necessary III.vii.13

necessite, necessiteis *n.* constraining power of circumstances XI.xvii.53. deprivation, situation of hardship I.ix.33

neddir *adj.* lower VIII.iii.124

neddyrmar *adj.* farther below VI.v.heading

nedis *impersonal v.* need III.vii.49; IV.i.103

neidlyngis *adv.* of necessity IV.Prol.5

neif *n.* fist X.vii.88

nemmyt *v.* named III.i.38

nemmyt *pa. p.* named III.iv.1. mentioned by name III.ix.62

neß *n.* headland, cape VI.viii.58

netheleß *adv.* nevertheless I.Prol.409; I.v.35

nevin *v.* name III.ii.144; VII.iv.60

nevis *n.* fists IV.xii.58; XII.xiii.186

nevo, nevoys *n.* nephew II.v.24. grandson I.v.103; IV.iv.70. posterity VI.xi.7; VII.i.168

newfangill *adj.* eager to adopt new fashions and ideas XIII.vi.141

newis *n.pl.* news IV.v.42

newlingis, newlyngis *adv.* just now, anew II.xi.117; III.vi.26; V.xiii.63

neyf *n.* fist XI.xvi.62

neyß *n.* nose IV.Prol.187

neyß *v.* sneeze VIII.Prol.124

nobilite *n.* nobleness or dignity of mind, excellence I.Prol.330

nocht *n.* nothing I.viii.96. **for** ~ in vain, fruitlessly VII.v.32; XIII.vi.141

nokkis *n.* the tips at the end of an archer's bow XI.xvi.60. tips of a yardarm III.viii.83; V.xiv.9

nokkyt *pa. p.* of an arrow, fitted to the bowstring V.ix.44; VII.viii.46

nold *v.* would not I.Prol.271

nolt *n.* cattle XI.xv.100

not *v.* know not I.Prol.64; II.i.40

not bot *adv. conj.* only *Conclusio*.5. unless *Directioun*.88

note *v.* affix blame or accusation to I.Prol.126; XIII.iii.135

noterly *adv.* notoriously or generally known XII.i.88

notis *n.* uses, offices, employments, practices VI.iv.26

notyfy, notyfyß *v.* make evident or conspicuous II.vii.108; IV.i.28; V.ix.67. publish, proclaim III.v.8; IV.Prol.33; IX.Prol.89

noveltis, novelty *n.* newness I.viii.58 (B **novellis**); I.viii.122

nowmyr *n.* number I.iv.61

noyn *adj.* no, none IV.i.10

noyt *v.* accuse, attach a stigma to XIII.iii.135

noyt *v.* use XIII.vi.64

nuke *n.* piece or fragment X.xii.27

nukit *pa. p.* having corners, referring to cakes scored into quadrants by two cuts across the top VII.ii.26

nummyn *pa. p.* taken, captured II.x.130; V.vi.92; VI.ii.13

nunis *n.* nuns, priestesses I.v.81, marginal note

nurys, nuryß *n.* nurse-maid I.v.80; IV.xi.99, 100, 102

nurysyng *vbl.n.* raising, training (representing **alendum**) III.i.94

nutrytyve *adj.* nourishing XII.Prol.228

nyce *adj. see* **nyß**. ignorant, foolish V.xiv.41. strange, rare, uncommon I.viii.2; I.i.52; II.vii.67; III.Prol.14. requiring exactness or precision III.iv.138. carefully adjusted V.iv.heading

nyddris *v.* straitens, oppresses VIII.viii.41

nyl *v.* will not VI.v.48

nyß *adj.* wanton, loose IV.Prol.100. strange VII.i.147

nyte *v.* deny, refuse a request IX.v.164

obesand *adj.* obedient I.Prol.507

obeys *v.* obey III.iii.78

obeysans *n.* action of obeying VII.xii.81; XII.x.36

obiectum *Latin n.* that which is acted upon I.Prol.373; *compare* **subiectum**

oblacionys, oblacioune *n.* offering, or rites in general II.i.7; III.vi.103

oblike *adj.* oblique I.xi.95

oblisit *pa. p.* agreed to as obligatory XIII.iii.83

oblivie *n.* oblivion VI.Prol.4

obseruyt *pa. p.* kept, followed as a rule or method I.Prol.362

obstant *adj.* standing against, resisting XII.ix.99

obumbrat, obumbrate *adj.* shaded,

darkened VI.ii.124; XII.Prol.66

occiane see *n.* the ocean I.v.100;
IV.ix.14

occident *adj.* situated in the west VII.
Prol.25

occisioun *n.* slaughter IX.ix.3

occupy *v.* make use of (a thing) VIII.vi.12

occupy *pa. p.* occupied *Directioun.*49

occupyis *v.* possesses VIII.iii.170

occur *v.* attack, intrude (representing **occur-rat**) III.vi.100

och *interj.* alas! IV.xii.62

odibill *adj.* hateful IV.Prol.246

ofspryng *n.* family, race, fact of descent
from an ancestor IV.vi.94

oly *n.* oil VI.iv.37

olyve *n.* olive VIII.iii.48. *See also* **dolyve**

ombekend *pa. p.* unknown (**ignarum**)
X.xii.44

omberauch *v.* surrounded II.x.155

omberaucht *pa. p.* surrounded VI.i.118

ombeset *v.* encompassed, beset I.ii.53

ombeset, ombesett *pa. p.* encompassed,
beset IV.viii.71; V.i.36

ombethynk *v.* think about, consider I.x.32

ombyschew *v.* avoid, shun III.vi.81

ombyset *pa. p.* surrounded, encompassed
IV.i.85

omdo *v.* undo IV.ix.53; IV.xii.117; VI.i.48

omdyd *v.* loosened VI.vi.45

omsemly *adj.* unseemly X.x.90

on *adj.* one V.vii.103; XIII.Prol.163

on *prefix, un-* ~ **rycht** incorrect
IX.x.62

on breid *phr.* opened, displayed XII.
Prol.113

on char *prep. and n.* ajar VII.Prol.129

onarmyt *pa. p.* unarmed II.ii.17

onassayt *pa. p.* untried IV.viii.16

onawarnyst *pa. p.* unwarned X.xii.110

onbegrave *pa. p.* unburied XI.i.54

onbet *pa. p.* unbeaten II.viii.122

onbodeit *pa. p.* deprived of bodies
III.v.42

onbydrew *v.* drew away XII.Prol.6

oncorn *n.* evil grain IV.Prol.13

oncunnandnes *n.* ignorance VIII.

Prol.87

oncun3eit *pa. p.* uncoined X.ix.53

ondantabill *adj.* indomitable I.vi.62

ondantit, ondantyt *pa. p.* undefeated
IV.i.84. undisciplined, unrestrained
IV.Prol.58

ondepys *n.* shallows V.ix.114

onderlowt *adj.* subjugated, submissive
XIII.iii.71

ondigest *adj.* undigested, confused
XI.iv.63

ondocht *n.* ineffective, worthless person VII.vii.33

ondowtit *pa. p.* undoubted, certain
II.vi.114

ondreich *adv.* at a distance II.xi.56. *See
also* **dreich**

ondyrtakyn *vbl.n.* undertaking, enterprise XII.vi.105

oneith *adv.* scarcely, not easily
I.Prol.270; III.iii.107

onenarmyt *pa. p.* unarmed XII.vi.3

onerdit, onerdyt *pa. p.* unburied
IV.xi.75; V.xiv.85; VI.ii.145

oneschewabill *adj.* inescapa-
ble XI.xiv.102; XII.v.116 (R
Vnscheveabill)

oneth, onethis *adv.* scarcely II.x.27;
III.v.41; IV.vi.8; V.Prol.17

onevenly, onevyn *adj.* uneven, rough
IV.v.135; XII.iv.147

onfald *v.* expose X.xiv.158

onfar *adj.* unfair, horrible (**letalem**)
XII.xiii.197

onfarrand *pr. p.* unattractive, unpleas-
ing IX.ix.52 E (C **evil farrand**)

onfensabill *adj.* incapable of defence
IX.xii.16

onfery *adj.* inactive X.xiv.70

onflocht *adj.* in flight, or figuratively, in
a flutter V.iii.67; V.xiii.33; X.xii.106;
XI.xv.38. afloat, spreading abroad
V.vii.52

onforlatit, onforlatyt *pa. p.* not drawn
off from one vessel to another
V.Prol.53; *Directioun.*90

onforleit *pa. p.* unsurrendered, not

abandoned XI.xi.16

onfrend *n.* enemy IX.vi.111

onfrendlych *adj.* unfriendly V.vii.96

onfructuus *adj.* unfruitful IV.Prol.19

onfylit *pa. p.* undefiled II.ii.153

onganand *adj.* unsuitable I.vii.102

ongrouf *adj.* grovelling XIII.v.24

onhabill *adj.* unable, lacking in some ability or power VI.v.162

onhalsyt *pa. p.* ungreeted IX.v.141

onhand *compound adv.* **tak** ~ undertake XIII.i.101

onhappy *adj.* unfortunate II.vi.89; III.ix.68; V.xi.51. unhappy in the modern sense IV.ii.34; V.i.6. ill-omened V.xi.71

onhappely *adv.* by ill chance V.vi.73

onheld *compound adv.* in a leaning position XII.viii.113

onhie *compound adv.* on high V.ix.42

onhyt *pa. p.* un-hit VI.xiv.87

onkend *pa. p.* unknown, unfamiliar I.iv.71; I.vi.136; III.vi.47

onknaw *pa. p.* unknown I.vi.heading; I.vi.49; IV.ii.43

onkouth *adj.* strange, foreign, outlandish II.iv.51; III.Prol.13, 38; III.iv.63. unnatural, unheard of I.viii.38; III.vi.117; V.ix.79. ignorant, unknowing V.x.80. unknown (with some sense of uncouth, lawless?) IV.Prol.267. novel, unusual (representing **novo**) III.iii.63

onkynd *adj.* in the modern sense, unkind I.i.44

onkyndly *adj.* unnatural VI.xiv.33

onkyndnes *n.* unnatural conduct I.Prol.441

onlace *v.* attach by means of a lace XI.Prol.102

onlappyt *pa. p.* unfolded XII.Prol.114

onleif *adj.* unlawful XII.xiii.48

onmeit *adj.* unequal, unevenly matched II.xi.76

onmensurabill *adj.* unmeasurable, infinite X.Prol.93

onmesurly *adv.* unmeasurably V.vii.70

onmysurly *adj.* unmeasurable XII.xii.33

onone *adv.* at once, directly I.vi.102; II.iii.60; III.ii.7

onplayn *adj.* uneven, rough, hilly VI.ii.112

onprovisitly *adv.* incautiously I.x.49; VI.iii.28

onpunyst *pa. p.* unpunished I.iii.71

onrebutit *pa. p.* unrepulsed IX.xiii.49

onrequerit, onrequirit *pa. p.* unbesought, unasked VI.ii.28. unbidden, unasked III.iii.16

onrestles *adj.* restless IV.x.13

onreturnabil *adj.* admitting of no return VI.i.44

onrovm *adv.* at a distance X.xiii.52

onrude *adj.* rude, violent V.i.24; VI.ii.114; VI.v.3

onrycht *adj.* not right, wrong IX.x.62

onsaucht *adj.* troubled, distressed XII.v.201

onsikkyr *adj.* unsafe II.i.19

onsilly *adj.* un-seely, unfortunate, unhappy IV.iii.52; VI.iii.109; VI.xiv.36

onsned *pa. p.* uncut IX.xi.44

onsound *adj.* wounded, unhealthy IV.i.1; IV.xii.92

onspulȝeit *pa. p.* unspoiled, unstripped XI.xi.134

onsubieckit *pa. p.* unsubjected VII.vi.67

onsure *adj.* unsafe III.vi.133

onsylle, onsylly *adj.* un-seely, unfortunate I.xi.36; IV.Prol.230; V.viii.86

onsyverit *pa. p.* not separated or scattered IX.viii.133

ontald *pa. p.* uncounted XI.Prol.197; hence, infinite XII.ii.85

ontelabill *adj.* indescribable (**infandum**) I.xii.6; XII.xiii.33

onthrall *pa. p.* freed, emancipated XII.iv.77

onthrift *n.* dissolute conduct IV.Prol.24

onthrifty *adj.* producing no gain, harmful IX.x.25

onthriftynes *n.* dissoluteness IV.Prol.174

ontraste *adj.* unreliable XII.xii.89

ontretabill *adj.* stubborn, implacable IV.viii.40; VI.Prol.116

ontymusly *adv.* in an inappropriate time

VI.vii.11

ontynt *pa. p.* untaken I.x.43

onvsyt *pa. p.* unaccustomed VI.i.17

onwarly *adv.* unwarily II.vii.23

onwarnyt, onwarnyst *pa. p.* unprepared, unwarned II.iv.3; VIII.iv.143

onwaryit *pa. p.* uncursed II.xi.108

onweilde, onweldy *adj.* awkward, slow, clumsy from age V.xii.92; V.xiii.11

onwemmyt *pa. p.* unstained I.Prol.52; X.Prol.106

onwrocht *pa. p.* undone, unfinished IV.vii.77

onwrokyn *pa. p.* unavenged II.x.197; III.ix.74; IV.xii.30

onwyttyng *pr. p.* unknowing III.ix.53; IV.vi.51

onyrkyt *pa. p.* unirked XIII.xi.35

oppetere *Latin v.* go to meet (especially death) I.Prol.350

oppone *v.* place oneself in opposition XII.xiii.19. set down in an entry IX.Prol.97: R (C **expone**)

opposit *n.* opposite point (astronomically) VII.Prol.2

oppressit *v.* ravished, raped I.i.75, marginal note

oppyn *adj.* open; bare, exposed I.vii.104

or *adv.* ere, before I.Prol.106; I.i.8; I.vii.69; III.ii.93; III.v.54; III.vi.65, 194; distinguished by context from **or**

or … or *phr.* either … or IV.vi.7

orator *n.* shrine, as seat of oracle VII.i.127

oratory *n.* small temple, shrine II.ii.103; VII.iv.172

oratry *n.* rhetoric I.Prol.308

ordand *v.* ordain V.ii.48

ordinance *n.* order, mode of disposition IX.iv.13

ordur *n.* filth, dirt III.ix.11

orient *adj.* eastern, from the East I.vii.125; I.ix.133

original *n.* origin V.xiii.81; VI.xii.17

oriʒont *n.* horizon VII.Prol.112

orlager, orleger *n.* proclaimer of the hours VII.Prol.113; XII.Prol.278

orlege *n.* time-piece; hence, measure of excellence I.Prol.340

ornat, ornate *adj.* embellished with flowers of rhetoric I.Prol.2, 149, 326, 361, 393

orpyt *adv.* stoutly, boldly X.i.49

oryson, orysoun *n.* orison, prayer III.iii.54; III.viii.40

ostis *n.* hosts I.v.28

other *pron.* one of the two I.vi.28

othersum *pron.* some others I.vii.18

our *adj.* over, beyond III.vi.161

our *adv.* over, excessively VI.iii.61

our *prep.* over I.i.22; IV.i.110; IV.xii.54

ourane *adv.* in one, together VI.viii.55; X.vii.89

ourblaw *v.* blow over the surface of VIII.iv.158

ourcharge *v.* lay an excessive burden upon XI.vii.111

ourchargit *v.* laid an excessive burden upon IV.x.54

ourcled *pa. p.* completely clothed IV.viii.130

ourcummyn *v.inf.* to overcome VI.xiv.84

ourdrewyn *pa. p.* driven or passed over V.xi.57

ouredynnyt *pa. p.* filled with uproar IV.xii.48: R

ourflet *pa. p.* overflowed X.v.135

ourfret *v.* cover over with ornaments (as frost on grass) VII.Prol.162

ourfret *pa. p.* covered with embroidery or ornaments VII.Prol.42

ourgilt *pa. p.* gold-plated V.v.30

ourgretlie *adv.* too greatly VI.xiv.21

ourhand *n.* supremacy X.viii.64

ourheild, ourheildis *v.* cover over, conceal III.iv.57; III.vi.98

ourheildis *v.intrans.* covers VII.Prol.38

ourheildit *pa. p.* covered III.i.86

ourheld, ourheldis *v.* cover over I.iv.17; VII.xi.8

ourhippit, ourhippyt *pa. p.* passed over, skipped I.Prol.154, 175

ourkest *v.* of sky, overcast V.xii.52

ourloft, ourloftis *n.* lowest deck of a ship V.xi.122; V.xii.159

ourquhelm, ourquhelmis *v.* overwhelms I.xii.15; II.i.63

ourquhelmar *n.* conqueror XII.ix.108

ourquhelmyt *v.* overwhelmed I.i.78

ourraucht *v.* overtook, overpowered

V.vi.122

ourrunnyn *pa. p.* overrun III.vii.54

oursalit *v.* sailed over VI.x.101

our set *v.* overthrow, upset IV.Prol.92

ourset *v.* overturn V.iv.73

ourset *pa. p.* oppressed I.iii.60

ourseyn *pa. p.* looked over, surveyed I.Prol.498

oursild *pa. p.* covered over, concealed VI.ix.46

ourslip *v.* slip by I.Prol.251

ourslyden *pa. p.* slid by I.v.94

ourspannand *pr. p.* travelling over, passing through III.iii.19

ourspynnerand *pr. p.* spinning over, rapidly traversing IV.iv.53

ourstudyus *adj.* too studious, over-critical I.Prol.499

ourthourt, ourthourtyr, ourthwort *adv.* across V.vi.84; V.xii.102; VIII.Prol.17. all around, here and there VI.ix.150

ourturnyt *pa. p.* turned over, reversed I.vii.107

ourvoluyt *v.* laid aside VII.Prol.154

ourwelt *pa. p.* turned over, threw over X.viii.137; XII.xii.80

ourweltis *v.pres.3 sg.* stumbles over X.vii.105

ourweltyt *pa. p.* turned over V.iii.77

outbullyrand *pr. p.* boiling out IV.xii.41

outhrow *prep.* throughout I.vi.87

outquent *pa. p.* quenched, extinguished IV.xii.121

outscrape *v.* escape V.xii.46

outsmyte *pa. p.* struck out V.vii.92

outtak *prep.* save, except V.xii.61

outthrou *prep.* right through III.vi.165

ouyrhand *n.* over-hand, victory XII.iv.68

ovir see *n.* the upper or Adriatic Sea VIII.iii.122

ovyr *adj.* upper III.vi.134

owdir *adj.* either I.vi.159

owrloft *n.* the deck of a ship above the hold IX.ii.98

owrreik *v.* stretch over or beyond VI.ix.136

owt harro *interj.* a cry of alarm VII.vi.135

owtak *prep.* except XIII.Prol.61

owtbrist *v.* burst out IV.i.61

owtgait, owtgatis *n.* path out, exit IX.vii.28; XII.vii.53

owtwith *prep.* outside II.iv.13

owtyn *prep.* without. **for ~ fail** without fail III.x.59

oystis *n.* victims, sacrifices X.xi.36

oyß *n.* use, custom V.x.99

oyß *v.* use I.Prol.117; IV.Prol.98; IX.Prol.15

pace *n.* peace III.iv.100; III.viii.72

pacient *n.* patient, invalid IV.Prol.118

page *n.* youth, lad (without the chivalric sense) I.Prol.112; V.Prol.24

pagen *adj.* pagan: Douglas's usual spelling is **payane** V.ii.71: 53

paill *adj.* white or faintly coloured XII.Prol.106

paill *n.* paling, palisade IX.viii.153; x.i.53

pailȝeon, pallȝeonys *n.* a large tent II.i.31; IX.vi.15

pair *n.* a set, a suit (of armour) VII.iii.74

pair *v.* impair IX.x.51

paithit *pa. p.* paved I.vii.9

pal *n.* fine or rich cloth IV.iv.12

palestral *adj.* athletic III.iv.136; VI.x.34

pall *n.* a rich cloth I.ix.106. a rich robe XI.xi.97

pallat *n.* head, pate X.x.29

palm *n.* palm leaf as a symbol of victory I.Prol.257

palmys *n.* the blades of oars V.iv.9; VII.i.8; X.iv.122

palt *n.* blow XIII.ii.15

palustrall *adj.* athletic I.Prol.374

palȝardy *n.* knavery IV.Prol.178

palȝeonys *n.* large tents VIII.x.20

pan *n.* the skull X.vii.131

panaces *n.* panacea, a mythical plant XII.vii.91 (R, 53 **panates**)

pand *n.* pawn, pledge XI.vii.164

pane *n.* suffering I.i.7. effort, trouble to accomplish something II.iv.28

pantis *n.* points IX.ix.62

pantyt *pa. p.* painted VII.xiii.25

pap *n.* breast I.vii.131

papis *n.* popes, used loosely for lords VIII. Prol.106

pappis *n.* breasts I.Prol.468; III.vi.74; IV.vii.12

papyngay *n.* parrot I.Prol.262

parage *n.* equality IV.Prol.44. value, worth III.vi.222

paramouris *n.* love, especially sexual love IV.Prol.147, 204

parkis *n.* enclosed tracts of land XII. Prol.176

parroch *adj.* parish VIII.Prol.108

parsmentis *n.* partiment, a division or company V.x.31

participate *pa. p.* having been made a partner XIII.Prol.71

partis man *n.* partner, sharer XII.vii.132

partit *pa. p.* of a dispute, dissolved, brought to an end I.viii.27

party *adj.* particoloured VIII.iv.201

party *n.* part III.iv.28; XII.iii.73

partyment *n.* division, company XII. iii.39

partyng *pr. p.* dividing VI.ii.89

paryngis *vbl.n.* parings, fragments VII. ii.22

pasand *adj.* heavy, forceful X.viii.13; XII. viii.34

passage *n.* travelling, voyaging III.Prol.3

passyngear *n.* ferry boat VI.vi.14

passynger *n.* passer. **thrynfald** ~ one who has three ways, as Ascensius supposes Diana Trivia to have VI.i.11

pastans *n.* recreation V.Prol.47; XII. Prol.212

pasys *v.* estimates the weight of, poises or lifts in the hand V.vii.84

pasyt *pa. p.* weighed XII.xii.77

patent *adj.* open, evident II.iv.62; IX.ii.53, 81

patermon *n.* patrimony, property VIII. Prol.106

patrellis, patrellys *n.* pieces of armour to protect the breast of a horse VII.iv.193;

IX.vi.122

patron *n.* lord or master I.Prol.128. a tutelary divinity VI.Prol.1; VI.ii.83. captain or master of a ship V.iii.36; V.iv.3

patterraris *n.* paternoster-sayers VIII. Prol.105

pavis, pavyß *n.* a convex shield, or any large shield or protection VII.xii.67; IX.viii.111, 130

pawkis *n.* wiles, cunning devices VIII. Prol.81

payan, payane *adj.* pagan I.Prol.460; V.ii.71; VI.Prol.60 (L misunderstands **payn**; B **vayn**)

payß *n.* course, way direction of movement III.ix.20

payß *n.* weight. **scheild of** ~ heavy shield X.x.25

payß *v.* pace, step steadily IV.ii.21

paysand *adj.* heavy, forceful V.v.37; VI.vi.61

paysit *pa. p.* having weight, pressing down heavily VIII.v.11

pecyt *pa. p.* brought to peace or silence X.ii.110

peddar *n.* pedlar VIII.Prol.55

peill *v.* plunder, rob VIII.Prol.55

peir *n.* equal I.Prol.339; III.vii.42

peirlys *n.* pearls I.ix.133

pelf *n.* wealth, possessions II.iii.89

pelit *pa. p.* peeled, bereft of hair XIII. Prol.33

pellok, pellokis *n.* missile thrown from a cross-bow VII.xi.111; IX.ix.138

penates *n.* household gods XIII.x.81; I.ii.27, marginal note

pendes *n.* pendants, ornaments XII.xiv.132

penetratyve *adj.* pungent, piercing VII. Prol.87; X.viii.105

pennys *n.* feathers XII.v.79

pennyß *n.* pennies, coins VIII.Prol.162

pensioun *n.* tribute, tax XI.Prol.24

pensyve *adj.* sorrowful, gloomy IV.vii.56; IX.iii.29

penuryte *n.* penury, insufficiency I.Prol.380

penys *v.* hammers out as at a forge

VII.x.72; VIII.Prol.93

per cace *adv.* by chance III.vi.99

per de *adv.* by God, a mild oath I.Prol.41, 312

per ordour *adv.* in due order III.i.130; III.iii.58

perbrake, perbrakit *pa. p.* broken up, shattered I.iv.25; I.vi.135; VI.vi.63

percace *adv.* by chance I.Prol.383; III.v.35; VIII.iii.14

perchance *adv.* by chance III.Prol.35; III.v.47

perdrawis *v.trans.* ? draws away from, separates VI.Prol.77: E (C **frawart our faith part drawis**)

peregale, peregall *adj.* fully equal VI.xiv.50; IX.x.152

perfay *interj.* verily, truly IV.iii.46

perform *v.* carry through to completion, finish VII.Prol.145

perfurnyst *pa. p.* finished, brought to completion III.viii.82 (53 **perfurmis**); VI.viii.68

perfyte *adj.* perfect, but not an absolute, since **mast** ~ is possible I.Prol.314

perkis *n.* poles, stakes XI.ii.65; XI.iv.76

perkit *v.* perched III.iv.72

perordour *adv.* in due order I.vii.68

perpetual *adj.* perpetual: *for Douglas's error, see the note to* VIII.iii.201

perß *adj.* of dark blue colour XII.Prol.106

persaue *pa. p.* perceived III.viii.24

persavit *v.* perceived III.iii.64

persewar *n.* persecutor VI.ii.22

person *n.* guise, semblance. person, parson **in** ~ **of** in the character of I.Prol.327

personage *n.* benefice or living of a parson VIII.Prol.36

persuading *v.inf.* to persuade XII.xiii.53

persyng *pr. p.* piercing IV.v.154

pertrubbil *v.* trouble greatly III.vi.181

pertrublans *n.* mental disturbance XII.xi.119

pertryk *n.* partridge IX.Prol.50

perturbance *n.* disturbance, molesta-

tion IV.viii.85

perturbe *v.* disturb greatly XIII.iii.78

perturble *v.* disturb greatly VII.vi.16

perturbyng *v.inf.* to disturb III.vi.101

peruersit *pa. p.* perverted VI.iv.88

perych *v.* die, especially violently III.ix.35

perych *v.trans.* destroy, cause to perish IV.Prol.180

perys *n.* peers, equals XI.iv.81

pest *n.* a thing or person that is destructive or troublesome XI.xv.59

pestiferus *adj.* mischievous, hurtful VII.ix.63

pestilenciall *adj.* baneful or harmful VII.viii.65

petuus *adj.* godly, devout III.iv.108. exciting pity I.iii.3

pevach *adj.* mischievous, harmful I.v.28, marginal note

pevagely *adv.* perversely, squalidly VI.v.14

pevych *adj.* epithet of dislike or contempt XI.viii.78

pew *n.* melancholy chirp of a bird VII.Prol.125

peyn *v.* beat thin with a hammer VIII.vii.128. *See also* **penys**

peyr *v.* pour VI.iv.37

peyß *n.* cup, especially a wine-cup VI.iv.27

phalarica *n.* falarica, a form of missile, a javelin wrapped in tow and set on fire IX.xi.88

picht *n.* pith; vigour, toughness V.ii.52

picht *pa. p.* adorned or set with jewels VII.i.111

piete *n.* pity III.v.61; IV.vii.18; VIII.ix.69

pietefull *adj.* pious I.iv.105

pig *n.* earthenware bottle, urn VII.xiii.25

piggeis *n.* sailyards to which pennons are attached III.vi.4

pight *pa. p.* decorated, as with jewels I.ix.133; IV.v.160

pike *v.* sail along closely III.Prol.35

pikis *n.* prickle, thorn III.iv.42

pikkyt *pa. p.* pitch-covered, caulked

VIII.ii.54

pile, pilis *n.* hair or fur, whiskers VI.iv.16; VII.v.115; VIII.iii.149

pilis *n.* pointed blades of grass XII. Prol.92; XIII.Prol.25

pipis *n.* the tubes leading to the heart VI.i.98; VI.ii.47; IX.vii.100

pipis *v.* of the wind, whistles III.viii.48

pissance *n.* puissance, power VIII.vi.37

placabill *adj.* pleasing, agreeable IX.ix.133

place *n.* house, place of residence IV.xii.7. a particular part or point in a book I.Prol.409

plagis *n.* zones, regions VII.iv.80

plaig *n.* blow, stroke XII.viii.23

plait *n.* armour plate II.viii.55

plakkis *n.* small copper coins, each worth 4d. Scots VIII.Prol.93

planand *pr. p.* gliding, soaring V.ix.109

plane *adj.* level IV.iv.53; VII.Prol.53. evident I.i.22. **in ~** plainly to be seen I.vi.36

plasch *n.* splash IX.xiii.82

plasmatour *n.* maker, creator X.Prol.1

plastyr *n.* an external curative application XII.vii.89

plat *adj.* flat, level IV.vii.59

plat *adv.* directly, exactly VI.vi.6; IX.ix.120; X.xiv.95. flatly II.x.164; III.ii.52. **Atlas baris hevins on his schulderis ~** possibly *n.* flat surface VIII.iii.96

plat *v.* slapped, struck IX.ix.117

platis *n.* flat places VIII.vi.111

play *n.* play; profligate indulgence IV.v.38

playand *pr. p.* glittering, rippling VI.iii.120

playntis *n.* complaints I.vi.139

plays *n.* games (not theatrical plays) I.Prol.174

pled *n.* pleading, controversy, dispute I.viii.27; IV.vi.119

plenand *pr. p.* mourning XI.xvi.16

plene *v.* complain I.ii.10

plenyst *v.* filled up, replenished,

stocked IV.Prol.42; VIII.v.11

plesance *n.* pleasure, delight IV.Prol.6; V.Prol.14, 19; VI.Prol.100

plesand *adj.* pleasant I.iii.57; I.iv.18, 85

plet *pa. p.* plaited, woven VII.viii.29; IX.ii.64

plettis *n.* plaits VIII.iv.203

pley *n.* suit or action at law XII.xiv.32

pleyn *v.* complain I.iv.104; I.vi.138

pleys *n.* debates, contentions III.iii.77

plewchmanis *n.* ploughman's I.Prol.509

pliabill *adj.* flexible I.ix.125

plukkit, plukkyt *pa. p.* stripped, plundered VI.Prol.23; VIII.Prol.86

plummet *n.* pommel on the hilt of a sword XII.xii.97

ply *n.* plight, condition I.iv.98, marginal note

plychting *vbl.n.* pledging, plighting IV.vi.69

poil, poill *n.* pole VI.i.18. pole, polestar XIII.Prol.67

pol ax, polax *n.* an ax used as a weapon of war III.Prol.25; XI.Prol.16

pollecy *n.* prudence, skill, sagacity I.Prol.97

pollut *pa. p.* polluted, defiled III.i.114

pollute *v.* polluted II.iii.45; VI.xiv.86

pome *n.* pomander, a mixture of aromatics carried in a small box XII. Prol.146

pompus *adj.* splendid, proud IX.vi.40

popill *n.* poplar V.iii.61; VIII.i.31; VIII. iv.201

popland *pr. p.* pouring in a bubbling stream VI.v.5

poplys, poplit *v.* pours out, gushes in a stream VII.vii.131. poured out in a stream III.ix.69; IX.xi.106; X.vii.131

port *n.* gate II.x.94; III.v.133; IV.iv.8; VI.Prol.56

port *n.* bearing, appearance VI.iv.84

portage *n.* cargo, baggage II.iii.64; III. ii.6

portis *n.* doors, gates I.v.113; I.vii.7; II.i.26; II.xii.81

portis *n.* harbours, ports IV.xi.61;

VI.v.147

portrature *n.* figure, appearance III. vi.134

porturat, porturate *pa. p.* portrayed, depicted I.vii.87; VI.i.31

porturit *v.* portrayed VI.i.36

porturyt *pa. p.* portrayed V.v.20

possand *pr. p.* pushing, thrusting with a weapon X.xii.116

possit *v.* pushed XII.v.203

postponyt *v.* subordinated, put in an inferior position I.i.27

pot, pote, pottis *n.* pit, abyss IV.i.53; IV.v.128; V.xii.125

pouste *n.* power, authority III.viii.43.

povn *n.* peacock XII.Prol.161

powder *n.* dust II.v.41

powis *n.* paws XI.xiii.70

powste *n.* power, authority X.i.40

poyd *adj.* vicious, evil IV.Prol.193

poynt *n.* sharp end V.vi.50. order; **to ~** into proper condition XIII.vi.33. **in ~ to** ready to IV.ix.93; IV.xi.55. **at ~** aptly, suitable IV.iv.40; V.iii.61

poyntalis *n.* daggers VII.xi.59. a plectrum for playing the harp VI.x.46

poyntment *n.* appointment XII.ii.148

poyse *n.* poetry VI.Prol.7

pra *v.* pray XII.ii.7

practike *adj.* requiring skill or experience I.Prol.290

pransand *pr. p.* of a person, dancing, swaggering V.v.48

prattik *n.* stealth, cunning X.xii.113

prattis *v.* tricks VIII.Prol.81

precident *n.* presiding deity I.i.14, marginal note

precordialis *n.* parts in front and over the heart VII.vi.14

predestinate *adj.* predestined III.iv.89

prefer *v.* surpass, excel *Directioun*.99

prekand *pr. p.* spurring (a horse) X.xiv.135

prekis *v.* spurs (a horse) IV.iv.59; IX.vii.25

prelaceis *n.* prelacies VIII.Prol.106

preparat *pa. p.* preparate, prepared

preß *n.* wine press V.Prol.52. urgency VI.ii.96. pressure, effort III.i.73

preß *v.* presume, take upon oneself I.Prol.401

presand *adj.* present III.ix.44

presciens *n.* foreknowledge VIII.ix.74

present *pa. p.* presented I.xi.4

president *n.* presiding patron, deity or guardian X.Prol.116; X.v.97

pressand *pr. p.* attempting V.v.61

prest *adj.* ready for action or use II.vi.10; VI.ii.50

preste *n.* priest II.vi.43

preste *v.* pressed II.vi.76

pretend *v.* portend, foreshow, purpose VIII.ix.82. intend, design, plan X.ii.38

pretending *pr. p.* portending X.v.147

pretendis *v.* portends III.viii.65; V.xii.75. intends IX.iv.93; XI.v.82. cherishes pretensions to VIII. Prol.106

pretermyt *v.* omit, neglect VI.viii.66; VI.xiv.88

prettykis *n.* tricks, stratagems XI.xiii.120

prevaly *adv.* privily, secretly III.iv.56

preve *adj.* privy, privately knowing VI.Prol.138

prevene, preveyn *v.* take in advance, prepossess I.xi.55; X.i.27

prevert *v.* go beyond, outstrip, without any moral sense VII.xiii.64

previdit, previdyt *pa. p.* provided by foresight III.vii.16; X.ii.92

previte *n.* private XII.Prol.213

prevyly *adv.* secretly III.x.23

prik *adj.* pricked up, erect IV.v.20

prik *v.* spur IX.i.29

principalis *n.* chieftains, governors VIII.iii.21

probatioun *n.* proof VII.xiii.21

proceß *n.* progress, course, onward movement I.Prol.379. discourse, argument XII.xiv.110

proclame *pa. p.* proclaimed I.vii.75

procur *v.* bring about, effect VII.i.72;

313

II.ii.48

producear *n*. creator XII.xiii.92

proferris *v*. puts forth, extends VI.iv.113

progenitouris *n*. forefathers III.ii.122

proheme, proheym *n*. preface, proem III.Prol.end; V.Prol.end

prolixit, prolixt *adj*. wordy, tedious I.Prol.167; XIII.ix.16

promittit *pa. p*. promised IX.i.20

promyt *n*. promise I.Prol.439; VI.v.105

pronosticate *v*. foretell V.ix.63

pronosticate *pa. p*. foretold III.vi.209

pronosticatioun *n*. forecast, prediction VII.Prol.122; VII.i.123

pronuba *n*. assistant in ceremonies of marriage IV.iv.78

pronȝe *v*. of a bird, trims the feathers with the beak V.iii.50

proper *adj*. one's own, personal II.Prol.18; VII.v.93; X.v.7

properte *n*. distinctive character (of words, style) I.Prol.121, 397

properteis *n*. distinctive qualities I.iii.75, marginal note

prophane *adj*. unhallowed, ritually unclean VI.iv.47

prophecy *n*. the action or function of a prophet IV.Prol.30

prophete *n*. prophet (usually masculine, feminine in III.iv.heading)

propheteß, prophetis *n*. prophetess II.iv.73; III.vi.190

propir *adj*. one's own, belonging to oneself, characteristic of I.ii.39; III.ii.140; III.iii.34, 48

proplexit, proplexte *pa. p*. perplexed IV.vii.68 (R **prolixte**); XI.ix.16

proplexite *n*. anxiety, confusion XI.vii.38

proponyng *pr. p*. putting forth, proposing I.i.heading

proponys *v*. proposes XI.vii.heading

proport *v*. mean, convey to the mind VI.Prol.28

proportionys *n*. musical harmonies, hence tunes VI.x.43

propyne *n*. present (of wine) V.Prol.52

prosper, prospir *adj*. prosperous, fortunate I.iv.4, 84; III.iv.86; III.vi.203 (53 **prosperus**)

protectrix *n*. protectress X.v.98 (E **protecteris**, 53 **protectour**)

protestatioun *n*. apologia, solemn affirmation of fact I.Prol.104, 137

prouocar *n*. instigator VI.viii.106

provest *n*. head of a collegiate church *Directioun*.31

provoke *v*. call forth, summon X.i.27

provyd, provyde *pa. p*. provided III.vi.25; VIII.ix.74

prowd *adj*. stately, magnificent III.vii.27

proyß *n*. prose I.Prol.139; V.Prol.51

prunȝeit *pa. p*. of persons, decked out or adorned IV.v.80

prymys *v*. equips, furnishes, loads III.vi.213

pryce *n*. prize V.ii.58; V.iii.14; V.ix.55

prygpenny *n*. ? one who haggles, drives a hard bargain VIII.Prol.98

prynnyt *pa. p*. sewed, embroidered III.vii.26; IV.v.163

pryß *n*. sign of capture. **blew the ~ triumphal** sounded the bugle to indicate taking or capture X.xii.123

prysaris *n*. appraisers *Exclamatioun*.40

puft *n*. puff IV.xii.122

puldir *n*. powder; funeral ashes III.v.40; VI.iii.135

pulderit *pa. p*. in heraldry, ornamented with small devices, spangled VIII.vii.150

pulpyt *n*. poop of a ship VIII.iii.46

punsys *n*. talons, claws XI.xiii.170

punsyt *pa. p*. of metalwork, embossed V.v.45

punte *n*. point, condition. **at nyce ~** in good condition III.iv.138

punȝe *n*. a small group of men IX.viii.129

purcheß *n*. concubinage IX.xi.72

purches *v*. obtain, procure II.Prol.6

purchesyng *pr. p*. purchasing, in the sense of pursuing, acquiring by effort or sacrifice III.vi.33

purgator, purgatory, purgatorye *n.* a place or state of suffering VI.Prol.91; VI.xii.heading, 47; XII.Prol.208

purge *v.* purify I.iv.38

purgit *v.* purified, sanctified VIII.iii.202

purpour *adj.* purple IV.iv.20

purpurat *adj.* purple-coloured XII. Prol.16

pursevant *n.* squire, follower, attendant IX.x.133

purvay *v.* prepare, attend to in advance VII.vii.146

purvayt *v.* arranged, prepared in advance IV.viii.15

purviance, purvyance, purvyans *n.* prearrangement, divine providence, plan I.xi.20; III.vi.42; III.vii.9; IV.i.93; VII.vi.57

puryfyde *pa. p.* purified; of metals, refined VIII.x.68

put *n.* butt IX.x.91

puyll *n.* pool I.Prol.376; VI.v.58

puyr *adj.* poor III.ix.51;VIII.vii.90

puyr *adj.* pure VII.Prol.87

pyk *n.* the act of sticking with something pointed II.ix.64

pyk *n.* pitch, tar III.viii.131; V.xii.56

pyke *v.* pick, prod II.viii.44; III.ix.88

pyke *v.* ? sail close to III.v.18; III.x.99

pyke thank *n.* flatterer VIII.Prol.98

pykky *adj.* pitchy, dark with smoke V.xii.32

pykland *pr. p.* pecking, nibbling XII. Prol.158

pykyt *pa. p.* fitted at the tip, pointed V.iv.94

pylchis *n.* outer garments of skins or fur VII.vi.126

pylotis *n.* pilots III.vi.224

pyn, pyne *n.* effort, trouble I.Prol.144; I.i.4. pain, distress, suffering I.ix.31; V.xii.43

pyn *n.* pin (see note) XI.x.15

pyngil, pyngill *v.intrans.* strive, exert oneself, contend I.iv.14; III.v.14; VII. ii.87; XII.x.55

pynglys *v.trans.* pushes hard in a contest

V.iv.122

pynglyt *v.* strove V.iv.75

pynsalis, pynsellis *n.* banners, streamers III.vi.4; VII.x.63; XI.x.72

pynyt *pa. p.* distressed III.ix.6

pyone *n.* a plant, the peony. **roys** ~ species of peony distinguished by red flowers VII.xii.158

pype *n.* wine-cask IX.vi.91

pyrat *n.* pirate VIII.Prol.55

pyrkis *v.* perches XII.Prol.237

pyssant *adj.* puissant, powerful V.Prol.65

pyt *n.* pit VI.ii.118

pythis *n.* strength, force VIII.vii.160

qhare *adv.* where III.i.30: 53

qhuais *pron.* whose (**qhu-** for **quh-** is not uncommon in 53) VII.i.157: 53

quafe *n.* coif, head-covering VII.xi.26

quakis *n.* shivers VII.viii.79

quakyng *v.inf.* to quake VI.xiii.97

qualm *n.* loss, damage X.i.31

quam *pron.* whom (irregular spelling) II.x.70

quarellis *n.* crossbow bolts, squareheaded arrows II.viii.52

quavir *n.* quiver VIII.iii.165

quayf *n.* coif, headdress IV.iv.19

quaynt *adj.* strange, unusual XI.Prol.88

quayntly *adv.* cleverly, ingeniously X.xi. heading

queith *n.* speech, address V.ii.102 (53 **queinth**)

quell *v.* kill V.xiii.21

quellys *v.* oppresses, vanquishes VIII. Prol.112

quellyt *v.* killed IX.vi.50

quent *adj.* wise, knowing, skilled; cunning, crafty II.ii.56; VI.iv.106. strange, unfamiliar, odd II.v.4, 36; III.Prol.12; III.i.108; VI.ii.60. of dress, fine or elegant I.ix.124; I.xi.35. of speech or ideas, clever or elaborated I.Prol.185, 196, 255. proud, fierce IV.ii.37; VII.v.117. beautifully contrived VIII.x.66

quent *v.intrans.* cease to burn

IV.xii.121

quent *pa. p.* quenched, extinguished IV.Prol.120

quently *adv.* skilfully, cleverly, ingeniously II.iv.85; IV.Prol.240

quernys *n.* grindstones I.iv.39

querral *n.* crossbow bolt IX.vii.98

querral stanys *n.* heavy stones, often mill stones IX.vii.98

querrell *n.* quarrel, dispute X.ii.98

querrellys *n.* stone quarries I.vii.22

queste *n.* baying of hounds V.v.26

quething, quethyng *pr. p.* bequeathing. ~ **word** last farewell II.x.145 (E, R **quenthing**); IX.viii.62 (R, 53 **quenthing**)

queym *adj.* convenient, suitable VIII. iv.66. closed against the wind VII.x.21. quiet, still IX.iv.60

quha *pron.* who

quhaill *n.* whale III.vi.137; X.iv.132

quhais *pron.* whose I.Prol.378

quhalis, quhalys *n.* whales V.xiii.132; VII.Prol.23

quham, quhame *pron.* whom I.ii.35; III.v.112

quhamof *compound* of whom IX.vii.116

quhamtill, quhamto *compound* to whom I.viii.51; II.ii.23; II.iv.93; III. vii.47. to which III.viii.125

quhar *adv.* where (**whare** spellings occur in 53, e.g. III.i.22; IV.i.77; **quhere** III.iii.67)

quharat *compound* where, in which place I.v.32

quharof *compound* whereof I.Prol.379

quharthrou *compound* through which III.x.33

quharto *compound* to which place I.ix.56

quhat, quhate *pron.* what I.Prol.370; XII.i.80 (**what** spellings occur in 53, e.g. III.vi.16; IV.i.69)

quhatkyn, quhatkynd *adj.* what kind of I.vi.6; V.xi.96; VII.i.27

quhatsumeuer *pron.* whatever I.pro

367, marginal note; IV.x.8

quhayngis *n.* thongs IX.xi.5: R, 53 (C **thwangs**)

quheil(l) *n.* wheel V.v.57; XII.Prol.162

quhelm *v.* turn upon something so as to cover it II.vii.54. throw down violently, overturn V.xii.18

quhelmyt *v.* turned upside down I.xi.90

quhen *adv.* when I.Prol.280 (**when** spellings occur in 53, e.g. V.xii.139; X.xiii.116)

quhet, quhete *n.* wheat I.iv.37; IV.vii.80; VII.v.80

quhew *n.* sound of passing quickly through the air VII.x.46

quhidder *adj. and pron.* which of two choices IV.v.65

quhidder *adv.* whither, towards what place III.ii.159; IV.viii.41

quhidder *conj.* whether III.i.74

quhidder *n.* violent, impetuous movement V.x.62

quhidderand *pr. p.* rushing V.vi.65; V.ix.29

quhiddir *n.* violent or impetuous movement or its sound VI.v.85

quhiddir *pron.* which (of the alternative choices) IV.i.65

quhiddir *interrog. adv.* whence VI.v.160

quhil, quhile *adv.* until I.ii.54; I.iv.60; VI.Prol.85. up to the time or state that III.v.52

quhile *n.* a portion of time IV.Prol.263; IV.x.53

quhilis *adv.* sometimes IV.vii.31

quhilk *pron.* which, who I.Prol.265, 360; I.i.51

quhilkis *pl.pron.* which, who I.Prol.369; III.iii.5

quhill *adv.* until I.Prol.498; I.ii.10

quhillis *v.* wheels XII.Prol.30: 53 (C **quhirlys**)

quhilum *adv.* once upon a time I.iii.35; III.vi.220

quhip *n.* whip VII.vi.88

quhir *n.* whirr XII.v.114

quhirk *v.* of a top, move in a sudden or jerky motion VII.vi.88: E (C **quhirl**)

quhirl *v.* whirl I.ii.52; VII.vi.88

quhirling *vbl.n.* swift turning VI.Prol.5

quhirlys *v.* whirls V.x.84

quhis *pron.* which (exceptional spelling) I.iii.75, marginal note

quhislyng *pr. p.* whistling II.iv.19

quhispirand *pr. p.* whispering III.v.65

quhissil *n.* whistle III.x.11 (B **quhissing**)

quhite *adj.* white I.Prol.447; III.ii.103; VIII.i.58, 64. of complexion, beautiful, fair (not pallid) I.vii.108. fair-seeming, plausible I.xi.34

quhitly *adj.* pale, light-complexioned XII.ii.34, 96

quhitstanys *n.* whetstones VII.x.62

quhou *adv.* how III.v.111

quhoyn *adj.* few I.iii.43; X.i.38; XII.i.66

quhoyn *n.* a few III.vi.45

quhryne *v.* whine, squeak I.ii.10; V.Prol.32

quhrynnys *n.* cries, whining VI.vi.36

quhy *adv.* why I.Prol.361

quhy *n.* reason XI.Prol.138

quhymperand *pr. p.* whimpering II.xii.15

quhympring *vbl.n.* whimpering VI.vii.6

quhyn *n.* boulder, hard dark-coloured stone IV.vii.8; VII.Prol.39; VIII.iv.110

quhyngeand *pr. p.* whining XIII.iii.28

quhyngyng *vbl.n.* whining XIII.iii.32

quhynnys *n.* boulders or slabs of hard stone V.iv.88; VIII.iv.17; XII.xii.14

quhyppyt *v.* cut quickly, slashed X.vii.128

quhyte *adj.* white, fair IV.Prol.266

quod *v.* quoth, said I.ii.34; II.iii.2

quoy *adj.* quiet, still II.viii.80

quy *n.* heifer IV.ii.19

quyis, quyiß *n.* heifers V.ii.106; VIII.iv.60

quyk *adj.* alive, lifelike VI.xv.6; VIII.viii.69

quykkyn *v.* bring to life X.Prol.128

quyknar *n.* one who brings to life XII.Prol.254

quynche *v.* stifle, suppress VI.viii.102

quynchit *v.* put out, extinguished IV.ii.60

quynchyng *v.inf.* to cease to shine XIII.Prol.29

quynkill *v.* of a light, to go out XIII.Prol.29: E (C **quynchyng**)

quynt essens *n.* quintessence, the fifth, non-material substance out of which the heavenly bodies were supposed to be composed VIII.Prol.95 (E **quent essens**, 53 **quentassence**)

quyok *n.* queyock, heifer VIII.iv.76

quyte *v.* requite I.ix.37

quytterand *pr. p.* quivering II.viii.63

quytteris *v.* chirps, twitters XII.Prol.241

qweir *adj.* suspicious, dubious VIII.Prol.43

qwel *v.* quell IV.xi.19

qwil *adv.* while VI.i.1

qwoyk *v.* quaked III.x.34

qwyk *adj.* alive I.v.81, marginal note

ra *n.* roe deer X.xii.91

ra *n.* sail yard V.xiv.8

rabandis *n.* ropes used to secure sails to the yard-arm III.iv.110

rabell *n.* rebel XI.Prol.80

rabill *n.* mob XIII.iv.63

race *n.* the course or path of a moving body VII.Prol.28

racht *v.* reached, handed VIII.Prol.146

rad *adj.* frightened, alarmed II.ii.18; XII.xii.182

raddour *n.* fear, dread IX.xii.67; XI.vii.147

ragiand *pr. p.* raging VI.ii.49

ragment, ragmentis *n.* gibberish, long rigmarole I.Prol.295; VIII.Prol.147. long writings (not necessarily pejorative) VI.Prol.32

rahatour *n.* a term of abuse for **impro-**

bus XIII.vi.117

raid *n*. road, piece of water near the shore where ships may ride in safety II.i.heading, 19; III.v.34; IV.xi.17

raif *v*. tore apart I.iii.49

raik *v*. proceed at a rapid pace VII.viii.35. *especially in the alliterative tag* ~ **on raw** IV.ii.20; VI.xv.36; VIII.vi.109

raik *v*. raked VIII.vii.90

raiosys *v*. rejoices VI.Prol.96

raip *n*. rope II.iv.66

rair *n*. roar I.ii.64

rair *v*. roar V.xi.26

raith *adv*. quickly I.iv.89; VII.vi.55; VIII.x.85

rak *n*. crash, collision XI.xii.41. storm X.v.127

rak *n*. driving mist, fog VII.Prol.131

rak *v*. reck, care, regard X.xiv.128

rakand *pr. p*. rapidly moving I.vi.heading; III.iv.23; VI.x.59

rakis *n*. rakes VII.xii.49

rakis *v*. proceeds rapidly XII.Prol.177

rakkis *v*. takes thought, care or heed II.vii.51; IV.Prol.149

rakles *adj*. careless, heedless VIII.Prol.21

raknys *v*. reckons, recounts III.x.69

rakyt *v*. proceeded rapidly VIII.ii.67

ralys *n*. rails, fences, enclosures IV.iv.4; X.xii.57

ralys *v*. flows, gushes XI.xiii.172

ralȝear *n*. one who rails, reviler VIII.Prol.66

ramand *pr. p*. shouting, screaming VIII.Prol.7

rammale, rammell *n*. brushwood, underwood IX.Prol.37; XI.ii.18

rammemorit *pa. p*. memorialized, commemorated VIII.vi.61

rammys *n*. battering-rams XII.xii.27

ramrayß *n*. headlong rush XI.xvii.49

ramyngis *vbl.n*. shouts, complaints V.vi.94

randoun *n*. impetuosity, force; hence, a straight course I.vi.149; V.ix.66; X.vi.115

rane *v*. demand with continuous cries VII.ix.90

rang *v*. reigned III.v.24

rangald *n*. common herd (of deer) I.v.37. disorder, disturbance VI.xii.73

range, rangis *n*. row or rank of hunters, fighters or animals IV.iii.56; IX.ix.58

rank *adj*. vigorous or luxuriant in growth II.vi.13. violent, virulent II.iv.37

ransonyng *vbl.n*. ransom, ransoming X.ix.65

ranys *n*. idle talk, rigmarole VIII.Prol.66

raparal *v*. rebuild, repair IV.vi.125

raparalyt *v*. repaired, made good (a loss) IV.vii.27

raport *v*. obtain, get for oneself IV.iii.7

rappis *v*. sends forth with a clap III.iii.96

rare *n*. roar I.ii.11

raschand *pr. p*. dashing, rushing violently VII.viii.108

rasch, raschis *n*. clashes or crashes IX.xii.60; XII.xii.74

raset *n*. refuge, harbour, shelter X.xiv.197

rasys *n*. races, tribes, kindred; course of life III.x.122

rasys *v*. rages, growls IX.ii.64

rat *n*. rut, wrinkle, furrow VII.vii.26

rat rane *n*. a piece of doggerel verse VIII.Prol.147

ratillyng *v.inf*. to rattle VII.xi.85

raucht *pa. p*. reached VI.vi.78

rave *v*. dragged, pulled up IV.x.112

rave *v*. cut, tore, pierced IV.xii.34

ravest *v*. clothed, apparelled IX.iv.37

ravestis *v*. clothes, apparels VI.x.30

ravyt *v*. talked wildly or foolishly VI.v.101

raw *n*. row, rank VIII.ii.30. row or rank of oars V.v.53. **on** ~ in a line (usually meaningless padding) I.viii.44, 124; III.viii.64; IV.ii.20

rawk *adj*. hoarse XI.ix.29

rax *v*. stretch, raise oneself up VI.xiv.45

raxit *v*. stretched or strained oneself

IV.xii.93; V.viii.47

ray *n.* king; error for man, person, or else used ironically VIII.Prol.157

rayd *n.* anchorage, road III.x.101

rayf *v.* tore apart III.ix.66

raym *v.* scream, shout V.xi.116; VII. ix.76; IX.viii.44

rays *n.* roe deer IV.iv.49; XII.Prol.182

rays *n.* sail yards III.viii.83

rays, **rayß** *n.* course taken by a moving body, journey III.vi.22; III.ix.21; IV.x.49

rays *v.* snatch, pluck XI.xi.126

rayß *v.* rose III.viii.27

rayt *pa. p.* arrayed VI.xiv.62

rebald daill, **rebalddaill** *n.* low company, rabble I.Prol.323 (see note); IX.Prol.43

rebellaris *n.* rebels VI.xv.18: R, 53

rebound *v.* leap up VII.vii.96; VII. Prol.112

rebund *n.* violent blow XI.xii.49

rebute *n.* rebuke, reproach XII.v.166

rebute, **rebutyt** *pa. p.* repulsed, driven back II.i.3 (53 **rebukit**); XI.vii.174

recollect *v.* collect, gather I.Prol.99

recollectis *n.* memoirs, collections I.v.2, marginal note

recontir, **recontris**, **recontyr** *v.* meet, encounter in battle I.vii.134; IV.v.165; IV.iv.62

recryand *n.* cowardly or faint-hearted person XI.Prol.119

recryant *adj.* surrendering VI.xv.17

recullys *v.* recoils IX.xiii.38

recuntyrrit *v.* met, encountered in battle XIII.v.13

red *n.* counsel, advice, plans II.xi.6; VII. vi.64; XIII.iii.137

red *v.* prepare, put into order V.i.28; VII. xi.86; X.vii.30

red *v.* prepared XII.vi.142

red *pa. p.* arranged, cleared up IX.vi.114

reddand *pr. p.* preparing, clearing a way X.x.139

rede *n.* counsel, advice, plans IX.viii.48

redis *n.* pieces of advice X.i.77

redoundis *v.* resounds, reverberates XI.vi.118

redoutit *pa. p.* feared, dreaded VIII.iv.43

reduce *v.* bring back to mind, recall VII.i.31. translate, render I.Prol.404. lead back VI.ii.84; VII.x.15. adapt to a purpose VIII.vi.68. restore to a previous condition, comfort IX.viii.69

reducit *pa. p.* led back XI.xi.135. translated. *Directioun.*127

reducyng *pr. p.* recalling to mind VII. Prol.45. bringing back XI.xvii.100

redymyt, **redymyte** *adj.* ornate, beautiful I.Prol.34; VI.xi.60; XII.Prol.128

referris *v.* reflexive, commit, entrust XII. xiii.100

reffell *n.* revel, riotous merrymaking IV.v.38

reflex *n.* reflection of light XII.Prol.61

refrenyng *pr. p.* restraining, checking IV.Prol.182

refrenys, **refreyn** *v.trans.* restrain, check I.ii.7; IV.Prol.154

regester *n.* someone or something that records the past for posterity I.Prol.6

reging *pr. p.* raging, being furious VII. Prol.12: 53

regnand *pr. p.* reigning VI.Prol.81

regrait, **regrate** *n.* lamentation, complaint, plaint II.ii.27; V.xiii.35

regratis *v.* laments I.iv.106

regratyng *pr. p.* mourning V.xi.25

reguler *n.* regulating power or principle; standard I.Prol.340

reherß, **rehersis** *v.* say, speak, give an account of III.v.7; IV.iii.36

rehersyng *v.inf.* to rehearse V.vii.86

rehersyng *vbl.n.* recital I.Prol.226

reif *n.* robbery, spoliation IV.v.81

reif *v.* rob, plunder II.iii.42; IV.vii.46

reik *n.* reach, the limit of one's grasp X.xii.65

reik *n.* smoke V.xii.5

reill *v.* whirl with dizziness or excitement III.Prol.35

reiosyt *pa. p.* filled with joy V.viii.103

reirding *v.inf.* to roar, resound VIII. iv.125

rekand *pr. p.* smoking X.i.102. smelling

strongly III.viii.131

rekand *pr. p.* reaching III.ix.12

reke *v.* reach, stretch VI.v.150. surrender IV.Prol.49

reky *adj.* smoky VII.i.114

reland *pr. p.* dancing reels XIII.ix.109

releifis *n.* cessation, release from occupation VIII.Prol.29

releschand *pr. p.* singing, carolling XII. Prol.246

relevand *pr. p.* returning or rallying in battle X.x.4

relevys *v.* returns or rallies in battle XI.xiv.16

religyus *adj.* bound by monastic vows IV.ix.74

religyus *n.* one bound by monastic vows, priestess IV.ix.53

reliqueis *n.* relics, remains V.ii.11; VI.iii.137

relis *v.* whirls about IV.vi.42

relit *pa. p.* caused to whirl, impelled II.vii.130

rellyk, rellykkis *n.* relic, applied to sacred objects in the pagan religion II.vi.45; II.iii.40

remanand *pr. p.* remaining, fixed III.ii.38

remand *pr. p.* foaming I.xi.89

remane *v.* continue to exist V.xi.34. await for a thing or person I.iv.84

remeid *n.* remedy III.ii.146; IV.iii.2

remembrance *n.* used as a *pl.* with **thir**. remembrances, souvenirs III.vii.32

remordis *v.* causes remorse VII.vi.140

removing *vbl.n.* the action of moving from place to place XIII.Prol.49

rendir *v.* give in return I.vi.173

rendrit *pa. p.* surrendered, gave up II.ii.5

renk *n.* path, route VII.xi.86; X.xi.139. course (of sun or river) VI.xiii.88; VII.xiii.51. act of running X.vii.142; XI.xiii.160. *See also* **rynk**

renown *n.* dissyllabic, renown IX.vii.172

renowne, renownee, renownye *n.* trisyllabic, renown IV.vi.81; VII.iv.88;

IX.x.149

rent, rentis *n.* profit, value I.Prol.82. income VIII.vii.92; IX.v.116

rent, rentis *v.* rend, tear apart I.Prol.281; III.i.77

rent *pa. p.* torn or pulled to pieces II.v.40

renys, renȝe, renȝeis *n.* reins I.iv.4; I.vii.105; III.viii.71; XII.vi.151

repair, repar *n.* the act of returning or going to a place VI.iv.12; VI.xvi.24

repatyrit, repatyrrit *pa. p.* fed VII. Prol.93 (R **recreate**); VIII.iv.70 (E **reparit**)

repfell *n.* revel (*irregular spelling in C and perhaps in E*) IV.v.38

repreif *n.* censure, reproach I.Prol.429

repreif, reprevis *v.* reprove, censure, condemn I.Prol.403, 411

reprochyng *v.inf.* to reproach XI.viii.37

repungnant *adj.* hostile, antagonistic X.i.70 (E, R, 53 **repugnant**)

reputtis *v.* considers, reckons to be VII.v.110

requer, requir *v.* sue for, ask (without any sense of demanding as a right) III.iv.100; IV.vi.10

rerd *n.* clamour, din I.xi.108; III.ii.51; III.viii.147

rerdis *v.* resounds II.vii.98

resistyng *v.inf.* to resist VIII.vii.172

resoundyng *v.inf.* to resound IV.viii.8

responsions *n.* replies, answers VII.i.129

resput *n.* respite X.xi.41

respyte *v.* spare, especially from death VIII.ix.79

ressavyt *pa. p.* accepted; received as a practice V.x.99

resset *n.* residence, place of refuge, haunt VI.viii.39, 54

resset *pa. p.* received, harboured VII.ix.81

resson, ressons *n.* reason. **of** ~ according to reason I.Prol.445. statement, narrative VIII.Prol.67

rest *n.* a contrivance fixed to the cuirass to support the butt-end of a lance

XI.Prol.180

restis *n.* ironwork on a gate VII.iii.78

restyng *v.inf.* to rest V.i.52

resursyng *pr. p.* flying up again IX.ix.84

resyng *v.* resign IV.Prol.213

retour *v.* return XI.i.101

retretit *pa. p.* turned backwards, reversed X.i.16

retrograde *adj.* of the planets, apparently moving backwards, or from east to west VII.Prol.25

returne *n.* trisyllabic, riming with **aduersyte**. return IX.iv.18

returnyt *v.* changed into something else IV.viii.100

reuerens *n.* the state or condition of being revered I.Prol.277

reuery *n.* noise, din X.vii.117

reuolue *v.* destine, purpose I.i.33

reuthful, reuthfull *adj.* compassionate (**pius**) I.Prol.442; I.vi.1; IV.vii.40. sometimes approaching dismal XII.xiii.209

reuthfully *adv.* dismally, piteously IV.xii.57

reutht *n.* pity IV.Prol.149

reuthtfull *adj.* ruth-producing, pitiful IV.Prol.71

revar *n.* thief, pirate VII.vi.48

revell *n.* riotous merry-making II.x.52

revengar *n.* avenger IV.xi.85

revengeabill *adj.* vengeful XII.iv.100

revertis *v.* of plants, springs up afresh XII.Prol.200

revestit *pa. p.* clothed VI.ix.46

revestre *n.* vestry, hence a private room VI.i.138

revestyng *v.pres.3 pl.* re-clothe XII. Prol.78

revis *v.* steals IV.v.130; VIII.Prol.111

revist *v.* ravished, carried away by force I.i.50

revist *pa. p.* ravished, carried away by force IV.v.48. ravished, smitten, enchanted VII.iii.88

revolue *v.* turn over in the mind IV.Prol.12

revoluyng *pr. p.* turning over in the

mind (**volvens**) III.ii.67

revyn *pa. p.* torn, ravelled VI.Prol.24

revyst *pa. p.* violently carried away VIII.x.93

rewis *n.* streets II.vi.69

rewland *pr. p.* guiding V.x.29

rewle *n.* order, pattern III.vi.176, 185

rewthfull *adj.* compassionate I.vi.125

rewyne *n.* ruin I.i.36; III.vii.10

rewyß *n.* streets II.xi.78

reyk *v.* offer, extend V.vii.42

richt *adj.* right, rightful IV.vii.43

richtfull *adj.* right-doing, moral IV.vii.40: R

riggyng *n.* back XIII.Prol.148

ring *n.* kingdom, realm I.ii.44, marginal note. **ringis** VI.i.128

ringis *v.* reigns VII.Prol.12

rispand *pr. p.* grating II.ii.142: R

roch, rochis *n.* rock I.iii.77; III.vi.166

rocht *pa. p.* cared for IV.vii.35

rod, roddis *n.* road, path I.vii.2; IV.vii.89; VI.vii.43

roddis *n.* shafts, boat-poles V.iv.94

roik *n.* fog XII.x.95

rok *n.* a distaff, spindle VII.xiii.58; VIII. vii.93

rokis *n.* clouds, fog VII.Prol.36

rolkis *n.* rocks I.iii.28. rock's III.iv.72

roll *n.* the rim (of a helmet) XII.vi.172

roll *v.* roll, wheel XII.Prol.31

roll, rollis, rollys *v.* row III.iii.113; V.iv.125; VI.v.52

rollyng *v.inf.* to roll XIII.xi.25

romans *n.* romance, chivalrous tale V.Prol.14; marvellous story VIII. Prol.157

ronk *adj.* rank, luxuriant in growth III.ix.4

ronnys, ronys *n.* brambles, thickets VII. Prol.69; IX.vii.31; XII.Prol.182

roset *n.* resin VI.iii.45, 113

rouch, roucht *adj.* rough III.ix.97; VII. Prol.132; VII.xi.63

roundalis *n.* roundels, in Scots used of various types of short poem VIII. Prol.67

roundis *n.* circular dances and the music

for such VII.ix.85

roundis *v.* whispers XI.vii.3

rout *n.* riot, disturbance I.ii.64. disorderly crowd I.ii.51

routhe, routht *n.* rowing V.iii.24; V.v.67

rovis *n.* in ships, the plates on which the point of a rivet is beaten down I.iii.49

rovm *v.* abandon, vacate X.viii.18

rovndis *n.* dances XII.Prol.193

rovste *n.* rust, hence moral corruption IV.Prol.167

rowand *pr. p.* rolling X.vii.4 (E, R, L, 53 **round**)

rowaris *n.* rowers III.viii.7

rowch, rought *adj.* rough II.vii.33; X.xii.95

rowkis *n.* rocks I.viii.77; III.vi.133

rowm *n.* room. **on ~** at a distance V.x.14

rowmyng *pr. p.* I.vii.63

rowmys *v.* clears (space, field) VII.xi.86

rowmys *v.* roam, wander XII.Prol.201

rowmys *n.* courses, beats, paths IX.iv.135

rowmyt *pa. p.* vacated, abandoned XII.xii.38

rown *v.* whisper IV.vi.37

rowndis *n.* round dances VIII.v.19

rownys *v.* whispers XII.Prol.211

rowp *v.* scream, croak IX.viii.44

rowpand *pr. p.* proclaiming aloud III.i.129; V.ii.109

rowpyt *v.* invoked loudly IV.viii.129; IV.ix.15

rowst *v.* scream, roar X.vi.79

rowstis *n.* roars, shouts IV.Prol.67; XII.ii.136

rowstyng *vbl.n.* roaring XII.xii.69

rowt *n.* rout, confused and disorderly crowd I.iv.51; I.vii.32; I.viii.8; IV.iv.26, 31. riot, disturbance I.iii.52

rowt *v.* resound, roar I.v.33; III.vi.146; IV.iv.64

rowtand *pr. p.* roaring I.iv.75; VII.i.132

rowth, rowthis, rowthys *n.* rowing III.viii.112; V.iii.95; V.iv.76; VIII.i.86. a stroke of the oar III.v.15; V.iv.10

rowting *pr. p.* roaring III.viii.95

rowtis *n.* heavy blows V.viii.25

rowtyng *v.inf.* to roar VIII.iv.73

royk *n.* fog III.iii.95

royn *adj.* ? roan, mixed red and white XII.Prol.121

royr *n.* cry I.iii.52

royß *n.* rose; hence a matchless person or paragon I.Prol.342

royst *v.* roast V.ii.117

royt *adj.* wild, disorderly VIII.Prol.67

roytast *adj.* most disorderly, wantonest VIII.Prol.147

roytnes *n.* wildness VIII.Prol.177

rubbaris *n.* robber's X.xiii.48

rubbis *v.* robs II.vii.26

rubbist *v.pres.2 sg.* robs IV.Prol.29

rubicund *adj.* reddish XII.Prol.68

rubric *n.* section heading I.i.heading

rud *n.* ruddy colour XII.ii.28

rude *adj.* severe, violent V.i.67

rude *n.* cross X.Prol.131; XI.Prol.108

ruffis *n.* roofs IV.xii.47

rug, ruggis *v.* pull violently, tear VI.ix.140; IX.x.53; X.i.34

rumesand *pr. p.* roaring VIII.iv.145

rummyll *n.* tumult, uproar V.xii.54

rummyll *v.* make an uproar or tumult III.viii.128; IV.iv.64

rummyß *v.* roar VI.iv.40

rummysand *pr. p.* roaring III.x.17

rummysing *v.inf.* to roar II.iv.41

rumour *n.* uproar, loud expression of opinion (**plausu**) V.ix.34

rumylling *pr. p.* rumbling I.ii.64

rumysand *pr. p.* roaring VI.ii.42

rumyst *v.* roared VII.Prol.22

runclys *n.* wrinkles VII.vii.26 (E **runchis**)

runge *v.* gnaw, chew III.iv.93 (R **ronie**)

rungeand *pr. p.* gnawing, with marginal explanation **gnyppand** IV.iv.11

rungyn *pa. p.* reigned I.v.66

rungyng *vbl.n.* gnawing III.vi.78

runtis *n.* decayed tree stump VIII.vi.10 (E, 53 **rutis**, R **ruttis**)

rurall *adj.* rustic, peasant-like I.Prol.316

rusyt *v.* praised, extolled I.ix.84

ruther *n.* rudder X.v.8

ruyd *n.* cross *Directioun*.146

ruyß *n.* boast VIII.Prol.50

ruyß *v.* praise, extol XI.ix.37

rwys *n.* roofs VII.v.135 (E **ruffis**, L **rwffis**, B **ruffys**; E in next line rimes **lwis**, loves)

rych *adj.* abounding in something e.g. game V.Prol.4

rycht *n.* the right. **al at** ~ suitably III. vi.156. **at** ~ by rights III.vi.22

ryfe *adj.* widespread, common I.Prol.375

ryfe *v.* tear VI.ix.140

ryfe *v.intrans.* split III.Prol.21; VII. xii.120

ryfe *pa. p.* riven III.vi.115

ryg *n.* back XI.xv.104

ryg bone *n.* the backbone X.vii.53

ryggis *n.* the elevations between each pair of plough-furrows VI.xiv.96

ryggyng *n.* the ridge or roof of a building V.iv.106

ryllyng *n.* a shoe made of undressed leather VII.xi.118

rym *n.* fog, chill mist XIII.Prol.31

rym *n.* rim XII.Prol.162

rynd *n.* bark (of tree) VII.Prol.135

rynde *n.* rind, the outer skin or surface IX.vii.99

ryng *n.* kingdom III.ii.106

ryng *v.* ring VI.xvi.26

ryng *v.* reign I.i.35; I.iii.80

ryng dansys *n.* round dances I.viii.11

ryng sangis *n.* choral dancing songs VII.vi.115; XII.Prol.193

rynggyt *pa. p.* ringed, encircled V.x.40

ryngis *n.* enclosed places V.x.91: L, B. circular dances IV.iv.31

ryngnyng *pr. p.* reigning IV.Prol.227

ryngnys *v.* reigns III.i.66

rynk, rynkis *n.* spell of running, a course in a tournament IV.iv.58; V.vi.57, 71; V.x.91

rynnyng *pr. p.* running III.ix.21; IV.iv.7

ryot *n.* wild revelry II.iv.95

rype *v.* search thoroughly, open up II.i.47; II.iii.29; XI.Prol.22; XII.vii.17

ryply *adv.* maturely, fully III.vi.197

ryppet *n.* tumult, uproar VIII.xii.104

rypys *v.* ripens IV.Prol.13

rysp *n.* sedge II.ii.142; XII.Prol.152

ryspy *adj.* grating XII.Prol.152: R (C **rysp and redis**)

ryspys *n.* reeds, sedge VI.vi.68

ryvage *n.* shore, riverbank VI.v.44

ryvand *pr. p.* tearing IV.xi.11

sa *v.* say I.Prol.478; III.iii.13; IV.v.98

sabyll *n.* the colour black VII.Prol.167

sacre *v.* dedicate VI.i.144

sacrifyis *n.* sacrifice VI.iv.heading

sacryfy *v.* offer sacrifice to I.i.85; II.iv.58

sad *adj.* mournful, with something of the sense of heavy III.iii.12. of blows, etc., heavy, violent, massive XI.xi.47; XII.vi.148

safron *adj.* saffron, yellow (for **croceis**) IV.xii.112; XI.xv.18

saikleß *adj.* unmolested XII.x.13

sail, saill *n.* salle, hall VII.iii.45; VIII. iv.129; XIII.viii.40

sailrife *adj.* abounding in sails I.v.3

saisit *v.* seized III.ii.15

saisyn *n.* possession XIII.vi.164

saisyt *pa. p.* endowed VII.x.85

sakleß *adj.* guiltless VI.vii.14

sal *v.* shall I.iv.72. as first element in compounds: ~**be** III.iv.92. ~**behald** VI.ii.157. ~**beir**, ~**ber** II.xi.55; V.vi.43; VII.v.92. ~**do** II.xi.52

salf *adj.* safe I.vi.146

salfand *prep.* except I.Prol.155

salfgard *n.* safeguard XII.Prol.96

salfte, salfty *n.* safety I.vi.147; III.iv.141; VI.ii.67

salt *adj.* salt II.ii.21; III.iii.19; hence, bitter, vexatious XIII.Prol.98

salt *v.* shalt, shall II.Prol.11; III.ii.96; III. vi.111; IV.x.85; VI.ii.27

salue *adj.* safe I.vi.135

salue *v.* save II.iii.31; III.Prol.45

salus *v.* salute, greet XIII.Prol.168

salust *v.* greeted XII.v.90

salve *adj.* safe III.iii.115

salve *v.* save III.ii.39

salwyt *pa. p.* saved II.x.140

same *n.* lard VII.x.61

samekill *adj.* so large II.i.36

sammyn *adj.* same VI.iii.6

sammyn *adv.* in the same manner, at the same time III.ix.78. together V.vi.16

samony *adj.* so many II.i.2; III.x.111

sane *v.inf.* to say VI.Prol.125, 133

sangler *n.* wild boar X.xii.47

sanguane *n.* a blood-red colour VII.i.4

sanguynolent *adj.* blood-coloured X.v.141

sangwane, sangwyne *n.* and *adj.* blood-red colour, or cloth of such a colour VIII.x.61; XI.xv.11; XII.Prol.16; XII.ii.38

sans *prep.* without I.Prol.67, 128; I.xi.81; XII.xiii.70

sant *n.* saint VI.ix.8

saplynnys *n.* shoots, branches III.i.47

sapour *n.* savour, taste V.Prol.54; XI.xv.118: E (C **purpour schene**)

sark *n.* shirt XII.Prol.269

sarris *v.* injures, wounds XI.xiii.170

sary *adj.* sorry, pitiful II.iv.26

sarys *n.* sores, wounds (mental, not physical) VIII.i.36

satis *n.* seats I.iv.22

satisfyit *pa. p.* satisfied V.xi.11 (E, R, 53 **satyfyit**); VIII.x.52 (E, 53 **satifyit**)

sattil *v.* of troops, to fall back IX.xiii.28

satyfy, satyffy *v.* satisfy V.Prol.36, *Directioun.*70

sauch *n.* sallow or willow tree VII.x.73

savoryng *vbl.n.* something that gives a faint notion I.Prol. 44.

saw *n.* speech, discourse III.i.76; IV.Prol.10

saw *v.* save XI.xiv.10

saw *v.* sow VI.xiv.96; VII.ix.28; XIII.ix.78

saw *pa. p.* sown, planted IV.Prol.8

sawch *n.* the sallow or willow tree VIII.i.54

sawchnyng *vbl.n.* reconciliation X.xiv.176

sawcht *adj.* in agreement II.vii.48

sawyn *pa. p.* sawed II.i.6

sawys *n.* wise sayings I.ix.10

sax *adj.* six V.x.30

saxt *adj.* sixth *Contentis*

sayar *n.* author IX.Prol.27; *Exclamatioun.*29

sayd *pa. p.* said, aforesaid II.vi.90; V.ii.30

saykles *adj.* blameless II.ii.150

saymyt *pa. p.* seamed VI.vi.62

sayn *v.inf.* to say VI.Prol.99

sayn *v.pres.1 sg.* say III.ix.96

sayng *vbl.n.* saying I.Prol.123; I.Prol.288

sayr *adj.* sore, grievous, unhappy III.vii.10; IV.vi.heading

sayr *adv.* sorely I.v.25; IV.vi.3

saysyng *pr. p.* seizing IV.vii.77

saysyng *n.* possession X.xi.116

scaill *v.* pour down, be spilled XIII.Prol.22

scaithfull *adj.* harmful II.i.34

scald *v.* be scorched or burned IV.x.89. figuratively I.Prol.258

scalit *pa. p.* scattered, dispersed X.i.58

scant *adv.* scarcely I.Prol.366

scartis *v.* scratches XII.x.129

scawbart *n.* scabbard IV.v.160; XI.i.27 (R **scawart**)

schaddis *n.* clots (of blood) V.viii.97

schaddowist *v.* casts a shadow IV.Prol.2

schaddowit *v.* enwrapped, enfolded (*figuratively*) I.x.70

schaif *n.* sheaf IV.Prol.14

schaik *v.* shake. **all to ~** shake savagely VII.Prol.17

schaik *pa. p.* shaken I.iii.heading; II.viii.95. **to ~** shaken to bits I.viii.103

schakaris, schakeris *n.* ornaments or trimming made of thin metal plates V.vii.8; VI.iii.102. vibrating drops of dew XII.Prol.131

schake *pa. p.* shaken II.vii.75

schald *adj.* shallow, shoal I.iii.31, 90; III.Prol.40; III.viii.99

schaldis *n.* shoals, shallows I.iii.55; III.x.99; V.iv.60

schame *n.* modesty IV.ii.5; VIII.iii.60

schank, schankis *n.* the legs from knee to ankle I.vi.57. the trunk of a tree IV.viii.70, 76

schap *v.* planned, made arrangements IX.iii.8

schape *pa. p.* shaped I.iv.82; II.ii.113; VI.i.42

schar *v.* shear, divide VIII.ii.68

schare *v.* sheared, cut I.iv.92

scharp *adj.* keen, violent I.xi.54. sharp, savage VIII.vi.18

scharp *v.* sharpen XII.xiii.141

scharpit *v.* sharpened, made fierce, aroused (**asperat**) III.v.2

scharpyt *pa. p.* sharpened III.ix.87

schauld *adj.* shallow VII.xii.57

schaw *n.* grove I.vi.heading, 10; I.vii.42; I.x.47, 68

schaw *v.* show III.ix.39; V.xiv.100

schaw *pa. p.* shown I.vii.48; IV.ix.20

schawd *adj.* shoal, shallow V.xi.56

schawmys *n.* musical instruments of the oboe class IX.x.67

schawyng *pr. p.* shaving, cutting lightly in passing VIII.i.97

schawys *n.* groves III.x.49; V.Prol.2

sched *n.* the parting of the hair, the top of the crown II.xi.7

sched *pa. p.* cut, divided VI.ix.13

scheir *n.* a shear-like structure, the division of the body into legs III.vi.135

scheir *v.* cut III.iv.66. reap VII.xiii.40

schene *adj.* shining, glittering, beautiful III.vi.11

schent *v.* disgrace IV.Prol.102. destroy II.iv.33; II.i.2

schent *v.* profaned IV.viii.37

schent *pa. p.* corrupted, destroyed I.iii.54; IV.Prol.199

scherald, scheraldis *n.* turf VIII.iii.190 (E **scherardis**); XII.Prol.88; XII.iii.14

scherand *pr. p.* cutting, dividing IV.v.109; V.i.3; V.iv.107

schet *v.* shut IV.v.127

schete, schetis *n.* the rope attached to the lower corners of a sail III.viii.28, 84, 108; V.i.30; V.xiv.7. a sail, for **vela**

III.iv.111; III.vi.193

scheyn *adj.* shining, glittering; hence beautiful I.i.82; III.ii.114

schidis *n.* chips VII.i.103

schil *adj.* shrill V.iii.90

schipbrokyn *pa. p.* shipwrecked III.viii.92

schippit *v.* shipped, took aboard ship I.iii.38

schire *adj.* clear, complete, utter VIII.Prol.78

schirris *n.* sirs I.Prol.502

schod *pa. p.* shod, applied to cart-wheels with iron rims V.v.57

schorand *pr. p.* threatening VIII.iv.13; XII.xii.166

schore *adj.* steep, precipitous X.xi.122

schort *n.* short. **at** ~ near at hand II.xii.82

schort, schortis *v.* to make (time or a journey) to appear short, to beguile VI.x.37; VIII.v.75

schortly *adv.* in short I.Prol.259, 334

schot, schot wyndo *n.* a window that can be opened or shut on its hinges VII.Prol.129, 138

schot *v.* dashed, pressed forward II.vii.39

schote *n.* the action of shooting with the bow, and missiles collectively III.i.85

schotyng *vbl.n.* shooting V.ix.heading

schour *n.* shower IV.iv.66

schow *v.* shove VI.v.15

schowyn *v.inf.* to shove V.iv.95

schoys *n.* shoes VIII.viii.10

schrenkis *v.* shuns, avoids VIII.Prol.61

schrew, schrewis *n.* a wicked, evil-tempered person VI.viii.106. villains, the wicked, the damned IV.vi.58; V.ix.64: R; VI.ix.20

schrewit *adj.* vicious, fierce II.iv.53; IV.v.29; VI.i.41

schrewitly *adv.* severely, harshly VII.vi.134

schrewyt *adj.* vicious, fierce IV.v.57; V.ix.64

schrowd, schrowde *pa. p.* shrouded

IV.i.14; IX.v.12

schrowit *adj.* vicious, fierce XI.x.90

schrynkis *v.* recoils from, draws back I.Prol.189

schuddir *v.* tremble X.vi.112. **schuddrit** trembled II.i.72

schuddris *v.* scatters, breaks apart XII. xi.152. **schuddrit** scattered IX.xiii.48

schuldir, schulder *n.* shoulder I.vi.24; X.xiv.95

schuldir *n.* **in** ~ into separate pieces and fragments IX.vii.98. *See also* **to schuldris**

schup, schupe *v.* planned, attempted, arranged I.v.1; III.i.73

schurtis *v.* beguiles oneself V.Prol.7 (R, L, 53 **schortis**)

schute *v.* press, rush, dart II.vi.105

schydis *n.* split pieces of logs IV.ix.65

schydit *pa. p.* cut, split VI.iii.48

schyne *pa. p.* shone XIII.Prol.22

schypbrokkyn *pa. p.* shipwrecked IV.vii.24

schyre *adj.* clear, bright IV.v.188; V.i.5

sclaik *v.* slacken X.v.34; XI.xvii.48

sclakand *pr. p.* slackening, relaxing VIII.xii.83

sclane *pa. p.* slain VII.ix.72

sclavys *n.* slaves IX.v.114; X.Prol.128

sclentis *v.* strikes obliquely X.xiii.51

sclentyng *pr. p.* striking obliquely VII. viii.112

sclentys *v.* slants VII.vi.87

sconnys *n.* scones, round cakes VII.ii.15

scor *n.* score, as in a game I.Prol.490

scoryt *pa. p.* fractured, wrecked V.iv.91

scowrand *pr. p.* passing rapidly I.i.65

scrabbis *n.* crab apples VII.ii.18

screke *n.* shriek VII.Prol.108

scriptour *n.* pencase XII.Prol.305

scroggis *n.* brushwood VIII.vi.88

scroggit *pa. p.* stunted, dwarfed VIII. ix.120: 53 (C **scroggy bussys**)

scroggy *adj.* rough, covered with brushwood VIII.ix.120

scry *n.* cry II.v.32; XI.xvi.14

scryk *v.* shriek X.viii.122

scryke *n.* shriek IV.viii.111; VII.vi.125

scummand *pr. p.* skimming XII.viii.73

scurryvagis *n.* vagabonds VIII.Prol.68

scuyll *n.* school I.Prol.375

secludand *pr. p.* prohibiting, precluding XII.xii.4

seclude, secludis *v.* shut out, exclude I.x.heading. prevent from doing something I.iv.41, marginal note

see *n.* dwelling-place, seat of authority I.i.28

seg, sege *n.* man (poetic) VIII.Prol.4, 19

sege *n.* seat I.xii.4; XII.Prol.41; XIII. Prol.65

sege *v.* besiege IV.viii.36

segyß *n.* seats VI.iii.89

seid *n.* posterity IV.v.182

seik *adj.* sick VI.iv.80

seik *v.* set out for, go to III.iii.42. ~ **about** examine III.vi.141

seill *n.* joy, happiness VIII.Prol.173; X.v.100; XIII.x.20

seir *adj.* sore, painful VI.xii.heading

seir *adj.* separate, distinct, several I.Prol.87, 351; I.ii.32

sekyng *v.pres.3 pl.* seek IV.ii.9

selcouth *adj.* uncommon, marvellous VII.i.106; VIII.Prol.4; XIII.iii.12

self *adj.* same, identical I.Prol.229; VII. iv.140

selis *n.* sells VIII.Prol.104

selkouth *adj.* rare, marvellous III. viii.103

sellet *n.* a light leather helmet (French **salade**) VII.x.89

selvage *n.* border V.v.12; VII.vi.26

selwyn *pron.* self I.Prol.119; II.ii.133

semabill *adj.* like, similar I.Prol.388

sembland, semblant *n.* semblance, appearance I.vi.171; I.xi.43; IV.ix.8

semmys *n.* seams I.iii.49

sen *conj.* since, considering that I.Prol.436; VIII.ix.41

send *pa. p.* sent (*rhyming with end*) I.ix.117; I.x.heading; III.v.92

sene *v.inf.* to see IX.viii.98

sennonys *n.* sinews IX.x.77

sens, senß *n.* incense III.iii.56; IV.viii.95; VII.viii.28

sensymentis *n.* opinions, judgments XI.v.89

sent *v.inf.* to send X.i.111

sentence, sentencis *n.* sense, substance, thought I.Prol.54, 396; V.Prol.41; VI.Prol.13

sentencyus *adj.* full of wisdom I.Prol.296; VI.Prol.75

sentens *n.* sense, substance, thought I.Prol.133, 147, 289, 309, 352, 356, 365

senȝeoreis, senȝeory *n.* lordship, estates, rule I.v.85; IV.v.104, 112; VII.i.99

sepulcre *n.* tomb VI.iii.40

sepultur, sepulture *n.* tomb V.xii.180; VI.iii.148; VI.v.145. burial-place (*strictly speaking, representing* **sepulto**, *the one buried*) III.i.78

sequestrate *v.* suppress, seclude XI.iii.76

serchyn *v.inf.* to examine VIII.v.78

sergis *n.* cierges, tapers, candles XIII.ix.103

sermond, sermondis *n.* general talk, discourse, speech I.iv.100; I.viii.50; I.xi.110

sermonyng *vbl.n.* speaking, talking V.xii.98

sermoun *n.* talk in general I.v.1

seroppys *n.* medicinal or preservative syrups XII.Prol.145

serpentyne *adj.* venomous (not crooked) VII.vi.22

serß *v.* search I.vi.5; II.i.48

seruyabill *adj.* eager to serve XII.ii.88

serve *v.* deserve I.Prol.78

serviatis *n.* table-napkins I.xi.17

servyt *pa. p.* deserved XI.xvi.36

seß *v.* cease II.ii.61

sesit *pa. p.* endowed with property, established in an office or dignity XII.xiii.13

sessing *v.inf.* or *vbl.n.* to cease, ceasing VI.ii.48

sesson *n.* an indefinite space of time III.v.35. **in the meyn** ~ meanwhile V.xiii.33

sesson *n.* of game, the time of finest condition I.iv.98, marginal note

sessonabil *adj.* suitable III.viii.48

sesyng *v.inf.* to cease IV.iii.16

sesyt *pa. p.* placed, fixed VII.Prol.80; VIII.iv.93

set *conj.* since II.iii,67. although I.iv.86, 104; I.vi.118

set *n.* seat, residence III.vi.188

set *n.* site III.ii.80

set *v.* spread out nets to catch animals IV.iii.58

set *v.* count, place value on III.iii.75; III.ix.118

set *v.* sat I.iv.30

set *pa. p.* having a specified disposition or inclination II.ix.58

sete *n.* site, location III.ii.108. mansion or house in the Zodiac XIII.Prol.2. **in** ~ in situ VII.xi.40

setis *n.* men posted to intercept game IV.iii.58

settis *n.* slips used for planting XII.Prol.133

seuch *n.* furrow V.xii.168

seuchand *pr. p.* ploughing VIII.xi.77

sew *v.* pursue, follow X.ii.125

sew *v.* sow VII.v.140

sew *v.* sowed II.ii.70; XII.ix.49

sewane *n.* name of a herb (see note) XII.Prol.145

seweris *n.* servers at table I.xi.25

sewch *n.* furrow VII.iii.20; IX.vii.147. trench, gap VIII.iv.134

sewch *v.* plough, literal or figurative III.vii.49; VIII.76; X.v.16

sewchquhand *pr. p.* ploughing V.iii.102 (R, 53 **souchand**)

sewyt *pa. p.* fastened, fixed III.x.13

sey *n.* the sea II.iii.60. a heavy swell I.iii.38

seyd *n.* seed (in various senses) IV.Prol.8; XI.Prol.199

seyk *adj.* sick V.xi.99

seyll *n.* joy IV.xii.26; V.i.46

seyr *adj.* many, several I.i.23; III.ii.139; III.

vi.36, 210

seys *v.* sees, watches, keeps guard III.iv.60

seysit *pa. p.* established VII.iv.190

seywart *n.* a position towards the sea III. viii.123

sich *adj.* such I.Prol.264

sichand *pr. p.* sighing I.vi.114

siclike, sik *adj.* such I.i.18; I.ix.89

sikane *pron.* such a one I.Prol.328; I.viii.17

sike *n.* brook VII.Prol.60

sikkyr *adj.* safe, secure VI.xi.72

sikkyrly *adv.* certainly I.Prol.445

silly *adj.* deserving of pity; helpless I.vi.69; V.xiii.53; VI.vii.21; IX.v.137. a conventional epithet applied to sheep VII.Prol.77; IX.vi.73

sillys *n.* large beams, here used as missiles IX.ix.19 (E **schillys**, L, B **schillis**, 53 **shotys**)

similitudes *n.* comparisons drawn between two things I.Prol.196

singular *adj.* of a fight or combat, single IX.vi.130

sipplyn *n.* sapling VII.xiii.85

sistir son *n.* sister's son I.v.76 and 102, marginal notes

skaill *v.* scatter, pour out, spill IV.iii.59; IV.v.32

skaill *pa. p.* scattered, spread IV.ix.74; XIII.i.14

skaith *n.* injury, harm II.i.61; III.v.115

skalis, skalys *v.* scatters IV.iv.67; IV.v.42

skalit *pa. p.* scattered, spread I.vii.109; VI.xi.58

skant *n.* scantiness, scanty supply I.iv.39

skar *adj.* frightened, shy XII.v.186

skar *v.* take fright, be scared VII.iv.166

skarrit *v.* took fright VII.xii.180

skarthis *n.* a kind of bird, the cormorant V.iii.49

skat *n.* tax, tribute XI.Prol.24

skath *n.* harm II.v.41; II.xi.9; VI.iv.9

skeich *adj.* skittish XII.vi.134

skeich *v.* take fright IX.iii.108

skeichit *v.* took fright, shied VII.xii.152

skelleis, skelleys *n.* shallows V.iv.89; V.xiv.70

skippar *n.* the captain of a ship, or the pilot I.iii.39

skowgis *n.* shadows VI.v.94

skowgit *pa. p.* shaded, sheltered, protected VIII.vi.90

skowgy *adj.* shady VII.ix.54; VIII.x.9

skowland *pa. p.* forbidding, threatening VII.xii.19

skoyr *n.* mark, finish line V.vi.70

skroggy *adj.* rough, covered with brushwood VIII.vi.84 (53 **skrokky**)

skrymmys *v.* darts XII.v.68 (R **skymmys**)

skug, skugg, skuggis *n.* shadow VI.iv.74; VII.Prol.47; VIII.iv.202

skuggyt *pa. p.* shaded, protected VII.i.24

skul *n.* a drinking vessel, goblet III.i.125; VII.ii.89

skummand *pr. p.* skimming, passing lightly over IV.v.149

skurgyng *vbl.n.* whipping VII.v.133

skynk, skynkis *v.* pour out and offer (wine) I.iv.67; VII.ii.62, 90; VIII.iv.200

skynnar *n.* ? flayer; brigand VIII. Prol.133

skyppar *n.* the captain or pilot V.iv.31

skyppyt *pa. p.* skipped (of men in a foot-race, for **transeat**) V.vi.69

skyrlys *n.* cries, screams II.xi.1

skyrt, skyrtis *n.* skirt I.x.54. edges, borders VII.ix.101; XI.vi.44

sla *v.* slay II.iii.43

sladis *n.* valleys, dells XI.xi.84

slaid *v.* slid VI.v.112

slaik *v.* relax, relieve I.iii.99

slak *n.* small valley VIII.x.91; XI.x.69; XII.Prol.46

slang *v.* slung, flung I.i.76; II.v.49

slakis, slakkis *v.* slackens, loosens III. viii.28; V.xiii.123

slaw *pa. p.* slain VI.vii.67

slays *n.* the instrument used in weaving to beat up the weft VI.xvi.29

sle *adj.* cunning, skilful, able, sly, in good and bad senses I.vii.66; I.x.i;

V.iii.95

sleip *v.* slip VII.vi.96

sleipry *adj.* inducing sleep V.xiv.52

sleipryfe *adj.* bringing sleep IV.ix.28 (R, 53 **slepery**)

slekie *adj.* smooth, sleek VII.Prol.38: 53 (C **slekit**)

slekit, slekyt *pa. p.* smoothed, polished VII.Prol.38; VII.xiii.79; XI.i.94. of words, specious, artful I.x.27; I.xi.34; IV.Prol.191

slely *adv.* slyly I.vi.77

slepy *adj.* sleep-producing VII.xii.127

slevit *v.* thrust, caused to slip into VI.iv.25

slew *v.* struck (fire from flint) I.iv.33

slewthit *pa. p.* delayed XII.ix.62

slewch *v.* slew XII.vi.105

sloggorn *n.* battle cry VII.x.87

sloknyng *vbl.n.* slackening, relaxing V.xii.heading

sloknyt *pa. p.* extinguished VIII.iv.183; VIII.ix.2

slokyt *pa. p.* quenched, made to burn less strongly V.xii.59 (E, R, 53 **sloknit**)

slonk *n.* a shallow depression XI.xi.84

slop *n.* breach, gap II.viii.77

slop *v.* breach, make gaps IX.viii.110

sloppand *pr. p.* breaching X.viii.6

sloppit *pa. p.* pierced, breached, left with gaps IX.viii.120

slotteris *v.* is slothful or slovenly IV.Prol.165

slottis *n.* door bars VII.iii.79; VII.x.22

slottry *adj.* sluggish VI.iv.87

slowch *n.* the outer skin of a snake II.viii.60

slowch *n.* a watery bog II.x.83

sloyk *v.* quench, extinguish II.xi.14

sluggardry *n.* sloth IV.Prol.165 (L, B **sluggardy**)

sluggart *adj.* sluggish, slovenly VI.v.9

slung *n.* sling IX.ix.134

slycht *adj.* smooth, adroit IV.Prol.240

slycht *n.* skill, in a good sense III. Prol.8. a ruse IV.iii.74. cunning,

deceit IV.vi.31

slyddir *adj.* slippery XIII.v.49

slyde *adj.* slippery; changeably, uncertain; sly VII.vi.28; X.v.173

slyde *pa. p.* slid V.iv.34

slydry *adj.* slippery II.viii.61; V.vi.80, 85

slyke *n.* mud, gravel VI.v.6. a beach of such I.viii.83

slyppis *v.trans.* causes to move with a slipping motion IX.ix.61

smake *n.* a mean fellow, a rascal VIII. Prol.133

smart *adj.* painful, severe, biting IV.Prol.71; V.v.59; V.xii.63

smertly *adv.* speedily VIII.iv.205

smor *v.* smother IX.Prol.85

smotterit *pa. p.* soiled, stained VI.v.13

smottyt *pa. p.* besmirched, befouled V.vii.91 (53 **smottin**)

smowt *adj.* of weather, fair, calm XIII. viii.30

smuyr *v.* smother, suppress XI.Prol.48

smy *n.* rogue XIII.Prol.131

smyddy *n.* blacksmith's forge, smithy VIII.vii.107

smyte *v.* XIII.i.42. *See* **to smyte**

smyte *pa. p.* smitten II.vii.111; IV.viii.76; V.xii.63; VI.v.120

smytht *n.* blacksmith VI.Prol.159

snak *n.* a short time, a snatch VIII. vii.86

sned *pa. p.* snipped, cut XI.i.14; XII. iv.126

sneith *adj.* polished XI.i.94

snell *adj.* bitter, keen, severe VII. Prol.43, 139

sneryng *pr. p.* of a horse, snorting VI.iv.201 (E **swermand**, R **swirlling**)

snod *n.* a fillet or band confining the hair V.xiii.24

snog *adj.* sleek, smooth, neat XII. Prol.186 (R, 53 **snod**)

snoif *v.* twirl, twist VIII.vii.100

snokis *v.* sniffs, smells V.ii.99

snor *n.* the snort of a horse X.x.72

snowtis *n.* the prows of ships VIII.xii.2

snyb *v.* check sharply X.Prol.15

snypand *pr. p.* cutting, biting VII. Prol.50

sobir, sobyr *adj.* poor, mean, trifling; moderate, not showy V.xii.47; X.xi.23

socery *n.* witchcraft I.Prol.208

soft *adv.* softly, silently IX.iii.203

soir *adj.* sorrel; a technical term of falconry applied to a hawk of the first year that has not moulted and still has its red plumage VII.Prol.125

sokkis *n.* ploughshares VII.x.79; XI.vii.55

solace *n.* pleasure, entertainment I.vi.34

solacius *adj.* giving pleasure or entertainment VIII.xii.106

solang *compound* so long VI.xiv.14

sold *n.* a sum or quantity III.i.91

solemnyt *adj.* solemn, ceremonious V.ii.24 (E **solempt**)

solemnytly *adv.* solemnly, ceremoniously V.xi.7

solist *adj.* characterized by solicitude or care VIII.vii.71

solist *v.* urge, importune II.x.132

solysting *vbl.n.* urging, importunity II.ii.74

somys *n.* the ropes or chains attaching a draught-horse to a plough VII.x.79

sond *n.* sound, a narrow bay VII.v.49

sondyr *phr.* **in ~** apart V.x.67

sonk, sonkis *n.* a. seat of turf III.iv.30; V.vii.44; VII.ii.14

sop *n.* a fragment VI.vi.75

sop *n.* sap IV.ix.85

sop *n.* a compact body or group III. viii.138; VII.xi.154; IX.viii.109. a cloud of mist or smoke I.vi.176; V.xii.51

sorand *pr. p.* soaring V.ix.48

sort *n.* kind, nature III.ix.66; IV.v.77. set, band, company IV.iv.7

sort *v.* allot III.viii.7

sory *adj.* miserable IV.i.42; dismal, painful VII.v.101

sossary, sossery *n.* enchantment, sorcery IV.vii.30; IV.ix.42 (R, 53 sorcery)

souchand *pr. p.* rushing, murmuring V.iii.102: R, 53

soundand *pr. p.* resounding, rustling III.vi.165

sours *n.* fountainhead I.Prol.9

soursand *pr. p.* of a bird, rising after seizing its prey XI.xiv.74; XII.v.63: L (C **sorand**)

sovir *adj.* safe, sure, certain I.iv.15; I.v.105; III.ii.20; III.v.57; IV.x.64

sovirly *adv.* safely, surely I.v.30; III. xi.46, 65

sovm *n.* load, charge XI.viii.88

sovn *n.* sound IV.i.50

sovyr *adj.* safe VIII.x.40; X.iv.45

sowchand *pr. p.* cutting, ploughing X.iv.11

sowchquhyng *vbl.n.* sighing, murmur XII.xi.9 (E **swouching**, R, 53 **souching**)

sowder *n.* solder VIII.vii.140

sowk *v.* suck III.vi.133; IV.xii.83

sowkand, sowking *pr. p.* sucking (of whirlpool sands) I.iii.42; III.vi.74; V.v.74; VII.v.45

sown *n.* sound IV.ii.66

sownd *adv.* soundly, profoundly I.x.45

sownd, sowndis *n.* a narrow channel III.vi.108; III.viii.8

sowne *n.* sound I.ii.4

sowpe *v.* weary, tire XII.xi.6

sowpit *pa. p.* exhausted, sunk (in sorrow, sleep) III.ix.80 (R **sowperit**)

sowpyt *pa. p.* soaked V.iv.35; VIII.Prol.5

sowr *adj.* sour, bitter, unpleasant X.vii.13

sowrssys *n.* springs, fountainheads VIII.ii.12

soyn *adv.* soon I.vii.127

soyr *adj.* reddish brown XII.Prol.27

spait *n.* spate, flood VII.Prol.19

spakis *n.* spokes VI.ix.185

spald, spaldis *n.* shoulder V.ii.118; X.xii.60; X.xiv.157

spaldyt *v.* laid flat on the ground XII.v.138; XII.v.204

spa men, spamen *n.* prophets IV.ii.29;

V.ix.63; VI.iii.77

span *v.* grasp, lay hold of III.iii.111; III.v.13; IV.x.98

spang *n.* jerk, a sudden movement V.ix.60; VII.viii.50

spang *v.* spring, leap V.ix.29

spangit *v.* struck, jerked, cast XII.vi.76

spanʒellis *n.* spaniels IX.Prol.50 (E **spalʒellis**, R **spanʒartis**, 53 **spanʒeartis**)

spar *n.* beam, rafter VIII.i.18

sparkand *pr. p.* issuing like sparks III. viii.132

sparkis *n.* sparks IX.ix.68; particles of light XII.Prol.39; drops XII.vi.76; men (in derogatory sense) VI.Prol.58. *See also* **sperkis**

sparkyt *adj. pa. p.* bespattered IX.xii.64. *See also* **sperklyt**

sparpellis *v.* scatters XI.xiii.8

sparpellit *pa. p.* sprinkled XI.xii.50

sparris *n.* rafters, roof beams I.xi.63

spaying *vbl.n.* prophecy I.vi.148

spayit *v.* prophesied II.iv.89

species *Latin n.* a classification based on the particular thing among many to which the looks are turned, hence a particular sort I.Prol.371

specify *v.* make definite and particular mention of IV.Prol.18

sped *v.* reflexive, went with speed I.iv.62, 96

speicht *n.* woodpecker VII.iii.91

speid *n.* **cum** ~ be successful I.Prol.383; VIII.i.69

speid hand *v.* hurry, make haste IV.x.91

speil, speill *v.* climb II.viii.11; IX.ii.10

speir *n.* spear VII.Prol.62

speir *n.* sphere II.v.1; IV.ix.18; VII. Prol.11; VIII.iii.104

speir *v.* ask, inquire, question I.vi.180; III.ii.155; IV.v.113. inquire one's way II.vi.52

speland *pr. p.* climbing VI.viii.80

speldit, speldyt *pa. p.* stretched, spread out V.vii.19; VI.ix.132, 185; VIII. viii.66

spelis *v.* climbs VII.viii.83

spell *v.* read slowly, with difficulty I.Prol.284

spelys *v.* climbs IV.vii.86

sper *v.* inquire one's way VII.iv.113

sperand *pr. p.* questioning I.vi.114

speris *v.* asks, questions VI.ix.73

sperkis *n.* small traces of feeling or sentiment IX.Prol.4

sperklyt *pa. p.* sprinkled, bespattered II.viii.114

sperris *n.* beams II.viii.19

spetis *n.* roasting-spits V.ii.117

spetit *pa. p.* spitted, transfixed IX.xii.90

speyr *n.* sphere III.viii.13

spicery *n.* spice-shop XII.Prol.143

spilis *n.* piles, stakes IX.x.20

spill *v.* put to death, destroy IV.Prol.54; IV.vi.73, 83

spill *v.intrans.* perish III.ii.39

spilt *v.* destroyed, killed XII.x.123

spilys *n.* splinters, chips IX.ix.42

spiretis *n.* spirits VI.Prol.82

spiritual *adj. and n.* (one) concerned with ecclesiastical things VIII. Prol.47; XI.xv.2

spleyn *n.* spleen, bad temper XIII.Prol.62

spousale *adj.* pertaining to marriage VII.ix.39

spowß *v.* marry IV.x.27

spousage, spowsage *n.* marriage, wedlock IV.iii.26; IV.iv.89; IV.vi.70

spowsit *pa. p.* married III.v.93

spowt *pa. p.* spouted III.viii.118

spraichis *n.* shrieks, screams XI.i.82

sprangis *n.* brightly coloured stripes XII. Prol.22

sprauch *n.* scream, outcry IV.xii.60

spray *n.* twig IV.x.9; VIII.Prol.30

sprayngis *n.* brightly coloured stripes VII. ii.82; IX.vi.58

spreit *n.* spirit III.ix.44

spreith *n.* plunder, booty II.vii.27

spreitleß *adj.* fainting (for **exanimis**) IV.xii.55

sprent *n.* leap, bound XI.xiv.68

sprent *v.* sped, sprinted, leaped III.iii.52;

V.ix.158; V.xiv.66

sprent *pa. p.* sprinkled (with blood) IV.i.43

spreth *n.* plunder I.viii.62; II.xii.6

sprete, spretis *n.* spirit, ghost I.Prol.274; III.v.150

spretely *adv.* with spirit IX.iii.116: R

sprety *adj.* vigorous, spirited XI.viii.26

sprewland *pr. p.* sprawling V.viii.115

springald, springaldis *n.* young man, stripling VI.v.28; VI.xiii.11; VII.iii.32

springis *n.* tunes VI.ii.86

sprutlis *n.* spots V.ii.90

sprutlit, sprutlyt *pa. p.* spotted II.iv.32; VII.iii.91

spryng *n.* tune, song V.xiii.135

spryng *pa. p.* sprung IX.iv.38

sprynkill *v.* wriggle, dart quickly XI.xiv.71. **sprynkland** *pa. p.* XII. Prol.56

spulȝe *n.* plunder I.v.106; I.vii.119; IV.iii.7. the individual piece of plunder ~ ... mony ane V.vii.54

spulȝe *v.* spoil, plunder I.viii.61; I.xii.7

spulȝeyt *pa. p.* robbed, plundered V.iv.119

spur *v.* hasten, hurry, proceed I.xi.31; VII.iii.19

spurrand *pr. p.* urging on IV.x.101

spyll *v.* destroy IV.vi.159

squair, squar *adj.* heavy, strong **charyot quhelys** ~ V.iii.22, 75, 107; VII.viii.17

squeil *v.* of cows, low, cry out VIII.vi.112

squeland *pr. p.* of cows, lowing VIII.iv.77

squyar *n.* squire, armour-bearer (for **armiger**) V.v.21

sqwat *n.* a heavy fall or bump, and the noise made by falling X.vii.108

stabill *v.* stabilize, calm, settle IV.viii.44; V.xiii.38

stabillyng *vbl.n.* of horses, stabling IX.vii.44

stablit *pa. p.* kept in stables VI.iv.102

stad *v.* stood V.vii.33

stad *pa. p.* stood, placed II.ii.17; V.xii.69; VI.x.65

staf slyng, staf slung *n.* type of ballista, catapult VII.xi.111; IX.ix.134

staffage *adj.* unruly, stubborn XII.vi.134

stage *n.* position, level, step in a process XII.i.112

stageis *n.* day's journeys I.vi.107, marginal note

stail, staill *n.* position, place of ambush IV.viii.123; XI.x.96; XI.xii.4

stair *n.* fixed, look, stare I.viii.3. condition of staring amazement or horror IV.ii.58

stair *v.* gaze I.iii.56

stair *v.* thrust (a weapon) into III.iv.56

stakit *pa. p.* struck, stuck through VII.v.48

stakyt *pa. p.* placed XII.iii.72

stallyt *pa. p.* installed X.iv.124

stalk *v.* walk with a stately and dignified stride (representing **progredior, subibant, discurrent**) III.v.33; VIII. vi.108; IX.iii.204

stalkand *pr. p.* moving softly VI.iii.82

stalkar *n.* one who moves softly, tending animals (**pastor**) IV.ii.40

stammyt *pa. p.* prowed IX.iii.104

stanch *v.* satisfy, extinguish III.iv.107; III.vi.33

stanche *v.intrans.* come to an end I.v.110

stanching *v.inf.* to repress, to extinguish I.ii.21

stand *n.* place of standing, boundary fence (for **limen**) V.vi.56

standyn *pa. p.* stood II.i.78

stangis *n.* stings II.iv.20, 25

stangyng *vbl.n.* stings VII.xii.124

stank *n.* stagnant pool VI.v.57; VIII.ii.48

stannand *pr. p.* standing III.v.43

stannyris *n.* gravel and stones at the edges of a river XII.Prol.60

stant *v.* stands I.Prol.493; IV.iii.50

stanyt *v.* stoned II.ii.47

stanyt *pa. p.* of fruit, having pits III. ix.111

stapillis *n.* pillars, columns; or the holds for a hasp, hook or bolt II.viii.72

star *adj.* rough, stiff, violent VI.vi.68

staris *n.* stairs XII.xi.132

stark *adj.* strong, substantial VIII.x.40;

XII.x.122

starn *n.sg.* star I.vi.119; III.viii.19

starnschoit *n.* meteor V.ix.69

starny *adj.* starry IX.vii.13

starnys *n.* stars III.iii.106; III.viii.30;
IV.v.8

starnyt *pa. p.* star-studded V.xiv.22

startland, **startling** *pr. p.* capering,
mettlesome IV.iv.57; XIII.ix.63

starve *v.* die (not specialized to dying
of hunger) IV.xii.33; X.xiv.127

staturis *n.* statues VI.xv.3

statut *v.* establish, ordain I.v.63

statw *n.* statue II.iii.80; II.v.20

staw *v.* stole V.xiii.104; VI.iv.205

stay *adj.* steep, sheer III.viii.56; XII.
xii.144

stayn *n.* stone V.iv.104

stayr *n.* stare I.xi.46

sted, stede, stedis, steid *n.* place I.i.5,
84; III.iv.71; III.viii.30; IV.vi.61;
VI.Prol.89

steid, steyd *n.* war horse IV.iv.10;
IX.ii.37

steir *n.* rudder, helm V.iv.31

steir *n.* stare I.xi.39

steir *v.* stir, rouse, wake I.iii.68; I.x.7;
IV.ii.26

steir *v.* steer I.xi.55

steir *v.* either stir or steer II.vi.93;
V.x.64

steirburd *n.* the right-hand side of a
ship V.iv.6

stek *n.* closing I.v.113, marginal note

stekit *pa. p.* closed VI.i.81

stekit *pa. p.* stuck, stabbed IV.xii.40;
IX.vi.60

stellyng *vbl.n.* a placing in position. ~
place place of shelter XI.x.95

stend, stendis *n.* leap X.x.72; XII.vi.59;
XII.xi.162

stent, stentis *v.* set up, erect III.viii.26;
IX.iv.120. extend, stretch out III.
iv.111. hang with curtains of garlands
IV.ix.67

stent *pa. p.* extended, distended
IX.vii.31

stentit *v.* stationed, fixed II.i.31

stentit *pa. p.* placed, fixed I.xi.7; VII.
iii.24

stentys *v.* erects XI.ii.22

stenyt *v.* stained III.i.55

step *pa. p.* advanced. **far ~ in age** old
VI.v.19; VII.xii.78

stepyt *pa. p.* steeped, soaked VI.vi.75

sterage *n.* motion, stirring II.xi.82; IV.v.4

sterand *pr. p.* full of energetic movement (of horses). ~ **stedys** coursers
V.Prol.10

steris *v.* stirs III.v.118; IV.v.109

sterit *pa. p.* steered VII.i.170

sterit *v.* stirred II.ii.27

sterrit *pa. p.* star-studded I.v.55

sterve *v.* die II.iii.88

sterysman *n.* steersman, pilot III.iv.114

stevin, stevyn *n.* voice, song III.iii.54;
III.vi.196, 208; VI.Prol.70

stevin, stevynnys *n.* prow, stem I.i.65;
III.viii.53; V.v.14, 137

stevin, stevyn *v.* steer V.i.57; VII.i.22

stew *n.* smoke, vapour, dust III.viii.139,
148; VII.vii.132; VIII.iii.23

steyng *n.* sharpened stake, stick III.ix.87

stikkit *v.* impaled I.i.80

stile *n.* style I.Prol.492; VII.xi.4

still *n.* stillness, silence II.v.7

stilland *pr. p.* distilling VIII.iv.32

stobys *n.* little branches, sticks XI.ii.18

stoir *n.* abundance, stock, supplies XIII.
Prol.8. stock, animals kept for breeding
XIII.Prol.44

stok *n.* stock, the trunk of a tree IV.viii.76:
R, L, 53 (*cancelled in* C, B). applied
contemptuously to a pagan idol or
sacred image X.Prol.154

stok swerd, stok swerdis *n.* stabbing, thrusting sword VII.xi.58; XII.v.205

stokis *n.* swords with blades of a triangular or
square section VII.xi.59

stokit *v.* stuck, thrust IX.vii.140

stokyn *pa. p.* stuck, stabbed II.viii.98

stomok *n.* taste, inclination, desire XIII.vi.76

stond, stondis *n.* pang, shock, thrill XII.vii.97.
time for doing something, hour (of death)

XI.xv.139

stonyst *v.* astonished III.iv.95

stonyt *pa. p.* of an animal, having testicles IV.Prol.59 (E **stonich**)

stoppyn *v.inf.* to stop XI.i.44

stormstad *adj.* stormstead III.iii.heading

storour *n.* keeper of livestock VII.viii.23, 75

stot *n.* act of rebounding IX.xi.10

stot *v.* rebound X.vi.96

stottis *n.* steers VI.i.79; VI.iv.16

stound *n.* moment II.x.80. time, opportunity XII.xii.82

stoundis *v.* throbs, becomes acutely painful X.x.135

stour *n.* battle VII.viii.117. tumult, uproar, storm I.iii.26; III.viii.57

stour *n.* stake, pole IX.viii.149

stouth *n.* an act done by stealth XII.Prol.212

stovis *n.* steam, mist; or heating apparatus? *see note to* VII.Prol.89

stovys *n.* vapours XII.Prol.46

stownd *n.* moment VI.v.75

stowr, stowris *n.* tumult, uproar, storm III.v.16; III.viii.100; IV.x.82. a cloud of spray III.vi.130

stowris *n.* poles, stakes VII.vi.128

stowris *v.* rises in a cloud II.iv.16

stowt *adj.* proud, haughty, hardy *Contentis*

stowtar *adj.* more strenuous or vigorous V.i.38

stowtnes *n.* pride, arrogance I.viii.64

stowyt *pa. p.* sheared, cut VI.viii.41

stra *n.* straw, used with reference to low value I.Prol.33

stragill *n.* at the ~ in straggling order XII.xi.4

straik *n.* blow II.i.72; IX.vi.46: R

strait *adj.* narrow III.vi.108; III.x.63. tight III.iv.111

strake, strakis *n.* blow II.iv.5; VI.ix.51; VII.v.133; XII.xiii.18

strakis *v.* strokes IV.Prol.189

strampand *pr. p.* treading heavily VIII.ix.124: E (C **stampand**)

strand, strandis *n.* stream I.Prol.342; VII.

xi.54; XII.Prol.60 and 188; XII.ii.104

strang, strange *adj.* strong IV.Prol.263; IV.x.18; VIII.viii.124

strange *adj.* strange I.Prol.269, 378; IV.x.29

strater *adj.* more narrow or confining I.Prol.290

straucht *v.* stretched, reached III.ix.81; IX.ix.81

strech *adv.* straightway VI.xiv.61

strecht *adj.* straight, narrow VII.viii.36

strecht *pa. p.* stretched out V.vii.25

strek *adj.* straight IX.vi.23

strek *adv.* in a straight course III.ii.123; V.i.58

strekand *pr. p.* stretching II.viii.62; III.iii.53; V.v.64

streke, strekis *v.* stretch, extend I.vii.121; III.vi.110; III.viii.102; III.ix.9

strekyng *pr. p.* stretching III.x.46

stremaris *n.* banners I.iv.46

strenth *n.* strength I.x.15. a stronghold, strong point (**arx**) III.ii.133; VI.i.3

strenthing *v.inf.* to strengthen II.viii.28

strenthing *pr. p.* strengthening, fortifying VI.Prol.60

strenthty, strenthy *adj.* strong VII.x.22; VIII.x.19 (E **strenthly**); XI.viii.13

strenthyast *adj.* strongest VII.xii.113

strenys *v.* constrains IV.Prol.37; IX.v.160

strenyt *v.* constrained, confined VI.vi.22

strike *v.* make one's way III.viii.9

strive *n.* strife VII.x.24

stro *n.* straw XII.xiv.22

strow *v.* strew VI.xv.89

strugling *pr. p.* struggling III.iv.138 (E **strongling**, R **strukling**)

stryfe *v.* strive V.iii.9

strynd, strynde *n.* strain (of descent), lineage VIII.viii.129. family line VI.x.47

stryngis *n.* strings, the eye-strings that were supposed to crack at death VI.v.131

strynkill *v.* sprinkle XI.ii.61

strynkillit *pa. p.* sprinkled VI.x.18

strynkland *pr. p.* sprinkling IV.ix.27

stude *n.* stud-horse VII.iv.202; XI.xi.87

stude *v.* was in a particular state or condition **scho ~ syk aw** III.v.49

studeis *v.* considers, applies one's mind to VII.vi.94

studeyng *vbl.n.* contemplation, mental effort XII.xi.113

studis *n.* stud-horses VII.viii.22. horse-stables XI.x.19

studyus *adj.* carefully attentive I.Prol.309

stuffyt *v.* garrisoned IX.ii.14

stummerit, **stummyrryt**, **stumryt** *v.* stumbled V.vi.80; X.ix.83; XII.xiv.45

stunnys *v.* shock, dismay XI.i.44

stupefac, **stupefak** *pa. p.* stupefied V.xi.87; VII.ii.34

sturt *n.* trouble, fighting, strife VII. vi.48; VII.viii.heading; VIII.ix.86. woe, vexation II.ii.59; IV.Prol.89

sturt *v.* attack VII.v.40

sturtyn *adj.* vexatious VIII.Prol.15

stuthis *n.* studs, knobs, ornaments XII. xiv.132

stuyr *adj.* big, powerful, violent V.viii.20; XI.xi.45

sty *n.* contemptuously, a habitation VI.Prol.168

styddeis, **styddeys** *n.* anvils VII.x.67; VIII.vii.116, 180

styf *adj.* stout, stalwart, massive IV.iv.5

stykkit *pa. p.* transfixed; garnished IV.v.163

styll *n.* style, name and titles I.vi.125, marginal note

styng, **styngis** *n.* club, spear IX.viii.126, 149

stynt, **styntis** *v.* stop, make pause, cut short I.iv.53, 59; III.v.41; IV.Prol.63, 261

styntyng *v.inf.* to stop XI.ii.91

styntyng *vbl.n.* stopping XI.xvii.14

styrkis *n.* young bullocks III.iv.78; V.ii.114; V.vi.75

styth *adj.* unyielding, stiff, stout, fierce V.iv.64 (53 **stif**); V.viii.5 (R **stiff**);

XI.xi.45

stythly *adj.* stiff VII.Prol.132

stythly *adv.* strongly, severely V.vii.109 (R, 53 **stifly**)

subcharge *n.* a second dish or course XIII.ix.118

subiectum *Latin n.* that which is spoken of I.Prol.373

substans *n.* essential nature, essence I.Prol.458

subtell *adj.* skilful, clever I.Prol.305. cunning, crafty IV.Prol.239

subtilite *n.* craftiness, cunning I.xi.48

subuersioun, **subvertioun** *n.* over-throw, demolition II.Prol.4; VIII. vii.61

succudrus *adj.* arrogant XIII.vi.111 (R **sucquedry**, 53 **sucquerdry**)

succurs, **succurß** *n.* succour, assistance III.ii.156 (E, R **succouris**, L **succuris**); III.x.22 (R, B, 53 **succour**); VIII.iii.54 (E **suckyr**, R **succoure**)

suddill *v.* soil, defile XII.ii.124

sudiornys *v.* sojourns XIII.xi.80

sudron *adj.* and *n.* southern; English as distinguished from Scots I.Prol.111, 113

sufferance *n.* sanction, permission I.iv.80

sufferis, **suffir**, **suffyr** *v.* permits VI.ii.35; V.xii.94. endure III.ix.75

suffysyt *v.* sufficeth V.Prol.58

sugurate *adj.* dulcet, sweet I.Prol.29

sukkyn *pa. p.* of breast-feeding, sucked VIII.x.81

suld *v.* should III.Prol.35

suldbe *compound* should be I.ii.35; I.ix.96; IV.v.100

suldist *v.pres.2 sg.* should VI.vii.84

suldyn *v.pres.3 pl.* should XI.viii.100

sulphuryus *adj.* sulphurous VII.viii.94

sulȝart *adj.* bright, dazzling XII.Prol.64

sulȝe *n.* soil IV.i.76; VII.Prol.132

sum, **summyn** *pron.* some I.Prol.282; IV.iii.42

superexpendyt *pa. p.* spent (time) wastefully *Directioun*.31

supernale *adj.* heavenly XII.Prol.50

suppit *v.* drank in VI.vi.64

supple *n.* assistance, succour I.Prol.465; I.viii.136; II.iii.70; III.x.105

suppoß *v.* imperative introducing a proposal or suggestion or a hypothetical case I.vii.105; III.Prol.27

suppovel, suppovell *n.* support, assistance, supplies VIII.iii.176; VIII.xii.24

suppowellyng *vbl.n.* victualling, supplying IV.x.32

suppys *v.* sucks in III.vi.128

surly *adv.* surely, safely VIII.vi.28; IX.iv.55

surmontyn *v.inf.* to surmount XII.xii.18

surname *n.* name (*representing* **cognomine**) III.ii.131; III.v.132; VI.v.182

surrigian, surrugyn, surrurgyne *n.* surgeon XII.vii.heading, 45, 92

surß *n.* source *Directioun*.57

surß *n.* rush, surge V.v.21

surte *n.* safety VI.v.128

suspek *adj.* suspect III.viii.85

sussy *n.* care, trouble IV.Prol.236

suttel *adj.* skilful V.v.15

suythfast *adj.* true, genuine III.v.68

suythly *adv.* truly I.Prol.89, 369; I.viii.113

suyr *adj.* safe, sure IV.ii.75

swagit *v.* assuaged I.iii.82

swagit *pa. p.* calmed IX.i.80

swail *adj.* ? fat (Gaelic **sul**) VI.x.62

swair *v.* swore IV.viii.34

swait *n.* sweat V.iv.81

swak *n.* a hard blow, a violent dash I.iii.22; V.viii.10; XI.xii.70; XII.v.169

swak, swakkis *v.* hurl, throw, dash, fling III.viii.114; IV.xi.32; V.iv.148

swakand *pr. p.* flinging V.vii.85

swane, swanys *n.* youth, young man attendant on a knight I.xi.23; VIII.Prol.68; XIII.iv.22

swankeis *n.* active young men VIII.Prol.68

swar *n.* neck, throat I.ii.37

sward *n.* the surface of the earth, turf VI.iii.65

swardit *pa. p.* covered with turf XII.Prol.65

swarffard *adj.* weakening, spent X.vi.5

swarffis *v.* faints XI.xv.116: R, 53 (C **swarthis**)

swarm *n.* group (of ants) IV.vii.83

swarthis *v.* faints away, swoons XI.xv.116

swax *v.* strikes XI.xiii.19. *See also* **swak**

swecht, swechtis *n.* weight, force, impetus VII.ix.100; IX.ix.36; XII.xi.159

sweir *adj.* slow, indolent III.viii.15; XII.x.27

sweit *n.* life blood VII.viii.130; sweat III.iii.51; XIII.Prol.136

swelch *n.* pit, abyss III.viii.117; VI.v.3. gullet, belly; sink of evil IV.Prol.243. the action of swallowing III.vi.128

swell *n.* wave VI.v.122, E

swelland *pr. p.* billowing, bulging I.iii.82; III.iii.19

swelly *adj.* swelling III.viii.113: 53

swelly *v.* swallow II.ii.21; IV.i.49. swallow, in the metaphorical sense of drinking in with the eyes IV.xii.35

swellyaris *n.* swallowers, feeders XIII.vi.222

swelt *v.* die VIII.Prol.5; VIII.ix.85

swelth *n.* whirlpool I.iii.42; I.iv.73; III.Prol.44

swengeouris *n.* rogues, rascals VIII.Prol.68, 171

swepyng *v.pres.3 pl.* sweep VI.xvi.22

swer *adj.* slow XI.Prol.4

swet *v.* sweated (tears) II.iii.54

swete *n.* the sweet (i.e. life) I.iii.10; VIII.vi.76

swete *n.* life blood I.iii.10; VIII.vi.76; sweat V.iii.84; IX.vii.196; XII.vi.71

swevyn *n.* dream II.xii.64

swevynnyng *vbl.n.* dreaming VIII.Prol.3

swevynnys, swewynnys *n.* dreams II.v.36; IV.i.17; VI.xv.111

swik *v.* cheat, ensnare IV.ii.72

swipperly *adv.* quickly, nimbly IX.ii.34

swippir *adj.* nimble, quick VI.v.20; XII. xiii.147

swith *adv.* quickly, forthwith I.ii.61; I.vi.181; IX.ii.9

sworland, sworlyng *pr. p.* swirling, whirling VII.i.13; VIII.ii.64

sworll *n.* eddy or coil of flame XII.xi.125

sworlys *n.* eddies, whirlpools IX.iii.66

swouch, swowch *n.* swoon, state of trance II.vi.11; VIII.i.22

swouchand, swowchand *pr. p.* rustling I.iii.24; I.vi.155; V.iii.76; VI.xi.51

swypir *adj.* active, nimble XII.xii.146

swyre *n.* valley, gentle depression IV.iv.50; VI.x.111; VIII.iv.104; XIII.Prol.38

swyrl *n.* eddy, whirlpool III.viii.113

swyth *adv.* at once, forthwith I.iii.20; I.ix.12

sychit *v.* sighed X.xiii.150

syde *adj.* large, extensive XIII.Prol.85; XIII.vi.18. ~ **garmont** XI.xi.97. ~ **rob** VI.x.42

syde *n.* side. **furth on** ~ dispersedly III. vi.172. ~ **hair** the hair on the temples VII.i.106

sydrapis *n.* the traces for a horse XII.xi.25

syiß *n.* times III.vi.132

sykane *adj.* such a one I.viii.17

sykkyn *adj.* such kind of V.xii.70

syklyke *compound* just like III.x.45

sykkyrly *adv.* surely VI.vii.15

syl *n.* beam IX.ix.92 (E **schyll**)

syld *pa. p.* hidden XIII.Prol.42

sylle, sylly *adj.* deserving of pity IV.iii.11. feeble-minded V.vi.18. simple, natural, innocent II.vi.19; IV.Prol.21; IX.iv.46

symmeris, symmyris *n.* summer's VII. Prol.3, 84

symmyr *n.* summer IX.xii.12

symylitude, symylitudes *n.* similitude, likeness I.Prol.256; III.vii.51; IV.vi.97; V.x.72; V.xi.41

syndris *n.* cinders XI.xv.50

syndry *adj.* sundry, several, having an existence apart I.v.4, 26; III.iv.45;

V.Prol.47. apart I.Prol.232

syne *adv. conj.* after, since I.Prol.283; I.i.35; III.i.119; III.iii.34

syng, syngis, syngnys *n.* sign III.ii.150; IV.viii.heading, 116; X.ix.91

synopar, *n.* cinnabar; some shade of brown. XII, Prol. 57

syoun, syonys *n.* branch III.i.71; XI.ii.17

sypir *n.* cypress II.xi.61

syß *n.* times II.iv.80; III.vi.132; III.viii.67

syß *n.* journeys VIII.Prol.60

syt *v.* endure, bear, put up with IV.vi.6

syte *n.* sorrow VI.vi.10; VI.ix.80; VIII. Prol.5; IX.ii.72

syth *adv.* afterwards IX.vii.117

syth *n.* scythe VII.xii.69

syth *n.* time III.i.11

sytting *v.inf.* to sit VIII.vi.127

ta *adj.* that one, the one IV.ix.91; V.v.63; XII.xii.123

tabillis *n.* boards, planks (Latin **tabulae**) I.iii.44

tachit *pa. p.* attached I.vi.31

tail *n.* the stern of a ship III.ii.123

taill *n.* tale IV.vi.11

taill *n.* ? account, reckoning; or story, tale I.Prol.178

tailȝeis *n.* cut pieces, slices 1.iv.92

tailȝeve *v.* rock to and fro V.xiv.77

tak *v.* take. ~ **on hand** undertake IV.iii.44, 48

tak *v.intrans.* make one's way, proceed V.vi.55

take *pa. p.* taken II.viii.heading

takill, takillis *n.* apparatus, instruments, equipment, especially instruments of war V.i.28; V.ix.59; IX.vii.110 the rigging of a ship I.iii.18

takill *v.* equip X.v.34

takilling *v.inf.* to handle or work the tackle of a ship III.ii.119

takis *v.* takes, grasps the sense of, understands I.Prol.318

takyn *n.* token, sign III.i.51; III.iv.61; III. viii.63

takynar, takynnar *n.* one who portends, portent I.v.114; I.vii.46

takynnyng *vbl.n.* token, proving II.v.13; V.i.9; V.ix.84

takynnyt *pa. p.* marked, decked with trophies XI.viii.23

talbert *n.* a loose upper garment without sleeves I.v.80

talent *n.* inclination, desire, disposition X.iv.12

talent, talentis *n.* a weight of money V.iii.18; X.ix.50; X.ix.61

talkyn *vbl.n.* talking XIII.ix.97

tallans *n.* talons XI.xiii.171

tallonyt, tallownyt *pa. p.* tallowed, greased IV.vii.74; IX.ii.97

talꝫeis *n.* pieces, slices XIII.ii.18

tane *pron.* [tha-]t one V.vi.25

tap *n.* a top, the toy VII.vi.87

tapetis, tapettis *n.* carpets I.xi.8, 30; IV.vii.62: R, 53 (C **carpettis**)

tapysry *n.* tapestry IX.vi.120 (E **tapystry**, R **tapesey**)

targe, targis *n.* light shield II.iii.59; III.iv.57; III.ix.90. anything resembling a shield in shape V.xi.122

target *n.* a light round shield VII.vii.171 (53 **tergane**)

tary *n.* a delay, interruption VI.Prol.52

tary *v.trans.* delay II.ii.77; IV.i.107

tarysum *adj.* delaying IV.xii.100

tasand *pr. p.* of weapons, stretching or bending, aiming, poising IX.x.79; XI.xi.51

tassis *n.* cups XIII.ix.25

tastyng *v.inf.* to taste *Directioun*.89

tatis *n.* tufts or locks of hair VI.v.11

taty *adj.* shaggy, matted VII.xi.63

tawbart *n.* a short sleeveless garment worn over armour (*translating* **chlamydem**) III.vii.27; III.ix.13

tawbronys *n.* tabors, drums IX.x.66

tawys *n.* whips for driving spinning tops VII.vi.91

tayll *n.* tail. **in the** ~ thereafter IV.iv.65

tayn *pa. p.* taken I.Prol.108

tayß *n.* tasse, bowl I.xi.84

tayß *v.* of weapons, bend, aim, poise

V.viii.III

tayt *adj.* cheerful, nimble VIII.x.84; XII.Prol.184

techit *v.* taught IV.Prol.48

techrys *n.* drops of liquid XIII.Prol.26

techyng *v.inf.* to teach XII.ix.1

teil *v.* till VII.xiii.40

telit *pa. p.* tilled VII.xii.106

tellyng *v.inf.* to tell XIII.ix.113

telys *v.* tills VI.xiv.96

temperit *adj.* temperate XII.Prol.268 (E, L, B **temperat**)

temys *v.* teems, is plentiful VIII.iii.198

tenchis *n.* ? taunts, reproaches IX.Prol.23: E, R, 53 (C **thewhes**)

tendir *adj.* friendly, well-disposed III.i.31; XI.Prol.174

tendis *n.* tithes VIII.Prol.107

tent, tentis *n.* attention I.ix.41; I.xii.2; III.x.124; VIII.Prol.170

tentit *pa. p.* covered with a tent, set out like a tent VIII.xii.84: R (C **payntit barge**); VIII.x.23: R, 53 (C **with tentis stentit**)

teppet, tepyt *adj.* tepid IX.vi.59. lukewarm, faint-hearted XI.Prol.60

terebynthyn *n.* terebinth, or turpentine tree X.iii.39

terget *n.* a small shield VIII.vii.148

term *n.* terminus, that which limits the extent of something V.iii.53

testify *v.trans.* give proof (of a fact) XI.xi.60; XII.viii.121

tewch *adj.* tough V.v.58; VI.ii.122; XII.xiii.213

text *n.* the whole work (as opposed to a verse or a short passage) III.Prol.31

teyn *adj.* angry VIII.Prol.170

teyn *n.* rage, anger I.i.68; II.iv.18; V.iii.83

teyr *adj.* difficult, toilsome XI.Prol.197

teyr *n.* tear XIII.iv.23

teys *n.* the ropes by which yard-arms are suspended V.xiv.6

teyt *pa. p.* tied XII.x.121

tha, thai *adj. pron.* those I.iii.64; III.iv.16, 47; III.ix.54

thak *n.* thatch I.vii.14; II.viii.7, 11; VII.

Prol.137. a thatched roof IV.xii.53

thankful *adj.* worthy of thanks, agreeable I.Prol.509; IV.x.34

tharat *adv.* thereat I.vi.53

tharby *adv.* thereby I.i.58

tharintill *prep.* therein II.iv.56

tharmys *n.* intestines VIII.xi.9

tharthrou *adv.* therewith VI.viii.102

tharwithall *adv.* therewith IV.xii.121; VI.vi.59

the *n.* thigh XII.vi.24

the *pron.* thee VI.ii.83

the *v.* prosper VI.vii.74

theatreis, theatry *n.* amphitheatre I.vii.20; V.vi.7; V.xii.1. perhaps stages IV.viii.128

thee *n.* thigh X.vi.123

theilk *adj.* that same I.ix.69

thekit *pa. p.* thatched, covered with a roof VIII.xi.30; IX.viii.130

theleß *compound* the less III.vii.23

thempyre *compound* the empire I.v.100

theolog *n.* theologian VI.Prol.75

thetis, thetys *n.* the ropes or traces by which a carriage or plough is drawn V.xiii.122; IX.vi.25; XII.viii.59

thewhes *n. obscure, and possibly a scribal error* IX.Prol.23 (*see note*)

thewis *n.* manners, customs I.viii.80; VIII.Prol.74. virtues, powers VII.i.98; VII.vii.149

thewleß *adj.* destitute of morals or virtues IV.Prol.162

thewys *n.* characteristics, attributes XI.vii.124

theyfage *adj.* thieving III.iv.75

theys *n.* thighs III.ix.38

thidderwart *adv.* thither I.viii.72

thiggyn *vbl.n.* begging VIII.Prol.74

thikkis *v.* thickens, clusters X.vii.31

thikkit *v.* crowded VI.v.30

thine *pron.* thine. ~ **alane** by yourself III.vi.69

thir *pron.* these III.Prol.34; III.iii.41

thirlage *n.* thraldom, servitude XI.iv.61

thirlys *n.* holes, openings VII.iv.201

thistory *compound* the history

I.Prol.324

tho *adv.* then I.iii.45; I.vi.70

thocht *adv.* though I.x.49; II.iv.89

thocht *v.* thought. **me** ~ it seemed to me I.Prol.504; IV.viii.123

thochtfull *adj.* pensive, musing IV.i.heading

thoftis *n.* rowers' benches V.iii.63

thoil, thoill *v.* endure, permit III. vi.heading; III.viii.71; IX.vii.89

thoilmude *adj.* submissive, patient V.vii.48

tholand *pr. p.* enduring V.xii.81

tholit, tholyt *v.* endured I.iv.103; X.Prol.128

thra *adj.* sturdy, bold, fierce VIII.xii.128

thra *n.* eagerness, keenness VIII.Prol.17

thraldom, thraldome *n.* slavery III.v.88; VIII.iii.120 (R, 53 **thirl dome**, L **thrildoun**)

thrall *n.* servant, bondman VIII.Prol.38

thraly *adv.* eagerly, keenly XII.x.55

thrang *n.* bustle, crowding VII.x.90

thrang *v.intr.* pushed one's way, crowded I.vii.41; VII.Prol.69

thrang *v.trans.* thrust V.iv.50

thrast, thrastis *v.* thrust II.vii.82. oppress, push against I.v.58

thraw *n.* twist, turn II.iv.9

thraw *n.* trice, instant anything happens, instance IV.Prol.241; IV.v.133

thraw *n.* struggle, contest XI.Prol.35

thraw *v.* twist V.ii.86

thrawartly *adv.* perversely VII.vi.133: 53 (C **thrawynly**)

thrawin *pa. p.* twisted VII.vi.19

thrawing *pr. p.* throwing III.viii.129

thrawis *v.* twists VI.iv.11

thrawyn *pa. p.* twisted II.i.70; III.ix.89; V.v.66

thrawynly *adv.* askew, perversely VII. vi.133

thrawys *n.* death throes V.viii.115

threpe, threpis *v.* scold, chide I.Prol.487. argue, dispute, contend III.Prol.18

threst *pa. p.* thrust I.vi.87

threswald *n.* threshold VI.i.84

threthis *v.* presses, throngs VIII.Prol.17

thretis, threyt *n.* throng, crowd. **in ~** together V.ii.117; XII.ix.78

threw *v.* twisted II.iv.30. fell with violence, sprang out of place VI.v.115

thrifty *adj.* prosperous, flourishing V.Prol.13

thrillage *n.* thraldom, bondage VIII. Prol.38

thring, thringis *v.* thrust, throw I.v.22; I.viii.121; IV.iv.2

thrist *n.* pushing, act of pressure VI.ii.33

thristis *v.* thrusts IV.vii.29

throuch *adv.* through. **~ and ~** entirely III.ix.98

througyrd *pa. p.* pierced through III.i.85

throwand *pr. p.* twisting, writhing IV.xii.102; IX.vii.185

throwgangis *n.* passages II.ix.38; II.viii.80

throwgyrd *v.* pierced through II.vii.118

thrung *pa. p.* thrust, pushed III.viii.141; V.vi.67 (E, R **thrungen**)

thryft *n.* thriving, prosperity VI.v.78

thrymland *pr. p.* pressing, crowding V.xiii.94

thrymlys *v.* squeezes, compresses X.xii.96

thrympand *pr. p.* pressing, pushing XI.xii.8

thrynfald *adj.* three-fold, three-ply III. vi.218; IV.ix.78; V.iii.33

thryng, thryngis *v.* throng, press, crowd V.iii.6. thrust, drive VI.Prol.115. confine, bind IV.iv.37

thryst *n.* thirst IV.i.88

thryst *v.* thrust III.viii.108

thrystyt *pa. p.* thrust V.x.22

thud *n.* blast of wind V.vi.60. a heavy blow (and its sound) I.i.80

thunderus *adj.* thundery, loud like thunder VI.ix.103: 53

thundir *n.* lightning bolt III.viii.142

thundir *n.* possessive, thunder's

V.xii.54

thusgatis, thus gaitis *adv.* thus wise, in this way II.xi.16; VIII.viii.177

thwangs *n.* thongs IX.xi.5

thy *adv.* **for ~** for that reason, therefore I.Prol.267

thyftuusly *adv.* stealthily IV.vi.113; IX.iii.177

thyg *v.* crave, ask VI.viii.110; VII.ix.75

thyn *adv.* scantily X.iii.10

thyne *adv.* thence

thynkyng *v.inf.* to think III.vii.33

thyrll *v.* penetrate, pierce X.i.32

thyrlyt *pa. p.* pierced III.viii.117; X.viii.114

thystory *compound n.* the history I.Prol.163

tide *n.* time V.xiv.22

til, till *prep.* to I.iv.65

tilbe *compound* to be I.v.134

tistys *v.* entices VII.vii.148

titil *v.* enrol V.xii.155

to baith *v.* bathe, wet copiously XII. xii.67

tobald *compound adj.* too bold I.Prol.411

to- *as first element in compounds.*
~basyt *pa. p.* abashed II.ii.132. **~be** I.iv.29; III.v.93. **~bedone** VI.ix.44. **~behald** I.ix.110; II.ii.11. **~beild** I.vii.11. **~beleif** II.vi.107. **~beseik** VIII.vii.27. **~bet** II.vii.84. **~bewail** XIII.i.90. **~brek** to interrupt VIII. iii.34. **~brok** *see* **all tobrok** XIII. iv.75. **~broke** VII.ix.111. **~bryng** II.ii.8. **~by** to buy I.vii.122. **~ byrstis** breaks up completely X.vi.37. **~cast** V.xi.85. **~changes** *see* **all tochangis** XII.i.93. **~come** *n.* approach, entrance V.viii.44; IX.ii.59; XI.xii.22. **~cum** I.viii.19; III.iii.21. **~cummyn, ~cummyng** *n.* approach, entrance X.v.173; X.viii.44. **~do** IV.x.41. **~feyn** IV.vi.115. **~for, ~forn** *adv. conj.* and *prep.* before I.Prol.413; I.ii.68; IV.vi.93. **~fruschit** crushed II.vii.83; IX.ix.102. **~get** II.iii.37. **~glyde**

V.iii.33

to granyt *pa. p.* two-branched IX.xi.95.

to-, *as first element in compounds.*
~**grund** to the ground II.vii.125.
~**haue** V.vi.121. ~ **holkyt** VIII.iv.116.
~ **hungyn** XII.xii.76. ~ **laym** VII.
viii.53. ~**leif** III.i.114

tomorn *adv.* tomorrow XIII.vi.202

tongit *pa. p.* tongued I.x.10

tonys *n.* musical tones XII.vii.29

tonys *n.* tunes VI.Prol.70

tonyt *v.* tuned I.Prol.506

topace *n.* topaz, a yellowish or bluish
semi-precious stone XII.Prol.37

top our tail *phrase* topsy-turvy VII.
vii.9

toppyt *pa. p.* equipped with towers,
lofty IV.x.86. pointed, peaked (of
hat) VIII.xi.52

to quakyng *v.inf.* to quake violently
VI.xiii.97

tor *v.* tear VI.ix.83

tor *pa. p.* torn VI.viii.38

toremane *v.inf.* to remain IV.vi.136

to rent *pa. p.* torn apart XIII.iii.84

torentis *v.* tears apart II.ii.140

tort *pa. p.* twisted, tortured X.xi.30;
XI.xiii.109.

to-, *as first element in compounds.* ~
schaik *pa. p.* shaken up IV.v.139. ~
schuldris *v.* fly asunder XI.xii.42.
~ **schyde** *v.pa. p.* split asunder.
~ **sparpillyt** *v.* scattered utterly
X.vii.165. ~**set** to set (a sail) III.x.53.
~**smyte** V.viii.48. ~ **smyte** *pa. p.*
completely struck XIII.i.42. ~**spil** to
spoil II.viii.124. ~**tell** IV.v.18

tother *adj.* [tha-]t other III.viii.89;
IV.vi.4

to tor *v.* tore up XII.x.129

to torn *pa. p.* torn up VIII.iv.116

tovme *n.* tomb VI.xv.70

tovn *n.* an enclosed place, a camp XII.
viii.6. an enclosure around a dwelling, a manor XII.xi.90

tow *n.* rope III.ii.119

towart *prep.* with reference to IV.vi.71

towartly *adj.* tractable III.viii.70

towartly *adv.* tractably, docilely
X.xiv.94

towis *n.* ropes V.xii.163

towk *n.* blow, tap VIII.iv.119

town *n.* an enclosure (? a battlefield)
XI.ix.4. a city (Troy) II.iv.96

toyn *n.* tune I.Prol.159

trace *n.* track V.xi.17

tragedy, tragedyis *n.* sad story,
unhappy fate IV.Prol.264; VIII.
Prol.83

traik *n.* plague, pestilence III.ii.141

traill *adj.* trailing XIII.vi.18

traist *adj.* trusty I.iv.55. faithful, devout
III.ii.88. trustworthy VI.vii.49: R

traist *n.* trust, a matter of belief (*for*
manifesta fides) III.vi.39

trake *n.* plague, pestilence IX.vi.46;
XI.xv.59

tralys *v.* drags behind VIII.iv.64

trane *n.* treachery, guile, deceit, trap I.x.32;
IV.Prol.26; XI.Prol.93

transcend *v.* be transcendent, excel
I.Prol.301

translait *v.* transfer from one region to
another I.v.73. translate (from one
language to another) I.Prol.402

translait *pa. p.* transferred II.vi.59

translate *v.* to alter the form of VII.v.112

trappouris, trappuris *n.* trappings
IX.x.60. coverings put over a horse,
trappings VII.iv.193

trast, traste, trastis *v.* trust, have confidence in, believe I.Prol.171, 271, 319

traste *adj.* firm, safe, secure I.Prol.401

trasting *v.inf.* to trust XI.viii.83

trasyng *v.inf.* to make one's way VIII.v.5

trasyng *pr. p.* moving, twisting XII.
Prol.293

trasyt *pa. p.* betrayed IX.iv.8 (53
betrasit)

trat *n.* old woman, crone IV.Prol.166;
IV.xi.114; VII.vii.25

tratlys *n.* idle talk, gossip VIII.Prol.83

trattes *n.* a trat, an old woman VII.vii.30

travaill, travell *n.* travel or travail I.i.16;

V.xi.32

travale, travel, travell *n.* travail I.i.60; I.v.27;
I.vi.45; III.x.105; IV.i.30; V.xii.43; V.xiii.16;
VIII.x.27; XII.xi.46

trayl *v.* walk with long trailing garments
V.Prol.11

trayß *n.* course V.x.84

tre *n.* pole, stake I.Prol.298

treilʒeis *n.* trellis XII.Prol.100

trelʒeis *n.* ? curry-comb XII.ii.92

trestis *n.* three-legged stools III.vi.11;
V.iii.13; IX.v.97

tretabill *adj.* tractable IV.viii.65

trety *n.* treatise XIII.Prol.113

treuth *n.* troth IV.vi.69; IV.vii.42

trewis *n.* truce V.ix.19

trewth plycht, treutht plyght *n.* betro-
thal X.ii.50; X.xii.87

trewys *n.* truce XII.ii.157

treyn *adj.* made of tree, wooden
XI.ii.65

tribbill *n.* harm, distress IV.Prol.247

trippis *v.* skips, prances III.iv.24

trist *adj.* sad VI.vii.49

triumphe *n.* triumph, triumphal pageant
I.vii.24

troch, trowch *n.* channel, bed of river
I.v.81, marginal note; IX.i.76. trough,
container for liquid VIII.vii.177

tropheall *adj.* pertaining to or adorned
with trophies XI.viii.24

trossyt *v.* trussed, tied V.xiv.6

trow *v.* believe, trust I.viii.69; IV.i.24

trowit *v.* believed II.iv.90

trowys *v.* trusts I.Prol.366

trowyt *pa. p.* believed, expected
IV.viii.22

troyn *n.* throne V.vi.9; VII.iii.44

trubly *adj.* troubled, disturbed IV.v.133

trufis *n.* trifles, jests VIII.Prol.170;
IX.Prol.52

trump *n.* trumpet V.xiii.135; VI.iii.16

trump *n.* trifle VIII.Prol.107

trump *v.* blow on the trumpet, blast
XI.viii.17

trump *v.* trick XI.xiii.99

trumpit *v.* deceived I.vi.82

trumpys *n.* trifles V.xii.47

trunschions, trunschon *n.* a fragment
of a spear or lance X.vi.120; XI.i.22

trunschuris *n.* trenchers I.xi.58

tryakill *n.* a medicinal compound XII.
Prol.144

tryg *adj.* trim, neat IX.x.89; XII.
Prol.184

tryggettis *n.* enchantments, deceitful
tricks IV.Prol.247

trygland *pr. p.* trickling IV.vi.66 (E
tringling)

trymlit *v.* trembled II.iv.50

trymlyng *pr. p.* trembling II.i.71; II.iii.59

trymmyl, trymmyll *v.* tremble III.ii.46;
III.ix.109; IV.ix.36

tryne *n.* train, procession VIII.xii.119;
XIII.viii.48

trynglyng, trynland *pr. p.* trickling
VI.xi.14; IX.xiii.78

trynschand *adj.* trenchant, cutting
*Conclusio.*3

trynschis *n.* trenches X.v.53

trynschit *pa. p.* cut IV.xi.35 (see also **all to
~** VI.iv.32)

trynschour, trynschouris *n.* a slice of
bread used instead of a plate VII.ii.17, 26

tryst *adj.* sad X.v.142

tuffyng *n.* caulking V.xii.31 (B **kuffyng**)

tun *n.* tun, barrel V.Prol.53

tunder, tundir *n.* tinder I.iv.34; VII.iv.78

tung *n.* language I.Prol.362, 494

turbacioun *n.* confusion, disturbance III.
ii.159

turcas, turcaß *n.* pincers, tongs VIII.
vii.185; XII.vii.55

turment *pa. p.* tormented VI.ix.161

turn *n.* activity V.xiv.102

turnament *n.* tournament VIII.x.96

turnay *n.* tournament V.v.10

turnyt *pa. p.* turned, as on a lathe VII.
vi.95; VIII.vi.114

turß *v.* carry, convey IV.xii.37; V.xii.116

tursand, tursyng *pr. p.* carrying II.vii.26;
IV.vii.84

tuskand *pr. p.* beating the bushes to
rouse game XII.xii.146: R. 53 (C **Tus-**

can hund)

tutand *pr. p.* peeping out, pushing out XII.Prol.123 (E, L, B, 53 **tetand**)

tvme *adj.* empty VIII.Prol.50

twa part *phrase* two parts out of three I.Prol.170

twan *adj.* two XIII.v.65

twenty *n.* a group of twenty. **a ~ chosyn men** IX.ii.36

twestis *n.* branches XII.Prol.165

twhangis *n.* thongs I.vi.107, marginal note

twich *n.* touch III.iv.36

twich *v.* touch I.Prol.259

twichyn *v.inf.* to touch VI.ix.157

twme *adj.* empty VI.iv.120

twn *n.* tun, a kind of cup VI.iii.140

twychis *pa. p.* (for **twichit**) touched I.iii.75, marginal note

twychyng *pr. p.* touching, referring to I.Prol.380

twyn *n.* one of two parts. **in ~** apart IX.x.79

twyn *v.* separate VI.vii.28

twyne *n.* twine IV.x.102

twynkland *pr. p.* flickering, twinkling II.iv.20; IV.xii.96

twynnyt *v.* separated VI.vii.11

twynris *n.* XII.vii.55: R (C **wynrys**)

twyntris, twyntyr, twyntyrris *n.* a sheep or cow two years old IV.ii.10; V.ii.71; V.ii.105; XII.iv.27

twynyt *pa. p.* entwined, twisted VII. vi.88

twyst, twystis *n.* branch III.i.58; VI.ii.122

twyte *v.* scrape, grate IV.Prol.70

tyar *n.* tiara VII.iv.125

tychirris *n.* drops of liquid IV.xii.5. *See also* **techrys**

tycht *adj.* tight V.v.30

tyd *v.* betided VI.v.98

tyde *n.* time, period, season I.vi.107; III. vi.190

tydy *adj.* in good condition, plump III. iv.23; V.ii.106; IX.x.89

tyght *adj.* tight III.viii.52

tygir, tygris *n.* tiger IV.vii.11; VI.xiii.105

tymbrall, tymbrellis *n.* crest of helmet VII.xiii.9; II.vii.88

tymbrete *n.* the crest of a helmet III. vi.219 (53 **timbrel**)

tyme *n.* thyme I.vii.35

tymmyr *n.* timber I.viii.105

tympane *n.* drum VIII.xii.55

tyndis *n.* the pointed branches of deer antlers I.iv.56; VII.viii.18

tyne *v.* lose III.v.17; IV.Prol.87

tynsell *n.* loss III.x.12; XI.vi.93; *Directioun.*33

tynt *pa. p.* lost III.iii.82; IV.x.39

tynys *v.* loses V.vi.118

typtays *n.* tiptoes IX.xii.53

tyrlyst *pa. p.* furnished with a lattice or grating III.iii.10 (E **tirlis**, R **trillist**)

tyrment *n.* burial XI.ii.heading

tyrrand *n.* tyrant XII.ii.59

tyrvit *pa. p.* overthrown IX.viii.78

tyrvyt *v.* tore off, stripped V.v.32

tyschay, tysche *n.* tissue I.vii.132. a girdle of rich fabric V.vi.49; IX.vi.125

tyste, tystis *v.* entice IV.Prol.140; VII.v.118; XI.xiv.13

tyt *v.* tied XII.xi.21

tyte *adv.* quickly, soon (usually padding) I.ix.13; III.iv.20; IV.viii.75; IV.x.98; VI.vi.9; XII.xiii.178

tythingis, tythyngis *n.* tidings II.ii.104; III.iii.41; III.v.21

tytillis *v.* furnishes with a title III.v.8

uith *prep.* with I.ix.1

vagabund *adj.* leading a wandering, irregular life VI.Prol.68

vagabund *n.* a wanderer IV.v.69

vail que vail, vail que vaill, vail que vailʒe *French phrase* be as it may, at all events VI.Prol.167; IX.Prol.86; X.xiii.129

vaill *n.* a more or less extensive level place between hills (**parte patientis**) IV.iv.53

vaill *v.* veil, shroud VIII.i.33

valᴣement *n.* the process of being walled or fenced VIII.viii.57: R (C **this land inhabyt, vale, mont and swyre**)

valle *n.* valley (disyllabic, not vale) I.iv.52

valᴣeand *adj.* valiant I.Prol.332

vantouris *n.* boasters IV.Prol.171

vareit *v.* altered, adapted I.Prol.485

variant *adj.* varied, variegated VIII.x.52 (E **variand**). inconstant, fickle XI.xiii.151

vary *v.* wander in mind, depart from the truth VI.Prol.53

vassalage, vassallage, vassyllage *n.* prowess, courage, strength IV.Prol.46; IX.Prol.32; X.vi.125; XI.iii.31

vauengeour, vavengeour, vavengouris *n.* vagabond IV.xi.13; VII.v.41; XII.v.99

vayage *n.* voyage I.Prol.436

vaynglor *n.* vainglory, ostentation VI.xiv.22

vaynhope *n.* false hope I.vi.82

vdyr *n.* udder VIII.x.81

vehement *adj.* intense, severe, violent IV.ix.32

veilys *n.* veals, calves XII.Prol.185

veir *n.* spring III.i.17; VI.Prol.110; X.Prol.11

velys *n.* calves, veals V.xiii.20

vengeabill *adj.* vengeful III.iv.102

venerall *adj.* venerable XIII.vi.188

veneryane *adj.* influenced by Venus, relating to sexual desire IV.Prol.93; XI.xiv.30

vennomys *n.* poisons VII.iii.88

vental *n.* the moveable part of the front of a helmet XII.vii.123

ventositeis *n.* blasts of wind VII. Prol.123

venust *adj.* pleasant, peaceful, elegant XII.Prol.87

verlettis *n.* attendants on knights, squires X.xiv.9. grooms XII.ii.87

vermel *adj.* vermilion XII.Prol.124; XII. ii.40

verray *adj.* true I.vi.167; VI.Prol.11

vertew *n.* merit, power, virtue, excel-

lence V.v.28; V.vi.100

vertuus *n.* virtues X.x.122

vervane *n.* wild verbena XII.iii.19

veschell *n.* vessels, containers, in collective singular I.iv.64

veyr *n.* spring VI.Prol.109

vgsum *adj.* ugly III.iii.89; III.iv.37; V.i.21

vgsumnes *n.* ugliness II.xi.124

victoriall *adj.* victorious VII.xi.38

vilyte *n.* meanness, debased conduct IX.Prol.4

vincus *v.* vanquish VI.xv.85

violait, violet *pa. p.* characterized by impurity, defiled II.iii.86; V.i.12 (E **violant**)

virago *n.* an amazon XII.viii.50

visseand *pr. p.* regarding, examining VIII.xii.114

visseit *v.* sought, visited I.vii.38; XII.v.95

vissy *v.* visit I.vi.182; III.v.32; IV.iv.30

vittaill, vittal, vittale, vittalle *n.* provisions, food, supplies I.iv.39; I.vii.50; I.viii.68; I.xi.20

vmast, vmaste *adj.* uppermost, highest I.vi.66; X.viii.96

vmbrage *n.* shaddow XII.Prol.72; XIII. Prol.40

vmquhil, vmquhile *adv.* once upon a time I.Prol.505; III.i.92; III.v.27

vncredyble *adj.* unbelieving, incredulous IV.viii.40: 53

vnderlowt *n.* underling, inferior X.vi.160

vndermyndand *pr. p.* undermining VIII.xi.38

vnderstand *pa. p.* understood I.Prol.132; XI.xiv.2

vndertak *v.* affirm I.Prol.336

vndirly *v.* under-lie, support, bear XII.v.20

vntellabil *adj.* indescribable VIII.viii.61 (R **intolerable**, 53 **vntollerabel**)

voduris *n.* trays or baskets for clearing a table I.xi.58

volt *n.* vault, ceiling; the sky I.viii.21; IX.viii.114, 132

voust *n.* boast XI.xiii.133

voustour *n.* boaster V.vii.62

voyd *adj.* empty II.v.70; III.v.43; IV.ii.65

voydis *v.* vomits X.vi.136

voydyt *pa. p.* emptied, cleared IV.ii.59.

vp-, *as first element in compounds.* ~**bet** *pa. p.* of fire, built XII.ix.51. ~**boltyt** *pa. p.* burst up to the surface V.iv.36. ~**bullyrris** *v.* boils up or over III. viii.100. ~**dryve** *pa. p.* driven up I.viii.147. ~**heit**, ~**heyt** *pa. p.* raised up IV.i.99; X.viii.153. ~**hesit** *v.* lifted, raised III.viii.113. ~**hie** *v.* raise up XIII.vi.132. ~**kyndilling** *pr. p.* catching fire V.xi.121. ~**pykyt** *v.* picked one's way up or along III.x.99. ~**set** *v.* set up, built III.vii.57. ~**sprent** *v.* sprang up III.viii.16. ~**stowryng** *pr. p.* stirring up IV.iv.54. ~**strak** *v.* struck up, rose II.viii.86. ~**strikis** *v.* rises III.viii.140. ~**tobend** *v.* of oars, to fit into position V.iv.75. ~**walxing** *pr. p.* growing up IV.v.181. ~**wark** *n.* **mak** ~ **heirof** cessation of work XIII.Prol.187 (E, R, L, B, 53 **mak vpwark**). ~**warpit** *pa. p.* thrown, flung I.vii.44. ~**weltris** *v.* stirs up III.x.25. ~**wreil**, ~**wrelis** *v.* lift up, raise IV.vii.85; V.v.52

vre *n.* ore X.iii.52

vrn *n.* urn VI.i.31

vrusum *adj. ? error for* **unrusum**, restless XIII.Prol.57

vsance, vsans *n.* usage IV.ii.27; VII.x.3

vsyng *v.pres.1 pl.* we use, we have the habit VIII.iii.181

vsyt *v.* was customary III.i.64

vtyr *adj.* outer VI.iv.95; VI.vii.7

vtyrance *n.* the uttermost V.iv.74

vtyrmest *adj.* uttermost II.vi.102; V.iv.122

vtyrrans *n.* the uttermost X.vii.169; XII. ix.126

vyre *n.* a bolt for the crossbow V.xi.16

vyssyand *pr. p.* examining, inspecting III.ix.113

wa *adv.* away. **do** ~ put away, refrain

from X.viii.32; XII.ii.52

wachand *pr. p.* watching, keeping watch II.vi.69; IV.v.25

wage *n.* pledge, security V.iv.132

wageour *n.* hireling, mercenary soldier III.ix.51; XI.Prol.71

wageouris *n.* prizes won in contests V.iii.10

waid *v.* proceed, advance VII.vii.119

waif *n.* coil, wreath, convolution VII.vi.25

waik *v.* weaken IX.x.50

wail *adv.* choicely, excellently VIII. Prol.42; IX.ii.38

wail, waill *n.* gunwale III.viii.27; V.iv.76; X.v.24

wail, waill *v.* choose V.xii.92; VII.iii.11

wailaway *interj.* alas! IX.vii.49

waill *n.* that which is chosen as the best VII.iv.188

waill *v.* avail V.xii.35

wailliant *adj.* valiant I.i.35

wair *n.* seaweed VII.ix.104

waist *adj.* void, destitute of XI.vii.177

waist *adv.* in vain XII.xii.152

waist *n.* waste, wasted labour IV.ii.64. **in** ~ fruitlessly V.viii.24

wait *n.* watcher, one who waits III.iv.60

wait *v.* know I.Prol.184, 337, 351, 389; V.xiii.44

waith *n.* stray, homeless wanderer VI.Prol.68

wak *adj.* watry, wet III.ix.2; IV.ix.27; V.x.89

wald *n.* plain, wold IX.xi.13

wald *v.* would, wished III.i.14; III.iii.13

waldbe *compound v.* would be VI.ii.24; VIII.Prol.136

waldyst *v.pres.2 sg.* wouldst X.xi.63

walis *v.* chooses VI.Prol.65

walit *pa. p.* chosen II.i.10; IV.ii.10

walit *v.* wailed III.v.61

walk *n.* **vundir** ~ clouded over III. viii.155

walkand *pr. p.* awake IX.vi.88

walkin *v.inf.* to walk VI.viii.24

walking *v.pres.3 pl.* walk VI.iv.66

walkryfe *adj.* wakeful, vigilant IV.v.17,

51; IV.ix.25

walkyn *v.inf.* to walk VI.x.14

walkyn *vbl.n.* waking, watching, being awake VI.viii.91

walkynnaris *n.* wakeners VIII.Prol.109

walkynnyt, walkyt *pa. p.* awakened III.x.38; VII.iv.68

wall, wallis, wallys *n.* walls I.iii.33; V.x.93; V.xi.48

wall, wallis, wallys *n.* waves (**undas**: *not to be confused with* wall) I.i.78; I.ii.55; I.iii.20, 23, 57; I.iv.10; II.iv.13; III.iii.91, 98, 115; III.iv.112; III.vi.113; V.iii.43; V.x.90; V.xi.60; XII.xii.182

wallaris *n.* wall-builders I.i.12

wallit *pa. p.* chosen (**optatae**) III.ii.128

walloppis *v.* gallops XI.x.23: R (C **walxis**, 53 **waloppis**)

walloway *interj.* alas! II.v.44; IV.Prol.78

wallowit, wallowyt *pa. p.* withered, faded, dried up, discoloured VII. Prol.55, 64; VII.vii.11

wallowyng *pr. p.* withering, fading III. ii.152

wally *adj.* swelling, stormy VI.v.84, 117

walx, walxis *v.* grow, increase III. viii.29; VI.ii.17; IV.Prol.248

walxin *v.inf.* to wax XI.v.13

walxy *adj.* waxy, waxen XII.x.91

walyng *vbl.n.* wailing II.vii.89; IV.i.70

walyt *v.* chose V.viii.2

walyt *pa. p.* chosen V.iv.58; IX.iii.167, 189

walyt *v.* wailed IV.vii.15

wame *n.* belly (*translating* **ventre** *in* Ascensius) II.i.70; III.vi.147; VIII. Prol.52

wamyt *pa. p.* wombed, having a womb II.iv.68

wand, wandis *n.* little sticks, faggots IX.ii.64; XI.ii.16. sceptre, hence rule XII.vi.67. a rod used as a symbol of office I.ix.131; III.v.25

wangrace *n.* want of propriety *Exclamatioun*.13

wanhap *n.* misfortune V.iv.89

want *v.* lack V.xi.100

wanthrift *n.* lack of thrift or economy

VIII.Prol.79

wanton, wantoun *adj.* unrestrained, sportive, gay, lively IV.Prol.196; V.Prol.11

wanwerd *n.* ill-fortune I.v.24; VI.ix.76, 102

wanys *n.* waggons XI.iii.87

wanys *n.* dwelling places X.iii.94; XII. viii.6. taken as a singular noun, a dwelling place XII.x.88 (cf. **that innys** XII.x.92)

wappand *pr. p.* throwing quickly or with violence VIII.iv.150: E (C **warpand**)

wappys *v.* throws quickly or with violence V.viii.116: L (C **warpys**)

war *adj.* aware II.iii.72; III.v.97. wary XII.i.96. *used as an interjection*, on guard! VI.Prol.168

war *adj.* worse VIII.vi.33

war *n.* a knot in a tree or in timber XII. xii.212

ward, wardis, wardys *n.* a place for guarding, station IV.x.98; VI.viii. heading.4. a company or garrison, a division of an army V.x.33. the guarded entrance, the inner circuit of the walls of a castle III.ii.39; IV.xii.7; VI.iii.7

wardly *adj.* worldly VI.xv.58

ware *v.* were (*rhymes* declare) III. viii.105

wareis *v.* curses III.vi.188

wareit *pa. p.* cursed II.iii.38; III.i.113; IV.ix.54

warin *v.pa.3 pl.* were VI.viii.3

waris *n.* sea-weed V.iv.10

warkand *pr. p.* paining, throbbing IX.vii.158; XI.xii.110

warld clerkis *n.* worldly scholars II.Prol.2: E, R

warly *adv.* cautiously, prudently I.Prol.107

warn *v.* refuse, deny V.xi.63

warrand *n.* protection, security XI.xvii.8

warris *v.* worsts, defeats V.iii.100

warryn *n.* a hard oak XI.iii.84

warryn *v.* were III.ii.130; V.x.32; VI.ix.165

warp, warpis *v.* throw, especially violently I.Prol.280; I.ii.33; III.iv.74. bend, twist, open VI.i.102

warp, warpit, warpyt *pa. p.* thrown, tossed about I.iii.13, 33; I.x.72; III.viii.123; III.x.118; V.xi.60

warpit *v.* wrapped VII.Prol.95

wary *v.* curse III.iv.121; VI.Prol.55

wasty *adj.* empty, desolated, waste XII.viii.6

wastyt *pa. p.* exhausted X.iv.28

watis *v.* watches over, takes care of IV.ix.96

waucht, wauchtis *v.* drinks, quaffs VII.ii.90; VIII.iv.198

wavand *pr. p.* waving; of hair, flowing IV.iv.37

wave *v.* waver XII.v.4

waverand *pr. p.* wandering I.iv.49; III.iii.98; VI.v.70

waverit *pa. p.* wandered, strayed III.x.71

wavyt *pa. p.* driven by waves VI.viii.113

waw, wawis *n.* waves I.iv.16; III.viii.114

wawland *pr. p.* of the eyes, revolving, rolling VIII.vii.154; X.vii.136

way *adv.* at a distance from, away III.viii.96

wayage *n.* voyage III.vi.40

wayd *v.* walk, especially through liquid III.x.78

wayfleyng *vbl.n.* taking flight IV.vi.93

waykly *adv.* weakly II.ix.63

wayll *n.* gunwale VI.vi.57

waym *n.* womb X.vi.64. belly XI.xv.105

wayn *n.* dwelling place V.iv.103

ways me *adv. phrase* woe is me XI.i.133; XIII.v.47

wedderis *n.* male sheep VII.i.195

weddir *n.* weather in its adverse or destructive conditions IV.iv.65

wedis *n.* weeds XIII.Prol.27

wery *adj.* irksome, wearisome, tedious XIII.iv.9

weffyng *vbl.n.* weaving V.v.76, marginal note

weggeis *n.* wedges VI.iii.48

weggyt *pa. p.* wedged XI.xv.85

weid *n.* clothing V.xi.39. defensive covering, armour XII.xii.45

weilaway *interj.* alas! III.x.110

weilbeknaw *pa. p.* well known II.vii.70

weilbelovit, weilbelovyt *pa. p.* well-beloved V.x.44; VI.v.141

weilbyknaw *pa. p.* well-known VII.i.17

weilfar *n.* well-being, happiness II.xi.53; X.Prol.174

weill *n.* good, well-being, weal II.iii.34; IV.Prol.148

weil willyng *adj.* favourably disposed V.xii.85

weir *n.* war I.i.24; V.x.102

weir *n.* doubt I.x.13; II.xi.11; IV.viii.23. in the phrase **but** ~ without doubt (*a filler*) I.iv.67; III.i.62, 115

weir *n.* wear; customary disposition V.vi.109

weirly *adj.* warlike III.i.27

weirly *adv.* for war, martially XII.xi.132

weit *n.* wetness IV.iii.60

wel *v.* weld VIII.vii.135

welch *adv.* having a sickly taste VI.vii.79

weld *v.* rule, govern I.v.81

welis *n.* eddies VII.i.13

well *v.* weld VIII.vii.128, 174

welt *v.* roll, turn over, bend down I.vii.13; III.v.16; V.xiii.32

welthis *n.* condition of prosperity, felicity VI.Prol.95

weltis *v.* rolls, turns up, overturns III.iii.114; IV.vii.76

weltris *v.* rolls, twists, writhes I.ii.55; III.iii.90

weltrit *pa. p.* turned over VIII.Prol.117

welys *v.* bends, curves VIII.ii.64

wemmys *n.* scars, injuries IV.i.46

wench *n.* a young woman (*without any pejorative connotation*) I.vi.20; VII.viii.9; VII.xiii.19; XI.xii.18

wend *v.* go II.iii.60; III.ii.91; III.vi.194

wend *v.* weened, thought XIII.v.46

wensch *n.* a young woman IV.v.31

went *n.* path III.iv.39; IV.vii.89. way, course I.Prol.378; III.i.119; III.iv.113; V.i.49; V.iv.157. course, state of affairs VIII.Prol.117

went *v.* wend, pass VI.ii,127; VII.ix.22

went *pa. p.* gone, wended II.iii.48; IV.vi.80, 88; V.xii.103

wentis *n.* courses, paths III.Prol.8; III. viii.heading

wenyng *pr. p.* thinking I.Prol.417; II.i.22

wenys *v.* believes, expects I.vii.81; VI.ii.38

werd, werdis *n.* fate I.i.30, 58; I.v.52; V.xiii.74

werefull *adj.* martial, bellicose XI.iv.40: R

weriouris *n.* detractors, critics *Directioun*.65

wernour *n.* miser, niggard VIII.Prol.96

werslyng *n.* wrestling VI.x.36

wersyll *v.* wrestle V.ii.52

weryit *v.* worried, attacked XI.xv.100

weryour *n.* pursuer, rival V.iv.51

wes *v.* was III.iii.47

weschin *v.inf.* to wash VI.iii.138

weschin *pa. p.* washed II.xi.70; VI.iii.121

weyand *pr. p.* considering, pondering on, regarding II.ii.60

weyf *pa. p.* woven V.v.15

weyn *v.* believe, think I.Prol.369; III. Prol.22

weyng *n.* a division of an army XI.xii.17

weyngyt *pa. p.* fitted with wings V.iv.109

weyr *n.* doubt III.vi.55

weyt *n.* wetness, rain V.xii.53

whare *adv.* where (**quh-** *spellings are usual*) III.i.22: 53; IV.i.77: 53

what *pron.* what (**quh-** *spellings are usual*) III.vi.16: 53; IV.i.69: 53

when *adv.* when (**quh-** *spellings are usual*) V.xii.139: 53; X.xiii.116

widdyrsyns *adv.* in a direction opposite to the usual II.xii.26

widequhar *adv.* at large, everywhere

I.ii.32; I.iv.42

wie *n.* a small quantity I.ix.61

wife *n.* a woman, especially of humble rank, not necessarily a *wedded* wife VIII.vii.90

wight *adj.* strong, stout I.vii.11; I.x.16; II.iv.43

wight, wightis *n.* a living being in general, persons without any disrespect or facetiousness III.i.43; III.v.64; III. vi.21

wightly *adv.* bravely, stoutly V.i.29

wil *adj.* lost, gone astray, at a loss II.xi.6

wilfully *adv.* willingly, readily II.ii.4

will *adj. adv.* astray, lost I.i.56; I.vii.49; VII.iv.15. out of the way, unfrequented IV.vi.61; XI.x.64. **wil of red** *phr.* at a loss of a plan II.xi.6

will *n.* determined state of mind (the Greeks were **in** ~) II.ii.91

will *v.* be desirous of III.ii.160; IV.vi.74, 84

wilsum *adj.* wandering, straying, desolate, doubtful I.viii.76; I.xi.124; III. Prol.38; III.iii.105

wily coyt *n.* a coat worn under the outer coat VII.Prol.90

wippit *pa. p.* twisted, entwined VII. vi.114

wirk *pa. p.* wrought VI.iv.58

wirschip *n.* good name, credit, honour I.Prol.330; V.iv.27

wiß *adj.* wise, sagacious VI.Prol.15

wissy *v.* visit, be present at VIII.v.58

wissyll *v.* exchange IX.iv.92

withdraw *v.trans.* elude, escape III. vi.200

withhawd *v.* withhold (*rhyming with* defraud) IV.vi.150

wittering *vbl.n.* knowledge IV.iv.79; IX.iv.66

wittir *n.* mark, sign V.iv.22

witty *adj.* wise, sagacious X.vii.132

wlgar *adj.* written in the ordinary language of a country I.Prol.492; IX.Prol.96; *Exclamatioun*.37. plebeian I.Prol.286

wlgat *pa. p.* spread, reported, divulged
I.vii.69

wlt, wltys *n.* face III.iv.14; IX.xiii.37;
X.xiii.147; XII.xi.93

wo *adj.* grieved, sorrowful XIII.xi.39

wobbis *n.* webs VI.xvi.30; IX.viii.73

wod, wode *adj.* mad (mad is used
XI.viii.55). I.iii.26, 93; I.v.32; II.viii.6,
102; IV.viii.122

wod *n.* wood X.xiv.142

wodman *n.* madman II.vi.49

wodneß *n.* madness II.i.55

woid *adj.* mad III.iii.114; III.ix.71

wollit, wollyt *pa. p.* wool-bearing,
wool-covered III.x.9; VII.i.155

wolt *v.pres.3 sg.* will IV.i.65: 53

wolx *v.* waxed, grew III.ii.152; III.iv.97;
IV.vii.90

woman *n.pl.* women VIII.ix.32

womanheid *n.* womanliness, connoting
chastity IV.vi.80

**womanting, womenting, womentyng,
womentyngis** *vbl.n.* lamentation
II.vii.18; II.viii.85; III.v.62; IV.viii.2;
IV.xii.46; VI.xv.55

wonder *adj.* wonderful, marvellous
I.vi.39

wonderly *adv.* wonderfully I.ix.107

wondir *adj.* wonderful, marvellous
VI.Prol.99

wondir *n.* wonder. **no** ~ without doubt
(*literal rendering of* **nimirum**) III.
viii.103

wondryng *vbl.n.* an object of wonder, a
marvel V.ix.61; VI.iv.92

wondyrfull *adj.* full of wonder, wonderful (*the strong sense is suggested
by the rhymes* dull, full, *and* pull) III.
Prol.10

wonnyt *v.* dwelt XI.xi.82

wont *v.* accustomed, used to. **robbis
quharwith he** ~ **wes cled** *as a
quasi-adverb*, he ordinarily was clad
VI.iii.126

worsum *n.* purulent matter, pus III.
ix.64; VIII.viii.71

worth *adv.* worthily II.vii.129

worth, worthis *v.* become III.Prol.21;
III.i.69; IV.Prol.245

wortis *n.* roots XII.Prol.157

woust *n.* boast X.vi.80

woustand *pr. p.* boasting IX.x.16

wow *interj.* oh! VI.Prol.19

wow *v.* woo XII.Prol.298

wowar *n.* used as *adj.* wooing, loving
XII.Prol.300

woweris *n.* wooers IV.Prol.196

woyd *v.* waded X.xiii.23

woyk *v.* awoke II.i.9

wra *n.* nook, sheltered corner
VI.Prol.158

wrabill *v.* wriggle VIII.x.84

wraik *n.* anger XI.vi.15. danger,
destruction I.i.73; II.ii.120; III.ii.142;
III.ix.60, 119

wraith *adj.* enraged I.Prol.437

wraith *n.* wrath (*with pun on* wraith?)
IV.Prol.233

wrake *n.* vengeance VI.i.27. punishment, disaster II.x.30

wrang *v.* squeezed, wrung III.ix.67

wrangis *n.* the ribs of a ship IX.ii.98

wrangwisly *adv.* unjustly II.ii.158

wrangwyß *adj.* wrongful, unrighteous
I.Prol.444

wrasyll *v.* wrestle, strive IV.Prol.248

wrassill *v.* twist or writhe about XIII.
iv.82

wrath, wrathys *n.* wraith X.x.111;
X.xi.127

wrayngis *n.* the ribs of a ship V.xii.58, 164

wreil *v.* struggle, move writhingly
I.Prol.298

wrek, wreke, wrekis *v.* avenge III.x.30;
IV.viii.132; IV.xi.53; VI.xiv.85

wrekar *n.* avenger VI.ix.81

wreland *pr. p.* twisting V.iv.114

wrelis *v.* struggles XII.xii.209

wriblys *n.* warblings VII.xi.147

wright *n.* artificer VI.i.13

wrikis *n.* twists, bends XIII.iv.86

wrinkillyt *pa. p.* twisted V.x.79

write *n.* writ, writing I.Prol.467; III.

vi.174; VI.Prol.131

write *pa. p.* written XIII.Prol.125

writh *v.trans.* turn or wrench around III.viii.83

writhand *pr. p.* twisting V.vi.67

writhis *v.trans.* twists, twists about IV.xi.95; VI.iii.130

writhyn *pa. p.* entwined, plaited V.v.12

writis *n.* writings III.vi.186

wrocht *v.* made, created X.Prol.20; XI.Prol.200

wroith *adj.* angry. **wod** ~ furiously angry IV.v.56

wrok *n.* hatred, malice V.xi.11

wrokin, wrokyn *pa. p.* avenged II.x.49; IV.xii.24; V.xiii.49

wry *v.* reveal, disclose, communicate IX.iii.5

wry *v.* twist, turn V.xiv.9

wryblis *n.* warblings VII.i.18

wryngis *v.* writhes, twists or turns in anguish VIII.Prol.53

wrynkillit *pa. p.* twisted VI.i.44

wrynklis, wrynklys *n.* turns in a path, curves V.v.62; XII.viii.69

wryth *n.* something twisted, a twisted band V.x.25

wryth *v.* twist I.iii.19

wy *n.* a warrior or fighting man (*poetic*) III.ix.7; VII.xii.174. a person V.xi.19; *Directioun*.36

wyce *adj.* wise VI.Prol.51

wycht *adj.* strong III.ii.78

wycht *n.* a living being I.Prol.331; III. ix.26

wydderit *pa. p.* shrivelled XII.ix.52

wyddyr synnys *adv.* in a direction opposite to the usual *Directioun*.29

wydequhar, wydquhar *adv.* everywhere, in or to various places I.i.35; IV.i.77; VI.x.58

wyfe *n.* a woman IX.v.137

wyfly *adj.* female (*? more like modern womanish than womanly*) IV.xii.46

wyght *adj.* strong IV.Prol.248

wyght *n.* a person II.ii.17; IV.i.54; IV.vii.8. a god IV.x.103

wykkyt *adj.* offensive, baleful V.iv.86

wyl *v.* wish, be desirous of X.vii.33

wylbe *compound* will be XI.viii.128

wyldfyre *n.* lightning I.v.12

wylsum *adj.* strange, desolate, dreary III.vi.57

wympil, wympill, wympillis, wymplis *n.* a garment folded to envelop the head, a veil I.vii.111; II.v.90; IV.xii.88. folds or wrinkles II.iv.30

wymplis *v.* coils around VI.iii.98

wymplit, wymplyt *v.* twisted up, folded X.xiii.134. enfolded VI.iv.93; VII. xiii.61

wyn *v.* ~ **away** find or make one's way, escape IX.vii.28

wynd *v.* twist, turn VIII.xii.81

wynde *v.* go, proceed, make one's way VI.xiii.85

wyndflaucht *adv.* sprawling, overthrown by the wind V.vi.86; XII.ix.75

wyndill strays *n.* dry withered stalks of grass VII.Prol.134

wynnyng *pr. p.* dwelling. ~ **wane** dwelling place V.iv.103

wynrys *n.* winners, ? pincers XII.vii.55 (R **twynris**)

wyntring *pr. p.* passing the winter IV.iv.28

wyrin *adj.* made of wire, wire-like IV.iv.19

wyrkis *v.* performs, executes IV.Prol.65

wyrreit *v.* worried, strangled VIII.v.26

wyß *n.* manner, mode, custom XII. xii.208

wyß for I ~ see under I III.viii.104; IV.iii.12

wyß *v.* wish XII.xiv.17

wysk *v.* sweep quickly through the air, dart III.iv.68; IV.vi.40

wyskyt *v.* moved suddenly IV.vii.55

wyskyt *pa. p.* moved away VIII.Prol.163

wysnand *pr. p.* causing to wither VI.xi.42

wysnyt *pa. p.* thin, shrivelled, parched VII.Prol.56, 124; IX.ii.70

wyssys *n.* wishes VIII.ix.31

wyt *n.* mental capacity, understanding

I.Prol.294

wyt *pa. p.* known III.vi.50

wyte *n.* blame, reproach, blame-worthiness I.Prol.313, 360, 448; IX.Prol.71

wyttir *n.* mark, sign, token V.iii.52

y *n.* the letter y VII.Prol.120

ybaik *pa. p.* baked, seasoned XI.xi.47

ybe *pa. p.* been XI.i.73

ybeldyt *pa. p.* built VIII.iii.192

ybent *pa. p.* of a bow, bent VII.viii.46

yberyit *pa. p.* buried II.v.28

ybocht *pa. p.* bought II.iv.53

ybond, ybondyn *pa. p.* bound II.vii.78; IV.Prol.39; IV.v.40

ybor, yborn, yborne *pa. p.* III.i.80: R, 53; VII.iv.35; VIII.iii.80; VIII.vi.9; X.Prol.58

ybrokkyn *pa. p.* broken XIII.vi.77

ybrynt *pa. p.* burnt III.i.7; III.v.84

ybund *pa. p.* bound I.Prol.299

yburnyst *pa. p.* burnished VIII.x.60

yclepit, yclepyt *pa. p.* named III.ii.9, 23, 73, 116; V.iii.29, 35

ycloß *pa. p.* closed VII.i.150

yconquest *pa. p.* conquered XI.ii.50

ydolatryis *n.* idolatry VI.Prol.10

ydoll *n.* idol, pagan god X.Prol.154

ydred *pa. p.* dreaded XII.iv.55

yfeir *adv.* together, in company I.vi.15; VI.v.83

yfettyrit *pa. p.* VI.xii.28

yforgyt *pa. p.* forged, wrought II.viii.73

ygrant *pa. p.* granted IV.v.96 (E, R, B I **grant**, L **a grant**, 53 I **grantit**)

ylowpit *pa. p.* looped XI.xiv.68: R, 53

ymagery *n.* imagery, pictures I.viii.83

ymerkit *pa. p.* marked VI.xiii.54 (R **thare merkit**)

ympnys *n.* hymns VI.x.70; VIII.v.21

yplet *pa. p.* plaited XII.ii.126

yschape *pa. p.* shaped VI.xi.69 (L, B **eschaip**)

yschit *v.* issued II.i.26; IV.iv.13

yschit *pa. p.* issued, emerged III.iii.21

yschrowd, yschrowdyt *pa. p.* shrouded XI.xv.36; XII.Prol.163

yset *pa. p.* set VI.xiii.65

yslane *pa. p.* slain XIII.ii.3

ysowpit *pa. p.* soaked VII.Prol.35

ysundir *adv.* asunder, apart I.iii.59

ythand *adj.* assiduous, busy VI.xvi.25

ythandly *adv.* diligently, constantly, busily V.xiv.74

ytwyn *adv.* apart IX.i.3

ywympillit, ywymplyt *pa. p.* wrapped up VIII.viii.15; XI.xi.48

ӡa *adv. interj.* yes, an introductory particle to emphasize the following statement XIII.Prol.176

ӡaip *adj.* eager, ready XII.ii.88

ӡaldin *pa. p.* yielded I.iii.9

ӡallow *adj.* yellow II.xi.73

ӡammering *vbl.n.* moaning, lamentation VI.xvi.38 (R **wammyring**)

ӡar *adv.* willingly, readily VII.vii.28

ӡardis *n.* enclosures VI.x.26

ӡarn *adv.* carefully, eagerly IV.vii.83; VI.vii.44

ӡarn clewis *n.* balls of yarn IX.viii.36

ӡeid *v.* went I.Prol.506; VII.vi.81

ӡeild *v.* yield, offer III.vi.97

ӡeill *n.* intent, purpose, will, disposition III.Prol.29

ӡeir *n.* year. **to ~** this year IV.vii.18

ӡeld *adj.* barren VI.iv.32

ӡeld *v.* yelled V.iii.85

ӡell *n.* yell I.vii.118

ӡelloch *n.* yell XII.xiv.100

ӡerd *n.* a yard, the measure of length III.ix.12

ӡeris *n.* years I.i.58

ӡet *n.* gate IV.viii.103. open door III.vi.181

ӡet *v.* pour V.iv.149

ӡet *pa. p.* poured IV.vii.17; V.xii.36

ӡettand *pr. p.* pouring forth III.iii.56

ӡettis *n.* gates I.xi.28; IV.iv.2; VI.xv.109

ӡheir *n.* year, used as a *pl.* **forteyn ~** IV.Prol.47

ӡheris *n.* years I.i.83

ӡiskis *v.* belches forth VIII.iv.154

ӡiskyt *v.* belched, vomited, poured

351

VIII.iv.36

ȝistreyn *adv.* last night V.vi.72.

ȝit *adv.* still, up to this time III.v.74

ȝoir *adv.* formerly, long ago, for a long time past II.xi.21; *Mension*.3

ȝok *n.* yoke; metaphorically, marriage IV.vi.118

ȝok, ȝokkit, ȝokkyt *pa. p.* yoked VII. iv.199. joined, i.e. in battle X.vi.164. yoked. **dowbill** ~ having two horses V.iii.80

ȝoldin *pa. p.* surrendered VI.xv.17.

ȝon *adj.* yonder I.x.52

ȝonder mar *adv.* farther VIII.xi.48

ȝondermast *adj.* most distant VIII.xii.31

ȝongker, ȝonkeir, ȝongkeris *n.* a young man, a young nobleman I.ix.19; I.xi.108; IV.ii.74; VI.xiii.11

ȝor *adj.* ready V.iv.97

ȝor *adv.* quickly, readily I.v.37; VI.i.150

ȝoustir *n.* the discharge from a wound III.ix.72

ȝouthhed *n.* youth IV.Prol.168

ȝowe *n.* ewe V.xiii.22

ȝowle *v.* yell, howl IV.viii.112; VII. Prol.106

ȝowstyr *n.* the discharge from a wound III.ix.82

ȝoyd *v.* went II.xii.21

ȝym *v.* care for, attend, keep VII.viii.23; VII.xi.94

ȝymmand *pr. p.* tending III.ix.97

ȝyng *adj.* young III.v.87

ȝyngkeris *n.* young men, young noblemen I.viii.7

ȝynglyng *n.* a youngster X.xiii.155

ȝyskis *v.* belches forth III.ix.82

Index of Proper Names

Awnus Aunus XI.xiii.heading, 111

Bachus Bacchus I.xi.80; III.v.138;
V.Prol.55
Bais Baiae IX.xi.99
Barbary Coast of Africa I.i.37, marginal
note
Barcen Barce IV.xi.98
Barchay Barcaea IV.i.89
Batall Battle, personified VI.iv.90
Batulane Batulum VII.xii.85
Bebrycy Bebrycia V.vii.21
Bellerophon I.iii.11, marginal note
Bellona VII.v.86; VIII.xii.71
Belus I.vi.60, marginal note; I.xi.68;
I.ix.75, 76
Bennacus Benacus X.iv.113
Berecynthia, Berecyntia Berecyntian
Cybele VI.xiii.64; IX.iii.11
Beroes, Beroys Beroes V.xi.40, 91, 98
Bethliam Bethlehem I.v.102, marginal
note
Bibill Bible I.Prol.100, marginal note
Bitias IX.xi.heading
Blithnes Frivolity, personified
VI.iv.88
Bocas, Bocaß, Iohn Bocas, Bochas
Boccaccio I.Prol.165, 204; I.i.82,
marginal note; I.ii.12, marginal
note; I.iii.54, marginal note; I.v.2,
marginal note; I.v.81, marginal note;
Directioun.68
Boetius Boethius XI.Prol.146
Bohem Bohemia I.v.29, marginal note
Bolan Bola VI.xiii.44
Boreas North wind I.ii.3, marginal
note; VII.Prol.67
Boryane Men of Boreas X.vi.138
Bractanys Bactrians (R has 'britanys')
VIII.xii.31
Brontes VIII.vii.127
Brutus Brutus, who expelled the Tar-
quins VI.xiv.24, 28
Bryareus Briareus VI.iv.104
Bucolykis, Bucolyqueys Virgil's *Bucol-
ics* I.v.102, marginal note; V.Prol.22;
VI.Prol.71

Buk of Kyngis Kings I.Prol.211, mar-
ginal note
Butes V.vii.18; IX.x.132
Butrot Buthrotum, a seaport in Epirus
III.v.20
Butys Butes XI.xiii.90
Butys Asbytes XII.vii.131
Byrsa I.vi.110
Bythyus, Bytias Bitias I.xi.88; IX.xi.
heading, 21; XI.viii.45

Cacus VIII.iv.22, 33
Caicus I.iv.46
Caiet Caieta, the port VI.xv.124
Caieta Aeneas' nurse VI.xvi.heading, 1
Calabar, Calabre Calabria X.i.64;
Epitaph.2
Calcas Calchas II.ii.74, 116; II.iii.61
Cales VII.xii.55
Calidone Calydon VII.v.58
Calliope IX.ix.1
Calydon XI.vi.110
Calybe VII.vii.30
Camerthes, Camertis Camers X.x.48;
XII.v.7
Cameryna Camerina III.x.89
Camilla XI.xvii.2
Camp Elyse the Elysian Fields
VI.Prol.100
Camyll, Camylla Camilla VIII.xiii.
heading, 53; XI.x.29; XI.xv.77
Camyllus Camillus VI.xiv.47
Caphareus Caphereus XI.vi.79
Capis Capys I.iv.46; II.i.42
Capitolie, Capitoll the Capitol at Rome
VIII.vi.83; VIII.xi.28; IX.vii.174
Capreas Capreae, Capri VII.xii.76
Capricorn VII.Prol.8
Capua Capena VII.xi.140
Capua Capua, the city founded by
Capys X.iii.58
Capys VI.xiii.27; IX.ix.114; X.iii.57
Caribdis Charybdis the whirlpool III.
Prol.44; VII.v.47
Carmentaill Carmental Gate VIII.vi.60
Carmentes Carmentis VIII.vi.52
Carras Carians VIII.xii.126

357

Erymanthus a mountain in Arcadia
V.viii.56; VI.xiii.101
Erymanthus Erymas, a Trojan IX.xi.81
Erynnys Erinys, a fury II.vi.77
Eryphyle Eriphyle VI.vii.49
Erypilus Eurypylus II.ii.101
Esacus Esacus, who was turned
into a waterfowl XII.Prol.286
Esperus Hesperus, the evening
star XIII.Prol.19
Ethikis Aristotle's 'Ethics'
XI.Prol.54
Ethiope Ethiopian IV.ix.16
Ethna Etna III.viii.94, 113, 128;
VI.Prol.160
Etholiane Aetolian XI.vi.28
Ethrurianys Etruscans VI.xiv.27
Euboica Euboea XI.vi.77
Euboycon Euboic IX.xi.98
Eufrates Euphrates VIII.xii.129
Eumedes XII.vi.92
Eurilly Euryalus IX.iv.heading
Euristeus Eurystheus VIII.v.31
Eurition Eurytus X.viii.146
Europ, Europe I.Prol.240; I.vi.137;
IV.Prol.80
Eurot Eurotas I.viii.9
Eurus the south-east wind I.ii.57;
I.iii.30, 63, 78
Euryalus IX.iv.33
Evadne VI.vii.51
Evander, Evandir, Evandrus I.Prol.225;
VIII.i.73; VIII.vi.56
Evantus Evanthes X.xii.34
Evomynos Euonymus, one of the Aeo-
lian Islands I.ii.3, marginal note
Evricyus Eurytion V.ix.17
Evrille Euryalus (*trisyllabic, rhyming
with* 'silly') V.vi.17
Ewboica Euboea V.xiv.89
Ewmenydes Eumenides IV.viii.124
Ewmenyus Euneus (1507 'Eumenium')
XI.xiii.39
Ewmolus Eumelus V.xii.2
Ewricion Eurytion V.ix.44
Ewrialus, Ewrill, Ewrillyus Euryalus
V.vi.18, 63, 83. IX.v.184

Ewrus Eurus, south-east wind I.ii.3, 57,
marginal notes
Ewrylly Euryalus IX.iv.45
Exanth, Exanthus Xanthus I.vii.99;
III.v.132; V.xi.69; V.xiii.88, 98

Fabarus Fabaris VII.xii.24
Fabius VI.xiv.100
Fabricius VI.xiv.93
Fabyus Fabius VI.xiv.98
Fabyus a follower of Romulus I.v.89,
marginal note
Fader God the Father X.Prol.51
Fadus IX.vi.86
Falyscy Falisci VII.xi.133
Fame Fame, personified IV.v.heading,
3; IV.vi.36; IX.viii.30
Fascenyum Fescennia VII.xi.132
Fastulus a shepherd I.v.81, marginal note
Fauonius the west wind I.ii.3, marginal
note
Fawnus Faunus, father of Latinus
VII.i.50; X.x.21; XII.xii.178
Feronya Feronia VII.xiii.47; VIII.ix.50
Fidena VI.xiii.40
Flagiton Phlegethon VI.Prol.3; VI.iv.59;
VI.ix.35
Flavynya Flavinia, part of Etruria VII.
xi.137
Flora XII.Prol.63
Forolas Foruli VII.xii.21
Forton, Fortune I.Prol.183; XIII.v.107
Franch French I.Prol.117; I.Prol.269;
VI.xv.31; VI.xiv.59. Gaulish VIII.
xi.36
Franchly Frenchly, like a Frenchman
I.Prol.270
Franchmen Gauls VIII.xi.35 (53 'gauls')
Frans France VIII.Prol.8
Frigia Phrygia V.xiii.48
Fureys Furies VI.ix.154; VIII.xii.67
Fuscynus Fucinus VII.xii.132

Gabios, Gabyne Gabii VI.xiii.39; VII.
xi.98
Gabyne Gabine VII.x.30
Galathea Galatea IX.iii.60

Galesus Galaesus VII.viii.132

Gallia Cysalpina Cisalpine Gaul I.v.29, marginal note

Ganges IX.i.73

Ganymede, Ganymedes I.i.50, 51, marginal note; V.v.16

Garamantas Garamant VI.xiii.86

Garamantida Garamantian, in error taken as a proper name IV.v.48

Gargane Garganus XI.vi.44

Gargarus Mount Gargara IX.iii.17

Gawinus Dowglas, Gawyn Gavin Douglas *Directioun*.3, tailnote; *Tyme, space and dait*.tailnote. See **Douglas**

Geddes, Master Matho Geddes, Douglas's secretary *Conclusio*. tailnote

Gela III.x.92

Gelones Gelonians VIII.xii.127

Geloy Gela III.x.91

Genealogi of Godis, Genealogie of Goddys, Genealogy of gentille Goddis, Genealogy of Goddis, Genology of Goddis Boccaccio's 'De Gen. Deorum' I.Prol.204, 205; I.i.82, marginal note; I.iii.54, marginal note; I.v.2, marginal note; I.v.81, marginal note; Directioun.68

Genyus, Genyvs Genius (*taken as a single god*) IV.i.38; V.Prol.26; V.ii.103; VII.ii.68

Georgikis Virgil's *Georgics* IV.Prol.58; VI.Prol.101

Gereon, Geryon VI.iv.110; VII.xi.49; VIII.iv.46

Gethys Getae VII.x.10

Getule, Getuly, Getulya Gaetulia IV.vi.91; V.ii.20; V.vi.115

Getulyanys Gaetulians IV.i.82

Getya Getae III.i.67

Gilip Gylippus XII.v.128

Gill a farm-girl XIII.Prol.175

Glaucus, Glawcus a sea-deity V.xiii.133; VI.i.64

Glawcus father of Deiphobe I.Prol.244

Glawcus Glaucus, son of Imbrasus XII.vi.84

Glawcus Glaucus, son of Antenor VI.viii.15

Gnosia, Gnosya Gnosia or Crete III. ii.97; VI.i.35

God I.Prol.76, 313, 449; III.Prol.8, 17; IV.Prol.38, 82, 129, 131; IV.vi.85; V.xi.33; VI.Prol.81, 153, 154. **God Fader** VI.Prol.80. as Jove I.Prol.443; I.iv.72. **Godhed** X.Prol.27

Gorgones Gorgons II.x.100; VI.iv.108

Gorgonyane Gorgonian VII.vi.2

Gower, Ihonne John Gower IV.Prol.213

Gracchus VI.xiv.89

Gradyus Mars Gradivus III.i.66; X.ix.92

Grauyssa Graviscae X.iv.54

Grece Greece I.Prol.235

Gregion Greek I.xii.11; V.vi.52. **Gregionys** Greeks II.vii.41; III.viii.85. **Gregioun** III.ix.90

Gregor, Sanct St Gregory I.Prol.395

Gregyus Greeks II.vii.22

Greik Greek III.v.24; III.ix.14. **Grekis** Greeks I.i.40, 73; III.ii.40; III.iii.30

Grew Greek I.Prol.115; III.iv.1. the Greek language I.i.13, marginal note (R, III.iv.1 *has what seems to be* 'grewkid', i.e. Greeked, *made into the Greek language*)

Gryneus refers to Apollo's temple at Gryneum in Asia Minor IV.vi.127

Gwydo de Columnis Guido delle Colonne I.v.28, marginal note

Gyan Gyas I.iv.110; I.ix.60

Gyara Gyaros, an island in the Aegean III.ii.16

Gyas V.iii.30, 92; XII.viii.37

Gyas a Latin X.vi.71

Gyges IX.xii.81

Hales Halys IX.xii.87

Halesus Halaesus VII.xii.45

Haly Gaist Holy Ghost X.Prol.32

Haly Scriptour Bible I.vi.151, marginal note

Halyus Halius IX.xii.91

Hamadriades wood-nymphs I.iv.24, marginal note; III.i.65

Ithis Itys IX.ix.110
Iubar the day-star XIII.Prol.156
Iulian XIII.xi.77
Iulius, Iuliuß Cesar Julius Caesar I.v.102
and marginal note
Iulus Julus Ascanius I.v.69, 103; II.xi.55
Iuno I.Prol.181; IV.i.93. **Iunois** Juno's
I.iii.62
Iupiter I.Prol.182; III.ii.72, 96. the planet
Jupiter XII.Prol.10
Iuturna X.viii.2
Ixion VI.ix.145

Katheryn a farm-girl XIII.Prol.175
Kyddis two small stars known as the
Kids IX.xi.15
Kyng of Kyngis God I.Prol.453

Laborynth, Laborynthus the Labyrinth
III.Prol.14; V.x.78; VI.i.43
Lacena Laconia VI.viii.72
Laces, Lachidemonya Lacedaemon, or
Sparta III.v.91; VII.vi.53
Lacon Virgil has 'Ladon' X.vii.125
Lacynya Lacinium, a Greek promontory
with a temple to Juno III.viii.90
Laertes III.iv.120
Lagus X.vii.47
Lamentatioun Lament, personified
VI.iv.78
Lamus IX.vi.61
Lamyrus IX.vi.61
Landinus Cristoforo Landino I.iii.100,
marginal note; I.iv.49, marginal
note; I.v.28, marginal note
Lang Alba the city of Alba VI.xiii.24
Laocon Laocoon II.i.52; II.iv.heading,
4, 22
Laodomya Laodamia VI.vii.51
Laomedon, Laomedone III.iv.75;
IV.x.40; VIII.iii.152
Lapytas, Lapythos Lapithae VI.ix.144;
VII.v.52
Larissyane from Larissa XI.viii.66
Laryd, Laryde Larides X.vii.73. 85
Laryna Larina XI.xiii.18

Larysseus the Laryssean, Achilles
II.iii.102
Latagus X.xii.24
Latinus VII.i.47
Latio, Latium I.i.8; I.v.65; I.viii.108
Latone Latona, mother of Diana
I.viii.15
Latonya Diana, Latona's daughter VII.
Prol.99; IX.vii.77
Latyn the Latin language I.Prol.359,
381, 493
Latyn, Latyne Latin, of the Latins I.i.10;
V.x.42
Latyn, Latyne Latinus VI.xv.105;
VII.i.58; X.ii.9
Laubour Labour, personified VI.iv.86
Lavinia VI.xiii.20. **Laviniais** Lavinia's
XIII.x.16
Lavyn, Lavyne Lavinium I.v.54, 73; XI.iv.67
Lavyne Lavinia VII.vii.61
Lavyne Lavinian, Italian I.i.3
Lavynya Lavinia VII.i.105; VII.v.76
Lawrens of the Vaill Lorenzo Valla
I.Prol.127
Lawrens Laurens X.xii.55
Lawrent Laurentum VII.i.51
Lawrent Laurentine V.xiii.71
Lawrentes Laurentians VII.i.84
Lawrentyn Laurentum VII.vi.4
Lawsus Lausus, son of Mezentius VII.
xi.22; X.vii.156
Lawsus Lausus, son of the king of Alba
I.v.81, marginal note
Leander IV.Prol.72
Leleganys Leleges VIII.xii.126
Lemnos VIII.viii.1
Lent Spring VIII.Prol.2
Lerna VI.iv.105; VI.xiii.102
Lethie Lethe VI.Prol.4
Lewcas Mount Leucata III.iv.123
Lewcaspis Leucaspis I.iii.39
Lewcata Leucate VIII.xii.4
Libiane Libyan I.ix.29; V.xiii.57
Libicanys Labicians VII.xiii.36
Liburnanys Liburni I.v.31
Libya IV.i.88
Libyane VI.v.89

365

Seruius, Seruyus Maurus Servius, the commentator I.Prol.350, marginal note; I.i.28, marginal note; I.iii.1, marginal note; I.v.2, marginal note; I.vi.107, marginal note; VI.Prol.28

Sestos the scene of Leander's disaster IV.Prol.79

Sevyn Starnys probably the Hyades, not the Pleiades I.xi.100; VIII.Prol.151

Sextus Rufus the name prefixed to an abridgment of Roman history prepared for the Emperor Valens I.v.29, marginal note

Seya the Scaean Gate III.v.133

Sicarbas the husband of Dido I.vi.60, marginal note

Sibil, Sibill, Sibilla, Sibilla Cumane the Sibyl I.Prol.242; V.xii.128; VI.Prol.8, 24, 135, 137, 146; VI.i.heading. the Virgin Mary VI.Prol.145. **Sibillais, Sibilys** Sibyl's VI.Prol.70; VI.iii.38

Silla Scylla I.iv.73

Siluius Silvius VI.xiii.17

Siluya Silvia VII.viii.27, 59

Siluyus Eneas Silvius Aeneas VI.xiii.29

Sisyphus VI.ix.184

Skynnar, Sym hangman. See note VIII. Prol.133

Sleip Sleep, personified VI.iv.87

Son of God X.Prol.28

Sonnys Sun's VI.xvi.23

Soractis Mount Soracte XI.xv.43

Span3e Spanish VII.xi.52

Spart, Sparta, Spartha I.vi.19; II.x.32; VII.vi.53; X.ii.85

Spyo Spio V.xiii.139

Steropes VIII.vii.127

Sthelenus, Sthenelus Sthenelus, a Greek II.v.22. a Trojan XII.vi.79

Sthenelus Sthenius X.vii.66

Stix Styx III.iv.13; V.xiv.54; VI.Prol.3

Stragile I.ii.3, marginal note

Strophades, Strophe the Strophades, islands in the Ionian Sea III.iii.115; III.iv.1

Strymone Strymon X.v.125

Strymonyus Strymonius X.vii.127

Stygian IV.xii.110

Subsolanus the east wind I.ii.3, marginal note

Sucron Sucro XII.ix.14

Sulmon Sulmo X.ix.27. **Sulmonys** Sulmo's IX.vii.97

Swytoneus Suetonius I.v.102, marginal note

Sybar Sybaris XII.vi.132

Sybil Sibyl III.vi.188

Sycany, Sycanys Sicanians VII.xiii.34; VIII.vi.38; XI.vii.52

Syche, Sychey Sychaeus I.vi.67; I.xi.52; IV.i.42; IV.x.62

Sycil Sicilian III.vi.59

Sycil, Sycill, Sycilly Sicily I.iv.66; I.viii.99; III.viii.94, 147. **Sycilyanys** Sicilians V.vi.16

Sydon Sidon I.ix.73; IV.x.47

Sydonas Sidoness I.vii.51

Sydony Sidon (*trisyllabic, rhyming with* 'haue I' *in* IV.xii.78) IV.ii.49; IV.iv.15

Sydycina Sidicinia VII.xii.54

Sygean of Sigeum II.vi.29

Syla Sila XII.xii.53

Sylla Scylla, the rock III.Prol.44

Syluanus Silvanus VIII.x.15

Sym Skynnar hangman. *See note* VIII. Prol.133

Symethus Symaethus IX.ix.131

Symoes, Symois Simois, a river near Troy I.iii.12; I.ix.72; III.v.37; X.i.140

Synon, Synone Sinon II.ii.heading, 41; II.iii.98

Synthea Cynthia, the moon VII.Prol.117

Syrene Siren V.xiv.71

Syrius Sirius, the dog-star X.v.144

Syrtis Syrtes IV.i.86; VII.v.45

Syryvs Sirius, the dog-star III.ii.149

Sysilly Sicily I.i.63

Taburn Taburnus XII.xii.52

Tagus an Italian soldier IX.vii.111

Talon Talos XII.ix.32

Tanais a river. See note I.Prol.239

Tanaus Tanais, a Rutulian XII.ix.31

Tantalus VI.ix.149

Vrsis, Vrsys Urses, the Great and Little Bear constellations I.xi.102; XIII.Prol.67

Watlyng Streit a name for the Milky Way III.viii.22

Werd Sisteris, Werd Systeris the fates III.vi.50; V.xiii.74

Weris Wars, personified XII.vi.66

Wlcan, Wlcane, Wlcanus Vulcan VI.Prol.156; VIII.vii.heading, 7; VIII.vii.122; XII.xii.109

Wlturnus Volturnus, the river VII.xii.57. The wind I.ii.3, marginal note

Wraith Wrath, personified XII.vi.67

Xanthus X.i.140

Ypocras Hippocras, a wine I.xi.67

Ytail Italy I.i.3

3acynth Zacynthus, an island in the Ionian Sea III.iv.116

3airmuth Yarmouth I.iii.29, marginal note

3epherus, 3ephirus, 3ephyrus Zephyr, the west wind I.iii.63; II.vii.96; XII.Prol.75; XII.vi.62